Advanced
Data Structures in C++

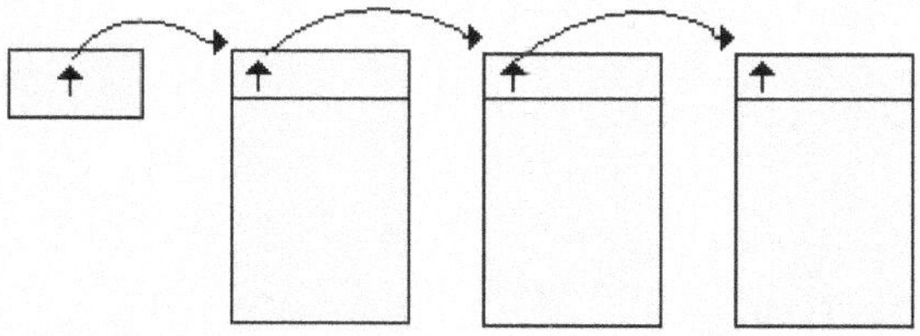

by Vic Broquard

Broquard eBooks

Advanced Data Structures in C++
3rd Edition

Vic Broquard

Advanced Data Structures in C++
3rd Edition
Vic Broquard

ISBN: 978-1-941415-55-9

Broquard eBooks
103 Timberlane
East Peoria, IL 61611
author@Broquard-eBooks.com

To all of my dedicated, persevering students,
and to L. Ron Hubbard, who taught me to "Simplify"

Table of Contents

Preface

This book assumes you have had a beginning course in data structures and are familiar with basic object oriented programming techniques, linked lists, stacks, and queues.

The book begins with a complete review of basic object oriented programming techniques with which you should be familiar. Then, step by step, more advanced principles are presented including full coverage of operator overloaded functions and inheritance. One chapter deals exclusively with C++ error handling methods. Next, templates are covered. After reviewing the basic data structures, ways of converting them into template container classes are discussed. This is followed by a complete treatment of binary files and hashing theory. It is illustrated by both inquiry and direct file update programs. Both the Remainder Method and ISAM files are programmed. A thorough presentation of the tree data structures comes next with some of the theory applied to sorting algorithms in the next chapter. The efficiencies of the different sorting methods are illustrated with a benchmark program.

When you have finished this book, you are fully prepared to tackle Windows MFC Programming I, to learn how to create Windows applications complete with toolbars, dialogs and child windows.

The book comes with a self-extracting zip file containing all of the sample programs in the book along with all of the test data required for the programming assignments. Download them at:
http://www.Broquard-eBooks.com/pb/advancedds and use the link there.

At the end of each chapter are **Review Exercises**, **Stop Exercises** and **Programming Problems**. Before you tackle any programming assignments, you should do both the Review and Stop Exercises. The Review Exercises are paper and pencil activities that assist in solidifying the basic design principles covered in the chapter. The Stop Exercises cover the new syntax of the language, illustrating many of the more common errors beginners make in coding the language. If you dutifully do these two sets of exercises **before** you start in on your programming assignments, you will have a much better chance of success with drastically lower frustration level.

If you find any errors or have any suggestions or comments, please email me at author@Broquard-eBooks.com

Chapter 1—A Review of Classes

Introduction

An object is "a thing," an entity. In this chapter we begin our study of advanced data structures by reviewing the basic principles of Object Oriented Programming and class construction. OOP is centered upon objects and how they interact.

Consider a computer emulation of a car object. Such a simulation would have a number of **properties** associated with it, the **data members**. Some car properties might be the number of doors, its color, the engine size, its mpg, gas tank capacity, a flag representing whether or not the motor is running, and its current speed. A car simulation would also have **methods** or **member functions** to perform actions upon a car object, such as, start, stop, drive, speed up, slow down, and turn.

A **class** is a model for the compiler to follow to create an object. A class usually has data members or properties that define its various characteristics and it has member functions or methods that perform requested actions. When one creates a specific instance of the car class in memory, one then has a real object. This is called **instantiating an object** Given an instance of a car, we can then request it to perform various actions, such as starting up and driving.

Recall that the data members and the functions to operate on those data are joined into an inseparable whole, a principle known as encapsulation. Normally, the outside world can utilize the object only through its provided member functions. How those actions are actually implemented and how the properties are actually stored are totally hidden from the outside world. With this black box approach, ideally one should be able to completely rework the internal algorithms and never touch the client's coding.

With the car, the user might invoke a **StartCar** function. How the car is actually started is never known nor is it ever a concern to the user. The benefit of encapsulation is large with perhaps the biggest being code reusability.

The member data and functions have a user **access attribute**: **public**, **private**, and **protected**. Specifying **public** access on a data item or function allows the user to use and refer to it directly by name. Only public data and functions can be accessed by the user of the object—the client program. Often, we do not wish the user to be able to directly access the member data and perhaps a few function members. Such items are given either **protected** or **private** access, meaning these are for our own internal use within our class.

For example, the manner in which we wish to keep track of whether the car is started or not is our own business. The user should not be given public access to that member; instead we give him a function **IsStarted** which returns **true** or **false**. If we do not like the way we are internally storing the started state, we can change it without affecting the user's code. It is unwise to make data members public, for that allows the user to be able to change object state directly; doing so removes a bit of the black box. For then we cannot change these public data members without impacting the users of our class. Member functions are often public so the user can perform actions with the object.

Class Syntax

A class is normally composed of a definition file and an implementation file—that is, a header file and a cpp file. The definition of a class begins with the keyword `class` which is followed by the name of the class and the begin brace. Class names are usually capitalized while the data member names it contains are usually lowercase. An end brace and semicolon end the definition.

Here is the basic syntax of a class definition.

```
/*****************************************************/
/*                                                   */
/* name: purpose, etc.                               */
/*                                                   */
/*****************************************************/

class name {

 /*****************************************************/
 /*                                                   */
 /* class data                                        */
 /*                                                   */
 /*****************************************************/

 public:
 protected:
 private:
  data definitions

 /*****************************************************/
 /*                                                   */
 /* class function                                    */
 /*                                                   */
 /*****************************************************/

 public:
 protected:
 private:
  function prototypes
};
```

Notice that I usually group all of the member data into one area and all of the member functions into another portion. This enables the reader to rapidly find things. If you intersperse data definitions and function prototypes, it becomes more difficult to rapidly find items of interest.

Suppose that we wanted to create a class to encapsulate a simple vehicle, such as a wagon or cart. We can code the following.

```
class Vehicle {
 // here the default access is private unless qualified
};
```

This definition is located in the file **Vehicle.h**; its implementation is in **Vehicle.cpp**.

The Three Access Qualifiers

Every data member and member function has an access qualifier associated with it: **public:** or **protected:** or **private:**.

Rule: By default, everything after the begin brace of the class definition is private.

Public items can be accessed directly by everyone, including the client programs. Certainly the class user interface (member functions) should be public. This represents the main user interface to the object. However, most all of the member data should not be given public access.

Private access is the most restrictive. No client program can ever access private items. Furthermore, if we derive a **Car** class from the **Vehicle** class, the **Car** class inherits all of the member data and functions of the **Vehicle** class. However, those items that are private cannot be accessed from the new derived **Car** class. In general this is way too restrictive. The whole idea of OOP is to create a good hierarchical collection of classes. Thus, one should really make private only those really critical items that even a derived class should not have access to.

If one were creating a linked list of items, the pointer to the head of the list should likely be given private access because if that pointer to the entire list should get messed up, the list is irrevocably corrupted. A reference count is sometimes maintained by a class, tracking how many instances of the class have been created. When that count becomes zero, the class may take special actions. For example, dynamic link libraries (dlls) and ActiveX controls often maintain a reference count so that when no applications are using them, they can unload themselves from memory. Reference counts, in my opinion, should be private in nature.

The third access qualifier is **protected**. Protected items are not accessible by client programs. However, a derived class does have direct access to them. Nearly all of my examples in this text use protected for data member access. Why? If one has done a great job creating a class, then someone else is highly likely to wish to extend it to help handle their situation, that is, to derive another class from it. Private items make the derived class very awkward to implement; the designer must find ways and means to work around the inability to access their own inherited members.

This is one fallacy that is rampant in the OOP textbook arena as well as many magazine articles. One frequently sees all of the data members having private access! Time and time again, I have seen this occur. It is terrible practice because if you have done your programming task well, someone else will want to reuse your class extending it to solve their problem. Private items become a real bane to class derivations. Thus, right here from the onset, I will make my data members protected, reserving private access for those items I really do not want even a derived class to have access.

For a **Vehicle**, what data members could be defined? Let's keep this simple and track whether or not the vehicle is in motion and how fast it is traveling. We have then the following.

vehicle.h

```
class Vehicle {

 protected:
  bool isMoving;
  int  speed;

 public:

};
```

Now we need some functions. Function fall roughly into three broad categories: constructors/destructor functions, access functions, and operations functions.

Constructors and Destructors

Generally, a class has one or more **constructor** functions and one and only one **destructor** function. The constructor function is called by the compiler when the object is being created and its job is usually to give initial values to this instance's data members. Think of the constructor as getting the object all ready for operations. The destructor function is called by the compiler when the object is being destroyed. Its purpose is to provide clean up actions, such as removal of dynamically allocated memory items or reference count decrementing. Both functions have the same name as the class, except that the destructor has a ~ character before its name.

Neither a constructor nor a destructor function can ever return any value of any kind, not even **void**. A destructor function cannot ever be passed any parameters, ever, and thus cannot ever be overloaded with multiple versions. However, the constructor function can have as many parameters as desired and often is overloaded so that the class can be initialized in a variety of ways. Note that "constructor" is often abbreviated as "**ctor**." Likewise, "destructor" is often called "**dtor**."

Rule: All classes must have at least one constructor function whose job is to initialize this instance's member data. It can be overloaded and is always called by the compiler.

Rule: All classes must have a destructor function whose job is to perform cleanup activities. It is called by the compiler when the object goes out of scope and must be deleted.

Rule: If a class has either no constructor or destructor function, the compiler provides a default constructor or destructor function for you. The provided constructor and destructor do nothing but issue a return instruction.

Remember that overloaded functions are functions whose names are the same but differ in the number and types of parameters being passed to the function. Return data types do not count. Here in the **Vehicle** class the constructor function and destructor function prototypes could be

```
Vehicle ();
~Vehicle ();
```

When designing the constructor functions, give some thought to how the user might like to create instances of your class. With a **Vehicle**, the user might want to create a default vehicle or they might like to create a specific vehicle that is moving down the road at 42 miles an hour. Thus, we should provide two different constructor functions in this case. Here is the class definition with the new functions added. Note that since there is no dynamic memory allocation involved in this class, there is no need to code the destructor function. Let the compiler create a default one which does nothing because there is nothing to delete.

vehicle.h

```
class Vehicle {

 protected:
  bool isMoving;
  int speed;

 public:
        Vehicle ();
        Vehicle (bool move, int sped);
};
```

The **default constructor** is a constructor that takes no parameters.

Rule: A class should always provide a default constructor as a matter of good practice.

This default constructor is called when the user wishes to create a default instance. Hence, this is most likely to be the most frequently invoked function in a client program.

The Implementation File

These functions are actually implemented in the **Vehicle.cpp** file; they are only defined in the header file. Think about the default constructor's implementation. What should it do? Suppose that in the **Vehicle.cpp** file we coded the following.

vehicle.cpp

```
#include "Vehicle.h"
Vehicle::Vehicle () {
 isMoving = false;
 speed = 0;
}
```

How does the compiler know that this function **Vehicle** is the constructor that is defined in the header file? To show that a data member or a member function is part of a class, we use the **class qualifier** which is the name of the class followed by a double colon—**classname::** To notify the compiler that this function belongs to the **Vehicle** class, we code

```
Vehicle::Vehicle () {
...
```

```
}
```

Rule: When you define the member function body, include the classname::

```
returntype  classname::functionname (parameter list) {
  ....
}
```

Rule: any member function has complete access to all member data and functions.

Outside that class, only public members are available (except with derived classes and friend functions). Here is how we could implement the two constructor functions of the **Vehicle** class.

vehicle.cpp

```
#include "Vehicle.h"

Vehicle::Vehicle () {
 isMoving = false;
 speed = 0;
}

Vehicle::Vehicle (bool move, int sped) {
 isMoving = move;
 speed = sped;
}
```

Of course, the implementation in the second constructor function is a bit shaky. Suppose that the caller passed **false** and 42 miles per hour. We are then storing a vehicle that is not moving at 42 miles an hour. Or suppose that the user passed **true** and 0? Ok. We could check on the speed and override the user's request so that the object was not in some silly state. But for simplicity, I am overlooking this situation.

Notice how that within the member functions, we have complete access to all of the member data.

One must be a bit careful of parameter variable names. Suppose that we had coded it this way. We run into a scope of names situation. Specifically, a parameter name hides member names of the same exact name.

```
Vehicle::Vehicle (bool isMoving, int speed) {
 isMoving = isMoving; // error
 speed = speed;       // error
}
```

What is happening is that the parameter variables hide the class member variables of the same name. These two lines are saying to copy the contents of the parameter **speed** and put it into the parameter **speed**. One way around this conflict is to use different names for the parameters as I originally did. However, you can also use the class qualifier to specify which variable is desired.

```
Vehicle::Vehicle (bool isMoving, int speed) {
 Vehicle::isMoving = isMoving;
 Vehicle::speed = speed;
}
```

Alternatively, recall that each member function is passed a pointer to the specific instance of the class; it is called the **this** parameter. Thus, one can alternatively use the **this** parameter to distinguish member data.

```
Vehicle::Vehicle (bool isMoving, int speed) {
 this->isMoving = isMoving;
 this->speed = speed;
}
```

Either way, this is a lot of extra coding; the simpler solution is to ensure the parameter names do not conflict with member names.

Access Functions

Because we do not want the user directly accessing any of the protected data members, we must provide some means for the user to access this protected data that we are storing for them. Functions that permit the user to retrieve and change protected data members are called **access functions**. Such functions commonly begin with the prefixes **Get . . .** and **Set . . .** If a class is encapsulating a lot of data, then there are a large number of these access type functions.

Consider our **Vehicle** class. What access functions do we need to provide? What data that we are storing would a user need to retrieve or change? In this example, a user of a **Vehicle** object probably needs to access the **isMoving** state and the vehicle's **speed**. Thus, the definition is expanded to include four more functions.

vehicle.h

```
class Vehicle {
 protected:
  bool isMoving;
  int speed;
 public:
        Vehicle  ();
        Vehicle  (bool move, int sped);

   // the access functions
   bool IsMoving ();
   void SetMoving(bool move);

   int  GetSpeed ();
   void SetSpeed (int sped);
};
```

These four new functions are implemented as follows.

vehicle.cpp:

```
#include "Vehicle.h"
bool Vehicle::IsMoving () {
 return isMoving;
}
void Vehicle::SetMoving(bool move) {
 isMoving = move;
}
int Vehicle::GetSpeed () {
 return speed;
}
void Vehicle::SetSpeed (int sped) {
 speed = sped;
}
```

Again, the implementations are oversimplified with respect to the interrelationship between **isMoving** and **speed**.

One could also overload the **SetSpeed** and pass two parameters. The definition and implementation are as follows.

```
void SetSpeed (bool move, int sped);
void Vehicle::SetSpeed (bool move, int sped) {
 is_moving = move;
 speed = sped;
}
```

Quite frequently, the implementation of a class consists of a rather large number of extremely short functions, many of which are one-liners!

Instantiating Classes

How are instances of a class instantiated or created in client programs? An instance is defined just like any other data type—just like you would create an instance of a structure. Objects can be of automatic storage type, static, constant and even dynamically allocated. Arrays can be created as well.

main.cpp

```
#include "vehicle.h"
int main () {
 Vehicle a;              // calls the default constructor
 Vehicle b (true, 42); // calls the overloaded version to create
                       // a vehicle that is moving at 42 mph

 const Vehicle c (true, 55);  // a constant vehicle
 static Vehicle d (true, 60); // a static vehicle

 Vehicle e[100];         // creates an array of 100 vehicles

 Vehicle* ptrv;
 ptrv = new Vehicle;     // dynamically allocate a vehicle calling
                         // the default ctor
 delete ptrv;

 ptrv = new Vehicle (true, 42); // dynamically allocate a vehicle
                                // and call the second ctor
 delete ptrv;

 Vehicle* array = new Vehicle [number]; // allocate an array
 delete [] array;
```

The next client program action is to access public data members and call public member functions. How is a member of a structure accessed? By using the dot (.) operator or the pointer operator (->), in the case of a pointer to a structure. We use

```
object_instance.function
```

or

```
object_instance.data_item
```

If one has a pointer to the object, use

```
ptr->function
```

or

```
ptr->data_item
```

The client program can now perform the following actions on its newly created vehicle **a** by coding the following.

```
a.SetSpeed (100);       // get the car moving
a.SetMoving (true);     // at 100 miles per hour
cout << a.GetSpeed (); // display a's speed
```

Or if using the vehicle that was dynamically allocated

```
ptrv->SetSpeed (100);       // get the car moving
ptrv->SetMoving (true);     // at 100 miles per hour
cout << ptrv->GetSpeed (); // display a's speed
```

Or if using element j of the array of 100 vehicles

```
e[j].SetSpeed (100);       // get the car moving
e[j].SetMoving (true);     // at 100 miles per hour
cout << e[j].GetSpeed (); // display a's speed
```

Or if using element j of the dynamically allocated array of vehicles

```
array[j].SetSpeed (100);       // get the car moving
array[j].SetMoving (true);     // at 100 miles per hour
```

```
cout << array[j].GetSpeed (); // display a's speed
```

Pointer operations for array accessing also work, yielding a faster execution. Define a pointer to the current vehicle and one that points to the last vehicle.

```
Vehicle *ptrThisVehicle = &e[0];
```

or

```
Vehicle *ptrThisVehicle = e; // name of array is const ptr to
                             // the first element as usual
Vehicle *ptrLastVehicle = e + 100;
```

Pointer arithmetic works as normal. Here **ptrLastVehicle** is given the address of the beginning of the array of **e** plus 100 * **sizeof** a **Vehicle** object. Similarly, the ++ and -- operators work as expected. The following sets all vehicles in the array moving at 50 miles per hour.

```
while (ptrThisVehicle < ptrLastVehicle) {
 ptrThisVehicle->SetMoving (true);
 ptrThisVehicle->SetSpeed (50);
 ptrThisVehicle++;
}
```

Only one of the many vehicles created in the **main** function above causes problems. Have you spotted which one it is? Look at the definition of vehicle **c** once more. This vehicle is defined to be a constant vehicle. If we coded these same function calls, compile time errors result.

```
c.SetSpeed (100);       // error trying to alter a const obj
c.SetMoving (true);     // error trying to alter a const obj
cout << c.GetSpeed (); // error trying to alter a const obj
```

The error message says that the compiler cannot convert a **const Vehicle** to a **Vehicle**. That is, it cannot call a function that may change the member data of an instance when that instance is supposed to be a constant instance. Certainly the compiler is correct on the first two calls above. If vehicle **c** is defined to be constant, then we should not be allowed to change its speed or moving state. However, we also cannot even access in a read-only manner the speed so that we can display it. This factor is addressed and handled below in the Constant Functions section.

Initializing Arrays of Objects

The client program can allocate an array of objects. In the example a few pages above, the **main** function created an array called **e** as follows.

```
Vehicle e[100];    // array of vehicles
```

In a similar manner, one can create arrays of structures or intrinsic data types, such as **temps** shown below.

```
double temps[100];
```

However, there is a significant difference between these two allocations. What is the content of each element in the array **temps** after it is defined above? No initialization is done and so all elements contain core garbage. Instances of classes behave differently.

Rule: When the compiler allocates each instance of a class, it also calls that instance's constructor function to permit that instance to initialize itself!

Thus, when the compiler allocates the memory for the array **e** above, it then calls the default **Vehicle** constructor 100 times, once for each instance in the array. Whenever an instance of a class is created, the compiler always gives it a chance to initialize itself.

The same is true when we dynamically allocate an array. Consider the allocation of the array of a variable number of vehicles. We had above

```
Vehicle* array = new Vehicle [number]; // allocate an array
```

Once the compiler has allocated space for **number** of **Vehicle** objects, it then calls the default constructor for each of the **Vehicles** in the array.

It is also possible to specify which constructor function is to be called during array initialization.

Vehicle has a second constructor that allows the user to specify the initial state. The syntax is shown below.

```
 Vehicle d[3] = {Vehicle(false,0), Vehicle(true,50),
                 Vehicle(true,30)};
```

Within braces {}, one specifically invokes the desired constructor function passing it the desired parameters. However, if one had a large array to initialize, the syntax would be cumbersome to say the least.

Assigning Instances

Just as one structure instance can be assigned to another structure instance as long as they both have the same structure tag, objects can be assigned as long as they are instances of the same class. Thus, the client program could make a copy of **Vehicle b** as follows.

```
     a = b;
```

When an assignment is done, the compiler looks to see if we have provided an assignment operator. If not, then the compiler itself copies all data members as is. The compiler does a byte-by-byte copy of all of **b**'s data into instance **a**, replacing all of the data stored in object **a**. In the case of the **Vehicle** class, this is just what is desired. This is called a **shallow copy**.

However, if a class has dynamically allocated memory, such as an array, then catastrophic trouble arises, because only the pointer to the memory is copied, not the array itself. Be extra careful when the constructor allocates memory and a destructor frees that memory. Consider this class called **Trouble** which stores a dynamically allocated character string as its member data.

Trouble.h

```
class Trouble {

protected:
 char *ourString;

public:
  Trouble (char* string);
 ~Trouble ();
};
```

Trouble.cpp

```
#include "Trouble.h"

Trouble::Trouble (char* string) {
 ourString = new char [strlen (string) + 1];
 strcpy (ourString, string);
}

Trouble::~Trouble () {
 delete [] ourString;
}
```

Now consider what happens in **main** when the assignment operator is required.

main.cpp

```
 ...
 Trouble s1 ("hello");
 Trouble s2 ("hi");
 s2 = s1;
 return 0;
} // here bad trouble
```

The assignment copies the contents of **s1**'s **ourString** and places it in **s2**'s **ourString**, without freeing **s2**'s initial string. Thus, it leaks all memory allocated by the original **s2** instance. Next, as **main** ends, both objects go out of scope and are destroyed in the reverse order they were created (both objects are automatic storage instances on **main**'s stack). The destructor for **s2** is called which deletes the memory to which **ourString** points, which is really the string held in object **s1**. Then, when the compiler calls the destructor for **s1**, it attempts to delete the memory pointed to by **ourString** which has already been deleted; a program crash results.

When dynamic memory allocations are part of class member data, we must provide an assignment operator to handle the situation. Obviously, our new assignment operator function will have to make a duplicate copy of the string. This is called a **deep copy**. We will examine this in great detail later on.

Objects (Instances of a Class) Can Be Passed to Functions and Returned

A function can return an instance of a class. A function can be passed a copy of a class instance. With structures returning a structure instance or passing a copy of a structure to a function is inherently inefficient in terms of both speed of execution and of memory usage. The same holds true when passing or returning class instances. In such cases, the compiler must allocate space for the object and then copy all of the data members. We removed these inefficiencies by passing pointers or references to a class whenever possible.

Consider the following client C function. Notice how it is passed a copy of a **Vehicle** object and also returns a copy of a **Vehicle** object.

```
Vehicle fun (Vehicle a) { // Vehicle a is a copy of the
                          // object that was passed
 Vehicle b = a;     // copy Vehicle a
 b.SetSpeed (42);   // and change its speed
 return b;          // return a copy of b on the stack
}
```

And the **main** function might call **fun** as follows.

```
 Vehicle newvehicle = fun (b);
```

Rule: When passing objects to functions, always pass them by reference whenever possible. Further, if that function is not going to alter the member data of a passed object, pass a constant reference to it.

In the above example, function **fun** does not change the passed vehicle **a**. Thus, the function should have been coded this way.

```
Vehicle fun (const Vehicle& a) {
```

Rule: When possible, a function should return a reference to an object instead of a copy of the object.

Again, returning a reference to an object avoids making a duplicate copy of the object to return.

However, it is not always possible to return a reference. Consider what would result if this was done in the preceding example.

```
Vehicle& fun (const Vehicle& a) {
 Vehicle b = a;
 b.SetSpeed (42);
 return b;
}
```

And the **main** function might call **fun** as follows.

```
 Vehicle newvehicle = fun (b);
```

When the return is executed, the compiler returns the memory address of the automatic storage instance of **fun**'s vehicle **b**. But when the end brace of **fun** is reached, the compiler then deletes all of the automatic storage for function **fun**. Specifically, vehicle **b** is destroyed. When the compiler next reaches the assignment portion, the reference it has now points to a destroyed, nonexistent vehicle. This rule of returning a reference to an object must be applied to objects that do not go out of scope when the function terminates.

Constant Member Functions

Consider the **Get...** type of access functions. A **Get...** function's purpose is simply to return the value of the indicated property that the class is encapsulating for the user. Under what circumstances could such a **Get...** type access function ever change the data that it is retrieving for the user? None!

> **Rule: Those member functions that do not in any way alter the data being stored in this class instance must be made constant member functions.**

Only member functions can be constant. They are so indicated by placing the keyword **const** after the end of the parameter list. In the **Vehicle** class, the **GetSpeed** and **IsMoving** functions should be constant functions. I have highlighted the new keyword in the header file below.

vehicle.h

```
class Vehicle {

 protected:
  bool isMoving;
  int speed;

 public:
         Vehicle  ();
         Vehicle  (bool move, int sped);

   // the access functions
   bool IsMoving () const;
   void SetMoving(bool move);

   int  GetSpeed () const;
   void SetSpeed (int sped);
};
```

Also, these functions must be specified as constant in the implementation file. I have highlighted this addition below.

```
bool Vehicle::IsMoving () const {
 return isMoving;
}

int Vehicle::GetSpeed () const {
 return speed;
}
```

Why do they have to be made constant functions? Users sometimes create constant objects whose properties are supposed to be held constant under all situations. In the case of a **Vehicle** class, suppose the user has created the "pace car" at a race track. Its properties are to be constant, since it is setting the initial launching of the race. The user might code

```
const Vehicle paceCar (true, 80);
cout << paceCar.GetSpeed();
```

If the user now calls **GetSpeed** on this object, the compiler generates an error unless this **GetSpeed** member function has been made constant.

If one does not specify **const** in the prototype (and function header), it does not matter whether or not you actually change any member data in the actual implementation file. Remember that when compiling the client program, the compiler sees only the **Vehicle** definition file with the prototype; it cannot look ahead into another cpp file to see if you are really not changing anything; it must depend upon the class function prototype.

Another way a constant object occurs is when the client program passes a constant reference (or pointer) to an object to a function that should not be altering that passed object. For example, suppose that the client race track program had an array of **Vehicle** objects and wanted to call a function, **CalcAverageSpeed**. It might do so as follows.

```
Vehicle array[100];
int numCars; // current array bounds
double avgSpeed = CalcAverageSpeed (array, numCars);
```

The function is coded as follows.

```
double CalcAverageSpeed  (const Vehicle array[],
                          int numCars) {
 double sum = 0;
 if (!numCars) return 0;
 for (int j=0; j<numCars; j++) {
  sum += array[j].GetSpeed();
 }
 return sum / numCars;
}
```

Here the call to **GetSpeed** is made on a series of constant objects. If **GetSpeed** was not a constant function, the compiler would issue an error message about this.

Default Arguments

Suppose that we chose to overload the Vehicle **SetSpeed** function with another version that allowed for modification of the moving state as well as the speed. We would have

```
void SetSpeed (int sped);
void SetSpeed (bool move, int sped);
```

A very powerful feature is the ability to specify default values for arguments should none be specified. One could also use default arguments on the second version as follows.

```
void SetSpeed (int sped);
void SetSpeed (bool move=false, int sped = 0);
```

Now, when this specific **SetSpeed** function is called, it can be invoked three ways:

```
a.SetSpeed ();
a.SetSpeed (true);
a.SetSpeed (true, 55);
```

But what would happen if we chose to use default arguments with both functions?

```
void SetSpeed (int sped = 0);
void SetSpeed (bool move=false, int sped = 0);
```

If **main** chose to call it passing two parameters, all is well, since there is only one overloaded function that takes the two parameters.

```
a.SetSpeed (true, 55);
```

But consider what happens at compile time for this one.

```
a.SetSpeed ();
```

Which function does the compiler invoke? Both versions are equally possible. Thus, an ambiguous function error message results.

Default arguments can also be used with the constructor functions. I could have coded them this way.

```
Vehicle  ();
Vehicle  (bool move = false, int sped = 0);
```

Had I done so, then I would have introduced function ambiguity with the default constructor that takes no parameters. Sometimes, a class designer deletes the default ctor function and uses another ctor function whose arguments are all defaulted. I could have used only this one ctor function.

```
Vehicle  (bool move = false, int sped = 0);
```

It would then serve dual duty, so to speak.

Operations Functions—Handling I/O Operations—A First Look

Under the category of "operations" functions come all those functions that client programs can use to manipulate the object. I/O operations are often the foremost actions that are usually needed. Comparison functions are frequently required so the client program can compare two instances. In addition, there can be a large number of specialized operations. If one created a **Rectangle** class, one might need a **GetArea** function and maybe even a **GetPerimeter** function.

How can an object be input or output to/from a text file? The insertion and extraction operators are certainly convenient with intrinsic data types, such as longs. However, those operators are discussed in the next chapter on operator overloaded functions. There is an alternate approach that is often used in place of and/or in addition to the insertion/extraction operators. Such member functions are commonly called **Input** and **Output**.

An **Input** member function has access to all of the member data. Thus, if it is passed the **istream&** from which to input the data, it can do so, filling up all the member data. Likewise, for the **Output** function. If it is passed the **ostream&** on which to display, it can display the data members as desired. However, would any output type function ever alter the member data being displayed? No. Thus, the **Output** function must be made constant.

For our **Vehicle** class, here are the two new prototypes in the header file.

vehicle.h

```
class Vehicle {

 protected:
  bool isMoving;
  int speed;

 public:
        Vehicle  ();
        Vehicle  (bool move, int sped);

   // the access functions
   bool IsMoving () const;
   void SetMoving(bool move);

   int  GetSpeed () const;
   void SetSpeed (int sped);

   istream& Input (istream& is);
   ostream& Output (ostream& os) const;
};
```

The implementation of **Input** has the additional problem of how to input the **bool isMoving**. The best way is not to input it at all, but input only the **speed**. Then, set **isMoving** based upon whether or not the vehicle is moving.

```
istream& Vehicle::Input (istream& is) {
 is >> speed;
 if (!is) {
  cerr << "Error on inputting vehicle's speed\n";
  speed = 0;
  isMoving = false;
  return is;
 }
 isMoving = speed ? true : false;
 return is;
}
```

The **Output** function can be written to match the form of display that the client desires. Let's say that the user wishes to see output similar to the following.

```
The vehicle is not moving.
The vehicle is moving at 42 miles per hour.
```

Then, the **Output** function would be as shown below.

```
ostream& Vehicle::Output (ostream& os) const {
 if (isMoving)
  os << "The vehicle is moving at " << speed
     << " miles per hour.\n";
 else
  os << "The vehicle is not moving.\n";
 return os;
}
```

Using Instances of Another Class as Data Members in Another Class

Commonly, one class may use an instance of another class as one of its data members. A class to encapsulate a circle would certainly have a radius data member. But it might also have an instance of a **Point** class which is used to mark the origin or center of the circle in a two-dimensional space.

For example, the definition file of the **Point** class might be as follows.

Point.h

```
class Point {
public:
 int x;
 int y;

public:
 Point ();
 ...
};
```

If the **Circle** class desires to have an instance of the **Point** class as one of its members, then the **Circle** definition file must include the **Point** class definition file so that the compiler knows how much memory a **Point** object requires.

Circle.

```
#include "Point.h"
class Circle {
protected:
 double radius;
 Point  origin;

public:
 Circle ();
...
};
```

Notice that the **Circle** class is actually a client of the **Point** class just as the **main** function has been a client of the classes discussed thus far. The **Circle** ctor can be coded as follows.

```
 Circle::Circle () {
  radius = 0;
  origin.x = origin.y = 0;
}
```

Practical Example 1—The Class Rectangle (Pgm01a)

Let's encapsulate a rectangle. First, we must decide upon what properties we should store. I have chosen to save the length and the width as **doubles** and a character string name of the rectangle.

Next, examine how a user might wish to construct an instance of a **Rectangle** class. Certainly, there must be a default constructor that takes no parameters. But also we should provide one that is passed the length and the width the user desires, defaulting then name parameter to "Rectangle."

Now examine what user access functions should be provided to allow the client to retrieve and alter the length and width we are storing for them. I have chosen to create Get/Set functions for both the length and the width. And I also chose to allow the user to change them both by providing **GetDimensions** and **SetDimensions** functions.

Some means must be provided for I/O operations. Thus, I have an **Input** and **Output** pair of functions. However, the client also wishes to have a fancier form of output that looks like this: [10.5, 22.5]. This function I called **OutputFormatted**.

Finally, what operations would you expect a user to wish to do with a rectangle? Most likely they wish to find the area or the perimeter of the rectangle. Hence, I added **GetArea** and **GetPerimeter**.

The next step is to code the **Rectangle** definition file. When all of the function prototypes have been coded, look them over and decide which functions must be made constant member functions and add that **const** keyword to them. Also, if you can see the need for helper functions, add them as protected. Here is the **Rectangle** definition file from **Pgm01a**.

Rectangle Class Definition

```
#pragma once
#include <iostream>
using namespace std;

/***************************************************************/
/*                                                             */
/* Rectangle: encapsulates a rectangle                         */
/*                                                             */
/***************************************************************/

const int MAXNAMELEN = 21;

class Rectangle {

 /***************************************************************/
 /*                                                             */
 /* class data                                                  */
 /*                                                             */
 /***************************************************************/

protected:
 double length;
 double width;
 char   name[MAXNAMELEN];

 /***************************************************************/
 /*                                                             */
 /* class function                                              */
 /*                                                             */
```

```
 /***************************************************************/

public:
 // makes a default rectangle
 Rectangle ();
 // makes a specific rectangle
 Rectangle (double len, double wid,
            const char* nam = "Rectangle");

 ~Rectangle ();

 // Access Functions

 // returns the name of this rectangle as a string
 const char* GetName () const;
 // change the name of this rectangle
 void   SetName (const char* nam);

 // returns the length of this rectangle
 double GetLength () const;
 // change the length of this rectangle
 void   SetLength (double len);

 // returns the width of this rectangle
 double GetWidth () const;
 // change the width of this rectangle
 void   SetWidth (double wid);

 // returns both the length and width of this rectangle
 void   GetDimensions (double& len, double& wid) const;
 // change both the length and width of this rectangle
 void   SetDimensions (double len, double wid);

 // Operational Functions
 // returns the area occupied by this rectangle
 double GetArea () const;
 // returns the perimeter of this rectangle
 double GetPerimeter () const;

 // I/O Functions
 // inputs a rectangle from any input stream
 istream& Input (istream& is);
 // outputs the rectangle in a formatted manner
 ostream& OutputFormatted (ostream& os) const;
 // outputs the rectangle
 ostream& Output (ostream& os) const;

protected:
 // helper functions
 // verifies that a length or width is valid and stores it
 void VerifyNumber (double& number, double val, const char* who);
 // verifies the new string name is valid and stores it
 void VerifyName (const char* newname);
};
```

Next, start the cpp file by copying all of the prototypes into the **Rectangle.cpp** file and removing the semicolons and inserting { } braces. Do not forget to add the **Rectangle::** qualifier to all functions. In this implementation, I chose to log an error message to **cerr** whenever I encountered a negative length or width. And I inserted a value of zero in its place in the corresponding data member. All of the coding is very simple and quite straightforward. Here is the **Rectangle.cpp** file. Notice how I handle the situation of the character string name variable.

Rectangle Class Implementation

```
#include <iostream>
#include <iomanip>
using namespace std;

#include "Rectangle.h"

/***************************************************************/
/*                                                             */
/* Rectangle: default constructor - sets all to 0              */
/*                                                             */
/***************************************************************/

Rectangle::Rectangle () {
 length = width = 0;
 name[0] = 0;
}

/***************************************************************/
/*                                                             */
/* VerifyNumber: helper function to verify val is not          */
/*               negative - displays error msg if so           */
/*                                                             */
/***************************************************************/

void Rectangle::VerifyNumber (double& number, double val,
                              const char* who) {
 if (val >= 0)
  number = val;
 else {
  number = 0;
  cerr << "Error: a rectangle's " << who
       << " cannot be less than 0\n";
 }
}

/***************************************************************/
/*                                                             */
/* VerifyName:  helper function to verify new name string*/
/*              is not 0 or too long - fills up name           */
/*                                                             */
/***************************************************************/

void Rectangle::VerifyName (const char* newname) {
 if (!newname) {
  cerr << "Error: a null pointer was passed for the name"
       << " instead of a character string\n";
```

```
  name[0]  = 0;
  return;
 }
 if (strlen (newname) > MAXNAMELEN - 1) {
  cerr << "Error: name exceeds " << MAXNAMELEN -1
       << " characters - truncation occurred\n";
  strncpy_s (name, sizeof(name), newname, MAXNAMELEN -1);
  name[MAXNAMELEN-1] = 0;
  return;
 }
 strcpy_s (name, sizeof (name), newname);
}

/***************************************************************/
/*                                                             */
/* Rectangle: makes a rectangle from user's data               */
/*            displays error if either is < 0                  */
/*                                                             */
/***************************************************************/

Rectangle::Rectangle (double len, double wid,
                      const char* nam) {
 VerifyNumber (length, len, "length");
 VerifyNumber (width, wid, "width");
 VerifyName (nam);
}

/***************************************************************/
/*                                                             */
/* ~Rectangle: destructor - does nothing                       */
/*                                                             */
/***************************************************************/

Rectangle::~Rectangle () { }

/***************************************************************/
/*                                                             */
/* GetName: returns the name property                          */
/*                                                             */
/***************************************************************/

const char* Rectangle::GetName () const {
 return name;
}

/***************************************************************/
/*                                                             */
/* SetName: sets our name property to a new string             */
/*                                                             */
/***************************************************************/

void Rectangle::SetName (const char* nam) {
 VerifyName (nam);
}

/***************************************************************/
```

```
/*                                                          */
/* GetLength: returns the length of a rectangle             */
/*                                                          */
/************************************************************/

double Rectangle::GetLength () const {
 return length;
}

/************************************************************/
/*                                                          */
/* SetLength: sets the length, displays error if < 0        */
/*                                                          */
/************************************************************/

void   Rectangle::SetLength (double len) {
 VerifyNumber (length, len, "length");
}

/************************************************************/
/*                                                          */
/* GetWidth: returns the width of the rectangle             */
/*                                                          */
/************************************************************/

double Rectangle::GetWidth () const {
 return width;
}

/************************************************************/
/*                                                          */
/* SetWidth: sets the width - displays error if < 0         */
/*                                                          */
/************************************************************/

void   Rectangle::SetWidth (double wid) {
 VerifyNumber (width, wid, "width");
}

/************************************************************/
/*                                                          */
/* GetDimensions: updates user's fields with length/width*/
/*                                                          */
/************************************************************/

void Rectangle::GetDimensions (double& len, double& wid) const {
 len = length;
 wid = width;
}

/************************************************************/
/*                                                          */
/* SetDimensions: sets the length and width - errors are */
/*                displayed if either is < 0                */
/*                                                          */
/************************************************************/
```

```

void   Rectangle::SetDimensions (double len, double wid) {
 VerifyNumber (length, len, "length");
 VerifyNumber (width, wid, "width");
}

/***************************************************************/
/*                                                             */
/* GetArea: returns the area of a rectangle                    */
/*                                                             */
/***************************************************************/

double Rectangle::GetArea () const {
 return length * width;
}

/***************************************************************/
/*                                                             */
/* GetPerimeter: returns the perimeter of a rectangle          */
/*                                                             */
/***************************************************************/

double Rectangle::GetPerimeter () const {
 return length * 2 + width * 2;
}

/***************************************************************/
/*                                                             */
/* Input: "name" len wid is the format expected                */
/*                                                             */
/***************************************************************/

istream& Rectangle::Input (istream& is) {
 char nam[MAXNAMELEN];
 char c;
 double val1, val2;
 is >> c;
 if (!is) return is;
 is.get (nam, sizeof (nam), '\"');
 is >> c >> val1 >> val2;
 if (!is) return is;

 VerifyName (nam);
 VerifyNumber (length, val1, "length");
 VerifyNumber (width, val2, "width");

 return is;
}

/***************************************************************/
/*                                                             */
/* OutputFormatted: displays as name [length, width]           */
/*                                                             */
/***************************************************************/

ostream& Rectangle::OutputFormatted (ostream& os) const {
```

```
 os << fixed << left << setw (MAXNAMELEN + 2) << name << right
  << " [" << setprecision (2) << length << ", " << width << "]";
 return os;
}

/***************************************************************/
/*                                                             */
/* Output: displays the name surrounded with " " and           */
/*         the length and width with 2 decimals                */
/*         separated by a blank                                */
/*                                                             */
/***************************************************************/

ostream& Rectangle::Output (ostream& os) const {
 os << fixed << '\"' << name << "\" " << setprecision (2)
    << length << " " << width;
 return os;
}
```

The last step is to design a testing program to **thoroughly** test the class before placing it into production by giving it to the user. A testing oracle is highly desirable. Ideally, one should test out all circumstances of the class usage. Specifically, this means at least testing every one of the member functions. In the case of those functions which can report an error or run into execution errors, such as inputting bad data from the input stream, several tests are needed. Please carefully examine the output from the tester program and the tester program (**Pgm01a.cpp**) and see if I did indeed test all of the possibilities. (In actual fact, I did not; I failed to thoroughly test this one. However, that is the topic of a Stop Exercise below.)

Pgm01a Tester Program

```
#include <iostream>
#include <iomanip>
#include <fstream>
#include <strstream>

#include "Rectangle.h"

using namespace std;

int main () {
 Rectangle a;                    // test default ctor
 cout << "Default ctor (0,0): " << a.GetLength() << " "
      << a.GetWidth() << endl;

 Rectangle b (42.42, 84.84); // test overloaded ctor
 cout << "b's overloaded ctor (should be 42.42, 84.84): "
      << b.GetLength() << " " << b.GetWidth() << endl << endl;

 double l, w;                    // test GetDimensions
 b.GetDimensions (l, w);
 cout << "GetDimemsions: should be the same: "
      << l << " " << w << endl;

 Rectangle c;                    // test assignment
 c = b;
 cout << "Rectangle c should be as b: " << c.GetLength()
```

```
     << " " << c.GetWidth() << endl;

Rectangle d (1, 2);            // test integers
cout << "Rectangle d should be 1,2: " << d.GetLength()
     << " " << d.GetWidth() << endl << endl;

Rectangle e (-1., 4);          // test error length
Rectangle f (1, -4.4);         // test error width
Rectangle g (-2, -4);          // test error both
a.SetLength (-1.1);            // test error length
a.SetWidth (-2);               // test error width
a.SetDimensions (-1, -2);      // test error both
cout << endl;

a.SetLength (4);               // test SetLength and SetWidth
a.SetWidth (8);
cout << "SetLen and width check (should be 4,8): "
     << a.GetLength() << " " << a.GetWidth() << endl;

a.SetDimensions (9, 10);       // test SetDimensions
cout << "SetLen and width check (should be 9,10): "
     << a.GetLength() << " " << a.GetWidth() << endl << endl;

// test GetArea and GetPerimeter
cout << "Check area (should be 90): " << a.GetArea()
     << endl;
cout << "Check perimeter (should be 38): "
     << a.GetPerimeter() << endl << endl;

// test Input function for good and bad data
char string[] = "\"Test Input 1\" 10.10 20.20   ";
istrstream is (string);
a.Input (is);
if (!is) {
 cerr << "Oops: input should be good\n"
      << a.GetName () << " " << a.GetLength() << " "
      << a.GetWidth() << endl;
}
cout << "Input test (should be Test Input 1 10.1 20.2):\n "
     << a.GetName () << " " << a.GetLength() << " "
     << a.GetWidth() << endl;

// test bad input
char stringbad[] = "\"Test Input 2\" 30 A";
istrstream isbad (stringbad);
if (a.Input (isbad).fail()) {
 cout << "bad data was correctly found\n";
}
else {
 cerr << "Oops - bad data not detected in Input function\n"
      << a.GetName () << " " << a.GetLength() << " "
      << a.GetWidth() << endl;
}

// testing Output function
cout << "\nTest Output: ";
```

```
 b.Output (cout) << endl;

 // testing OutputFormatted function
 cout << "Test OutputFormatted: ";
 b.OutputFormatted (cout) << endl << endl;

 Rectangle m (42,42, "Test name");
 m.Output (cout) << endl;

 Rectangle n (42, 42, "too long a nameeeeeeeeeeeeeeeeeee");
 n.Output (cout) << endl;

 cout << "n's truncated name is |" << n.GetName () << "|" <<endl;
 n.SetName (0);
 cout << "Should have seen null pointer for name error\n";
 n.SetName ("A new Name");
 cout << "n's new name is |" << n.GetName () << "|" << endl;


 // test file operations
 cout << "\nTest reading a file\n";
 ifstream infile ("RectangleTest.txt");
 while (a.Input (infile)) {
  a.OutputFormatted (cout) << endl;
 }
 infile.close ();
 cout << "tests done\n";

 return 0;
}
```

```
Output from the Tester Program
```

```
Default ctor (0,0): 0 0
b's overloaded ctor (should be 42.42, 84.84): 42.42 84.84

GetDimemsions: should be the same: 42.42 84.84
Rectangle c should be as b: 42.42 84.84
Rectangle d should be 1,2: 1 2

Error: a rectangle's length cannot be less than 0
Error: a rectangle's width cannot be less than 0
Error: a rectangle's length cannot be less than 0
Error: a rectangle's width cannot be less than 0
Error: a rectangle's length cannot be less than 0
Error: a rectangle's width cannot be less than 0
Error: a rectangle's length cannot be less than 0
Error: a rectangle's width cannot be less than 0

SetLen and width check (should be 4,8): 4 8
SetLen and width check (should be 9,10): 9 10

Check area (should be 90): 90
Check perimeter (should be 38): 38

```

```
Input test (should be Test Input 1 10.1 20.2):
 Test Input 1 10.1 20.2
bad data was correctly found

Test Output: "Rectangle" 42.42 84.84
Test OutputFormatted: Rectangle                [42.42, 84.84]

"Test name" 42.00 42.00
Error: name exceeds 20 characters - truncation occurred
"too long a nameeeeee" 42.00 42.00
n's truncated name is |too long a nameeeeee|
Error: a null pointer was passed for the name instead of a charac
Should have seen null pointer for name error
n's new name is |A new Name|

Test reading a file
 2
3 4
5 6
.5 .5
123    [45.00, 678.99]
tests done
```

Practical Example 2—The Interval Timer Class (Pgm01b)

Suppose that we wished to time how long some action took to execute. The C Standard Library has built-in support for timing. The function **clock** returns the number of clock cycles that have taken place since the computer was started. The returned data type is **clock_t** which is a **typedef** name for a **long**. The library also provides a constant, **CLOCKS_PER_SEC**, which, if divided into a **clock_t** value, converts it into seconds. The header files are **ctime** or **time.h**.

To construct an interval timer class, what data items are required? It should store the start and ending **clock_t** times. The class constructor can initialize these to 0 or perhaps the current time. The operational functions are **StartTiming**, **EndTiming**, and **GetInterval**. The idea is to invoke **StartTiming** to initialize the start time member. Then, do the processing we wish to time. When it is finished, invoke **EndTiming** to set the end time. And call **GetInterval** to obtain the number of seconds the process required. With these functions, one only needs to allocate a single instance of the **Timer** class in order to be able to time many events.

Here are the **Timer** class definition and implementation files. It is a very simple class but highly useful for timing things.

Timer Class Definition

```
#pragma once

#include <ctime>
using namespace std;

/***************************************************************/
/*                                                             */
/* Timer: encapsulates an elapsed time in clock cycles         */
/*                                                             */
/***************************************************************/
```

```

class Timer {

protected:
 clock_t startTime;    // the starting time of the interval
 clock_t endTime;      // the ending time of the interval

public:
 Timer();              // initializes the two times to 0

 // reset the starting time value to begin monitoring
 void StartTiming ();

 // resets the ending time value at the end of the interval
 void EndTiming ();

 // returns the measured interval in seconds
 double GetInterval () const;

};

```

Timer Class Implementation

```
#include "Timer.h"

/***************************************************************/
/*                                                             */
/* Timer: ctor that sets the two times to 0 clock cycles       */
/*                                                             */
/***************************************************************/

Timer::Timer() {
 startTime = endTime = 0;
}

/***************************************************************/
/*                                                             */
/* StartTiming: sets startTime to the current time at the      */
/*              beginning of the interval to monitor           */
/*                                                             */
/***************************************************************/

void Timer::StartTiming () {
 startTime = clock ();
}

/***************************************************************/
/*                                                             */
/* EndTiming: sets endTime to the current time at the end      */
/*            of the interval to be monitored                  */
/*                                                             */
/***************************************************************/

void Timer::EndTiming () {
```

```
 endTime = clock ();
}

/***************************************************************/
/*                                                             */
/* GetInterval: returns the interval just timed in seconds    */
/*                                                             */
/***************************************************************/

double Timer::GetInterval () const {
 return ((double) (endTime - startTime)) / CLOCKS_PER_SEC;
}
```

Next, we need something to time. I have chosen to find out just how much faster it is to use a pointer to access the elements in an array of objects than using the traditional subscript approach. The objects are rectangles. I have simply copied the **Rectangle** class definition and implementation files from **Pgm01a** into this new project folder, **Pgm01b**. No changes are required in the **Rectangle** class.

The code to time consists of setting the dimensions of 1000 **Rectangle** objects and outputting the resultant area. The first version uses subscripts to access each element in the **Rectangle** array. The second version uses a pointer to point to each successive element; to move to the next element in the array, I use **ptrThis++**.

I create a single instance of the **Timer** class and invoke the **StartTiming** method. After the subscript processing loop is finished, I call the **EndTiming** method to set the ending time and invoke **GetInterval** to acquire the total elapsed time for the loop in seconds. Then, the process is repeated for the pointer version. When that loop has finished and its interval acquired, the program then prints a short report of the results.

Here is **Pgm01b** and a sample output run that is abbreviated showing the last few lines. Are the results what you expected?

Pgm01b Timing Subscript Versus Pointer Array Access

```
#include <iostream>
#include <iomanip>
using namespace std;

#include "Timer.h"
#include "Rectangle.h"

/***************************************************************/
/*                                                             */
/* Pgm01b: measure the difference in execution speed          */
/*         between using subscript array accesses and         */
/*         using pointer array accessing methods              */
/*                                                             */
/***************************************************************/

const int MAXRECTS = 1000; // maximum number of rectangles

int main () {
 Rectangle array[MAXRECTS];
 int i;

 Timer timer;              // the single Timer object
 timer.StartTiming ();     // begin timing the subscript version

```

```
 for (i=0; i<MAXRECTS; i++) {
  array[i].SetDimensions (i, i);
  cout << array[i].GetArea() << endl;
 }

 timer.EndTiming ();        // mark the end of the subscript timing
 double subscripts = timer.GetInterval (); // get its duration

 timer.StartTiming ();      // begin timing the pointer version

 i = 0;
 Rectangle* ptrThis = array;
 Rectangle* ptrEnd = array + MAXRECTS;
 while (ptrThis < ptrEnd) {
  ptrThis->SetDimensions (i, i);
  cout << ptrThis->GetArea () << endl;
  ptrThis++;
  i++;
 }

 timer.EndTiming ();        // mark the end of the pointer timing
 double pointers = timer.GetInterval (); // get its duration

 // display a simple report of the results
 cout << endl << "Release Build Run Timings\n";
 cout << "Subscripts version total time: " << subscripts
      << " seconds\n";
 cout << "Pointers version total time:   " << pointers
      << " seconds\n";
 cout << "Elapsed time difference:       " << subscripts-pointers
      << " seconds\n";

 return 0;
}
```

Results of Timing Subscript Versus Pointer Array Access

```
...
996004
998001

Release Build Run Timings
Subscripts version total time: 3.424 seconds
Pointers version total time:   0.902 seconds
Elapsed time difference:       2.522 seconds
```

Review Questions

1. Reflecting upon member data and member functions, how do member data obviate the need for global variables or the passing a large amounts of data to a series of functions?

2. Why should most member data have the protected (or private) access qualifier?

3. How does encapsulation impact class design? What is its benefit to the programmer of a class and to the client of the class?

4. What is meant by polymorphism? Of what use is it in class function design?

5. What are the parallels in coding syntax between **struct CostRec** and **class CostRec**?

6. What is a constructor function? What is its purpose? How many constructors can a class have?

7. What is a destructor? What is its purpose? How many destructors can a class have? Why?

8. Why is the class qualifier, such as **Vehicle::**, needed in the implementation file?

9. What is the purpose of access type member functions? Give an example. Why are they needed?

10. What is the purpose of operation type member functions? Give an example.

11. Ignoring the initialization aspect, compare how a client program can create instances of a structure called **CostRec** and a class called **InventoryRec**.

12. Why is the use of default arguments useful? What problems does the use of default arguments pose when such functions are overloaded?

13. What is the difference between the two uses of the **const** key word shown below?

```
class Point {
protected:
 int x;
 int y;
public:
 Point ();
 long AvgPoints (const Point& p);
 long SumPoints () const;
};
```

14. What happens if a class has no constructor functions? What happens if it has no destructor functions?

15. What is meant by a default constructor? For a class **Dog**, write the prototype for the default ctor. Why should every class have a default ctor?

16. If the parameter names being passed to a member function are the same as member data names, how can that function access its members with the same names as the parameters?

17. Assuming **Dog** is a class, the **main()** function codes the following.

```
      Dog dogs[1000];
```

Is any ctor called? If so, how many times is the ctor called?

18. Assuming the array of dogs in question 17, is the following legal, assuming the subscripts are within range? If so, what does it do?

```
      dogs[i] = dogs[i+1];
```

19. What is the difference between a shallow copy and a deep copy operation when assigning objects?

20. Why is it preferable to always pass a reference or a constant reference to an object to a function instead of passing a copy of that object?

21. What is a constant member function? Why do some member functions need to be constant? Could not all member functions be made constant?

Stop! Do These Exercises Before Programming

1. Look over the **Pgm01a** testing program. What major feature covered in this chapter concerning the use of instances of objects did I fail to test in any way whatsoever? What about constant objects? Sketch out some additional tests and perhaps a client function call that would guarantee that **Rectangle** is properly supporting constant objects.

2. A programmer decided to encapsulate a geometric point object by writing a class called **Point**. He began with the following design. There are several design flaws with what has been actually coded thus far. Point out these flaws and show a more optimum way to code the definition.
Point.h

```
Class Point {
 int x;
 int y;
public:
 Point ();
 Point (int x, int y);

 Point GetPoint ();
 void  SetPoint (int x, int y);
 void  SetPoint (Point& p);
}
```

3. The programmer decided to add the ability to I/O a point. He added the following two member function prototypes. What is wrong with them and how should they be corrected?

```
class Point {
...
 void InputPoint (istream infile, int x, int y);
 void OutputPoint (ostream outfile, Point& p);
```

4. The programmer decided to use overloaded functions with default arguments. He added the following member prototypes. What is inherently non-optimum with these new functions as coded? Could they be repaired to be productive?

```
class Point {
...
 void SetPoint (int xx, int yy);
 void SetPoint (int xx, int yy = 0);
 void SetPoint (int xx = 0, int yy = 0);
```

5. The programmer created two tester functions to be called from the **main** function. What is non-optimum about the coding? How can it be repaired?

```
void SumPoints (Point& p, long& totalX, long& totalY,
                long& count) {
 totalX += p.x;
 totalY += p.y;
 count++;
```

```
}

Point MakePoint (int x, int y) {
 Point p (x+42, y+42);
 return p;
}
```

6. The programmer gave up on overloaded functions and wrote the following implementations. What is wrong with the coding and how can it be fixed?
Point.cpp

```
void SetPoint (int xx, int yy) {
 x = xx;
 y = yy;
}
void GetPoint (int xx, int yy) const {
 xx = x;
 yy = y;
}
```

7. Next the programmer attempted to implement the constructors but failed. How can they be corrected so that the constructors work fine?
Point.cpp

```
void Point::Point (int x, int y) {
 x = x;
 y = y;
}

void Point::Point () {
 x = y = 0;
}
```

Programming Problems

Problem Pgm01-1 —A Date Class—I

The objective is to construct a class to encapsulate a calendar date. I provide the interface that you must meet; the internal details of how you wish to support that interface are completely up to you. However, do not store the date as three integers. In future chapters, you will be asked to modify this beginning problem to add new features. Eventually, the **Date** class will be able to handle addition and subtraction of a number of days from the date and so on. If you store the data as three integers, future programs will be very hard to implement. It is highly recommended that you store the date as a long serial date; see below.

The Interface for the Date Class

The name of the class is **Date** and it is to store and manipulate a calendar date. The user creates a **Date** object as follows. (Note in the next chapter, other alternate methods of constructing a **Date** will be added.) There are no constructor or destructor functions in the class at this time.

```
Date date;
```

or

```
Date *ptrdate = new Date;
```

Provide the Following Public Member Functions

```
void SetDate (int month, int day, int year);
```

SetDate should set your internal date to the passed date. If the year is less than 100, then add 1900 to the year; thus, a year of 97 would really be 1997. (It is not "year 2000" compliant.)

```
void GetDate (int &month, int &day, int &year);
```

GetDate should return the current date you are storing converted into month, day and year filling up the three reference parameters. The year should be a 4-digit number.

```
void FormatDate (char *string, unsigned int max_string_len);
```

FormatDate fills the string with a formatted date, such as " 01/10/1997". The parameter, **max_string_len**, contains the maximum length of the caller's string including the null terminator. If the string is too small to hold the formatted date, place as much as will fit including a null terminator. The idea is to avoid overwriting memory should the user give the function too small a string to fill. There are a number of ways you can handle this. However, the easiest method is to utilize an instance of **ostrstream** wrapped around the user's string.

```
long DateToSerial (int month, int day, int year);
```

DateToSerial returns the number of days since November 25, 4713 BC.

```
void SerialToDate (int &month, int &day, int &year);
```

SerialToDate fills up the month, day and year from a long serialized date which is assumed to be a class member.

Serialized Dates

When comparing, adding a number of days to a date, and finding the number of days between two dates, it is very convenient to convert the date into a long integer number of days from some given point in time. In this case I use November 25, 4713 BC as the starting point. I am providing two C style helper functions that you may use as models for your above two member functions. You may cannibalize them as you see fit. The C functions are located in the **TestDataForAssignments Pgm01-1** folder.

Additional Requirements for the Date Class

Create two files: **Date.h** and **Date.cpp**. Cannibalize the **datehlpr.cpp** file—do not include this file nor its C style functions in your project. Rework them into your two member functions.

You may assume that all dates are correct so no error checking need be done. You may write any additional helper functions to simplify the main interface actions and to avoid repetitious coding.

Make sure you use the **const** keyword where appropriate. That is, make all parameter pointers or references that are not changed constant. Make all member functions that do not alter the object constant as well. This means the above prototypes I have given you could be changed by adding in **const** where you deem appropriate.

Write a Main Program Tester Application

Also, located in the **TestDataForAssignments Pgm01-1** folder is the testing file, **dates1.txt**. Write a main program that thoroughly tests your class. You may add additional test lines to the testing file. The **dates1.txt** file consists of one date per line in month, day and year order, separated by a blank. Assuming that you read in the date 1 2 1601, for each of these dates printout the following.

```
date          date from    date from    date to   date from
input         GetDate      FormatDate   serial    serial

 1  2 1601    01/02/1601   01/02/1601   9999999   01/02/1601
```

Note: in the date to serial column, the 99999's represent whatever that number should be.

You may add in any additional testing as you deem appropriate to thoroughly test your class. When using **cin** or an **ifstream** instance to input an integer that can have leading 0's as in 02 or 08 month numbers, one time only do

```
cin >> dec;
```

or

```
infile >> dec;
```

This tells the input stream class that the data with leading zero's are really decimal numbers. The default is leading 0's imply octal numbers.

Additionally, the date to serial column in the main program is problematical. **main()** should not have access to the protected/private data members. You may handle this in any way you see fit. You could temporarily make that data member public or provide a constant member function that just returns that long value.

Here is the C style coding to convert dates to and from the long serial date. It has been adapted from FORTRAN coding *Communications of the ACM*, Vol 11, No 10 October 1968, page 657 by Fliegl and Van Flanders.

```
/***************************************************************************/
/*                                                                         */
/* date2serial: converts a calendar date to a serial number that may be    */
/*              used in date arithmetic.                                   */
/*                                                                         */
/* Arguments:   a month, a day, and a year (in that order, all int's).     */
/*                                                                         */
/* Returns:     a long int representing the same calendar date as          */
/*              the number of days elapsed since November 25, 4713 B.C.    */
/*                                                                         */
/***************************************************************************/

long   date2serial (int mo, int day, int yr) {
 return day - 32075L + 1461L * (yr + 4800 + (mo - 14L) / 12L) / 4L
        + 367L * (mo - 2L - (mo - 14L) / 12L * 12L) / 12L
        - 3L * ((yr + 4900L + (mo - 14L) / 12L) / 100L) / 4L;
}

/***************************************************************************/
/*                                                                         */
/* serial2date:  converts a date serial number to the date's               */
/*               month, day, and year.                                     */
/*                                                                         */
/* Arguments:    a date serial number (long int) and pointers to           */
/*               month, day, and year variables (int*)                     */
/*                                                                         */
/* Results:      the month, day, and year variables are assigned           */
/*               the calendar date corresponding to the date serial number */
/*                                                                         */
/***************************************************************************/

void   serial2date (long serial, int *ptrmo, int *ptrday, int *ptryr) {
 long t1, t2, m, y;

 t1 = serial + 68569L;
 t2 = 4L * t1 / 146097L;
 t1 = t1 - (146097L * t2 + 3L) / 4L;
 y  = 4000L * (t1 + 1) / 1461001L;
 t1 = t1 - 1461L * y / 4L + 31;
 m  = 80L * t1 / 2447L;
 *ptrday = (int)(t1 - 2447L * m / 80L);
 t1 = m / 11L;
 *ptrmo = (int)(m + 2L - 12L * t1);
```

```
 *ptryr = (int)(100L * (t2 - 49L) + y + t1);
}
```

Problem Pgm01-2 —A Circle Class

Design, implement, and test a class that encapsulates a **Circle** object. It should have three data members: its radius and the integer x, y coordinates of its center. There should be a default constructor and a constructor that takes the necessary three parameters to define a circle object. Provide proper access functions for the user to retrieve and modify the three properties. **Circle** operations include obtaining the area of the circle, its circumference, and the ability to input and output a **Circle** object.

The input stream containing a **Circle** object consists of two integers for the coordinates (x, y) followed by a **double** representing the radius. The output is more formalized. It should appear as follows:

```
Circle at [xxx, yyy] of radius rrrr.rr
```

Always show two decimals in the radius.

Next, add a function, **CompareRadius**, which returns an **int** as follows.

0 means the two circles have the same radius
+ value means the member circle has a larger radius than the passed circle
– value means the member circle has a smaller radius than the passed circle

Its prototype is

```
int CompareRadius (const Circle& c) const;
```

Now write a tester program to thoroughly test the **Circle** class.

Problem Pgm01-3 —An Employee Class

Acme Corporation wishes a class to encapsulate their employee workforce. The **Employee** class contains the employee first and last name strings which should include a maximum of 10 and 20 characters respectively. The date that he or she was hired should be stored as three **short**s. His/her job title is a string of up to 20 characters. His/her age and sex should be stored as **char** fields. His/her pay rate is stored in a **double** and the pay type is a **char** containing an H or S for hourly or salaried. If he or she is an hourly worker, the pay rate is the hourly rate. If he or she is a salaried worker, the pay rate is the uniform amount that he or she is paid each week. Finally, his or her employee id number is stored as a **long**.

The class should have a default constructor and a constructor that is passed all of the relevant data needed to initialize an employee object. Provide access functions for all of the data members.

Write an **Input** function that is passed a reference to an **istream** from which to input the data. One blank separates each field on input. All strings are padded with blanks to the maximum length of that particular string. That is, if the first name was Sam, on the input it would appear as Sambbbbbbb where the b represents a blank. The order of the fields on input is as follows.

id number, first name, last name, job title, mm/dd/yyyy, age, sex, pay rate, pay type

Note that there are / separating the elements of the hired date.

Write a **Pay** function that calculates and returns the employee's weekly pay. Its prototype should be

```
double Pay () const;
```

Write a tester program to thoroughly test the class functions.

When that is working properly, then write the client Weekly Pay Program. Use the file that came with the book called **Problem1-3-WeeklyPay.txt** as the input file. The pay program inputs all of the employee records into an array of **Employee** objects. Allow for a maximum of 50 employees in the array. Then, for each employee in the array, calculate and print their pay as shown below.

```
                         Acme Weekly Payroll Report
Employee  First      Last                      Date       Weekly
   Id     Name       Name                      Hired      Pay
```

```
 1123123  John      Jones                  05/12/1994 $9999.99
...
Total Payroll ----------------------------------> $999999.99
```

The last line represents the total amount that all of the employees are paid.

Problem Pgm01-4 —A Bank Account Class

Acme First National Bank wishes a new basic **BankAccount** class to be written. The class contains a long account number, the current balance and the accumulated total fees for this month.

Provide a default constructor and one that takes the three parameters necessary to properly initialize an account. Create access functions to get and set each of the three properties. Create input and output functions to handle I/O of a bank account. On input, the account number comes first, followed by the balance and fees. On output, display the fields in the same order, but with each field 10 columns wide and separated by five blanks.

The operations member functions consist of **Deposit** and **Withdrawal**. We are ignoring any possible interest in this overly simplified problem. The **Deposit** function is passed a positive amount to be added to the current balance and it returns the new balance.

The **Withdrawal** function is more complicated; it is passed the withdrawal amount and a reference to the service charge that will be applied to the account for this transaction. The function returns **true** if the withdrawal was successful or **false** if there are insufficient funds for this transaction. The service charge is $0.10 per withdrawal as long as the balance is below $500.00. There is no service charge if the balance is $500.00 or above. If the withdrawn amount plus any service charge would take the balance below $0.00, then the withdrawal is not made; instead a service charge of $25.00 is applied to the account and the function returns false. Note that the service charges are always applied to the balance with each transaction. They are accumulated as well for later monthly display. The service charge for this transaction is stored in the passed reference variable for the client program's use.

Next, write a tester program to thoroughly test the new class.

When you are satisfied that the class is working correctly, write the client program to process a day's transactions. There are two files provided with this text. The first file, **Problem1-4-BankAccounts.txt,** contains the initial bank accounts at the start of the day. The program should load these into an array of up to 50 bank account objects. Next, the program should input the transaction's file, **Problem1-4-Transactions.txt**. Each line in the transaction's file contains a character, D for deposit or W for withdrawal. This letter is followed by the account number and then the monetary amount to be deposited or withdrawn. For each transaction, attempt to process it. Display the results in a report as shown below. When the end of the file is reached, then output a new version of the bank accounts for use in the next day's processing.

```
Account  Type Amount    Status  Service Charge
1234567   W   $ 100.00   Okay      $ 0.10
1234546   D   $  50.00   Okay      $ 0.00
1234556   W   $1000.00  Failed     $25.00
```

Problem Pgm01-5 —A Distance Class – I

Write a **Distance** class to encapsulate linear distances. You may store the distance in any format you choose. For example, you might save the distance as a **double**, the total distance in millimeters. The header file should be called **Distance.h** and the implementation file **Distance.cpp**.

Provide the Following Constructors

a default constructor with no parameters, use 0 as the distance
accept a **long** number of millimeters
accept a trio of **long**s containing meters, centimeters, and millimeters

accept a pair of **int**s containing feet first and inches second
accept a **double** representing miles

There is no destructor.

Create Public Member Functions as Follows

GetDistance returns a **double** which is the distance you are storing converted to millimeters
SetDistance which accepts a **double** millimeters – set the stored distance accordingly
MtoE which returns a **double** representing the feet that this distance represents
EtoM which is given two **int**s, feet and inches, and returns the **double** millimeters
EtoM which is given a **double** miles and returns the **double** millimeters
Paint which is given a **char** which is used to determine how to print the distance
display the distance as "Distance is nnn units\n"

```
M or m -> print in millimeters
F or f -> print in feet
I or i -> print in meters and millimeters
L or l -> print in miles
```

for example:

```
cout << "Distance is = " << mm << " millimeters\n";
```

Unless you have an alternative, use the following to convert meters to feet

```
const double MTF = 3.280833;
```

The Main Testing Program

Create a main program to thoroughly test the **Distance** class. Include at least the following tests as well as your additional ones:

```
Distance a;
Distance b (1000.);
Distance c (100L, 50L, 8L)
Distance d (10, 11);
Distance f (1.23);
a.SetDistance (1234.);
cout << "1234 mm equals " << a.MtoE () << " feet\n";
cout << "Testing GetDistance for object a - 1234 mm = "
     << a.GetDistance () << " mm\n";
```

Now use these 5 objects and thoroughly test the **Paint** function. Next, test assignment:

```
a = b;
cout << "a should now be the same as b:\n"
a.Paint ('M');
b.Paint ('M');
```

Now test passing and returning objects to functions.

```
a = fun (c);
cout << "a should now be the same as c:\n"
a.Paint ('M');
c.Paint ('M');
```

Use the following for the function.

```
Distance  fun  (const Distance &x) {
 Distance y, z;
 cout << "fun: passed value: ";
 x.Paint ('M');
 y = z = x;
 y.SetDistance (1234.);
 cout << "fun: altered value: ";
 y.Paint ('M');
 return z;
}
```

Chapter 2—Advanced Features of Classes

Introduction

When coding header files, **#ifndef-#define** or **#pragma once** logic should always be used to avoid accidental circular definitions. We must examine the impact of having a class which includes an instance of another class versus one which uses a reference or pointer to an instance of another class. Next, we must examine just how a member function can actually find the member data on which to operate.

Enumerated data types are extremely useful for adding clarity to a program. An **enum** can be physically a part of a class definition. That is, the **enum** itself may belong to a class and is called a **class enum**. In OOP programming, the use of **class enums** is widespread and becomes a very powerful feature. We will see how an ordinary C style nonmember function can be granted the ability to access a class's private member data.

Classes may have constant data members as well as static data members and reference variables to other items. However, their usage imposes some restrictions upon class initialization. A class may also have static member functions which can utilize the static data members.

We examine how short member functions can have their execution speed increased. The compiler does perform some amazing implicit type conversions when classes are involved. In the practical example, all of the new principles are put to use as an operational dice rolling set of classes are built. Finally, we explore how production libraries of operational classes can be built.

Using #ifndef-#define or #pragma once Logic in Class Header Files

When coding header files, we must guarantee that a specific definition does not get accidentally included multiple times in a given cpp file.

Consider for example, designing an **Employee** class. One of its data members would likely be a date, such as their hired date. Very often, a company already has an existing **Date** class to encapsulate a date and provide standardized support for date operations. Notice that the **Employee** class is now considered a client of the **Date** class, just like the **main** function has been the client program thus far. However, duplicate **Date** class definitions can very easily occur when **#ifndef** logic is not used. Consider the following skeletal class coding.

Date.h
```
class Date {
...
};
```
Employee.h
```
#include "Date.h"
class Employee {
...
 Date hiredDate;
...
};
```
main.cpp
```
#include "Date.h"
#include "Employee.h"
int main () {
```

```
 Date today;
 Employee employee;
...
}
```

As you can see, in **main.cpp**, two copies of the definition of the **Date** class are brought in by the compiler which results in a compile-time error. Okay, in this overly simplified example, **main** does not need to include **Date.h** because it is coming in from **Employee.h**. True. However, let's add another class to **main.cpp**, **YTDPay** (year to date pay), which encapsulates the yearly accumulated pay of the employees. This class would also have one or more **Date** instances as data members and would be also including **Date.h** in its header. Now, **main.cpp** has no way to avoid duplicate definitions when it includes **Employee.h** and **YTDPay.h**. The solution is use **#ifndef** logic around the entire class definition.

Rule: Always wrap a class definition with #ifndef logic or #pragma once to avoid any future possibility of duplicate definitions.

Thus, the above example should have been coded as follows. This method works with all compilers.

Date.h

```
#ifndef DATEH
#define DATEH
class Date {
...
};
#endif
```

Employee.h

```
#ifndef EMPLOYEEH
#define EMPLOYEEH
#include "Date.h"
class Employee {
...
 Date hiredDate;
...
};
#endif
```

main.cpp

```
#include "Date.h"
#include "Employee.h"
int main () {
 Date today;
 Employee employee;
...
}
```

Now only one copy of the **Date** class definition is included by the compiler in **main.cpp**.

The #pragma once logic is unique to Microsoft Visual Studio. Here is how it could be done using this method.

Date.h

```
#pragma once
class Date {
...
};
```

Employee.h

```
#pragma once
#include "Date.h"
class Employee {
...
```

```
 Date hiredDate;
...
};
```

main.cpp

```
#include "Date.h"
#include "Employee.h"
int main () {
 Date today;
 Employee employee;
...
}
```

The **this** Pointer

Suppose I had four instances of the **Vehicle** class from chapter 1 called, **a**, **b**, **c** and **d**. There is only one code area for each of the member function; the machine instructions of the functions are the same for every instance of the class. However, there must be four separate member data areas, one for each of the four **Vehicle** objects. It does not make sense to carry along a copy of constant code (member functions) with each object instance. Figure 2.1 shows the layout of memory for these four **Vehicle** objects.

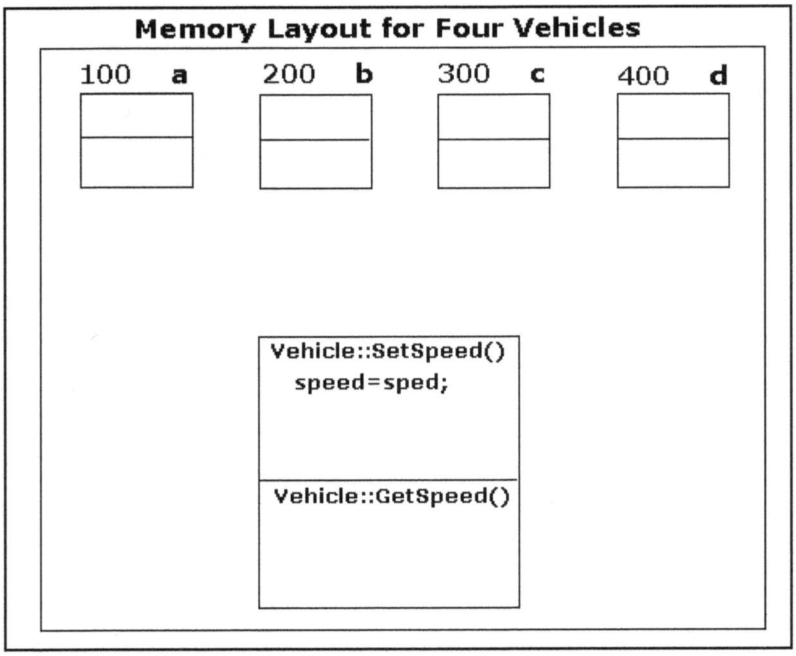

Figure 2.1 Memory Layout of Four Vehicles

Here **Vehicle a** is located at memory location 100. Its two member data, **isMoving** and **speed**, are shown. Similarly the other three vehicles are at locations 200, 300 and 400. Consider what happens when the **main** function does

```
a.SetSpeed (50);
```

How does that common code, the **SetSpeed** member function in this case, know where to find the data for object **a**—that is to set **a**'s **speed**? Without some help, it cannot know where object **a** is located and thus cannot place a new value into **a**'s **speed**!

The C++ language handles this situation by defining and passing a very special constant pointer that contains the memory location of the object in question. The pointer is called **this** and it is automatically passed to any member functions by the compiler. Actually, it is a hidden first parameter to member functions. When we code

```
a.SetSpeed (50);
```

The compiler obtains the address of **Vehicle a**, here location 100, and passes that address into the **this** parameter of the **SetSpeed** function. Our prototype for this function is

```
void SetSpeed (int sped);
```

But when the compiler compiles the class, it modifies our prototypes of member functions to include the **this** parameter. What the compiler actually creates is shown below with the additions by the compiler in bold/italics.

```
void SetSpeed (const Vehicle* this, int sped);
```

Now in the implementation of **SetSpeed**, we code

```
void Vehicle::SetSpeed (int sped) {
 speed = sped;
}
```

But the compiler alters our coding as follows.

```
void Vehicle::SetSpeed (const Vehicle* this, int sped) {
 this->speed = sped;
}
```

This clever scheme allows the compiler to automatically access the member data of any object from within member functions. In fact, the **this** parameter is also available for our use as well, when the need arises. We could also have implemented the function this way.

```
void Vehicle::SetSpeed (int sped) {
 this->speed = sped;
}
```

But why do the compiler's work for it? However, suppose that we had called the parameter **speed** instead of **sped**? We saw in the last chapter that we cannot just code

```
void Vehicle::SetSpeed (int speed) {
 speed = speed;
}
```

But now we have two ways to specify the member data **speed**. Either of the following is correct.

```
void Vehicle::SetSpeed (int speed) {
 Vehicle::speed = speed;
 this->speed = speed;
}
```

When the situation of conflicting parameters and member names occur, programmers use either one of these methods to avoid the name conflict. However, the major use of the **this** pointer occurs when we implement operator overloading.

When Classes Contain References or Pointers or Instances of Other Classes—Forward References

Classes can be interrelated and contain instances of other classes or pointers or references to other classes. With the **Employee** class, an actual **Date** instance is being used. Thus, the **Employee** header file must also include the **Date** header file so the compiler knows how to create the needed **Date** member. However, in other circumstances, only a reference or pointer to another class is used. And this brings up additional considerations.

We already have a class to encapsulate vehicles. Suppose that we also needed some kind of class to monitor the traffic flow of vehicles. Consider this additional class, **Monitor**, whose job is to track counts of moving and nonmoving vehicles.

In this example, a pointer to a **Vehicle** object is being passed to the **AddVehicle** function. In the **Monitor.h** file, the compiler must know what the identifier **Vehicle** is. True, the actual parameter is just a pointer, but the compiler still must know that **Vehicle** is a class. With pointers and references to other classes, all that is really required by the compiler is notification that this identifier is a class. This can be done by using a **forward reference** to the class. A forward reference is just the keyword class followed by the name of the class and a semicolon.

Monitor.h

```
class Vehicle; // forward reference to class that's not
               // defined at this point
class Monitor {
 protected:
  int moving;
  int stationary;

 public:
       Monitor ();
 void  AddVehicle (const Vehicle* ptrv);
};
```

On the other hand, if this **Monitor** class contained an actual instance of the **Vehicle** class, then in the **Monitor** header file, the **Vehicle** class definition must be included so that the compiler can determine how much memory must be reserved for this **Vehicle** instance within a **Monitor** instance.

When only a reference or a pointer to another class is used within another header file, a forward reference suffices. However, one could also include the actual other class header file instead of the forward reference.

In all cases, in the implementation file, the other class header file must be included. So in **Monitor.cpp**, we must include **Vehicle.h,** unless it has already been included in **Monitor.h**.

Monitor.cpp

```
#include "Monitor.h"
#include "Vehicle.h"

void Monitor::AddVehicle (const Vehicle* ptrv) {
 if (ptrv->IsMoving ()) moving++;
 else stationary++;
}
```

Notice that a forward reference in **Monitor.h** is required so that the identifier **Vehicle** is known to be a class. However, in **Monitor.cpp**, the actual **Vehicle** header file must be included so code can be created.

Now examine the **Vehicle** class once more. In the **SetSpeed** function and **Vehicle** constructors, a call to the monitor class **AddVehicle** is needed. We must add an additional parameter as follows.

Vehicle.h

```
class Monitor;  // forward reference

class Vehicle {
 protected:
  bool is_moving;
  int  speed;

 public:
       Vehicle ();
       Vehicle (bool move, int sped, Monitor* ptrm);
  bool IsMoving  () const;
  void SetMoving ();
  int  GetSpeed  () const;
  void SetSpeed  (bool, int, Monitor* ptrm);
};
```

In the **Vehicle.cpp** file, we must add an include for the **Monitor** class. Now a new problem arises.

In the **Vehicle** ctor, the **Monitor**'s **AddVehicle** function must be called passing the address of this new **Vehicle** object. How can the ctor pass the address of this object to **AddVehicle**? Remember that member functions are always passed the hidden **this** parameter which is a pointer to this object. Notice how the **this** parameter is used.

Vehicle.cpp

```
#include "Monitor.h"

Vehicle::Vehicle (bool move, int sped, Monitor *ptrm) {
 is_moving = move;
 speed = sped;
 ptrm->AddVehicle (this);
}

void Vehicle::SetSpeed (bool move, int sped, Monitor* ptrm){
 is_moving = move;
 speed = sped;
 ptrm->AddVehicle (this);
}
```

So far so good. But now we have the potential for the common C++ header file—circular class definitions problem. The compiler creates a complete class definition whenever the class is included in the cpp files. Consider the **main** function, for here is where the problem occurs; **main** must include both class headers. If only forward references were used, no problem. However, if the actual header files were used instead of a forward reference, then **main** would wind up with multiple class definitions.

```
#include "Vehicle.h"
#include "Monitor.h"

Monitor m;
Vehicle a, b, c (true, 50, &m);
a.SetSpeed (true, 50, &m);
b.SetSpeed (false, 0, &m);
```

Notice how the address of the **Monitor** class instance is passed to the **Vehicle** constructor and member function **SetSpeed**.

To be totally safe in all circumstances, always use **#ifndef/#define** or **#pragma once** logic in all class definition files. Here is a far better way to define the two classes.

Monitor.h

```
#pragma once

class Vehicle; // forward reference to class that's not
               // defined at this point
class Monitor {
 protected:
  int  moving;
  int  stationary;
public:
       Monitor ();
 void  AddVehicle (const Vehicle *);
};
```

Vehicle.h

```
#pragma once

class Monitor;  // forward reference

class Vehicle {
```

```
 protected:
  int  is_moving;
  int  speed;
 public:
       Vehicle ();
       Vehicle (int move, int sped, Monitor *ptrm);
  int  IsMoving  ();
  void SetMoving ();
  int  GetSpeed  ();
  void SetSpeed  (int, Monitor *ptrm);
};
```

In OOP programming, references are preferred to pointers wherever possible. If I had used references, the **Vehicle** class would appear as follows

```
#include "Monitor.h"

Vehicle::Vehicle (bool move, int sped, Monitor& m) {
 is_moving = move;
 speed = sped;
 m.AddVehicle (this);
}

void Vehicle::SetSpeed (bool move, int sped, Monitor& m) {
 is_moving = move;
 speed = sped;
 m.AddVehicle (this);
}
```

Further, suppose that in the **Monitor** class, I wanted a reference to the **Vehicle** instance. Monitor.cpp

```
#include "Vehicle.h"
void Monitor::AddVehicle (const Vehicle& v) {
 if (v.IsMoving ()) moving++;
 else stationary++;
}
```

Ah, now I have added an error to the **SetSpeed** function and the **Vehicle** constructor. Can you spot it?

I used the **this** parameter to pass this instance of the **Vehicle** class to **AddVehicle**. Yet the function requires a reference! I would now have to recode the **Vehicle** functions using ***this** to convert the pointer to a reference.

```
Vehicle::Vehicle (bool move, int sped, Monitor& m) {
 is_moving = move;
 speed = sped;
 m.AddVehicle (*this);
}
void Vehicle::SetSpeed (bool move, int sped, Monitor& m) {
 is_moving = move;
 speed = sped;
 m.AddVehicle (*this);
}
```

Rule: When a reference to the current object is needed, use *this.

This conversion from a pointer to a reference and vice versa is found with great frequency in OOP programming situation.

Using Class enums

Suppose that we desired to make a class to encapsulate pets for a pet store. One of the data members would have to be the pet's type, such as dog, cat, snake, hamster or mouse. While one could use **#define**s or **const int**s to create good identifiers for the pet types, we know that an **enum** is a much better approach. We could easily define **PetType** as follows.

```
enum PetType {Dog, Cat, Snake, Hamster, Mouse};
```

From a design point of view, this new **PetType** really belongs with our new **Pet** class. It does not likely make any sense if used outside of the **Pet** class and such operations. So if we just defined the **enum** as above, then there is nothing to show that it really is used in conjunction with **Pet** objects.

A **class enum** is an enumerated data type that is defined within the class definition and thus belongs to the class. As such, all uses outside the class require the class qualifier. Usually, a **class enum** has the **public** access qualifier so that it can be broadly used. Here is how the **Pet** class could be defined.

Pet.h

```
#pragma once
class Pet {
 public:
  enum PetType {Dog, Cat, Snake, Hamster, Mouse};
  enum Gender {Male, Female};
 protected:
  PetType type;
  Gender  sex;
 public:
  Pet ();
  Pet (PetType t, Gender g);
  PetType GetPetType () const;
  Gender  GetPetGender () const;
};
```

And here is how it could be implemented. Notice how the **Pet::** class qualifier is used with both the return data types and with actual **enum** values.

Pet.cpp

```
Pet::Pet () {
 type = Dog;
 sex = Female;
}

Pet::Pet (PetType t, Gender g) {
 type = t;
 sex = g;
}

Pet::PetType Pet::GetPetType () const {
 return type;
}

Pet::Gender Pet::GetPetGender () const {
 return sex;
}
```

Notice that within the **Pet** class member functions, the **Pet::** qualifier is not needed on the two class **enum** variables or values. However, when class **enums** are used as a return value, we must use the class qualifier as shown in bold face above.

Here is how a client program may use the class **enums**. Since the **enum** is **public**, it can even allocate instances of the **enum.** However, it must use the **Pet::** class qualifier for both instances of the **enums** and for the values.

```
int main () {
 Pet::PetType t = Pet::Cat;
 Pet p (Pet::Dog, Pet::Male);
 if (p.GetPetGender() == Pet::Male &&
     P.GetPetType() == Pet::Cat) {
```

Class **enums** are widely used in class designs. All of the **ios::** identifiers you have been coding are class **ios enums**! Try opening up the **ios.h** header file and there you will find all of the **ios::** identifiers you are familiar with—all are **ios** class **enums**.

Friend Functions

A friend function is not a member of the class of which it is a friend. But it is granted the rights to access private member data as if it were. Its primary use is to aid operator overloading and I/O streaming as discussed later on. It also is a means for a function to be able to access member data of several classes to be able to do its work.

For example, we could add a friend function to Vehicle, **Compare** as follows

```
class Vehicle {
 ...
 public:
 friend int Compare (const Vehicle &a, const Vehicle &b);
};
```

The keyword **friend** appears only in the class definition on the function prototype. It never is present in the actual cpp file. Here, **Compare** is not a member function, rather it is an ordinary C style function. However, because it is a friend function, it can access all **Vehicle** data and functions, independent of access qualifiers.

We could implement the **Compare** function as follows. Notice that friend functions also are located in the class implementation file along with member functions.

Vehicle.cpp

```
int Compare (const Vehicle &a, const Vehicle &b) {
 return a.speed>b.speed ? 1 : a.speed==b.speed ? 0 : -1;
}
```

We would invoke it in **main** this way.

```
if (Compare (a, b) > 0) // is vehicle a faster than b?
```

Note that inside a friend function, all references to data members and functions must be qualified by which object instance, such as **a.speed**. It is a separate function outside of the class. It is meaningless to refer to data member without a reference to a specific object. That is, this would be a compile time error: **speed**. Whose speed is being referred to?

Friend functions offer us a way to handle several situations that arise in OOP design that otherwise would have no possible solution. Frequently these occur in operator overloading as we will see in the next chapter.

In this specific case there is no real reason to make **Compare** a friend function. In fact, it is more awkward for the client programs when it is a friend function. Here is how it could have been written as a member function.

Vehicle.h

```
class Vehicle {
  . . .
 public:
  int Compare (const Vehicle &b) const;
};
```

Vehicle.cpp

```
int Vehicle::Compare (const Vehicle &b) const {
 return speed>b.speed ? 1 : speed==b.speed ? 0 : -1;
}
```

We would invoke it in **main** this way.

```
if (a.Compare (b) > 0) // is vehicle a faster than b?
```

Constant Data Members

Suppose that we wanted to encapsulate a deck of playing cards. Certainly enumerated data types would greatly aid the design and implementation. We might use the following.

```
enum Suit {Clubs, Diamonds, Hearts, Spades};
enum Rank {Ace, Deuce, Trey, Four, Five, Six, Seven, Eight,
           Nine, Ten, Jack, Queen, King};
```

If we now create a **Card** class to encapsulate a single playing card, a new problem in design arises. Suppose that this card is created to be the **Ace** of **Spades**. That is, the class contains an instance of both **Suit** and **Rank**. Once created, this card instance cannot ever be changed. It cannot suddenly become the **King** of **Hearts**. Such is otherwise known as "cheating." Once a card instance has been created or initialized, its **Suit** and **Rank** data members can never be changed. These are called **constant data members**.

A class may desire certain data members to be constant. Once these items have their initial values, they can never be changed. To indicate that a class data member is to be held constant, simply prefix the data definition with the const **keyword**. Here is how the **Card** class can be partially defined.

Card.h

```
#pragma once
class Card {
public:
 enum Suit {Clubs, Diamonds, Hearts, Spades};
 enum Rank {Ace, Deuce, Trey, Four, Five, Six, Seven, Eight,
           Nine, Ten, Jack, Queen, King};

protected:
 const Suit suit;
 const Rank rank;

public:
 Card (Suit s, Rank r);
...
};
```

When we try to implement the class, a new problem arises. Consider this attempt to implement the constructor. It fails utterly.

Card.cpp

```
#include "Card.h"
Card::Card (Suit s, Rank r) {
 suit = s;
 rank = r;
}
```

Rule: Upon block entry of the constructor, all constant data members must already have their values.

When the compiler reaches the begin brace of the ctor for **Card**, the **suit** and **rank** constant members must already have their values. They cannot ever be assigned their values within the block of coding. This leaves only one single location at which constant data members can be assigned their values. Recall the scope of parameter variables and when they come into existence. Their scope is from their point of definition within the function header to the end of the defining block of coding, the end of the function. Parameter variables are given their values as the function is called and before reaching that actual function body. Thus, parameter variables can be utilized after the parameter list and before the begin brace of the function body. This is shown at "x" marks the spot below.

```
Card::Card (Suit s, Rank r) x {
```

C++ allows a new style of initialization not only for class instances but also for all of the intrinsic built-in data types. The initialization parallels that of constructor invocation. The following are legal.

```
int x (0);      // define x and initialize it to 0
double z (42); // define a double z and set it too 42
```

This new form produces identical and is interchangeable with the following with which you are familiar.

```
int x = 0;
double z = 42;
```

If **main** was creating the Ace of Spades, we have as expected the following.

```
Card ace (Card::Spades, Card::Ace);
```

How does this help us in providing the proper initialization of the constant data members?

C++ provides the base class and member initialization list mechanism. After the parameter list and before the begin brace of the function body (at point "x" in the above example), code a single colon. This says here comes the base class and member initialization list. Base class initialization refers to derived classes and inheritance and is covered in a later chapter. Here we are after member initialization. We must use the new form of initialization. Separate each member initialization with a comma. Here is how we must code the Card constructor. It is the only way to initialize constant data members.

```
Card::Card (Suit s, Rank r) : suit (s), rank (r) {}
```

Notice that now there is nothing left in the actual function body.

This member initialization list can be used for any data member's initialization, not just constant members.

Rule: All constant data members must be initialized in the constructor function by using the base class and member data initialization mechanism.

Consider the **Rectangle** class from the last chapter. The default ctor could have been coded this way.

```
Rectangle::Rectangle () : length(0), width(0) { }
```

Likewise, the **Timer** class ctor could have been written this way.

```
Timer::Timer() : startTime(0), endTime (0) { }
```

The ctor for a **Point** could be done this way.

```
Point::Point (int xx, int yy) : x (xx), y (yy) { }
```

Certainly, this base class and member initialization mechanism can shorten the normal coding for constructor functions besides providing the only method for initializing constant data members.

The Copy Constructor and How to Forbid Certain Operations

There is one very special constructor function. It is called the copy constructor. As its name implies, it is used by the compiler to create copies of an object.

Rule: The copy constructor is a constructor that is passed a constant reference to this same class.

The copy constructor for the **Card** class would be given by the following.

```
Card (const Card& c);
```

The copy ctor for a **Rectangle** class is

```
Rectangle (const Rectangle& r);
```

The copy ctor for a **Point** class is
```
Point (const Point& p);
```
The copy ctor for the **Timer** class is
```
Timer (const Timer& t);
```
When does the compiler call the copy constructor? It is called whenever the compiler must make a duplicate copy of an instance. Here are the possibilities.
```
Point Fun(Point w);// makes a parameter and return copies
Point p;           // default ctor
Point q (p);       // copy ctor
Point r = p;       // copy ctor not the assignment operator
Point e;           // default ctor
e = p;             // the assignment operator, not copy ctor
Point s = Fun (p); // copy p into parameter w
                   // then copy the returned value into s
Point Fun (Point w) {
  Point t;
  return t;        // copy t as the return value
}
```
In general, just as a class should always define a default constructor, it should also define a copy constructor. In fact, a copy constructor is mandatory when the class has dynamic memory allocation of member data. This is examined in detail in the next chapter.

How is the copy constructor implemented? It only has to copy the passed object's data. Here is the implementation for the **Point** copy constructor.
```
Point::Point (const Point& p) {
 x = p.x;
 y = p.y;
}
```
Alternatively, it could be implemented this way using the base class and member initialization method.
```
Point::Point (const Point& p): x(p.x), y(p.y) { }
```
It is a lot shorter this way.

For the **Circle** class, the copy constructor can be implemented this way.
```
Circle::Circle (const Circle& c) {
 radius = c.radius;
 origin = c.origin;
}
```
Or it may be done this way.
```
Circle::Circle  (const  Circle&  c)  :
radius(c.radius),origin(c.origin){}
```
Now, what has all this to do with our **Card** class? Ah, let's examine some **main** function coding.
```
#include "Card.h"
int main () {
 Card ace (Card::Hearts, Card::Ace);
 Card anotherAce (ace);
 Card moreAce = ace;
 Card whatIsIt;
```
At this point, we now have three aces of hearts! Oops. Cheating again. With a deck of cards, a single card must not be allowed to be duplicated. How can we prevent this from happening?

When you wish to prevent a specific function from being called by the client programs or the compiler, simply make it a protected or private function. The compiler cannot call protected or private constructor functions. We can protect against accidental copying of a card by defining a private copy constructor.

Card.h
```
#pragma once
class Card {
```

```
public:
 enum Suit {Clubs, Diamonds, Hearts, Spades};
 enum Rank {Ace, Deuce, Trey, Four, Five, Six, Seven, Eight,
            Nine, Ten, Jack, Queen, King};
protected:
 const Suit suit;
 const Rank rank;

public:
 Card (Suit s, Rank r);

private:
 Card (const Card& c);
 Card ();
...
};
```

Notice that I also took care of another illegal detail, the creation of a card with no rank or suit defined. In the **main** function above, the last instance called **whatIsIt** should also not be allowed, for it would have no suit or rank specified. There cannot be a "default" card when creating a deck of cards. Thus, I made that ctor also private.

When a function has been made private or protected and the client or the compiler (in the case of the constructors) attempts to invoke it, the compiler generates an error message stating that "cannot call a protected or private function." Here is an implementation of the **Card** copy ctor function that cannot be called because its access is private.

```
Card::Card (const Card& c) : suit(c.suit), rank(c.rank) {
 cerr << "Error cannot call the copy constructor\n";
}
```

Reference Variables as Data Members

A class can also have **reference variables** as data members. To see why we might need reference variables as class members, let's continue developing the playing card example. The next step is to create the actual deck of cards class.

Class **Deck** contains the number of cards in the deck along with an array of the remaining cards in the deck. Exactly how the cards are created and stored and used is very specific to the intended use. Here, I just want to illustrate some basic actions. Thus, I store the cards in an array of Card pointers so that I can individually dynamically allocate and initialize each card.

```
Deck.h
#pragma once
class Card;    // forward reference to the Card class

class Deck {
protected:
 Card* *cards; // going to be single dim array of pointers to the
               // card objects
 int    numcards;

public:
 Deck (int number_of_cards = 52);
 ~Deck ();

private:
 Deck (const Deck& d); // do not permit duplicate decks
```

```
};
```

Notice that I have provided a default of 52 cards in the deck since this is very often the correct number. I have disallowed making duplicate decks by making the copy constructor private. Obviously the next step is to add some action functions to the deck class, such as deal cards and so on. However, here is what I have for the basic implementation. Notice, a much better method for card creation should be devised, since the method I use here is really only satisfactory for a 52-card deck.

Deck.cpp

```
#include <iostream>
#include "Deck.h"
#include "Card.h"
using namespace std;

Deck::Deck (int number_of_cards) {
 numcards = number_of_cards;
 if (numcards <= 0) {
  cerr << "Error in Deck: you cannot create an empty deck\n";
  cards = 0;
  ret;
 }
 cards = new Card* [numcards];
 int i = 0;
 for (int j=0; j<4 && i<numcards; j++) {
  for (int k=0; k<13 && i<numcards; k++) {
   cards[i] = new Card ((Card::Suit)j, (Card::Rank)k);
   i++;
  }
 }
}

Deck::~Deck () {
 if (!cards) return;
 for (int i=0; i<numcards; i++) {
  delete cards[i];
 }
 delete [] cards;
}
Deck::Deck (const Deck& d) {
 cards = 0;
 numcards = 0;
}
```

Finally we need a **Player** class. However, the **main** function will create the one and only actual **Deck** instance. Each **Player** instance should have a reference to this single deck. So here is the start of the **Player** class.

```
#pragma once
class Deck;      // forward reference to the Deck

class Player {
protected:
 Deck& thisdeck;

public:
 Player (Deck& deck);
};
```

So here is an example of a class that has a reference variable as member data. How can the constructor be implemented?

Rule: Upon block entry of the constructor, all reference data members must already have their values.

Rule: All reference data members must be initialized in the constructor function by using the base class and member data initialization mechanism.

Here is the **only** way that the constructor can be implemented.

Player.cpp
```
#include "Player.h"
#include "Deck.h"
Player::Player (Deck &deck) : thisdeck (deck) {}
```
Finally, to tie these three classes together, here is a simple **main** function that creates the single deck and allocates some players. This shell coding can be found in the sample programs under the **Pgm02Cards** folder.

Main.cpp
```
#include <iostream>
#include "Card.h"
#include "Deck.h"
#include "Player.h"
using namespace std;
int main () {
 Deck thedeck;
 Player player1 (thedeck);
 Player player2 (thedeck);
 Player player3 (thedeck);

 return 0;
}
```

Static Data Members and Static Member Functions

Static Member Data

A **static member variable** belongs to the entire class. It acts as if it were a global variable to this entire class. Only **one** instance of the static member exists and it is independent of whether or not any actual instances of the class have ever been or are or ever will be allocated. They are often used as a "reference count" tracking the number of class instances that are currently allocated.

But why do we need static data members? Consider the design of a **Circle** class to encapsulate a circle object. As soon as we begin to add operational functions, such as **GetArea** or **GetCircumference**, we need **PI**. So we might code the following for the **Circle** class.

Circle.h
```
#pragma once
class Circle {
protected:
 double radius;
 const double PI;
public:
 Circle (double rad = 0);
 double GetArea () const;
 double GetCircumference () const;
};
```
Notice that I made **PI** be a constant member. Then, we proceed to implement the **Circle** as follows.

Circle.cpp
```
#include <math.h> // for acos() function for PI
#include "Circle.h"

Circle::Circle (double rad) : PI(acos(-1.)), radius(rad) {}

double Circle::GetArea () const {
 return PI * radius * radius;
}

double Circle::GetCircumference () const {
 return 2 * PI * radius;
}
```

I cleverly initialized **PI** to the most accurate value of **PI** that can fit in a **double**. Geometrically, the arc cosine of –1 is, by definition, **PI.** All works fine, until you think about memory requirements. Suppose that the drawing program allocates 1,000 **Circle** objects. How many **PI** instances are created? 1,000! That is 999 PI's too many! We only need a single **PI** to service all of these instances. Now one could insert a global constant in the **Circle.cpp** file this way.

Circle.cpp
```
#include <math.h> // for acos() function for PI
#include "Circle.h"

const double PI = acos (-1.); // a global PI

Circle::Circle (double rad) : radius(rad) {}
...
```

However, when we define global items, we run the risk of collision with other globals defined in other cpp files. A way around this is to use the **static** keyword on the global item. A **static global item** is global in scope within this cpp file. It is not known beyond this cpp file. So a somewhat better approach is this way.

Circle.cpp
```
#include <math.h> // for acos() function for PI
#include "Circle.h"

const static double PI = acos (-1.); // a PI for this cpp file

Circle::Circle (double rad) : radius(rad) {}
...
```

But a class can have a **static data member**. So here is a far better OOP way of handling **PI.**

Circle.h
```
#pragma once
class Circle {
protected:
 double radius;
 const static double PI;
public:
 Circle (double rad = 0);
...
```

When new instances of the class that contains the static data members are allocated, no additional instances of the static members are created. In fact, the compiler, at compile time, allocates and initializes the static data members. However, since the compiler must reserve space for the static variables in the program, they must appear in the cpp file. Hence, we must include the definitions there as well. Although it looks like we are redefining **PI**, we are not: we are just providing a place holder for the compiler and perhaps to initialize it as well. But we must use the class qualifier so the compiler recognizes this as the same

variable that is defined in the class definition
Circle.cpp

```
#include <math.h> // for acos() function for PI
#include "Circle.h"

const double Circle::PI = acos (-1.); // a static PI member

Circle::Circle (double rad) : radius(rad) {}
...
```

Reference counting is another example of static data members. Suppose that a class needs to know how many instances of that class are in existence at any point. A static counter can be added as a data member. It is incremented in the constructor functions and decremented in the destructor.

tally.h

```
class Tally {
protected:
static int count;
public:
  Tally ();
 ~Tally ();
};
```

tally.cpp

```
int Tally::count = 0;  // initialize count

Tally::Tally () {
 count++;
}

Tally::~Tally () {
 count--;
}
```

Static Member Functions

Static member functions operate similarly. Only **one** instance of the function exists and it can operate on **no** class instance! That is, it applies to the entire class independent of whether or not any objects of the class are yet allocated. It has no **this** parameter, hence no instance data. It is often used for global class initializations. What static functions can operate on are static member data.

Static member data and functions provide the OOP way to handle having some data available application-wide.

For example, suppose our application needed access to the running full path location of several folders so that it could automatically save report files in the **\Reports** folder, update some accounting files located in the **\Accounts** folder, and file some notices in the **\Pending** folder. These folders are assumed to be located beneath the folder wherever the user has installed our program and we do not have control over where the user has installed us. Assume that the user installed our application to the **\SuperApp** folder located on **D:** drive under the folder **\Program Files**. It would be very convenient if one time only, our application constructed these paths and had them readily available for all the functions that needed to use them. This is an ideal application for a special **SysInfo** class which contains only static data members and static member functions.

We can define the **SysInfo** class this way.

```
SysInfo Class Definition
```

```
#pragma once
#include <iostream>
using namespace std;

class SysInfo {
public:
 static char reports[_MAX_FNAME];
 static char accounts[_MAX_FNAME];
 static char notices[_MAX_FNAME];

 static bool InitSysInfo (const char* exePath);
};
```

Notice that the class has no instance data, only static data. It does not even have a constructor, however, the compiler will supply one for us that does nothing. No function is ever going to allocate any instances of this class. Instead, all of our program functions are just going to use the data. The purpose of the single static member function, **InitSysInfo** is to initially construct these three paths for us. The define **_MAX_FNAME** contains the maximum length a path can be on the platform for which you are compiling. For a Win32 platform, this is 256 bytes. I made the three strings public so that the users could have direct access to them. If you wish additional protection, then make them protected and provide three static access functions, such as **GetReportPath**.

SysInfo.cpp

```
char SysInfo::reports[_MAX_FNAME];
char SysInfo::accounts[_MAX_FNAME];
char SysInfo::notices[_MAX_FNAME];

bool SysInfo::InitSysInfo (const char* exePath) {
 ...
}
```

The real question is how can we actually implement **InitSysInfo**? Recall that the first string that is passed to the **main** function always contains the full drive and path and filename of the program itself. Thus, if we remove the program name and exe extension, we have the installed path of our application. We only need to append the three subfolders. Thus, one time only in **main** before our application really begins its work, we need to invoke **InitSysInfo** to fill up these three strings.

Main Function to Test SysInfo Class

```
#include <iostream.h>

#include "SysInfo.h"

void Tester ();

int main (int argc, char* argv[]) {

 // initialize the three application path strings
 if (!SysInfo::InitSysInfo (argv[0])) {
    cerr << "Initialization failure:\n"
       << "Unable to create needed report subfolders\n";
  return 1;
 }

 // go write a sample test file
 Tester ();
```

```
 return 0;
}
```

Now any function anywhere within the entire application can have direct access to the paths simply by including the **SysInfo.h** header file! Here is the **Tester** function that writes a test file. The concatenation assumes that the **reports SysInfo** string ends with a backslash.

```
Tester Function
```

```
#include <fstream>
#include <string>
using namespace std;

#include "SysInfo.h"

void Tester () {
 char file[_MAX_FNAME];

 // construct the file name
 strcpy_s (file, sizeof(file), SysInfo::reports);
 strcat_s (file, "TestFile.txt");

 // attempt to open the output file
 ofstream outfile (file);
 if (!outfile) {
  cerr << "Error - unable to open test file: "
       << file << endl;
  return;
 }

 // write a test message
 outfile << "This is a test message.\n";
 outfile.close ();
}
```

The only really remaining question is how to actually implement the **InitSysInfo** function. A C library function, **_splitpath_s** takes a fully qualified path with filename and extension and splits it into four strings: the drive string, the path, the filename and the extension. Once that is done, we merely have to rejoin the drive and path strings to obtain the full path to the folder in which our application executable is installed. We can then append the three various subfolders that the application requires to this full path.

Another C library function, **_mkdir**, makes a directory. It is passed the character string containing the full path to make. If it is not successful, it returns a –1. One reason it could fail is that the folder already exists. The function automatically sets a global error field, **errno**, if it fails. If we test **errno** for the value **EEXIST**, we can rule out that the folder already exists. Here is the complete **SysInfo** implementation.

```
SysInfo Class Implementation
```

```
#include <iostream>
using namespace std;
#include <io.h>
#include <string>
#include <direct.h>
```

```
#include <errno.h>

#include "SysInfo.h"

char SysInfo::reports[_MAX_FNAME];
char SysInfo::accounts[_MAX_FNAME];
char SysInfo::notices[_MAX_FNAME];

/***************************************************************/
/*                                                             */
/* InitSysInfo: build the three application subfolders         */
/*              beneath the exe folder, if not already there   */
/*                                                             */
/***************************************************************/

bool SysInfo::InitSysInfo (const char* exePath) {

 char drive[_MAX_DRIVE];
 char dir [_MAX_DIR];
 char file[_MAX_FNAME];
 char ext[_MAX_EXT];

 // split the exe path into its parts - pitch the file.exe parts
 _splitpath_s (exePath, drive, sizeof(drive), dir, sizeof(dir),
               file, sizeof(file), ext, sizeof(ext));
 // form up the drive and path parts
 strcpy_s (file, sizeof(file), drive);
 strcat_s (file, sizeof(file), dir);

 // copy to each of the needed folder strings and append the
 // appropriate subfolder name
 strcpy_s (reports, sizeof(reports), file);
 strcat_s (reports, sizeof(reports),"Reports");
 strcpy_s (accounts,sizeof(accounts), file);
 strcat_s (accounts,sizeof(accounts), "Accounts");
 strcpy_s (notices, sizeof(notices), file);
 strcat_s (notices,sizeof(notices), "Pending");

 // attempt to make the reports folder
 if (_mkdir (reports) == -1) { // was there an error?
  if (errno == EEXIST); // folder already there? yes do nothing
  else {                // no, so display error message
   cerr << "Error: The desired folder cannot be created\n";
   cerr << "The path was: " << reports << endl;
   return false;
  }
 }

 // attempt to make the accounts folder
 if (_mkdir (accounts) == -1) { // was there an error?
  if (errno == EEXIST); // folder already there? yes do nothing
  else {                // no, so display error message
   cerr << "Error: The desired folder cannot be created\n";
   cerr << "The path was: " << accounts << endl;
   return false;
  }
```

```
 }

 // attempt to make the notices Pending folder
 if (_mkdir (notices) == -1) { // was there an error?
  if (errno == EEXIST); // folder already there? yes do nothing
  else {                // no, so display error message
   cerr << "Error: The desired folder cannot be created\n";
   cerr << "The path was: " << notices << endl;
   return false;
  }
 }

 // for later convenience, append the trailing backslash
 strcat_s (reports, sizeof(reports), "\\");
 strcat_s (accounts, sizeof(accounts), "\\");
 strcat_s (notices, sizeof(notices), "\\");

 return true;
}
```

In the right circumstances, static data and static functions are quite handy. They obviate the need for anything global/external in your OOP programming!

Inline Functions

An **inline** function is a function for which the compiler actually substitutes the function body in the calling program and does not actually create a function of that name in the resulting program. In other words, the compiler bypasses all of the function calling overhead by placing what would have been the function's body directly in the client's code at the point the function would have been invoked. The idea is to speed up the client program by reducing the function calling overhead of that function. However, please use caution with inline functions. In the client program, wherever that inline function is used, the compiler places another copy of the function body. Thus, if the client calls an inline function from 100 locations, then there are 100 copies of that function's body in the client program. Its exe size has grown but it runs faster.

Inlining should only be used on very short functions, such as constructors. Inlining is only a request of the compiler. If the compiler feels it is not worth it or is too complex a body to inline, it will not inline that function.

A function can be inlined in one of two ways. One is to code its body right there in the header file. In the industry, this **automatic inlining** is frowned upon because the clients of the class are going to have a copy of the header file. Thus, part of the actual class implementation is visible to the customers of the class. Inlining by coding the body directly in the header file is found in short magazine articles, academic areas and book examples. It is not done in the real world of production.

Circle.h

```
#pragma once
class Circle {
protected:
 double radius;
 const static double PI;
public:
 Circle (double rad = 0) : radius(rad) {}
...
```

Circle.cpp

```
#include <math.h> // for acos() function for PI
#include "Circle.h"
```

```
const double Circle::PI = acos (-1.); // a static PI member
...
```

The preferred, second method of inlining still has the function coded in an inl file which is included after the class definition. We use the **inline** identifier on the function prototype in the class definition file. Here is an example of how inlining can be requested in a header file. Notice the use of the **inline** identifier.

Circle.h

```
#pragma once
class Circle {
protected:
 double radius;
 const static double PI;
public:
 inline Circle (double rad = 0);
...
};
#include "Circle.inl"
```

Circle.inl

```
Circle::Circle (double rad) : radius(rad) {}
...
```

Circle.cpp

```
#include <math.h> // for acos() function for PI
#include "Circle.h"

const double Circle::PI = acos (-1.); // a static PI member
...
```

Note that the **inline** keyword is not found in the implementation file. The actual coding is found in the .inl (inline) file which is included after the class definition in the Circle.h file.

If you want to use inline functions, first get the entire class fully operational and error free. Then simply add the **inline** keyword before the function prototypes that you wish to inline (in the header file). However, when debugging, one cannot step into inline functions to examine things. There is no function there to step into! Thus, debugging inline functions is best done before they are actually inlined.

Implicit Type Conversions

The compiler does implicit type conversions fully utilizing all of your class member functions in an attempt to build the client program. To see just how this works, let's examine a **Circle** class once again, adding a **Compare** function. To keep the illustration short, I have automatically inlined all functions.

Circle.h

```
class Circle {
protected:
 double radius;
public:
 Circle() : radius (0) {}
 Circle (const circle& c) : radius(c.radius) {}
 Circle (double rad) : radius (rad) {}
 bool Compare (const Circle& c) {return radius == c.radius;}
};
```

Here is a client program.

Main.cpp

```
#include "Circle.h"
int main () {
 Circle a, b (42.0), c (b); // uses all three ctors
 if (a.Compare (b))
```

```
   cout << "Circle a equals circle b\n";
  if (b.Compare (42.0))
   cout << "Circle b has a radius of 42.\n";
  return 0;
}
```

The first invocation of the **Compare** function calls our member function passing a constant reference to **Circle b**. But what about the second call to **Compare**? The parameter is a double. We have not written a **Compare** function with the necessary prototype.

```
bool Compare (double r);
```

Nevertheless, this not only compiles fine, but also executes properly outputting the fact that **Circle b** does have a radius of 42! How can this be?

The compiler first examines our **Circle** class looking for a **Compare** function that takes a double. It does not find one. Then, it sees that if it somehow had another **Circle** object, there is a **Compare** function it could call. So the compiler now asks is there any way to turn a **double** into a **Circle** object? Yes, there is a constructor function that is passed a single **double** parameter. The compiler then constructs a temporary **Circle** object, calls the **double** ctor function to initialize it, calls the **Compare** function passing a reference to this temporary **Circle** object, calls the **Circle** destructor for this temporary **Circle** object, and finally deletes the memory occupied by the temporary **Circle** object. This is what is meant by implicit type conversion. It is a very powerful capability of OOP compilers.

Summary of Constructor and Destructor Functions

A constructor (ctor) is a special nonstatic member function whose purpose is to initialize this instance's member variables.

1. It is automatically called by the compiler whenever an instance of the class comes into existence, whether it is on the stack (automatic or parameter), in the data segment (static or global), on the heap (dynamically allocated with **new**), or contained inside another class.
2. It is not invoked when the compiler is creating a pointer or a reference to an instance; these are memory addresses, not instances that the compiler is creating.

3. It must be the same name as the class.
4. It can have no return value, not even **void**.
5. It cannot be static or constant.
6. It may be public, protected or private. The compiler can only call public ctors.
7. If there is no constructor for a class, the compiler makes a default one which does nothing but issue a return instruction.
8. It can be overloaded and very often is overloaded.
9. The default constructor is one that has no parameters.
10. The copy constructor is one that is passed only a constant reference to another instance of the same class.
11. It is never called directly by programs.

The destructor (dtor) is a special member function that is called by the compiler whenever an instance of a class goes out of existence. Its purpose is to provide clean up actions, such as deleting dynamically allocated memory.

1. It is a function with the same name as the class but with a ~ prefix.
2. It can have no return value, not even **void**.
3. It cannot be static or constant.
4. It cannot be overloaded.
5. It cannot have any parameters.
6. It must have public access. A destructor cannot be protected or private.

7. If a class has no destructor, the compiler supplies one; it only issues a return instruction.
8. If a function aborts the program by calling exit (1); only global objects' dtors are called.

Practical Example 1—Dice and Die Rolling

Many games involve the rolling of one or more dice. Imagine that you hold a group of dice of various number of sides in your hand. You shake them and roll them. Each time you roll the dice, you get a "random" set of results. This is what we wish to simulate with a series of classes.

The starting point is the generation of random numbers. The C library has two functions to assist us in creation of random numbers: **rand** and **srand**. Each time **rand** is called, it returns a random integer. Well, the value is not really random. It begins with a seed integer and generates a pseudo random sequence of integers from that seed value. Given the same seed, **rend** produces the same sequence of random numbers. **srand** is used to provide the initial seed value. For debugging, it is helpful if the same sequence of numbers is generated. However, from a game playability point of view, we need to generate very different sequences of numbers each time the application starts. This is commonly done by using the current time as the seed value.

```
srand ((unsigned) time (0));
```

The **Random** class is very simple. It has a constructor that initializes the seed value and a **GetRandom** function to obtain a die roll for a die. The number must be between 1 and the passed number of sides of the die.

Random Class Definition

```
#pragma once
/***************************************************************/
/*                                                             */
/* Random: obtain a random number between 1 and the number of  */
/*         die sides passed                                    */
/*                                                             */
/***************************************************************/

class Random {

public:
       // seeds the random number generator with current time
       Random ();

       // for debugging, seed with a specific repeatable sequence
       Random (unsigned int x);

          // gets a random number between 1 and num_sides
 unsigned GetRandom (int num_sides) const;

};
```

The **Random** class implementation is also very simple.

Random Class Implementation

```
#include <ctime>
#include <iostream> // for the random number functions
using namespace std;
#include "Random.h"
```

```

/***************************************************************/
/*                                                             */
/* Random: initialize the random number generator              */
/*         using the current time as the seed value            */
/*                                                             */
/***************************************************************/

         Random::Random () {
 srand ((unsigned) time (0)); // use the current time as the seed
}

/***************************************************************/
/*                                                             */
/* Random: for debugging, use the passed seed value            */
/*                                                             */
/***************************************************************/

         Random::Random (unsigned int x) {
 srand (x); // use the passed repeatable seed value
}

/***************************************************************/
/*                                                             */
/* GetRandom: obtain a random number between 1 and numsides    */
/*                                                             */
/***************************************************************/

unsigned  Random::GetRandom (int num_sides) const {
 return (rand () % num_sides) + 1;
}
```

Next, we must encapsulate a **Die** object. A die has a fixed number of sides. Once the number of sides is known, that die cannot ever change its number of sides. So the number of sides should be a constant. Further, the minimum number of sides is 4, but 6-sided dice are more commonly found. The two instance data members are the constant number of sides and the current die roll of the die. In order to actually roll the die, an instance of the Random class is needed. But notice only a single instance of the **Random** class is needed to service all instances of the die class. Hence, the instance of **Random** is a static data member.

```
Die Class Definition
```

```
#pragma once
#include "Random.h"

/***************************************************************/
/*                                                             */
/* Die: encapsulates the behavior of one die-sides must be >=4 */
/*                                                             */
/* Toss gets the next die roll and saves it in current_roll    */
/*                                                             */
/* If the number of sides is not specified, 6 is used.         */
/*                                                             */
/* It has only 1 copy of the Random number generator object    */
/*                                                             */
/***************************************************************/
```

```

class Die {

public:
 static const int DefaultNumSides; // = 6 used if not given
 static const int MinimumNumSides; // = 4 the smallest allowed

 static Random random; // one copy of the actual number generator
                       // to service all dice roll requests

 const int numberSides;      // number of sides for this die
       int currentRoll;      // the current die roll value

public:
       // construct a die, default to 6 sides
       Die (int sides = DefaultNumSides);

       // throw the die, save result in currentRoll
Die&   Toss (); // allows for chaining of events

       // returns value last rolled
int    GetRollValue () const;

       // returns the number of sides of this die
int    GetNumberSides () const;
};
```

In the **Die** implementation, notice how the constant **static** members are coded and given their values of 4 and 6 respectively. Also notice how the constant instance member, **number_sides**, is initialized in the constructor.

Die Class Implementation

```
#include "die.h"

/***************************************************************/
/*                                                             */
/* Die Class: simulates the action of rolling a die of sides>=4*/
/*                                                             */
/***************************************************************/

// all static data members must be defined in the cpp file
// so the compiler can create space for them in the exe file
// we can initialize them here

const int  Die::DefaultNumSides = 6; // used if number not given
const int  Die::MinimumNumSides = 4; // min allowed number sides
   Random  Die::random;        // one copy of the number generator


/***************************************************************/
/*                                                             */
/* Die: construct a die with a given number of sides           */
/*      must be 4 or more                                      */
/*                                                             */
```

```
/***************************************************************/

Die::Die (int sides) : numberSides (sides < MinimumNumSides ?
                       DefaultNumSides : sides) {
 // constant data members must be initialized PRIOR to ctor block
 // entry - do a preparatory die roll - not really needed, but it
 // ensures that currentRoll also has a value
 Toss ();
}

/***************************************************************/
/*                                                             */
/* Toss: emulates the effect of rolling the die                */
/*       result is in currentRoll                              */
/*                                                             */
/***************************************************************/

Die&      Die::Toss () {
 currentRoll = random.GetRandom (numberSides);
 return *this; // permits chaining Die events by the user
}

/***************************************************************/
/*                                                             */
/* GetRollValue: returns the current die roll value            */
/*                                                             */
/***************************************************************/

int       Die::GetRollValue () const {
 return currentRoll;
}

/***************************************************************/
/*                                                             */
/* GetNumberSides: returns the number of sides of this die     */
/*                                                             */
/***************************************************************/

int    Die::GetNumberSides () const {
 return numberSides;

```

Now we can define a **Dice** class to encapsulate a bunch of dice. The Dice class needs to store how many die objects it holds and an array of the Die objects. It is much simpler if we dynamically allocate the array and store Die pointers instead of Die objects in the array. Hence the data member is

```
Die* *dieArray; // an array of pointers to the Die objects
```

Further, the collection of dice may not all have the same number of sides. The easy way to handle this is to let the constructor just set the array to NULL or 0. A member function, **AddDie()**, is then called by the client to add in a number of dice of the same number of sides. In AddDie(), we just grow the array by allocating a new array as big as it needs to be, copying the pointers of the previously added die objects into this larger array, and then allocating and adding in the new requested Die objects. This will give us a production version of these classes, one that you can use in your games.

For operations, we can provide several methods of obtaining the results. After a **Roll()** is finished, **GetTotal()** returns the sum of all the individual die values. Often this is all that is required. However, the **Display()** function makes a nice printout such as 1 + 3 + 5 = 9 for the user to clearly see what the roll produced. In other situations, the caller may desire to have an array of integers filled with the actual numerical value of each **Die**. **GetDieValues()** does this. To avoid overwriting memory should the passed user array of integers to be filled be too small to hold all of the values, the user must specify the maximum array bounds of the array they pass.

Additionally, we can provide a function to return the number of Die in the array and another to return the number of sides of each die, should the client need such. Finally, once this set of dice has been created, it would be illegal to make duplicates of it; that's called cheating. Hence, we can make the copy constructor private along with the assignment operator. However, although we have not yet discussed this function, the assignment function, I have included it here on line 22 so that the class is complete as it stands. You may take this function prototype on faith for a short while.

Dice Class Definition

```
 1 #pragma once
 2 #include <iostream>
 3 using namespace std;
 4 #include "Die.h"
 5
 6 /***************************************************************/
 7 /*                                                             */
 8 /* Dice: simulates rolling a collection of dice                */
 9 /*       the array of die is growable                          */
10 /*       so that any number of any kind can be housed          */
11 /*                                                             */
12 /***************************************************************/
13
14 class Dice {
15
16 protected:
17
18  int    numberOfDice;   // this instance's number of dice
19  Die*   *dieArray;      // the growable array of die*
20
21 public:
22         // creates an empty array of dice
23         Dice ();
24        ~Dice ();
25
26 private: // don't allow any copying of any instance of this class
27         Dice (const Dice& d) {}
28         Dice& operator= (const Dice& d) {return *this;}
29
30 public:
31         // add numDie of this die sides to the array
32  bool   AddDie (int numDie, int numSides = Die::DefaultNumSides);
33
34         // roll the dice - allows chaining
35  Dice&  Roll ();
36
37         // retrieve total value of all dice
38  int    GetTotal () const;
39
40               // displays each die value
41  const Dice&  Display (ostream& os = cout) const;
42
```

```
        // fills users array of count ints with the die results
 void   GetDieValues (int die[], int count) const;

        // gets the number of die in the array
 int    GetNumberOfDice () const;

        // fills users array of the number of sides on each die
 void   GetDieSides (int dieSides[], int count) const;
};
```

Dice Class Implementation

```
#include <iostream>
using namespace std;
#include "Dice.h"

/***************************************************************/
/*                                                             */
/* Dice: simulates rolling a collection of dice                */
/*                                                             */
/***************************************************************/

/***************************************************************/
/*                                                             */
/* Dice: construct an empty growable array of die              */
/*                                                             */
/***************************************************************/

Dice::Dice () {
 dieArray = 0;
 numberOfDice = 0;
}

       // add a die of this type to the array
bool   Dice::AddDie (int numDie, int numSides) {
 if (numSides < Die::MinimumNumSides)
  numSides = Die::MinimumNumSides;

 if (numDie < 0) {
  cerr << "Error: trying to add too few new dice\n";
  return false;
 }

 // allocate a new array of Die pointers to hold numDie more
 Die** temp = new (std::nothrow) Die* [numberOfDice + numDie];
 if (!temp) {
  cerr << "Error: out of memory making the Die array in Dice\n";
  return false;
 }

 int i, j;
 // copy existing Die pointers into the larger array
 for (i=0; i<numberOfDice; i++) {
  temp[i] = dieArray[i];
 }
```

```
 // allocate and store all newly added dice
 for (i=0, j=numberOfDice; i<numDie; i++, j++) {
  temp[j] = new (std::nothrow) Die (numSides);
  if (!temp[j]) {
   // ran out of memory, so remove only those we've added
   cerr << "Error out of memory in Dice - allocating die\n";
   for (int k=numberOfDice; k<j; k++) {
    if (temp[k]) delete temp[k];
   }
   delete [] temp;
   return false;
  }
 }

 // delete old array and reset new one and its count
 delete [] dieArray;
 dieArray = temp;
 numberOfDice += numDie;
 return true;
}

/***************************************************************/
/*                                                             */
/* ~Dice: remove the allocated die_array and individual dice   */
/*                                                             */
/***************************************************************/

Dice::~Dice () {
 for (int i=numberOfDice-1; i>=0; i--) delete dieArray[i];
 delete [] dieArray;
}

/***************************************************************/
/*                                                             */
/* Roll: roll all the dice at one time - use GetTotal, Display */
/*       or GetDieValues to retrieve the results of this roll  */
/*                                                             */
/***************************************************************/

Dice&     Dice::Roll () {
 if (!numberOfDice) {
  cerr << "No Dice have been allocated!\n";
 }
 else {
  for (int i=0; i<numberOfDice; i++) dieArray[i]->Toss ();
 }
 return *this;
}

/***************************************************************/
/*                                                             */
/* GetTotal: returns the sum of all the dice in this roll      */
/*                                                             */
/***************************************************************/

int       Dice::GetTotal () const {
```

```
 int total = 0;
 for (int i=0; i<numberOfDice; i++) {
  total += dieArray[i]->GetRollValue ();
 }
 return total;
}

/***************************************************************/
/*                                                             */
/* Display: show the results like this: 2 + 4 + 5 = 11         */
/*                                                             */
/***************************************************************/

const Dice&  Dice::Display (ostream& os) const {
 if (!numberOfDice) {
  os << "No Dice have been allocated";
  return *this;
 }

 for (int i=0; i<numberOfDice; i++) {
  os << dieArray[i]->GetRollValue ();
  if (i < numberOfDice -1) os << " + ";
 }
 os << " = " << GetTotal ();
 return *this;
}

/***************************************************************/
/*                                                             */
/* GetDieValues: fill up the user's array with the individual  */
/*               die roll values but avoid overwriting memory  */
/*               if user's array is too small                  */
/*                                                             */
/***************************************************************/

void      Dice::GetDieValues (int die[], int count) const {
 int num_to_do = count < numberOfDice ? count : numberOfDice;
 for (int i=0; i<num_to_do; i++)
  die[i] = dieArray[i]->GetRollValue ();
}

/***************************************************************/
/*                                                             */
/* GetNumberOfDice: returns the number of dice in the array    */
/*                                                             */
/***************************************************************/

int    Dice::GetNumberOfDice () const {
 return numberOfDice;
}

/***************************************************************/
/*                                                             */
/* GetDieSides:  fill up the user's array with the individual  */
/*               die number of sides,avoid overwriting memory  */
/*               if user's array is too small                  */
```

```
/*                                                                 */
/*******************************************************************/

void   Dice::GetDieSides (int dieSides[], int count) const {
 int num_to_do = count < numberOfDice ? count : numberOfDice;
 for (int i=0; i<num_to_do; i++)
  dieSides[i] = dieArray[i]->GetNumberSides ();
}
```

Finally, here are a small tester program that illustrates the actions and its output.

Pgm02Dice Tester Program

```
#include <iostream>
using namespace std;

#include "Dice.h"

#include <crtdbg.h> // for memory leak checking

void ShowSides (int a[], int num);
void ShowDieValues (int a[], int num);


int main () {
 {
 int a[20];

 Dice d;  // empty set
 cout << "Should get empty array error message\n";
 d.Roll ();
 cout << endl;
 d.AddDie (2, 6);
 d.GetDieSides (a, sizeof (a));
 ShowSides (a, d.GetNumberOfDice());
 d.Roll ();
 cout << "Should see 2 6-sided dice\n";
 d.Display ();
 cout << "\nThe total of this roll is: " << d.GetTotal() << endl;
 d.GetDieValues (a, sizeof (a));
 ShowDieValues (a, d.GetNumberOfDice());
 cout << endl;

 cout << endl;
 d.AddDie (4, 8);
 d.GetDieSides (a, sizeof (a));
 ShowSides (a, d.GetNumberOfDice());
 d.Roll ();
 cout << "Should see 2 6-sided + 4 8-sided dice\n";
 d.Display ();
 cout << "\nThe total of this roll is: " << d.GetTotal() << endl;
 d.GetDieValues (a, sizeof (a));
 ShowDieValues (a, d.GetNumberOfDice());
 cout << endl;
 }

```

```
 // check for memory leaks
 if (_CrtDumpMemoryLeaks())
  cerr << "Memory leaks occurred!\n";
 else
  cerr << "No memory leaks.\n";

 return 0;
}

void ShowSides (int a[], int num) {
 cout << "Number of dice: " << num  << endl << "Sides: ";
 for (int i=0; i<num; i++)
  cout << a[i] << " ";
 cout << endl;
}

void ShowDieValues (int a[], int num) {
 for (int i=0; i<num; i++) {
  cout << a[i] << (i < num -1? " + " : "\n");
  }
}
```

Output of Pgm02Dice Tester Program

```
Should get empty array error message
No Dice have been allocated!

Number of dice: 2
Sides: 6 6
Should see 2 6-sided dice
5 + 4 = 9
The total of this roll is: 9
5 + 4


Number of dice: 6
Sides: 6 6 8 8 8 8
Should see 2 6-sided + 4 8-sided dice
1 + 2 + 8 + 1 + 5 + 3 = 20
The total of this roll is: 20
1 + 2 + 8 + 1 + 5 + 3

No memory leaks.
```

Review Questions

1. Why is **#ifndef/#define** logic used in header files? Show an example of circular headers that absolutely must have this logic in them or **main.cpp** will not compile.

2. Explain why a class might wish to have an instance of some other class as one of its data members.

3. What is a forward reference? If, in the definition of class A, an instance of class B is used as a data

member or as a parameter copy, can a forward reference be used? Why or why not. If in the definition of class A a reference to an instance of class B is used as a parameter, can a forward reference be used?

4. Under what circumstances does the class definition of class B have to be included in the definition file for class A?

5. What is the **this** pointer? How does it get a value? What value does it get?

6. What use is the **this** parameter to us as we code our member functions? When would we absolutely need the **this** parameter?

7. What is a class **enum**? Why are they useful? How does a class **enum** differ from an ordinary **enum**?

8. What is a friend function? Does a friend function have a **this** parameter? Is a friend function a class member function?

9. What is meant by constant data members? Give an example of a constant data member in some class not mention in this chapter.

10. By what point in the constructor coding must all constant data members have their values?

11. What is meant by the term base class and member initialization mechanism? When can it be used? What purpose does it serve at this point in our studies of OOP?

12. What is a copy constructor? Give three situations in which it is called by the compiler.

13. How can we make certain constructors unavailable for client programs to use?

14. Why would a class need or desire a reference member variable? How can a constructor initialize a reference variable?

15. What is a **static** data member? Under what circumstances would a **static** data member be useful for a class?

16. If 100 instances of a class are created which also has a **static** data member, how many instances of the **static** data member are created? If there are no instances yet created of that same class, how many instances are there of that **static** data member?

17. Can a member function access a **static** data member?

18. What is a **static** member function? What purpose do **static** member functions serve? Do they have a this parameter? Can a **static** member function access instance data of an instance of the class?

19. What is an inline function? Why do inlined functions execute more quickly? What is the price that one pays for having inline functions? Why cannot you use the debugger to step through the instructions in an inline function?

20. What is meant by implicit type conversion that the compiler performs? How is it useful? How can it be confusing when debugging a program that has errors in it?

21. What is meant by a lib project? How are production libraries of OOP classes useful?

22. What happens if the client program codes the following?

```
Point p;
this->SetCoordinates (42,10);
```

23. Write a class **enum** called **Month** for use in a **Date** class. The **enum** values contain three letter abbreviations for the 12 month names such as Jan for example.

Stop! Do These Exercises Before Programming

1. Look over the **Dice** series of three classes. These three classes are not robust or bulletproof. That is, client programs can easily still perform "illegal" actions with them. List all of the potential error situations that could create program crashes or illegal operations with a set of dice.

2. A programmer decided to implement a class called **Line**. He began with a simple header file shown below. What is syntactically wrong with it and what is non-optimum about the header file? Show how these can be corrected.

Line.h

```
struct Point {
 double x;
 double y;
}
class Line {
protected
 Point left;
 Point right;
public
 Line ();
 Line (const Point& l, const Point r);
}
```

3. A different programmer decided to implement a class called **Line** in an alternate way. He began with the following. What is syntactically wrong with it and what is non-optimum about the header files? Show how these can be corrected.

Point.h

```
class Point {
 double x;
 double y;
}
```

Line.h

```
class Line {
protected
 Point left;
 Point right;
public
 Line ();
 Line (const Point& l, const Point r);
}
```

4. A third programmer tried his hand at creating a more optimum design and coded it this way. What is wrong with this version and how can it be corrected?

Point.h

```
class Point {
 double x;
 double y;
}
```

Line.h

```
class Line {
protected
 Point& left;
 Point& right;
public
 Line ();
 Line (const Point& l, const Point r);
}
```

5. A programmer tried to implement the **Point** class constructor but it does not compile. Show four different approaches to making it work, only one of which should use the base class and member initialization mechanism.

```
Point::Point (int x, int y) {
 x = x;
 y = y;
}
```

6. Write a definition for a **Client** class that defines a class **enum ClientType** to store the values **SmallBusiness**, **Corporation**, and **Chain**. In the class, define an instance of this type. Code the prototype for a constructor that takes such an **enum**. Code the prototype for a function **GetClientType** which returns the corresponding member variable. Then, write a **main** function that creates three instances of the **Client** class each with a different type.

7. Assume the definition of the **Point** class given at the beginning of this chapter. Write a **Compare** member function that returns true if the two points are equal, that is, if both their x and y values match each other. Then write a **compare** friend function to do the same thing. Show the prototypes and then the function bodies. Show how a client could call each of the two comparison functions.

8. Write the class definition and inline the constructor function as described below. The class is called Car. It has two data members. One is the constant long integer vinNumber and the other is its speed. The constructor function takes a long number and the integer current speed.

9. In the class definition in question 8 above, show how one could prevent a client program from car cloning by coding

```
Car a (123445, 42);
Car b (a);
```

10. Modify the **Point** class given at the very start of this chapter. Add a static data member called **counter** whose initial value is 0. Add a static member function called **GetPointInstances** which returns this counter's value. Modify the constructors to increment this counter and add a destructor to decrement this count. Show the modified header and definition files. Also show how a client program can track how many **Point** instances are in existence at any point in time.

Programming Problems

Problem Pgm02-1 —A Date Class—II

Modify the **Date** class of Problem **Pgm01-1** as follows to make it more efficient and useful.

Modifications to the Interface for the Date Class

Create 3 constructors:

One version takes 3 integers for month, day, and year in that order

One takes a constant character string of the form "9/1/1997" (meaning September 1, 1997)

A default constructor with no arguments

The default ctor initializes the date to the current computer system date. There is a short example at the end of these specifications that shows you how to access the local time on your PC. Note that, if you wish to use a constructor that takes a **long** serial date, it must be made private. It is not required that you have a constructor that takes a **long**, however.

Compare function:

This function, **Compare**, takes another **Date** object and compares it to this date. It returns a positive integer when this date is greater than the passed date, 0 if the same, and a negative integer if less. Neither date is altered by this function.

usage: `int result = mydate.Compare (otherdate);`

Difference function:

This function, **Difference**, returns the **long** number of days from the this date to the passed date. It is negative when this date is before the passed date. Neither this date nor the passed date are altered.

usage: `long diff = mydate.Difference (otherdate);`

Add function:

This function, **Add**, allows one to add a **long** number of days onto this date, returning the new date. It does not alter the date object itself.

usage: `Date z = mydate.Add (100L); // add 100 days to this date`

Subtract function:

This function, **Subtract**, allows one to subtract a **long** number of days from this date, returning the new date. It does not alter the date object itself.

usage: `Date z = mydate.Subtract (100L); // subs 100 from this date`

Note that for both Add and Subtract, the passed **long** could be positive or negative.

Input function:

This function, **Input**, takes a reference to an **istream** and inputs a date of the form mm/dd/yy or mm/dd/yyyy. It should return a reference to the passed **istream**. Again, if the year is of the form 99, add 1900 to it. Ignore the fact that this is not year 2000 compliant.

Output function:

This function, **Output**, takes a reference to an **ostream** and outputs the formatted date: 01/01/1997 for example. It should return a reference to the passed **ostream**. Always print 2 digits for the month and day and 4 digits for the year with a slash between them.

Remember that **Date** arguments should be passed by reference. Decide on how to use the **const** qualifier.

Here is how you can get the current date from your PC:

```
#include <time.h>
...
time_t now;
```

```
tm      *ptrtime;
now = time (NULL);
ptrtime = localtime (&now);

int mo, da, yr;
mo = ptrtime->tm_mon + 1;
da = ptrtime->tm_mday;
yr = ptrtime->tm_year + 1900;
```

I would suggest you write a simple testing main program to test the **Date** class until you feel it is working. Then, try to add in the provided **main** program below. The source is in the **TestDataForAssignments** folder.

Test your class by running the provided **Pgm02-1.cpp** tester **main** program. It inputs the file **Pgm02-1.txt** and writes a results file, **Pgm02-1Output.txt**. The correct output should be as follows:

```
 DATE 1          DATE 2        DIFFERENCE

01/01/1996      01/01/1996            0
01/02/1996      01/01/1996            1
01/02/1995      01/01/1996         -364
02/01/1996      01/01/1996           31
02/01/1995      01/01/1996         -334
03/01/1996      01/01/1996           60
03/01/1995      01/01/1996         -306
12/31/1996      01/01/1996          365
12/31/1995      01/01/1996           -1
01/01/1997      01/01/1996          366
01/01/1994      01/01/1996         -730
03/01/1997      01/01/1996          425
03/01/1994      01/01/1996         -671
06/15/1997      01/01/1996          531
06/15/1994      01/01/1996         -565
09/20/1999      01/01/1996         1358
09/20/1993      01/01/1996         -833
01/01/2000      01/01/1996         1461
01/01/1990      01/01/1996        -2191
04/21/2000      01/01/1996         1572
04/21/1990      01/01/1996        -2081
12/31/2400      01/01/1996       147923
12/31/1601      01/01/1996      -143906
01/01/1900      01/01/1900            0
12/31/2400      01/01/1601       292193
01/01/2000      12/31/1899        36525
01/01/2000      12/31/2400      -146462
07/01/2049      01/01/1900        54603
07/01/1750      01/01/1900       -54605
01/01/1601      12/31/2100      -182620

conDateA = 12/31/1899
conDateB = 01/01/2000
date_1   = 12/31/1899
date_2   = 01/01/2000
```

Problem Pgm02-2 —The Piggy Bank Class

Write a class to encapsulate a child's piggy bank. Allow for pennies, nickels, dimes, quarters, half dollars and dollar coins. Also allow for unknown type coins because children often insert any kind of coin token into their piggy banks. Create a class **enum** called **CoinType** that defines a coin's type (dime, nickel and so on). The **PiggyBank** class needs to keep track of the number of each type of coin in the bank. Thus, you can make a **Coin** structure that contains the coin type, number of those coins and string name of the coin type and store an array of these in the **PiggyBank** class. Or you can design a class **Coin** that encapsulates this same information and store an array of **Coin** objects in the **PiggyBank** class.

Next, decide what member functions the **PiggyBank** class would need to have. Certainly it must have an **AddCoin** function and some means of displaying the entire contents of the **PiggyBank**. There must also be some way to remove a coin from the **PiggyBank**. See what other functions a **PiggyBank** ought to have.

After writing the class, create a testing oracle. Then write a client program to thoroughly test your **PiggyBank** class.

Problem Pgm02-3—A Checkbook Class

With electronic checking becoming more popular, design a **Checkbook** class to manage an account electronically.

Assume that a check contains the person's name and account number, the check number, to whom the check is written, the date, and the amount. A deposit slip contains the person's name and account number, the deposit number, the date, and the amount.

The default constructor, **Checkbook**, initializes all fields to reasonable defaults, such as zero. Additionally, no other operations on an account whose account number is 0 are permitted until **Setup** is called. **Setup** is passed the person's name, account number, and the initial deposit. Provide an overloaded constructor that takes the person's name, account number, and the initial deposit.

With all financial type operations, a transaction's log is essential to maintain an account's history. Thus, the overloaded constructor and **Setup** must take an additional parameter, the name of this customer's transaction log file. The first line in the log file should contain the information passed to **Setup** or the overloaded constructor. Thus, after initializing the member data, these functions should open the transaction's log file and write that first line of data and then close the file.

Assume check and deposit numbers begin with number 100. Member operational functions consist of **GetBalance**, **MakeDeposit** and **WriteCheck**. These functions should perform the indicated actions. In addition, **MakeDeposit** and **WriteCheck** must also reopen the transaction's log and append an additional line with the relevant deposit or check information.

Another operation is **DisplayHistory**. This function opens the transaction log file and displays a report of the initial state and the account activities.

Write a tester program that thoroughly tests the **Checkbook** class.

Problem Pgm02-4—A Distance Class—II

Review Problem **Pgm01-5—A Distance Class—I**. We are going to make a number of revisions to it in Part A.

Part A. Revise the Distance class as follows.

1. Create two public class **enums**. The first is called **Type** whose values are **Metric** and **English**. The second **enum** is **ShowAs** whose values are **Mm**, **Feet**, **Meter**, **Miles**.
2. The default constructor remains unchanged. However, change all the other constructors to accept the **enum Type** as the **first** parameter. The other constructors and their **additional** parameters are now to be

accept a **double** number of millimeters
accept a **double** representing miles—careful with this one
accept a **long** meters, **long** centimeters, and **double** millimeters (it was 3 **longs**). Also, default the millimeters parameter to 0
accept a **long** feet and **double** inches, defaulting inches to 0 (it was 2 **ints**)

3. Modify member functions:
GetDistance is now passed the **Type enum** and based on its value returns the distance as a **double** millimeters or inches.
SetDistance is now passed the **Type enum** as a first parameter and then a **double** which represents either mm or inches according to the **enum** value.
Paint is now passed the **enum ShowAs** instead of the **char** and is used to determine how to print the distance. Default it to display in millimeters.
4. Remove **MtoE** and **EtoM** as class member functions. They are now to be stand-alone C style utility or helper functions.
MtoE is passed a **double** millimeters measurement and returns that value converted into a **double** inches.
MtoE is passed a reference to a **Distance** object. It returns the object's distance as a **double** inches.
EtoM is passed a **double** inches measurement and returns that value converted to a **double** millimeters.
EtoM is passed a reference to a **Distance** object and a **double** inches. After converting the inches into millimeters, it stores that measurement in the **Distance** object and returns the millimeters as a **double**.
5. Once again, decide which upon where the **const** keyword should be applied on both functions and parameters.
6. Create a main program to **thoroughly** test the **Distance** class. Be sure to illustrate **EtoM** actually alters the passed **Distance** object.

Part B. Construct a class Path Class that Has Distance Objects as Data Members

We wish to construct a **Path** class that encapsulates a trajectory a moving object might take. For now, ignore the starting point and direction of travel. Instead, just store the line segment distances traveled along the path of movement.
1. The two private data members consist of an integer count of the number of **Distance** objects in the array and the array **path** which is a dynamically allocated array of **Distance** objects, for example

```
Distance *path;
int      count;
```

2. The **Path** constructor sets **path** to NULL and the **count** to 0.
3. The **destructor** deletes the array of **Distances**, if any.
4. The public member function, **AddPath**, allocates a new array of **count + 1 Distance** objects using the **new** operator, storing the pointer in say **temp**. Then, for each of the original **Distance** objects in the original array, it copies the original data into the new array's objects. Then, it copies the new **Distance** object's values into the last array object. The old array (which is pointed to by **path)** is then deleted and **path** is assigned the new array (**temp**) and **count** is incremented. (Yes, there are other far better ways of avoiding this awkward copying, but save them for later on. For now, you are after the experience of working with arrays, **new**, and **delete**.) Note that this is basically a growable array type of data structure.
The prototype for **AddPath** is

```
void AddPath (Distance &d);
```

5. The last member function of **Path** is **ShowPath** which takes no parameters. It should display a series of messages that trace the complete path array of distance. If there were three distances in the path array, your

output might be

```
      Tracing this path of 3 segments
        Segment 1: 45 mm
        Segment 2: 105 mm
        Segment 3: 9 mm
```

6. Your first main tester program should look something of the order of this

```
int main ()  {
 Distance d[3];
 d[0].SetDistance (Distance::Metric, 45);
 d[1].SetDistance (Distance::Metric, 105);
 d[2].SetDistance (Distance::Metric, 9);
   { // allow destructor to be called before main ends
       Path p;
       p.AddPath (d[0]);
       p.AddPath (d[1]);
       p.AddPath (d[2]);
       p.ShowPath ();
   }
 return 0;
}
```

7. Once you have this basic main testing program working, then run the **Pgm02-4.cpp** testing main program I have provided. Be very alert for memory leaks, that is, failing to free allocated memory. Note that you will need to insert compiler specific memory leak check coding at the indicated location in the tester program.

Turn in the test runs from both main programs (from Step 6 and 7). Your output from **Pgm02-4** should appear as:

```
Displaying Path1 Results:
Tracing this path of 6 segments
Segment 0: Distance is =        1000.50 millimeters
Segment 1: Distance is =  1610152055.90 millimeters
Segment 2: Distance is =      100086.30 millimeters
Segment 3: Distance is =        1181.10 millimeters
Segment 4: Distance is =       10010.00 millimeters
Segment 5: Distance is =        1524.00 millimeters


Displaying Path2 Results:
Tracing this path of 5 segments
Segment 0: Distance is =        1000.50 millimeters
Segment 1: Distance is =        1000.00 millimeters
Segment 2: Distance is =        1000.00 millimeters
Segment 3: Distance is =        1000.00 millimeters
Segment 4: Distance is =          42.00 millimeters
```

Pgm02-5—An Employee Class I (Using the Date Class)

The purpose of this assignment is to write and use a class which has a member variable from another class. Specifically, it uses the Date II class from **Pgm02-1** above.

The Employee Class Interface

Design an **Employee** class to contain the employee name, identification number and date hired. The id number is a one- to nine-digit integer; the name is a maximum of 20 characters; the date hired is in mm/dd/yyyy format. Note that you should have a **Date** object for the hired date as one of the three **Employee** data members.

Create the following public member functions:

The **default constructor** sets the id number to 0, the name to a null string ("") and the date hired to 01/01/2400.

The **Input** function is passed a reference to any kind of input stream and returns that reference. The data order is id number followed by name and then the date hired. The name is enclosed in quote marks ("") so that blanks can be part of the name. Do not retain the quote marks in the name member variable. Typical invocations might be as follows.

```
emp.Input (infile);
```

The **OutputToFile** function is passed a reference to any kind of output stream and it returns that reference. It displays on the output stream the contents of the employee record. Show the id number first with leading 0's as needed for a length of 9 digits (use the **setfill** function). Then, have one blank separating the id number from the employee name. Surround the outputted employee name with leading and trailing quote marks. Lastly, display the date hired beginning in column 34 always. Display the date in the usual format mm/dd/yyyy. Typical invocations might be as follows.

```
emp.Output (outfile);
```

The **CompareDate** function is passed another **Employee** object and returns an **int** that is 0 if the two hire dates are the same. It returns a positive integer if this employee's hire date is greater than the passed date; a negative integer if less than. Typical invocations might be as follows.

```
if (emp.CompareDate (other_emp)) ...
```

The **GetId** function returns the employee's identification number.

```
long id = emp.GetId ();
```

The **GetName** function returns the employee's name as a **const char***.

```
const char *name = emp.GetName ();
```

The **GetHireDate** function returns the employee's hire date.

```
Date hiredate = emp.GetHireDate ();
```

There are **no** other public member functions. You may have any protected or private member functions you wish. Create a separate **Employee.h** and **Employee.cpp** set of files. Include the **Date.h** file as needed. Notice that in the **Employee** class, you will have an instance of the **Date** class as a member variable.

The Main Program Client

Create the main client program that uses the **Employee** class. All functions described below belong in the **main.cpp** file and **not** in the **Employee** class.

1. Call a load array function that inputs a file of employee data (**employee1.txt**) into an array. The file is in the test data folder as usual.

2. Call an output file function that outputs the array (via calls to the **Employee**'s **OutputToFile**) to a file on disk called **employee_new.txt**. Output the 9-digit id number first followed by 1 blank, followed by the name surrounded by quote marks. Start the date field in column 34 always. When done, do a file compare of the original data with your new file—they should be the same.

```
c:>fc  employee1.dat   employee_new.dat
```

3. Now make a **Date** object to hold the report date of December 31, 2010. Make a printed report (output redirection is ok) with appropriate column headings as shown in the attached printout. Put the report date at the top. Calculate the years hired and display that in the fourth column on the report. Convert the report date and the hired date into days and subtract to find the total days of employment. Then divide by 365.25 to get the years employed. Your report should be similar to the sample output shown below.

Turn in a screen shot of your file compare along with the printed report from step 3.

```
Report Date: 12/31/2010

ID Number  Employee Name          Date Hired     Years
                                               Employed

333445555  AILSHIE, LARRY         01/01/1990     21.00
444662000  ANDERSON, J. DENNIS    11/16/1985     25.12
555770001  BENSON, JAMES          12/04/1982     28.07
000008888  BOLDEN, EDWARD         01/05/1977     33.98
011111111  BRAHAM, JOSEPH         08/19/1986     24.37
444562001  BROWN, CLAYTON         03/07/1988     22.82
000002001  CALLAM, LARRY          10/15/1991     19.21
666779003  COPELAND, LINDA        01/02/1994     16.99
000000011  DARNELL, FREDERICK     07/22/1975     35.44
444561001  FREY, WILLIAM          05/29/1986     24.59
444562000  HANNAH, CAROL          04/28/1987     23.68
000666666  HERLAN, WILLIAM        02/28/1995     15.84
000000001  HOOP, JEANETTE         05/16/1968     42.63
445660001  JARETT, PAUL           09/14/1992     18.29
000667777  LACEY, JAMES           02/06/1989     21.90
444557000  MCCLEARY, JANE         12/31/1988     22.00
000007777  NOBEL, WILLIAM         04/01/1979     31.75
666778888  NOONCASTER, BRENDA     07/18/1987     23.46
555777777  NUTTING, TERESA        11/03/1983     27.16
666778889  RAINTREE, VICTORIA     06/17/1988     22.54
444560002  REEVES, WILLA          08/23/1993     17.36
555777778  RICHARDSON, O. SUSAN   10/02/1984     26.25
000779001  SEVERNS, JERRY         03/04/1992     18.83
445661000  STEARNS, KENNETH       06/21/1995     15.53
000778888  TYNER, CHARLES         09/10/1985     25.31
666779000  WATASHE, KENNETH       04/05/1991     19.74
000000099  WOOD, STEVEN           07/22/1972     38.44
444556667  WOODS, REBECCA JANIE   01/02/1995     15.99
666779002  YOUNG, RICHARD         02/03/1993     17.91
```

Chapter 3—Operator Overloading

Introduction

The C++ operators, such as +, -, [], ==, >>, and <<, can be overloaded just as ordinary functions can be overloaded. These are called **operator overloaded** functions. The syntax is a bit unusual because of the "name of the function" is + for example. Assume that the **Point** class has two protected data members **x** and **y**. By providing overloaded operator functions, we can extend the functionality of the **Point** class. Here are some likely operations a client program might desire.

```
Point a, b, c;
c = a + b;
a++;
c = a;
if (a == b) ;
cin >> a;
cout << b;
```

While each of the above do not look like function calls, they are, in fact, operator overloaded function calls. The general syntax of these unusual looking functions is as follows.

```
return type  classname::operatorZ (argument list);
```

where "Z" is the operator. The name of the functions in the above **Point** examples are

operator+, **operator++**, **operator==**, **operator=**, **operator>>**, and **operator<<**

The return type is most frequently the class for which the function is defined, such as **Point** in this case. However, you can return most anything desired. In fact, the implementation is totally up to the programmer. That is, one can define **operator+** for the **Point** class to actually add 42 to both coordinates, plot this point on a graph, output this point's distance from the origin while returning the square root of that distance!

However, a cardinal rule applies to OOP operator overloading.

Rule: Always maintain the spirit of the C++ operator.

When implementing the operator overloaded function, the actions it performs should parallel what would occur if the intrinsic C++ operator was being invoked on intrinsic types. That is, when implementing **operator+**

```
c = a + b;
```

the actions you take for the **Point**'s **operator+** should parallel that that would occur if the data types of the three variables were **int**. Maintain the spirit of C++ usage of operators when overloading them.

Which operators in the C++ language can be overridden? It is easier to state which operators cannot be overridden. The only operators that cannot be overridden are **. :: ? :** and any of the preprocessor directives. Yes, **[]** and even **()** function call operators can be overridden! Even **new** and **delete** can be overridden.

Rule: The precedence of C++ operators neither can be altered nor can the number of parameters an operator requires be altered.

Corollary: Thus, operator overloaded functions cannot have default arguments.

Examine the series of operations on the three **Point** objects above. Notice the similarities. The operator overloaded functions break down into two categories: **binary operators** and **unary operators**. A binary operator function has two parameters; a unary operator has only one. In the above examples with the three **Point** objects, only the increment operator is a unary operator. The others are binary in nature. One cannot say the following.

```
c = a *
a /
a =
a -
```

The compiler as well as the reader says multiply **a** by what? Divide **a** by what? Assign what to **a**? Subtract what from **a**?

First, let's examine the overloading of the binary operators and then the unary operators.

Overloading Binary Operators

Overloading the Math Binary Operators (such as + and –)

Suppose our **Point** class is defined this way.

```
class Point {
protected:
 int x;
 int y;
public:
 Point () : x(0), y(0){}
 Point (int xx, int yy) {x = xx; y = yy;}
 Point (const Point& p) : x(p.x), y(p.y) {}
};
```

We want to be able to write such operations as these.

```
Point a (5, 10), b (10, 20), c;
c = a + b;
c = c + 42;
c = 42 + c;
```

Rule: When overloading binary operators, there is only one parameter—the item that is to the right of the operator! It is the object on the left of the operator that generates the function call. The *this* parameter is used to pass the left side object to the function.

In the above desired addition operation,

```
c = a + b;
```

it is object **a** that invokes the **operator+** function passing object **b** as a parameter to the **operator+** function. So in the **Point::operator+** function, ***this*** points to object **a**. Thus, we would expect to need a prototype of the following.

```
Point   operator+ (Point b);
```

In the second case,

```
c = c + 42;
```

here object **c** is passed with the ***this*** parameter and the **42 int** is passed as the single argument. We would expect to need a prototype of the following.

```
Point   operator+ (int i);
```

In the third case,

```
c = 42 + c;
```

the integer class's **operator+** is invoked passing object **c** as its parameter; immediately we have a problem! There is no integer class **operator+** function! In this case we have no choice but to write an ordinary C style nonmember function that is a friend of the **Point** class.

Let's look at each of these in turn. Let's take them in order. The simplest case is

```
Point   operator+ (Point p);
```

for

```
c = a + b;
```

However, we know passing copies of objects is slow and inefficient, especially if the class has dynamically allocated memory or contains a lot of member data. We can immediately try this variation.

```
Point   operator+ (Point& p);
```

But wait a moment. If the three objects were integers, would the value of integer **b** be altered in the statement? No. Thus, we should pass a constant reference.

```
Point   operator+ (const Point& p);
```

Further, if the three objects were integers, would integer **a** be changed by the instruction? Nope. And since object **a** is providing the ***this*** parameter, the function itself should be constant indicating that it is not changing the **this** object.

```
Point   operator+ (const Point& p) const;
```

Now what about the return data type? Consider the following line.

```
c = d = e = a + b;
```

If these were integers, we know that **c**, **d**, and **e** are all being assigned the same value. Chaining the assignment operator must therefore be considered at all times. This is why we must always try to return an instance of the class data type, here **Point**. But can we return a reference to a Point in order to make it more efficient? Remember, the object that the reference is pointing to must exist after the function terminates and returns. Specifically, we cannot return a reference to a temporary automatic (or stack) instance that is defined within the operator function. Since neither **a** or **b** are being changed, we must construct a temporary **Point** object within the **operator+** function to hold the sum result. Thus, a reference cannot be returned.

These are the three considerations you must always make when creating the operator overloaded function prototype.

Can it be passed a constant reference to the parameter?
Can the entire function be constant?
Can it return an object or a reference to an object?

Thus, our prototype is

```
Point   operator+ (const Point& p) const;
```

Now how can it be implemented? The answer is that there are many ways it can be done, assuming that the addition of two points means to add the corresponding coordinate values. Let's examine several implementations. Here is the simplest way.

```
Point   Point::operator+ (const Point& p) const {
 Point ret;
 ret.x = x + p.x;
 ret.y = y + p.y;
 return ret;
}
```

It could also be implemented this way by making use of existing constructor functions.

```
Point   Point::operator+ (const Point& p) const {
 Point ret (x, y);
 ret.x += p.x;
 ret.y += p.y;
 return ret;
}
```

But we could also go a bit farther by coding only this.

```
Point   Point::operator+ (const Point& p) const {
 Point ret (x + p.x, y + p.y);
 return ret;
}
```

And finally, we could shorten it to just this.

```
Point   Point::operator+ (const Point& p) const {
 return Point (x + p.x, y + p.y);
```

```
}
```

Here, we are constructing an unnamed temporary **Point** object and initializing it to the desired two values and returning it to the caller.

Let's also examine an error version. What would this have done?

```
Point    Point::operator+ (const Point &p) { // error!
 x = x + p.x;
 y = y + p.y;
 return *this;
}
```

In this case the ***this*** object is **altered**. Coding **c = a + b;** yields both **c** and **a** now containing the sum of **a** + **b**! However, coding **c = c + b;** would have first altered **c** to being **c + b** and then copied that value back into **c**, clearly redundant.

Now consider the second case.

```
c = a + 42;
```

What is the prototype this time?

```
Point operator+ (int j) const;
```

What does it mean to add a single integer to a **Point** object? If the user defines this operation as meaning "add the integer to both coordinates," we can then implement it very straightforwardly this way.

```
Point    Point::operator+ (int j) const {
 Point ret;
 ret.x = x + j;
 ret.y = y + j;
 return ret;
}
```

Again, we can shorten it by making use of the constructor functions we already have.

```
Point    Point::operator+ (int j) const {
 Point ret (x, y);
 ret.x += j;
 ret.y += j;
 return ret;
}
```

Or even shorter this way.

```
Point    Point::operator+ (int j) const {
 Point ret (x + j, y + j);
 return ret;
}
```

Or even shorter this way.

```
Point    Point::operator+ (int j) const {
 return Point (x + j, y + j);
}
```

However, there is also another way we can implement this one. Notice that we already have written the function to add two point objects. Can that coding be reused? Yes, all we need to do is to construct a **Point** object from the integer and call the existing function.

```
Point    Point::operator+ (int j) const {
 Point p (j, j);
 Point ret = *this + p;
 return ret;
}
```

Here I use ***this** to obtain a **Point** object to use. However, it could be shortened to just this.

```
Point    Point::operator+ (int j) const {
 return *this + Point (j, j);
}
```

So what is the significant difference between writing two separate implementations versus reusing an existing implementation? Speed of execution and complexity of the implementation are the two design considerations. In both methods, a constructor for **Point** is called to create the return **Point** object. However, the code reuse second version has the additional overhead of making a second function call to the original **operator+** function with its additional constructor call, not to mention the copying of the returned objects. If the design of the class requires that these **operator+** functions execute as quickly as possible, then the second version that reuses the original **operator+** function will run more slowly. However, sometimes the addition process is quite complex, requiring many lines of coding to carry it out. In such a case, writing the lengthy addition code once and then reusing it makes good sense.

Using Friend Functions to Handle Overloading Normal Data Types

This handles the first two cases of addition above. But we must still deal with the third version.

```
a = 42 + b;
```

As it stands, it appears that the integer addition operator is called passing an instance of **b**. This is, of course, an impossibility, We solve this circumstance by using a friend function. In the class definition, add a new public prototype.

```
friend Point operator+ (int j, const Point &p);
```

Its implementation can also be done several ways. Here is the simplest.

```
Point operator+ (int j, Point const &p) {
 Point ret;
 ret.x = p.x + j;
 ret.y = p.y + j;
 return ret;
}
```

It can be shortened this way by making use of the constructor.

```
Point operator+ (int j, const Point &p) {
 Point ret (p.x + j, p.y + j);
 return ret;
}
```

Or just

```
Point operator+ (int j, const Point &p) {
 return Point (p.x + j, p.y + j);
}
```

It can also be implemented by reusing the addition of two points member function this way.

```
Point operator+ (int j, const Point &p) {
 Point q (j, j);
 Point ret = p + q;
 return ret;
}
```

Or even simpler

```
Point operator+ (int j, const Point &p) {
 return p + Point (j, j);
}
```

The Subtraction Operator

With subtraction, three similar cases arise.

```
c = a - b;
c = a - 42;
c = 42 - a;
```

In the first and second lines, the **this** parameter points to **a**'s instance. Neither objects involved in the subtraction are altered by the subtraction process. Thus, the parameter **Point** reference and the member function are constant. Here it the first subtraction prototype.

```
Point operator- (const Point& p) const;
```

It can be implemented in several ways. The simplest is this.

```
Point Point::operator- (const Point &p) const {
 Point ret;
 ret.x = x - p.x;
 ret.y = y - p.y;
 return ret;
}
```

It can be shortened by using another constructor.

```
Point Point::operator- (const Point &p) const {
 Point ret (x - p.x, y - p.y);
 return ret;
}
```

Or even

```
Point Point::operator- (const Point &p) const {
 return Point (x - p.x, y - p.y);
}
```

The function to subtract an integer from a point would have the following prototype.

```
Point operator- (int j) const;
```

And it can be implemented this way.

```
Point   Point::operator- (int j) const {
 Point ret;
 ret.x = x - j;
 ret.y = y - j;
 return ret;
}
```

Or shorter

```
Point   Point::operator- (int j) const {
 Point ret (x - j, y - j);
 return ret;
}
```

Or just

```
Point   Point::operator- (int j) const {
 return Point (x - j, y - j);
}
```

Or in terms of the existing subtraction of two points, it can be done this way.

```
Point operator- (int j, const Point &p) {
 return p - Point (j, j);
}
```

However, the third case of subtracting a point from an integer must be done with a friend function.

```
friend Point operator- (int j, const Point &p);
```

Its implementation can also be done several ways. Here is the simplest.

```
Point operator- (int j, const Point &p) {
 Point ret;
 ret.x = j - p.x;
 ret.y = j - p.y;
 return ret;
}
```

or

```
Point operator- (int j, const Point &p) {
 Point ret (j - p.x, j - p.y);
 return ret;
}
```

or

```
Point operator- (int j, const Point &p) {
```

```
 return Point (j - p.x, j - p.y);
}
```

or

```
Point operator- (int j, const Point &p) {
 return Point (j, j) - p;;
}
```

What about the other math operators such as multiplication, division, and the remainder operator? They are overloaded in a similar manner. However, always design first. What would it mean to multiply or divide two points? Nothing. These are most likely undefined operations for a **Point** class, since they have no meaning. (Unless you want to consider math vector operations.)

Overloading the += and Similar Operators

Suppose that the client wanted to have the following be supported.

```
a += 5;
a += b;
```

The **Point** object to the operator's left supplies the ***this*** parameter and the parameter to the function lies to the right of the operator. In this case, the ***this*** object is being modified while the parameter object is not. Here are the two prototypes.

```
Point& operator+= (int j);
Point& operator+= (const Point& p);
```

Notice this time I am returning a reference to a **Point** object. The ***this*** object is changed but it does not go out of scope. Hence, a reference to it can be returned.

Here is a way these two can be implemented.

```
Point& Point::operator+= (int j) {
 x += j;
 y += j;
 return *this;
}
```

and

```
Point& Point::operator+= (const Point& p) {
 x += p.x;
 y += p.y;
 return *this;
}
```

Notice how the ***this*** pointer is turned into a reference by coding ***this**.

The other similar operators, such as –=. *=, /=, and %=, are coded in parallel ways. But again, they are provided only if they have some meaning. Certainly *= for **Point** objects has no meaning. How would you multiply a point times a point, for example?

Overloading the Relational Operators

The six relational operators, ==, !=, <, >, <=, and >=, can easily be overloaded so that client programs can do comparisons such as these.

```
if (a == b)
```

where both **a** and **b** are **Point** instances. Again, the object to the left of the operator provides the ***this*** parameter while the object to the right of the operator becomes the parameter. In a comparison operation, neither operand is modified, so both are constant. Here is the prototype for the equality relational operator.

```
bool operator== (const Point& p) const;
```

It is easily implemented by checking for identical coordinates.

```
bool Point::operator== (const Point& p) const {
 return x == p.x && y == p.y;
```

```
}
```

The not equals operator is similarly coded. However, what would it mean to say

```
if (a > b)
```

or is one point larger than another point? Sometimes a class does not have to support all of the relational operators. In this case, the client's specifications might say that one point is larger than another if its distance from the origin of the coordinate system is greater than the other point.

Overloading the Insertion and Extraction Operators—<< and >>

Again, assuming we are dealing with instances of the **Point** class, client programs greatly desire to be able to code the following.

```
cin >> a;
cout << a;
infile >> a;
outfile << a;
```

Following the guidelines, the item to the left of the operator provides the ***this*** parameter and the item to the right of the operator is passed as the parameter. So in this case, the **operator<<** function belongs in the **istream** class because **cin** or **outfile** is to the left! Oops. The only way that these functions can be implemented is by once again using an ordinary C nonmember function that is granted friendship with the class so that it can access the protected data members. Here are the two required prototypes.

```
friend istream& operator>> (istream& is, Point& p);
friend ostream& operator<< (ostream& os, const Point& p);
```

Notice that outputting a **Point** object should not alter its value, so it has been made a constant reference.

How do we implement the functions? Well, that depends upon how the client wishes the output of a point to appear and what is desired for input. Suppose that the specifications call for a point to be displayed this way.

```
(10, 541)
```

Then, it is our task to implement **operator<<** to provide this format. Here is how it can be accomplished.

```
ostream& operator<< (ostream& os, const Point& p) {
 os << "(" << p.x << ", " << p.y << ")";
 return os;
}
```

Or it could be shortened to just this.

```
ostream& operator<< (ostream& os, const Point& p) {
 return os << "(" << p.x << ", " << p.y << ")";
}
```

Suppose that on input, the point data also was in the same format. Then, the **operator>>** function could be done this way.

```
istream& operator>> (istream& os, Point& p) {
 char c;
 is >> c >> p.x >> c >> p.y >> c;
 return is;
}
```

The first character in **c** is the leading (; the second is the comma; the third is the trailing).

The Assignment Operator

The assignment **operator=** overloaded function can be quite useful, especially when the class needs to dynamically allocate memory for member variables or has constant data members. Continuing with the **Point** examples, the client may wish to do the following.

```
a = b;
a = b = c;
```

In this example of **Point** objects, is an overloaded **operator=** really needed? No. The compiler automatically can do a shallow copy by making a duplicate copy of the data members. In this case, that is perfectly fine. However, let's see how we could implement it. Here is the prototype.

```
Point&  operator= (const Point &p);
```

Here is its implementation. When dynamic memory is involved, we must take additional precautions. But that is discussed in the next chapter.

```
Point&  Point::operator= (const Point &p) {
 x = p.x;
 y = p.y;
 return *this;
}
```

Notice that the return value is a reference and ***this** is used. This is done so one can chain multiple assignments. Also, the reference is needed to prevent making a copy of the right side of the assignment.

Overloading the Unary Operators

With unary operators, there are no parameters passed to the functions except the hidden ***this*** parameter.

Overloading the Inc and Dec Operators

The increment and decrement operators are very often overloaded to add or subtract one from the object. With the **Point** objects, the client desires the ability to write the following.

```
a++;
++a;
```

The first problem is to be able to distinguish between these two functions. Following the guidelines for constructing prototypes, we have the following.

```
Point operator++ ();
Point operator++ ();
```

Oops. Both of these have the same prototype! Hence, the C++ language steps in to provide a means of distinguishing between prefix increment and postfix increment. Here are the correct versions.

```
Point operator++ ();       // ++a;
Point operator++ (int x);  // a++
```

Note that the parameter **x** will always be 0. To avoid compiler warnings about unused parameter variables, it is often not coded as shown below in the implementations.

However, there is still a subtle difference in return values that we are overlooking. Certainly in both cases the object being incremented is in fact incremented or changed. But with the after (postfix) increment, the function must return the previous value of the **Point**, not the new one. We must save the initial point contents so that they can be returned in a temporary **Point** object. With the before (prefix) increment, the function must return the new value. Thus, we could return a reference to the **Point**. Here are the revised prototypes.

```
Point& operator++ ();     // ++a;
Point  operator++ (int); // a++
```

Here are the two implementations.

```
Point& Point::operator++ () { // ++a;
 x++;
 y++;
 return *this;
}
Point Point::operator++ (int) { // a++
 Point ret (*this);
 x++;
 y++;
```

```
 return ret;
}
```

The decrement operator is handled similarly.

Overloading the Unary – Operator

To handle the negation of a **Point** object, the prototype is

```
Point operator- () const;
```

where the client writes

```
c = -a;
```

And it is implemented this way, since **a**'s values are not changed.

```
Point Point::operator- () const {
 Point ret(-x, -y);
 return ret;
}
```

or

```
Point Point::operator- () const {
 return Point(-x, -y);
}
```

The Time Class—A Complete Programming Example

In order to fully illustrate many of these operator overloaded functions, I have used one of the classes from my World War II game, the **Time** class. Since the basic turn interval is in minutes, in my game, time is tracked only in minutes since midnight. Further, since there are likely to be a huge number of **Time** instances used throughout the game, I wanted to keep the actual memory requirements for these instances as small as possible. Thus, the **Time** class stores only a single 24-hour time in a **short** representing the number of minutes since midnight. Obviously, a large number of operations can then be performed upon a time instance.

The game also has a **Date** class and a combined **DateTime** class. When a time in incremented past the 24-hour limit, another day is added to the **DateTime** instance and the **Time** instance is rolled back into the required 24-hour period of the next day. Similarly, if a **Time** instance is decremented past midnight (that is, it goes negative), the **DateTime** day is decremented and the **Time** instance is rolled back into the proper range for the previous day. However, in this sample program, only the **Time** class is used to illustrate the many operator overloaded functions.

Here is the **Time** class definition. Notice how I have grouped the various function definitions into sections for ease and clarity of reading. The copy constructor and assignment operator are not really needed in this class, but are shown to illustrate how they can be coded.

Time Class Definition

```
#pragma once
#include <iostream>
using namespace std;

/***************************************************************/
/*                                                             */
/* Class: Time - chronometer class handling time in minutes    */
/*                                                             */
/***************************************************************/


class Time {
```

```

 /*************************************************************/
 /*                                                           */
 /* Data Member: stores the number of minutes from midnight   */
 /*                                                           */
 /*************************************************************/

protected:

 short time;    // the time in minutes

 /*************************************************************/
 /*                                                           */
 /* Functions:                                                */
 /*                                                           */
 /*************************************************************/

public:

      Time (long hrs, long mns);
      Time (short hrs, short mns);
      Time (double t);
      Time ();
      Time (const Time &t);

     ~Time () {}

void  SetTime (long t);
void  SetTime (short t);
void  SetTime (long hrs, long mns);
void  SetTime (short hrs, short mns);
void  SetTime (double t);

short GetTime () const;
void  GetTime (short &h, short &m) const;
void  GetTime (double &t) const;

        Time& operator=  (const Time &t);

        bool  operator== (const Time &t) const;
        bool  operator>  (const Time &t) const;
        bool  operator<  (const Time &t) const;
        bool  operator>= (const Time &t) const;
        bool  operator<= (const Time &t) const;
        bool  operator!= (const Time &t) const;

        Time  operator+  (long n) const;
        Time  operator+  (const Time& t) const;
 friend Time  operator+  (long n, const Time &t);

        Time  operator-  (long n) const;
        Time  operator-  (const Time &t) const;
 friend Time  operator-  (long n, const Time &t);

        Time& operator+= (long n);
        Time& operator+= (const Time& t);
```

```
        Time& operator-= (long n);
        Time& operator-= (const Time& t);

        Time& operator++ ();
        Time  operator++ (int);
        Time& operator-- ();
        Time  operator-- (int);

        void  FormatHM (char *string, int maxlen) const;
        void  FormatH  (char *string, int maxlen) const;

friend  ostream& operator<< (ostream& os, const Time& t);
friend  istream& operator>> (istream& is, Time& t);

protected:
        void  RollIt (); // get a time back into a 24-hour range
};
```

The **FormatHM** function converts the short time into a client provided character string in the format of hh:mm. The client must also pass the length of its string so that I can avoid overwriting memory should the string be too small to hold all of the characters. Similarly, the **FormatH** function converts it into a string in the decimal format of hh.hhh.

As you look over these definitions, make sure you understand the use of the **const** keyword both on the parameters and on the member functions. These are critical. Likewise, observe which functions return a **Time** copy versus which are able to return a **Time** reference.

Here is the implementation of the **Time** class. Notice that most all of the functions are actually quite simple. Whenever a time value is altered, **RollIt** is called to force that value back into the proper range for a 24-hour time.

Time Class Implementation

```
#include <iostream>
#include <strstream>
#include <iomanip>
#include "time.h"
using namespace std;

/***************************************************************/
/*                                                             */
/* Time implementation: tracks minutes since midnight          */
/*                                                             */
/* RollIt() forces time back into 24 hour range                */
/*                                                             */
/***************************************************************/

// the constructor series

Time::Time (long hrs, long mns) {
 time = (short) (hrs * 60 + mns);
 RollIt ();
}

Time::Time (short hrs, short mns) {
 time = (short) (hrs * 60 + mns);
```

```
 RollIt ();
}

Time::Time (double t) {
 long h = (long) t;
 time = (short) ((t - h) * 60.+ .5 + h * 60);
 RollIt ();
}

Time::Time () {
 time = 0;
}

Time::Time (const Time &t) { // copy ctor
 time = t.time;
}


// the modifications series

void   Time::SetTime (long t) {
 time = (short) t;
 RollIt ();
}

void   Time::SetTime (short t) {
 time = t;
 RollIt ();
}

void   Time::SetTime (long hrs, long mns) {
 time = (short) (hrs * 60 + mns);
 RollIt ();
}

void   Time::SetTime (short hrs, short mns) {
 time = (short) (hrs * 60 + mns);
 RollIt ();
}

void   Time::SetTime (double t) {
 int h = (long) t;
 time = (short) ((t-h) * 60.+ .5 + h * 60.);
 RollIt ();
}


// retrieval series

short int Time::GetTime () const {
 return time;
}

void      Time::GetTime (short &h, short &m) const {
 h = (short) (time / 60);
 m = (short) (time % 60);
```

```
}

void      Time::GetTime (double &t) const {
 t = time / 60.;
}


// the assignment operator - not really needed...

Time&  Time::operator=  (const Time &t) {
 if (*this == t)
  return *this;
 time = t.time;
 return *this;
}


// the relational operator series

bool   Time::operator== (const Time &t) const {
 return time == t.time;
}

bool   Time::operator>  (const Time &t) const {
 return time >  t.time;
}

bool   Time::operator<  (const Time &t) const {
 return time <  t.time;
}

bool   Time::operator>= (const Time &t) const {
 return time >= t.time;
}

bool   Time::operator<= (const Time &t) const {
 return time <= t.time;
}

bool   Time::operator!= (const Time &t) const {
 return time != t.time;
}


// time addition series

Time   Time::operator+ (long n) const {
 Time t  (*this);
 t.time = (short) (t.time + n);
 t.RollIt ();
 return t;
}

Time   Time::operator+ (const Time &tt) const {
 Time t;
 t.time = (short) (time + tt.time);
```

```
 t.RollIt ();
 return t;
}

Time   operator+ (long n, const Time &t) {
 Time tt;
 tt.time = (short) (t.time + n);
 tt.RollIt ();
 return tt;
}


// time subtraction series

Time   Time::operator-  (long n) const {
 Time t;
 t.time = (short) (time - n);
 t.RollIt ();
 return t;
}

Time   Time::operator-  (const Time &t) const {
 Time tt;
 tt.time = (short) (time - t.time);
 tt.RollIt ();
 return tt;
}

Time   operator-  (long n, const Time &t) {
 Time tt;
 tt.time = (short) (n - t.time);
 tt.RollIt ();
 return tt;
}


// the += and -= series

Time&  Time::operator+= (long n) {
 time = (short) (time + n);
 RollIt ();
 return *this;
}

Time&  Time::operator+= (const Time& t) {
 time = (short) (time + t.time);
 RollIt ();
 return *this;
}

Time&  Time::operator-= (long n) {
 time = (short) (time - n);
 RollIt ();
 return *this;
}

```

```
Time&   Time::operator-= (const Time& t) {
 time = (short) (time - t.time);
 RollIt ();
 return *this;
}


// the inc and dec series

Time&   Time::operator++ () { // before inc
 time++;
 RollIt ();
 return *this;
}

Time    Time::operator++ (int) { // after inc
 Time t = *this;
 time++;
 RollIt ();
 return t;
}

Time&   Time::operator-- () { // before dec
 time--;
 RollIt ();
 return *this;
}

Time    Time::operator-- (int) { // after dec
 Time t = *this;
 time--;
 RollIt ();
 return t;
}


// the fancy formatting series


void    Time::FormatHM (char *string, int maxlen) const {
 // display as hh:mm
 short int h, m;
 GetTime (h, m);
 ostrstream os (string, maxlen);
 os << setfill ('0') << setw (2) << h << ":" << setw (2)
    << m << ends;
 if (maxlen < 6) // guard against too small a client string
  string[maxlen-1] = 0;
}

void    Time::FormatH  (char *string, int maxlen) const {
 // display as nn.nnn
 double x;
 GetTime (x);
 ostrstream os (string, maxlen);
 os << fixed << setw (6) << setprecision (3) << x << ends;
```

```
 if (maxlen < 7) // guard against too small a client string
  string[maxlen-1] = 0;
}


// the I/O series

ostream& operator<< (ostream& os, const Time& t) {
 char msg[8];
 t.FormatHM (msg, sizeof (msg));
 return os << msg;
}

istream& operator>> (istream& is, Time& t) {
 char c;
 long h, m;
 is >> h >> c >> m;
 if (!is)
  return is;
 t.SetTime (h, m);
 return is;
}


// RollIt() forces an out of range time back into a 24 hour range
void   Time::RollIt () {
 if (time < 0)
  time = (short) (1440 + (time % 1440));
 else if (time >= 1440)
  time = time % (short) 1440;
}
```

Next, we need a thorough tester program to guarantee that all functions are working properly. This is a major undertaking because of the volume of operator overloaded functions as well as the use of **const** and the use of **Time** and **Time&** return values. Each of these must be tested.

My philosophy when testing classes is to have the output set up so that at a glance I can tell if things are correct or not. So I tend to display messages such as this.

"Such and such should be this and it is that"

One quick glance at the output tells all.

With this many functions and variations to test, it is best to do it methodically from top to bottom, testing each function in the **Time** definition. A couple functions are automatically tested by the other functions: **RollIt** and **FormatHM**. Most of the tests are obvious and straightforward—insert a unique time into an object and add to it and display the results.

However, there are several circumstances that are not necessarily obvious that must be tested and which are often overlooked in testing. The first of these is the subtle difference between the prefix and postfix inc and dec operators. Assume that **a** is a **Time** instance storing 1 minute. What should the output from the following two lines be?

```
cout << ++a << "  " << a;
cout << a++ << "  " << a;
```

In the first line, the prefix inc takes place before any use of the object is made. Thus, 00:02 00:02 should be displayed. However, the postfix inc is done after usage is made of the current object's value. Thus, it should display 00:01 00:02.

The two formatting functions also have some special testing requirements. What happens if the client provides too small a string? Only those characters that can fit should be in the string along with a null terminator. So this situation is tested as well.

Finally, several constant **Time** objects are created and all of the possible **Time** functions that can be called using constant objects are invoked. Here are the **Pgm03a** tester program and its output.

Pgm03a Time Tester

```
#include <iostream>
#include <iomanip>
using namespace std;
#include "Time.h"

/***************************************************************/
/*                                                             */
/* Tester Program for Time Class                               */
/*                                                             */
/***************************************************************/

int main () {
 short shrs = 1;
 short smin = 42;
 Time a;
 Time b (1L, 42L);
 Time c (shrs, smin);
 Time d (1.5);
 Time e (d);
 Time f (48L, 42L);
 Time g (-72L, -2L);
 cout << "Testing constructors\n";
 cout << "a = 00:00 and is: " << a << endl;
 cout << "b = 01:42 and is: " << b << endl;
 cout << "c = 01:42 and is: " << c << endl;
 cout << "d = 01:30 and is: " << d << endl;
 cout << "e = 01:30 and is: " << e << endl;
 cout << "\nTesting RollIt ()\n";
 cout << "f = 00:42 and is: " << f << endl;
 cout << "g = 23:58 and is: " << g << endl;

 cout << "\nTesting SetTime()\n";
 a.SetTime (1.5);
 cout << "a = 01:30 and is: " << a << endl;
 a.SetTime (1L, 30L);
 cout << "a = 01:30 and is: " << a << endl;
 a.SetTime (shrs, smin);
 cout << "a = 01:42 and is: " << a << endl;
 a.SetTime (102L);
 cout << "a = 01:42 and is: " << a << endl;
 a.SetTime ((short) 102);
 cout << "a = 01:42 and is: " << a << endl;

 cout << "\nTesting GetTime\n";
 cout << "a = 102 and is: " << a.GetTime() << endl;
 a.GetTime (shrs, smin);
 cout << "a = 1:42 and is: " << shrs << ":" << smin << endl;
 double td;
 d.GetTime (td);
```

```
cout << "d = 1.5 and is " << td << endl;

cout << "\nTesting Assignment\n";
a = f;
cout << "a = 00:42 and is: " << a << endl;

cout << "\nTesting relational operators\n";
cout << (a == f ? "a is == f\n" : "error: a == f\n");
cout << (b > a ? "b is > a\n" : "error: b > a\n");
cout << (b >= a ? "b is >= a\n" : "error: b >= a\n");
cout << (a < c ? "a is < c\n" : "error: a < c\n");
cout << (a <= f ? "a is <= f\n" : "error: a <= f\n");
cout << (a != c ? "a is != c\n" : "error: a != c\n");

cout << "\nTesting Addition operators\n";
a.SetTime (1.0);
b.SetTime (1.0);
c.SetTime (1.0);
c = a + 30;
cout << "c = 01:30 and is " << c << endl;
c = a + b;
cout << "c = 02:00 and is " << c << endl;
c = 30 + a;
cout << "c = 01:30 and is " << c << endl;

cout << "\nTesting Addition operators\n";
a.SetTime (1.0);
b.SetTime (1.0);
c = a + 30;
cout << "c = 01:30 and is " << c << endl;
c = a + b;
cout << "c = 02:00 and is " << c << endl;
c = 30 + a;
cout << "c = 01:30 and is " << c << endl;

cout << "\nTesting Subtraction operators\n";
a.SetTime (1.0);
b.SetTime (1.0);
c = a - 30;
cout << "c = 00:30 and is " << c << endl;
c = a - b;
cout << "c = 00:00 and is " << c << endl;
c = 30 - a;
cout << "c = 23:30 and is " << c << endl;

cout << "\nTesting += and -= operators\n";
c.SetTime (0L, 42L);
a += 42;
cout << "a = 01:42 and is " << a << endl;
a -= c;
cout << "a = 01:00 and is " << a << endl;
a += c;
cout << "a = 01:42 and is " << a << endl;
a -= 42;
cout << "a = 01:00 and is " << a << endl;

```

```
cout << "\nTesting inc and dec operators\n";
a++;
cout << "a = 01:01 and is " << a << endl;
++a;
cout << "a = 01:02 and is " << a << endl;
a--;
cout << "a = 01:01 and is " << a << endl;
--a;
cout << "a = 01:00 and is " << a << endl;
cout << "old a = 01:00 and new a = 01:01 - old a is "
     << a++ << " and new a is " << a << endl;
a--;
cout << "old a = 01:01 and new a = 01:01 - old a is "
     << ++a << " and new a is " << a << endl;

cout << "\nTesting FormatH and FormatHM\n";
a.SetTime (1.567);
char msg[10];
a.FormatH (msg, sizeof (msg));
cout << "a = 1.567 and is " << msg << endl;
char msg2[4];
a.FormatH (msg2, sizeof (msg2));
cout << "a is 1. and is " << msg2 << endl;
d.FormatHM (msg, sizeof (msg));
cout << "d is 01:30 and is " << msg << endl;
d.FormatHM (msg2, sizeof (msg2));
cout << "d is 01: and is " << msg2 << endl;

const Time ca (10L, 30L);
const Time cb (5L, 30L);
cout << "\nTesting GetTime on constant objects\n";
cout << "ca = 630 and is: " << ca.GetTime() << endl;
ca.GetTime (shrs, smin);
cout << "ca = 10:30 and is: " << shrs << ":" << smin << endl;
cb.GetTime (td);
cout << "cb = 5.5 and is " << td << endl;

cout << "\nTesting relational ops on constant objects\n";
cout << (ca == cb ? "error ca is != f\n" : "ca is != cb\n");
cout << (ca > cb ? "ca is > cb\n" : "error: ca > cb\n");
cout << (ca >= cb ? "ca is >= cb\n" : "error: ca >= cb\n");
cout << (cb < ca ? "cb is < ca\n" : "error: cb < ca\n");
cout << (cb <= ca ? "cb is <= ca\n" : "error: cb <= ca\n");
cout << (ca != cb ? "ca is != cb\n" : "error: ca != cb\n");

cout << "\nTesting op+ and op- on constant objects\n";
c = ca + 30;
cout << "c is 11:00 and is " << c << endl;
c = ca + cb;
cout << "c is 16:00 and is " << c << endl;
c = 30 + ca;
cout << "c is 11:00 and is " << c << endl;
c = ca - 30;
cout << "c is 10:00 and is " << c << endl;
c = ca - cb;
cout << "c is 05:00 and is " << c << endl;
```

```
 c = 640 - ca;
 cout << "c is 00:10 and is " << c << endl;

 cout << "\nTesting FormatH and FormatHM on constant objects\n";
 ca.FormatH (msg, sizeof (msg));
 cout << "ca = 10.500 and is " << msg << endl;
 ca.FormatHM (msg, sizeof (msg));
 cout << "ca is 10:30 and is " << msg << endl;

 return 0;
}
```

Output from Pgm03a Time Tester

```
Testing constructors
a = 00:00 and is: 00:00
b = 01:42 and is: 01:42
c = 01:42 and is: 01:42
d = 01:30 and is: 01:30
e = 01:30 and is: 01:30

Testing RollIt ()
f = 00:42 and is: 00:42
g = 23:58 and is: 23:58

Testing SetTime()
a = 01:30 and is: 01:30
a = 01:30 and is: 01:30
a = 01:42 and is: 01:42
a = 01:42 and is: 01:42
a = 01:42 and is: 01:42

Testing GetTime
a = 102 and is: 102
a = 1:42 and is: 1:42
d = 1.5 and is 1.5

Testing Assignment
a = 00:42 and is: 00:42

Testing relational operators
a is == f
b is > a
b is >= a
a is < c
a is <= f
a is != c

Testing Addition operators
c = 01:30 and is 01:30
c = 02:00 and is 02:00
c = 01:30 and is 01:30

Testing Addition operators
c = 01:30 and is 01:30
```

```
c = 02:00 and is 02:00
c = 01:30 and is 01:30

Testing Subtraction operators
c = 00:30 and is 00:30
c = 00:00 and is 00:00
c = 23:30 and is 23:30

Testing += and -= operators
a = 01:42 and is 01:42
a = 01:00 and is 01:00
a = 01:42 and is 01:42
a = 01:00 and is 01:00

Testing inc and dec operators
a = 01:01 and is 01:01
a = 01:02 and is 01:02
a = 01:01 and is 01:01
a = 01:00 and is 01:00
old a = 01:00 and new a = 01:01 -
old a is 01:00 and new a is 01:01
old a = 01:01 and new a = 01:01 -
old a is 01:01 and new a is 01:01

Testing FormatH and FormatHM
a = 1.567 and is  1.567
a is 1. and is  1.
d is 01:30 and is 01:30
d is 01: and is 01:

Testing GetTime on constant objects
ca = 630 and is: 630
ca = 10:30 and is: 10:30
cb = 5.5 and is 5.5

Testing relational ops on constant objects
ca is != cb
ca is > cb
ca is >= cb
cb is < ca
cb is <= ca
ca is != cb

Testing op+ and op- on constant objects
c is 11:00 and is 11:00
c is 16:00 and is 16:00
c is 11:00 and is 11:00
c is 10:00 and is 10:00
c is 05:00 and is 05:00
c is 00:10 and is 00:10

Testing FormatH and FormatHM on constant objects
ca = 10.500 and is 10.500
ca is 10:30 and is 10:30
```

Classes with Dynamic Memory Allocation

When a class has dynamically allocated data members, that class should define three specific functions: the destructor, the copy constructor, and the assignment operator. Failure to do so most likely leads to memory leaks at best and client program crashes at worst. During normal construction or at any other point in the class operations, memory gets dynamically allocated. When the class instance goes out of scope, the destructor is called. The destructor's task is to delete that dynamically allocated memory. However, if during client program operations a copy of an instance is made, without the copy ctor and the assignment operator implementations, the compiler just makes a shallow copy, copying only the memory addresses. Thus, two or more instances point to the same memory. The client program crashes when the second destructor tries to delete the already deleted memory.

To illustrate these principles, let's examine the start of a **String** class designed to make operations with character strings easier for client programs. The class has a single data member, the pointer to the string. When working with classes with dynamic memory data members, it is most convenient to guarantee that under all situations, the pointer does point to something. So the default constructor allocates a null string—that is, a string of one byte containing the null terminator. This is quite different from a null pointer—that is, a pointer whose value is zero. Why?

If the string pointer always points to some kind of null terminated string, then all other class operations can proceed knowing that it does point to a valid string. If, on the other hand, the pointer could itself be zero, then all of the other member functions must begin their coding by querying the existence of the pointer before attempting to use it.

```
if (!string) {
 // oops it does not yet exist - so now what?
}
else {
 // do the requested operations on the string
}
```

Here is the start of the **String** class definition.

```
class String {
protected:
 char* string;
public:
 String ();
 String (const char* str);
 ~String ();
};
```

The three functions can be implemented this way. Notice that some method must be provided to handle the out of memory situation. Until the chapter on C++ Error Handling, we will totally ignore the possibility that the program is out of memory.

```
String::String () {
 string = new char[1];
 string[0] = 0;
}

String::String (const char* str) {
 if (!str) {
  string = new char[1];
  string[0] = 0;
  return;
 }
 string = new char [strlen (str) + 1];
 strcpy (string, str);
}
```

```
String::~String () {
 if (string)
  delete [] string;
}
```

With this simple start, let's examine the copy constructor and assignment operator needs. Suppose that the client program did the following.

```
String Fun (String s); // prototype
...
String s1 ("Hello World");
String s2 ("Good-Bye");
String s3 (s1); // the copy ctor
String s4 = s1; // the copy ctor
String s5;
s5 = s1; // the assignment operator
String s6;
s6 = Fun (s1); // s1 is passed by copy ctor and returned by
               // copy ctor and assignment op to s6
}
...
String Fun (String s) {
 String ret (s); // copy ctor
 return ret;     // copy ctor
}
```

Figure 3.1 illustrates all of the instances of the **String** class just prior to the end brace of the function **Fun** before the return value is assigned to **s6.** The moment the end brace is executed, troubles begin because the compiler then begins to call the destructors for the instances that go out of scope. The destructor for **ret** is called first, followed by the destructor for the parameter **s** which tries to delete the same memory as **ret**.

If the end brace of the **main** function were to also execute, then the compiler would be attempting to delete the string at memory location 100 eight times, including **s6**. Further, because of the shallow copy to **s5**, memory is leaked at location 300. This leads to the following two rules.

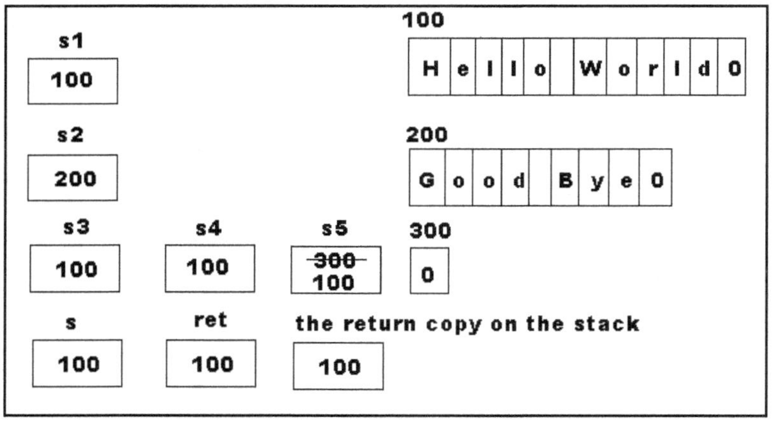

Figure 3.1 Memory Prior to the End } of Fun

Rule: Both the copy constructor and operator= must duplicate the data that is dynamically allocated.

Rule: Operator= must first delete the dynamically allocated memory before it makes the duplicate copy.

Coding the Copy Constructor and Operator= Functions

The first thing to notice about these two functions is that both are making a duplicate copy of the passed object, including any dynamic memory allocated items. Rather than code these actions twice, once within each function, a protected helper function ought to be used, called say **Copy**.

With the copy constructor, the ***this*** instance does not yet exist so there is nothing to delete yet. It can simply invoke the **Copy** helper function. The **operator=** must first delete any dynamically allocated memory that the ***this*** instance points to before it can call the **Copy** helper function. However, there is a further situation that must be examined with **operator=**. Suppose the client codes this.

```
String s1 ("Hello World");
String s2 ("Good Bye");
s1 = s1; // oops, the client meant s2 = s1;
```

If **operator=** begins by deleting the memory pointed to by the passed parameter, which is the instance to the right of the equal sign, then, when the copy operation begins, there is no string left to copy. It has just been deleted!

The prototype for **operator=** is this.

```
String& operator= (const String& s);
```

So the very first thing the function must do is guard against silly user errors such as the above assignment to itself. In this case, the ***this*** parameter contains the memory address of **String s1** while the parameter reference variable also contains the memory address of **String s1**. We need to verify that ***this*** and **s1** are not the same object. This is done by comparing the two memory addresses.

```
if (this == &s1)
  return *this;
```

What would result if we coded the test this way?

```
if (*this == s1)
  return *this;
```

***this** now is a **String** object. Thus, the compiler attempts to call the **operator==** function to find out if the two objects are equivalent. Notice equivalent objects are not necessarily the **same** object! We must determine if these two are in fact the same object.

Here are how the copy constructor and the **operator=** functions can be implemented for the **String** class. Note I am ignoring all errors that can occur if there is insufficient memory to allocate the items.

```
class String {
protected:
 char* string;
public:
 String ();
 String (const char* str);
 String (const String& s);
 String& operator= (const String& s);
 ~String ();
protected:
 void Copy (const String& s);
};
String::String (const String& s) {
 Copy (s);
}
String& String::operator= (const String& s) {
 if (this == &s)
  return *this;
 delete [] string;
 Copy (s);
 return *this;
}
```

```
void String::Copy (const String& s) {
 string = new char [strlen (s.string) + 1];
 strcpy (string, s.string);
}
```

Overloading the [] Operator

The array subscript operator can also be overloaded. With our **String** class, this would be a prudent operator to provide since it then allows the client programs to directly access individual characters within the array. The **operator[]** is a binary operator and thus has one parameter the value the client has coded within the brackets. With subscripts, this is usually an integer but it does not have to be so. But before we try to write the prototype, let's examine the slight problem the operator presents.

A client program can write either of the following statements.

```
String s1 ("Hello World");
char c = s1[0];
s1[0] = 'J';
```

Can you see the difficulty? The first usage is simply copying the indicated character while the second is replacing that character with the letter J. If our **operator[]** function returns the character at the indicated subscript location, then the first usage in the above coding works well; the letter H is stored in variable **c**. However, if we just return the indicated character, then the second usage fails because the letter J cannot be stored back into the string. However, if instead we return a reference to the indicated character, then the second usage works as expected because the compiler now has the memory location of the first element in the string and can replace the letter H with the letter J. Further, in the first usage, the compiler can dereference the reference character to get the actual letter H to store into variable **c**.

Rule: When overloading the operator[], always return a reference to the data so that the operator can be used either as a l-value or a r-value.

Here is the prototype for the **String** class **operator[]**.

```
char& operator[] (int j);
```

Its implementation is done this way. Notice how we can protect from subscript out of range errors.

```
char& String::operator[] (int j) {
 if (j < 0 || j >= (int) strlen (string)) {
  cerr << "Error: subscript out of range: " << j << endl;
  exit (2);
 }
 return string[j];
}
```

Overloading the & Address Operator

The address & operator can be overloaded. Why would anyone want to do so? Let's consider the following coding a client can make using our **String** class.

```
String s1 ("Hello World");
if (_stricmp (s1, "Hello World")...
```

Here, the string function requires a pair of **const char*** parameters. **s1** is a **String** object and so the compiler generates an error on this instruction. So next, the client tries the following.

```
if (_stricmp (&s1, "Hello World")...
```

But now **&s1** is a constant pointer to a **String** object not **const char*** and again issues a compiler error.

Certainly, we could provide an access function to return the needed address for the user.

```
const char* GetString () const {
 return string;
}
```

But this forces some awkward coding in the client program.

```
if (_stricmp (s1.GetString(), "Hello World")...
```

Here is a good situation where overloading the address operator is valuable. It is a unary operator and thus takes no parameters.

```
const char* operator& () const;
```

And it is very simply implemented as follows.

```
const char* String::operator& () const {
 return string;
}
```

Notice that the return value must be constant. If it were not constant, the client could store data into the string and could possibly overwrite memory, for example, by storing more characters than there is space available.

There is a side effect to overloading the address operator. Suppose that we have provided the above address operator overloaded function that returns the string's location. What then occurs when the client program does the following?

```
String* ptrstring = &s1;
```

This now fails as the address operator is now returning a **const char*** not a **const String***! In other words, the client programs can never again take the address of the **String** object itself! We cannot fix this by making a second version whose prototype is this.

```
const String* operator& () const;
```

Why? Overloaded functions cannot differ only in return data type. So if you expect that client programs would like to take the address of **String** objects, then you cannot overload the address operator. Instead, use the **GetString** access function above to provide the **const char***. However, there is another way around this.

Operator Conversion Functions

An operator conversion function is a function that is used to convert from some user-defined type, such as a class instance, into some other user defined type or into an intrinsic data type. With instances of our **String** class, client programs most certainly would like to be able to insert them to an output stream. While we could provide the insertion operator friend function in the **String** class, we can also provide an operator conversion function to convert a **String** class instance into a **const char*** instance, which points to the **string** data member.

The syntax for operator conversion function prototypes is **operator** followed by the type to which it is to be converted. Such functions take no parameters. Since the instance is being converted to the indicated data type, there is also no return data type coded. Here is the **String** operator **const char*** conversion function prototype.

```
operator const char* () const;
```

It is implemented this way.

```
String::operator const char* () const {
 return string;
}
```

While this looks promising, in fact when client programs use it, the syntax is awful. Here is how the client can insert an instance of our **String** class to **cout**.

```
cout << s1.operator const char*() << endl;
```

This is not elegant coding for the client programs.

However, this concept does have a singularly powerful usage. Recall how we usually utilize the extraction operator when reading a set of data.

```
while (cin >> x) {
```

We know that this is saying while the stream is still okay do the body of the loop. But how is this accomplished? We also know the extraction operator returns a reference to the original input stream. So the above becomes the following once the extraction is complete.

```
while (cin) {
```

How does this actually work?

The compiler calls an operator conversion function. It is coded within the **ios** class this way.

```
ios::operator void* () {
 return fail () ? 0 : this;
}
```

In other words, the compiler calls a conversion function to try to convert the **cin** instance into a void pointer. And the compiler can test the pointer to obtain the **bool** value, **true** if the pointer is not 0. (The fail bit is on if any kind of non-good event has occurred.)

Can we make use of this with our **String** class? Perhaps. Unlike the futile attempt to allow a conversion to a **const char***, we can readily convert to a **void***. Suppose that the client programs frequently wished to know if a given **String** instance contained a null string, that is, a string of length 1 containing only the null terminator. We could have this operator **void*** return this state.

```
operator void* () const;
String::operator void* () const {
 return string[0] == 0 ? 0 : string;
}
```

Clients could now test for null strings this way.

```
if (!s1) ...
```

This approach of using a **void*** conversion function can be useful in certain circumstances in which clients wish to somehow "test" an instance of a class for some purpose.

Pgm03b—String Class Thus Far

Here is the **String** class to this point in its design.

String Class Definition

```
#pragma once

/***************************************************************/
/*                                                             */
/* String Class: encapsulate a character string                */
/*                                                             */
/***************************************************************/

class String {
protected:
 char* string; // the client's string

public:
 String ();                          // makes a null string
 String (const char* str);           // copies the passed string
 String (const String& s);           // copies a String object
 String& operator= (const String& s); // assigns a String object
 ~String ();                         // deletes the string array

 const char* GetString () const; // returns ptr to the string
 char& operator[] (int j);       // handles array subscripting
 operator void* () const;  // true if string is not a null string

protected:
```

```
 void Copy (const String& s); // performs deep copy of the String
};

```

String Class Implementation

```
#include <iostream>
#include <string>
using namespace std;

#include "String.h"

/***************************************************************/
/*                                                             */
/* String: allocates a null string, aborts if out of memory    */
/*                                                             */
/***************************************************************/

String::String () {
 string = new (std::nothrow) char[1];
 if (!string) {
  cerr << "Error: out of memory in String ctor\n";
  exit (1);
 }
 string[0] = 0;
}

/***************************************************************/
/*                                                             */
/* String: stores passed string, aborts if out of memory       */
/*                                                             */
/***************************************************************/

String::String (const char* str) {
 if (!str) {
  string = new (std::nothrow) char[1];
  if (!string) {
   cerr << "Error: out of memory in String ctor\n";
   exit (1);
  }
  string[0] = 0;
  return;
 }
 string = new (std::nothrow) char [strlen (str) + 1];
 if (!string) {
  cerr << "Error: out of memory in String ctor\n";
  exit (1);
 }
 strcpy_s (string, strlen (str) + 1, str);
}

/***************************************************************/
/*                                                             */
/* ~String: deletes the array of char                          */
/*                                                             */
```

```
/***************************************************************/

String::~String () {
 if (string)
  delete [] string;
}

/***************************************************************/
/*                                                             */
/* String: copy ctor duplicates the passed string              */
/*                                                             */
/***************************************************************/

String::String (const String& s) {
 Copy (s);
}

/***************************************************************/
/*                                                             */
/* operator=: assigns passed string to this instance           */
/*                                                             */
/***************************************************************/

String& String::operator= (const String& s) {
 if (this == &s)
  return *this;
 delete [] string;
 Copy (s);
 return *this;
}

/***************************************************************/
/*                                                             */
/* Copy: actually duplicates the passed string, abort if out   */
/*                                              of memory      */
/*                                                             */
/***************************************************************/

void String::Copy (const String& s) {
 string = new (std::nothrow) char [strlen (s.string) + 1];
 if (!string) {
  cerr << "Error: out of memory in String Copy\n";
  exit (1);
 }
 strcpy_s (string, strlen (s.string) + 1, s.string);
}

/***************************************************************/
/*                                                             */
/* GetString: returns the address of the stored string         */
/*                                                             */
/***************************************************************/

const char* String::GetString () const {
 return string;
}
```

```

/*****************************************************************/
/*                                                               */
/* operator[]: provides access to jth element of the array       */
/*             aborts if subscript is out of range               */
/*                                                               */
/*****************************************************************/

char& String::operator[] (int j) {
 if (j < 0 || j >= (int) strlen (string)) {
  cerr << "Error: subscript out of range: " << j << endl;
  exit (2);
 }
 return string[j];
}

/*****************************************************************/
/*                                                               */
/* operator void* - returns 0 if string is a null string         */
/*                  or addr of string is it is not null          */
/*                                                               */
/*****************************************************************/

String::operator void* () const {
 return string[0] == 0 ? 0 : string;
}
```

Pgm03b tests these functions that we have coded thus far. One of the programming assignments will extend this class by adding many very useful operator functions.

Pgm03b String Class Tester

```
#include <iostream>
#include <iomanip>
#include <string>
#include <crtdbg.h>
using namespace std;

#include "String.h"

/*****************************************************************/
/*                                                               */
/* Pgm03b: String Tester Program                                 */
/*                                                               */
/*****************************************************************/

String Fun (String s);

int main () {
 {
 String s1 ("Hello World");
 String s2 ("Good-Bye");
 String s3 (s1); // the copy ctor
 String s4 = s1; // the copy ctor
 String s5;
 s5 = s1; // the assignment operator
```

```
 String s6;
 s6 = Fun (s1); // s1 is passed by copy ctor and returned by
                // copy ctor and assignment op to s6
 String s7;

 cout << "s1 should be |Hello World| and is\n"
      << "             |" << s1.GetString() << "|\n\n";
 cout << "s2 should be |Good-Bye| and is\n"
      << "             |" << s2.GetString() << "|\n\n";
 cout << "s3 should be |Hello World| and is\n"
      << "             |" << s3.GetString() << "|\n\n";
 cout << "s4 should be |Hello World| and is\n"
      << "             |" << s4.GetString() << "|\n\n";
 cout << "s5 should be |Hello World| and is\n"
      << "             |" << s5.GetString() << "|\n\n";
 cout << "s6 should be |Hello World| and is\n"
      << "             |" << s6.GetString() << "|\n\n";
 cout << "s7 should be || and is\n"
      << "             |" << s7.GetString() << "|\n\n";

 if (s7)
  cout << "s7 is not null - error\n";
 else
  cout << "s7 is null and is correct\n";

 if (s2)
  cout << "s2 is not null and is correct\n";
 else
  cout << "s2 is null - error\n";

 cout << "\nFirst character of s1 should be H and is "
      << s1[0] << endl;
 s1[0] = 'J';
 cout << "\nFirst character of s1 should be J and is "
      << s1[0] << endl;
 }

 // check for memory leaks
 if (_CrtDumpMemoryLeaks())
  cerr << "Memory leaks occurred!\n";
 else
  cerr << "No memory leaks.\n";

 return 0;
}

String Fun (String s) {
 String ret (s); // copy ctor
 return ret;     // copy ctor
}
```

```
Output from Pgm03b String Class Tester
```

```
s1 should be |Hello World| and is
             |Hello World|
```

```

s2 should be |Good-Bye| and is
             |Good-Bye|

s3 should be |Hello World| and is
             |Hello World|

s4 should be |Hello World| and is
             |Hello World|

s5 should be |Hello World| and is
             |Hello World|

s6 should be |Hello World| and is
             |Hello World|

s7 should be || and is
             ||

s7 is null and is correct
s2 is not null and is correct

First character of s1 should be H and is H

First character of s1 should be J and is J
No memory leaks.
```

Reviewing the Basic Generic Growable Array Class

In Beginning Data Structures, we created a **container class** for an array that grows in size as the number of items are added. The limit on the array size is the amount of memory available. In order to gain reusability, the growable array stored void pointers to the user's data.

A **void*** is independent of data type, Such pointers cannot be dereferenced. However, if all that our class is doing is maintaining an array of such pointers and providing access to those pointers, we do not need to dereference such pointers.

When a user wishes to gain access to a specific element and calls say **GetAt (i)** to acquire the ith one, our function returns to the user a **void***. For the user to be able to do anything with that data, he or she must typecast the pointer back to the specific data type to which it is pointing. The user, of course, knows what kind of data to which it is supposed to be pointing. This, of course, places an extra burden on the programmer. However, the benefits of using a generic array container are many. We can also implement **operator[]** as an alternative method to accessing elements.

There is also a significant side effect of storing only **void** pointers. The programmer must allocate the items they wish the container to store and they must delete those items before any class destructor is called. When the programmer calls the **Add** function, they must pass the address of the item to be stored. Frequently, they will have already dynamically allocated that item and filled it up with relevant data. Later, **before** any destructor of the **Array** class is called, they must traverse all elements in the array, retrieve each pointer from the **Array** and then delete the memory occupied by that item.

Another side effect is copying of the array. The copy ctor and the assignment operator have no way to actually make a deep copy of a passed array because the data items are **void** pointers. So in this case, these two functions will make a duplicate copy of the array of pointers, but not the client's data that is being stored.

It is then up to the client to traverse the array, acquiring and then deleting each of the objects the array is storing before the destructor is called.

Here are the **Array** class definition and implementation files. Please note that I am ignoring the out of memory error situation.

Array Class Definition

```
#pragma once

/***************************************************************/
/*                                                             */
/* Array: container for growable array of void* items        */
/*        it can store a variable number of elements          */
/*                                                             */
/*        since elements stored are void*, they can           */
/*        point to anything desired, intrinsic types,         */
/*        structures, other classes, for example              */
/*                                                             */
/*  limited by amount of memory and swap drive size           */
/*                                                             */
/*  errors are logged to cerr device                          */
/*                                                             */
/*  Note on destruction: before calling RemoveAt or           */
/*  RemoveAll or the destructor, the user is responsible */
/*  for the actual deletion of the items the void*            */
/*  pointers are actually pointing to                         */
/*                                                             */
/*  Typical clean up coding might be as follows:              */
/*  MyData* ptrd;                                              */
/*  for (i=0; i<array.GetNumberOfElements(); i++) {           */
/*   ptrd = (MyData*) array.GetAt (i);                        */
/*   if (ptrd)                                                 */
/*    delete ptrd;                                             */
/*  }                                                          */
/*  array.RemoveAll ();                                        */
/*                                                             */
/***************************************************************/

class Array {

 /**************************************************************/
 /*                                                            */
 /* class data                                                 */
 /*                                                            */
 /**************************************************************/

protected:
 void** array;
 long  numElements;

 /**************************************************************/
 /*                                                            */
 /* class functions                                            */
 /*                                                            */
 /**************************************************************/
```

```

public:
  // default constructor - makes an empty array
  Array ();

  // be sure to delete what the void* are pointing to before
  // the destructor is called
 ~Array ();
      // add the element to array end, returns true if successful
 bool Add (void* ptrNewElement);

      // adds this element at subscript i
      // if i < 0, it is added at the front
      // if i >= numElements, it is added at the end
      // otherwise, it is added at the ith position
      // returns true if successful
 bool InsertAt (long i, void* ptrNewElement);

       // returns element at the ith pos
       // if i is out of range, it returns 0
 void* GetAt (long i) const;

       // returns element at the ith pos, if out of range
 void* operator[] (long i);

      // removes the element at subscript i, element actually
      // pointed to is not deleted
 bool RemoveAt (long i);

      // removes all elements - what is pointed to is not deleted
 void RemoveAll ();

      // returns the number of elements in the array
 long GetNumberOfElements () const;

 // copy constructor duplicates the array, but not the items
 Array (const Array& a);

        // duplicates the array, but not the items
 Array& operator= (const Array& a); //

protected:
      // performs the actual deep copy
 void Copy (const Array& a);
};

```

Array Class Implementation

```
#include <iostream>
using namespace std;
#include "Array.h"

/*********************************************************/
/*                                                       */
```

```
/* Array: constructs an empty array                          */
/*                                                           */
/*************************************************************/

Array::Array () {
 numElements = 0;
 array = 0;
}

/*************************************************************/
/*                                                           */
/* ~Array: deletes dynamically allocated memory              */
/*         It is the client's responsibility  to delete      */
/*         what the void* are pointing to before the         */
/*         destructor is called                              */
/*                                                           */
/*************************************************************/

Array::~Array () {
 RemoveAll ();
}

/*************************************************************/
/*                                                           */
/* Add: Adds this new element to the end of the array        */
/*      if out of memory, displays error message to cerr     */
/*                                                           */
/*************************************************************/

bool Array::Add (void* ptrNewElement) {
 // allocate new temporary array one element larger
 void** temp = new (std::nothrow) void* [numElements + 1];

 // check for out of memory
 if (!temp) {
  cerr << "Array: Add Error - out of memory\n";
  return false;
 }

 // copy all existing elements into the new temp array
 for (long i=0; i<numElements; i++) {
  temp[i] = array[i];
 }

 // copy in the new element to be added
 temp[numElements] = ptrNewElement;

 numElements++;  // inc the number of elements in the array
 if (array) delete [] array; // delete the old array
 array = temp;   // point out array to the new array
 return true;
}

/*************************************************************/
/*                                                           */
/* InsertAt: adds the new element to the array at index i*/
```

```
/*  if i is in range, it is inserted at subscript i      */
/*  if i is negative, it is inserted at the front        */
/*  if i is greater than or equal to the number of       */
/*     elements, then it is added at the end of the array*/
/*                                                       */
/*  if there is insufficient memory, an error message    */
/*     is displayed to cerr                              */
/*                                                       */
/*******************************************************/

bool Array::InsertAt (long i, void* ptrNewElement) {
 void** temp;
 long j;
 // allocate a new array one element larger
 temp = new (std::nothrow) void* [numElements + 1];

 // check if out of memory
 if (!temp) {
  cerr << "Array: InsertAt - Error out of memory\n";
  return false;
 }

 // this case handles an insertion that is within range
 if (i < numElements && i >= 0) {
  for (j=0; j<i; j++) { // copy all elements below insertion
   temp[j] = array[j];  // point
  }
  temp[i] = ptrNewElement; // insert new element
  for (j=i; j<numElements; j++) { // copy remaining elements
   temp[j+1] = array[j];
  }
 }

 // this case handles an insertion when the index is too large
 else if (i >= numElements) {
  for (j=0; j<numElements; j++) { // copy all existing elements
   temp[j] = array[j];
  }
  temp[numElements] = ptrNewElement; // add new one at end
 }

 // this case handles an insertion when the index is too small
 else {
  temp[0] = ptrNewElement;        // insert new on at front
  for (j=0; j<numElements; j++) { // copy all others after it
   temp[j+1] = array[j];
  }
 }

 // for all cases, delete current array, assign new one and
 // increment the number of elements in the array
 if (array) delete [] array;
 array = temp;
 numElements++;
 return true;
}
```

```

/*********************************************************/
/*                                                       */
/* GetAt: returns the element at index i                 */
/*        if i is out of range, returns 0                */
/*                                                       */
/*********************************************************/

void* Array::GetAt (long i) const {
 if (i < numElements && i >=0)
  return array[i];
 else
  return 0;
}

/*********************************************************/
/*                                                       */
/* operator[]: returns the element at index i            */
/*             if i is out of range, returns 0           */
/*                                                       */
/*********************************************************/

void* Array::operator[] (long i) {
 if (i < numElements && i >=0)
  return array[i];
 else
  return 0;
}

/*********************************************************/
/*                                                       */
/* RemoveAt: removes the element at subscript i          */
/*                                                       */
/* If i is out of range, an error is displayed on cerr   */
/*                                                       */
/* Note that what the element actually points to is not  */
/*      deleted                                          */
/*                                                       */
/*********************************************************/

bool Array::RemoveAt (long i) {
 void** temp;
 if (numElements > 1) {
  if (i >= 0 && i < numElements) { // if the index is in range
   // allocate a smaller array
   temp = new (std::nothrow) void* [numElements - 1];
   long j;
   for (j=0; j<i; j++) {              // copy all elements up to
    temp[j] = array[j];               // the desired one to be
   }                                  // removed
   for (j=i+1; j<numElements; j++) { // copy all the elements
    temp[j-1] = array[j];             // that remain
   }
   numElements--;               // dec the number of elements
   delete [] array;             // delete the old array
   array = temp;                // and assign the new one
```

```
   return true;
  }
 }
 else if (numElements == 1 && i == 0) {
  delete [] array;
  numElements = 0;
  array = 0;
  return true;
 }
 cerr << "Array: RemoveAt Error - element out of range\n"
      << "       It was " << i << " and numElements is "
      << numElements << endl;
 return false;
}

/***************************************************************/
/*                                                             */
/* RemoveAll: empties the entire array, resetting it to        */
/*            an empty state ready for reuse                   */
/*                                                             */
/* Note that what the elements actually points to are          */
/*      not deleted                                            */
/*                                                             */
/***************************************************************/

void Array::RemoveAll () {
 if (array) delete [] array; // remove all elements
 numElements = 0;            // reset number of elements
 array = 0;                  // and reset array to 0
}

/***************************************************************/
/*                                                             */
/* GetNumberOfElements: returns the number of elements         */
/*                      currently in the array                 */
/*                                                             */
/***************************************************************/

long Array::GetNumberOfElements () const {
 return numElements;
}

/***************************************************************/
/*                                                             */
/* Array: copy constructor, makes a duplicate copy of a        */
/*                                                             */
/* Note: what the elements actually point to are not           */
/* duplicated only our pointers are duplicated                 */
/*                                                             */
/***************************************************************/

Array::Array (const Array& a) {
 Copy (a);
}

/***************************************************************/
```

```
/*                                                           */
/* operator=: makes a duplicate array of passed array a      */
/*                                                           */
/* Note: what the elements actually point to are not .       */
/* duplicated only our pointers are duplicated               */
/*                                                           */
/*************************************************************/

Array& Array::operator= (const Array& a) {
 if (this == &a) // avoids silly a = a assignemnts
  return *this;
 if (array) delete [] array; // remove existing array
 Copy (a);                   // duplicate array a
 return *this;         // return us for chaining assignments
}

/*************************************************************/
/*                                                           */
/* Copy: helper function to actual perform the copy          */
/*                                                           */
/*************************************************************/

void Array::Copy (const Array& a) {
 if (a.numElements) { // be sure array a is not empty
  numElements = a.numElements;
  // allocate a new array the size of a
  array = new (std::nothrow) void* [numElements];

  // check for out of memory condition
  if (!array) {
   cerr << "Array: Copy function - Error out of memory\n";
   numElements = 0;
   return;
  }

  // copy all of a's pointers into our array
  for (long i=0; i<numElements; i++) {
   array[i] = a.array[i];
  }
 }
 else { // a is empty, so make ours empty too
  numElements = 0;
  array = 0;
 }
}
```

Review Questions

1. What is meant by operator overloading? Why is operator overloading an important feature of a class?

2. Why cannot a programmer overload the operator+ and have it output the object to a disk file? Is there anything in the language prohibiting it?

3. Which operators cannot be overloaded?

4. Can the precedence of C++ operators be modified to better suit a class design when needed?

5. What is the difference between a binary operator and a unary operator? Give an example of each.

6. Why should operator overloaded functions be passed a constant reference to objects whenever possible instead of a totally safe copy of that object?

7. When would an operator overloaded member function be a constant function?

8. Under what circumstances should an operator overloaded function return a copy of an object instead of a reference to an object?

9. Write the prototype for the multiply operator function in the **Point** class such that the client can write

```
c = a * 10;
```

where **c** and **a** are **Point** instances.

10. Why must the insertion and extraction operator overloaded functions be friend functions and not member functions?

11. Why must a class that has dynamic memory allocation occurring within its data members always provide the copy ctor and the assignment operator functions? Is a destructor function really needed? Why?

12. Why should a function that is dynamically allocating a data member take some kind of action when the returned pointer from the **new** function is 0?

13. Assume the following definition for a class **Fun**. What is the inherent design glitch?

```
class Fun {
protected:
 int* x;
public:
 Fun () : x(0) {}
...
```

14. Why must a **operator=** function first check to see it this instance is the same as the passed instance? Why doesn't this work to do so?

```
if (*this == s)
```

where **s** is the passed object to be copied.

15. What are the benefits of using a **Copy** function when implementing the copy ctor and assignment operator functions?

16. A programmer coded the following prototype for **operator[]** to access a specific element in an array of integers. What is wrong with this definition and how can it be fixed?

```
int operator[] (int i);
```

17. If one overloads the address operator for a class **Fun** to return the address of the start of an array of integers, why does the following then fail?

```
Fun array;
Fun* ptrThisOne = &array;
```

18. What is the purpose of coding an operator conversion function to convert a class into a **void***?

Stop! Do These Exercises Before Programming

This series of exercises uses a **Date** class. In my World War II game, a date is stored as a **short** number of days since the war began on 1 September 1939. The class definition begins as follows.

```
class Date {
protected:
 short days;
public:
...
```

1. Write the function prototype and then the function header and body to implement **operator+** such that all of the following are valid.

```
date2 = date1 + 42;
date2 = 42 + date;
```

2. Write the function prototype and then the function header and body to implement **operator+=** such that the following is valid.

```
date2 += 42;
```

3. Write the function prototype and then the function header and body to implement **operator==** and **operator<** such that all of the following are valid.

```
if (date2 == date1)...
while (dateNow < dateEnd) {
```

4. Write the function prototype and then the function header and body to implement **operator++** such that all of the following are valid.

```
date2 = date1++;
date2 = ++date1;
```

5. Write the function prototype and then the function header and body to implement **operator=** such that all of the following are valid. Note that the assignment operator is not really necessary for this class.

```
date2 = date1;
date2 = date2;
```

6. Write the function prototype and then the function header and body to implement **operator>>** such that all of the following are valid.

```
cin >> date2 >> date3;
while (infile >> date2) {
```

On input, the date is in the form of mm/dd/yyyy. There is a helper function called **Serial** that is passed three integers, month, day, and year, and it returns the short number of days since September 1, 1939. You do not need to code the **Serial** function, just use call it.

7. Write the function prototype and then the function header and body to implement **FormatDate** which is passed a client's string and its length. There is a helper function called **GetDate** that is passed three integer references (month, day, and year) and it fills these references with the calendar date this short date represents. You do not need to code the **GetDate** function, rather call it. The string should contain a date in the form of mm/dd/yyyy. Avoid overwriting memory if the passed string is too small to hold all of the characters. Under all circumstances the string should be null terminated.

8. Write the function prototype and then the function header and body to implement **operator<<** such that all of the following are valid.

```
cout << date2;
outfile << date2;
```

Reuse your **FormatDate** function from question 7 above to assist in displaying the string date on the output stream.

9. Consider this class definition for a complex number array class.

```
class Cmplx {
protected:
 double* realPart;
 double* imagPart;
 long count;
public:
 Cmplx (double* realArray, double* imagArray, long num);
 Cmplx&  operator= (const Cmplx& c);
...

Cmplx::Cmplx (double* realArray, double* imagArray, long num) {
 realPart = new double [count];
 inagPart = new double [count];
 count = num;
 for (long j=0; j<num; j++) {
  realPart[j] = realArray[j];
  imagPart[j] = imagArray[j];
 }
}

Cmplx& Cmplx::operator= (const Cmplx& c) {
 realPart = new double [c.count];
 inagPart = new double [c.count];
 count = c.count;
 for (long j=0; j<count; j++) {
  realPart[j] = c.realPart[j];
  imagPart[j] = c.imagPart[j];
 }
}
```

What is wrong with the design of the **operator=** function and how can it be fixed?

10. Code a copy constructor for the above **Cmplx** number class.

11. Code an **operator[]** function for the above **Cmplx** number class. It should be able to handle both l-values and r-values. Display an error message to **cerr** if the subscript is out of range and abort the program.

12. Code an operator conversion **void*** function for the above **Cmplx** number class. It returns 0 if the array contains no elements. Otherwise, it returns the address of the **realPart** array.

Programming Problems

Problem Pgm03-1—A Date Class—III

Modify the **Date** class of Problem **Pgm02-1** as follows to make it more efficient and useful.

Modifications to the Interface for the Date Class

Remove the **Add**, **Subtract**, **Difference**, **Compare**, **Input**, and **Output** functions from the **Date** class and add in new operator functions to make the class much easier to use.

Alterations to the Date Class

For the following discussion, assume the following variables have been defined in **main**.

```
Date date, olddate, newdate;
long  n;
```

1. Replace the **Input** function with the extraction (>>) operator, deleting the old function. Typical use now is as follows.

```
cin >> date;
```

2. Replace the **Output** function with the insertion operator (<<), deleting the old function. Typical use now is as follows.

```
cout << date;
```

3. Replace the **Add** function with **operator+**, deleting the old function. The following addition instructions should work.

```
newdate = date + n;
newdate = n + date:
```

4. Replace the **Subtract** function with **operator–**, deleting the old function. The following is a typical subtraction.

```
olddate = date - n;
```

5. Replace the **Difference** function with **operator–**, deleting the old function. The following is typical use.

```
n = newdate - date;
```

6. Provide support for comparisons by adding the operators: ==, !=, >, >=, <, <=. Each operator returns a **bool** which is **true** when the condition is true. If you wish, you may keep and use the old **Compare** function. Typical use might be as shown.

```
if (date == newdate)
if (newdate < olddate)
```

7. Add support for **operator++**. Both prefix and postfix forms are required so that either of these two are valid.

```
newdate = date++;
newdate = ++date;
```

8. Add support for **operator--**. Both forms are required so that either of these two are valid.

```
olddate = date--;
olddate = --date;
```

9. Add support for **operator+=**. Typical use is as shown.

```
newdate += n;
```

10 Add support for **operator–=**. Typical use is as shown.

```
olddate -= n;
```

11. Provide three access functions for retrieving the date components. All return an integer: **GetMonth**, **GetDay**, and **GetYear**. Typical use is as follows.

```
int month = date.GetMonth ();
```

Remember to watch for the use of **const**. Note that there is no public function to create a **Date** object from a **long** serial date number, because that conversion from **long** back into a date is an implementation detail subject to change.

Test your class using the provided pair of programs and test data, **Pgm03-1A.cpp** and **Pgm03-1B.cpp** which use **Pgm03-1A.txt** and **Pgm03-1B.tx**t test data files respectively. Build a project for each of these. Both programs create no screen output; all results are written to disk files, namely **Pgm03-1A-results.txt** and **Pgm03-1B-results.txt**. You should get the results shown in the next two figures, Figure 3.2 and Figure3.3.

```
DATE 1         DATE 2         DIFFERENCE

01/01/1996     01/01/1996           0
01/02/1996     01/01/1996           1
01/02/1995     01/01/1996        -364
02/01/1996     01/01/1996          31
02/01/1995     01/01/1996        -334
03/01/1996     01/01/1996          60
03/01/1995     01/01/1996        -306
12/31/1996     01/01/1996         365
12/31/1995     01/01/1996          -1
01/01/1997     01/01/1996         366
01/01/1994     01/01/1996        -730
03/01/1997     01/01/1996         425
03/01/1994     01/01/1996        -671
06/15/1997     01/01/1996         531
06/15/1994     01/01/1996        -565
09/20/1999     01/01/1996        1358
09/20/1993     01/01/1996        -833
01/01/2000     01/01/1996        1461
01/01/1990     01/01/1996       -2191
04/21/2000     01/01/1996        1572
04/21/1990     01/01/1996       -2081
12/31/2400     01/01/1996      147923
12/31/1601     01/01/1996     -143906
01/01/1900     01/01/1900           0
12/31/2400     01/01/1601      292193
01/01/2000     12/31/1899       36525
01/01/2000     12/31/2400     -146462
07/01/2049     01/01/1900       54603
07/01/1750     01/01/1900      -54605
01/01/1601     12/31/2100     -182620

conDateA  = 12/31/1899
conDateB  = 01/01/2000
date_1    = 12/31/1899
date_2    = 01/01/2000
```

Figure 3.2 Output from Pgm03-1A

```
DATE 1         DATE 2         DIFFERENCE

01/01/1996     01/01/1996           0
01/02/1996     01/01/1996           1
01/02/1995     01/01/1996        -364
02/01/1996     01/01/1996          31
02/01/1995     01/01/1996        -334
03/01/1996     01/01/1996          60
03/01/1995     01/01/1996        -306
12/31/1996     01/01/1996         365
12/31/1995     01/01/1996          -1
01/01/1997     01/01/1996         366
01/01/1994     01/01/1996        -730
03/01/1997     01/01/1996         425
03/01/1994     01/01/1996        -671
06/15/1997     01/01/1996         531
06/15/1994     01/01/1996        -565
09/20/1999     01/01/1996        1358
09/20/1993     01/01/1996        -833
01/01/2000     01/01/1996        1461
01/01/1990     01/01/1996       -2191
04/21/2000     01/01/1996        1572
04/21/1990     01/01/1996       -2081
12/31/2400     01/01/1996      147923
12/31/1601     01/01/1996     -143906
01/01/1900     01/01/1900           0
12/31/2400     01/01/1601      292193
01/01/2000     12/31/1899       36525
01/01/2000     12/31/2400     -146462
07/01/2049     01/01/1900       54603
07/01/1750     01/01/1900      -54605
01/01/1601     12/31/2100     -182620
12/31/1899     01/01/1900          -1
03/01/1900     02/28/1900           1
10/31/1999     10/30/1999           1
02/29/2000     02/28/2000           1
07/01/1995     06/30/1995           1
```

Figure 3.3 Output from Pgm03-1B

Problem Pgm03-2—Distance Class—III

This problem modifies **Pgm02-4—Distance Class II**.
Modifications to the Interface for the Distance Class

1. Add two friend functions, **operator<<** and **operator >>** so that we can input a distance object and output a distance object. The extraction operator displays a prompt to **cout** and then uses **cin** to input the distance as follows.

```
Enter a distance in millimeters: 3.456
```

The insertion function displays the following format on the passed output stream.

```
Distance is nnnnnn.nn millimeters
```

Always use a precision of two digits and a total width of 12 bytes.

2. Add operator functions so that the following are valid (all numbers are in millimeters)

```
Distance a, b, c;
c = a + b;
c = a + xxx;    // where xxx is an int, long or double
c = xxx + a;    // where xxx is an int, long or double
c = a;          // make an assignment operator
```

```
if (a == b)     // also valid are !=, <, >, <=, and >=
c++; and  ++c;
c--; and  --c;
```

Create a main program to thoroughly test the **Distance** class similar to **Pgm03a Time Class Tester**.

Problem Pgm03-3—Extensions to the String Class

Modify the **String** class of **Pgm03b** in this chapter as follows to make it more efficient and useful.

Add support for **operator+=** which should concatenate the passed string onto the end of the string data member.

Add support for the insertion and extraction operators to input or display a string. Assume that the maximum length of any string on input is 100.

Add support for **operator+** in which the passed parameter is a **const char***. Usage would be similar to this.

```
s1 = s2 + "Hello";
```

Add support for **operator+** in which the passed parameter is another **String** object. Usage would be similar to this.

```
s1 = s2 + s3;
```

Extend the tester program, **Pgm03b**, to include thorough testing of all the new functions.

Chapter 4—Inheritance

Introduction

One of the most powerful features of OOP is inheritance—the ability to derive a new class from an existing class, forming a hierarchy of classes. Inheritance is the process by which a class is derived from a base or parent class so that it can inherit the data and functions of that base class to avoid "re-inventing the wheel" and to add or expand upon the base class functionality. In the real world of OOP programming, once you have created a terrific class, someone else will undoubtedly see it also as valuable and wish to reuse it by extending it a bit further to solve their problems.

The nomenclature that is used with these interdependent classes is as follows.

```
base   class     derived class
parent class     child   class
super  class     sub     class
```

In this text, I will use the terms base class and derived class exclusively.

Let's take an example from my WWII game. Assume that we have a complete implementation for a **Vehicle** class that encapsulates the movement of a basic vehicle. Now we can derive a **Car** class from the **Vehicle** class and inherit all of the data members and member functions of the **Vehicle** class. That is, all of those can be reused as is in the **Car** class. Of course, a **Car** class would add in some additional member data such as the size of the gas tank, the number of gallons of gas, the miles per gallon the car gets, and whether or not the engine is started. The **Car** class would also define additional member functions, if only to provide access to these new properties. However, should the base **Vehicle** class functions no longer provide the exact implementation, they can be overridden by a similarly named member function in the **Car** class. This certainly would be the case with the **SetSpeed** function because one cannot have the car moving along at 50 miles per hour unless the car is started and has gas.

Now once the **Car** class is operational, what is a truck but a car with cargo carrying capacity? So now we can derive a **Truck** from a **Car** class and add in a new data member, the cargo capacity. Further, what is an armored car but a **Car** with a gun? So we can derive the **ArmoredCar** class from the **Car**. Similarly, a **Halftrack** class can be derived from the **Truck** class, adding in a machine gun and ammunition. Likewise, we can derive class **Tank** from the **Halftrack** by adding in a big gun.

Ah, but what is an airplane? Is it also not a vehicle that moves? So we can define class **Plane** from the **Vehicle**. And from class **Plane** we can extend to class **Fighter** and **Bomber**. Likewise, a boat is a **Vehicle** that moves on water. So class **Boat** can be derived from a **Vehicle**. And from **Boat**, we can derive **AircraftCarrier**, **Battleship**, **Cruiser**, **Destroyer**, and **Submarine**. Even class **Infantry** can be derived from the **Vehicle** class!

In short, every item used in an "army" in the war game can ultimately be derived from the lowly **Vehicle** class! You see, we can provide the basic implementation of movement activities and then inherit that functionality in every one of the additional classes. Of course, there will be times that we need to provide a replacement function because the **Vehicle** implementation does not apply, as with the motored vehicles.

Besides the large amount of code reuse, there is another terrifically important ability that this class hierarchy provides us. Suppose that our task is to manage a fleet of company vehicles. The company's fleet certainly would have instances of a **Car** and **Truck** class, but would also likely have instances of classes **Limo** and **Bus**. If a program must maintain a fleet of such vehicles, then the main function would need to define the following fields.

```
Car cars[100];
Truck trucks[100];
Limo limos[100];
Bus buses[100];
```

```
int numCars;
int numTrucks;
int numLimos;
int numBuses;
```

What would the prototype for a **FillFleetWithGas** function look like? It would have to be passed all four arrays and the current number in each array. This becomes very awkward indeed.

However, since each of these new classes is derived from a lowly **Vehicle**, one could define the fleet this way.

```
Vehicle* fleet[1000];
int numFleet;
```

The eight variables have been reduced to a single array of pointers to **Vehicle** objects and the number in that array. One would then allocate individual vehicles as needed.

```
fleet[0] = new Car;
fleet[1] = new Truck;
fleet[2] = new Limo;
fleet[3] = new Bus;
numFleet = 4;
```

Operations can then be performed using the pointer operator. For example,

```
fleet[0]->SetSpeed (42);
```

Rule: A pointer declared as a pointer to a base class can also be used to point to any class derived from that base class.

This is indeed where we are headed with inheritance. By storing an array of pointers to the base class, a tremendous reduction in client programming complexity is removed.

Principles of Inheritance

The syntax to derive a new class from an existing class is as follows.

```
class derived : access base_class {
};
```

where *access* is **public**, **protected**, or **private**.

Protected access allows one to retain the base class access types for all base class data and member functions. Yet, these base class items are still accessible directly within the derived class. In other words, if an item is public in the base class, it remains public in the derived class. If it is protected, it is still protected in the derived class though the derived class only can directly access it. If it is private in the base class, it remains private in the derived class which means the derived class cannot directly access it.

The following table 4.1 illustrates the options and their effects.

Table 4.1 The Derivation Table

derived from base class as:	access qualifier for base class data and functions		
	public:	protected:	private:
public	public	protected	inaccessible
protected	protected	protected	inaccessible
private	private	private	inaccessible

The most common derivation used is public. If one derives **Car** publically from **Vehicle**, then whatever is public in the **Vehicle** class remains public in the **Car** class. Whatever was protected remains protected. And private **Vehicle** items remain inaccessible both in the derived class as well as the client programs.

On the other hand, if you derive **Car** protected or private from **Vehicle**, then all those public items in the **Vehicle** class cannot be used by the client programs anymore! That is, the client programs can no longer call **GetSpeed** or **SetSpeed** unless the **Car** class writes replacement functions that are public in access. This is generally way too severe an approach to take. Hence, the vast majority of the time, a class derives itself publically from the base class.

Here is the basic **Vehicle** class from which we can derive other classes.

Vehicle.h

```
class Vehicle {
protected:
 bool isMoving;
 int  speed;

public:
      Vehicle ();
      Vehicle (bool move, int sped);
     ~Vehicle ();
 bool IsMoving  () const;
 void SetMoving ();
 int  GetSpeed  () const;
 void SetSpeed  (int);
 void SetSpeed  (bool mov, int sped);
};
```

We can then derive the **Car** class from it as follows.

Car.h

```
#include "Vehicle.h"

class Car : public Vehicle {
protected:
 bool   isStarted;
 double mpg;
 double gallons;

 public:
    Car ();
    Car (bool move, int sped, bool start,
         double mpgs, double gals);
   ~Car ();
 ...
};
```

Here the new **Car** class defines three additional data members in addition to the two in the **Vehicle** class that it inherits. **Car** also inherits the five **Vehicle** access functions for getting and setting the speed and is moving state.

What about the base class constructors and destructors? Notice that both the base and derived classes have constructors and may also have a destructor function as well.

Rule: The constructors are always executed in the order of the derivation.

Here the base class **Vehicle** constructor must be called first and then the derived class **Car** constructor.

Rule: Destructors should always be executed in the reverse order; the derived class destructor is called first then the base class.

A special syntax is used to force the proper order of constructor calls. It is the base class and member initialization sequence which we have already been using to initialize constant data members.

```
derived_constructor (arg_list) : base_constructor (arg_list) {
}
```

For the **Car** constructor, whose prototype is

```
Car (bool move, int sped, bool start, double mpgs, double gals);
```

we must code the following.

```
Car::Car (bool move, int sped, bool start, double mpgs,
          double gals)  : Vehicle (move, sped) {
  isStarted = start;
  mpg = mpgs;
  gallons = gals;
 }
```

Or code it this way.

```
Car::Car (bool move, int sped, bool start, double mpgs,
          double gals)  : Vehicle (move, sped),
          isStarted(start), mpg(mpgs), gallons(gals) {}
```

This sequence guarantees that the base class constructor is called before the implementation of the derived class constructor.

The **Car** default constructor is called this way.

```
Car::Car () : Vehicle (), isStarted(false), mpg(20),
              gallons(10) {}
```

With destructor functions, the compiler automatically called the class destructors in reverse sequence for us. Even though the destructors for the **Vehicle** and **Car** classes have nothing to do, here is how they are coded.

```
Vehicle::~Vehicle () {}
Car::~Car () {}
```

Notice that we make no reference to the base class destructor in the **Car** class. The compiler handles it for us.

Rule: Constructors and destructor functions are never inherited.

Rule: Constructors must be explicitly called by the derived class constructors in the base class and member initialization list.

Rule: Destructors are called in the reverse order of derivation automatically by the compiler.

All other functions are inherited. Friend functions are never inherited. A friend of yours is not necessarily a friend of mine, even though we may be friends.

Next, let's derive class **Truck** from the **Car** class. Here is how it might be done.

Truck.h

```
#include "Car.h"
class Truck : public Car {
protected:
 double cargo;
public:
 Truck ();
 Truck (bool move, int sped, bool start,
        double mpgs, double gals, double cargos);
```

```
~Truck ();
 ...
};
```

Here is the implementation of the two constructor functions and the destructor.

```
Truck::Truck () : Car (), cargo(4000) {}
Truck::Truck (bool move, int sped, bool start,
              double mpgs, double gals, double cargos)
     : Car (move, sped, start, mpgs, gals), cargo(cargos) {}
Truck::~Truck () {}
```

Now, let's derive the **Bus** class from the **Car** class.

Bus.h

```
#include "Car.h"
class Bus : public Car {
protected:
 int passengers;
public:
 Bus ();
 Bus (bool move, int sped, bool start,
        double mpgs, double gals, int pass);
~Bus ();
 ...
};
```

Here is the implementation of the two constructor functions and the destructor.

```
Bus::Bus () : Car (), passengers(10) {}
Bus::Bus (bool move, int sped, bool start,
              double mpgs, double gals, int pass)
  : Car (move, sped, start, mpgs, gals), passengers(pass) {}
Bus::~Bus () {}
```

Figure 4.1 illustrates what memory looks like in a client program that has allocated an instance of each of these classes.

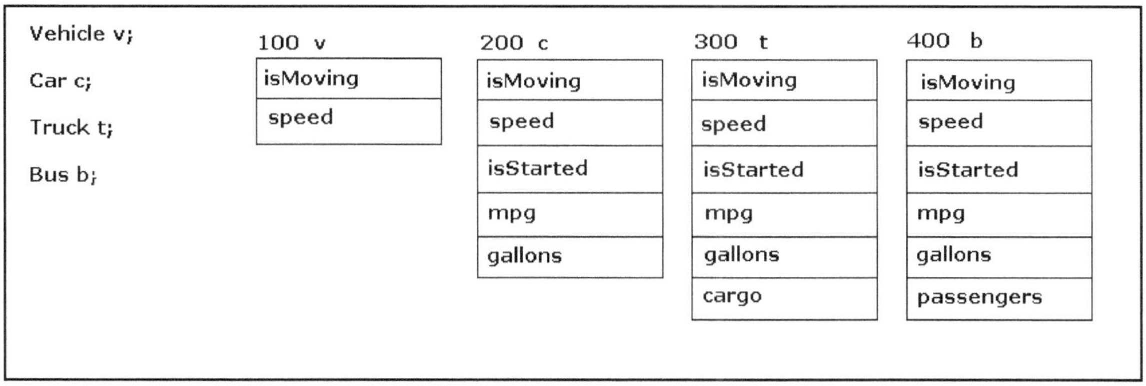

Figure 4.1 Memory Occupied by a Vehicle, Car, Truck, and Bus Object

Notice how memory is laid out. In all cases, the storage for the **Vehicle** base class data items is first. This is then followed by all the data members for the **Car** class. And these are followed by that of the **Truck** and **Bus** classes. This figure clearly shows why we must involve the base class constructors first. The **Truck** instance is built upon the **Car** portion which is built upon the **Vehicle** portion. When the Truck constructor is called, the base class initialization list gets executed before the compiler executes the rest of the Truck ctor coding.

```
Truck::Truck () : Car (), cargo(4000) {}
```

But when it gets to the **Car** ctor, it must first call the **Vehicle** ctor.

```
Car::Car () : Vehicle (), isStarted(false), mpg(20),
```

```
                         gallons(10) {}
```

Thus, the **Vehicle** ctor actually executes first building the **Vehicle** data members properly. When **Vehicle::Vehicle** returns, then the remainder of the **Car** initialization is finished. When **Car::Car** then returns, the remainder of the **Truck** initialization is done.

It's like building a house. The basement (**Vehicle**) must be built first before the first floor (**Car**) can be added which must be done before the second floor (**Truck**) can be built. You cannot build the second floor hanging in space and then try to build the first floor beneath it and then try adding a basement below that.

Working With Inherited Member Functions

In this example, the **Car** class inherits five access functions from the **Vehicle** class: **IsMoving**, **SetMoving**, **GetSpeed**, **SetSpeed(int)**, and **SetSpeed (bool, int)**. Thus, as it stands at this point, any **Car** member function and or the client program can call these five functions on a **Car** object.

```
Car c;
c.SetSpeed (42);
cout << c.GetSpeed();
```

However, with the addition of a motor and a gas tank, the **Car** class may wish to modify the behavior involved with setting the car's speed. That is, the speed can be set only if the motor is running and there is gas in the tank.

Rule: If one or more functions of the base class are redeclared in the derived class, all functions with that name in the base class become hidden and not directly accessible in the derived class. (Virtual functions, see below, are an exception.)

This is saying that if we declare this version of **SetSpeed(int)** in the **Car** class, that the other version of **SetSpeed(bool, int)** is hidden.

```
class Car : public Vehicle {
...
 void SetSpeed (int);
}
```

In the client program,

```
Car c;
c.SetSpeed (42); // works
c.SetSpeed (true, 42); // fails - it is hidden
```

or

```
void Car::SetSpeed (int sped) {
 if (gallons) {
  isStared = true;
  SetSpeed (true, sped); // fails - it is hidden
 }
}
```

There are two ways around this "hidden" rule.

1. Re-declare the hidden versions of that function in the derived class
2. Explicitly call the hidden function using the base class qualifier.

Using way 2, we could implement the **SetSpeed** function this way.

```
void Car::SetSpeed (int sped) {
 if (gallons) {
  isStared = true;
  Vehicle::SetSpeed (true, sped);
 }
}
```

This concept of hiding base class functions is useful when the base class function has no meaning for a derived class object. One then just hides these meaningless base class functions. The new implementation could output an error message, for example. Usually, when a derived class reimplements a base class function, it also reimplements the other variations of that function. So realistically, in the **Car** class, we would be reimplementing both versions of **SetSpeed**.

Copy Constructors

How are copy constructors handled? Since a copy ctor is another version of the constructor, the same rules apply. If we added copy constructors to each of these four classes, their implementation parallels the other ctor functions.

```
Vehicle::Vehicle (const Vehicle& v)
        : speed(v.speed), isMoving(v.isMoving) {}

Car::Car (const Car& c) : Vehicle (c),
          isStarted(c.isStarted), mpg(c.mpg),
          gallons(c.gallons) {}

Truck::Truck (const Truck& t) : Car(t), cargo(t.cargo) {}

Bus::Bus (const Bus& b) : Car(b), passengers(b.passengers){}
```

The Assignment Operator Implementation

The assignment operator must make a duplicate copy of an object. Thus, it too must follow the same sequence of handling the base class first.

Rule: The operator= must first invoke the base class assignment before it can copy the derived class items.

You must explicitly call that base class **operator=** function. This yields a rather strange-looking syntax. Suppose that we implemented **operator=** for the **Vehicle** class.

```
Vehicle& Vehicle::operator= (const Vehicle& v) {
 if (this == &v)
  return *this;
 // nothing to delete
 isMoving = v.isMoving;
 speed = v.speed;
 return *this;
}
```

Now consider the **Car operator=** function. It begins like this.

```
Car& Car::operator= (const Car& c) {
 if (this == &c)
  return *this;
 // nothing to delete
```

Now how do we call the base class function?

```
 Vehicle::operator= (c);
```

Or alternatively one can code this.

```
 *((Vehicle*) (this)) = c;
```

Personally, I prefer the first approach, directly invoking the base class function. The remainder of the assignment function is as follows.

```
 isStarted = c.isStarted;
```

```
 mpg = c.mpg;
 gallons = c.gallons;
 return *this;
}
```

The **Truck operator=** function is coded this way.

```
Truck& Truck::operator= (const Truck& t) {
 if (this == &t)
  return *this;
 // nothing to delete
 Car::operator= (t);
 cargo = t.cargo;
 return *this;
}
```

The **Bus operator=** function is coded this way.

```
Bus& Bus::operator= (const Bus& b) {
 if (this == &b)
  return *this;
 // nothing to delete
 Car::operator= (b);
 passengers = b.passengers;
 return *this;
}
```

Problems When Client Programs Use Base Class Pointers

Let's return to the client program that must perform operations on a company's fleet of vehicles. We had originally written the following.

```
Vehicle* fleet[1000];
int numFleet;
fleet[0] = new Car;
fleet[1] = new Truck;
fleet[2] = new Bus;
numFleet = 3;
for (int i=0; i<numFleet; i++)
 cout << fleet[i]->GetSpeed() << endl; // works fine
 fleet[i]->SetSpeed (42); // oops calls Vehicle::SetSpeed
 delete fleet[i];          // oops calls Vehicle::~Vehicle
}
```

The function calls to **GetSpeed** work fine because neither of the three derived classes redeclared the **GetSpeed** function. The **fleet[i]** pointer is a base class pointer and it only knows about base class, **Vehicle**, functions. Thus, the calls to **SetSpeed** end up going to the base class function and not to the **Car::SetSpeed** which is to replace it. Since the Truck and Bus classes have not redeclared **SetSpeed**, they inherit and expect to use **Car**'s **SetSpeed** function. When it is time to destroy the objects, the delete only deletes the **Vehicle** portion of the objects because it is a **Vehicle*** and only knows about the base class. Clearly we are in big trouble with our implementation at this point.

What is needed is a mechanism in which a base class pointer or reference knows what kind of object it is pointing to so that the correct derived class functions can be called. This is the virtual function mechanism.

Virtual Functions

We saw earlier that a pointer declared as a pointer to a base class can also be used to point to any class derived from that base class.

Rule: The base class pointer or reference variable, when used to point to the derived class, can only access those members inherited from the base class; it knows nothing of new items added in the derived class.

A **virtual** function is a class member function that is declared **virtual** in a base class and then later redefined by the derived class without changing parameters or return type.

Rule: A base class pointer or reference variable can be used to access functions that are declared to be virtual in the base class. Calls go to the derived class, overridden virtual function.

Let's examine a very simple situation. Here is a base and derived class.

```
class base {
public:
int fun ();
};
class derived : public base {
public:
int fun (); // redeclared version of fun()
};
```

In the client program, we can code the following.

```
base    b;
derived d;
base    *ptrbase = &b;
derived *ptrderived = &d;
ptrbase->fun();      // invokes base class fun
ptrderived->fun (); // invokes derived class fun
ptrbase = &d;
ptrbase->fun();      // invokes base class fun => error!
```

We have an error on the last call to function **Fun**; it should go to the derived class version but does not because of the first rule above. Yet by making the base class function **Fun virtual**, the problem is rectified.

```
class base {
public:
virtual int fun ();
};
class derived : public base {
public:
int fun ();
};
```

Now in the client, we have the same coding as before.

```
base    b;
derived d;
base    *ptrbase = &d;
ptrbase->fun();          // invokes derived class fun()
```

This is known as **run-time polymorphism**. In other words, at run time, the compiler determines which **virtual** function to call based on what the object really is!

Rule: Virtual functions must have the same prototypes in the base and derived classes!

If not, they represent overloaded functions.

Rule: Virtual functions are hierarchical in order of inheritance.

Rule: If a derived class does not override a base class virtual function, then the base class implementation is used in its place.

Let's examine these three rules. Consider the following hierarchy of derived classes from **Pgm04a**. I defined a base class with five functions, **Fun1** through **Fun5**. Notice that I forgot the **virtual** keyword on **Fun5**. Then, I created a **Derived1** class from **Base** and a **Derived2** class from **Derived1.**

Base and Derived Class Definitions

```
#include <iostream>

using namespace std;

class Base {
public:
virtual void Fun1 () {cout << "Base::Fun1\n";}
virtual void Fun2 (int) {cout << "Base::Fun2\n";}
virtual void Fun3 (int, int) {cout << "Base::Fun3\n";}
virtual void Fun4 (double) {cout << "Base::Fun4\n";}
        void Fun5 (short) {cout << "Base::Fun5\n";}
};

class Derived1 : public Base {
public:
virtual void Fun1 () {cout << "Derived1::Fun1\n";}
virtual void Fun2 (double) {cout << "Derived1::Fun2\n";}
virtual void Fun4 (double) {cout << "Derived1::Fun4\n";}
virtual void Fun5 (short) {cout << "Derived1::Fun5\n";}
};

class Derived2 : public Derived1 {
public:
 void Fun1 () {cout << "Derived2::Fun1\n";}
 void Fun2 (int) {cout << "Derived2::Fun2\n";}
 void Fun3 (int, int) {cout << "Derived2::Fun3\n";}
 void Fun5 (short) {cout << "Derived2::Fun5\n";}
};
```

Now consider a client program that uses a base class pointer to invoke all five functions. Certainly when the base pointer is set to the address of the **Base** object, all five of the **Base** class functions are invoked. However, see if you can predict which versions are called when the base pointer is set to the address of the **Derived1** object and then to that of **Derived2.** Finally, I created a **Derived1** pointer and invoked the five functions and then used that pointer to point to the **Derived2** object and called them again.

Pgm04a - Illustrates Virtual Functions

```
#include <iostream>
#include <iomanip>
#include "Base.h"

```

```
using namespace std;

int main () {
 short s = 10;
 Base      b;
 Derived1  d1;
 Derived2  d2;
 Base*     ptrbase;
 Derived1* ptrd1;

 cout << "ptrbase-> where it is the address of Base b\n";
 ptrbase = &b;
 ptrbase->Fun1 ();
 ptrbase->Fun2 (42);
 ptrbase->Fun3 (42, 42);
 ptrbase->Fun4 (42.);
 ptrbase->Fun5 (s);
 cout << endl;

 cout << "ptrbase-> where it is the address of Derived1 d1\n";
 ptrbase = &d1;
 ptrbase->Fun1 ();
 ptrbase->Fun2 (42);
 ptrbase->Fun3 (42, 42);
 ptrbase->Fun4 (42.);
 ptrbase->Fun5 (s);
 cout << endl;

 cout << "ptrbase-> where it is the address of Derived2 d2\n";
 ptrbase = &d2;
 ptrbase->Fun1 ();
 ptrbase->Fun2 (42);
 ptrbase->Fun3 (42, 42);
 ptrbase->Fun4 (42.);
 ptrbase->Fun5 (s);
 cout << endl;

 cout << "ptrd1-> where it is the address of Derived1 d1\n";
 ptrd1 = &d1;
 ptrd1->Fun1 ();
 ptrd1->Fun2 (42);
 ptrd1->Fun3 (42, 42);
 ptrd1->Fun4 (42.);
 ptrd1->Fun5 (s);
 cout << endl;

 cout << "ptrd1-> where it is the address of Derived2 d2\n";
 ptrd1 = &d2;
 ptrd1->Fun1 ();
 ptrd1->Fun2 (42);
 ptrd1->Fun3 (42, 42);
 ptrd1->Fun4 (42.);
 ptrd1->Fun5 (s);
 cout << endl;

 return 0;
```

```
}
```

Here is the output showing which exact functions are invoked in each case.

```
Output of Pgm04a - Illustrates Virtual Functions

ptrbase-> where it is the address of Base b
Base::Fun1
Base::Fun2
Base::Fun3
Base::Fun4
Base::Fun5

ptrbase-> where it is the address of Derived1 d1
Derived1::Fun1
Base::Fun2
Base::Fun3
Derived1::Fun4
Base::Fun5
```

Derived1 does reimplement **Fun2** but uses a different parameter type, so this **Fun2** is not the virtual one. Thus, it uses **Base::Fun2**. **Derived1** does not implement **Fun3** so **Base::Fun3** is invoked. Having forgotten the **virtual** on **Base::Fun5**, it is not virtual so it does not call the **Derived1::Fun5** version.

```

ptrbase-> where it is the address of Derived2 d2
Derived2::Fun1
Derived2::Fun2
Derived2::Fun3
Derived1::Fun4
Base::Fun5
```

Derived2's **Fun1** reimplements **Fun1** and is called. It also implements **Fun1** with the same prototype as the **Base** class and so **Derived2::Fun2** called. Even though **Derived1** did not reimplement **Fun3**, since **Derived2** did so, **Derived2::Fun3** is then called. Since **Derived2** did not reimplement **Fun4**, **Derived1::Fun4** is then called. Again, having forgotten the **virtual** on **Base::Fun5**, it is not virtual so it does not call the **Derived2::Fun5** version.

```

ptrd1-> where it is the address of Derived1 d1
Derived1::Fun1
Derived1::Fun2
Base::Fun3
Derived1::Fun4
Derived1::Fun5
```

Using a **Derived1** pointer causes all of the **Derived1** versions to be called directly. However, since there is no provided **Derived1::Fun3** function, the inherited **Base::Fun3** is used as usual.

```

ptrd1-> where it is the address of Derived2 d2
Derived2::Fun1
Derived1::Fun2
Derived2::Fun3
Derived1::Fun4
Derived2::Fun5
```

Finally, using the **Derived1** pointer with a **Derived2** object calls the **Derived2::Fun1** as expected. Since **Derived1**'s **Fun2** function has a different prototype from **Base** and **Derived2** class versions, it is **Derived1::Fun2** that is invoked. Now even though there is no reimplemented **Fun3** in the **Derived1** class, there is one in **Base**, so thus **Derived2::Fun3** is called. **Derived2** does not reimplement **Fun4** and so **Derived1::Fun4** is called.

If you understand these situations, you will have no trouble with virtual functions.

I/O Operations with Derived Classes Demand Virtual Functions

When one has a hierarchy of classes, handling I/O operations for all situations requires careful design and must utilize virtual functions. Let's see how this comes about. Let's add the ability to input and output **Vehicle**, **Car**, **Truck**, and **Bus** objects. This means that we must add friend **operator>>** and **operator<<** functions to all four classes. Skeletally, we have the following.

```
class Vehicle {
 ...
 friend istream& operator>> (istream& is, Vehicle& v);
 friend ostream& operator<< (ostream& os, const Vehicle& v);
};

class Car : public Vehicle {
 ...
 friend istream& operator>> (istream& is, Car& v);
 friend ostream& operator<< (ostream& os, const Car& v);
};

class Truck : public Car {
 ...
 friend istream& operator>> (istream& is, Truck& v);
 friend ostream& operator<< (ostream& os, const Truck& v);
};

class Bus : public Car {
 ...
 friend istream& operator>> (istream& is, Bus& v);
 friend ostream& operator<< (ostream& os, const Bus& v);
};
```

But before you charge ahead and implement these eight functions, consider how the client programs can perform the I/O operations. Certainly these operators are all called in the following client program situations.

```
Vehicle v;
Car c;
Truck t;
Bus b;
Vehicle* ptrv = &v;
Car* ptrc = &c;
Truck* ptrt = &t;
Bus* ptrb = &b;
cin >> v >> c >> t >> b >> *ptrv >> *ptrc >> *ptrt >> *ptrb;
```

However, suppose that the client program was written this way.

```
Vehicle* fleet[100];
fleet[0] = new Vehicle;
fleet[1] = new Car;
fleet[2] = new Truck;
fleet[3] = new Bus;
for (j=0; j<4; j++) {
  cin >> *fleet[j];
  cout << *fleet[j];
```

```
}
```

Now we are in big trouble. In all cases, since ***fleet[j]** is a **Vehicle**, only the **Vehicle** insertion and extraction functions are called! Our design must be able to handle the fleet situation, using a base class pointer or reference to input or output the derived class object.

How do we get this insertion and extraction operator situation to work properly? Actually, this is an extremely important detail, vital to inheritance programming. The key is to notice what the two operator functions are given as the second parameter. In all eight cases, the functions are presented with a **reference** to an object. Virtual functions take effect when pointers or references are used. True, if we are using the **Vehicle** base class reference with which to input or output a derived class object, the **Vehicle** insertion or extraction operator function is what is directly called by the compiler. However, when we implement these functions, because a reference to that object is given to the function, our implementation must then use that reference to invoke a **virtual** function of the **Vehicle** class so that the virtual function mechanism then invokes the proper derived class function.

Often these virtual functions are called **Input** and **Output**. When these are added to the classes, we have the following revisions.

```
class Vehicle {
 ...
 virtual istream& Input (istream& is);
 virutal ostream& Output (ostream& os) const;
 friend istream& operator>> (istream& is, Vehicle& v);
 friend ostream& operator<< (ostream& os, const Vehicle& v);
};

class Car : public Vehicle {
 ...
 virtual istream& Input (istream& is);
 virutal ostream& Output (ostream& os) const;
 friend istream& operator>> (istream& is, Car& c);
 friend ostream& operator<< (ostream& os, const Car& c);
};

class Truck : public Car {
 ...
 virtual istream& Input (istream& is);
 virutal ostream& Output (ostream& os) const;
 friend istream& operator>> (istream& is, Truck& t);
 friend ostream& operator<< (ostream& os, const Truck& t);
};

class Bus : public Car {
 ...
 virtual istream& Input (istream& is);
 virutal ostream& Output (ostream& os) const;
 friend istream& operator>> (istream& is, Bus& b);
 friend ostream& operator<< (ostream& os, const Bus& b);
};
```

Notice how the insertion and extraction operator functions for the **Vehicle** class are implemented. They must only invoke the **Input** or **Output** member functions using the reference that is passed.

```
istream& operator>> (istream& is, Vehicle& v) {
 return v.Input (is);
}
ostream& operator<< (ostream& os, const Vehicle& v) {
 return v.Output (os);
}
```

```
istream& Vehicle::Input (istream& is) {
 is >> speed;
 if (is)
  isMoving = speed ? true : false;
 else {
  speed = 0;
  isMoving = false;
 }
 return is;
}
ostream& Vehicle::Output (ostream& os) const {
 if (isMoving)
  os << "Vehicle is moving at " << speed << " mph\n";
 else
  os << "Vehicle is not moving\n";
 return os;
}
```

Notice that if the reference is really to a **Vehicle** object, the insertion operator correctly calls **Vehicle::Output** and the extraction operator correctly calls **Vehicle::Input**. However, it the reference is to a derived class, the **Vehicle** insertion and extraction operator ends up calling the redeclared derived class **Input** and **Output** functions instead, assuming that these functions are present.

Now, let's examine the **Car** implementation of these.

```
istream& operator>> (istream& is, Car& c) {
 return c.Input (is);
}
ostream& operator<< (ostream& os, const Car& c) {
 return c.Output (os);
}
```

The insertion and extraction friend functions again call the virtual pair of functions. If this is a **Car** object, then the **Car** versions are called. However, if this reference is that of a **Truck** or **Bus** object, then those classes' virtual functions are invoked, if present.

To implement the **Car**'s pair, notice that I first call the **Vehicle** base class versions of these functions to input or output the basic **Vehicle** data. Then, I input or output the additional **Car** properties. This reuses the coding already present in the base class. Sometimes, however, one might not desire the input or output format delivered by the base class. In this case, do not call the base class versions; instead, input all of the data members here.

```
istream& Car::Input (istream& is) {
 Vehicle::Input (is);
 is >> mpg >> gallons;
 isStarted = (speed > 0 && gallons > 0) ? true : false;
 return is;
}
ostream& Car::Output (ostream& os) const {
 Vehicle::Output (os);
 if (!isStarted)
  os << "Car with " << gallons
     << " gallons of gas and that gets " << mpg
     << " miles per gallon is not started\n";
 else
  os << "Car with " << gallons
     << " gallons of gas and that gets " << mpg
     << " miles per gallon is started\n";
 return os;
}
```

In this case, one might not like the resulting output because the first line talks of a **Vehicle** moving or not moving and this is a **Car**. So one does not have to call that base class function. It could be done this way without reusing the **Vehicle::Output** function.

```
ostream& Car::Output (ostream& os) const {
 if (!isStarted)
  os << "Car with " << gallons
     << " gallons of gas and that gets " << mpg
     << " miles per gallon is not started\n";
 else
  os << "Car with " << gallons
     << " gallons of gas and that gets " << mpg
     << " miles per gallon is started and is moving at "
     << speed << " miles per hour\n";
 return os;
}
```

The **Truck** is derived from a **Car**. Notice how its functions are implemented.

```
istream& operator>> (istream& is, Truck& t) {
 return t.Input (is);
}
ostream& operator<< (ostream& os, const Truck& t) {
 return t.Output (os);
}
istream& Truck::Input (istream& is) {
 Car::Input (is);
 if (is)
  is >> cargo;
 return is;
}
ostream& Truck::Output (ostream& os) const {
 Car::Output (os);
 os << "The Truck can carry " << cargo << " pounds\n";
 return os;
}
```

Notice that the operator functions invoke the **Input** and **Output** virtual functions. If the object **t** is a **Truck**, then the **Truck**'s functions are actually invoked. However, if this **t** object is a **Halftrack**, then the **Halftrack**'s versions are called instead.

The implementation of the **Input** and **Output** functions call the immediate base class versions, **Car**. If this is a **Truck** object, then **Car::Input** is called first which in turn calls **Vehicle::Input** to input the **speed** data. When the Vehicle function is done, it returns to **Car::Input** which then inputs the **mpg** and **gallons** and sets the **isStarted bool**. **Car::Input** then returns to **Truck::Input** which finally inputs the **cargo** property.

Similarly **Truck::Output** calls **Car::Output** which immediately calls **Vehicle::Output** which outputs the speed and moving properties. It returns to **Car::Output** which then displays the **Car** portions and returns to **Truck** which then displays the cargo information.

Given this situation, can you figure out how to implement the **Bus** versions of these functions? They are the topic of a Review Question below.

Destructors

If a class is going to be used as a base class, then, since a client program could be using pointers to the base class to store dynamically allocated derived class objects (as in the fleet array of **Vehicles**), when the destructor is called using the base class pointer, the compiler must know to call the derived class destructor before calling the base class destructor. Hence, we have the following rule.

Rule: The destructor function should always be a virtual function if this class is used as a base class.

Failure to do so causes the compiler to bypass the derived class destructor function. This can cause problems if the derived class destructor actually has some tasks to perform, such as deleting dynamic memory allocations.

How the Virtual Function Mechanism Is Implemented

Just how can the compiler generate code that, given an unknown pointer or reference at run time, determines which virtual function is to be called? It is done by using what is called a **Virtual Function Table**, or **v-table** for short. The compiler cannot know at compile time what kind of object a given pointer or reference will be at run time. So it creates a table of all possibilities, the v-table.

The v-table contains an array of function addresses to call. With a **Car** instance, there is a **Vehicle** base class v-table that contains an array of if this virtual function is called, then actually use this **Car** function instead. Pictorially, the **Vehicle** base class v-table for a **Car** object looks like this.

```
If calling this function    Use this function
Input()                     Car::Input()
Output()                    Car::Output()
```

The v-table for a **Truck** instance is more complex because not only can virtual functions be called using a **Vehicle** pointer but also a **Car** pointer. Thus, there are two sections of the v-table, depending upon which base class pointer is being used. The v-table for the **Truck** appears this way.

```
Vehicle* If calling this function    Use this function
         Input()                     Truck::Input()
         Output()                    Truck::Output()
Car*     If calling this function    Use this function
         Input()                     Truck::Input()
         Output()                    Truck::Output()
```

Thus, depending upon which base class pointer is used, at runtime, the compiler can loop up in the v-table which function should be actually be called.

Caution. As the size of the v-table grows, the amount of time at execution that is required to look up and find the correct function to call increases. Thus, if you have 200 member functions in a base class, do not make them all virtual. If you do, then the v-table look up process significantly slows down the program execution. Further, notice that the v-table is carried along with each instance of the class. So if one allocates 1,000 Truck objects, then each of those objects has a v-table as part of the instance data! With 200 virtual functions, the memory requirements for each object increases sharply.

Early Binding and Late Binding

When the compiler knows what function to call at compile-time, it creates a direct call to that function. Such is the case for normal functions, overloaded functions and operators and friend functions—that is, anything without the virtual tag. This is the most efficient method and is called **early binding**.

Late binding occurs when the compiler does not necessarily know what is to be actually called at compile time. This is the case with virtual functions. When a virtual function is accessed via a base pointer, the compiler can only figure out which function to call at run time. The advantage of late binding is greater flexibility; the price paid is greater overhead in making the call. The compiler maintains a virtual table look up mechanism to facilitate dynamic translation.

Animals—A Complete Example with Dynamic Memory Allocation and Virtual Functions—Pgm04b

When dynamic memory allocations are part of the inheritance picture, virtual destructor functions are needed to ensure that the derived class destructor gets called when deleting the object using a base class pointer. To illustrate the effect of virtual functions as well as inheritance, let's examine another series of classes. This time, we pick on animals. Our pets are often dogs and cats. While one could easily write **Dog** and **Cat** classes as totally separate classes, they both share some animal properties. Hence, frequently both pet classes are derived from a base **Animal** class.

What kinds of properties could an **Animal** class contain? Rather, what properties do all animals share in common? If these classes were for a veterinarian, the list might be rather extensive. Sex, age, weight, color, height, its name, the sound it makes, and even the type of animal could be some such properties. But to keep these classes from mushrooming in size, let's just have the **Animal** class store a string that identifies the type of animal, such as "Dog" or "Cat." The derived **Dog** and **Cat** classes will store the sound that they make, such as "Ruff! Ruff!" Both of the strings will be dynamically allocated to use mo more memory than is needed to hold each specific string. Memory is, then, going to be allocated in both the base and the derived classes.

Here is the start of the **Animal** class definition. Notice that there are now a copy ctor, a destructor, and an assignment operator—all required because of the dynamic allocation of the **name** member.

```
class Animal {
protected:
 char* name;   // the name of the animal, such as Dog or Cat

public:
          Animal ();                  // default ctor - "Unknown"
          Animal (const char* n);     // make specific animal
          Animal (const Animal& a); // copy ctor duplicate animal

 Animal& operator= (const Animal& a); // assignment op

 virtual ~Animal ();                    // delete name
```

Here is the start of the derived **Dog** class. It allocates the string to store the sound that the dog makes. Notice that it also has a copy ctor, a destructor, and an assignment operator.

```
class Dog : public Animal {
protected:
 char* sound; // the sound it makes, such as "Ruff! Ruff!"

public:
          Dog ();                 // default dog
          Dog (const char* s);  // dog with a specific sound
          Dog (const Dog& d);   // copy ctor
 Dog& operator= (const Dog& d); // assignment op

 virtual ~Dog ();               // dtor to remove sound
```

Here is the start of the **Cat** class. It closely parallels the **Dog**.

```
class Cat : public Animal {
protected:
 char* sound;   // the sound that a cat makes

public:
          Cat ();                 // default cat "Meow! Meow!"
          Cat (const char* s);  // cat with specific sound
```

```
         Cat (const Cat& c);    // copy ctor duplicate Cat
 Cat& operator= (const Cat& c); // assignment op

 virtual ~Cat ();               // removes sound string
```

Before we get too involved with virtual functions and the I/O situation, let's see how just this much can be implemented. For the **Animal** class, it is fairly straightforward. The default ctor is problematical because **name** should point to a string and not be initialized to a null pointer or 0. Otherwise, every time a member function wanted to access the string, it would first have to check if **name** was not 0. So I choose to install the string "Unknown" because no one should be allocating an instance of the base class. Look over the coding. All of the **Animal** implementation should be familiar or as you would expect to see it at this point.

```
Animal::Animal () {
 name = new char[8];
 strcpy (name, "Unknown");
}

Animal::Animal (const char* n) {
 if (!n) {                         // guard against 0 being passed
  name = new char[8];              // if so, make default Unknown
  strcpy (name, "Unknown");
 }
 else {                            // make name be passed name
  name = new char[strlen(n) + 1];
  strcpy (name, n);
 }
}

Animal::Animal (const Animal& a) {
 name = new char[strlen(a.name) + 1];
 strcpy (name, a.name);
}

Animal& Animal::operator= (const Animal& a) {
 if (this == &a)    // guard against a = a;
  return *this;
 delete [] name;                        // remove current name
 name = new char[strlen(a.name) + 1]; // make new name
 strcpy (name, a.name);
 return *this;
}

Animal::~Animal () {
 delete [] name;
}
```

Now we must implement the two derived classes. The **Dog** default ctor passes the string "Dog" on to the default **Animal** ctor. Once the base class is constructed, the default dog **sound** string is created.

```
Dog::Dog () : Animal ("Dog") {
 sound = new char [12];
 strcpy (sound, "Ruff! Ruff!");
}

Dog::Dog (const char* s) : Animal ("Dog") {
 if (!s) {                         // guard against 0 sound
  sound = new char [12];           // if so, install default sound
  strcpy (sound, "Ruff! Ruff!");
```

```
 }
 else {                               // store the new sound
  sound = new char [strlen(s) + 1];
  strcpy (sound, s);
 }
}
```

Notice how the **Dog** object **d** is passed to the **Animal** copy ctor. Since it is expecting a reference to an **Animal** and since a **Dog** is an **Animal**, the compiler passes the address of the base class.

```
Dog::Dog (const Dog& d) : Animal (d) {
 sound = new char [strlen(d.sound) + 1];
 strcpy (sound, d.sound);
}
```

With the assignment operator, things get a bit trickier. The **Animal** base class must first be given a chance to make its copy. Since the **Animal** assignment operator is expecting a reference to an **Animal**, the address of the base class is passed. Once the base class performs its copy, then the **Dog** class can remove the old sound string, allocate and copy the new one.

```
Dog& Dog::operator= (const Dog& d) {
 if (this == &d)              // guard against a = a;
  return *this;
 Animal::operator= (d);       // copy Animal portion of dog
 delete [] sound;             // remove old sound
 sound = new char [strlen(d.sound) + 1]; // create and copy
 strcpy (sound, d.sound);                // new sound
 return *this;
}

Dog::~Dog () {
 delete [] sound;
}
```

Notice that the destructor for **Dog** only deletes **Dog** items. The compiler first calls the **Dog** destructor and when it returns, the compiler then calls the **Animal** destructor. The Cat implementation is nearly identical except the default for the sound a cat makes is "Meow! Meow!"

Next, let's examine how a dog or cat could be input. Remember that a client can do either of these.

```
Dog d;
cin >> d;
```

or

```
Animal* ptrpet = new Dog;
cin >> *ptrpet;
```

In the first situation, the compiler calls the **Dog**'s friend **operator>>** function. In the second case, the compiler calls **Animal**'s friend **operator>>** function. Hence, to make both work for client programs, a virtual **Input** function is needed.

In the **Animal** class, add these two prototypes.

```
 virtual istream& Input (istream& is);
 friend istream& operator>> (istream& is, Animal& a);
```

In the **Dog** class, add these two prototypes. The **Cat** class is similar.

```
 virtual istream& Input (istream& is);
 friend istream& operator>> (istream& is, Dog& d);
```

The implementation of the extraction operators are parallel. All call the virtual **Input** function using the reference variable. Here is the **Animal** extraction implementation.

```
istream& operator>> (istream& is, Animal& a) {
 return a.Input (is); // invoke virtual Input
}
```

And here is the **Dog** version. The **Cat** version parallels the **Dog** implementation.

```
istream& operator>> (istream& is, Dog& d) {
```

```
 return d.Input (is); // call the virtual Input()
}
```

Now how do we actually implement the **Input** functions? Here is where novice OOP programmers sometimes fail. The input of a **Dog**, **Cat** or **Animal** object must always input the name string. The actual input of the name string should be done one time in the **Animal::Input** function. It should **not** be done three times, once in each of the **Input** functions. Code it once and reuse it. At this point, we must know of what the input is to consist. In this overly simplified case, I assume that the first item input is the name string and that it contains no blanks so it can easily be extracted. Further, I assume that no animal name can exceed 99 characters. There must be a real array of characters in which to store the data being extracted, a temporary string. Of course, we could also run into the end of file situation as well. If it is EOF, I store the usual "Unknown" as the name string. Finally, do not forget to delete the current **name** string before allocating space for the new **name**! To get to this function, the compiler has had to already call a constructor which has already allocated a **name** string.

```
istream& Animal::Input (istream& is) {
 char n[100];                // arbitrary maximum length of name
 is >> n;                    // input the new name
 delete [] name;             // remove current name
 if (!is) {                  // if failed to input, make unknown
  name = new char[8];
  strcpy (name, "Unknown");
 }
 else {                      // allocate and copy the new name
  name = new char[strlen(n) + 1];
  strcpy (name, n);
 }
 return is;
}
```

With the **name** input successfully, the derived class can input the **sound** that the critter makes. The **sound** string is assumed to be enclosed in double quote marks. Here is the **Dog::Input** function. Notice that first it calls back to the **Animal::Input** to input the common name string. If the stream is still in the good state, the **sound** is extracted. Again, do not forget to delete the old **sound** string before allocating a new string. The **Cat** is done similarly.

```
istream& Dog::Input (istream& is) {
 if (!Animal::Input (is))  // attempt to input the name portion
  return is;               // if fails, abort
 char s[100];              // arbitrary max length of dog's sound
 char c;
 is >> c;                  // input the "
 if (!is)
  return is;
 is.getline (s, sizeof(s), '\"');  // input the sound it makes
 delete [] sound;                  // remove old sound
 sound = new char [strlen(s) + 1]; // copy in the new sound
 strcpy (sound, s);
 return is;
}
```

Finally, we can turn our attention to the output of a critter. Suppose that the output should be like this.

```
The Dog says Ruff! Ruff!
The Cat says Meow! Meow!
```

Just as with the input operations, the client has two ways to output instances.

```
     Dog d;
     cout << d;
```

or

```
Animal* ptrpet = new Dog;
cout << *ptrpet;
```

This once again dictates that a friend **operator<<** function must be found in both the base and derived classes. It also implies that all must call a virtual **Output** function using the passed reference variable instance so that the correct version of **Output** is called.

However, thinking ahead, when additional members are added, such as height and weight, other types of output may be required than the "speak" line. So I added a third function, one that handles the speech aspect. Here are the **Animal** class prototypes.

```
 virtual ostream& Speak (ostream& os) const;
 virtual ostream& Output (ostream& os) const;
 friend ostream& operator<< (ostream& os, const Animal& a);
```

The corresponding ones for the **Dog** class are these. The **Cat** is similar.

```
 virtual ostream& Speak (ostream& os) const;
 virtual ostream& Output (ostream& os) const;
 friend ostream& operator<< (ostream& os, const Dog& d);
```

The **Animal** insertion operator just calls the virtual **Output** function as does the **Dog** and **Cat**.

```
ostream& operator<< (ostream& os, const Animal& a) {
 return a.Output (os); // invoke virtual Output
}
ostream& operator<< (ostream& os, const Dog& d) {
 return d.Output (os); // call the virtual Output
}
```

The **Animal Output** function displays a generic identification that can be used with several types of output. The generic message, "The Dog," can be followed by its weight and height or by its age and sex or, in this case by "says Ruff! Ruff!"

```
ostream& Animal::Output (ostream& os) const {
 return os << "The " << name;
}
```

The **Dog Output** function controls the action by choosing to use the **Speak** version. It calls **Animal Output** to begin the message and then calls **Speak** to display the dog's sound.

```
ostream& Dog::Output (ostream& os) const {
 Animal::Output (os); // display The dog says portion
 return Speak (os);   // display the sound
}
ostream& Dog::Speak (ostream& os) const {
 return os << " says " << sound << endl;
}
```

The **Cat** is done similarly.

Finally, we need a client program to thoroughly test all of this coding. **Pgm04b** does this. It creates numerous instances of the **Dog** and **Cat** classes, outputs them and then reads a small file of objects. Here is the output from **Pgm04b**.

Output of Pgm04b Animals Tester Program

```
 1 The Dog says Ruff! Ruff!
 2 The Dog says Bark! Bark!
 3 The Dog says Bark! Bark!
 4 The Dog says Bark! Bark!
 5
 6 The Cat says Meow! Meow!
 7 The Cat says Prrrrrrr
 8 The Cat says Prrrrrrr
 9 The Cat says Prrrrrrr
10
```

```
11 The Dog says Ruff!! Ruff!!
12 The Cat says Pfssssttttt!
13 No memory leaks
```

Lines 11 and 12 are coming from the input file which consists of the following two lines.
```
d Dog "Ruff!! Ruff!!"
c Cat "Pfssssttttt!"
```
The importance of the input file is great. It is designed to show you a very common technique that is used when the client program wishes to use only pointers to the base class to do the processing, such as the fleet of vehicles. In this case, we could have an array of animals. Here is the client program, **Pgm04b**.

```
Pgm04b Animals Tester Program

 1 #include <iostream>
 2 #include <iomanip>
 3 #include <fstream>
 4 #include <string>
 5 #include <cctype>
 6 #include <crtdbg.h>
 7 using namespace std;
 8 #include "Dog.h"
 9 #include "Cat.h"
10
11 /******************************************************************/
12 /*                                                                */
13 /* Tester for the Animals Series of Classes                       */
14 /*                                                                */
15 /******************************************************************/
16
17 int main () {
18   {
19   Dog d1;
20   Dog d2 ("Bark! Bark!");
21   Dog d3 (d2);
22   Dog d4;
23   d4 = d2;
24   cout << d1 << d2 << d3 << d4 << endl;
25
26   Cat c1;
27   Cat c2 ("Prrrrrrrr");
28   Cat c3 (c2);
29   Cat c4;
30   c4 = c2;
31   cout << c1 << c2 << c3 << c4 << endl;
32
33   ifstream infile ("animals.txt");
34   if (!infile) {
35    cerr << "Error: cannot open file animals.txt\n";
36    return 1;
37   }
38   char type;
39   Animal* ptranimal;
40   while (infile >> type) {
41    type = toupper (type);
42    if (type == 'D')
```

```
43     ptranimal = new Dog;
44    else
45     ptranimal = new Cat;
46    infile >> *ptranimal;
47    cout << *ptranimal;
48    delete ptranimal;
49   }
50   infile.close ();
51   }
52
53   // check for memory leaks
54   if (_CrtDumpMemoryLeaks())
55    cerr << "Memory leaks occurred!\n";
56   else
57    cerr << "No memory leaks.\n";
58
59   return 0;
60
```

Pay particular attention to lines 38 through 49. The input loop is controlled by an attempt to input the animal type character. If a letter was input, then the body of the loop executes. Notice how the **ptranimal** gets one of two addresses assigned to it on line 43 or 45. It stores either a new dog or a new cat object. Then, notice line 46 and 47 to see how that base class pointer is turned into a reference to an **Animal** and passed to the **Animal** extraction or insertion operators. This is a very common method to handle this type of situation.

For your reference, here are the complete definitions and implementation of the three classes.

```
Class Animal Definition
```

```
#pragma once
#include <iostream>
using namespace std;

/***************************************************************/
/*                                                             */
/* Animal: stores name of the animal and provides I/O ops      */
/*                                                             */
/***************************************************************/

class Animal {
protected:
 char* name;  // the name of the animal, such as Dog or Cat

public:
          Animal ();                 // default ctor - "Unknown"
          Animal (const char* n);    // make specific animal
          Animal (const Animal& a); // copy ctor duplicate animal

 Animal& operator= (const Animal& a); // assignment op

 virtual ~Animal ();                    // delete name

 // displays "The 'name' says "
 virtual ostream& Speak (ostream& os) const;

```

```
 virtual istream& Input (istream& is);
 virtual ostream& Output (ostream& os) const;

 friend istream& operator>> (istream& is, Animal& a);
 friend ostream& operator<< (ostream& os, const Animal& a);

protected:
 void AllocString (char*& dest, const char* src,
                  const char* errmsg);
};
```

```
Class Animal Implementation
```

```
#include <iostream>
#include <iomanip>
#include <string>
using namespace std;
#include "Animal.h"

/***************************************************************/
/*                                                             */
/* AllocString: dyn allocate new string and copy in src        */
/*                                                             */
/***************************************************************/
void Animal::AllocString (char*& dest, const char* src,
                          const char* errmsg) {
 dest = new (std::nothrow) char[strlen (src) + 1];
 if (!dest) {
  cerr << "Error - out of memory in " << errmsg << endl;
  exit (1);
 }
 strcpy_s (dest, strlen (src) + 1, src);
}

/***************************************************************/
/*                                                             */
/* Animal: create a default "Unknown" animal                   */
/*                                                             */
/***************************************************************/

Animal::Animal () {
 AllocString (name, "Unknown", "Animal Constructor");
}

/***************************************************************/
/*                                                             */
/* Animal: create an animal with this name                     */
/*                                                             */
/***************************************************************/

Animal::Animal (const char* n) {
 if (!n)                          // guard against 0 being passed
  AllocString (name, "Unknown", "Animal Constructor");
 else                             // make name be passed name
  AllocString (name, n, "Animal Constructor");
```

```
}

/***************************************************************/
/*                                                             */
/* Animal: duplicate an animal object                          */
/*                                                             */
/***************************************************************/

Animal::Animal (const Animal& a) {
 AllocString (name, a.name, "Animal Copy Constructor");
}

/***************************************************************/
/*                                                             */
/* Operator= copy passed animal into this one                  */
/*                                                             */
/***************************************************************/

Animal& Animal::operator= (const Animal& a) {
 if (this == &a)    // guard against a = a;
  return *this;
 delete [] name;                     // remove current name
 AllocString (name, a.name, "Animal Operator =");
 return *this;
}

/***************************************************************/
/*                                                             */
/* ~Animal: remove the name array                              */
/*                                                             */
/***************************************************************/

Animal::~Animal () {
 delete [] name;
}

/***************************************************************/
/*                                                             */
/* Speak: placeholder for derived classes - shouldn't be called*/
/*                                                             */
/***************************************************************/

ostream& Animal::Speak (ostream& os) const {
 return os << "nothing\n"; // oops - so display a goof message
}

/***************************************************************/
/*                                                             */
/* Input: input the animal's name from the input stream        */
/*                                                             */
/***************************************************************/

istream& Animal::Input (istream& is) {
 char n[100];                // arbitrary maximum length of name
 is >> n;                    // input the new name
 delete [] name;             // remove current name
```

```
 if (!is)                      // if failed to input, make unknown
  AllocString (name, "Unknown", "Animal Input");
 else                          // allocate and copy the new name
  AllocString (name, n, "Animal Input");
 return is;
}

/***************************************************************/
/*                                                             */
/* Output: display "The 'name' says " string                  */
/*                                                             */
/***************************************************************/

ostream& Animal::Output (ostream& os) const {
 return os << "The " << name;
}

/***************************************************************/
/*                                                             */
/* extraction: input an animal                                 */
/*                                                             */
/***************************************************************/

istream& operator>> (istream& is, Animal& a) {
 return a.Input (is); // invoke virtual Input
}

/***************************************************************/
/*                                                             */
/* insertion: display an animal                                */
/*                                                             */
/***************************************************************/

ostream& operator<< (ostream& os, const Animal& a) {
 return a.Output (os); // invoke virtual Output
}
```

Class Dog Definition

```
#pragma once
#include "Animal.h"

/***************************************************************/
/*                                                             */
/* Class Dog:                                                  */
/*                                                             */
/***************************************************************/

class Dog : public Animal {
protected:
 char* sound; // the sound it makes, such as "Ruff! Ruff!"

public:
          Dog ();                 // default dog
          Dog (const char* s);    // dog with a specific sound
```

```
          Dog (const Dog& d);    // copy ctor
 Dog& operator= (const Dog& d); // assignment op

 virtual ~Dog ();                // dtor to remove sound

 // Speak displays the entire output line
 virtual ostream& Speak (ostream& os) const;

 virtual istream& Input (istream& is);
 virtual ostream& Output (ostream& os) const;

 friend istream& operator>> (istream& is, Dog& d);
 friend ostream& operator<< (ostream& os, const Dog& d);
};
```

```
Class Dog Implementation
```

```
#include <iostream>
#include <iomanip>
#include <string>
using namespace std;
#include "Dog.h"

/***************************************************************/
/*                                                             */
/* Dog: make a default dog with the sound Ruff! Ruff!          */
/*                                                             */
/***************************************************************/

Dog::Dog () : Animal ("Dog") {
 AllocString (sound, "Ruff! Ruff!", "Dog Constructor");
}

/***************************************************************/
/*                                                             */
/* Dog: make a dog with this specific sound                    */
/*                                                             */
/***************************************************************/

Dog::Dog (const char* s) : Animal ("Dog") {
 if (!s)      // guard against 0 sound
 AllocString (sound, "Ruff! Ruff!", "Dog Constructor");
 else         // store the new sound
 AllocString (sound, s, "Dog Constructor");
}

/***************************************************************/
/*                                                             */
/* Dog: duplicate this dog                                     */
/*                                                             */
/***************************************************************/

Dog::Dog (const Dog& d) : Animal (d) {
 AllocString (sound, d.sound, "Dog Copy Constructor");
}
```

```

/***************************************************************/
/*                                                             */
/* Operator= copy the passed dog into this dog                 */
/*                                                             */
/***************************************************************/

Dog& Dog::operator= (const Dog& d) {
 if (this == &d)            // guard against a = a;
  return *this;
 Animal::operator= (d);     // copy Animal portion of dog
 delete [] sound;           // remove old sound
 AllocString (sound, d.sound, "Dog Operator =");
 return *this;
}

/***************************************************************/
/*                                                             */
/* ~Dog: remove sound array                                    */
/*                                                             */
/***************************************************************/

Dog::~Dog () {
 delete [] sound;
}

/***************************************************************/
/*                                                             */
/* Speak: display the sound the dog makes                      */
/*                                                             */
/***************************************************************/

ostream& Dog::Speak (ostream& os) const {
 return os << " says " << sound << endl;
}

/***************************************************************/
/*                                                             */
/* Input: input a dog                                          */
/*                                                             */
/***************************************************************/

istream& Dog::Input (istream& is) {
 if (!Animal::Input (is))  // attempt to input the name portion
  return is;               // if fails, abort
 char s[100];              // arbitrary max length of dog's sound
 char c;
 is >> c;                  // input the "
 if (!is)
  return is;
 is.getline (s, sizeof(s), '\"');  // input the sound it makes
 delete [] sound;                  // remove old sound
 AllocString (sound, s, "Dog Input");
 return is;
}

```

```
/***************************************************************/
/*                                                             */
/* Output: display the dog says 'sound'                        */
/*                                                             */
/***************************************************************/

ostream& Dog::Output (ostream& os) const {
 Animal::Output (os); // display The dog says portion
 return Speak (os);   // display the sound
}

/***************************************************************/
/*                                                             */
/* extraction: input a dog object                              */
/*                                                             */
/***************************************************************/

istream& operator>> (istream& is, Dog& d) {
 return d.Input (is); // call the virtual Input()
}

/***************************************************************/
/*                                                             */
/* insertion: output a dog object                              */
/*                                                             */
/***************************************************************/

ostream& operator<< (ostream& os, const Dog& d) {
 return d.Output (os); // call the virtual Output
}
```

```
Class Cat Definition
```

```
#pragma once
#include "Animal.h"

/***************************************************************/
/*                                                             */
/* class Cat                                                   */
/*                                                             */
/***************************************************************/

class Cat : public Animal {
protected:
 char* sound;  // the sound that a cat makes

public:
          Cat ();               // default cat "Meow! Meow!"
          Cat (const char* s);  // cat with specific sound
          Cat (const Cat& c);   // copy ctor duplicate Cat
 Cat& operator= (const Cat& c); // assignment op

 virtual ~Cat ();               // removes sound string

 // displays the entire output line
```

```
 virtual ostream& Speak (ostream& os) const;

 virtual istream& Input (istream& is);
 virtual ostream& Output (ostream& os) const;

 friend istream& operator>> (istream& is, Cat& c);
 friend ostream& operator<< (ostream& os, const Cat& c);
};
```

Class Cat Implementation

```
#include <iostream>
#include <iomanip>
#include <string>
using namespace std;
#include "Cat.h"

/***************************************************************/
/*                                                             */
/* Cat: make a default cat with sound Meow! Meow!              */
/*                                                             */
/***************************************************************/

Cat::Cat () : Animal ("Cat") {
 AllocString (sound, "Meow! Meow!", "Cat Constructor");
}

/***************************************************************/
/*                                                             */
/* Cat: make a cat with this sound                             */
/*                                                             */
/***************************************************************/

Cat::Cat (const char* s) : Animal ("Cat") {
 if (!s)       // guard against 0 sound
  AllocString (sound, "Meow! Meow!", "Cat Constructor");
 else          // otherwise use this new sound
  AllocString (sound, s, "Cat Constructor");
}

/***************************************************************/
/*                                                             */
/* Cat: duplicate the passed cat                               */
/*                                                             */
/***************************************************************/

Cat::Cat (const Cat& c) : Animal (c) {
 AllocString (sound, c.sound, "Cat Copy Constructor");
}

/***************************************************************/
/*                                                             */
/* Operator= copy cat c into this cat                          */
/*                                                             */
/***************************************************************/
```

```

Cat& Cat::operator= (const Cat& c) {
 if (this == &c) // guard against a = a;
  return *this;
 Animal::operator= (c);           // copy Animal base portion
 delete [] sound;                 // remove old sound
 AllocString (sound, c.sound, "Cat Operator =");
 return *this;
}

/***************************************************************/
/*                                                             */
/* ~Cat: delete the sound array                                */
/*                                                             */
/***************************************************************/

Cat::~Cat () {
 delete [] sound;
}

/***************************************************************/
/*                                                             */
/* Speak: output the Cat's sound                               */
/*                                                             */
/***************************************************************/

ostream& Cat::Speak (ostream& os) const {
 return os << " says " << sound << endl;
}

/***************************************************************/
/*                                                             */
/* Input: input a Cat object                                   */
/*                                                             */
/***************************************************************/

istream& Cat::Input (istream& is) {
 if (!Animal::Input (is)) // try to input the name portion
  return is;              // here it failed, so abort
 char s[100];             // arbitrary sound string max length
 char c;
 is >> c;                 // input the leading "
 if (!is)
  return is;
 is.getline (s, sizeof(s), '\"');  // get the sound
 delete [] sound;                  // remove old sound
 AllocString (sound, s, "Cat Input");
 return is;
}

/***************************************************************/
/*                                                             */
/* Output: display a Cat                                       */
/*                                                             */
/***************************************************************/

```

```
ostream& Cat::Output (ostream& os) const {
 Animal::Output (os); // display "The Cat says" part
 return Speak (os);    // display its sound
}

/***************************************************************/
/*                                                             */
/* extraction: input a Cat                                     */
/*                                                             */
/***************************************************************/

istream& operator>> (istream& is, Cat& c) {
 return c.Input (is); // invoke virtual Input
}

/***************************************************************/
/*                                                             */
/* insertion: display a Cat                                    */
/*                                                             */
/***************************************************************/

ostream& operator<< (ostream& os, const Cat& c) {
 return c.Output (os); // invoke virtual Output
}
```

Review Questions

1. Suppose that you were a botanist and needed a program to help classify a number of vegetables. How could inheritance assist you?

2. Assume that you have created a base Plant class and then derived Tree, Grass, and Flower classes from Plant. Why would a client program consider operations using an array of Plant pointers? How does this impact the design of the Plant class? How would it impact the Tree class if one then derived Oak, Maple, and Ash from the Tree class?

3. What is the impact on member functions if a pointer to a base class is used to point to any instance of a derived class?

4. What is the impact on the Tree class if it is derived privately from the Plant class? Be specific in the analysis.

5. Why must the constructor functions be executed in the order of derivation? What would happen if they were not so executed? What mechanism guarantees that they are so executed? Can a programmer violate this rule? If so, how?

6. Why must the destructor functions be executed in the reverse order, from derived to base? What mechanism guarantees that this occurs? Can a programmer violate this rule? If so, how?

7. What does the rule "Constructors and destructor functions are never inherited" mean? How is this different from ordinary member functions?

8. If a base class defines three versions of function **Fun** that take an integer, **long**, and a **double** respectively

and if a derived class defines a new version of **Fun** that takes an integer, can a client program that has an instance of the derived class call the **double** version of **Fun**? If not, why not?

9. When making copies of a derived class, why must the copy ctor and the assignment operator explicitly invoke the base class ctor? At what point in the coding sequence must it do so?

10. Assume that a base class defines a function **Fun** and the derived class also redefines **Fun**. If a client program uses a pointer to the base class of a derived object to invoke **Fun**, which version of **Fun** is invoked? If the derived class version of **Fun** was made **virtual**, would that impact which was called? If the base class version of **Fun** was made **virtual**, would that impact which was called?

11. What does the rule that "virtual functions must have the same prototypes in the base and derived classes" mean? What does it mean that if not, they represent overloaded functions?

12. What does it mean that virtual functions are hierarchical in order of inheritance mean?

13. What happens if a derived class does not override a virtual base class function?

14. When implementing the insertion and extraction operators in base and derived classes, what is the impact of a client program using a pointer to the base class of a derived class to invoke the insertion and extraction operator have on the design? What would happen in this case if there were no virtual functions involved? Show an example of this.

15. Explain how the virtual **Input** and **Output** functions work with the insertion and extraction operators of a base and derived class.

16. What is meant by the terms "early binding" and "late binding?" Is there any execution time difference between these two methods?

Stop! Do These Exercises Before Programming

1. Revise the **Animal**, **Dog**, and **Cat** classes as follows. In the **Animal** class, add two new members, **height** and **weight**, both doubles. Modify the input operations to accept these new items after the name field. Then, add a new **bool** member called **showSound** to the **Animal** class and add a **SetSound** function that sets the **showSound** to the passed **bool**. Modify the derived **Dog** and **Cat** classes to output either of the following depending upon the **showSound bool**.

```
The Dog says "Ruff! Ruff!"
```

or

```
The Dog weighs 40.5 pounds and is 44.5 inches tall
```

2. Write a base class called **Plant** that stores the dynamically allocated name of the plant string and its **double** height in inches. Provide a default ctor that sets the height to zero and the name to "Unknown." Provide another ctor that is passed these two values. Provide a copy ctor and an assignment operator along with a destructor.

3. For class **Plant**, provide an **Input** function that input the plant's name which is surrounded by double quote marks and the plant's height. Write an **Output** function that displays
"The name is height inches tall" where name and height are the data values being stored. Provide appropriate insertion and extraction operator functions that call these two functions.

4. Write class **Tree** that is derived from **Plant**. Add a new **double** data member called **girth**. Provide a default ctor that sets the **girth** to zero. Provide another ctor that is passed the necessary three values. Provide a copy ctor and an assignment operator along with a destructor.

5. For class **Tree**, provide an **Input** function that input the tree's name which is surrounded by double quote marks, the tree's height and girth. Write an **Output** function that displays
"The name is height inches tall and girth inches around" where name, height, and girth are the data values being stored. Provide appropriate insertion and extraction operator functions that call these two functions.

6. Make the **Tree** class insertion and extraction operations work when a client program uses a **Plant** pointer with the insertion and extraction operators.

Programming Problems

Problem Pgm04-1—Distance Class IV

Part A.
Revise the Distance class from Pgm03-2—Distance III as follows.
Look over the **Distance** class members and functions. Decide which should be private, protected and public and make the requisite changes. We are going to be deriving from this class.
The Derived Ruler Class
Now derive a **Ruler** class from the **Distance** class. The only **Ruler** data member is just the **Type** (**English** or **Metric**); the base class holds the actual distance. There are two constructors

```
Ruler ();
Ruler (Distance::Type, double length);
```

The default is to use **Metric** of length 1 meter.

Create two friend functions operator << and >>. The input dialog in the Ruler extraction operation is as follows.

```
Enter Ruler Type E or M: x
Enter Ruler Length:      y
```

where x is either E, e, M, or m. If it is neither, re-prompt until the user gets it right. The output dialog from the Ruler insertion operation appears this way.

```
The Ruler is nnn.nn units long.
```

where nnn.nn has a width of 12 and 2 decimals. The "units" is either inches or millimeters.
The Tester Program
Write a main tester program that creates a yardstick and a meter stick and any other test cases you deem needed to thoroughly test the **Ruler** class. Ignore the inherent problems of all of the **Distance** math operators working on a Ruler instance. Only consider input and output of **Ruler** objects.

Part B.
In this part, we are going to make the **Distance::Paint** function virtual and move the **Ruler** display actions into a **Ruler::Paint** function.
Modifications to the Interface for the Distance Class
1. Revise the Distance class to make its **Paint** function virtual.
Modifications to the Interface for the Ruler Class
Add a **Paint** function to the **Ruler** class, overriding the inherited virtual **Paint**. **Ruler::Paint** should take the same parameters as **Distance::Paint**.

Ruler's **Paint**, based on **ShowAs**, will now say: "The Ruler is nnn.nn units long" where "units" is either millimeters or inches.

In the testing main program construct several instances of **Distance** and **Ruler** objects with known lengths you can debug.

Now define in the main program a pointer to a **Distance** object.

```
Distance *ptrbase;
```

Assign it an instance of one of the **Distance** objects and then call its **Paint** function.

```
Distance a;
...
ptrbase = &a;
ptrbase->Paint (Distance::Mm);
```

Assign it an instance of one of the **Ruler** objects and test its **Paint** function.

```
Ruler r (Distance::Metric, 1000.);
...
ptrbase = &r;
ptrbase->Paint (Distance::Mm);
```

Repeat for other **Distance** and **Ruler** objects to verify the virtual function works as expected. Be sure to check for some constant objects.

Problem Pgm04-2—Planets

Create a base class called **Planet** which has the following data members.

```
double mass;
double radius;
double distance;
char*  name;
```

Provide a default ctor, a ctor that is passed these four parameters, a copy ctor, a destructor, and an assignment operator. Default all parameters to zero except the name which defaults to the string "Unknown."

Create three derived classes called **Asteroid**, **Jovian**, **Terrestrial**. The Asteroid class adds a new member called **minerals** which is a dynamically allocated string such as "Iron and Platinum". The **Jovian** class adds a new member called **gasType** which is a dynamically allocated character string, such as "Ammonia and Methane". The **Terrestrial** class adds two new **double** members called **percentOcean** and **temperature**.

For the derived classes, create the appropriate constructors and destructor functions as well as the assignment operator.

Finally, add support for insertion and extraction operators. The client program can perform any of these operations for example.

```
Planet* ptrPlanet;
Jovian jupiter ();
Asteroid eros ();
Terrestrial earth ();
cin >> jupiter >> earth >> eros;
cout << jupiter << earth << eros;
ptrPlanet = &jupiter;
cin >> *ptrPlanet;
ptrPlanet = earth;
cout >> *ptrPlanet;
```

Create a tester program to fully test these classes.

Problem Pgm04-3—Bank Accounts

Part A.

Create a base class called **BankAccount**. The class has two data members, the **long** account number and the **double** balance. The default ctor sets these two to zero. An overloaded ctor accepts these two arguments and assigns the data members accordingly. However, if the ctor is passed an account number that is less than or equal to zero, display an error message to **cerr** and assign 0 to the account number. If the passed balance is below zero, also display an error message to **cerr** and assign zero to the balance.

Next, provide access functions to get the account number and get the balance. There are no Set... type of functions for these.

Next, write an **Input** function to input a bank account. The account number is input first followed by the balance. Then write an **Output** function to display the account number and balance. The account number is displayed with a width of 9 while the balance is displayed with a width of 9 and a precision of 2.

Write a **Deposit** function that is passed the new amount to be deposited. If the amount to be deposited is less than zero, display an error message on **cerr** and return the integer called **INVALID_AMOUNT**. Otherwise, update the balance and return the integer **SUCCESSFUL**.

Write a **Withdraw** function that is passed the amount to withdraw. If the amount to be withdrawn is less than 0, return **INVALID_AMOUNT**. If there are insufficient funds in the account, return the integer **INSUFFICIENT_FUNDS**. Otherwise, withdraw the funds and return **SUCCESSFUL**.

Finally, write a **GetMessage** function that is passed the return code from **Deposit** and **Withdraw** and it returns a **const char*** pointer to the correct message for that passed integer:
SUCCESS return “”
INVALID_AMOUNT return “Invalid amount”
INSUFFICIENT_FUNDS return “Insufficient funds”
Otherwise, return “Unknown outcome code”

Part B.

Derive a **BankAccountWithInterest** class from **BankAccount**. It contains a new **double** member the year to date interest earned. The class also has a **static double** called **AnnualInterestRate** and a **static** member function **SetRate** to set that rate to a value between 0 and .20. Also provide a **static** member function **GetRate** to retrieve that rate.

The default ctor sets the year to date interest to 0. The second ctor which is passed the account number and initial amount also sets the year to date interest to 0.

The **Input** function should input the year to date interest after the account number and balance fields. The **Output** function should display the year to date interest with a width of 8 and precision of 3 and display it after the account number and balance.

Additionally, create an **EarnInterest** function that is passed the number of **days** and a reference to the amount of **interest** earned this time. If the number of days is less than or equal to zero, return **INVALID_DAYS**. Otherwise calculate the earned interest as follows.

```
double dailyRate = AnnualRate / 365;
interest = days * dailyRate * GetBalance();
balance += interest;
year to date interest += interest;
return SUCCESS;
```

You need to modify the **GetMessage** function to also return the new message:
INVALID_DAYS return "Invalid days"

Part C.

Write a **BankAccountWithCompoundInterest** class derived from **BankAccountWithInterest**. This type of account earns compounded interest. It has no new data members. It has one new member function, **EarnInterest**. When this function is called, it is passed the number of **days** that have elapsed and a reference to **interest** earned this time. If the number of days is less than or equal to zero, return **INVALID_DAYS**. Otherwise calculate the earned compounded interest as follows.

```
double dailyRate = AnnualInterestRate / 365;
interest =  pow ( 1. + dailyRate, days ) - 1 ) * GetBalance();
balance += interest;
year to date interest += interest;
return SUCCESS;
```

Part D.

Write a tester program to ensure these classes are working correctly. When they are working, then do the final part.

Part E.

Write a tester program to determine the effects of a compound interest versus simple interest on two bank accounts. Create a bank account with interest and one with compound interest for two customers. Their account numbers and initial balances are shown below.
123456789 5000.00
333333333 5000.00

Apply the **transactions.txt** file to each of these two accounts. The first character of each transaction line contains a letter type code, W for withdrawal, D for deposit, and I for calculate interest. The next field on each line is the account number and that is followed by the amount to be deposited or withdrawn or it represents the number of days for this interest calculation.

The output should display the running effects of the transactions on the account and a final line outputting the total year to date interest earned on that account. One can then compare the resulting corresponding interest amounts earned to decide which type account is best for them.

Chapter 5—Abstract Base Classes

Abstract Base Class, Shapes, a Complete Example, Pgm05a

Sometimes, a base class wants to provide the framework for derived class functionality, yet has no idea of how to implement that functionality. Such a base class cannot stand alone—that is, because it has no idea of how to implement a function, it really cannot itself be instantiated. Only classes derived from it which can provide an implementation for that function can be instantiated. Such functions in the base class are called **pure virtual functions** and the class that define pure virtual functions is known as an **abstract base class**, abstract, because no instances of that base class can ever be allocated.

To create a pure virtual function, add = 0; to the end of its declaration:

```
virtual double GetArea () = 0;
```

The main purpose of a pure virtual function is to force the derived class to implement it and not overlook it by accident. If so, a compiler error results. Let's examine in detail just such a situation.

The Abstract Base Class Shape and Its Derived Classes Development Steps

Geometric shapes are commonly encapsulated in a series of hierarchical classes which make extensive use of virtual functions. The base class called **Shape** provides the basic model from which to derive common geometrical shapes. This discussion will be evolutionary in that I present a basic framework at first and then see what changes are needed for additional operations and so on. This way, you can better see the need and the usage of virtual functions and see why abstract base classes can be very useful.

Also, I implement all member functions inline as we go along. This is done for two reasons. It conserves pages and it makes the total implementation picture easier to follow because far less physical space is needed to see what is going on. The final version contained on disk and shown at the end of the chapter contains no inlined functions.

An abstract shape will contain two dimensions called **x** and **y**. Constructors are needed to initialize the two members. Thus, initially the **Shape** class begins as follows.

```
class Shape {
protected:
 double x;
 double y;
public:
 Shape (double xx, double yy) : x(xx), y(yy) {}
 Shape () : x(0), y(0) {}
 Shape (const Shape& s) : x(s.x), y(s.y) {}
};
```

Next, a **Rectangle** class can be easily derived from **Shape** as follows. No new data members are required. However, we do need to document which base class data members correspond to the height and width which define the rectangle.

```
class Rectangle : public Shape {
// x = height, y = width
public:
 Rectangle (double height, double width) : Shape(height, width){}
 Rectangle () : Shape () {}
 Rectangle (const Rectangle& r) : Shape (r.x, r.y) {}
};
```

Next, a **Triangle** class can be derived from **Shape**. This time, a third variable is added because the three sides are to be stored.

```
class Triangle : public Shape {
// x = side1, y = side2
protected:
 double side3;
public:
 Triangle (double s1, double s2, double s3)
   : Shape (s1, s2), side3(s3) {}
 Triangle () : Shape (), side3(0) {}
 Triangle (const Triangle& t)
   : Shape (t.x, t.y), side3(t.side3) {}
};
```

Now a **Square** can be similarly derived. It could come from a **Shape** or even from a **Rectangle**. Let's derive it from **Rectangle**. Since a square has only one dimension, either we can store it in say **x** and ignore **y** or we can save it in both **x** and **y** and reuse more of the **Rectangle** operational functions later on. I intentionally chose to do the latter.

```
class Square : public Rectangle {
// x = side, y = side
public:
 Square (double side) : Rectangle (side, side) {}
 Square () : Rectangle () {}
 Square (const Square& s) : Rectangle (s.x, s.y) {}
};
```

Now we can create a **Circle** also derived from **Shape** and use the **x** member to store the radius.

```
class Circle : public Shape {
// x = radius
public:
 Circle (double radius) : Shape (radius, 0) {}
 Circle () : Shape () {}
 Circle (const Circle& c) : Shape (c.x, c.y) {}
};
```

Finally, a **Sphere** can be derived from a **Circle**. No new data members are required.

```
class Sphere : public Circle {
// x = radius
public:
 Sphere (double radius) : Circle (radius, 0) {}
 Sphere () : Circle () {}
 Sphere (const Sphere& s) : Circle (s.x) {}
};
```

Adding Operational Functions

So far so good. Now let's define some operations that a client might wish to perform on these. Two actions come to mind at once, obtaining the area of the shape and the perimeter of the shape. Certainly, we can add these two functions to all of the classes except **Shape** because they have meaning for these classes. However, these two functions have no real method of implementation for the rather abstract **Shape** class. Consider what can happen if we do not put these functions in the base **Shape** class.

If a client program manages an array of geometric shapes, it is highly likely that an array of base class pointers will be used instead of numerous arrays of each specific type. Thus, calls to these two operational functions would fail unless they are defined as virtual in the **Shape** base class. Okay. So we can define **GetArea** and **GetPerimeter** in the **Shape** class as virtual functions. But then how do we implement them? Well, we could just display an error message such as "You should not be doing this", but that is rather tacky. We could have them return the area and perimeter assuming that the abstract **Shape** was a rectangle, but that would create mostly working software. Someone might actually call them and use their results! We could display an error message and abort the program, but that is quite drastic. No, the best possible solution is to make these two functions pure virtual functions. **Shape** becomes an abstract base class.

If **GetArea** and **GetPerimeter** are pure virtual, then the **Shape** class becomes an abstract class. No instances of **Shape** could ever be allocated. But that is fine, no one should be allocating an abstract shape in the first place. So here is the revised **Shape** class.

```
class Shape {
protected:
 double x;
 double y;
public:
 Shape (double xx, double yy) : x(xx), y(yy) {}
 Shape () : x(0), y(0) {}
 Shape (const Shape& s) : x(s.x), y(s.y) {}
 virtual double GetArea () const = 0;
 virtual double GetPerimeter () const = 0;
};
```

Each derived class must provide an implementation for both these functions.

Rule: If a derived class fails to implement a pure virtual function, then that derived class also becomes an abstract base class; no instances of it can be created.

In a complex hierarchy of classes, there could be several layers of abstract base classes providing a range of functionality for further classes.

The **Rectangle** class implements these as follows. Since I expect to derive another class from this one, I made the two functions virtual here as well.

```
class Rectangle : public Shape {
// x = height, y = width
public:
 Rectangle (double height, double width) : Shape(height, width){}
 Rectangle () : Shape () {}
 Rectangle (const Rectangle& r) : Shape (r.x, r.y) {}
 virtual double GetArea () const {return x * y;}
 virtual double GetPerimeter () const {return 2*x + 2*y;}
};
```

The **Triangle** implements these two functions as follows. To figure the area based upon the lengths of the three sides, first calculate the semi perimeter which is ½ the sum of the three sides. Since this class is not derived from, the two functions are not virtual.

```
class Triangle : public Shape {
// x = side1, y = side2
protected:
 double side3;
public:
 Triangle (double s1, double s2, double s3)
   : Shape (s1, s2), side3(s3) {}
 Triangle () : Shape (), side3(0) {}
 Triangle (const Triangle& t)
   : Shape (t.x, t.y), side3(t.side3) {}
 double GetArea () const {
       double s = .5 * (x + y + side3); // semiperimeter
       return sqrt (s * (s-x) * (s-b) * (s-c));}
 double GetPerimeter () const {return x + y + side3;}
};
```

The **Square** does not have to implement either of these functions because it is derived from a **Rectangle** and since we stored the side length in both **x** and **y**, the **Rectangle** calculations totally handle the **Square**. **Square** is unchanged.

```
class Square : public Rectangle {
// x = side, y = side
public:
 Square (double side) : Rectangle (side, side) {}
 Square () : Rectangle () {}
 Square (const Square& s) : Rectangle (s.x, s.y) {}
 // uses Rectangle's GetArea() and GetPerimeter()
};
```

Here is the **Circle**'s implementation. Note **acos(–1.)** is PI. The area is PI times the radius^2 while the circumference is 2 times PI times the radius.

```
class Circle : public Shape {
// x = radius
public:
 Circle (double radius) : Shape (radius, 0) {}
 Circle () : Shape () {}
 Circle (const Circle& c) : Shape (c.x, c.y) {}
 virtual double GetArea () const {return acos(-1.) * x * x;}
 virtual double GetPerimeter () const {return 2 * acos(-1.) * x;}
};
```

Finally, the **Sphere** area formula is 4 PI radius^2. The circumference is the same as the circle. So only the area function is defined here. Notice how I choose to reuse the base class calculation. Further, since **Sphere** is not being used as a base class, it is not virtual.

```
class Sphere : public Circle {
// x = radius
public:
 Sphere (double radius) : Circle (radius, 0) {}
 Sphere () : Circle () {}
 Sphere (const Sphere& s) : Circle (s.x) {}
 double GetArea () const {return 2 * Circle::GetArea();}
};
```

Handling Input and Output

Now how do we handle inputting and outputting of these objects? Each of the classes must define the insertion and extraction operators because clients can be expected to directly input and output these objects. However, because the client could also use a base class pointer with the insertion and extraction operations, virtual functions must be implemented in all the classes, just like was done with the vehicle series of classes. So each class must define the virtual **Input** and **Output** functions and have the insertion and extraction friend operator functions call them. However, how would one implement these for a Shape? Once again, **Shape**'s virtual **Input** and **Output** functions will be pure virtual in nature.

But before we charge forward implementing all of these functions, let's give some thought to the client output being produced. Here is a possible report produced by a client program.

```
Shape        Side(s)             Area   Perimeter
Rectangle    10.0  20.0          200.0    60.0
Triangle     40.0  50.0  60.0    992.2   150.0
Square       10.0                100.0    40.0
Circle       10.0                314.2     6.3
Sphere       10.                 628.4     6.3
```

Can you spot the new detail? Each object ought to be able to identify itself by producing the string naming its shape type, such as **Rectangle**. How can we implement this?

One solution would be to define a string member in each of the derived classes and provide a pure virtual **GetName** function in the **Shape** class. It would have to be a virtual function in **Shape** so that base class pointers would call the correct derived class **GetName** function. However, and this is a major however, each of the five classes would end up coding roughly the same coding to input the name and to output the name. This would be repetitive, redundant coding! OOP to the rescue. There is no reason why **Shape** cannot implement the inputting and outputting of the string name of the shape. This way, we write it once and the other derived classes reuse it.

To keep this simple, **Shape** defines the actual array of characters for the name. The first ctor is passed the string name. The default ctor simply assigns it a null string. An access function, **GetName** is provided to retrieve the name. I also added the virtual destructor.

```
class Shape {
protected:
 double x;
 double y;
 char name[10];
public:
 Shape (double xx, double yy, const char* n) : x(xx), y(yy) {
    strcpy_s (name, sizeof(name), n);}
 Shape () : x(0), y(0) {name[0] = 0;}
 Shape (const Shape& s) : x(s.x), y(s.y) {
        strcpy (name, sizeof(name), s.name);}
 virtual ~Shape () {}
 const char* GetName() const {return name;}
 virtual double GetArea () const = 0;
 virtual double GetPerimeter () const = 0;
};
```

The **Rectangle** class implements these changes by passing the name string to the base class as follows. Since **Rectangle** is being derived from, the destructor is added as well as a default third parameter. Square is going to be calling this base ctor and needs to pass it the string “Square”. By defaulting the third parameter to the string “Rectangle” clients can still construct a rectangle from two dimensions.

```
class Rectangle : public Shape {
// x = height, y = width
public:
 Rectangle (double height, double width,
            const char* n = "Rectangle")
     : Shape(height, width, n){}
 Rectangle () : Shape (0, 0, "Rectangle") {}
 Rectangle (const Rectangle& r) : Shape (r.x, r.y, "Rectangle"){}
 virtual ~Rectangle () {}
 virtual double GetArea () const {return x * y;}
 virtual double GetPerimeter () const {return 2*x + 2*y;}
};
```

The **Triangle** is coded as follows. It is simpler because it is not being used as an additional base class.

```
class Triangle : public Shape {
// x = side1, y = side2
protected:
 double side3;
public:
 Triangle (double s1, double s2, double s3)
   : Shape (s1, s2, "Triangle"), side3(s3) {}
 Triangle () : Shape (0, 0, "Triangle"), side3(0) {}
 Triangle (const Triangle& t)
   : Shape (t.x, t.y, "Triangle"), side3(t.side3) {}
```

```
 double GetArea () const {
       double s = .5 * (x + y + side3); // semiperimeter
       return sqrt (s * (s-x) * (s-y) * (s-side3));}
 double GetPerimeter () const {return x + y + side3;}
};
```

The **Square** is coded this way. Notice that the default and copy ctors now call a different **Rectangle** ctor.

```
class Square : public Rectangle {
// x = side, y = side
public:
 Square (double side) : Rectangle (side, side, "Square") {}
 Square () : Rectangle (0, 0, "Square") {}
 Square (const Square& s) : Rectangle (s.x, s.y, "Square") {}
 // uses Rectangle's GetArea() and GetPerimeter()
};
```

Circle's implementation parallels that of **Rectangle** because **Sphere** is derived from it.

```
class Circle : public Shape {
// x = radius
public:
 Circle (double radius, const char* n = "Circle")
        : Shape (radius, 0, n) {}
 Circle () : Shape (0, 0, "Circle") {}
 Circle (const Circle& c) : Shape (c.x, c.y, c.name) {}
 virtual ~Circle () {}
 virtual double GetArea () const {return acos(-1.) * x * x;}
 virtual double GetPerimeter () const {return 2 * acos(-1.) * x;}
};
```

Finally, the **Sphere** is simple and parallels the **Square**.

```
class Sphere : public Circle {
// x = radius
public:
 Sphere (double radius) : Circle (radius, "Sphere") {}
 Sphere () : Circle (0, "Sphere") {}
 Sphere (const Sphere& s) : Circle (s.x, s.name) {}
 double GetArea () const {return 2 * Circle::GetArea();}
};
```

Does the assignment operator need to be provided? No, there are no dynamically allocated memory items or constant data members. So now we can proceed to implement the I/O functions. Let's begin with **Shape**. On input, the input format will be similar to the following.
[Rectangle 10 20] or [Circle 10]. So **Shape**'s **Input** must extract what it can, namely the beginning angle bracket and the name. The **Output** function just displays the name.

```
class Shape {
protected:
 double x;
 double y;
 char name[10];
public:
 Shape (double xx, double yy, const char* n) : x(xx), y(yy) {
    strcpy_s (name, sizeof(name), n);}
 Shape () : x(0), y(0) {name[0] = 0;}
 Shape (const Shape& s) : x(s.x), y(s.y) {
    strcpy_s (name, sizeof(name), s.name);}
 virtual ~Shape () {}
 const char* GetName() const {return name;}
 virtual double GetArea () const = 0;
```

```
 virtual double GetPerimeter () const = 0;
 virtual istream& Input (istream& is) {
        char c;
        is >> c >> name;// no blanks allowed and not too long
        return is;}
 virtual ostream& Output (ostream& os) const {
        return os << left << setw(12) << name << right;}
 friend istream& operator>> (istream& is, Shape& s) {
        return s.Input (is);}
 friend ostream& operator<< (ostream& os, const Shape& s) {
        return s.Output (os);}
};
```

The **Rectangle** class implements these changes by having its insertion and extraction operator friend functions invoke the virtual **Input** and **Output** functions. Within these functions, the base class is invoked first to input and output the name.

```
class Rectangle : public Shape {
// x = height, y = width
public:
 Rectangle (double height, double width,
            const char* n = "Rectangle")
     : Shape(height, width, n){}
 Rectangle () : Shape (0, 0, "Rectangle") {}
 Rectangle (const Rectangle& r) : Shape (r.x, r.y, "Rectangle"){}
 virtual ~Rectangle () {}
 virtual double GetArea () const {return x * y;}
 virtual double GetPerimeter () const {return 2*x + 2*y;}
 virtual istream& Input (istream& is) {
        char c;
        Shape::Input (is);
        if (!is) return is;
        return is >> x >> y >> c;}
 virtual ostream& Output (ostream& os) const {
        Shape::Output (os);
        return os << setw (6) << x << setw(6) << y;}
 friend istream& operator>> (istream& is, Rectangle& r) {
        return r.Input (is);}
 friend ostream& operator<< (ostream& os, const Rectangle& r) {
        return r.Output (os);}
};
```

The **Triangle** is coded as follows.

```
class Triangle : public Shape {
// x = side1, y = side2
protected:
 double side3;
public:
 Triangle (double s1, double s2, double s3)
   : Shape (s1, s2, "Triangle"), side3(s3) {}
 Triangle () : Shape (0, 0, "Triangle"), side3(0) {}
 Triangle (const Triangle& t)
   : Shape (t.x, t.y, "Triangle"), side3(t.side3) {}
 double GetArea () const {
       double s = .5 * (x + y + side3); // semiperimeter
       return sqrt (s * (s-x) * (s-y) * (s-side3));}
 double GetPerimeter () const {return x + y + side3;}
 virtual istream& Input (istream& is) {
```

```
        char c;
        Shape::Input (is);
        if (!is) return is;
        return is >> x >> y >> side3 >> c;}
 virtual ostream& Output (ostream& os) const {
        Shape::Output (os);
        return os <<setw(6)<< x <<setw(6)<< y <<setw(6)<< side3;}
 friend istream& operator>> (istream& is, Triangle& t) {
        return t.Input (is);}
 friend ostream& operator<< (ostream& os, const Triangle& t) {
        return t.Output (os);}
};
```

The **Square** cannot reuse the **Rectangle Input** and **Output** functions and is coded this way.

```
class Square : public Rectangle {
// x = side, y = side
public:
 Square (double side) : Rectangle (side, side, "Square") {}
 Square () : Rectangle (0, 0, "Square") {}
 Square (const Square& s) : Rectangle (s.x, s.y, "Square") {}
 // uses Rectangle's GetArea() and GetPerimeter()
 virtual istream& Input (istream& is) {
        char c;
        Shape::Input (is);
        if (!is) return is;
        is >> x >> c;
        y = x;
        return is;}
 virtual ostream& Output (ostream& os) const {
        Shape::Output (os);
        return os <<setw(6)<< x;}
 friend istream& operator>> (istream& is, Square& s) {
        return s.Input (is);}
 friend ostream& operator<< (ostream& os, const Square& s) {
        return s.Output (os);}
};
```

Here is **Circle**'s implementation.

```
class Circle : public Shape {
// x = radius
public:
 Circle (double radius, const char* n = "Circle")
       : Shape (radius, 0, n) {}
 Circle () : Shape (0, 0, "Circle") {}
 Circle (const Circle& c) : Shape (c.x, c.y, c.name) {}
 virtual ~Circle () {}
 virtual double GetArea () const {return acos(-1.) * x * x;}
 virtual double GetPerimeter () const {return 2 * acos(-1.) * x;}
 virtual istream& Input (istream& is) {
        char c;
        Shape::Input (is);
        if (!is) return is;
        return is >> x >> c;}
 virtual ostream& Output (ostream& os) const {
        Shape::Output (os);
        return os <<setw(6) << x;}
 friend istream& operator>> (istream& is, Circle& c) {
```

```
        return c.Input (is);}
 friend ostream& operator<< (ostream& os, const Circle& c) {
        return c.Output (os);}
};
```

Finally, the **Sphere** derived from a **Circle** can, in fact, simply reuse **Circle**'s **Input** and **Output** functions because there are no new data members. It still must implement the friend insertion and extraction operators, though.

```
class Sphere : public Circle {
// x = radius
public:
 Sphere (double radius) : Circle (radius, "Sphere") {}
 Sphere () : Circle (0, "Sphere") {}
 Sphere (const Sphere& s) : Circle (s.x, s.name) {}
 double GetArea () const {return 2 * Circle::GetArea();}
 friend istream& operator>> (istream& is, Sphere& s) {
        return s.Input (is);}
 friend ostream& operator<< (ostream& os, const Sphere& s) {
        return s.Output (os);}
};
```

The Actual Implementation of Shape and Its Derived Classes

While every function in all of these classes could be inlined as given above, it's not practical to do so. First, if every function is inlined, then the client program's file size is much larger than needed because every time any of these functions is called, all of the coding is present in the client at that point. Second, the client must include the header file. With everything in it, the header takes longer to compile and the client gets to see all of your implementation coding.

Okay. So we split the definition and implementation into a header and cpp file. Now do we create six headers and six cpp files, one for each of the classes? Well, that all depends. In this particular case, each of the classes is quite small and they are very closely related. Thus, I chose to have only one header and one cpp file. The benefit for client programs is that only one header file must be included to gain access to any and all of the various shape classes.

Here are the definition and implementation files that are really used by client programs.

Shape Classes Definition

```
#pragma once
#include <iostream>
using namespace std;

/***************************************************************/
/*                                                             */
/* Shape class - abstract base class holds 2 dimensions & name */
/*                                                             */
/* derived classes must implement GetArea, GetPerimeter        */
/*                                                             */
/***************************************************************/

class Shape {
protected:
 double x;
 double y;
 char name[10];

```

```
public:
                  Shape (double xx, double yy, const char* n);
                  Shape ();
                  Shape (const Shape& s);
 virtual         ~Shape ();

 const char*      GetName() const;

 virtual double   GetArea () const = 0;
 virtual double   GetPerimeter () const = 0;

 virtual istream& Input (istream& is);
 virtual ostream& Output (ostream& os) const;

 friend  istream& operator>> (istream& is, Shape& s);
 friend  ostream& operator<< (ostream& os, const Shape& s);
};


/***************************************************************/
/*                                                             */
/* Rectangle class                                             */
/*                                                             */
/***************************************************************/


class Rectangle : public Shape {
// x = height, y = width
public:
                  Rectangle (double height, double width,
                             const char* n = "Rectangle");
                  Rectangle ();
                  Rectangle (const Rectangle& r);
 virtual         ~Rectangle ();

 virtual double   GetArea () const;
 virtual double   GetPerimeter () const;

 virtual istream& Input (istream& is);
 virtual ostream& Output (ostream& os) const;

 friend  istream& operator>> (istream& is, Rectangle& r);
 friend  ostream& operator<< (ostream& os, const Rectangle& r);
};


/***************************************************************/
/*                                                             */
/* Triangle class                                              */
/*                                                             */
/***************************************************************/


class Triangle : public Shape {
// x = side1, y = side2
protected:
```

```
 double side3;
public:
                  Triangle (double s1, double s2, double s3);
                  Triangle ();
                  Triangle (const Triangle& t);
 virtual         ~Triangle ();

         double   GetArea () const;
         double   GetPerimeter () const;

 virtual istream& Input (istream& is);
 virtual ostream& Output (ostream& os) const;

 friend  istream& operator>> (istream& is, Triangle& t);
 friend  ostream& operator<< (ostream& os, const Triangle& t);
};


/***************************************************************/
/*                                                             */
/* Square class                                                */
/*                                                             */
/***************************************************************/


class Square : public Rectangle {
// x = side, y = side
public:
                  Square (double side);
                  Square ();
                  Square (const Square& s);
 virtual         ~Square ();

 // uses Rectangle's GetArea() and GetPerimeter()

 virtual istream& Input (istream& is);
 virtual ostream& Output (ostream& os) const;

 friend  istream& operator>> (istream& is, Square& s);
 friend  ostream& operator<< (ostream& os, const Square& s);
};


/***************************************************************/
/*                                                             */
/* Circle class                                                */
/*                                                             */
/***************************************************************/


class Circle : public Shape {
// x = radius
public:
                  Circle (double radius, const char* n="Circle");
                  Circle ();
                  Circle (const Circle& c);
```

```
 virtual         ~Circle ();

 virtual double   GetArea () const;
         double   GetPerimeter () const;

 virtual istream& Input (istream& is);
 virtual ostream& Output (ostream& os) const;

 friend  istream& operator>> (istream& is, Circle& c);
 friend  ostream& operator<< (ostream& os, const Circle& c);
};


/***************************************************************/
/*                                                             */
/* Sphere class                                                */
/*                                                             */
/***************************************************************/


class Sphere : public Circle {
// x = radius
public:
                  Sphere (double radius);
                  Sphere ();
                  Sphere (const Sphere& s);
 virtual         ~Sphere ();

         double   GetArea () const;
 // uses Circle's GetPerimeter
 // uses Circle's Input and Output

 friend  istream& operator>> (istream& is, Sphere& s);
 friend  ostream& operator<< (ostream& os, const Sphere& s);
};
```

In the implementation file below, please examine lines 17 through 22. When a class is storing a string as a fixed sized array of char, you cannot just do a **strcpy_s** of the user's string into your array. What happens if the user gives you a string that is too long? You would clobber memory! Thus, if the user's string is too long, simply truncate it. Use **_strncpy** to copy the maximum number of characters your string can hold and then insert the null terminator.

Shape Classes Implementation

```
 1 #include <iostream>
 2 #include <iomanip>
 3 #include <string>
 4 #include <cmath>
 5 using namespace std;
 6 #include "Shape.h"
 7
 8 /***************************************************************/
 9 /*                                                             */
10 /* Shape Implementation                                        */
11 /*                                                             */
```

```
/***************************************************************/

Shape::Shape (double xx, double yy, const char* n)
      : x(xx), y(yy) {
 strcpy_s (name, sizeof(name), n);
}

Shape::Shape () : x(0), y(0) {
 name[0] = 0;
}

Shape::Shape (const Shape& s) : x(s.x), y(s.y) {
 strcpy_s (name, sizeof (name), s.name);
}

Shape::~Shape () {
}

const char* Shape::GetName() const {
 return name;
}

istream& Shape::Input (istream& is) {
 char c;
 is >> c >> name; // inputs the leading [ and the name
 return is;
}

ostream& Shape::Output (ostream& os) const {
 return os << left << setw(12) << name << right;
}

istream& operator>> (istream& is, Shape& s) {
 return s.Input (is);
}

ostream& operator<< (ostream& os, const Shape& s) {
 return s.Output (os);
}


/***************************************************************/
/*                                                             */
/* Rectangle Implementation                                    */
/*                                                             */
/***************************************************************/

Rectangle::Rectangle (double height, double width, const char* n)
          : Shape(height, width, n) {
}

Rectangle::Rectangle () : Shape (0, 0, "Rectangle") {
}

Rectangle::Rectangle (const Rectangle& r)
         : Shape (r.x, r.y, r.name) {
```

```
}

Rectangle::~Rectangle () {
}

double Rectangle::GetArea () const {
 return x * y;
}

double Rectangle::GetPerimeter () const {
 return 2*x + 2*y;
}

istream& Rectangle::Input (istream& is) {
 char c;
 Shape::Input (is); // input [Rectangle portion
 if (!is)
  return is;
 return is >> x >> y >> c; // input h w] portion
}

ostream& Rectangle::Output (ostream& os) const {
 Shape::Output (os);
 return os << setw (8) << x << setw(8) << y;
}

istream& operator>> (istream& is, Rectangle& r) {
 return r.Input (is);
}

ostream& operator<< (ostream& os, const Rectangle& r) {
 return r.Output (os);
}


/***************************************************************/
/*                                                             */
/* Triangle Implementation                                     */
/*                                                             */
/***************************************************************/

Triangle::Triangle (double s1, double s2, double s3)
         : Shape (s1, s2, "Triangle"), side3(s3) {
}

Triangle::Triangle () : Shape (0, 0, "Triangle"), side3(0) {
}

Triangle::Triangle (const Triangle& t)
         : Shape (t.x, t.y, t.name), side3(t.side3) {
}

Triangle::~Triangle () {
}

double Triangle::GetArea () const {
```

```
 // calculate the semi-perimeter
 double s = .5 * (x + y + side3);
 // now calc the area using semi-perimeter
 return sqrt (s * (s-x) * (s-y) * (s-side3));
}

double Triangle::GetPerimeter () const {
 return x + y + side3;
}

istream& Triangle::Input (istream& is) {
 char c;
 Shape::Input (is); // input [Triangle portion
 if (!is)
  return is;
 return is >> x >> y >> side3 >> c;
}

ostream& Triangle::Output (ostream& os) const {
 Shape::Output (os);
 return os <<setw(8)<< x <<setw(8)<< y <<setw(8)<< side3;
}

istream& operator>> (istream& is, Triangle& t) {
 return t.Input (is);
}

ostream& operator<< (ostream& os, const Triangle& t) {
 return t.Output (os);
}


/***************************************************************/
/*                                                             */
/* Square Implementation                                       */
/*                                                             */
/***************************************************************/

Square::Square (double side)
       : Rectangle (side, side, "Square") {
}

Square::Square () : Rectangle (0, 0, "Square") {
}

Square::Square (const Square& s)
       : Rectangle (s.x, s.y, s.name) {
}

Square::~Square () {
}

istream& Square::Input (istream& is) {
 char c;
 Shape::Input (is); // input [Square portion
 if (!is)
```

```
  return is;
 is >> x >> c;
 y = x;
 return is;
}

ostream& Square::Output (ostream& os) const {
 Shape::Output (os);
 return os <<setw(8)<< x;
}

istream& operator>> (istream& is, Square& s) {
 return s.Input (is);
}

ostream& operator<< (ostream& os, const Square& s) {
 return s.Output (os);
}


/***************************************************************/
/*                                                             */
/* Circle Implemenation                                        */
/*                                                             */
/***************************************************************/

Circle::Circle (double radius, const char* n)
       : Shape (radius, 0, n) {
}

Circle::Circle () : Shape (0, 0, "Circle") {
}

Circle::Circle (const Circle& c) : Shape (c.x, c.y, c.name) {
}

Circle::~Circle () {
}

double Circle::GetArea () const {
 return acos(-1.) * x * x;
}

double Circle::GetPerimeter () const {
 return 2 * acos(-1.) * x;
}

istream& Circle::Input (istream& is) {
 char c;
 Shape::Input (is); // input [Circle portion
 if (!is)
  return is;
 return is >> x >> c;
}

ostream& Circle::Output (ostream& os) const {
```

```
 Shape::Output (os);
 return os <<setw(8) << x;
}

istream& operator>> (istream& is, Circle& c) {
 return c.Input (is);
}
ostream& operator<< (ostream& os, const Circle& c) {
 return c.Output (os);
}


/***************************************************************/
/*                                                             */
/* Sphere Implementation                                       */
/*                                                             */
/***************************************************************/

Sphere::Sphere (double radius) : Circle (radius, "Sphere") {
}

Sphere::Sphere () : Circle (0, "Sphere") {
}

Sphere::~Sphere () {
}

Sphere::Sphere (const Sphere& s) : Circle (s.x, s.name) {
}

double Sphere::GetArea () const {
 // 4 PI r squared - so 2 * circle's area
 return 2 * Circle::GetArea();
}

istream& operator>> (istream& is, Sphere& s) {
 return s.Input (is);
}

ostream& operator<< (ostream& os, const Sphere& s) {
 return s.Output (os);
}
```

Writing the Client Tester Program Pgm05a

Now let's turn our attention to how a client program can make excellent usage of these classes. Two subtle key issues are raised. See if you can spot them. Here is the input file of shapes that the client program must input. It is followed by the report that is generated.

Input to Pgm05a Shapes Tester

```
[Rectangle 50 50]
[Circle    15]
[Circle    10]
```

```
[Square     42]
[Circle     7]
[Circle     5]
[Triangle    35 20 20]
[Triangle    15 30 40]
[Sphere     10]
[Triangle 15 20 30]
[Triangle    30 30 30]
[Rectangle  15 30]
[Rectangle  20 5]
[Square      88]
[Rectangle 10 20]
[Sphere     100]
[Rectangle  20 15]
[Circle      12]
[Triangle  5 5 5 ]
[Triangle  50 50 50 ]
```

```
Output from Pgm05a Tester of Shape Classes
```

```
Shape Type  <-----   Dimensions ----->        Area    Perimeter

Rectangle       50.00   50.00              2500.00      200.00
Circle          15.00                       706.86       94.25
Circle          10.00                       314.16       62.83
Square          42.00                      1764.00      168.00
Circle           7.00                       153.94       43.98
Circle           5.00                        78.54       31.42
Triangle        35.00   20.00   20.00       169.44       75.00
Triangle        15.00   30.00   40.00       191.11       85.00
Sphere          10.00                       628.32       62.83
Triangle        15.00   20.00   30.00       133.32       65.00
Triangle        30.00   30.00   30.00       389.71       90.00
Rectangle       15.00   30.00               450.00       90.00
Rectangle       20.00    5.00               100.00       50.00
Square          88.00                      7744.00      352.00
Rectangle       10.00   20.00               200.00       60.00
Sphere         100.00                     62831.85      628.32
Rectangle       20.00   15.00               300.00       70.00
Circle          12.00                       452.39       75.40
Triangle         5.00    5.00    5.00        10.83       15.00
Triangle        50.00   50.00   50.00      1082.53      150.00
No memory leaks.
```

The first detail is how can the client input the file of shapes? Recall that the **Shape::Input** function inputs the leading [and the name, such as "[Rectangle". Certainly, the client program can input the shape data into an array of base class pointers.

```
Shape* shapes[MAX]; // the array of shapes
```

and

```
infile >> *shapes[i];   // input the shape
```

But the problem facing the client is **shapes[i]** must already contain an instance of the correct derived class for which the line to be inputted represents. The client must know in advance which kind of shape is coming. In earlier examples, this can be done by having a single character code as the first item on the line, identifying what kind of shape the line contains. But that is not the way the input file is structured in this case.

The client program can input the first three characters of the line. Why three? The first is the useless leading [. In order to determine which shape is on the line, two characters are needed because of **Sp**here and **Sq**uare. If the client inputs these first three characters to determine what kind of shape is coming, then, if nothing else is done, the **Shape::Input** function does not have the proper data in the stream for it to input!

The input stream has another function, **putback**, that puts back into the input stream the character that it is passed. In other words, after the client has extracted the first three characters of a line, it can put those characters just read back into the stream so that **Shape::Input** can actually input them properly!

Thus, the client's main loop can be written like this.

```
while (infile >> b >> c >> d) { // ie. input [Re of [Rectangle
  infile.putback (d);           // and put those chars back
  infile.putback (c);           // into the stream so they can
  infile.putback (b);           // be extracted by Shape::Input
```

And here it can switch on the character **c** and use character **d** to assist in sorting out **Sphere** and **Square** objects. It can now dynamically allocate the correct new shape and store that pointer in the base class pointer array, **shapes**.

The second hurdle is the output formatting. Examine the report to be generated as shown above once again. Can you spot this new difficulty? Consider what happens when one of the **Output** function is called. Compare the output results of **Triangle::Output** and **Circle::Output**. What is the difference? The triangle output contains three numerical side values while the circle only has one. So the problem is one of columnar alignment of all fields after the dimensions of the shape are displayed. We must force the area field to be aligned in a specific column.

This can be done in a clever way. If we make up an **ostrstream** wrapped around a sufficiently large character string and pass that stream to the shape's **Output** functions, then the output fills up the string. We can then display that resultant string left justified in a sufficiently wide width to get good column alignment. We can use coding like this.

```
ostrstream os (leftPart, sizeof (leftPart));
os << fixed << setprecision (2);
os << *shapes[i] << ends;
// now display that string left adjusted in wide field
cout << left << setw (36) << leftPart << right;
// and display the area and perimeter columns
cout << setw(12) << shapes[i]->GetArea()
     << setw(12) << shapes[i]->GetPerimeter() << endl;
```

Here is the complete **Pgm05a** tester program. Since memory is dynamically allocated, I included memory leak checking as usual.

Pgm05a Tester of Shape Classes

```
#include <iostream>
#include <iomanip>
#include <fstream>
#include <string>
#include <cctype>
#include <strstream>
#include <crtdbg.h>
using namespace std;
#include "Shape.h"

const int MAX = 100;

int main () {
 {
```

```
// setup floating point output format
cout << fixed << setprecision (2);

// open input file od shapes
ifstream infile ("testdata.txt");
if (!infile) {
 cerr << "Error: cannot open testdata.txt file\n";
 return 1;
}

Shape* shapes[MAX]; // the array of shapes
int numShapes;      // number of shapes currently in array
int i = 0;
char b, c, d;       // stores first three chars of each line

while (infile >> b >> c >> d) { // ie. input [Re of [Rectangle
 infile.putback (d);            // and put those chars back
 infile.putback (c);            // into the stream so they can
 infile.putback (b);            // be extracted by Shape::Input

 c = toupper(c);                // remove case sensitivity
 d = toupper(d);
 shapes[i] = 0;                 // initialize this Shape pointer

 switch (c) {                   // allocate a new shape based on
  case 'R':                     // what type it is
   shapes[i] = new Rectangle;
   break;
  case 'T':
   shapes[i] = new Triangle;
   break;
  case 'S':
   if (d == 'Q') {
    shapes[i] = new Square;
    break;
   }
   else if (d == 'P') {
    shapes[i] = new Sphere;
    break;
   }
  case 'C':
   shapes[i] = new Circle;
   break;
 };

 if (shapes[i] == 0) {  // check for unknown shape type error
  cerr << "Error: unknown shape encountered on input: "
       << c << d << endl;
  infile.close ();
  return (2);
 }

 infile >> *shapes[i];  // input the shape
 i++;
}
numShapes = i; // save number of shapes in the array
```

```
 infile.close ();

 // display report heading
 cout << "Shape Type  <-----  Dimensions ----->"
      << "          Area    Perimeter\n\n";

 char leftPart[80];

 for (i=0; i<numShapes; i++) {
  // build the basic shape output string portion
  ostrstream os (leftPart, sizeof (leftPart));
  os << fixed << setprecision (2) << *shapes[i] << ends;

  // now display that string left adjusted in wide field
  cout << left << setw (36) << leftPart << right;
  // and display the area and perimeter columns
  cout << setw(12) << shapes[i]->GetArea()
       << setw(12) << shapes[i]->GetPerimeter() << endl;
 }

 // clean up action - remove all shapes that were allocated
 for (i=0; i<numShapes; i++) {
  delete shapes[i];
 }
 }

 // check for memory leaks
 if (_CrtDumpMemoryLeaks())
  cerr << "Memory leaks occurred!\n";
 else
  cerr << "No memory leaks.\n";

 return 0;

```

Multiple Inheritance

It is possible for a derived class to have more than one immediate base class. This is known as **multiple inheritance**. For example going back to the **Vehicle** class, the **Tank** class could be derived from a **Truck** class to get **Vehicle** aspects and also be derived from a **Gun** class to inherit gun properties and methods.

```
class Tank : public Truck, public Gun {
```

The syntax for multiple inheritance is

```
class derived : access base1, access base2, ... access basen {
```

The constructor functions must then invoke all of the base classes.

```
Tank::Tank () : Truck(), Gun() {
```

When a tank is constructed, the **Truck** base class is called first, followed by the **Gun** base class ctor, followed by the **Tank** constructor's body. When the tank destructors are called, first **~Tank** is called, then **~Gun** is called and finally **~Truck** is invoked—the reverse order of construction.

Multiple base classes offer powerful class design capabilities as you can imagine with the **Tank** class. However, there is one small catch that sometimes can arise. Let's see how this can occur. The **Gun** class could also be derived from a **Vehicle** because a gun can be moved. Small caliber machine guns can be carried by a squad of men. Smaller field pieces can be manhandled by the gun crew for short distances if needed. Thus, we might have the following pictorial derivation, Figure 5.1.

Notice that two copies of the **Vehicle** base class are included in a **Tank** object. This causes ambiguity when a member of **Vehicle** is referenced by **Tank**. This problem is resolved by another C++ mechanism, a **virtual base class**.

By adding the virtual keyword before the access qualifier in the derivation, only a single copy of such virtual base classes is included in the derived class. If we code the class definitions as follows, then only a single copy of the **Vehicle** class is included in class **Tank**.

```
class Gun : virtual public Vehicle { ...
class Car : virtual public Vehicle { ...
class Truck : virtual public Car { ...
class Tank : public Gun, public Truck { ...
```

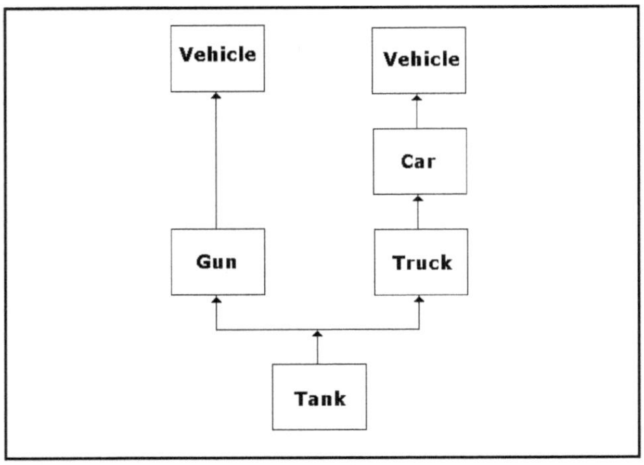

Figure 5.1 Multiple Inheritance of Tank

Adding Multiple Base Classes to Shapes

Returning to the series of geometrical shape classes, each object would also likely have an origin point or center coordinates in two-dimensional space. That origin point could be defined by a class called **Point**.

```
class Point {
protected:
 int coordx;
 int coordy;
...
};
```

Given this definition of **Point**, the **Rectangle** class could be defined this way. Assume for input the x and y coordinates precede the height and width values and similarly for output.

```
class Rectangle : public Shape, public Point {
// x = height, y = width
public:
 Rectangle (double height, double width, int x, int y,
            const char* n = "Rectangle")
     : Shape(height, width, n), Point (x, y) {}
 Rectangle () : Shape (0, 0, "Rectangle"), Point (0,0) {}
 Rectangle (const Rectangle& r) : Shape (r.x, r.y, "Rectangle"),
            Point (r.coordx, r.coordy) {}
 virtual ~Rectangle () {}
 virtual double GetArea () const {return x * y;}
 virtual double GetPerimeter () const {return 2*x + 2*y;}
```

```
 virtual istream& Input (istream& is) {
        char c;
        Shape::Input (is);
        if (!is) return is;
        return is >> coordx >> coordy >> x >> y >> c;}
 virtual ostream& Output (ostream& os) const {
        Shape::Output (os);
        return os << setw (4) << coordx << setw (4) << coordy
                  << setw (6) << x << setw(6) << y;}
 friend istream& operator>> (istream& is, Rectangle& r) {
        return r.Input (is);}
 friend ostream& operator<< (ostream& os, const Rectangle& r) {
        return r.Output (os);}
};
```

The use of multiple base classes can add a new dimension in class design and corresponding hierarchy.

The Microsoft I/O Stream Classes

At this point in our studies of OOP, we know enough to grasp the basics of how Microsoft defines the I/O stream classes—that is, if advanced complexities are removed from the files and if we examine the Old Style streams. In the following two listings, I have removed a large number of complex #defines and other items, leaving a more understandable definition. The objective of this section is to gain a better overall understanding of the stream classes, not an in depth understanding.

In the definition of the **ios** class below, notice that there is also a forward reference for another class, **streambuf**, line 16. Essentially, **streambuf** handles the actual keyboard character buffer in which DOS places incoming characters from the keyboard. For our purposes of gaining an initial overview of the stream classes, this is as far as we will go with how characters are actually extracted or inserted into the buffers and so on.

Line 19 defines the **ios** class proper. And the first items in it are a number of public **enums** for all of the **ios::** identifiers that we have been using. First come **io_state** and **open_mode**, lines 22 through 34. Notice the notation of the values, such as 0x01. The 0x prefix specifies that the following value is in hexadecimal. For example,

```
    enum open_mode { in        = 0x01,
                     out       = 0x02,
                     ate       = 0x04,
                     app       = 0x08,
                     trunc     = 0x10,
                     nocreate  = 0x20,
                     noreplace = 0x40,
                     binary    = 0x80 };
```

We know that these are the various flag values that we OR together when defining or opening a file or stream, such as

```
    ifstream infile ("test.txt", ios::in | ios::nocreate);
```

This example illustrates a very common coding technique of flags. Suppose that some function could be passed any number of flag values—say six were possible. Rather than making that function take six parameters, one for each possible flag setting, by carefully specifying individual flag values, it is possible to pass a single flag parameter that contains those six flag values. To see how this is done, let's examine the eight bits within a byte value.

```
  The 8 Bits          Decimal Value   Hex Value
  0 0 0 0   0 0 0 1         1            0x01
  0 0 0 0   0 0 1 0         2            0x02
  0 0 0 0   0 1 0 0         4            0x04
```

```
0 0 0 0   1 0 0 0      8        0x08
0 0 0 1   0 0 0 0     16        0x10
0 0 1 0   0 0 0 0     32        0x20
0 1 0 0   0 0 0 0     54        0x40
1 0 0 0   0 0 0 0    128        0x80
```

If each bit position represents a single flag value (true/false), then a single byte could contain eight different flags as shown below.

```
1 1 1 1   1 1 1 1
```

Since the values are passed as a **long** or 32-bit value, theoretically, one **long** could contain up to thirty-two different flag values!

This concept is further illustrated by the next anonymous enumerated series in the **ios** class beginning on line 38. Here we find the actual definition of most all of the other values we have been using, such as **ios::left**, **ios::right**, and **ios::fixed**.

Next notice that the definitions of **basefield**, **adjustfield**, and **floatfield** (lines 55 through 57) are storing whether numbers with leading zeroes are to be considered decimal or octal, left or right justification is in force, and how floating point numbers are to be displayed (scientific or fixed). These fields are **static**; one setting services all class instances.

Line 59 defines the single constructor function that is passed a pointer to the stream buffer instance that holds the actual characters to be input or output. What about other possible constructor functions? Look down to line 94. Here are several other constructor functions including the copy ctor and the assignment operator. However, these others are all protected. This prevents someone from trying to do the following.

```
istream myIn = cin;
```

For if this were allowed, we would now effectively have two keyboards and total confusion!

The group of member function prototypes beginning on line 62 defines many of the familiar functions that we have used, such as **setf**. Notice in particular the two functions defined on lines 84 through 87. These functions are called when we write

```
while (cin)
if (!infile)
```

These functions test the state of the stream. Remember that the fail bit is on if there is bad data encountered, it is EOF, or there has been a physical I/O error.

Finally, notice how Microsoft handles the inlining of functions. The **inline** keyword appears before the prototype. And after the class definition, the functions are implemented here in the header file. If a function is to be implemented here in the header file, the function header must have the **inline** keyword before it.

Modified Microsoft ios.h Header File

```
 1 /***
 2 *ios.h - definitions/declarations for the ios class.
 3 *
 4 *       Copyright (c) 1990-1997, Microsoft Corporation.
 5 *  All rights reserved.
 6 *
 7 *Purpose:
 8 *       This file defines the classes, values, macros, functions
 9 *       used by the ios class.
10 *       [AT&T C++]
11 *
12 *       [Public]
13 *
14 ****/
15 ...
16 class streambuf;
```

```
class ostream;

class ios {

public:
    enum io_state {  goodbit = 0x00,
                     eofbit  = 0x01,
                     failbit = 0x02,
                     badbit  = 0x04 };

    enum open_mode { in        = 0x01,
                     out       = 0x02,
                     ate       = 0x04,
                     app       = 0x08,
                     trunc     = 0x10,
                     nocreate  = 0x20,
                     noreplace = 0x40,
                     binary    = 0x80 };

    enum seek_dir { beg=0, cur=1, end=2 };

    enum {   skipws      = 0x0001,
             left        = 0x0002,
             right       = 0x0004,
             internal    = 0x0008,
             dec         = 0x0010,
             oct         = 0x0020,
             hex         = 0x0040,
             showbase    = 0x0080,
             showpoint   = 0x0100,
             uppercase   = 0x0200,
             showpos     = 0x0400,
             scientific  = 0x0800,
             fixed       = 0x1000,
             unitbuf     = 0x2000,
             stdio       = 0x4000
                                 };

    static const long basefield;        // dec | oct | hex
    static const long adjustfield;      // left | right | internal
    static const long floatfield;       // scientific | fixed

    ios(streambuf*);                    // differs from ANSI
    virtual ~ios();

    inline long flags() const;
    inline long flags(long _l);

    inline long setf(long _f,long _m);
    inline long setf(long _l);
    inline long unsetf(long _l);

    inline int width() const;
    inline int width(int _i);

    inline ostream* tie(ostream* _os);
```

```
    inline ostream* tie() const;

    inline char fill() const;
    inline char fill(char _c);

    inline int precision(int _i);
    inline int precision() const;

    inline int rdstate() const;
    inline void clear(int _i = 0);

    operator void *() const {
                   if(state&(badbit|failbit) ) return 0;
                   return (void *)this; }
    inline int operator!() const;

    inline int  good() const;
    inline int  eof() const;
    inline int  fail() const;
    inline int  bad() const;
...
protected:
    ios();
    ios(const ios&);                    // treat as private
    ios& operator=(const ios&);
    void init(streambuf*);

    int     state;
    long    x_flags;
    int     x_precision;
    char    x_fill;
    int     x_width;
...
};



inline long ios::flags() const { return x_flags; }
inline long ios::flags(long _l) {
                  long _l0; _l0 = x_flags;
                  x_flags = _l; return _l0; }

inline long ios::setf(long _l,long _m) {
                  long _l0; lock(); _l0 = x_flags;
                  x_flags = (_l&_m) | (x_flags&(~_m));
                  unlock(); return _l0; }
inline long ios::setf(long _l) {
                  long _l0; lock(); _l0 = x_flags;
                  x_flags |= _l; unlock(); return _l0; }
inline long ios::unsetf(long _l) {
                  long _l0; lock(); _l0 = x_flags;
                  x_flags &= (~_l); unlock(); return _l0; }

inline int ios::width() const { return x_width; }
inline int ios::width(int _i) {
                  int _i0; _i0 = (int)x_width;
```

```
                      x_width = _i; return _iO; }

inline char ios::fill() const { return x_fill; }
inline char ios::fill(char _c) {
                      char _cO; _cO = x_fill;
                      x_fill = _c; return _cO; }

inline int ios::precision(int _i) {
         int _iO; _iO = (int)x_precision;
         x_precision = _i; return _iO; }
inline int ios::precision() const { return x_precision; }

inline int ios::operator!() const{return state&(badbit|failbit);}

inline int  ios::bad() const { return state & badbit; }
inline void ios::clear(int _i){ lock(); state = _i; unlock(); }
inline int  ios::eof() const { return state & eofbit; }
inline int  ios::fail() const {return state &(badbit | failbit);}
inline int  ios::good() const { return state == 0; }
```

With class **ios** defined, the **istream** class is derived from it as shown in line 16 below in the **istream.h** file.

```
class istream : virtual public ios {
```

(The **virtual** keyword is used with multiple base classes to ensure only a single copy of **ios** is included in derived classes.) Line 19 defines the only constructor that is allowed, one that is passed a pointer to the actual stream buffer containing the characters coming from the keyboard.

This is followed by a huge number of extraction operator overridden functions. Here we can actually see what function is being called when we write

```
double x;
int y;
cin >> x >> y;
```

Remember the operator overloaded function rule. The item to the left of the operator >> provides the **this** parameter and the item to the right becomes the single parameter to the function. The above example first calls the **operator>>** function that is passed a **double&** and then calls the **operator>>** function that is passed an **int&**.

Next, beginning on line 41 the various overloaded forms of the **get** and **getline** functions are defined. Notice how the last parameter is defaulted to a newline code.

Finally, on line 120, class **istream_withassign** is defined, derived from **istream**. And on line 131 comes the actual definition of **cin** as an instance of **istream_withassign**. Notice that it is in the global namespace and would be included in any file that includes **iostream.h** which in turn includes **istream.h**. This is reason that **cin** seems to be available everywhere we need it—it is a global variable.

Modified Microsoft istream.h Header File

```
  1 /***
  2 *istream.h - definitions/declarations for the istream class
  3 *
  4 *        Copyright (c) 1990-1997, Microsoft Corporation.
  5 *  All rights reserved.
  6 *
  7 *Purpose:
  8 *        This file defines the classes, values, macros, functions
  9 *        used by the istream class.
 10 *        [AT&T C++]
```

```
*
*        [Public]
*
****/

class istream : virtual public ios {

public:
    istream(streambuf*);
    virtual ~istream();

    istream& operator>>(char *);
    inline istream& operator>>(unsigned char *);
    inline istream& operator>>(signed char *);
    istream& operator>>(char &);
    inline istream& operator>>(unsigned char &);
    inline istream& operator>>(signed char &);
    istream& operator>>(short &);
    istream& operator>>(unsigned short &);
    istream& operator>>(int &);
    istream& operator>>(unsigned int &);
    istream& operator>>(long &);
    istream& operator>>(unsigned long &);
    istream& operator>>(float &);
    istream& operator>>(double &);
    istream& operator>>(long double &);
    istream& operator>>(streambuf*);

    int get();

    inline istream& get(         char *,int,char ='\n');
    inline istream& get(unsigned char *,int,char ='\n');
    inline istream& get(  signed char *,int,char ='\n');

    istream& get(char &);
    inline istream& get(unsigned char &);
    inline istream& get(  signed char &);

    istream& get(streambuf&,char ='\n');
    inline istream& getline(         char *,int,char ='\n');
    inline istream& getline(unsigned char *,int,char ='\n');
    inline istream& getline(  signed char *,int,char ='\n');

    inline istream& ignore(int =1,int =EOF);
    istream& read(char *,int);
    inline istream& read(unsigned char *,int);
    inline istream& read(signed char *,int);

    int gcount() const { return x_gcount; }
    int peek();
    istream& putback(char);

    istream& seekg(streampos);
    istream& seekg(streamoff,ios::seek_dir);
    streampos tellg();

```

```
    void eatwhite();

protected:
    istream();
    istream(const istream&);    // treat as private
    istream& get(char *, int, int);

private:
    istream(ios&);
    int getint(char *);
    int getdouble(char *, int);
};

    inline istream& istream::operator>>(unsigned char * _s) {
                         return operator>>((char *)_s); }
    inline istream& istream::operator>>(  signed char * _s) {
                         return operator>>((char *)_s); }

    inline istream& istream::operator>>(unsigned char & _c) {
                        return operator>>((char &) _c); }
    inline istream& istream::operator>>(  signed char & _c) {
                        return operator>>((char &) _c); }

    inline istream& istream::get(         char * _b, int _lim,
                             char _delim) {
      return get(        _b, _lim, (int)(unsigned char)_delim); }
    inline istream& istream::get(unsigned char * _b, int _lim,
                             char _delim) {
      return get((char *)_b, _lim, (int)(unsigned char)_delim); }
    inline istream& istream::get(signed   char * _b, int _lim,
                             char _delim) {
      return get((char *)_b, _lim, (int)(unsigned char)_delim); }

    inline istream& istream::get(unsigned char & _c) {
                         return get((char &)_c); }
    inline istream& istream::get(  signed char & _c) {
                         return get((char &)_c); }

    inline istream& istream::getline(         char * _b,int _lim,
                                 char _delim) {...
    inline istream& istream::getline(unsigned char * _b,int _lim,
                                 char _delim) {...
    inline istream& istream::getline(  signed char * _b,int _lim,
                                 char _delim) {...

    inline istream& istream::ignore(int _n,int _delim) {...

    inline istream& istream::read(unsigned char * _ptr, int _n) {
                            return read((char *) _ptr, _n); }
    inline istream& istream::read(  signed char * _ptr, int _n) {
                            return read((char *) _ptr, _n); }


class istream_withassign : public istream         {
        public:
            istream_withassign();
```

```
             istream_withassign(streambuf*);
             ~istream_withassign();
      istream& operator=(const istream& _is) {
                 return istream::operator=(_is); }
      istream& operator=(streambuf* _isb) {
                 return istream::operator=(_isb); }
};

extern istream_withassign cin;
```

If you examine the actual source files provided with your compiler, you will find that there is more complexity wrapped around these definitions. But the above simplified view is sufficient to get us familiar with the streams. (The newer I/O streams are implemented as template classes. Templates are covered in chapter 7.)

Review Questions

1. What is meant by an abstract base class? If class **Plant** is an abstract base class, what ramifications does this have on client programs?

2. What is a pure virtual function? How does one differ from an ordinary virtual function?

3. If a class has just one pure virtual function defined in it, what impact does that have on that class?

4. In class derivations, when should one consider using a pure virtual function?

5. What does multiple inheritance involve? How can it be effectively used?

6. What is the problem with having two or more copies of the same base class in a multiple inheritance derived class? How can one force only one instance of a specific base class being included?

Stop! Do These Exercises Before Programming

1. Acme sells appliances and services them. They need a billing program to display a customer's bill. Excited about inheritance, management decided to give multiple inheritance a try. Create a base class called **BillItem** that contains a 30-character **description** string and a double **amount** field. If this item was a new refrigerator, the **description** string would contain "refrigerator" and the **amount** would represent its total cost, $750.00. If this item was a service call, then the **description** string would contain "Service Call" and the **amount** would represent total charges, such as $90.00. Create appropriate constructors, a destructor, and a **Print** function. Since this class does not know how the bill is to be printed, **Print** is a pure virtual function.

2. Create a derived class called **ServiceCall** that encapsulates a service repairman's charges. It is derived from **BillItem** and contains one new data member, the hours worked. Its **Print** function outputs a line such as this.

```
Service Call        2.5 hours labor      $90.00
```

3. Create a derived class called **Appliance** that encapsulates the sale of an appliance. It is derived from **BillItem** and contains one new member, the quantity sold. Its **Print** function outputs a line such as this.

```
Acme Refrigerator quantity 1            $750.00
```

4. Create a derived class called **Installation** that encapsulates the sale of a new appliance and the service charge for setting it up. It is derived from **Appliance** and from **ServiceCall**. Only a single **BillingItem** instance should be contained in the derived class. Its **Print** function should look like this.

```
Purchase and Install 1 Refrigerator  $800.00
```

Programming Problems

Problem Pgm05-1—Employee Class II—Using Derived Classes

The Employee Payroll Program

In the **Employee** class from **Pgm02-5—Employee Class I**, remove the **Date** object data member for the date hired and remove all traces of that object from the class. Remove the **GetHireDate** and **CompareDate** functions. The **Input** and **Output** functions may be kept as utility functions as you see fit.

The Larger Picture

Employees of the Acme Company are paid either an hourly wage, a piece-rate, or a fixed salary. Thus, there are three kinds of employee classifications. Common to all employee classifications is the need for the employee name and social security number. All other retained employee compensation details vary by the class they are in.

Thus, the **Employee** class becomes the base class encapsulating the basic functionality and the name and social security number. Three other classes are to be derived from the **Employee** class, **HourlyEmp**, **PieceEmp**, and **SalariedEmp**.

The actual implementation is broken down into three smaller sections that can be compiled and run and tested in smaller units so you do not have to implement the entire project at one time. There should be a single header file, Employee.h and a single cpp file that contain all four classes. In reality, these classes are tightly coupled and are very small in size.

The other three classes require additional information. The hourly wage employees are paid for each hour worked and are paid "time and a half" for all overtime hours (any hours above 40). Salaried employees are paid a fixed annual rate; thus, their pay is found by dividing the yearly amount by 52 weeks and then multiplying by the number of weeks in the pay period. The piece-rate employees are paid based on the number of pieces produced; they are paid a fixed amount on each piece made up to their production quota and then a bonus rate for each piece above that quota. Thus, each of the three employee classes stores different additional information beyond the base class's name and id number.

On this programming assignment, I am minimizing the "specifications" so that you may have a greater level of creativity. Your fundamental design rule is simple: make your classes work with the three provided main programs without altering the three main programs. Pay particular attention to what functions must be virtual. Your header file should define the four classes and your cpp file should implement the four classes.

Pgm05-1A: Tests the constructors and operator<<

The **HourlyEmp** class constructor takes the long ID, the employee name, and the hourly pay rate. The id number may be up to nine digits long and the name may be up to 25 characters long.

The **PieceEmp** class constructor takes the ID number, employee name, the base rate, the bonus rate, and the production quota.

The **SalariedEmp** class constructor takes the ID number, employee name, and the annual salary.

All constructor parameters have a 0 as their default value. Pgm09-1A uses no input file.

The **operator<<** function prints the ID number as a zero-filled nine-digit integer followed by one blank space. The employee name is printed enclosed within a pair of double quote marks and there are sufficient blank spaces after the trailing double quote marks to complete a total of 28 columns. The next item output maybe hourly pay rate, the base piece rate or the annual salary, depending upon the employee class. In each case, the number is printed in an 8-column field with two decimal digits after the decimal point. For piece-rate employees, there are two more fields printed, the bonus rate and then the production quota. The bonus rate is printed in a five-column field preceded with one blank space; it is printed with two digits after the decimal point. The production quota is a whole number and is printed with one preceding blank space in a three-column field.

Finally, **do not write repetitive coding**. That is, there should only be a single function to input the employee's name and id. That coding should not be in three different functions. It belongs only in the base class. **Pgm05-1A.cpp** is found in the test data folder under **Pgm05-1**. Here is what that tester program looks like.

```
// Pgm05-1A.CPP

#include <iostream.h>
#include <iomanip.h>
#include "employee.h"


main()
   {
   HourlyEmp
      hEmp1 (333456789L, "JONES, W.", 7.25),
      hEmp2 (45698L, "BROWN, SARA L.", 10.50);
   PieceRateEmp
      prEmp1(123445566L, "MILLER, ROBERT JONATHON", 1.5, .1, 50),
      prEmp2(2L, "ROW, ANN", 3.0, .75, 30);
   SalariedEmp
      sEmp1 (3549876L, "ABERNATHY, ALEXANDER", 28000.0);

   Employee
      *pEmp[] = { &hEmp1, &prEmp2, &sEmp1, &hEmp2, &prEmp1 };
   int count = sizeof(pEmp) / sizeof(pEmp[0]);

   cout << "EMPLOYEE LISTING\n\n";

   for (int i = 0; i < count; i++)
      cout << *pEmp[i] << '\n';
   return 0;
   }
```

The output of **Pgm05-1A** should be as shown in Figure 5.2.

```
333456789 "JONES, W."                  7.25
000000002 "ROW, ANN"                   3.00 0.75  30
003459876 "ABERNATHY, ALEXANDER"
000045698 "BROWN, SARA L."            10.5
```

```
123445566 "MILLER, ROBERT JONATHON"          1.50 0.10  50
```
Figure 9.2 Output from Pgm09-1A

Pgm05-1B: Tests operator>>

This program inputs the **Pgm05-1.txt** data file. On input, the ID number can be nine digits long and represents the social security number. This can be entered in one of two ways. It can be a series of nine digits or as 999-99-9999 where a dash is the separator.

On input, the employee name is always enclosed in double quote marks to handle the presence of blanks in the name field. Do not store the leading and trailing double quote marks. It is up to 25 characters long, not counting the two double quote marks. The data following the name depends upon the employee class. If this is a salaried employee, the next field is the annual pay. For hourly employees, the next field is the hourly pay rate. For piece-rate employees, there is the base rate, the bonus rate and then the production quota.

When testing your program, run the program against the provided **Pgm05-1.txt** data file. Save the display output to a file. You can then input the output as the input and produce the exact same output as from using **Pgm05-1.txt**. In other words the output of **Pgm05-1B** is compatible with the input file for this program.

```
// Pgm05-1B.CPP

#include <iostream.h>
#include <iomanip.h>
#include "employee.h"

enum { HOURLY = 'H', SALARIED = 'S', PIECE_RATE = 'P' };

main()
   {
   ifstream infile ("Pgm05-1.txt", ios::in | ios::nocreate);
   if (!infile) {
    cerr << "Error: unable to open file Pgm05-1.txt\n";
    return 1;
   }

   Employee *emp;
   char type;

   while (infile >> type)
      {
      switch (type)
         {
         case HOURLY:      emp = new(HourlyEmp);    break;
         case PIECE_RATE:  emp = new(PieceRateEmp); break;
         case SALARIED:    emp = new(SalariedEmp);  break;
         default:          cerr << "Bad employee type\n";
                           return 1;
         }
      infile >> *emp;
      infile.ignore(100, '\n');
      cout << type << ' ' << *emp << '\n';
      delete emp;
      }
```

```
    infile.close ();
    return 0;
    }
```

Notice that **Pgm05-1B** inputs the employee type as a character, H, S or P.

Pgm05-1C: The full implementation of the Employee Pay Program

Now that you have the constructors and I/O operators working, you can add in the payroll calculation portion. **Pgm05-1C** inputs the data similarly to **Pgm05-1B** but adds in another field, **work_amount**. For salaried employees, **work_amount** is the number of weeks in the pay period. For hourly workers, this field contains the number of hours worked. For piece-rate employees, this represents the number of items made.

Provide two new functions, **id** and **name**, that return the employee's id and name. Note that the name string returned should be **const char***. Finally create the **pay** function which is passed the **work_amount** field and returns the employee's pay. Here is what **Pgm05-1C** looks like.

```
// Pgm05-1C.CPP

#include <iostream.h>
#include <iomanip.h>
#include <fstream.h>
#include "employee.h"

enum { HOURLY = 'H', SALARIED = 'S', PIECE_RATE = 'P' };

main()
   {
   Employee *emp;
   char type;
   float work_amount;

   ifstream infile ("Pgm05-1.txt", ios::in | ios::nocreate);
   if (!infile) {
    cerr << "Error: unable to open file Pgm05-1.txt\n";
    return 1;
   }

   cout.setf(ios::fixed, ios::floatfield);
   cout.setf(ios::showpoint);
   cout.precision(2);

   cout << "   ID                   NAME                     PAY\n\n";

   while (infile >> type)
      {
      switch (type)
         {
         case HOURLY:      emp = new(HourlyEmp);    break;
         case PIECE_RATE:  emp = new(PieceRateEmp); break;
         case SALARIED:    emp = new(SalariedEmp);  break;
         default:          cerr << "Bad employee type\n";
                           return 1;
         }
      infile >> *emp >> work_amount;
      cout.fill('0');
```

```
    cout << setw(9) << emp->id() << "      ";
    cout.fill(' ');
    cout.setf(ios::left, ios::adjustfield);
    cout << setw(30) << emp->name();
    cout.setf(ios::right, ios::adjustfield);
    cout << '$'
         << setw(7) << emp->pay(work_amount) << '\n';
    delete emp;
    }

 infile.close ();
 return 0;
}
```

Figure 5.3 shows the output your program should produce.

```
   ID                 NAME                          PAY

333456789     DARNELL, FREDERICK              $ 961.54
456123456     NOBEL, WILLIAM                  $ 510.00
111223333     WOOD, STEVEN                    $ 735.81
345671234     NUTTING, TERESA ELAINE          $ 100.00
123456789     HOOP, JEANETTE                  $2307.69
678654321     BOLDEN, EDWARD D.               $ 272.70
555667777     MCCLEARY, JANE                  $ 486.06
004556666     HERLAN, WILLIAM BART            $ 384.62
001020003     ANDERSON, J. DENNIS             $ 437.50
777889999     HANNAH, CAROL                   $ 323.20
888990000     RAINTREE, VICTORIA LYNN         $ 461.54
467010002     NOONCASTER, BRENDA              $ 240.00
321456789     YOUNG, RICHARD                  $1750.00
333040005     FRESH, GAIL                     $1076.92
234854321     KINGSLEY, JACKIE                $ 550.00
012998877     BRAHAM, JOSEPH                  $ 512.50
```

Figure 5.3 Output from Pgm05-1C

Problem Pgm05-2—A Revised Shapes Set of Classes

Revise the sample shapes' classes given in this chapter to use multiple base classes. The **Point** base class has two members, **coordx** and **coordy**, both integers. Create appropriate constructor functions as desired. Create an **Input** function that extracts two integers from the input stream. Create an O**utput** function that displays the coordinates as follows.

(100, 100)

The format is a leading (followed by the **coordx** value with a width of four digits followed by a comma and one blank followed by the **coordy** value with a width of four digits followed by a trailing).

The **Shape** class is unchanged. Derive all of the remaining classes from both **Shape** and **Point**. Modify their **Input** functions to input the coordinates before the remaining dimensions of the shape. Modify their **Output** functions to display the location after the name and before the dimensions.

Rewrite the tester program **Pgm05a** to now display the point locations after the name and before the dimensions. Note that you will need to add some testing x and y values after the names and before the dimensions in the input test file.

Chapter 6—C++ Error Handling

Introduction

C++ adds a new methodology toward the handling of error situations that arise during a program's execution. This chapter's purpose is to examine this new approach with emphasis on how we can best handle error situations that develop while a program is running. The discussion begins with an examination of typecasting.

Typecasting—Static and Dynamic

Undoubtedly you have used typecasting in programming probably from the beginning of your C++ training. It is often used to force a conversion into the proper data type so that a calculation can be done correctly or to remove warning messages. Consider the following two situations.

```
int points;
int number;
float grade = (float) points / number;

double dollars;
int pennies = (int) (dollars * 100 + .5);
```

In the first equation, the typecast is required in order to obtain the correct result while in the second equation, the possible loss of precision warning is being eliminated. These are called static casts. A **static cast** always performs the indicated conversion no matter whether or not it makes any sense as long as the conversion is actually possible. I jokingly call a static cast the "idiot cast."

Suppose that we had a base class, called **BaseObj**, from which several other classed were derives. Specifically, assume that the classes **PhoneDirectory** and **YellowPages** were derived from **BaseObj**. The client program dynamically allocates many of these two derived classes and stored them in an array of BaseObj pointers.

```
BaseObj* phoneStuff[100];
```

Next, the client program needs to actually convert the **BaseObj** pointer back into a **PhoneDirectory** pointer. They might code the following.

```
PhoneDirectory* ptrpd = (PhoneDirectory*) phoneStuff[i];
```

What would result if the ith pointer in the array was not a **PhoneDirectory** pointer but instead was actually a **YellowPages** pointer? The above static cast assumes that you know what you are doing and it goes ahead and makes the assignment. As soon as the program makes use of **ptrpd**, any number of runtime errors occur, especially if the program attempts to assign values to **PhoneDirectory** members pointed to by **ptrpd**! It is actually a **YellowPages** object.

What is needed is a way to make an "intelligent" cast, one that fails to make the cast if the source pointer is not of the correct data type. This type of cast is called a **dynamic cast**. A dynamic cast is made at runtime, not at compile time as the static cast. If the source pointer is not of the correct data type, the dynamic cast assigns 0 or NULL to the resulting pointer.

The syntax is a bit awkward.

```
dynamic_cast<desired pointer datatype>(pointer to typecasted)
```

The **PhoneDirectory** cast could be done this way using a dynamic cast.

```
PhoneDirectory* ptrpd;
ptrpd = dynamic_cast<PhoneDirectory*> (phoneStuff[i]);
if (!ptrpd) {
 cerr << "Pointer is not a PhoneDirectory pointer\n";
}
```

Incidentally, the static cast can be coded in a similar manner as the dynamic cast.

```
static_cast<desired pointer datatype>(pointer to typecasted)
```

However, it is far easier to use the **(datatype*)** format.

Invoking Derived Class Functions That Are Not Virtual or Defined in the Base Class

The dynamic cast also provides a way for us to get a pointer to the derived class from a pointer to a base class. Consider the fleet array of **Vehicle** pointers from chapters 4 and 5.

```
Vehicle* fleet[100];
```

It is unlikely that any pointer in the array is actually a **Vehicle***. Rather, the elements are **Car***, **Truck***, **Limo***, **Bus***, and so on. Further, only virtual or **Vehicle** base class functions can be invoked using the **fleet[i]** pointer. Thus, if the **Truck** class had a function called **LoadCargo**, it could not be called this way

```
fleet[i]->LoadCargo(); // error
```

unless **LoadCargo** was present in the **Vehicle** base class, which it is highly unlikely to so be.

However, if the **fleet[i]** pointer was actually a **Truck***, then the following would work well.

```
Truck* ptrt = dynamic_cast<Truck*> (fleet[i]);
if (ptrt) {
  ptrt->LoadCargo();
```

This is a vital detail, for it now permits us to safely get a pointer to the derived class from a pointer to a base class.

This feature is turned on by default with the .NET 2005 compiler. In previous versions, one had to enable it this way. In order to use the dynamic cast with Microsoft's VC 6 compiler, for example, a project setting must be made. Go to Project Settings—C/C++ tab—C++ Language combo box choice—check the box entitled "Enable Run-Time Type Information."

Run-Time Type Information

Run-Time Type Information is a new feature which obtains the object's data type at runtime. It is often used with base class pointers in order to find out what kind of object that pointer is really pointing to at this instant. However, this mechanism can be used with any kind of data, including the built-in data types, such as a **double**. In order to use run-time type information, the header file **<typeinfo>** is included.

To get the data type of an item, use the function **typeid**. The syntax is simple.

```
typeid (object)
```

typeid returns a reference to an instance of **type_info** that is used to describe the object. This class has three commonly used member functions: **name**, **operator==**, and **operator!=**. The **name** function returns the character string name of the data type. For example,

```
double cost;
Vehicle v;
Car c;
cout << "The data type of cost is " << typeid(cost).name ()
     << endl;
cout << "The data type of v is " << typeid(v).name ()
     << endl;
cout << "The data type of c is " << typeid(c).name ()
     << endl;
```

gives this output.

```
The data type of cost is double
The data type of v is class Vehicle
The data type of c is class Car
```

When dealing with base class pointers, the data type returned is that of the derived class, if any.

Further, since **typeid** requires an object, pointers must be dereferenced. For example, the following sequence produces the indicated output.

```
Vehicle* ptrv;
Car c;
Truck t;
ptrv = &c;
cout << "The data type of ptrv is " << typeid(*ptrv).name ()
     << endl;
ptrv = & t;
cout << "The data type of ptrv is " << typeid(*ptrv).name ()
     << endl;
```

the output:

```
The data type of ptrv is class Car
The data type of ptrv is class Truck
```

What happens if the pointer is 0 or NULL? The class throws a **bad_typeid** exception. Thus, we must examine next the new C++ error handling system and find out what these exceptions are all about.

The C++ Error Handling System

Let's establish the groundwork for the need of a new method for handling error situations detected at run time. Suppose that we have written an **Image** class that encapsulates a graphical image such as a bitmap or JPG file. We would expect one of the constructor functions to be passed the filename to open and load into this class instance. Consider the following snippet of coding.

main:

```
Image pic ("MyImage.bmp");
pic.Display();
```

Image.h

```
class Image {
...
Image (const char* file) {
 ifstream infile (file);
 if (!infile) {
   // oops! Now what do we do????
```

The constructor is in big trouble if the file that is to be loaded cannot be opened. What does the ctor do next? If it only displays an error message, what then happens when **main** then calls the **Display** function? Disaster strikes.

This is the very common problem constructor functions have—a constructor function cannot return any value, not even **void**. Thus, it has no way to indicate that it failed to construct the object in question! We arrive at the same situation if the constructor must dynamically allocate some memory and the system cannot provide the necessary memory.

One common solution to the situation is to maintain an **isValid bool** member variable. One might implement it this way.

Image.h

```
class Image {
protected:
 bool isValid;
public:
bool IsValid () const { return isValid; }
...
Image (const char* file) {
 ifstream infile (file);
 if (!infile) {
  cerr << ....
```

```
   isValid = false;
  }
  ...
  isValid = true;
 }
 void Display () {
  if (!IsValid())
   return;
  ...
```

The ctor sets **isValid** to **true** or **false**. Then, every other function must first test **isValid** before it attempts any operations on the image. While this is effective, when there are a large number of functions in the class, it is awkward to have to check **isValid** at the start of every function body!

Indeed the C++ error handling system provides a much better way to handle error situations that can occur at run time. However, a new philosophy for handling errors must be observed. The philosophy is this.

A. a function checks for errors and signals their presence

B. the caller then decides what to do about those errors

In other words, the function that detects that an error has occurred does **not** attempt to handle the error. Rather, the function merely signals the C++ system and thereby the caller that an error of a specific nature has occurred. It is totally up to the caller to decide what to do about that error—whether to abort the program or attempt some kind of recovery process. Should the caller choose to ignore the error, then the standard C++ error system handles it for the caller and terminates and aborts the program.

The function signals the presence of errors by using the **throw** statement, while the caller checks and handles the errors using the **try-catch** statements. Let's examine these within a simple context first. Consider the following **Quadratic** function. What types of run time errors could occur?

```
double Quadratic (double a, double b, double c) {
 double determinant = b * b - 4 * a * c;
 return ( - b + sqrt (determinant) ) / (2 * a);
}
```

Suppose that **a** contains 0? What happens if the determinant is less than zero? These are the two situations that can arise at run time. If they should occur, what action should this function take? Obviously, this function is totally ignorant of the program logic of which it is a part. There is no way that this function could "handle" these two error situations. Instead, it can signal their presence and let the caller make the determination about what to do about the errors.

The **throw** statement syntax is very simple.

```
throw item;
```

Here item can be any intrinsic data type (variable or constant) or any instance of any user defined data type, such as a structure or class instance. For example, consider the following statements.

```
throw 0;      // throws an int whose value is 0
throw 42.;    // throws a double whose value is 42.
throw "This is an error."; // throws a const char* string
char message[80];
throw message; // throws a char* string
class Error {
...
};
Error e;
throw e;      // throws an instance of class Error
```

When a function intends to use the throw statement, it should notify the compiler what data types it intends to throw. These are added to the function header using the keyword **throw** followed by a parentheses list of data types that could be thrown separated by a comma.

```
void fun () throw (int, double, const char*, Error) {
```

Here **fun** is defined as possibly throwing an **int**, **double**, **const char***, and an instance of the **Error** class.

The **Quadratic** function can be rewritten this way.

```
double Quadratic (double a, double b,
                  double c) throw (int, const char*) {
 if (a == 0)
  throw 0;
 double determinant = b * b - 4 * a * c;
 if (determinant < 0)
  throw "Imaginary Roots";
 return ( - b + sqrt (determinant) ) / (2 * a);
}
```

What happens if a function should throw an exception that is not in the indicated series in the header? That is, what would happen if **Quadratic** threw 42.—a **double**? When a function throws something that was not expected, the C++ Error Handler in turn throws the "Unexpected Exception" exception. And these unexpected exceptions can also be checked for in the caller.

The caller must wrap the possible instructions that could raise an exception within a **try-catch** block. Wrapping the instructions within a **try** block notifies the compiler that this caller function wishes to be notified of thrown exceptions that these instructions might raise. The syntax of the **try-catch** block is

```
try {
 1 or more statements that could raise an exception
}
catch (item1) {
...
}
catch (item2) {
...
}
...
```

If a statement is outside of the **try** block and if that statement in turn raises an exception, then the C++ Error Handler does not notify it of the exceptions. Instead, the Error Handler looks to the caller of this function for possible handling.

Here is how **main** could be coded.

main:

```
double a, b, c, ansr;
// get a set of a, b, c values
...
try {
 ansr = Quadratic (a, b, c);
}
catch (int num) {
 if (num == 0)
  cerr << "a's value is 0 which results in division by 0\n";
 else
  cerr << "Unknown integer error value raised\n";
}
catch (const char* msg) {
  cerr << msg << endl;
}
// get next set of a, b, c values
```

Notice that if an operation could result in several different error situations, using different values of an integer to identify each type is common practice. That is, in this situation, **Quadratic** could have thrown 1 instead of the string error message when the determinant was less than zero.

The other common method is to have all exceptions throw a string error message. This then simplifies the caller's reporting of the error. That is, **Quadratic** could have thrown "Division by 0" instead of the integer value 0. Then, the single **catch (const char* msg)** could have displayed both messages.

If a caller does not have a catch block for something that was thrown, then the Error Handler looks on up the calling sequence to see if the caller of the caller wishes to handle this exception. If the Error Handler can find no one in the calling sequence that wishes to handle a given exception, then the Error Handler calls the **terminate** and **abort** functions to shut the program down.

Consider this sequence of function calls and where each of **Quadratic**'s exceptions would be handled.

main:

```
try {
 ansr = funA ();
}
catch (const char* msg) {
  cerr << msg << endl;
}
```

funA:

```
double funA () {
 double a, b, c, ansr;
 // get a set of a, b, c values
 ...
 try {
  ansr = Quadratic (a, b, c);
 }
 catch (int num) {
  if (num == 0)
   cerr <<"a's value is 0 which results in division by 0\n";
  else
   cerr << "Unknown integer error value raised\n";
 }
 return ansr;
}
```

If **Quadratic** throws a zero integer, then it is handled in function **funA**'s **catch** block. However, if the **const char*** message is thrown, then the Error Handler looks to see if **funA** wishes to handle it. It does not. So then the Error Handler looks to see if the caller of **funA**, **main** wishes to handle it. Again, if no one handles it, then the Error Handler calls the **terminate** and **abort** functions to shut the program down.

Sometimes, one might not be sure what all a subsystem of function calls can **throw**. In this case, there is the ellipsis form of the **catch** statement that can **catch** any thrown exception.

```
catch (...) {
 // catches all throws here
}
```

However, note that the catch statements are searched in the order that they are coded. What would be the result of this sequence?

```
try {
 ansr = Quadratic (a, b, c);
}
catch (...) {
 cerr << "An Error Occurred\n";
}
catch (const char* msg) {
  cerr << msg << endl;
}
```

The **catch** of the string would never be called because **catch (...)** already caught it. Reserve **catch (...)** as the last item for which to check.

Details of the try-catch-throw Mechanism

The code that you wish to monitor for errors must be wrapped in a **try-catch** block. Exceptions thrown by that code are then possibly caught by the **catch** statements that immediately follow the end of the **try** block. The statements to be monitored can be as simple or as vast in scope as desired. One can even wrap the entire **main** function in a **try** block!

throw exception; this generates or raises the exception at the point of the **throw** statement. The Error Handler then looks back up the calling sequence function by function looking for a **catch** block that can handle what was thrown. If none are found, it calls **terminate** or **unexpected**.

When a **catch** block finishes execution, program flow then continues at the first line after all of the **try-catch** blocks. Control never is returned to the statement that threw the error in the first place.

When terminating a program, you can either call **abort** or **exit**. The **abort** function does not return a return code back to DOS while **exit** does return a value.

You can control what, if any, exceptions are thrown by including the **throw** clause on the function's header. In this example

```
void fun (int x) throw (double) {
```

fun is restricted to only being able to **throw** a **double**. If it tries to **throw** any other type of exception, the system raises the Unexpected Exception exception instead.

However, if you code

```
void fun (int x){
```

fun is not allowed to throw any kind of exception whatsoever.

Exceptions can be rethrown! For example, if a **catch** block decides that it does not have enough information with which to recover from the exception, it can rethrow the exception by simply coding **throw;** (with no item after the **throw** keyword). In effect, this **catch** block is passing the original exception on up the calling sequence to the next higher block. A **catch** may also **throw** a different exception as well. Consider the results of this sequence.

```
void funA (int x) throw (int) {
 if (!x)
  throw 0;
 ...
}
void funB (int x) throw (int) {
 try {
  int y = funA (x);
 }
 catch (int j) {
  // cannot handle it so pass it on up to main
  throw;
 }
 ...
}
int main () {
 int x;
 try {
  int z = funB (x);
 }
 catch (int) {
  cerr << ...
 }
 // get a new value for x and repeat
```

First, **main** calls **funB** and **funB** calls **funA**. If the passed integer is 0, then **funA** throws an integer whose value is 0. Now **funB**'s **catch** block gets control but it does not know what to do about it and merely rethrows the original exception, an integer whose value is 0. Finally, **main**'s **catch** block is called to handle the original exception thrown in **funA**.

Replacing the Default terminate Function and the Default unexpected Functions

In certain circumstances, one might desire to replace the default **terminate** and **unexpected** functions which display an error message and call the **abort** function. Suppose that you intended to "borrow" or reuse a subsystem of functions that performed folder manipulation operations. Some of these functions could raise errors. If the system is well documented, great, go ahead and program in the **try-catch** blocks. However, if you do not have any ideas what can get thrown and you do not want the program automatically aborted when they are raised, then you can supply your own replacement functions for the **terminate** and **unexpected** functions.

The prototypes for these two functions are as follows

```
void terminate ();
void unexpected ();
```

Two functions are provided to allow you to install your replacement functions.

```
set_terminate (your replacement function name);
set_unexpected (your replacement function name);
```

Commonly, the last line of your replacement functions should invoke **abort;** if the program is to terminate.

This first example shows how to replace the **terminate** function.

```
#include <iostream>
using namespace std;
void myTerminate () {
 cerr << "Error - in my terminate function\n";
 abort ();
}
int main () {
 set_terminate (myTerminate);
 throw 1;
 return 0;
}
```

This second example shows how to replace the **unexpected** function.

```
#include <iostreamh>
using namespace std;
void myUnexpected () {
 cerr << "Error - in my unexpected throw function\n";
 terminate ();
}
void fun () throw (int) {
 throw "Error Message"; // throws const char* instead
}
int main () {
 set_unexpected (myUnexpected);
 try {
  fun ();
 }
 catch (int x) {
  ...
 }
 return 0;
}
```

Overloading the new and delete Functions

The **new** and **delete** dynamic memory allocation functions can also be overloaded. However, their behavior differs between the Old Style and New Style headers. In the Old Style headers, if memory could not be allocated, the **new** function returned a 0 or NULL value for the pointer. However, in the New Style, the **new** function raises the **bad_alloc** exception when it fails. The header file **<new>** must be included to gain access to **bad_alloc**.

Historical note: exactly what the exception is called that is raised when **new** fails has changed frequently over time as the compiler manufacturers scrambled to meet the ever changing C++ guidelines before the language was finally standardized. One earlier name for this exception was **xalloc**.

Thus, when checking on dynamic memory allocations, the method used should match the style of headers in use.

Old Style
```
#include <iostream.h>
int main () {
 double* array = new double [1000];
 if (!array)
 cerr << ...
```
New Style
```
#include <iostream>
#include <new>
using namespace std;
int main () {
 double* array;
 try {
  array = new double [1000];
 }
 catch (bad_alloc bad) {
  cerr << ...
 }
```
Finally, if you wish the New Style new function to behave as it does in the Old Style, that is, return a 0 for the memory address if it fails instead of throwing an exception, you can pass the new function another option, **nothrow**. When you pass **nothrow**, the New Style **new** function does not raise the **bad_alloc** exception but returns 0 instead. This is useful when reworking older C or C++ coding that is not making use of try-catch logic.

New Style
```
#include <iostream>
#include <new>
using namespace std;
int main () {
 double* array = new(nothrow) double [1000];
 if (!array)
  cerr << ...
```
What are the prototypes of **new** and **delete** should one want to overload them?
```
void* operator new (size_t size) {
 void* ptrMemory;
 // you allocate memory as you wish
 // the compiler will subsequently call any class ctor needed
 return ptrMemory;
}
void operator delete (void* ptrObject) {
 // you free up the memory pointed to by ptrObject
```

```
 // and class dtor will automatically be called by the compiler
}
```

Why would you want to overload them? In a large project that uses the New Style headers, not all programmers are familiar with exception handling or have coding that allows for exception processing. Further, it is hard to guarantee that all calls to **new** are passed **nothrow**. Thus, you could rewrite **new** to return 0 when it fails instead of throwing the exception. Or perhaps your program must continue to operate even when the computer is out of memory. In this case you could detect this situation and allocate memory from disk and use it in place of real memory. In fact, this is very easy to do in Windows C++ programming; there are some API functions that allow your program to create its own "swap" drive as "real" memory. In this manner, a program could act as if it had access to 40G or more of memory. (I'll show you how this is done in the next book in this series, Windows Programming.)

Finally, when overloading **new** and **delete**, if you make these functions global in scope, they replace the C++ default **new** and **delete**. However, if you make these functions member functions of a class, then they are only used in conjunction with allocation/deletion of instances of that class.

Throwing Class Instances

Up to this point, we have examined throwing intrinsic items, such as an **int** or **char*** (string). In reality, these are very easy to use and **int** or **char*** items are by far the most commonly thrown items. A program could throw thousands of different integer values representing the numerous run time errors that that program could generate. Thrown integer values can be switched upon and alternative recovery implemented. Or even easier, strings can be thrown. Strings have the advantage that the **catch** block can simply display the thrown error message. However, in more advanced situations, class instances can be thrown. This approach is often found in larger systems, such as the Microsoft Foundation C++ Windows Classes (the MFC).

When class instances are thrown, quite often the actual instance thrown is a derived class instance. Then the **catch** block catches a reference to the base class. In this manner, a single **catch** block can catch all of the possible items thrown. To see how this clever approach works, let's return to the **Quadratic** function example.

What functionality would be desirable in the base class say called **Quad_Error**? Certainly, it should store the error message so that catch blocks can easily display the error message. Additionally, it might be very useful to client programs if the negative value of the discriminant was also automatically displayed. Thus, the base class should hold an error message and provide a means to display that message. The derived class can add in the discriminant value. Here are the base class definition and implementation.

```
class QuadError {
private:
 char message[256];
public:
 QuadError (const char* msg);
 virtual ostream& Display (ostream& os = cerr) const;
 friend ostream& operator<<(ostream &os, const QuadError& qe);
};
```

Notice that the **catch** block will be getting a reference to this base class and will call either the **Display** function or attempt to directly output the **QuadError** reference using the insertion operator.

```
QuadError::QuadError (const char* msg) {
 strcpy (message, msg);
}
ostream& QuadError::Display (ostream& os) const {
 return os << message;
}
ostream& operator<< (ostream &os, const QuadError& qe) {
 return qe.Display (os);
}
```

Notice too that the insertion operator of this base class calls the **virtual Display** function which then will invoke the derived class's **Display** function.

Next, here is the first of the two derived classes, **NonQuadError**. This class handles the division by zero error situation. Since no additional information must be stored beyond the division by zero message, then the ctor only has to pass the message on down to the base class which in turn copies the message ("division by zero") into the base class **message** member. I also implement the virtual **Display** function. However, the **NonQuadError** version of **Display** does nothing more than the base class. In fact, **Display** does not even need to be defined or implemented for **NonQuadError**!

```
class NonQuadError : public QuadError {
public:
  NonQuadError (const char* msg) : QuadError (msg) {}
  virtual ostream& Display (ostream& os = cerr) const;
};
ostream& NonQuadError::Display (ostream& os) const {
  return QuadError::Display (os);
}
```

Here is the second derived class, **ImagRootsError**. This class must store the double discriminant value and also display it. Thus, this class must reimplement the **Display** function.

```
class ImagRootsError : public QuadError {
private:
 double discriminant;
public:
 ImagRootsError (const char* msg, double d) :
      QuadError (msg), discriminant (d) {}
 virtual ostream& Display (ostream& os = cerr) const;
};
ostream& ImagRootsError::Display (ostream& os) const {
 return QuadError::Display (os) << "\nDiscriminant = "
        << discriminant << endl;
}
```

Given these three classes, here is how **Quadratic** can be rewritten to **throw** instances of these derived classes.

```
double Quadratic (double a, double b, double c)
                 throw (QuadError) {
 if (!a)
  throw NonQuadError ("Non-quadratic equation");
 double discriminant = b*b - 4*a*c;
 if (discriminant < 0)
  throw (ImagRootsError ("Imaginary roots", discriminant));
 return (-b + sqrt (discriminant)) / (2*a);
}
```

Notice that within the **throw** statement itself, a new instance of either **NonQuadError** or **ImagRootsError** is created and then thrown.

Finally, here is how **main** can utilize these.

```
int main () {
 double a, b, c;
 cout << "Enter the three coefficients: ";
 while (cin >> a >> b >> c) {
  try {
   double x = Quadratic (a, b, c);
   cout << "The first root is at " << x << endl;
  }
  catch (const QuadError& qe) {
   cout << qe << endl;
```

```
  }
  cout << "Enter the three coefficients: ";
 }
 return 0;
}
```

This complete example is contained in **Pgm06a** in the **Samples** folder. I have not included a complete listing for it here since the above coding is it. Here is a sample test run.

```
Output From Pgm06a - Quadratic() Errors
```

```
Enter the three coefficients: 1 2 3
Imaginary roots

Discriminant = -8

Enter the three coefficients: 0 1 2
Non-quadratic equation

Enter the three coefficients: 1 9 1
The first root is at -0.112518
Enter the three coefficients: ^Z
```

One footnote. When compiling **Pgm06a**, the warning "warning C4290: C++ Exception Specification ignored" is generated. This is because Microsoft does not yet fully implement standardized C++. This warning will be eliminated in the future when they do in fact follow the standard for C++. The warning is on the line

```
double Quadratic (double a, double b, double c)
                  throw (QuadError) {
```

Handling Error Situations Where Multiple Dynamic Memory Allocations Exist

The final situation to be examined is what must be done when a constructor must dynamically allocate several data members, any one of which could fail.

Beginning with the .NET versions, the **new** function as implemented in the old header files (those with the .h extension) returned 0 if an allocation failed. However, the new namespace std version throws and exception, **std::bad_alloc**.

Care must be taken so that all memory that has been previously allocated just before the failing allocation is deleted. To illustrate this, suppose that we need a **BigArray** class which is to encapsulate two large arrays of x and y integers.

The class begins in this manner.

```
class BigArray {
protected:
 int* x;
 int* y;
 int  xcount;
 int  ycount;
public:
 BigArray (int xc = 0, int yc = 0) throw (const char*);
 BigArray (const BigArray&) throw (const char*);
~BigArray ();
```

```
BigArray& operator= (const BigArray& b);
```

The constructor must allocate two arrays containing **xcount** and **ycount** number of elements. The assignment operator must also allocate the two arrays, of course after deleting any existing arrays.

The problem arises when the second allocation fails. Suppose that we implemented the ctor this way. Under older compiler implementations, **new** returns null if out of memory.

```
BigArray::BigArray (int xc, int yc) throw (const char*) {
 xcount = xc;
 ycount = yc;
 x = new (std::nothrow) int [xcount];
 y = new (std::nothrow) int [ycount];
 if (!x || !y)
  throw "Out of memory";
}
```

Back in the caller function, we then have the following **try-catch** logic.

```
 try {
  BigArray big (100000, 100000);
 }
 catch (const char* msg) {
  cerr << msg << endl;
 }
```

If the system obtains memory for array **x** and then runs out of memory for array **y**, the exception is raised. However, all memory for array **x** is leaked. The destructor for **big** has never been called.

Certainly, we must free up unneeded memory before the exception is thrown. And since this same process is needed in two constructor functions and the assignment operator, I chose to add two protected helper functions, **Allocate** and **Release**. Notice that **Allocate** is passed the error string to throw if it cannot obtain the required memory. If the allocation for array **y** is unsuccessful, before throwing the string exception, memory just allocated for array **x** is deleted. In this version for VC7, notice that if anything goes wrong, I leave the object in a stable state with the pointers containing 0 as well as the counts.

```
void BigArray::Allocate (const char* msg) throw (const char*) {
 try {
  x = new int[xcount];
 }
 catch (std::bad_alloc e) {
  xcount = ycount = 0;
  x = y = 0;
  throw msg;
 }
 try {
  y = new int[ycount];
 }
 catch (std::bad_alloc e) {
  delete [] x;
  xcount = ycount = 0;
  x = y = 0;
  throw msg;
 }
}
void BigArray::Release () {
 if (x) delete [] x;
 if (y) delete [] y;
}
```

Given these helper functions, then the implementation of the remaining member functions is straightforward. Each of the functions passes to **Allocate** a string that identifies where the error arose.

```
  BigArray::BigArray (int xc, int yc) throw (const char*) :
```

```
                        x(0), y(0), xcount (xc), ycount (yc) {
 Allocate ("Default constructor failed");
}
BigArray::BigArray (const BigArray& b) throw (const char*) :
               x(0), y(0), xcount(b.xcount), ycount(b.ycount){
 Allocate ("Copy constructor failed");
}
BigArray::~BigArray () {
 Release ();
}
BigArray& BigArray::operator= (const BigArray& b)
                                throw (const char*) {
 if (this == &b)
  return *this;
 Release ();
 x = y = 0;
 xcount = b.xcount;
 ycount = b.ycount;
 Allocate ("Assignment operator failed");
 return *this;
}
```

The **Pgm06b** tester program is very simple—just ask for more memory than exists.

```
int main () {
 int a, b, c;
 try {
  BigArray g (1000000000, 1000000000);
 }
 catch (const char *msg) {
  cout << msg << endl;
 }
...
```

This tester displays the message "Default constructor failed." Complete coding is contained in the **Pgn06b** folder under the **Samples** folder.

The bottom line under VC7 is to wrap all calls to **new** with try-catch logic to avoid runtime crashes when out of memory. This differs from the VC6 methodology of just returning null pointers.

Review Questions

1. How does a dynamic cast differ from a static cast?

2. Consider an array of void pointers. When the elements are assigned their values, statements such as this are used.

```
CostRec* ptrrec = new CostRec;
array[i] = ptrtrec;
```

What is inherently wrong with later retrieval statements such as this?

```
ptrrec = (CostRec*) array[i];
```

How can a dynamic cast remedy the deficiency? Code an appropriate dynamic cast for the above.

3. Consider the Shapes program discussed in chapter 9. If the client program stored all the derived shape class instances in an array of type **Shape***, how could dynamic casting assist the client program in accessing the ith shape?

4. What is meant by RTTL—Run-Time Type Information? How can RTTL be utilized in programs? What

is its value in an application that utilizes many derived classes with pointers to their base classes?

5. What is meant by the philosophy of C++ Error Handling?

6. Consider function **Fun1**. If the passed parameter contains 0, what occurs?
```
int Fun1 (int num) throw (int) {
 if (!num)
  throw 42;
 ...
}
```

7. Consider function **Fun2**. If the passed parameter contains 0, what occurs?
```
int Fun2 (int num) throw (int) {
 if (!num)
  throw 42.;
 ...
}
```

8. Consider function **Fun3**. If the passed parameter contains 0, what occurs?
```
int Fun3 (int num) {
 if (!num)
  throw 42;
 ...
}
```

9. Consider function **Fun4**. If the passed parameter contains 0, what occurs?
```
int Fun4 (int num) throw (int, const char*) {
 if (!num)
  throw "Error: num is 0";
 ...
}
```

10. Assume **Fun1** is defined as given in question 6 above and that its parameter is 0. What occurs in the following code? What is displayed?
```
try {
 int y = Fun1 (x);
}
catch (int) {
 cerr << "An error has occurred\n";
 y = 0;
}
cout << y << endl;
```

11. Assume **Fun1** is defined as given in question 6 above and that its parameter is 0. What occurs in the following code? What is displayed?
```
try {
 int y = Fun1 (x);
}
catch (const char* msg) {
 cerr << msg;
 y = 0;
}
cout << y << endl;
```

12. Assume **Fun1** is defined as given in question 6 above and that its parameter is 0. What occurs in the following code? What is displayed?

```
try {
 int y = Fun1 (x);
}
catch (...) {
 cerr << "An error has occurred\n";
 y = 0;
}
cout << y << endl;
```

13. When would a **catch** block ever rethrow the same exception? Give an example. When might a **catch** block desire to **throw** a different exception? Give an example.

14. When might an application desire to supply its own terminate handler?

15. How can the New Style **new** function be directed to return a NULL pointer instead of throwing an exception? How can this behavior change be valuable in an application?

16. When a constructor function must allocate three member arrays and the third allocation fails due to lack of memory, what must that function do before any exceptions are raised?

Stop! Do These Exercises Before Programming

1. Consider the function **ReciprocalSum**. This function is passed an integer representing the maximum value to be used in the summation of reciprocals. For example, if the function is passed 5, then it returns the sum of 1/1 + 1/2 + 1/3 + 1/4 + 1/5. Determine what errors could possibly occur. Then design and code this function, checking for and throwing appropriate errors. You may determine what is thrown when.

2. The constructor for the **PhoneBookArray** class is passed a filename. The class stores an array of **PhoneBook** structures. The array size is a constant, **MAXNUM**. The constructor opens the file and fills the array. Consider what events could go wrong in this possibility and create a series of exceptions that can be thrown. The class begins in this manner.

```
const int MAXNUM = 42;
class PhoneBookArray {
protected:
 PhoneBook array[MAXNUM];
 int count;
public:
 PhoneBookArray (const char* filename);
```

Alter the constructor to throw your chosen exceptions. Then write the shell coding of the constructor, throwing the exceptions as they are detected. Finally, show how a **main** function could call this ctor.

3. A programmer attempted to utilize C++ exceptions with the **Image** class discussed at the start of this chapter. He has coded the following.

main.cpp

```
Image pic ("MyImage.bmp");
pic.Display();
```

Image.h

```
class Image {
unsigned char* imageData;
```

```
...
Image (const char* file);
}
```

Image.cpp

```
Image::Image (const char*file) {
 ifstream infile (file);
 if (!infile) {
  throw 1;
 }
 ...
 // size contains the number of bytes in the image file
 imageData = new unsigned char [size];
 if (!imageData)
  throw 2;
 ...
}
```

Correct all syntax errors so that the C++ exceptions are properly handled in all three files.

4. A program maintains various shapes by storing a pointer to the **Shape** base class. Write a block of coding to convert **ptrshape,** which is a **Shape** pointer, into either a **Rectangle***, **Square***, **Triangle***, or a **Circle*** depending upon what the true derived class actually is.

Programming Problems

Problem Pgm06-1—The Vehicle-Car-Truck-Limo Program

This is fundamentally a design problem.

Step One. Use the basic shell coding for the **Vehicle** class given in chapter 5. It maintains a **double speed** and **bool isMoving** members. Create **virtual** access functions for these members.

Step Two. Create a **Car** class derived from **Vehicle**. The **Car** class maintains a **bool isStarted**, **double gallons**, and **double mpg**. Provide **virtual** access functions for these as well. Override the SetSpeed access function to do nothing is the car is not started.

Step Three. Create a **Truck** class derived from **Car**, adding the double cargo data member and corresponding access functions.

Step Four. Create a **Limo** class derived from **Car**, adding the integer number of possible passengers and a **bool isTV_On**. Also, provide access functions for these.

Step Five. Write a **main** function that has an array of 4 **Vehicle** pointers called **fleet**. Dynamically allocate one each of the four classes and store them in the **fleet** array. The design problem to overcome is this. For each of the four elements in the **fleet** array, invoke each of the corresponding access functions. Note, do NOT provide pure **virtual** or **virtual** functions for all of these derived class access functions down in the **Vehicle** class. Keep **Vehicle** down to its minimum number of functions required to manipulate a **Vehicle** object. This means, at run time, you need to discover what derived class each **fleet** element actually is and dynamically cast each **fleet** element pointer back into the appropriate derived class pointer and use that pointer to call the derived class functions.

Problem Pgm06-2—The LoadArray Function with Exceptions

The **LoadArray** function is passed an array of **CostRecord** structures and the integer maximum array size and a **const char*** filename. **LoadArray** opens the passed filename, inputs the cost records, closes the file, and returns the number of records now actually in the array. A **CostRecord** structure can be of your own design, but it should include at least the item number, character string description, a quantity, and a cost.

Consider what errors can possibly occur within **LoadArray**—there are several. For each of the possible errors that can occur, throw an exception at the appropriate point within the actual function coding. Thus, you must add the **throw** list to the prototype and header of **LoadArray**. When you have written **LoadArray**, it should return the number in the array or throw an exception. Thus, the only direct way back to the calling program is when all goes well and no errors occur.

Now write a **main** function to call **LoadArray**. Wrap this call in a **try-catch** block. Be sure that you **catch** all of the error situations and display an appropriate error message stating the exact cause of the error. All displays of error messages must occur from within a **catch** block in **main**. That is, no error messages are ever displayed from within **LoadArray**.

Finally, thoroughly test the program using as many test files as needed to trigger each of the errors that can occur.

Chapter 7—A Review of the Basic Container Classes

Introduction

A container class is a class that holds a collection of user data items, for example, in an array or list. In Beginning Data Structures, the basic container classes were introduced and include the growable array, the double linked list, the stack and the queue. In this chapter, all four are presented in the format of a simple review of their basic coding techniques for your ready reference in the ensuing chapters.

Container Class Design Principles

To be robust, a container class should be able to grow in size as the user inserts more items. The practical limits on a container's size should be the amount of memory available for the application, never some arbitrary fixed limit. This implies dynamic memory allocation as the underlying methodology.

Any container class must provide means for insertion and extraction of items to and from the container itself. These methods should be intuitive by the user of the class. For example, back in Chapter 3, we had an **Array** class. Here users would expect to find **GetAt**, **SetAt**, **InsertAt**, and **RemoveAt** (or possibly **DeleteAt**) type of methods to allow them to retrieve, store, insert and remove items from the array. (While you could implement a **GrabThisItem** function instead of **GetAt** or **GetCurrentItem** method, your class users will complain about the non-intuitive method names.) One could also implement operator[] if desired. Also, some means of traversing each item in the container must be provided. Quite commonly, "**Find**" methods are needed to allow the user to find a specific item that the container is storing for them.

However, you should also expect that your **Array** class users may want to be able to code the following.

```
Array array;
. . .
item = array[i];
array[i] = item;
```

So the **[] operator** function should also be implemented.

Users are also known to do things such as this.

```
Array array1;
Array array2;
. . .
array2 = array1;
```

And this should tell you at once that the assignment operator and the copy ctor should be implemented as well.

So always design the class with your expected users in mind. What are they going to need this container to be able to do? User's expectations must also be tempered with the next design feature.

A container class must be generic in nature. In other words, the class should be totally reusable from application to application. This is the "write it once and use it over and over" principle at work. A well designed, generic container class can be used in countless applications in which that form a container is needed. The client program merely adds the container header file to their project file (and perhaps the cpp file or they must link to your .lib file) and begins creating and using instances of the container.

The generic aspect means that nothing in the container can be application-specific in nature. Otherwise, that container could not be reused in other applications. And this directly impacts how we can store the user's data within the container. (In the next chapter, we will see how this can be circumvented.)

For example, suppose that the user wanted our **Array** class to store their **CostRec** structures. The following is totally verboten. Such an **Array** class would only be reusable in other applications that want to store **CostRec** structures.

```
class Array {
protected:
 CostRec* array; // our growable array of CostRec structures
...
};
```

Likewise, we cannot even store an array of pointers to **CostRec** structures this way.

```
class Array {
protected:
 CostRec* array[]; // our growable array of pointers to
                   // the user's CostRec structures
...
};
```

This also means that we cannot store copies of the user's data but must resort to storing only pointers to their data items. And those pointers must be **void** pointers. Here is how we **must** define our internal array.

```
class Array {
protected:
 void** array; // our growable array of pointers to
               // the user's data
...
};
```

That is, our array contains **void*** elements each of which points to the user's data.

A positive side benefit of storing only **void** pointers to the user's data is that the amount of memory that the container uses is very small, since a pointer occupies only four bytes on a Win32 platform. Thus, in the Beginning Data Structure containers, reusability was obtained by always storing **void** pointers to the user's data.

But this choice has two other side effects. Since the container cannot know what the data being stored really is, a deep copy cannot be performed. There would be no way for the container to allocate additional instances of the user's data items and copy them. The best we can do is to make a duplicate copy of the array of void pointers.

The other side effect directly impacts the user who now must dynamically allocate each new item and insert its pointer into the container. Further, before the destructor of the container is called, the user must traverse the container and delete every item that is being stored in the container. Failure to do so results in major memory leaks. Additionally, every time the client program retrieves a **void** pointer from the container, it must typecast that pointer to the actual kind of data to which it points. For example,

```
CostRec* ptrcrec = (CostRec*) array.GetAt (i);
```

Finally, storing the user's data as a **void** pointer allows the container to store many different kinds of objects! Normally, we think of an array as storing like items, such as an array of **CostRec** structures. But by using **void** pointers, our containers could care less what each pointer was really pointing to! This allows the user to do the following.

```
// allocate and store an instance of the Inventory class
Inventory* ptrInvItem = new Inventory;
array.Add (ptrInvItem);
// allocate and store an instance of the AirTravel class
AirTravel* ptrATrec = new AirTravel;
array.Add (ptrATrec);
// allocate and store an instance of the BusTravel class
BusSchedule* ptrbus = new BusSchedule;
array.Add (ptrbus);
```

How would they regain access to the class pointers from our returned **void** pointers? By using a dynamic cast, they can determine what each pointer actually is.

```
void* ptritem = array.GetAt(i);
Inventory* ptri = dynamic_cast<Inventory*> (ptritem);
```

```
if (ptri) {
 // here it is an instance of the Inventory class
}
else {
 AirTravel* ptra = dynamic_cast<AirTravel*> (ptritem);
 if (ptra) {
  // here it is an instance of the AirTravel class
 }
 else {
  BusSchedule* ptrb = dynamic_cast<BusSchedule*> (ptritem);
  if (ptrb) {
   // here it is an instance of the BusSchedule class
  }
 }
}
```

Given these pros and cons, let's review how each of the basic four container classes could be implemented.

The Growable Array Container Class

Arrays are a linear, direct access type of data structure whose elements are homogeneous. Table 7.1 shows the definition of the array data structure. Note that here I am using the array as an ADT, not as the built-in C++ array definition.

Data Type	Array as an Abstract Data Type
Domain	An array consists of 1). A collection of a fixed number of components that are of the same data type 2). A set of integer index values that permit a one-to-one correspondence with the array elements
Structure	It consists of a linear, direct access structure that has a one-to-one relationship between each integer index and an array element. The first subscript accesses the first element in the array. That first index does not have to be 0.
Operations	
[k] or GetAt(k)	Retrieve the value of the array element at the kth index
[k] or InsertAt(k)	Store a value in the array element at the kth index

Table 7.1 The Array Data Structure Definition

The two data members are the array of void pointers and the number of elements in the array. In this example, I did not overload the [] operator. This is the topic of one of the Stop Exercises.

Since the users include the header file for the container, your header files should contain good documentation about the class and its usage. Since the user is required to traverse the array and delete the actual items we are storing before the destructor is called, some sample coding can help immensely.

What is the difference between this version and the version back Chapter 3? In Chapter 3, the dynamic allocations used std::nothrow so that if we ran out of memory, the new function returned a NULL or 0 pointer. In all of these versions here in Chapter 7, the new function is allowed to throw C++ exceptions which are then caught, using the try-catch logic.

Array Definition - Growable Array Class

```
#pragma once

/*********************************************************/
/*                                                       */
/* Array: container for growable array of void* items    */
/*        it can store a variable number of elements     */
/*                                                       */
/*        since elements stored are void*, they can      */
/*        point to anything desired, intrinsic types,    */
/*        structures, other classes, for example         */
/*                                                       */
/*  Limited by amount of memory and swap drive size      */
/*                                                       */
/*  errors are logged to cerr device                     */
/*                                                       */
/*  Note on destruction: before calling RemoveAt or      */
/*  RemoveAll or the destructor, the user is responsible */
/*  for the actual deletion of the items the void*       */
/*  pointers are actually pointing to                    */
/*                                                       */
/*  Typical clean up coding might be as follows:         */
/*  MyData* ptrd;                                        */
/*  for (i=0; i<array.GetNumberOfElements(); i++) {      */
/*   ptrd = (MyData*) array.GetAt (i);                   */
/*   if (ptrd)                                           */
/*    delete ptrd;                                       */
/*  }                                                    */
/*  array.RemoveAll ();                                  */
/*                                                       */
/*********************************************************/

class Array {

 /********************************************************/
 /*                                                      */
 /* class data                                           */
 /*                                                      */
 /********************************************************/

protected:
 void** array;
 long  numElements;

 /********************************************************/
 /*                                                      */
 /* class functions                                      */
 /*                                                      */
 /********************************************************/

public:
 Array ();    // default constructor - makes an empty array
 ~Array ();   // be sure to delete what the void* are pointing
              // to before the destructor is called

```

```
 bool Add (void* ptrNewElement); // add the element to array end
                                 // returns true if successful
 bool InsertAt (long i, void* ptrNewElement);
      // adds this element at subscript i
      // if i < 0, it is added at the front
      // if i >= numElements, it is added at the end
      // otherwise, it is added at the ith position
      // returns true if successful

 void* GetAt (long i) const; // returns element at the ith pos
                    // If i is out of range, it returns 0

 bool RemoveAt (long i); // removes the element at subscript i
                    // if i is out of range, an error is
                    // displayed on cerr - Note what the
                    // element actually points to is not deleted
                    // returns true if successful

 void RemoveAll (); // removes all elements - Note what the
                    // elements actually point to are not deleted

 long GetNumberOfElements () const; // returns the number of
                                    // elements in the array

 Array (const Array& a);            // copy constructor
 Array& operator= (const Array& a); // duplicates the array
 // Note that neither the copy constructor or the assignment op
 // makes a copy of what the pointer elements are actually
 // pointing to. Displays an error msg to cerr if out of memory

protected:
 void Copy (const Array& a); // performs the actual deep copy
};
```

From the implementation viewpoint, I chose to return **bool** values to indicate success or failure of the add and remove functions. With the **Add** and **InsertAt** functions, the only way **false** can be returned is if the computer is out of memory. The implementation of **InsertAt** reflects my own personal consideration that a function should try to do its job in all cases. If the index is out of range, I still add the item. If the index is negative, I insert it at the front of the array; if the index is too large, I insert it at the end of the array. **RemoveAt** must return false if the index is out of range because there is no way to second-guess the programmer's intention.

Also pay careful attention to the try-catch logic.

Array Implementation - Growable Array Class

```
#include <iostream>
#include "Array.h"
using namespace std;

/***************************************************************/
/*                                                             */
/* Array: constructs an empty array                            */
/*                                                             */
/***************************************************************/

```

```
Array::Array () {
 numElements = 0;
 array = 0;
}

/*******************************************************/
/*                                                     */
/* ~Array: deletes dynamically allocated memory        */
/*         It is the client's responsibility  to delete */
/*         what the void* are pointing to before the    */
/*         destructor is called                         */
/*                                                     */
/*******************************************************/

Array::~Array () {
 RemoveAll ();
}

/*******************************************************/
/*                                                     */
/* Add: Adds this new element to the end of the array   */
/*      if out of memory, displays error message to cerr */
/*                                                     */
/*******************************************************/

bool Array::Add (void* ptrNewElement) {
 void** temp = 0;
 try {
  // allocate new temporary array one element larger
  temp = new void* [numElements + 1];
 }
 catch (std::bad_alloc e) {
  // check for out of memory
  cerr << "Array: Add Error - out of memory\n";
  return false;
 }

 // copy all existing elements into the new temp array
 for (long i=0; i<numElements; i++) {
  temp[i] = array[i];
 }

 // copy in the new element to be added
 temp[numElements] = ptrNewElement;

 numElements++;  // increment the number of elements in the array
 if (array) delete [] array; // delete the old array
 array = temp;    // point out array to the new array
 return true;
}

/*******************************************************/
/*                                                     */
/* InsertAt: adds the new element to the array at index i*/
/*  if i is in range, it is inserted at subscript i      */
/*  if i is negative, it is inserted at the front        */
```

```
/*  if i is greater than or equal to the number of        */
/*     elements, then it is added at the end of the array*/
/*                                                        */
/*  if there is insufficient memory, an error message     */
/*     is displayed to cerr                               */
/*                                                        */
/**********************************************************/

bool Array::InsertAt (long i, void* ptrNewElement) {
 void** temp;
 long j;
 try {
  // allocate a new array one element larger
  temp = new void* [numElements + 1];
 }
 catch (std::bad_alloc e) {
  // check if out of memory
  cerr << "Array: InsertAt - Error out of memory\n";
  return false;
 }

 // this case handles an insertion that is within range
 if (i < numElements && i >= 0) {
  for (j=0; j<i; j++) { // copy all elements below insertion
   temp[j] = array[j];  // point
  }
  temp[i] = ptrNewElement; // insert new element
  for (j=i; j<numElements; j++) { // copy remaining elements
   temp[j+1] = array[j];
  }
 }

 // this case handles an insertion when the index is too large
 else if (i >= numElements) {
  for (j=0; j<numElements; j++) { // copy all existing elements
   temp[j] = array[j];
  }
  temp[numElements] = ptrNewElement; // add new one at end
 }

 // this case handles an insertion when the index is too small
 else {
  temp[0] = ptrNewElement;         // insert new on at front
  for (j=0; j<numElements; j++) { // copy all others after it
   temp[j+1] = array[j];
  }
 }

 // for all cases, delete current array, assign new one and
 // increment the number of elements in the array
 if (array) delete [] array;
 array = temp;
 numElements++;
 return true;
}

```

```
/***************************************************************/
/*                                                             */
/* GetAt: returns the element at index i                       */
/*        if i is out of range, returns 0                      */
/*                                                             */
/***************************************************************/

void* Array::GetAt (long i) const {
 if (i < numElements && i >=0)
  return array[i];
 else
  return 0;
}

/***************************************************************/
/*                                                             */
/* RemoveAt: removes the element at subscript i                */
/*                                                             */
/* If i is out of range, an error is displayed on cerr         */
/*                                                             */
/* Note that what the element actually points to is not        */
/*      deleted                                                */
/*                                                             */
/***************************************************************/

bool Array::RemoveAt (long i) {
 void** temp;
 if (numElements > 1) {
  if (i >= 0 && i < numElements) {     // if index is in range
   try {
    temp = new void* [numElements - 1]; // allocate smaller array
   }
   catch (std::bad_alloc e) {
    cerr << "Error: out of memory\n";
    return false;
   }
   long j;
   for (j=0; j<i; j++) {              // copy all elements up to
    temp[j] = array[j];               // the desired one to be
   }                                  // removed
   for (j=i+1; j<numElements; j++) { // then copy all elements
    temp[j-1] = array[j];             // that remain
   }
   numElements--;               // decrement  number of elements
   if (array) delete [] array; // delete the old array
   array = temp;                // and assign the new one
   return true;
  }
 }
 cerr << "Array: RemoveAt Error - element out of range\n"
      << "       It was " << i << " and numElements is "
      << numElements << endl;
 return false;
}

/***************************************************************/
```

```
/*                                                       */
/* RemoveAll: empties the entire array, resetting it to  */
/*            an empty state ready for reuse              */
/*                                                       */
/* Note that what the elements actually points to are   */
/*      not deleted                                      */
/*                                                       */
/*********************************************************/

void Array::RemoveAll () {
 if (array) delete [] array; // remove all elements
 numElements = 0;            // reset number of elements
 array = 0;                  // and reset array to 0
}

/*********************************************************/
/*                                                       */
/* GetNumberOfElements: returns the number of elements   */
/*                      currently in the array           */
/*                                                       */
/*********************************************************/

long Array::GetNumberOfElements () const {
 return numElements;
}

/*********************************************************/
/*                                                       */
/* Array: copy constructor, makes a duplicate copy of a  */
/*                                                       */
/* Note: what the elements actually point to are not     */
/* duplicated only our pointers are duplicated           */
/*                                                       */
/*********************************************************/

Array::Array (const Array& a) {
 Copy (a);
}

/*********************************************************/
/*                                                       */
/* operator=: makes a duplicate array of passed array a  */
/*                                                       */
/* Note: what the elements actually point to are not     */
/* duplicated only our pointers are duplicated           */
/*                                                       */
/*********************************************************/

Array& Array::operator= (const Array& a) {
 if (this == &a) // avoids silly a = a assignemnts
  return *this;
 delete [] array; // remove existing array
 Copy (a);        // duplicate array a
 return *this;    // return us for chaining assignments
}
```

```
/*********************************************************/
/*                                                       */
/* Copy: helper function to actual perform the copy      */
/*                                                       */
/*********************************************************/

void Array::Copy (const Array& a) {
 if (a.numElements) { // be sure array a is not empty
  numElements = a.numElements;
  try {
   // allocate a new array the size of a
   array = new void* [numElements];
  }
  catch (std::bad_alloc e) {
   // check for out of memory condition
   cerr << "Array: Copy function - Error out of memory\n";
   numElements = 0;
   return;
  }

  // copy all of a's pointers into our array
  for (long i=0; i<numElements; i++) {
   array[i] = a.array[i];
  }
 }
 else { // a is empty, so make ours empty too
  numElements = 0;
  array = 0;
 }
}
```

The Double Linked List Container

A list is a linear data structure that is accessed sequentially. The first item in the list is located at the **head** of the list, while the last item in the list is located at the **tail**. Each item in the list points to the next item in the list and in some lists. each item also points to the previous item in the list. There is no arbitrary maximum number of items in a list. Table 7.2 shows the ADT definition of the linked list.

Data Type	List Data Structure
Domain	Each list has 1). A collection of component values each of the same data type 2). A cursor to mark the current position in the list and whose values can range from 1 to N+1 where N is the number of items currently in the list.
Structure	A linear, sequential access data structure of varying length
Operations	Note: the C++ function names I have used can be called by many similar names.
Initialize()	Initialize to an empty list
AddAtHead()	Add an item at the head of the list
AddAtTail()	Add an item at the tail of the list

InsertAt()	Add an item at the cursor location
Next()	Move sequentially to the next item in the list
Previous()	Move sequentially to the previous item in the list
ResetToHead()	Reset the cursor to the beginning of the list
ResetToTail()	Reset the cursor to the last item in the list
IsHead()	Is the cursor at the head of the list?
IsTail()	Is the cursor at the tail of the list?
RemoveAt()	Remove the item at the cursor from the list
GetCurrent()	Get the item at the cursor
IsEmpty()	Is the list empty?
Empty()	Remove all items from the list

Table 7.2 The List Data Structure Definition

Typical implementations of a list data structure maintain a pointer that points to the first item in the list, say called **headptr**. A **double linked list** contains a list of items and is implemented by storing the user's data in a node structure that also contains a forward and a back pointer to the next and the preceding list items. Any node then points both forward to the next node in the list and points backwards to the previous node in the list. When either of these pointers are null or 0, such indicates that there is no previous or no next node and we are either at the beginning of the list or the end.

The class that implements a double linked list would have both a head pointer as well as a tail pointer that points to the last node in the list. The current pointer member can be used to traverse the list in either direction. These pointers are of the data type of the "node." The class could also maintain a count of the number of nodes in the list for convenience. However, specification of the client's data that is to be stored in a node is the variable factor. Again to be generic, we store the user's data as a void pointer.

The definition of a node can be done using a structure or a simple class;

```
struct LinkNode {
 LinkNode* fwdptr;
 LinkNode* backptr;
 void*     dataptr;
};
```

or

```
class LinkNode {
public:
 LinkNode* fwdptr;
 LinkNode* backptr;
 void*     dataptr;
};
```

By storing **void** pointers to the client's data, we have removed all dependencies upon client data. Thus, we can write a single implementation of the double linked list that can be used to store any kind of client data.

Once more, by storing **void** pointers to the client's data, we are normally forcing the client program to dynamically allocate instances of their data to be stored in the list. However, now we no longer know the data type of the client's data. And this factor does indeed impact the client programming significantly. Let's see how.

One of the more significant results of using **void** pointers is that the linked list class can no longer be responsible for the deletion of the client's data portions whenever **EmptyList** or the destructor is called. All that the linked list class can do is delete the **LinkNode** instances. Thus, it becomes the full responsibility of the client program to traverse the list and delete all of the client's data before the client program calls **EmptyList** or a linked list destructor!

There is another major impact on client programs. When copying lists either by use of the copy constructor or the assignment operator, a deep copy cannot be performed. The linked list class can only make duplicate copies of the **LinkNode** instances. Each of these new copies will contain the original client's data pointers. There is no way we can make duplicate copies of the actual client's data in the list. This is generally not a serious problem as long as the client program is aware of this side effect.

The four private data members are as follows.

```
LinkNode* headptr;     // points to first node in list
LinkNode* currentptr;  // points to the current node
LinkNode* tailptr;     // points to last node in list
long      count;       // the number of nodes in list
```

The class should have a constructor and destructor, the latter of which calls the usual **EmptyList** function which could also be called by client programs. What kinds of add new node functions are needed? Because the list has both a head and a tail pointer, additions can be made at both locations; these are called **AddAtHead** and **AddAtTail**. With the current pointer marking the current node in the list, the user may wish to add either before or after this specific node. This is often the case when they wish to maintain a sorted list. We have then another pair of functions: **InsertAfterCurrentNode** and **InsertBeforeCurrentNode**.

We should also provide a means of deleting the current node, **DeleteCurrentNode**. We can add some convenience functions such as **GetSize**, which returns the number of items in the list, **IsHead**, which returns **true** if the current pointer is pointing to the first item in the list, and **IsTail**, which returns **true** if the current pointer is pointing to the last item in the list.

What iterator functions are required for list traversal? They include **ResetToHead**, **ResetToTail**, **Next**, **Previous** and **GetCurrentNode**. Thus, a client program can move both forward and backwards through the list.

Providing a Find Matching List Item Function

Look over the functionality that the linked list class provides. Is anything missing? Well, yes, as a matter of fact, there is something missing. How would a client program find a specific item in the list? Suppose that the list contained instances of the **Student** structure. How could a client program find the student whose id number was 123456789? As the class design currently stands, the client program would have to manually iterate sequentially through the list from either end looking for a matching id number in the list.

Can we provide a **FindNode** function to assist client programs in locating a specific item? Yes, however, this single function poses a major problem in design. Certainly, we can iterate sequentially through the list, setting **currentptr** as we go along. But how do we compare the current node's user data with the user's matching criteria when we know nothing about the client's data? In fact, we cannot. Instead, we must rely on the user to notify our **FindNode** function if a specific node matches their criteria. The user criteria can be anything so **FindNode** must accept that criteria using a constant **void** pointer. The user can typecast it back into the actual matching criteria data type. For each node in the list, we must call a function back in the client program and give it the current user data and the criteria in use on this search. This is known as a **call back function** because our function (which is viewed as "system" coding by the client program) must repeatedly call a function back in the client program to perform the actual comparison list item by list item. This process is diagramed in Figure 7.1 below.

What would the user call back function prototype be? It is given two constant **void** pointers, the pointer to the specific criteria for matching and the pointer current node's item. For example, suppose that the client program needed to match on student id numbers. They would have coded the function **MatchOnId**.

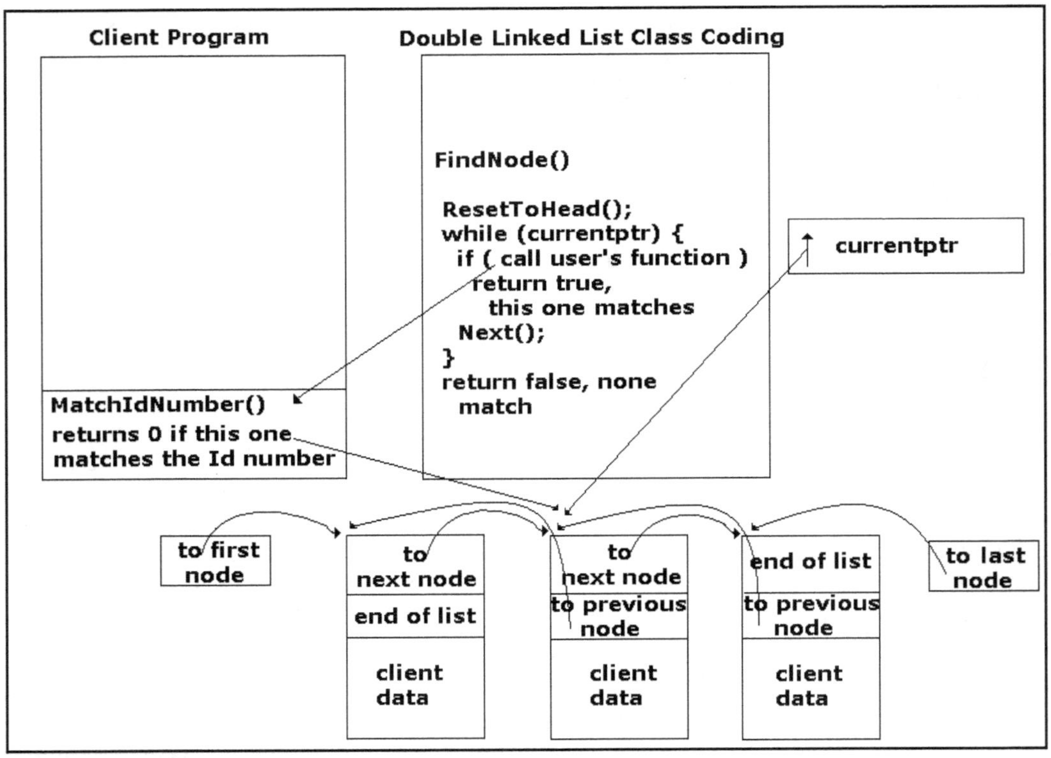

Figure 7.1 The Callback Function Process

```
int MatchOnId (const void* ptrmatchData,
               const void* ptrthis);
```

On the other hand, suppose the client program wanted to match on the student's name. The matching function prototype is

```
int MatchOnName (const void* ptrmatchData,
                 const void* ptrthis);
```

Sample client coding to perform these actions might be as follows.

```
long idToFind;
char nameToFind[NAMELEN];
...
if (roster.FindNode (&idToFind, MatchOnId)) {
...
if (roster.FindNode (nameToFind, MatchOnName) {
...
```

Notice how the client must pass the address of the matching data item as the first parameter. However, it is the second parameter that causes the complexity. The client must pass into our **FindNode** function the function for us to actually use.

This raises a most interesting question. What is the data type of the name of a function? We need this information to code our own prototype for **FindNode**. The data type of the name of a function is a pointer to a function that has the same prototype. In the following prototype of the matching function, the parentheses around the * are required.

```
int (*FINDFUNCT) (const void* ptrmatchData, const void* ptrthis);
```

This reads, **FINDFUNCT** is a pointer to a function that returns an **int** and is passed two constant **void** pointers. If the parentheses (*) are omitted as in this next one,

```
int *OOPS (const void* ptrmatchData, const void* ptrthis);
```

This says that **OOPS** is a function that returns a pointer to an **int**!

Ok. Then how do we code our **FindNode** prototype. The easiest way is to use the **typedef** statement to define **FINDFUNCT** as a new kind of data, one that is a pointer to a function that returns an **int** and is passed two constant **void** pointers.

```
typedef int (*FINDFUNCT) (const void* ptrmatchData,
                          const void* ptrthis);
```

Then, the **FindNode** prototype in our class is simply

```
      bool  FindNode (const void* ptrmatchData, FINDFUNCT Find);
```

Within **FindNode**, how do we actually call the passed function pointer, **Find**?

Ok. Now how do we actually call this passed function pointed to by parameter **Find**? Normally, to get to the value pointed to by a pointer, we dereference the pointer; again the parentheses are required.

```
      (*Find) (x, y); // the hard way to invoke the Find function
```

If we had coded it as

```
      *Find (x, y); // error
```

The dereference operator is applied to the return value of the **Find** function, a **bool** in this case, causing a compile-time error.

But wait a minute. All names of all functions in C/C++ are pointers to the coding that they represent. We never do the following.

```
      x = (*sqrt) (z);
      y = (*sin) (angle);
```

The compiler automatically performs function pointer dereference for us. Thus, we can call the passed **Find** function by coding just this.

```
      Find (x, y); // the easy way to invoke the Find function
```

In reality, by having the **typedef** for the call back function, the **FindNode** function is easily implemented. Here is the shell of our generic **DoubleLinkedList** class showing the implementation of **FindNode**.

```
typedef int (*FINDFUNCT) (const void* ptrmatchData,
                          const void* ptrthis);
class DoubleLinkedList {
 bool  FindNode (const void* ptrmatchData, FINDFUNCT Find);
...
bool  DoubleLinkedList::FindNode (const void* ptrmatchData,
                                  FINDFUNCT Find) {
 if (!count)      // is the list is empty
  return false;   // yes, so leave doing nothing with no match
 ResetToHead (); // begin at the first node in the list
 while (currentptr) { // for each node, see if it matches
  if (Find (ptrmatchData, currentptr->dataptr) == 0)
   return true; // yes, this one matches, return true to caller
  Next ();      // move to the next item in the list
 }
 return false;  // here no item matched the user's criteria
}
```

Handling the Insertions into the List

Now let's examine how items are added to the list with the four functions. The functions **AddAtHead** and **AddAtTail** are the simpler ones to implement because we are always at one end of the list, never in the middle. Adding at the head of the list presents only two circumstances—either the list is empty or there are one or more items already in the list. Figures 7.2 and 7.3 illustrates what must be done to insert a new node at the head. For both cases, allocate a new node and fill it as shown.

```
 LinkNode* ptrnew = new LinkNode;
 ptrnew->dataptr = ptrdata; // copy the passed client pointer
 ptrnew->backptr = 0;       // back pointer is 0 because at head
 count++;                   // increment total number of nodes
```

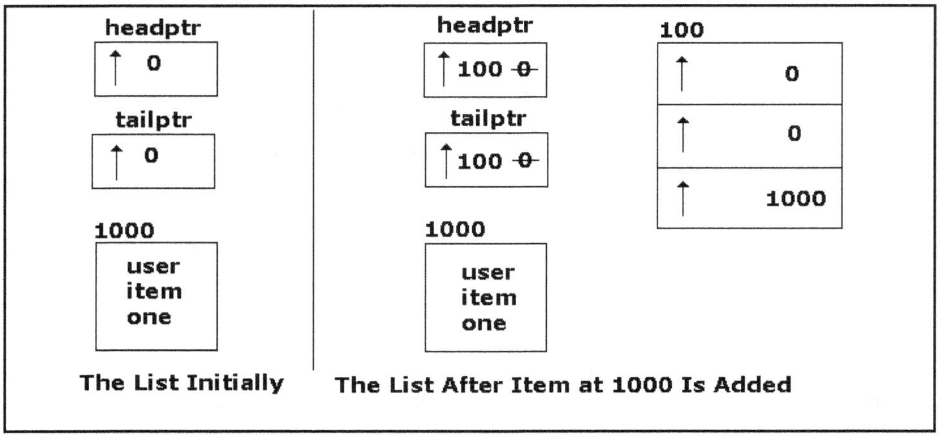

Figure 7.2 Adding a New Item at the Head to an Empty List

For an empty list, we just set the head and tail pointers to the new node.

```
headptr = tailptr = ptrnew; // this new node
ptrnew->fwdptr = 0;         // and no forward nodes yet
```

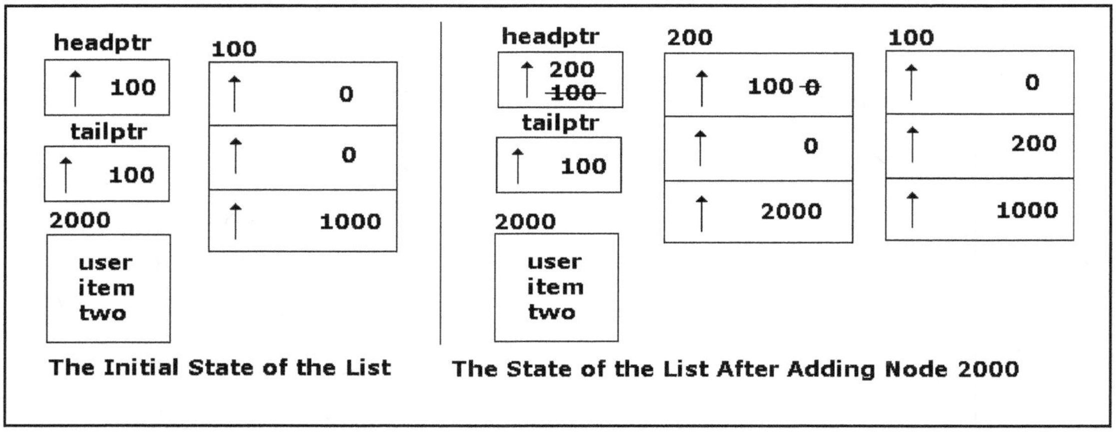

Figure 7.3 Adding a New Item at the Head with Items Already in the List

If there are items in the list, we must set the new node's forward pointer to the previous node that was at the front of the list. We must also set the previous first node's back pointer to point to the new first node. And **headptr** now stores the new node's address.

```
ptrnew->fwdptr = headptr; // fwdptr contains the previous one
headptr->backptr = ptrnew;// prev node's backptr is us now
headptr = ptrnew;         // set headptr to newly added node
```

When adding at the tail, once again, two cases arise: an empty list and a list with items in it. The situation of an empty list is the same as it is with adding at the head when the list is empty. When there are items in the list, adding at the tail is shown in Figure 7.4.

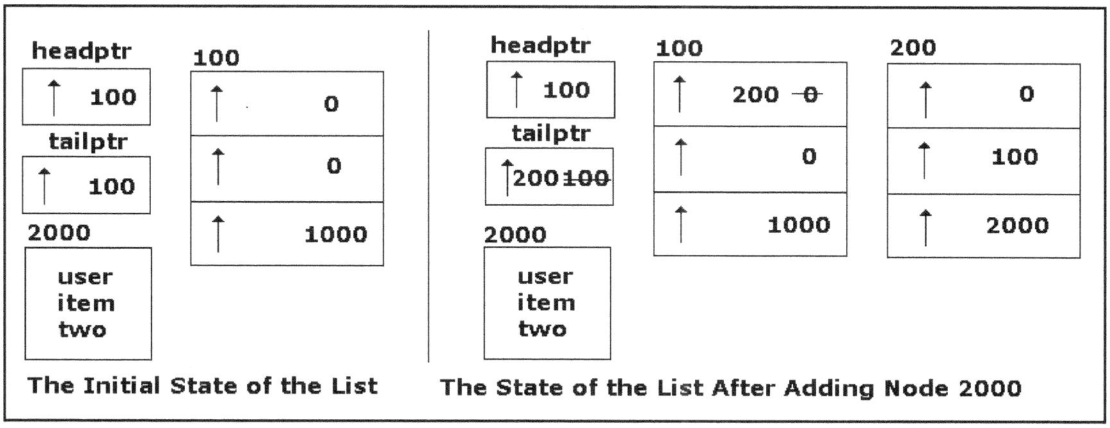

Figure 7.4 Adding a Node at the Tail of the List When There Are Items in the List

The current last node's forward pointer must now point to the new one being added at the tail. The new one being added must have its backwards pointer pointing to the previous last node. And the **tailptr** is updated to point to the new one being added at the tail.

```
tailptr->fwdptr = ptrnew; // yes, prev tail node points to us
ptrnew->backptr = tailptr;// us points back to the prev node
tailptr = ptrnew;         // tail is now us
```

Handling the insertion either before or after the current node raises additional complexities because a node could exist on either side of the insertion point. If the list is empty, **headptr** is 0, then reuse the **AddAtHead** function. If the current pointer is 0, then I chose to also call **AddAtHead**. However, one could signal an insertion error in this case if you so desire or even add at the tail. That leaves two remaining possibilities.

If we are inserting after the current node, then there must be a previous node from the viewpoint of this new one we are adding. If the current pointer is actually the last node in the list, then in effect we are adding at the tail and I chose to simple call **AddAtTail** to carry out the insertion. That leaves only the one remaining possibility, we are inserting between two nodes. Figure 7.5 shows this more complicated case. Notice carefully how the forward and back chains on the list must be broken as the new node is inserted in between them. The code begins by allocating a new node and storing the user's data pointer and incrementing the count of the number of items in the list.

```
LinkNode* ptrnew = new LinkNode;
ptrnew->dataptr = ptrdata;
count++;
```

The new node must point forward to the node on the right and back to the node on the left of it. The node to its left must point forward to this new node while the node to its right must point back to the new node.

The first two assignments are easy. Remember that **currentptr** is pointing to the node just before the new node.

```
ptrnew->backptr = currentptr;
ptrnew->fwdptr = currentptr->fwdptr;
```

The next two lines break the existing chain, inserting the new node into the chain.

```
currentptr->fwdptr = ptrnew;
ptrnew->fwdptr->backptr = ptrnew;
currentptr = ptrnew;
```

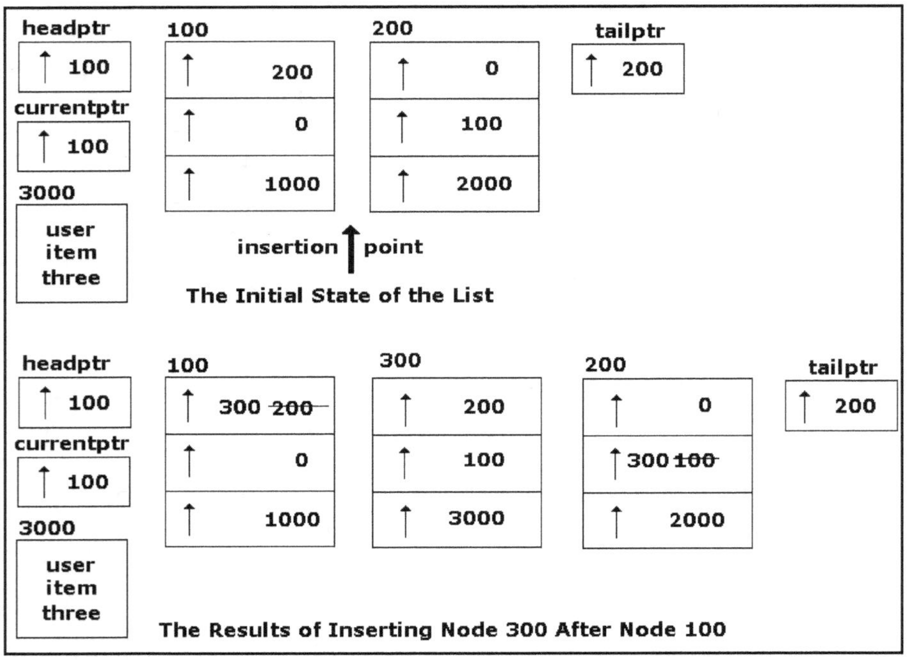

Figure 7.5 Inserting a Node After the Current Node at Location 100

The insert before the current node is handled in a similar fashion. If the list is empty or the current pointer is 0, I call **AddAtHead** to insert the new node. This leaves two remaining cases to handle. Since we are inserting before the current node, then there will always be a node to the new node's right. But if the current node is actually the first node, then there is no node to its left and we are in effect adding at the head once again. The coding begins the same way as before. Allocate a new node, copy the user's pointer and increment the number of items in the list.

```
LinkNode* ptrnew = new LinkNode;
ptrnew->dataptr = ptrdata;
count++;
```

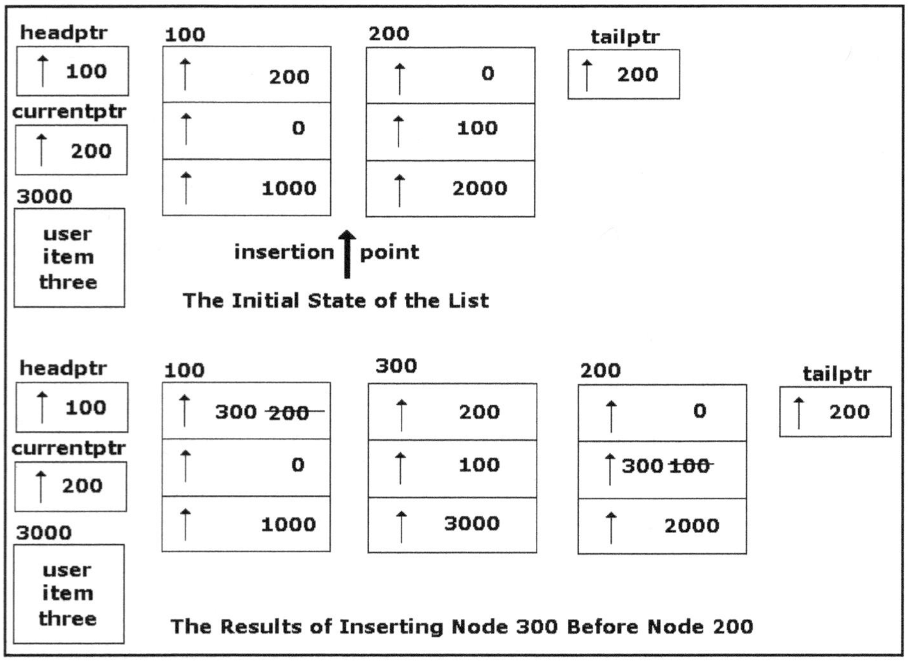

Figure 7.6 Inserting Node 300 Before Node 200

The new node's forward pointer is set to **currentptr** while the new node's back pointer is set to the current node's back pointer.

```
ptrnew->backptr = currentptr->backptr;
ptrnew->fwdptr = currentptr;
```

Then, the current pointer's back pointer must be set to point to the new node. And the previous node's forward pointer must now point to the new node.

```
currentptr->backptr = ptrnew;
ptrnew->backptr->fwdptr = ptrnew;
currentptr = ptrnew;
```

Deleting the Current Node

When we wish to delete the current node, five situations arise. If the current node is 0, then there is nothing to do. The function should return **false** to alert the client program. Next, suppose that there is only one node in the list which is the current one to delete. This case is easy, we simply delete the node and reset all pointers and the count to 0. The remaining three cases deal with the location of the current node to delete in the list. The current node to delete could be the first node or the last node or one in the middle. Let's examine each of these three remaining cases in detail beginning with the node to delete being the first node in the list. Figure 7.7 illustrates the deletion process for the first node in the list.

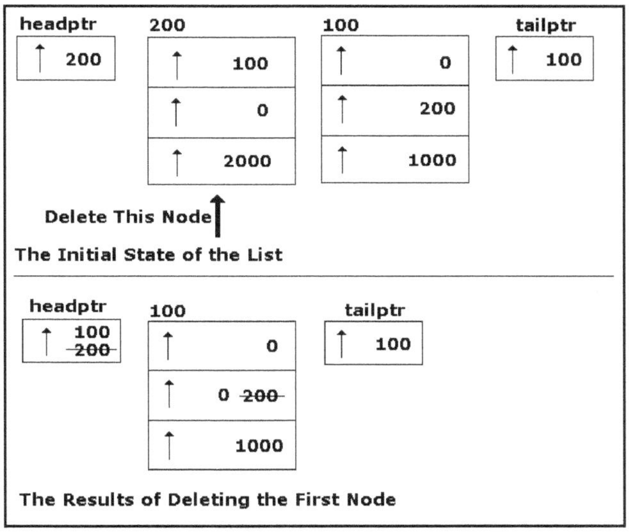

Figure 7.7 Deleting the First Node in a List

To delete the first node in the list, we must set the next node's back pointer to 0 and the **headptr** to the next node in order to remove the first node from the chain.

```
LinkNode* ptrtodelete = currentptr;
if (IsHead()) {                     // deleting first node? if so,
 currentptr->fwdptr->backptr = 0;// set next node's back to none
 headptr = currentptr->fwdptr;    // set head to next node
 currentptr = headptr;            // and current to next node
}
```

Next, suppose we are deleting the last node in the list. Figure 7.8 shows the situation. We must set the previous node's forward pointer to 0 and reset the tail pointer to that one.

```
else if (IsTail()) {                // deleting last one, if so,
 currentptr->backptr->fwdptr = 0;// set prev node's fwd to none
 tailptr = currentptr->backptr;   // set tail to prev node
 currentptr = tailptr;            // set current to prev node
```

```
}
```

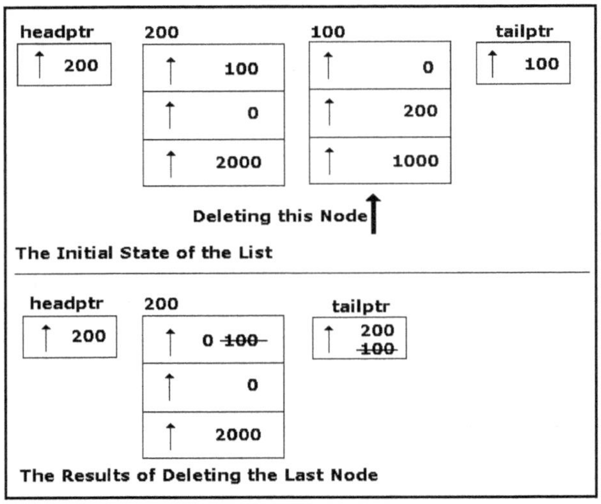

Figure 7.8 Deleting the Last Node in a List

The final situation is deleting a node that is in the middle with a node on either side. Figure 7.9 illustrates how the chain of pointers must be adjusted to remove a middle node.

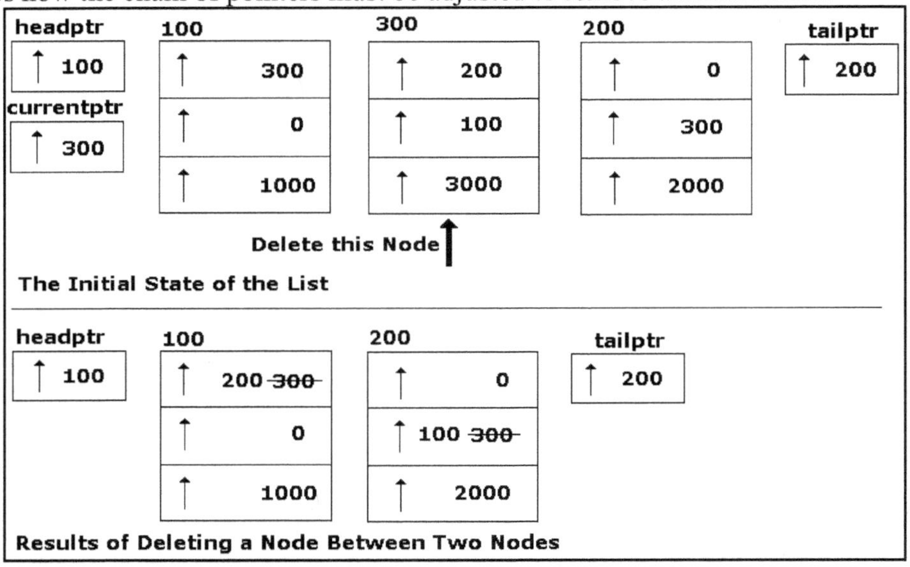

Figure 7.9 Deleting a Node from the Middle of the List

Examine the following two key coding lines and compare them to the above figure. Make sure you understand how the node at 300 is removed from the forward and back chains.

```
else { // here the node to delete is in the middle
  // set next node's back to previous node
  currentptr->fwdptr->backptr = currentptr->backptr;
  // set previous node's fwd to next node
  currentptr->backptr->fwdptr = currentptr->fwdptr;
  // leave current pointing to previous node
  currentptr = currentptr->backptr;
}
delete ptrtodelete; // now delete the requested node
return true;
```

Here is the header file for our generic **DoubleLinkedList** class. Notice that I placed numerous comments and some coding samples for the users in the header file.

```
Definition of a Generic DoubleLinkedList Class
 1 #pragma once
 3 #include <iostream>
 4
 5 using namespace std;
 6
 7 /***************************************************************/
 8 /*                                                           */
 9 /* DoubleLinkedList Class                                    */
10 /*                                                           */
11 /* A generic double linked list that can be reused          */
12 /*                                                           */
13 /***************************************************************/
14
15 /***************************************************************/
16 /*                                                           */
17 /* LinkNode: the link list node structure                    */
18 /*                                                           */
19 /***************************************************************/
20
21 struct LinkNode {
22   LinkNode* fwdptr;   // points to the next node in the list
23   LinkNode* backptr;  // points to the previous node
24   void*     dataptr;  // points to the client data stored
25 };
26
27 typedef int (*FINDFUNCT) (const void* ptrmatchData,
28                           const void* ptrthis);
29
30 class DoubleLinkedList {
31
32   /***************************************************************/
33   /*                                                           */
34   /* class data                                                */
35   /*                                                           */
36   /***************************************************************/
37
38 private:
39   LinkNode* headptr;      // points to first node in list
40   LinkNode* currentptr;   // points to the current node
41   LinkNode* tailptr;      // points to last node in list
42   long      count;        // the number of nodes in list
43
44   /***************************************************************/
45   /*                                                           */
46   /* class functions                                           */
47   /*                                                           */
48   /***************************************************************/
49
50 public:
51         DoubleLinkedList (); // constructs an empty list
52        ~DoubleLinkedList (); // deletes the total list
```

```
void  EmptyList ();         // removes all items from the list
// Note: client program must ensure that all client data are
// deleted before calling EmptyList() or the destructor
// Example: suppose the list contains CostRec structures
// list.ResetToHead();
// CostRec* ptrdata = (CostRec*) list.GetCurrentNode();
// while (ptrdata) {
//  delete ptrdata;
//  list.Next();
//  ptrdata = (CostRec*) list.GetCurrentNode();
// }
// list.EmptyList();

// the add new node functions
bool  AddAtHead (void* ptrdata); // add node at the head
bool  AddAtTail (void* ptrdata); // add node at the tail

// add node after the current node - if current node is 0,
// it is added at the head
bool  InsertAfterCurrentNode (void* ptrdata);

// add node before the current node - if the current node is 0,
// it is added at the head
bool  InsertBeforeCurrentNode (void* ptrdata);

// deletes the current node. If there is no current node,
// it returns false; otherwise it returns true.
bool  DeleteCurrentNode ();

// sets the current pointer to the node whose data matches
// the criteria set by the caller.
bool  FindNode (const void* ptrmatchData, FINDFUNCT Find);
// example of usage. Suppose that user data are double pointers
// client's prototype is:
//  int MatchDbl(const void* ptrmatchData, const void* ptrthis);
// double findThis = 2;
// if (test.FindNode (&findThis, MatchDbl)) {
//  double* ptrMatched = (double*) test.GetCurrentNode();
//  cout << "Found: " << *ptrMatched << " should find 2\n";
// and the function is coded:
// int MatchDbl (const void* ptrmatchData, const void* ptrthis){
//  double* ptrMatchThisOne = (double*) ptrmatchData;
//  double* ptrQuery = (double*) ptrthis;
//  if (*ptrQuery == *ptrMatchThisOne) return 0;
//  if (*ptrQuery > *ptrMatchThisOne) return -1;
//  return +1;
// }

long  GetSize () const; // get number of items in the list
bool  IsHead () const;  // is list at the start?
bool  IsTail () const;  // is list at the end?

// list iterator functions
void  ResetToHead ();   // set current back to start of the list
void  ResetToTail ();   // set current to the end of the list
void  Next ();          // moves current to the next item
```

```
 void  Previous ();      // moves current to  previous item

 // returns user data stored in the current node, 0 if none
 void* GetCurrentNode () const;

 // functions to copy or assign this list
 DoubleLinkedList (const DoubleLinkedList& r);
DoubleLinkedList& operator= (const DoubleLinkedList& r);

 // debugging test case display of all nodes and their values
 void  DebugDisplay (ostream& os, const char* title) const;

protected:
 void  CopyList (const DoubleLinkedList& r); // duplicate list
};
```

Here is the actual implementation. The major coding has already been discussed. You should look over the smaller functions as well as the more complex ones.

Implementation of a Generic DoubleLinkedList Class

```
#include <iomanip>
#include "DoubleLinkedList.h"

using namespace std;

/***************************************************************/
/*                                                             */
/* DoubleLinkedList: constructs an empty list                  */
/*                                                             */
/***************************************************************/

DoubleLinkedList::DoubleLinkedList () {
 headptr = tailptr = currentptr = 0;
 count = 0;
}

/***************************************************************/
/*                                                             */
/* ~DoubleLinkedList: destructor to remove all nodes           */
/*                                                             */
/***************************************************************/

DoubleLinkedList::~DoubleLinkedList () {
 EmptyList ();
}

/***************************************************************/
/*                                                             */
/* EmptyList: remove all nodes from the list                   */
/*                                                             */
/***************************************************************/

void  DoubleLinkedList::EmptyList () {
 if (!headptr) return;
 LinkNode* ptrnext = headptr; // pointer to traverse the list
```

```
 LinkNode* ptrdel;             // the node to delete
 // traverse the list - ends when there are no more nodes
 while (ptrnext) {
  ptrdel = ptrnext;          // save the current one to be deleted
  ptrnext = ptrdel->fwdptr; // point to the next node
  delete ptrdel;             // and delete the previous node
 }
 headptr = currentptr = tailptr = 0;
 count = 0;
}

/*********************************************************/
/*                                                       */
/* AddAtHead: insert new node at the beginning of list   */
/*                                                       */
/*********************************************************/

bool  DoubleLinkedList::AddAtHead (void* ptrdata) {
 // allocate a new node and fill it up
 LinkNode* ptrnew;
 try {
  ptrnew = new LinkNode;
 }
 catch (std::bad_alloc e) {
  cerr << "Error: out of memory\n";
  return false;
 }
 ptrnew->dataptr = ptrdata; // copy the passed client pointer
 ptrnew->backptr = 0;       // back pointer is 0 because at head
 count++;                   // increment total number of nodes
 // now chain this one into the list
 if (headptr) {             // if headptr exists, then the new
  ptrnew->fwdptr = headptr; // fwdptr contains the previous one
  headptr->backptr = ptrnew;// prev node's backptr is us now
  headptr = ptrnew;         // set headptr to newly added node
 }
 else {                     // empty list, so all ptrs point to
  headptr = tailptr = ptrnew; // this new node
  ptrnew->fwdptr = 0;       // and no forward nodes yet
 }
 currentptr = ptrnew; // leave the current one at the new one
 return true;
}

/*********************************************************/
/*                                                       */
/* AddAtTail: insert new node at the end of the list     */
/*                                                       */
/*********************************************************/

bool  DoubleLinkedList::AddAtTail (void* ptrdata) {
 LinkNode* ptrnew;
 try {
  ptrnew = new LinkNode;
 }
 catch (std::bad_alloc e) {
```

```
  cerr << "Error: out of memory\n";
  return false;
 }
 count++;                        // increment total number of nodes
 ptrnew->dataptr = ptrdata; // store the client pointer in node
 ptrnew->fwdptr = 0;           // at end, cannot be forward node
 if (tailptr) {                  // is there anything in the list yet?
  tailptr->fwdptr = ptrnew; // yes, prev tail node points to us
  ptrnew->backptr = tailptr;// us points back to the prev node
  tailptr = ptrnew;             // tail is now us
 }
 else {                          // no - list is empty,
  headptr = tailptr = ptrnew; // so set all to point to us
  ptrnew->backptr = 0;         // and there is no prev node
 }
 currentptr = ptrnew;          // leave with current node set to us
 return true;
}

/*******************************************************/
/*                                                     */
/* InsertAfterCurrentNode: add new node after the      */
/*                         current node                */
/*                                                     */
/*******************************************************/

bool  DoubleLinkedList::InsertAfterCurrentNode (void* ptrdata) {
 if (!headptr)          // list is empty so add at head
  return AddAtHead (ptrdata);
 else if (!currentptr) // current ptr is 0, so also add at head
  return AddAtHead (ptrdata);
 else if (IsTail())     // current ptr is the last node, so
  return AddAtTail (ptrdata); // reuse add at the tail
 else {                 // here we are inserting in the middle
  LinkNode* ptrnew;
  try {
   ptrnew = new LinkNode;
  }
  catch (std::bad_alloc e) {
   cerr << "Error: out of memory\n";
   return false;
  }
  ptrnew->dataptr = ptrdata;
  count++;
  // set new node's back pointer to current node to insert us
  ptrnew->backptr = currentptr;
  // set new node's forward ptr to the next node to the right
  ptrnew->fwdptr = currentptr->fwdptr;
  // set current's forward ptr to us to insert us
  currentptr->fwdptr = ptrnew;
  // set the node to the right of us to point back to us
  ptrnew->fwdptr->backptr = ptrnew;
  currentptr = ptrnew; // make the newly added node the current
 }
 return true;
}
```

```

/*****************************************************/
/*                                                   */
/* InsertBeforeCurrentNode: add new node before current  */
/*      node.                                        */
/*                                                   */
/*****************************************************/

bool  DoubleLinkedList::InsertBeforeCurrentNode (void* ptrdata) {
 if (!headptr)          // no nodes in list - so add at head
  return AddAtHead (ptrdata);
 else if (!currentptr)// no current ptr, so add at head too
  return AddAtHead (ptrdata);
 else if (IsHead())    // current ptr is the last node - so
  return AddAtHead(ptrdata); // add this one at the tail
 else {                 // here we are adding in the middle of list
  LinkNode* ptrnew;
  try {
   ptrnew = new LinkNode;
  }
  catch (std::bad_alloc e) {
   cerr << "Error: out of memory\n";
   return false;
  }
  ptrnew->dataptr = ptrdata;
  count++;
  // set new node's back ptr to current's back
  ptrnew->backptr = currentptr->backptr;
  // set new node's forward ptr to current node
  ptrnew->fwdptr = currentptr;
  // set current node's back ptr to point to us
  currentptr->backptr = ptrnew;
  // set prevous node's forward ptr to point to us
  ptrnew->backptr->fwdptr = ptrnew;
  currentptr = ptrnew; // set current pointer to the new node
  return true;
 }
}

/*****************************************************/
/*                                                   */
/* DeleteCurrentNode: removes the current node       */
/*    returns false if there is no current node      */
/*                                                   */
/*****************************************************/

bool  DoubleLinkedList::DeleteCurrentNode () {
 if (!currentptr) // if no current node, abort
  return false;
 count--;
 if (!count) { // will list now be empty? if so reset to 0
  delete currentptr;
  headptr = tailptr = currentptr = 0;
  return true;
 }
 LinkNode* ptrtodelete = currentptr;
```

```
 if (IsHead()) {                    // deleting first node? if so,
  currentptr->fwdptr->backptr = 0;// set next node's back to none
  headptr = currentptr->fwdptr;   // set head to next node
  currentptr = headptr;           // and current to next node
 }
 else if (IsTail()) {               // deleting last one, if so,
  currentptr->backptr->fwdptr = 0;// set prev node's fwd to none
  tailptr = currentptr->backptr;  // set tail to prev node
  currentptr = tailptr;           // set current to prev node
 }
 else { // here the node to delete is in the middle
  // set next node's back to previous node
  currentptr->fwdptr->backptr = currentptr->backptr;
  // set previous node's fwd to next node
  currentptr->backptr->fwdptr = currentptr->fwdptr;
  // leave current pointing to previous node
  currentptr = currentptr->backptr;
 }
 delete ptrtodelete; // now delete the requested node
 return true;
}

/***************************************************************/
/*                                                             */
/* GetSize: returns the number of nodes in the list            */
/*                                                             */
/***************************************************************/

long  DoubleLinkedList::GetSize () const {
 return count;
}

/***************************************************************/
/*                                                             */
/* IsHead: returns true if current node is the first node*/
/*                                                             */
/***************************************************************/

bool  DoubleLinkedList::IsHead () const {
 return currentptr == headptr;
}

/***************************************************************/
/*                                                             */
/* IsTail: returns true if current node is the last one        */
/*                                                             */
/***************************************************************/

bool  DoubleLinkedList::IsTail () const {
 return currentptr == tailptr;
}

/***************************************************************/
/*                                                             */
/* ResetToHead: sets current pointer to start of list          */
/*                                                             */
```

```
/***************************************************************/

void  DoubleLinkedList::ResetToHead () {
 currentptr = headptr;
}

/***************************************************************/
/*                                                             */
/* ResetToTail: sets current pointer to last node in list*/
/*                                                             */
/***************************************************************/

void  DoubleLinkedList::ResetToTail () {
 currentptr = tailptr;
}

/***************************************************************/
/*                                                             */
/* Next: move forward one node in the list                     */
/*                                                             */
/***************************************************************/

void  DoubleLinkedList::Next () {
 if (currentptr)
  currentptr = currentptr->fwdptr;
}

/***************************************************************/
/*                                                             */
/* Previous: backs up one node in the list                     */
/*                                                             */
/***************************************************************/

void  DoubleLinkedList::Previous () {
 if (currentptr)
  currentptr = currentptr->backptr;
}

/****************************************************************/
/*                                                              */
/* GetCurrentNode: returns user data at current node or 0 */
/*                                                              */
/****************************************************************/

void* DoubleLinkedList::GetCurrentNode () const {
 return currentptr ? (void*) currentptr->dataptr : 0;
}

/***************************************************************/
/*                                                             */
/* DoubleLinkedList: copy constructor - duplicate a list */
/*                                                             */
/***************************************************************/

DoubleLinkedList::DoubleLinkedList (const DoubleLinkedList& r) {
 CopyList (r);
```

```
}

/***************************************************************/
/*                                                             */
/* operator=: Make a duplicate copy of a list                  */
/*                                                             */
/***************************************************************/

DoubleLinkedList& DoubleLinkedList::operator= (
                  const DoubleLinkedList& r) {
 if (this == &r) return *this; // avoid a = a; situation
 EmptyList ();  // remove all items in this list
 CopyList (r);  // make a copy of r's list
 return *this;
}

/***************************************************************/
/*                                                             */
/* CopyList: Make a duplicate copy of a list                   */
/*                                                             */
/***************************************************************/

void  DoubleLinkedList::CopyList (const DoubleLinkedList& r) {
  // handle the empty list first
 if (!r.headptr) {
  headptr = currentptr = tailptr = 0;
  return;
 }
 count = r.count;
 LinkNode* ptrRcurrent = r.headptr;
 // previousptr tracks our prior node so we can set its
 // forward pointer to the next new one
 LinkNode* previousptr = 0;
 // prime the loop so headptr can be set one time
 try {
  currentptr = new LinkNode;
 }
 catch (std::bad_alloc e) {
  cerr << "Error: out of memory\n";
  return;
 }
 headptr = currentptr;  // assign this one to the headptr

 // traverse list r's nodes
 while (ptrRcurrent) {
  // copy r's student info into our new node
  currentptr->dataptr = ptrRcurrent->dataptr;
  currentptr->fwdptr = 0;  // set our forward ptr to 0
  currentptr->backptr = 0; // set our back ptr to 0
  // if previous node exists, set its forward ptr to the new one
  if (previousptr) {
   previousptr->fwdptr = currentptr;
   currentptr->backptr = previousptr;
  }
  // save this node as the prevous node
  previousptr = currentptr;
```

```
  // and get a new node for the next iteration
  try {
   currentptr = new LinkNode;
  }
  catch (std::bad_alloc e) {
   previousptr->fwdptr = 0; // end chain
   cerr << "Error: out of memory\n";
   return;
  }
  // move to r's next node
  ptrRcurrent = ptrRcurrent->fwdptr;
 }
 tailptr = previousptr;
 delete currentptr; // delete the extra unneeded node
 // leave list at the beginning
 ResetToHead ();
}

/*********************************************************/
/*                                                       */
/* FindNode: find the node whose data matches users      */
/*           specifications - calls user's Find Function */
/*                                                       */
/*********************************************************/

bool  DoubleLinkedList::FindNode (const void* ptrmatchData,
                                  FINDFUNCT Find) {
 if (!count) // empty list => not found
  return false;
 ResetToHead ();       // begin at the start of the list
 while (currentptr) {  // examine each node in turn
  if (Find (ptrmatchData, currentptr->dataptr) == 0)
   return true;        // return true if this one matches
  Next ();             // move to the next node in the list
 }
 return false;         // did not find it in whole list
}

/*********************************************************/
/*                                                       */
/* DebugDisplay: make nicely formatted display of list   */
/*                                                       */
/*********************************************************/

void  DoubleLinkedList::DebugDisplay (ostream& os,
                                      const char* title) const {
 os << endl << title << endl << dec;
 if (!headptr) {
  os << "head: " << setw(10) << headptr << endl;
  os << "tail: " << setw (10) << tailptr << endl;
  os << "curr: " << setw(10) << currentptr << endl;
  os << "count: " << setw(9) << count << endl << endl << endl;
  return;
 }
 LinkNode* ptr1, *ptr2, *ptrcur = headptr;
 os << "head: " << setw(10) << headptr;
```

```
 ptr1 = ptrcur;
 ptr2 = ptr1->fwdptr;
 os << "   Node At: " << setw(10) << ptr1;
 if (ptr2)
  os << "   Node At: " << setw(10) << ptr2;
 os << endl;
 os << "tail: " << setw (10) << tailptr;
 os << "       fwd: " << setw (10) << ptr1->fwdptr;
 if (ptr2)
  os << "       fwd: " << setw (10) << ptr2->fwdptr;
 os << endl;
 os << "curr: " << setw(10) << currentptr;
 os << "       bck: " << setw(10) << ptr1->backptr;
 if (ptr2)
  os << "       bck: " << setw(10) << ptr2->backptr;
 os << endl;
 os << "count: " << setw(9) << count;
 os << "       dat: " << setw(10) << ptr1->dataptr;
 if (ptr2)
  os << "       dat: " << setw(10) << ptr2->dataptr;
 os << endl << endl;
 while (ptr2 && ptr2->fwdptr) {
  ptr1 = ptr2->fwdptr;
  if (ptr1)
   ptr2 = ptr1->fwdptr;
  else
   ptr2 = 0;
  os << "                ";
  os << "   Node At: " << setw(10) << ptr1;
  if (ptr2)
   os << "   Node At: " << setw(10) << ptr2;
  os << endl;
  os << "                ";
  os << "       fwd: " << setw (10) << ptr1->fwdptr;
  if (ptr2)
   os << "       fwd: " << setw (10) << ptr2->fwdptr;
  os << endl;
  os << "                ";
  os << "       bck: " << setw(10) << ptr1->backptr;
  if (ptr2)
   os << "       bck: " << setw(10) << ptr2->backptr;
  os << endl;
  os << "                ";
  os << "       dat: " << setw(10) << ptr1->dataptr;
  if (ptr2)
   os << "       dat: " << setw(10) << ptr2->dataptr;
  os << endl << endl;
 }
 os << endl << endl;
}

```

The Stack Container

A stack is a linear, sequential access data structure. It has the property that the last item pushed or stored onto the stack is the first item that can be popped or removed from the stack. That is, a stack is LIFO. It is basically a very restricted version of a list in which all additions and removals occur at one end of the list.

One often sees stacks in operation is at a buffet restaurant where the plates are on a recessed, spring loaded, stainless steel dispenser cart. The bottom plate rests upon a spring. Customers take a plate from the stack from the top and the spring pushes the stack up. New plates are added at the top of the stack, pushing the spring and whole stack down. A multiple car family with a single car-wide driveway has experienced stack operations. If your car is at the bottom of the stack that is closest to the garage, then you have to move all the other cars out of the way, that is, pop them off of the stack, so you can get yours out.

Automatic and parameter variables in C++ are stored on a stack data structure. Undo operations in word processing and paint programs are implemented by storing the changes onto a stack. Stacks also are used in "artificial intelligence" type programs. For example, the problem of finding your way through any maze by trial and error is inherently a stack problem. The two major operations that a stack provides are called **Push** and **Pop** which puts a new item onto the top of the stack and removes the top item from the stack. Stacks are often implemented as a specialized single linked list. Table 7.3 shows the definition of a stack data structure.

Data Type	Stack
Domain	A stack is a collection of component whose values are all of the same data type
Structure	A list that is maintained in LIFO order so that only the most recently added item is available
Operations	
Initialize()	Creates an empty stack
Push()	Place a new item on the top of the stack
Pop()	Remove the current item from the top of the stack
IsEmpty()	Returns true if the stack is empty

Table 7.3 The Definition of the Stack Data Structure

If we implement the stack as a linked list, we can define the head of the list to be the top of the stack. Thus, we only need to implement **AddAtHead** and **RemoveAtHead** for **Push** and **Pop**. Here is the generic **Stack** class definition file.

The Generic Stack Definition File

```
#pragma once
#include <iostream>
using namespace std;

typedef ostream& (*DISPLAY) (ostream& os, const void* ptrdata);

/***************************************************************/
/*                                                             */
/* StackNode: contains the forward pointer and this item data  */
/*                                                             */
/***************************************************************/

```

```
struct StackNode {
 StackNode* fwdptr;
 void*      dataptr;
};

/*****************************************************************/
/*                                                               */
/* Stack: a generic stack class                                  */
/*                                                               */
/*****************************************************************/

/*****************************************************************/
/*                                                               */
/* Usage Notes: This class stores client data in void pointers */
/*   thus, before the destructor is called, the client pgm      */
/*   must delete the actual data being stored.                   */
/*                                                               */
/*   A sample destruction sequence might be as follows           */
/*   MyData* ptrd;                                               */
/*   while (!stack.IsEmpty()) {                                  */
/*    ptrd = (MyData*) stack.Pop();                              */
/*    delete ptrd;                                               */
/*   }                                                           */
/*                                                               */
/* If a copy of the stack is made, a shallow copy is done.      */
/* Only the pointers to the client data are copied.              */
/* The actual client data being stored is not duplicated.        */
/*                                                               */
/*****************************************************************/

class Stack {
protected:
 StackNode* headptr;     // the top of the stack pointer
 long       count;       // the number of items in the stack

public:
 Stack ();               // construct an empty stack
 Stack (const Stack& s); // the copy constructor
 Stack& operator= (const Stack& s); // the assignment operator

 ~Stack ();              // delete the stack

 bool Push (void* ptrdata); // store this new node on the stack
 void* Pop ();           // removes top node from the stack
 void* GetCurrentData () const; // returns user's data on top
 long GetCount () const; // returns the number of nodes in stack

 bool IsEmpty () const;  // returns true if stack is empty
 void RemoveAll ();      // removes all nodes in the stack

 // display all items on the stack nicely formatted
 ostream& DebugDisplay (ostream& os, DISPLAY Display) const;

protected:
 // helper function to duplicate the stack
 void CopyStack (const Stack& s);
```

```
};
```

Here is the actual implementation of the generic **Stack** class.

The Generic Stack Implementation File

```
#include "Stack.h"

/***************************************************************/
/*                                                             */
/* Stack: create an empty stack                                */
/*                                                             */
/***************************************************************/

Stack::Stack () {
 headptr = 0;
 count = 0;
}

/***************************************************************/
/*                                                             */
/* ~Stack: deletes the stack                                   */
/*                                                             */
/***************************************************************/

Stack::~Stack () {
 RemoveAll ();
}

/***************************************************************/
/*                                                             */
/* RemoveAll: deletes all nodes of the stack                   */
/*                                                             */
/***************************************************************/

void Stack::RemoveAll () {
 while (!IsEmpty()) Pop ();
}

/***************************************************************/
/*                                                             */
/* Push: store new node on the top of the stack                */
/*       returns false when out of memory                      */
/*                                                             */
/***************************************************************/

bool Stack::Push (void* ptrdata) {
 StackNode* ptrnew;
 try {
  ptrnew = new StackNode;
 }
 catch (std::bad_alloc e) {
  cerr << "Error: out of memory\n";
  return false;
 }
 ptrnew->dataptr = ptrdata;
```

```
 ptrnew->fwdptr = headptr;
 headptr = ptrnew;
 count++;
 return true;
}

/***************************************************************/
/*                                                             */
/* Pop: remove the top item from the stack                     */
/*                                                             */
/***************************************************************/

void* Stack::Pop () {
 if (!headptr) return 0;
 StackNode* ptrtodel = headptr;
 headptr = headptr->fwdptr;
 void* ptrdata = ptrtodel->dataptr;
 delete ptrtodel;
 count--;
 return ptrdata;
}

/***************************************************************/
/*                                                             */
/* GetCurrentData: returns a pointer to user data on the top   */
/*                 of the stack or 0 if it is empty            */
/*                                                             */
/***************************************************************/

void* Stack::GetCurrentData () const {
 return !IsEmpty () ? headptr->dataptr : 0;
}

/***************************************************************/
/*                                                             */
/* IsEmpty: returns true when there are no items on the stack  */
/*                                                             */
/***************************************************************/

bool Stack::IsEmpty () const{
 return headptr ? false : true;
}

/***************************************************************/
/*                                                             */
/* GetCount: returns the number of nodes on the stack          */
/*                                                             */
/***************************************************************/

long Stack::GetCount () const {
 return count;
}

/***************************************************************/
/*                                                             */
/* Stack: copy constructor - make a duplicate copy of passed s */
```

```
/*                                                                */
/******************************************************************/

Stack::Stack (const Stack& s) {
 CopyStack (s);
}

/******************************************************************/
/*                                                                */
/* operator=: assignment op - makes a copy of passed stack        */
/*                                                                */
/******************************************************************/

Stack& Stack::operator= (const Stack& s) {
 if (this == &s) return *this; // avoid a = a; situation
 RemoveAll ();  // remove all items in this stack
 CopyStack (s);  // make a copy of stack s
 return *this;
}

/******************************************************************/
/*                                                                */
/* CopyStack: helper that makes a duplicate copy                  */
/*                                                                */
/******************************************************************/

void Stack::CopyStack (const Stack& s) {
 if (!s.headptr) { // handle stack s being empty
  headptr = 0;
  count = 0;
  return;
 }
 count = s.count;
 StackNode* ptrScurrent = s.headptr;
 // previousptr tracks our prior node so we can set its
 // forward pointer to the next new one
 StackNode* previousptr = 0;
 // prime the loop so headptr can be set one time
 StackNode* currentptr;
 try {
  currentptr = new StackNode;
 }
 catch (std::bad_alloc e) {
  cerr << "Error: out of memory\n";
  return;
 }
 headptr = currentptr;  // assign this one to the headptr

// traverse s stack's nodes
 while (ptrScurrent) {
  // copy node of s into our new node
  currentptr->dataptr = ptrScurrent->dataptr;
  currentptr->fwdptr = 0;  // set our forward ptr to 0
  // if previous node exists, set its forward ptr to the new one
  if (previousptr)
   previousptr->fwdptr = currentptr;
```

```
  // save this node as the prevous node
  previousptr = currentptr;
  // and get a new node for the next iteration
  try {
   currentptr = new StackNode;
  }
  catch (std::bad_alloc e) {
   cerr << "Error: out of memory\n";
   return;
  }
  // move to s's next node
  ptrScurrent = ptrScurrent->fwdptr;
 }
 delete currentptr; // delete the extra unneeded node
}

/***************************************************************/
/*                                                             */
/* DebugDisplay: display all items on stack nicely formatted   */
/*                                                             */
/***************************************************************/

ostream& Stack::DebugDisplay (ostream& os, DISPLAY Display)const{
 os << "Debug display of the stack from top to bottom\n";
 StackNode* ptrnext = headptr;
 while (ptrnext) {
  Display (os, ptrnext->dataptr);
  ptrnext = ptrnext->fwdptr;
 }
 os << "\nDebug display finished\n";
 return os;
}
```

The Queue Container Class

Recall that a queue is a linear, sequential data structure with the properties that new items are added at one end of the list, the front, while items are removed from the other end of the list, the rear of the list. Queues are usually implemented as a variation of a double linked list data structure. A queue supports two key operations, **Enqueue** and **Dequeue** for the insertion of a new item and the removal of an existing item.

Examples of queues abound in the real world. The line of ticket purchasers at a movie theater is a queue. New arrivals are enqueued at the rear of the line. Tickets are sold only to those at the front of the queue. When purchasing your flight tickets at an airport, you stand often in a long queue waiting your turn. Similarly, the waiting room of a doctor can be modeled as a queue.

Programs that model assembly line operations use queues to simulate the line's action. A new car's engine appears at the end of the line. Workers then do various actions to it as it moves along the line. It is then removed from the other end of the line when they are finished.

Farmers who are loading cattle into a cattle truck force the cows into a queue to enter the truck. Students registering for school classes are formed into queues. Your car is forced into a queue behind the teller window when you go to the drive up window of a bank to make a deposit or withdrawal.

Table 7.4 gives the definition of the queue data structure. Queues are often called FIFO, first in, first out lists.

Data Type	Queue
Domain	A queue is a collection of component whose values are all of the same data type
Structure	A queue is a list that is maintained in first in, first out order. That is, insertions are done at the rear of the list, and removals are done at the head of the list.
Operations	
Initialize()	Create an empty queue
Enqueue()	Add an item at the rear of the queue
Dequeue()	Remove an item from the head of the queue
IsEmpty()	Returns true if the queue is empty

Table 7.4 The Queue Data Structure Definition

The enqueue function is basically adding a new node at the tail. So we really have **AddAtTail** renamed to **Enqueue**. The **Dequeue** function is just removing a node from the head of the list which is simpler to do than removing a node from the middle of the list. Hence, a queue class based on a double linked list is actually much simpler to implement than a double linked list. There are far fewer functions and possibilities.

In addition to the constructor, **Enqueue**, and **Dequeue** functions, we must support list traversal. The functions **ResetToHead**, **GetCount** and **GetNext** allows anyone to write loops to process all items in the queue. The destructor removes all items from the queue as usual, However, I provide a **RemoveAll** function to actually empty the queue. The destructor calls this function and a client program can also invoke it to empty the queue for its reuse.

To be robust, the **Queue** class must also support the copy constructor and the assignment operator. As usual, since both must copy a given queue, the helper function **CopyQueue** actually does the work of duplicating a queue. Here is the **Queue** class definition file.

The Queue Definition File

```
#pragma once

/***************************************************************/
/*                                                             */
/* QueueNode: stores the double linked list's fwd/back ptrs    */
/*            and the user's data ptr                          */
/*                                                             */
/***************************************************************/

struct QueueNode {    // a double linked list
 QueueNode* fwdptr;
 QueueNode* backptr;
 void*      dataptr; // the user's object being stored
};

/***************************************************************/
/*                                                             */
/* Queue Container Class                                       */
/*                                                             */
/* stores void pointers to user's objects                      */
/* before deleting an instance, the user MUST traverse and     */
```

```
/* delete any objects whose pointers are being stored           */
/*                                                              */
/****************************************************************/

class Queue {

public:
 Queue ();                             // makes an empty queue
 Queue (const Queue& q);               // copy constructor
 Queue& operator= (const Queue& q); // assignment operator
 // VITAL NOTE: when a copy is made, the copy contains the SAME
 // pointers as the original Queue - be careful not to delete
 // them twice

 ~Queue ();            // the destructor removes the queue
 void  RemoveAll (); // but not the user objects being stored!

 bool  Enqueue (void* ptrdata);// add another object to the queue
 void* Dequeue ();             // return and remove current node
 long  GetSize () const;       // returns the size of the queue

 void  ResetToHead (); // reset current to the start of the queue
 void* GetNext ();     // returns next user object or 0 when at
                       // the end of the queue
 // for cleanup operations, traverse the queue and delete the
 // objects the queue is saving for you before you destroy or
 // empty the queue

/****************************************************************/
/*                                                              */
/* for Queue's internal use only                                */
/* Queue uses a double linked list                              */
/*                                                              */
/****************************************************************/

private:
 QueueNode* headptr;    // pointer to first node
 QueueNode* tailptr;    // pointer to last node
 QueueNode* currentptr; // the current node when traversing
 long       count;      // the number of nodes

 // helper function to copy a Queue
 void  CopyQueue (const Queue& q);
};
```

Here is the complete **Queue** class implementation. It is very straightforward.

The Queue Implementation File

```
#include <iostream>
#include "queue.h"

using namespace std;

/****************************************************************/
/*                                                              */
```

```
/* Queue: construct an empty queue                                   */
/*                                                                   */
/*********************************************************************/

Queue::Queue () {
 headptr = currentptr = tailptr = 0;
 count = 0;
}

/*********************************************************************/
/*                                                                   */
/* ~Queue: remove all QueueNode objects - but does not delete        */
/*         any user objects                                          */
/*                                                                   */
/*********************************************************************/

Queue::~Queue () {
 RemoveAll ();
}

/*********************************************************************/
/*                                                                   */
/* RemoveAll: removes all QueueNode Objects, leaving the queue       */
/*            in an empty but valid state                            */
/*                                                                   */
/*********************************************************************/

void Queue::RemoveAll () {
 if (!headptr) return;          // nothing to do case
 QueueNode* ptrnext = headptr; // start at the front of the queue
 QueueNode* ptrdel;
 while (ptrnext) {            // for all QueueNodes,
  ptrdel = ptrnext;           // save pointer for later deletion
  ptrnext = ptrnext->fwdptr;// set for next node in the queue
  delete ptrdel;              // remove this node
 }
 // leave queue in a default, valid , empty state
 currentptr = tailptr = headptr = 0;
 count = 0;
}

/*********************************************************************/
/*                                                                   */
/* Queue Copy Constructor: duplicate the passed Queue object         */
/*                                                                   */
/* VITAL: we will not duplicate the user's actual data               */
/*                                                                   */
/*********************************************************************/

Queue::Queue (const Queue& q) {
 CopyQueue (q);               // call helper function to do the work
}

/*********************************************************************/
/*                                                                   */
/* Operator= - Assignment operator: duplicate this Queue object*/
```

```
/*                                                                  */
/* VITAL: we will not duplicate the user's actual data              */
/*                                                                  */
/********************************************************************/

Queue& Queue::operator= (const Queue& q) {
 if (&q == this) return *this; // avoid silly case of x = x;
 if (count != 0) RemoveAll (); // if we are not empty, empty us
 CopyQueue (q);                // call helper function to do it
 return *this;                 // return us so user can chain
}

/********************************************************************/
/*                                                                  */
/* CopyQueue: make a shallow copy of the passed queue               */
/*                                                                  */
/* VITAL: we will not duplicate the user's actual data              */
/*                                                                  */
/********************************************************************/

void  Queue::CopyQueue (const Queue& q) {
 // initialize queue so that we can use Enqueue to add the nodes
 currentptr = tailptr = headptr = 0;
 count = 0;
 if (!q.count) // if there are none, queue is now initialized
  return;
 QueueNode* ptrqcurrent = q.headptr;// point to their head
 while (ptrqcurrent) {              // while there's another node
  if (!Enqueue (ptrqcurrent->dataptr)) // add it to our queue
   return;                             // abort if out of memory
  ptrqcurrent = ptrqcurrent->fwdptr;// point to next one to copy
 }
}

/********************************************************************/
/*                                                                  */
/* Enqueue: Add a new node to the tail of the queue                 */
/*                                                                  */
/********************************************************************/

bool  Queue::Enqueue (void* ptrdata) { // Add at Tail
 QueueNode* ptrnew;
 try {
  ptrnew = new QueueNode;    // make new node
 }
 catch (std::bad_alloc e) {
  cerr << "Error: out of memory\n";
  return false;
 }
 ptrnew->dataptr = ptrdata;     // insert user's object
 count++;                       // increment number of nodes
 if (tailptr) {                 // if there are other nodes,
  tailptr->fwdptr = ptrnew;     // last one now points to us
  ptrnew->backptr = tailptr;    // us points to previous last one
  ptrnew->fwdptr = 0;           // us points to none
  tailptr = currentptr = ptrnew;// reset tail to us
```

```
 }
 else { // queue is currently empty, so just add us
  headptr = tailptr = currentptr = ptrnew;
  ptrnew->fwdptr = ptrnew->backptr = 0;
 }
 return true;
}

/***************************************************************/
/*                                                             */
/* Dequeue: return object at the head and delete that node     */
/*                                                             */
/***************************************************************/

void* Queue::Dequeue () { // remove at head
 if (!headptr) return 0;       // we are empty, so do nothing
 currentptr = headptr;         // reset to the head object
 if (headptr->fwdptr)          // is there more than one node?
  headptr->fwdptr->backptr = 0;// yes,set next one's back to none
 headptr = headptr->fwdptr;    // reset head ptr to the next one
 count--;                      // decrement count of nodes
 if (count == 0) tailptr = 0;  // reset tailptr if queue is empty
 void* retval = currentptr->dataptr;// save object to be returned
 delete currentptr;            // remove previous head object
 currentptr = headptr;         // reset the current node ptr
 return retval;                // give the user their object
}

/***************************************************************/
/*                                                             */
/* GetSize: returns the number of items in the queue          */
/*                                                             */
/***************************************************************/

long  Queue::GetSize () const {
 return count;
}

/***************************************************************/
/*                                                             */
/* ResetToHead: reset currentptr to head pointer for queue     */
/*              traversal operations                           */
/*                                                             */
/***************************************************************/

void  Queue::ResetToHead () {
 currentptr = headptr;
}

/***************************************************************/
/*                                                             */
/* GetNext: returns next user object & sets currentptr for next*/
/*                                                             */
/***************************************************************/

void* Queue::GetNext () {
```

```
 if (!currentptr) return 0;       // queue is empty, so do nothing
 void* retval = currentptr->dataptr;// save object to be returned
 currentptr = currentptr->fwdptr;// set currentptr to next in one
 return retval;                   // give the user the current obj
}
```

Review Questions

1. What is meant by a growable array? Why does storing the data as **void*** lead to a generic reuseable class?

2. What are the pro's and con's of storing the user's data as a void pointer in a container class?

3. Explain the concept of a double linked list. How does it work? Illustrate your answer with a drawing of how it operates.

4. What is the impact on client programs when the linked list class stores a copy of the client's data in the link nodes versus storing only a **void*** to that data? Be specific.

5. If a linked list class is storing only **void** pointers to the user's data, how can the linked list class ever be able to find any node that matches the user's criteria? Illustrate your answer with a drawing showing how this works.

6. What is meant by a call back function?

7. When loading data from a file into a linked list, what is the difference between always calling **AddAtHead** versus always calling **AddAtTail**?

8. Explain the concept of how a stack works. Illustrate your answer with a drawing of what happens when an item is pushed onto the stack and when an item is popped from the stack.

9. A stack is often implemented as a linked list. What are the differences between a linked list and a stack? How does this affect operations on the list and stack?

10. What is the effect on a client program when the stack nodes are storing a copy of the user's data (or pointer to) or storing a **void** pointer to the user's data? Is there any impact on the client program's clean up activities?

11. Under what circumstances would a programmer opt to implement a stack class using an array of stack nodes whose array bounds was fixed at compile-time?

12. Since a queue is implemented using a double linked list, how does queue processing differ from that of a linked list?

13. What is the difference between a stack's **Push** function and a queue's **Enqueue** function? What functions of a double linked list class correspond to these two functions?

14. Why is it sometimes reasonable to implement a queue with a built-in array instead of a linked list of dynamically allocated nodes?

Stop! Do These Exercises Before Programming

1. Revise the **Array** container class above and implement the **[] operator** as an alternative to **GetAt** function.

2. After much work a programmer finally has his **Line** class operational. Now he turns his attention to the client drafting program which must store an unknown number of lines. He decides to use our **Array** container. Here is his beginning of the client program. When it runs, there is a massive memory leak. Correct his errors.

```
...
#include "Array.h"
int main () {
 {
  Array a;
  Line* ptrl;
  for (int k=0; k<100; k++) {
   ptrl = new Line;
   a.Add (ptrl);
  }
  a.RemoveAll();
 }
 memory leak checking here
```

3. This time our programmer decided to be wise and use our **DoubleLinkedList** class as his container class in his latest programming project. He thought, “What can possibly go wrong this time?” His application needs to perform real time inquiry and update of automobile parts for Acme’s Finest Cars company. He created an initial test data file, corresponding structure and then attempted to load the input file into the array. The following coding failed miserably. Why? How can it be repaired so that it works?

```
...
struct PARTS {
 long partNum;
 int qtyOnHand;
 double cost;
};

int main () {
 DoubleLinkedList parts;
 ifstream infile ("parts.txt", ios::in | ios::nocreate);
 PARTS part;
 while (infile >> part.partNum >> part.qtyOnHand >> part.cost) {
  parts.AddAtTail (&part);
 }

 parts.ResetToHead();
 PARTS* ptrp = parts.GetCurrentNode ();
 while (ptrp) {
  cout << ptrp->partNum << "  " << ptrp->qtyOnHand << endl;
  parts.Next();
  ptrp = parts.GetCurrentNode ();
 }
 return 0;
}
```

4. With your assistance, he now has encapsulated the loading of the file in a function and gotten it to load properly and display fine. However, he now finds that he has a memory leak. He tried to fix it as follows. It did not work. Help the programmer out, correct his errors.

```
int main () {
 DoubleLinkedList parts;
 LoadParts (parts, "parts.txt");
 DisplayParts (parts);
 parts.EmptyList ();
 return 0;
}
```

5. Having gotten his program to load, display and clean up properly, he now has written the main menu and has embarked upon implementing the various menu choices. He has written the following for his **FindAPart** function. It does not work and he begs you for assistance once more. Find his errors so that this function works properly.

```
int main () {
 DoubleLinkedList parts;
...
 FindAPart (parts);
...
 parts.EmptyList ();
 return 0;
}

void FindAPart (DoubleLinkedList p) {
 char c;
 long num;
 cout << "Enter the number of the part to find: ";
 cin >> num;
 if (p.FindNode (&num, FindPart)) {
  PARTS* ptrpart = (PARTS*) p.GetCurrentNode ();
  cout ... this ptrpart fields...
 }
 else
  cout << "Error: part not found\n";
}

int FindPart (const void* ptrmatch, const void* ptrthis) {
 LinkNode* ptrpart = (LinkNode*) ptrthis;
 long* ptrnum = (long*) ptrmatch;
 if (ptrnum == ptrpart->ptrdata)
  return 0;
 else
  return 1;
}
```

6. Our programmer is confronted with a time-critical application. In real-time, his application helps predict space shuttle engine burns to move the shuttle out of the way of space debris that is on a collision course with the shuttle. That is, his application must execute quickly or there would be insufficient time for the shuttle to dodge the debris. He knows that his stack will never hold any more than 100 items. Thus, he has chosen to implement his **SpaceStack** by using an array of **StackNodes**. He began his class definition as follows.

```
struct SpaceData {
... // contents are not important to the problem at hand
};
```

```
struct SpaceNode {
 int forward;
 SpaceData spaceData;
};

const int MAX = 100;

class SpaceStack {
protected:
 SpaceNode array[MAX];
 int headIdx;
public:
  SpaceStack ();
 ~SpaceStack ();
  void Push (SpaceData& data);
  SpaceData Pop ();
  bool IsEmpty () const;
};
```

His documentation indicates that the **headIdx** stores the subscript of the top item on the stack. The stack is empty when the **headIdx** contains –1. The stack is full when it contains the value of **MAX**. He has written the following thus far.

```
SpaceStack::SpaceStack () {
  headIdx = -1;
}

bool SpaceStack::IsEmpty () const {
  return headIdx < 0 ? true : false;
}
```

Unfortunately, just at this point in the programming project, he became ill and the project manager has asked you for some assistance on this critical program.

Write the coding required to implement the **Push** function.

7. Write the coding to implement the **Pop** function.

8. Write the coding to implement the destructor.

9. Using the generic **Queue** class, implement a new function, **BailOut**. Sometimes when people are involved in a queue situation, they decide not to wait it out and just leave the queue. Thus, applications need a method of removing an arbitrary node from the queue. The function's prototype is

```
void* BailOut (void* ptrMatchCriteria,
               BAILFUNCT FindThisNode);
```

and the **typedef** for the user call back function is

```
typedef int (*BAILFUNCT) (const void* ptrMatchCriteria,
                          const void* ptrdata);
```

Specifically, the **FindThisNode** function returns 0 if this data matches the criteria, a negative value if this data is less than the matching criteria and a positive number if greater.

BailOut should find the matching node and delete it, returning a pointer to the user's data. This way, the client can then delete their data. If the node is not found, return 0.

Programming Problems

Problem Pgm07-1 The Revised Array Container Class

The **Array** class as presented in this chapter is very inefficient when storing large numbers of items. Consider the **Add** function implementation. Suppose that 10,000 items were consecutively added by the client program. How many times is the temporary array allocated and all previous items copied? Worse still, during the add process, we have allocated in memory both the current array and the temporary larger array before the current array gets deleted. The result is that as the number of items in the array increases, the poorer the performance of our **Array** class add operations.

This serious design problem can be rectified by adding two new members to the class. If a user knew that there were likely to be at least 10,000 items to be added when they initially allocate the array, allow them to specify an initial size for the array. Further, every time the array needs to be grown, we are adding only one element. Suppose we let the user specify a grow by value. Here is how the default constructor's prototype should be redesigned.

```
Array (long initialSize = 0, long growBy = 1);
```

By using the default arguments, the client can create instances as follows.

```
Array a;                // initial size = 0, grow by 1
Array b (10000);        // initial size = 10000, grow by 1
Array c (10000, 100);   // initial size = 10000, grow by 100
```

Redesign the **Array** class to store two additional member variables, **initialSize** and **growBy**. You have two choices for the handling of the initial size. If an array begins with space allocated for say 100 pointers, how do they get filled? One method is to provide a SetAt function and let the user call it to set the data items until SetAt returns an indicator that the array size has been exceeded at which point the user would have to call the Add function to cause the array to grow. The other method is to have the array class itself track where the next available array location is at and to grow the array when necessary. The second method is preferable from the user's viewpoint since the array is handling all of the details.

Thoroughly test your new array class.

Problem Pgm07-2 The Acme Music Store's Sheet Music in Stock Program

Acme Music Store carries a wide line of sheet music, much of which is always in stock. They desire a program to allow them to perform real time inquiries while the customer is waiting.

Each piece of sheet music carries their stock number on it. They maintain a data base of sheet music in stock called **music.txt** located in the **TestDataForAssignments Pgm07-2** folder. Each line contains the stock number (4 numerical digits), composer's name (21 characters), the title (31 characters), the quantity in stock at the moment and the cost of the music.

When the program begins, it should allocate an instance of the **DoubleLinkedList** class. Make no changes in that class. Input the file of music in stock into that linked list instance, always adding at the tail. Then display the main menu.

```
Acme Music Store - Sheet Music Inventory Program

1. Check on availability of a piece of music by stock number
2. Find a piece of music given the composer
3. Find a piece of music given the title
4. Exit the program

Enter the number of your choice: _
```

When choice 1 is made, prompt the user to enter the four digit stock number and then look it up in the list. If the item is found, display its information nicely formatted on the screen. If it is not found, so state.

When choice 2 or 3 is made, prompt the user to enter the composer or music title. Then search the list for any matches. The search should be case insensitive. If one is found, display that item's information nicely formatted along with an option to continue the search. Remember, that there can be more than one piece of music written by any specific composer and some works may have duplicate titles.

Thoroughly test your program. You may add additional data to the music.txt file to ensure that your program is working perfectly.

Problem Pgm07-3 Balanced () and [] in a C++ Program

One coding problem that sometimes occurs in writing expressions or a program statement is that of mismatched pairs of parentheses or square brackets. Acme wishes you to develop a "Programmer's Helper" program that finds mismatched items. The program is given a file consisting of one or more lines of coding of any type. The program then identifies the mismatched pairs.

Create a stack to hold one character which can be (or) or [or]. Input the data line by line. Then, process each character of that line. If the current character is a begin symbol (or [, then push it onto the stack. If the current character is an ending parenthesis, then pop the current symbol off the stack. Match the current ending one with the beginning one. If they form a matching pair, all is well. If they do not match, such as a [with), then display an error message that is appropriate. The following is an example of how the results can be displayed.

```
X = (y[2[ + (x - y) * (sin(angle)));
        ^                          ^

expected ]
extra )
```

Here is another example.

```
if ((x == (y/2)] && a]2] > (x - y)) {
               ^     ^ ^          ^

expected )
expected )
expected )
extra )
  R = s * 42 * sin[angle));
                        ^^

expected ]
extra )
}
```

Sometimes there is no real way you can easily tell what is really wrong as in the series of "expected)" messages where the] brackets are out of sync with each other.

You may place the error messages onto another message list instance to facilitate their proper display after the line and the ^ line are displayed.

Consider each line as a separate entity—that is, do not attempt to continue the process across line boundaries. The following is an example.

```
  R = s * 42 * sin(angle)(;
                         ^

missing )
```

Thoroughly test your program.

Problem Pgm07-4 Announcing the Galactic Treaty Game

The Galactic Omega Confederation, consisting of a number of planets scattered across a vast space, was at war. However, at Planet X, a peace treaty was signed. However, none of the rulers of the various planets will believe the treaty unless they see it with their own eyes. Thus, you have been hired to fly a space ship to each planet and show the signed treaty to each planetary ruler. The objective is to travel the minimum total distance and thus complete the process in the shortest amount of time thereby ending the war as fast as possible. Simplifying the process, all of the planetary systems lie in a common two-dimensional plane of the galaxy.

Each planet is located by its (x, y) coordinates. The distance between planet1 and planet2 whose coordinates are (x1, y1) and (x2, y2) respectively, is given by the following formula.

$$\text{Distance} = \text{sqrt} \; (\; (x2-x1)^2 + (y2-y1)^2 \;)$$

The program inputs a file of planet information and then displays the minimum total distance traveled along with the order of the planets.

Each line contains the planet's name, x and y coordinates. All coordinate values are in the same units. The name is abstract, such as "Planet 1" and can contain nine characters maximum. All coordinates are doubles. Further, the very first line is the location of Planet X, the starting point where the treaty was signed.

The program output should be something like the following.

```
Planet Visited    Total Distance Thus Far
Planet X                   0.0
Planet A                  10.3
Planet E                  15.3
...
Total Distance Traveled: 1000.2
```

Test your program using the provided file called **Planets.txt** which is located in the **TestDataForAssignments** folder under the **Pgm07-4** folder.

Problem Pgm07-5 The Veterinarian's Patient Processing Program

A veterinarian needs a program to manage his processing of his patients. When a person arrives with their pet, the pet information is input into a **Pet** structure. Next, the pet record is entered into his queue of patients at the proper location. The pet information consists of the owner's name (20 characters), the pet's name (20 characters), and an integer emergency code (0 = normal, 1 = emergency).

When the vet finishes with a patient, that animal is removed from the queue. The vet then takes the next patient in the queue unless there is an emergency patient in the queue. His algorithm to choose the next patient is to take the next patient in the queue unless there is another patient in the queue whose emergency code is 1. Should there be more than one emergency, he handles them in the order that they arrived.

To simulate the day's operations, a transaction file is used. Each record in the file consists of four fields:

action code (1 character) A (add this patient) or H (handle next patient)
owner's name
pet's name
emergency code (0 or 1)

If the action code is H, then the other three fields are not present. If the action code is A, then the other three fields are present.

In the **TestDataForAssignments** folder under the **Pgm07-5** folder is a test data file called **patients.txt**. Your program should input this file and process them. Your program output should be similar to the following.

```
Added:   Samuel Spade          Fido       0
Added:   John Jones            Rover      0
Added:   Betsy Ann Smithville  Jenny      0
Treated: Samuel Spade          Fido       0
Treated: John Jones            Rover      0
Added:   Lou Ann deVille       Kitty      1
Treated: Lou Ann deVille       Kitty      1
Added:   Tom Smythe            Fifi       0
Added:   Marie Longfellow      Jack       1
Treated: Marie Longfellow      Jack       1
Treated: Betsy Ann Smithville  Jenny      0
Treated: Tom Smythe            Fifi       0
```

Chapter 8—Templates

Introduction

A **template** is a model or blueprint for the compiler to follow when the compiler needs to create a function or a class. The idea is to write a generic model for a function or even a whole class and then let the compiler use this model to create specific instances tailored to the specific data types that the compiler encounters in a program.

Footnote: the syntax for templates is just awful. In the industry, programmers either love or detest templates. There seems to be no middle ground. My personal opinion is that templates are hideous in nature and a nightmare to debug and get working. They are definitely an advanced C++ topic. However, I will do my best to present templates in an understandable manner and to effectively illustrate their need and uses.

To see the need for templates, let's examine an extremely simple C function, **max**, which returns the larger of two values. Suppose first that your application needed to obtain the maximum of two integers and this capability was needed in numerous places within the application. One would not hesitate a moment to create a **max** function such as this.

```
int max (int x, int y) {
 return x>y ? x : y;
}
```

Now later on, the data types change and you find that you need **max** written for a pair of doubles. So you code

```
double max (double x, double y) {
 return x>y ? x : y;
}
```

And then you need one for a pair of long values and then unsigned short values and then a pair of char values and then for a pair of strings. So you write these additional versions of **max**.

```
long max (long x, long y) {
 return x>y ? x : y;
}
unsigned short max (unsigned short x, unsigned short y) {
 return x>y ? x : y;
}
char max (char x, char y) {
 return x>y ? x : y;
}
char* max (char* x, char* y) {
 return x>y ? x : y;
}
```

Oops. With strings, we cannot compare memory addresses. It must be rewritten as follows.

```
char* max (char* x, char* y) {
 return stricmp (x, y) > 0 ? x : y;
}
```

There is really no problem doing this repetitive coding; functions can be overloaded. So when a **max** function is needed for **CostRecord** structures, we go ahead and write yet another version.

```
CostRecord& max (CostRecord& x, CostRecord& y) {
 return x.qty > y.qty ? x : y;
}
```

With the exception of the last two versions of **max**, the coding of the function bodies is identical. Only the data types have changed. This is where a template **max** function shines. The objective is to write a model for compiler to follow and let it build the actual function for the specified data types it encounters in this particular program. The syntax of a template function is as follows.

```
template<list of generic types>
the function header using these generic types
  and the corresponding function body implemented using
  these generic types
```

The generic type is called **name** after the keyword class "name"—often it is coded as T. If there are more than one generic type of data, then the subsequent types are usually called U, V and so on. In the syntax notation found with templates, the keyword **class** means type of data and has absolutely nothing to do with OOP classes. (I find this most confusing for beginners.) Thus, the "list of generic types" becomes

```
class T, class U, int, double
```

Generic types can be interspersed with intrinsic types or even hard-coded classes and structures.

To implement **max** as a template function, in the header file we code the following.

```
template <class T>
const T& max (const T& x, const T& y) {
 return x>y ? x : y;
}
```

The first line says that here comes a single template function. This function has one generic data type, **T**. The second line is the function header written in terms of this generic type **T**. Notice that constant references are used. Why? Because when the compiler creates specific instances of this function, any kind of data can be passed. It is more efficient in the long run to use constant references unless you know for certain that only intrinsic built-in types such as **char**, **short**, **int**, or **long** will ever be used. The third line then provides the implementation written in terms of the parameters. However, other variables could have been defined within the body, including those of type **T**.

Now in the cpp files, such as the **main** function, the programmer codes the following.

```
int a, b, c;
c = max (a, b);
double d, e, f;
f = max (d, e);
```

The compiler looks over all known prototypes to find one for a function **max** that takes two integer parameters. It does not find one. However, it does find a template version of **max**. Here the program is passing **max** two integer parameters. So the compiler examines the template version to see what it is passed. It also is passed two items of the same data type, **T**. Thus, if the compiler substitutes **int** for **T**, it can generate the required **max** function and so does. Next, the compiler encounters another version of **max** which is passed two **doubles**. Again, it makes a **double** version of **max** by substituting **double** for **T** in the template version.

All template definitions must be in a header file. The template statement must precede each and every function definition. The function body follows the template function's definition.

One can instruct the compiler to use a particular form of a function by coding the data type(s) to be substituted for the template parameters by coding the data types desired separated by commas inside a pair of angle brackets. In the following line, the compiler is told to generate a **double** version of **max**.

```
f = max<double>(d, e);
```

This variation is useful when the actual parameters differ. It is also required when at least one of the types is not a formal argument and cannot therefore be deduced. This usually happens when that type is used as the return data type. Consider the following template for a **compare** function.

```
template <class T, class U>
T  compare (const U& a, const U& b) {
 return a < b ? -1 : a > b;
}
```

The return data type is the province of the compiler for it can often convert a result into many different data types. If the user codes the following,

```
int res;
```

```
double a, b;
res = compare(a, b); // error T = kind???
res = compare<int, double>(a, b);
```

then in the first case, the compiler cannot tell what the return data type is to be and thus generates the error message. However, by explicitly telling the compiler what the data types for **T** and **U** are to be, the compiler can successfully generate and use the function.

Since these are models, the template functions must be made available where the compiler can find them. Thus, they are in the header files not cpp files. Note that there is no actual code in them; they are blueprints only. The actual code is generated by the compiler when it encounters their use within a cpp file. Thus, if we were to actually implement **max**, we would have the following.

File: max.h

```
#pragma once
template <class T>
const T& max (const T& x, const T& y) {
 return x>y ? x : y;
}
```

One can mix parameterized and non-parameterized items within the formal argument list. For example, consider this version of a **largest** function which returns the largest element within an array of type **T**. Such a function must also be passed the number of elements in the array.

```
template <class T>
const T& largest (const T* array, unsigned int size) {
 unsigned int answer = 0, i;
 for (i=1; i<size; i++) {
  if (array[i] >  array[answer])
   answer = i;
 }
 return array[answer];
}
```

Specializing a Template

A single template function usually cannot handle all possible types of data. This is often true when pointers are being passed. Consider this next need for function **max**.

```
char* s1 = "A";
char* s2 = "B";
const char* s3 = max (s1, s2);
// error: this compares pointer values not strings
```

The way around this dilemma is to provide specialized version of **max** in the header file.

add to max.h

```
template <>
const char* max (const char* s1, const char* s2) {
 return stricmp (s1, s2) > 0 ? s1 : s2;
}
```

Now the user can successfully code the following.

```
cout << max (s1, s2);
```

Another form of trouble can arise when the parameters actually being passed differ in type. Consider this case.

```
long a;
unsigned int b;
cout << max (a, b); // error
```

No version of **max** can take two different data types. However, just declaring and not defining a version of **max** permits the compiler to handle data conversion. If we add this one line to the header, the compiler can use it.

```
inline const long& max (const long& x, const long& y);
```

This one now allows the compiler to convert **unsigned int** to **long** and then to create a **max** that is passed two **long** parameters. Caution. Since references are being passed, it is going to pass a reference to the temporary **long** that into which it converted the **unsigned int**; if the temporary **long** is the larger, its address is returned. Addresses of temporary variables are very short in duration. One may end up with a reference to memory that has already been destroyed.

Template Classes

An entire class can be templatized. Such classes must have at least one parameterized type. Template classes are often used with abstract container types such as link lists, queues, stacks, and arrays. The New Style I/O stream classes are also template classes.

To illustrate a template class, let's consider how a class can be constructed to encapsulate a complex number. Recall from mathematics that a complex number has two portions, a real part and an imaginary part. Such numbers are often notated this way.

$1.5 + 3.9i$

$x + y\,i$

where i represents the square root of -1.

A complex number class would have two numerical members, the real and imaginary parts. Certainly both parts would be of the same data type. Often doubles are used, but longs or ints may work as well, depending upon the application. It is this data type to which the class **T** in the template refers. Here is the class definition portion.

```
template <class T>
class ComplexNumber {
protected:
 T realpart;
 T imagpart;
 static int counter;
public:
 ComplexNumber (const T& = T(), const T& = T());
 ComplexNumber (const ComplexNumber&);
same as
 ComplexNumber<T>(const T& = T(), const T& = T());
 ComplexNumber<T>(const ComplexNumber<T>&);
};
```

Note first that the class qualifier is now technically **ComplexNumber<T>**. However, since we expect to code the class qualifier many times, the compiler allows a short cut of just **ComplexNumber**. Next, note how the default values are coded. For example, in a non-template version, one might desire to code a constructor prototype like this.

```
ComplexNumber (double x = 0, double y = 0);
```

The syntax **= `T()`** is used to indicate the insertion of the 0 value for this data type **T** whatever **T** actually is.

When a template class is written, the header file as usual contains the class definition. However, it also must include the template member functions as well. In other words, the entire class and its template implementation must be in the header file! Thus, after the above **ComplexNumber** definition come all of the following.

```
template <class T>
ComplexNumber<T>::ComplexNumber (const T& r, const T& i) :
                  realpart (r), imagpart (i) {}
template <class T>
ComplexNumber<T>::ComplexNumber (const ComplexNumber& c) :
             realpart (c.realpart), imagpart (c.imagpart) {}
```

```
int ComplexNumber<T>::counter = 0;
```

I used the **static** member variable to illustrate how **static** data members are handled in a template class.

In the **main** function, entire instances of the entire **ComplexNumber** class can be created this way.

```
ComplexNumber<int> c1 (1,2);
ComplexNumber<double> c2 (42., 99.);
```

Because the syntax is awful and since these class instances are likely to be passed to functions, to avoid constant use of `ComplexNumber<double>`, a **typedef** is nearly always used to streamline the syntax.

```
typedef ComplexNumber<double> ComplexDouble;
ComplexDouble c3 (42., 99.);
```

Double Linked List: Practical Example of a Template Class

To see how this all works, I chose to rewrite our Double Linked List container class as a template class. The **LinkNode** is redefined as follows.

```
template<class T>
class DoubleLinkedList {

/***************************************************************/
/*                                                             */
/* LinkNode: the link list node structure                      */
/*                                                             */
/***************************************************************/

struct LinkNode {
 LinkNode* fwdptr;  // points to the next node in the list
 LinkNode* backptr; // points to the previous node
 T*  dataptr;       // points to the client data stored
};
```

Notice that we are now storing a pointer to the user's actual data and not a **void** pointer.

There are many ramifications to using this template version. First, the actual data type of the object to be stored in the list is **known**, it is of type **T**. Thus, this class can now be smart in its handling of the client's data. This means that the class can perform a **deep** copy because it can allocate new instances this way.

```
dataptr = new T;
```

The user is not required to clean up stored instances of type **T** because the **EmptyList** function can delete them directly. The user now, when they wish access to the data of a node, no longer must perform a typecast to get it back. The **GetCurrentNode** function returns a **T***. The client program must still provide matching functions, though, for we do not know how to "find" a specific instance of type **T** in our list.

In short, by using a template double linked list class, we gain all of the benefits associated with knowing **precisely** what kind of data the client is storing in the list! Further, the class can be used to store any kind of data. It is reusable. Well, reusable in the sense that we write the template class once. Then, for each type of client data to be stored, the compiler generates the entire class and all its functions for us. If a client program needed six lists to store six different kinds of objects, with the template version, there would be six total classes with all of their functions included in the executable file. However, with the generic void pointer version, there would only be one set of class functions in the executable, all shared by the six different instances. So the price of using templates in a program is that of a larger executable file along with the huge size of the header files.

Here is the complete template Double Linked List class. Please note how the try-catch logic works with dynamic memory allocation. This class has no idea what should be done when this error occurs, so the handling is up to the client program.

```
Template Double Linked List Class
```

```
 1 #pragma once
 3 #include <iostream>
 4 using namespace std;
 5
 6 /**************************************************************/
 7 /*                                                          */
 8 /* DoubleLinkedList Template Class                          */
 9 /*                                                          */
10 /* A double linked list that stores objects                */
11 /*                                                          */
12 /**************************************************************/
13
14 template<class T>
15 class DoubleLinkedList {
16
17 /**************************************************************/
18 /*                                                          */
19 /* LinkNode: the link list node structure                  */
20 /*                                                          */
21 /**************************************************************/
22
23 struct LinkNode {
24  LinkNode* fwdptr;   // points to the next node in the list
25  LinkNode* backptr;  // points to the previous node
26  T*  dataptr;        // points to the client data stored
27 };
28
29 /**************************************************************/
30 /*                                                          */
31 /* class data                                               */
32 /*                                                          */
33 /**************************************************************/
34
35 private:
36  LinkNode* headptr;      // points to first node in list
37  LinkNode* currentptr;   // points to the current node
38  LinkNode* tailptr;      // points to last node in list
39  long      count;        // the number of nodes in list
40
41 /**************************************************************/
42 /*                                                          */
43 /* class functions                                          */
44 /*                                                          */
45 /**************************************************************/
46
47 public:
48         DoubleLinkedList (); // constructs an empty list
49        ~DoubleLinkedList (); // deletes the total list
50  void  EmptyList ();         // removes all items from the list
51
52  // the add new node functions
53  bool  AddAtHead (T* ptrdata); // add node at the head
54  bool  AddAtTail (T* ptrdata); // add node at the tail
55
56  // add node after the current node - if current node is 0,
```

```
 // it is added at the head
 bool  InsertAfterCurrentNode (T* ptrdata);

 // add node before the current node - if the current node is 0,
 // it is added at the head
 bool  InsertBeforeCurrentNode (T* ptrdata);

 // deletes the current node. If there is no current node,
 // it returns false; otherwise it returns true.
 bool  DeleteCurrentNode ();

 // sets the current pointer to the node whose data matches
 // the criteria set by the caller.
 bool  FindNode (const void* ptrmatchData);

 long  GetSize () const; // get number of items in the list
 bool  IsHead () const;  // is list at the start?
 bool  IsTail () const;  // is list at the end?

 // list iterator functions
 void  ResetToHead ();   // set current back to start of the list
 void  ResetToTail ();   // set current to the end of the list
 void  Next ();          // moves current to the next item
 void  Previous ();      // moves current to  previous item

 // returns user data stored in the current node, 0 if none
 T* GetCurrentNode () const;

 // functions to copy or assign this list
 DoubleLinkedList (const DoubleLinkedList& r);
 DoubleLinkedList& operator= (const DoubleLinkedList& r);

protected:
 void  CopyList (const DoubleLinkedList& r); // duplicate list
};


/***************************************************************/
/*                                                             */
/* DoubleLinkedList: constructs an empty list                  */
/*                                                             */
/***************************************************************/

template<class T>
DoubleLinkedList<T>::DoubleLinkedList () {
 headptr = tailptr = currentptr = 0;
 count = 0;
}

/***************************************************************/
/*                                                             */
/* ~DoubleLinkedList: destructor to remove all nodes           */
/*                                                             */
/***************************************************************/

template<class T>
```

```
DoubleLinkedList<T>::~DoubleLinkedList () {
 EmptyList ();
}

/***************************************************************/
/*                                                             */
/* EmptyList: remove all nodes from the list                   */
/*                                                             */
/***************************************************************/

template<class T>
void  DoubleLinkedList<T>::EmptyList () {
 if (!headptr) return;
 LinkNode* ptrnext = headptr; // pointer to traverse the list
 LinkNode* ptrdel;            // the node to delete
 T*        ptrdatadel;        // pointer to the data to delete
 // traverse the list - ends when there are no more nodes
 while (ptrnext) {
  ptrdatadel = ptrnext->dataptr; // save client's data to delete
  ptrdel = ptrnext;          // save the current one to be deleted
  ptrnext = ptrdel->fwdptr; // point to the next node
  delete ptrdel;             // and delete the previous node
  delete ptrdatadel;         // and delete the client's data
 }
 headptr = currentptr = tailptr = 0;
 count = 0;
}

/***************************************************************/
/*                                                             */
/* AddAtHead: insert new node at the beginning of list         */
/*                                                             */
/***************************************************************/

template<class T>
bool  DoubleLinkedList<T>::AddAtHead (T* ptrdata) {
 // allocate a new node and fill it up
 LinkNode* ptrnew;
 try {
  ptrnew = new LinkNode;
 }
 catch (std::bad_alloc e) {
  cerr << "Error: out of memory\n";
  return false;
 }
 ptrnew->dataptr = ptrdata; // copy the passed client pointer
 ptrnew->backptr = 0;       // back pointer is 0 because at head
 count++;                   // increment total number of nodes
 // now chain this one into the list
 if (headptr) {             // if headptr exists, then the new
  ptrnew->fwdptr = headptr; // fwdptr contains the previous one
  headptr->backptr = ptrnew;// prev node's backptr is us now
  headptr = ptrnew;         // set headptr to newly added node
 }
 else {                     // empty list, so all ptrs point to
  headptr = tailptr = ptrnew; // this new node
```

```
  ptrnew->fwdptr = 0;        // and no forward nodes yet
 }
 currentptr = ptrnew; // leave the current one at the new one
 return true;
}

/***************************************************************/
/*                                                             */
/* AddAtTail: insert new node at the end of the list           */
/*                                                             */
/***************************************************************/

template<class T>
bool  DoubleLinkedList<T>::AddAtTail (T* ptrdata) {
 LinkNode* ptrnew;
 try {
  ptrnew = new LinkNode;
 }
 catch (std::bad_alloc e) {
  cerr << "Error: out of memory\n";
  return false;
 }
 count++;                    // increment total number of nodes
 ptrnew->dataptr = ptrdata; // store the client pointer in node
 ptrnew->fwdptr = 0;         // at end, cannot be forward node
 if (tailptr) {              // is there anything in the list yet?
  tailptr->fwdptr = ptrnew; // yes, prev tail node points to us
  ptrnew->backptr = tailptr;// us points back to the prev node
  tailptr = ptrnew;          // tail is now us
 }
 else {                      // no - list is empty,
  headptr = tailptr = ptrnew; // so set all to point to us
  ptrnew->backptr = 0;       // and there is no prev node
 }
 currentptr = ptrnew;        // leave with current node set to us
 return true;
}

/***************************************************************/
/*                                                             */
/* InsertAfterCurrentNode: add new node after the              */
/*                         current node                        */
/*                                                             */
/***************************************************************/

template<class T>
bool DoubleLinkedList<T>::InsertAfterCurrentNode(T* ptrdata){
 if (!headptr)          // list is empty so add at head
  return AddAtHead (ptrdata);
 else if (!currentptr) // current ptr is 0, so also add at head
  return AddAtHead (ptrdata);
 else if (IsTail())     // current ptr is the last node, so
  return AddAtTail (ptrdata); // reuse add at the tail
 else {                 // here we are inserting in the middle
  LinkNode* ptrnew;
  try {
```

```
   ptrnew = new LinkNode;
  }
  catch (std::bad_alloc e) {
   cerr << "Error: out of memory\n";
   return false;
  }
  ptrnew->dataptr = ptrdata;
  count++;
  // set new node's back pointer to current node to insert us
  ptrnew->backptr = currentptr;
  // set new node's forward ptr to the next node to the right
  ptrnew->fwdptr = currentptr->fwdptr;
  // set current's forward ptr to us to insert us
  currentptr->fwdptr = ptrnew;
  // set the node to the right of us to point back to us
  ptrnew->fwdptr->backptr = ptrnew;
  currentptr = ptrnew; // make the newly added node the current
  return true;
 }
}

/***************************************************************/
/*                                                             */
/* InsertBeforeCurrentNode: add new node before current        */
/*      node.                                                  */
/*                                                             */
/***************************************************************/

template<class T>
bool DoubleLinkedList<T>::InsertBeforeCurrentNode(T* ptrdata){
 if (!headptr)         // no nodes in list - so add at head
  return AddAtHead (ptrdata);
 else if (!currentptr)// no current ptr, so add at head too
  return AddAtHead (ptrdata);
 else if (IsHead())    // current ptr is the last node - so
  return AddAtHead(ptrdata); // add this one at the tail
 else {                // here we are adding in the middle of list
  LinkNode* ptrnew;
  try {
   ptrnew = new LinkNode;
  }
  catch (std::bad_alloc e) {
   cerr << "Error: out of memory\n";
   return false;
  }
  ptrnew->dataptr = ptrdata;
  count++;
  // set new node's back ptr to current's back
  ptrnew->backptr = currentptr->backptr;
  // set new node's forward ptr to current node
  ptrnew->fwdptr = currentptr;
  // set current node's back ptr to point to us
  currentptr->backptr = ptrnew;
  // set previous node's forward ptr to point to us
  ptrnew->backptr->fwdptr = ptrnew;
  currentptr = ptrnew; // set current pointer to the new node
```

```
  return true;
 }
}

/*****************************************************/
/*                                                   */
/* DeleteCurrentNode: removes the current node       */
/*    returns false if there is no current node      */
/*                                                   */
/*****************************************************/

template<class T>
bool  DoubleLinkedList<T>::DeleteCurrentNode () {
 if (!currentptr) // if no current node, abort
  return false;
 T* ptrdatadel;
 count--;
 if (!count) { // will list now be empty? if so reset to 0
  ptrdatadel = currentptr->dataptr;
  delete currentptr;
  delete ptrdatadel;
  headptr = tailptr = currentptr = 0;
  return true;
 }
 LinkNode* ptrtodelete = currentptr;
 ptrdatadel = currentptr->dataptr;
 if (IsHead()) {                     // deleting first node? if so,
  currentptr->fwdptr->backptr = 0;// set next node's back to none
  headptr = currentptr->fwdptr;    // set head to next node
  currentptr = headptr;            // and current to next node
 }
 else if (IsTail()) {                // deleting last one, if so,
  currentptr->backptr->fwdptr = 0;// set prev node's fwd to none
  tailptr = currentptr->backptr;   // set tail to prev node
  currentptr = tailptr;            // set current to prev node
 }
 else { // here the node to delete is in the middle
  // set next node's back to previous node
  currentptr->fwdptr->backptr = currentptr->backptr;
  // set previous node's fwd to next node
  currentptr->backptr->fwdptr = currentptr->fwdptr;
  // leave current pointing to previous node
  currentptr = currentptr->backptr;
 }
 delete ptrtodelete; // now delete the requested node
 delete ptrdatadel;  // delete the client's data too
 return true;
}

/*****************************************************/
/*                                                   */
/* GetSize: returns the number of nodes in the list  */
/*                                                   */
/*****************************************************/

template<class T>
```

```
long  DoubleLinkedList<T>::GetSize () const {
 return count;
}

/***************************************************/
/*                                                 */
/* IsHead: returns true if current node is the first node*/
/*                                                 */
/***************************************************/

template<class T>
bool  DoubleLinkedList<T>::IsHead () const {
 return currentptr == headptr;
}

/***************************************************/
/*                                                 */
/* IsTail: returns true if current node is the last one   */
/*                                                 */
/***************************************************/

template<class T>
bool  DoubleLinkedList<T>::IsTail () const {
 return currentptr == tailptr;
}

/***************************************************/
/*                                                 */
/* ResetToHead: sets current pointer to start of list    */
/*                                                 */
/***************************************************/

template<class T>
void  DoubleLinkedList<T>::ResetToHead () {
 currentptr = headptr;
}

/***************************************************/
/*                                                 */
/* ResetToTail: sets current pointer to last node in list*/
/*                                                 */
/***************************************************/

template<class T>
void  DoubleLinkedList<T>::ResetToTail () {
 currentptr = tailptr;
}

/***************************************************/
/*                                                 */
/* Next: move forward one node in the list         */
/*                                                 */
/***************************************************/

template<class T>
void  DoubleLinkedList<T>::Next () {
```

```
 if (currentptr)
  currentptr = currentptr->fwdptr;
}

/*********************************************************/
/*                                                       */
/* Previous: backs up one node in the list               */
/*                                                       */
/*********************************************************/

template<class T>
void  DoubleLinkedList<T>::Previous () {
 if (currentptr)
  currentptr = currentptr->backptr;
}

/**********************************************************/
/*                                                        */
/* GetCurrentNode: returns user data at current node or 0 */
/*                                                        */
/**********************************************************/

template<class T>
T* DoubleLinkedList<T>::GetCurrentNode () const {
 return currentptr ? currentptr->dataptr : 0;
}

/*********************************************************/
/*                                                       */
/* DoubleLinkedList: copy constructor - duplicate a list */
/*                                                       */
/*********************************************************/

template<class T>
DoubleLinkedList<T>::DoubleLinkedList (
                                 const DoubleLinkedList<T>& r) {
 CopyList (r);
}

/*********************************************************/
/*                                                       */
/* operator=: Make a duplicate copy of a list            */
/*                                                       */
/*********************************************************/

template<class T>
DoubleLinkedList<T>& DoubleLinkedList<T>::operator= (
                   const DoubleLinkedList& r) {
 if (this == &r) return *this; // avoid a = a; situation
 EmptyList ();  // remove all items in this list
 CopyList (r);  // make a copy of r's list
 return *this;
}

/*********************************************************/
/*                                                       */
```

```
/* CopyList: Make a duplicate copy of a list                   */
/*                                                             */
/***************************************************************/

template<class T>
void  DoubleLinkedList<T>::CopyList (
                                  const DoubleLinkedList<T>& r) {
  // handle the empty list first
 if (!r.headptr) {
  headptr = currentptr = tailptr = 0;
  return;
 }
 count = r.count;
 LinkNode* ptrRcurrent = r.headptr;
 // previousptr tracks our prior node so we can set its
 // forward pointer to the next new one
 LinkNode* previousptr = 0;
 // prime the loop so headptr can be set one time
 try {
  currentptr = new LinkNode;
 }
 catch (std::bad_alloc e) {
  cerr << "Error: out of memory\n";
  return;
 }
 headptr = currentptr;  // assign this one to the headptr

 // traverse list r's nodes
 while (ptrRcurrent) {
  // copy r's student info into our new node
  currentptr->dataptr = new T;
  *(currentptr->dataptr) = *(ptrRcurrent->dataptr);
  currentptr->fwdptr = 0;  // set our forward ptr to 0
  currentptr->backptr = 0; // set our back ptr to 0
  // if previous node exists, set its forward ptr to the new one
  if (previousptr) {
   previousptr->fwdptr = currentptr;
   currentptr->backptr = previousptr;
  }
  // save this node as the prevous node
  previousptr = currentptr;
  // and get a new node for the next iteration
  try {
   currentptr = new LinkNode;
  }
  catch (std::bad_alloc e) {
   cerr << "Error: out of memory\n";
   return;
  }
  // move to r's next node
  ptrRcurrent = ptrRcurrent->fwdptr;
 }
 tailptr = previousptr;
 delete currentptr; // delete the extra unneeded node
 // leave list at the beginning
 ResetToHead ();
```

```
}

/***************************************************************/
/*                                                             */
/* FindNode: find the node whose data matches users            */
/*           specifications - calls user's Find Function       */
/*                                                             */
/***************************************************************/

template<class T>
bool  DoubleLinkedList<T>::FindNode (const void* ptrmatchData) {
 if (!count) // empty list => not found
  return false;
 ResetToHead ();         // begin at the start of the list
 while (currentptr) {   // examine each node in turn
  if (*(currentptr->dataptr) == ptrmatchData)
   return true;          // return true if this one matches
  Next ();               // move to the next node in the list
 }
 return false;           // did not find it in whole list
}
```

Creating a Client Program Using the Template Double Linked List

Acme has a contract to produce an inquiry/update type of program to process telephone directory information. Initially, the directory should contain the person's first and last names, the area code and phone number. If the concept proves acceptable to their client, then the additional fields that a phone directory has will be added. The specifications call for drawing a text box graphic around the actual listing. A sample is shown below.

My Phone Directory

Record Number	First Name	Last Name	Area Code	Phone Number
1	Tom	Jones	(309)	699-9999
2	Betsy	Smith	(309)	699-4444
3	Annie	Cringle	(309)	696-4242
4	Henry	Albright II	(309)	694-5555
5	Lorri Ann	Spieldt	(309)	676-6666
6	Harry	Durch	(309)	688-4325
7	Rusty	Earls	(309)	676-5551
8	Jennifer	Smallville	(309)	688-5321

The ASCII codes to use when drawing the box are from the upper ASCII sequence and thus must be defined as **unsigned char**. Each of these displays one character, such as the upper left corner angle.

```
unsigned char upleft = 218;
unsigned char upright = 191;
unsigned char botleft = 192;
unsigned char botright = 217;
unsigned char horiz = 196;
unsigned char vert = 179;
unsigned char leftright = 195;
unsigned char rightleft = 180;
```

```
unsigned char cross = 197;
unsigned char topdown = 194;
unsigned char botup = 193;
```

The program, upon startup, loads the current test file of directory entries and displays the above report. Next, the main menu is shown as follows.

```
Friends Phone Book

1 Add new friend
2 Delete an entry
3 Display the phone listing
4 Display phone listing to a file
5 Save into a new file
6 Exit

Enter the number of your choice: 1
```

The program should only accept a valid menu choice. The entry of a non-numeric character should not halt the program but be rejected and the menu re-shown.

When "Add new friend" is chosen, the following is a sample of the conversational dialog required.

```
Enter first name (10 characters):   Jenny
Enter last name (20 characters):    Heart-Smith
Enter the area code (3 numbers):    309
Enter the phone number (999-9999): 699-7777
Addition was successful
```

When "Delete an entry" is chosen, a new problem arises. How should the user indicate which directory entry is to be deleted? Rather than asking the user to enter the person's name (first and last), the program should maintain a record number id that begins at one. Thus, when the original file is loaded, as the records are being added to the list, the program adds a consecutive numerical id to each directory record. Thus, to delete an entry, the user is prompted to enter the record number id. The conversational dialog is shown below.

```
Enter the number of the phone book entry to delete: 8
Confirm deletion of the following entry
   8   Jennifer   Smallville            (309)  688-5321

Enter Y to confirm deletion or N to abort: y

Record deleted
```

If a matching list entry matches the user's number, that directory entry is then displayed and a "confirm deletion" query is made. The only acceptable reply is Y or N; the user is re-prompted until either y or n is entered. When the deletion is made, a new problem arises with the record numbers. To avoid a "hole" in the numbers, all records that come after the deleted one in the list must be renumbered.

When "Display phone listing to a file" is chosen, prompt the user for the filename. However, the program should accept long filenames and filenames that contain blanks. To handle the blanks, force the user to surround the filename with double quote marks.

```
Enter the filename on which to display the report
If there are blanks in the filename,
place double quotemarks around the whole filename.
for example, "My Phone Book.txt"
"My Phone Book.txt"

Report written to: My Phone Book.txt
```

When "Save into a new file" is chosen, use a similar dialog to obtain the new filename.

```
Enter the new filename to use
If there are blanks in the filename,
place double quotemarks around the whole filename.
```

```
for example, "My Phone Book.txt"
NewPhoneBook.txt
File Saved
```

Finally, if any changes have been made to the original data, then any attempt to exit the program should force a query of the user as shown below.

```
Note: you have made changes to the phone database
and have not yet saved those changes
Do you want to quit and discard those changes?
Enter Y or N: n
```

Again, accept only y or n and re-prompt until a valid entry is made. If the user does not want to quit, re-show the main menu.

I began the solution to the problem by using Top-down design to functionally decompose the problem into functional modules. Figure 8.1 shows the design I used.

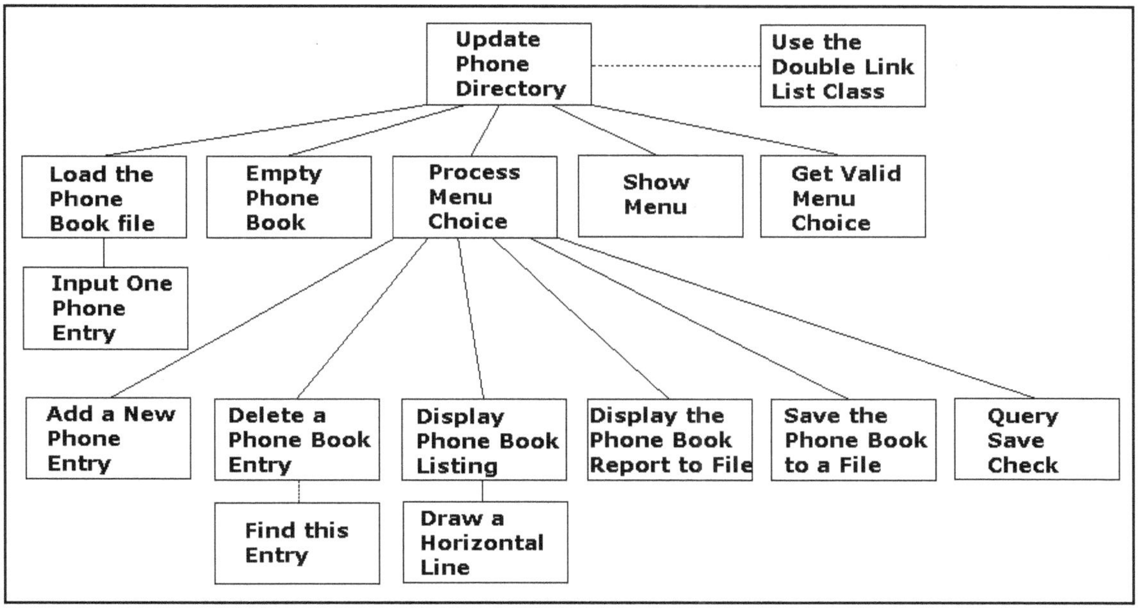

Figure 8.1 Top-down Design of Pgm08a - Update Phone Directory

In order to use the template linked list class, we must supply the type T. Thus, I chose to have a **PhoneDirectory** class that encapsulates the data itself. The link list will contain instances of **PhoneDirectory**. A series of **Get/Set** access functions are provided to retrieve and change the encapsulated data. To avoid overwriting memory when copying in the user data strings, I provided a protected helper function, **CopyString**. Here are the client **PhoneDirectory** class definition and its implementation.

Phone Directory Class Definition

```
#pragma once
#include <string>
#include <fstream>
using namespace std;

const int MAX_FNAME_LEN = 11;
const int MAX_LNAME_LEN = 21;
const int MAX_AREA_LEN = 4;
const int MAX_PHNUM_LEN = 9;

/***********************************************************/
```

```
/*                                                        */
/* class PhoneDirectory - encapsulates a Phone Book entry */
/*                                                        */
/**********************************************************/

class PhoneDirectory {

protected:
 int  recordNumber; // these are added by the pgm for id purposes
 char firstName[MAX_FNAME_LEN];
 char lastName[MAX_LNAME_LEN];
 char areaCode[MAX_AREA_LEN];
 char phoneNumber[MAX_PHNUM_LEN];

public:
 PhoneDirectory ();
 PhoneDirectory (const char* first, const char* last,
                const char* area, const char* pnum, int num = 0);

 // the access functions
 int         GetRecordNumber () const;
 const char* GetFirstName () const;
 const char* GetLastName () const;
 const char* GetAreaCode () const;
 const char* GetPhoneNumber () const;

 void SetRecordNumber (int num);
 void SetFirstName (const char* first);
 void SetLastName (const char* last);
 void SetAreaCode (const char* area);
 void SetPhoneNumber (const char* phnum);

 // provide implementations of the pure virutal functions
 bool MatchObject (const void* ptrtarget) const;
 bool operator==  (const void* ptrtarget) const;

protected:
 // helper function to copy strings and avoid overlaying memory
 void CopyString (char* des, const char* src, unsigned int max);
};
```

Phone Directory Class Implementation

```
#include <cstring>
#include "PhoneDirectory.h"
using namespace std;

/**********************************************************/
/*                                                        */
/* PhoneDirectory: default ctor                           */
/*                                                        */
/**********************************************************/

PhoneDirectory::PhoneDirectory () {
 recordNumber = 0;
```

```
 firstName[0] = 0;
 lastName[0] = 0;
 areaCode[0] = 0;
 phoneNumber[0] = 0;
}

/**********************************************************/
/*                                                        */
/* PhoneDirectory: make an instance from these values    */
/*                                                        */
/**********************************************************/

PhoneDirectory::PhoneDirectory (const char* first,
               const char* last, const char* area,
               const char* pnum, int num) {
 recordNumber = num;
 CopyString (firstName, first, MAX_FNAME_LEN);
 CopyString (lastName, last, MAX_LNAME_LEN);
 CopyString (areaCode, area, MAX_AREA_LEN);
 CopyString (phoneNumber, pnum, MAX_PHNUM_LEN);
}

/**********************************************************/
/*                                                        */
/* CopyString: copy a string into member string without   */
/*             overlaying memory                          */
/*             if src is too big, copies what will fit    */
/*                                                        */
/**********************************************************/

void PhoneDirectory::CopyString (char* des, const char* src,
                                 unsigned int max) {
 if (strlen (src) >= max) {
  strncpy_s (des, max, src, max-1);
  des[max-1] = 0;
 }
 else
  strcpy_s (des, max, src);
}

/**********************************************************/
/*                                                        */
/* The Get... access functions                            */
/*                                                        */
/**********************************************************/

int         PhoneDirectory::GetRecordNumber () const {
 return recordNumber;
}

const char* PhoneDirectory::GetFirstName () const {
 return firstName;
}

const char* PhoneDirectory::GetLastName () const {
 return lastName;
```

```
}

const char* PhoneDirectory::GetAreaCode () const {
 return areaCode;
}
const char* PhoneDirectory::GetPhoneNumber () const {
 return phoneNumber;
}

/***************************************************************/
/*                                                             */
/* The Set... Access functions                                 */
/*                                                             */
/***************************************************************/

void PhoneDirectory::SetRecordNumber (int num) {
 recordNumber = num;
}

void PhoneDirectory::SetFirstName (const char* first) {
 CopyString (firstName, first, MAX_FNAME_LEN);
}

void PhoneDirectory::SetLastName (const char* last) {
 CopyString (lastName, last, MAX_LNAME_LEN);

}

void PhoneDirectory::SetAreaCode (const char* area) {
 CopyString (areaCode, area, MAX_AREA_LEN);
}

void PhoneDirectory::SetPhoneNumber (const char* phnum) {
 CopyString (phoneNumber, phnum, MAX_PHNUM_LEN);
}

/****************************************************************/
/*                                                              */
/* MatchObject: return true if this object matches target */
/*                                                              */
/****************************************************************/

bool PhoneDirectory::MatchObject (const void* ptrtarget) const {
 return recordNumber == *((int*) ptrtarget);
}

/***************************************************************/
/*                                                             */
/* operator== return true if this object matches target   */
/*                                                             */
/***************************************************************/

bool PhoneDirectory::operator== (const void* ptrtarget) const {
 return recordNumber == *((int*) ptrtarget);
}
```

Finally, here is the revised client program, **Pgm08a**. Key usages of the template class are highlighted in bold face.

```
Pgm08a - Phone Directory Program Using Template Double Linked List
```

```
#include <iostream>
#include <iomanip>
#include <fstream>
#include <crtdbg.h>
#include <cstring>
#include <cstdlib>
#include "PhoneDirectory.h"
#include "DoubleLinkedList.h"
using namespace std;

/***************************************************************/
/*                                                             */
/* Pgm08a: Maintaining a Phone Directory Application           */
/*                                                             */
/***************************************************************/

typedef DoubleLinkedList<PhoneDirectory> DoubleLL;

// the prototypes
bool LoadPhoneBook (DoubleLL& pb, const char* filename);
istream& InputPhoneData (istream& is, PhoneDirectory& pd);

ostream& DisplayPhoneListing (DoubleLL& pb, ostream& os);
void DrawLine (ostream& os, unsigned char c, int count);
void DisplayPhoneBookToFile (DoubleLL& pb);

void ShowMenu ();
int  GetMenuChoice ();
bool ProcessMenuChoice (DoubleLL& pb, int choice,
                        bool& needToSave, ostream& os);

void AddEntry (DoubleLL& pb, bool& needToSavePb);
void DeleteEntry (DoubleLL& pb, bool& needToSavePb);
int  FindEntry (const void* ptrmatchData, const void* ptrthis);
void SavePhoneBook (DoubleLL& pb, bool& needToSavePb);
bool SaveCheck (DoubleLL& pb, bool needToSavePb);


int main () {
 {
  DoubleLL phoneBook; // create the phonebook list

  // load the book from a file
  if (!LoadPhoneBook (phoneBook, "phoneBook.txt"))
   return 1;
  // display the listing using fancy box drawing characters
  DisplayPhoneListing (phoneBook, cout);

  bool needToSavePb = false; // true when data has been changed
  bool quit = false;         // true when it is safe to quit
```

```

  // main loop shows a menu, gets a valid choice and process it
  while (!quit) {
   quit = ProcessMenuChoice (phoneBook, GetMenuChoice (),
                             needToSavePb, cout);
  }
 }

 if (_CrtDumpMemoryLeaks())
  cout << "\nOops! Memory Leaks!!\n";
 else
  cout << "\nNo Memory Leaks\n";

 return 0;
}

/***************************************************************/
/*                                                             */
/* LoadPhoneBook: loads the list from a database file          */
/*                                                             */
/***************************************************************/

bool LoadPhoneBook (DoubleLL& pb, const char* filename) {
 ifstream infile (filename);
 if (!infile) {
  cerr << "Error: unable to open file: " << filename << endl;
  return false;
 }

 int i = 1; // this will be the record id number value

 // allocate a new phone directory structure
 PhoneDirectory* ptrpd;
 try {
  ptrpd = new PhoneDirectory;
 }
 catch (std::bad_alloc e) { // check for out of memory
  cerr << "Error - out of memory\n";
  exit (1);
 }

 // for each set of input data, insert the id number, add to list
 // and allocate another phone directory structure for the next
 // input opperation
 while (InputPhoneData (infile, *ptrpd)) {
  ptrpd->SetRecordNumber (i++);
  pb.AddAtTail (ptrpd);
  try {
   ptrpd = new PhoneDirectory;
  }
  catch (std::bad_alloc e) { // check for out of memory
   cerr << "Error - out of memory\n";
   exit (1);
  }
 }

```

```
 delete ptrpd;   // delete the unneeded structure - eof was found
 infile.close ();
 return true;
}

/***************************************************************/
/*                                                             */
/* InputPhoneData: input a single phone directory entry        */
/*                                                             */
/***************************************************************/

istream& InputPhoneData (istream& is, PhoneDirectory& pd) {
 char c;
 is >> c;  // input the leading " of first name
 if (!is)
  return is;
 char str[80];
 is.getline (str, sizeof(str), '\"');
 pd.SetFirstName (str);
 is >> c; // get leading " of last name
 is.getline (str, sizeof(str), '\"');
 pd.SetLastName (str);
 is >> str;
 pd.SetAreaCode (str);
 is >> str;
 pd.SetPhoneNumber (str);
 return is;
}

/***************************************************************/
/*                                                             */
/* DisplayPhoneListing: display in a fancy fashion the         */
/*                      complete phone listing                 */
/*                                                             */
/***************************************************************/

ostream& DisplayPhoneListing (DoubleLL& pb, ostream& os){
 // the text graphics codes to draw fancy boxes
 unsigned char upleft = 218;
 unsigned char upright = 191;
 unsigned char botleft = 192;
 unsigned char botright = 217;
 unsigned char horiz = 196;
 unsigned char vert = 179;
 unsigned char leftright = 195;
 unsigned char rightleft = 180;
 unsigned char cross = 197;
 unsigned char topdown = 194;
 unsigned char botup = 193;

 os << "                        My Phone Directory\n\n";

 // draws the top line
 os << upleft;
 DrawLine (os, horiz, 6);
 os << topdown;
```

```
DrawLine (os, horiz, 12);
os << topdown;
DrawLine (os, horiz, 22);
os << topdown;
DrawLine (os, horiz, 7);
os << topdown;
DrawLine (os, horiz, 10);
os << upright << endl;

// display a pair of column heading lines
os << vert << "Record" << vert << " First      " << vert
   << " Last                 " << vert << " Area  "
   << vert << " Phone    " << vert << endl;
os << vert << "Number" << vert << " Name       " << vert
   << " Name                 " << vert << " Code  "
   << vert << " Number   " << vert << endl;

// display another horizontal line
os << leftright;
DrawLine (os, horiz, 6);
os << cross;
DrawLine (os, horiz, 12);
os << cross;
DrawLine (os, horiz, 22);
os << cross;
DrawLine (os, horiz, 7);
os << cross;
DrawLine (os, horiz, 10);
os << rightleft << endl;

// for each set of data, display all values within the boxes
pb.ResetToHead ();
PhoneDirectory* ptrpd = pb.GetCurrentNode ();
while (ptrpd) {
 os << vert << ' ' << setw(4) << ptrpd->GetRecordNumber() << ' '
    << vert << ' ' << left << setw(10) << ptrpd->GetFirstName()
    << ' ' << vert << ' ' << setw(20) << ptrpd->GetLastName()
    << ' ' << vert << " (" << setw(3) << ptrpd->GetAreaCode()
    << ") " << vert << ' ' << setw(8) << ptrpd->GetPhoneNumber()
    << ' '  << vert <<endl << right;
 pb.Next ();
 ptrpd = pb.GetCurrentNode ();
}

// display the bottom line of the box
os << botleft;
DrawLine (os, horiz, 6);
os << botup;
DrawLine (os, horiz, 12);
os << botup;
DrawLine (os, horiz, 22);
os << botup;
DrawLine (os, horiz, 7);
os << botup;
DrawLine (os, horiz, 10);
```

```
 os << botright << endl;
 os << endl;
 return os;
}

/***************************************************************/
/*                                                             */
/* DrawLine: helper function to draw a horizontal line         */
/*                                                             */
/***************************************************************/

void DrawLine (ostream& os, unsigned char c, int count) {
 // displays character c count times to the stream
 for (int i=0; i< count; i++) {
  os << c;
 }
}

/***************************************************************/
/*                                                             */
/* ShowMenu: displays the main menu of choices                 */
/*                                                             */
/***************************************************************/

void ShowMenu () {
 cout << "\n\n"
      << "Friends Phone Book\n\n"
      << "1 Add new friend\n"
      << "2 Delete an entry\n"
      << "3 Display the phone listing\n"
      << "4 Display phone listing to a file\n"
      << "5 Save into a new file\n"
      << "6 Exit\n"
      << "\nEnter the number of your choice: ";
}

/***************************************************************/
/*                                                             */
/* GetMenuChoice: gets a valid menu choice                     */
/*                                                             */
/***************************************************************/

int GetMenuChoice () {
 // get only a valid number between 1 and 6
 int choice = 7;
 while (choice < 1 || choice > 6) {
  ShowMenu ();
  cin >> choice;
  if (!cin) {    // check for non-numeric data entered
   cin.clear (); // yes, so reset cin state flags to good
   char c;
   cin.get(c);   // and get the offending character
  }
 }
 cout << endl;
 return choice;  // choice is a number between 1 and 6
```

```
}

/*******************************************************/
/*                                                     */
/* ProcessMenuChoice: driver to process that menu choice */
/*                                                     */
/*******************************************************/

bool ProcessMenuChoice (DoubleLL& pb, int choice,
                        bool& needToSavePb, ostream& os) {
 switch (choice) {
  case 1:
   AddEntry (pb, needToSavePb);
   return false;
  case 2:
   DeleteEntry (pb, needToSavePb);
   return false;
  case 3:
   DisplayPhoneListing (pb, os);
   return false;
  case 4:
   DisplayPhoneBookToFile (pb);
   return false;
  case 5:
   SavePhoneBook (pb, needToSavePb);
   return false;
  case 6:
   return SaveCheck (pb, needToSavePb);
 };
 return false;
}

/*******************************************************/
/*                                                     */
/* AddEntry: Adds a new person to the phone directory  */
/*                                                     */
/*******************************************************/

void AddEntry (DoubleLL& pb, bool& needToSavePb) {
 PhoneDirectory* ptrpd;
 try {
  ptrpd = new PhoneDirectory;
 }
 catch (std::bad_alloc e) { // check for out of memory
  cerr << "Error - out of memory\n";
  exit (2);
 }

 char c;
 cin.get (c); // eat the crlf from the previous cin

 char str[80];
 // acquire the data on the new person to be added
 cout << "Enter first name (10 characters):  ";
 cin.get (str, sizeof (str));
 ptrpd->SetFirstName (str);
```

```
 cin.get (c);
 cout << "Enter last name (20 characters):    ";
 cin.get (str, sizeof (str));
 ptrpd->SetLastName (str);
 cin.get (c);
 cout << "Enter the area code (3 numbers):    ";
 cin.get (str, sizeof (str));
 ptrpd->SetAreaCode (str);
 cin.get (c);
 cout << "Enter the phone number (999-9999): ";
 cin.get (str, sizeof (str));
 ptrpd->SetPhoneNumber (str);
 cin.get (c);

 // set its record id to one larger than is in the list
 ptrpd->SetRecordNumber (pb.GetSize() + 1);

 // and add it to the list
 pb.AddAtTail (ptrpd);

 // set the data has been modified flag
 needToSavePb = true;
 cout << "Addition was successful\n";
}

/*********************************************************/
/*                                                       */
/* DeleteEntry: removes a person from the phone directory */
/*    Note: use the record id number as the key id field  */
/*                                                       */
/*********************************************************/

void DeleteEntry (DoubleLL& pb, bool& needToSavePb) {
 char c;
 cout << "Enter the number of the phone book entry to delete: ";
 int num;
 cin >> num;

 // now see if that number is in the list
 if (pb.FindNode (&num)) {
  // here we found the number in the list, so get that set
  // and display it to the user and get a verification that
  // they really do want to delete this one
  PhoneDirectory* ptrpd = pb.GetCurrentNode ();
  cout << "Confirm deletion of the following entry\n";
  cout << setw(4) << ptrpd->GetRecordNumber() << "    " << left
       << setw(10) << ptrpd->GetFirstName() << "  "
       << setw(20) << ptrpd->GetLastName() << "  ("
       << setw(3) << ptrpd->GetAreaCode() << ")  "
       << setw(8) << ptrpd->GetPhoneNumber() << endl << right;

  // do not accept anything but a Y or N
  c = ' ';
  while (c != 'Y' && c != 'N') {
   cout << endl << "Enter Y to confirm deletion or N to abort: ";
   cin >> c;
```

```
   c = toupper (c);
  }
  if (c == 'N')
   cout << endl << "Nothing done\n";
  else {
   // here it has been verified as the one to delete, so do it
   pb.DeleteCurrentNode ();
   // now handle renumbering all list items....
   if (pb.IsHead()) // if deleted first one,
    num = 1;         // renumbering begins at 1
   else              // if we have not deleted the first one,
    pb.Next ();      // move current to the first that may need it

   // get current next one after the deleted one, if any
   ptrpd = pb.GetCurrentNode ();
   while (ptrpd) { // for each phone directory, change its record
    ptrpd->SetRecordNumber (num++); // id number down one
    pb.Next ();
    ptrpd = pb.GetCurrentNode ();
   }
   cout << endl << "Record deleted\n";
   // set the data has been modified flag
   needToSavePb = true;
  }
 }
 else
  cout << endl
       << "No such number in the phone book - try again\n";
}

/***************************************************************/
/*                                                             */
/* DisplayPhoneBookToFile: displays report to a file           */
/*           Note: can handle long filenames and those         */
/*           with blanks in them                               */
/*                                                             */
/***************************************************************/

void DisplayPhoneBookToFile (DoubleLL& pb) {
 char filename[_MAX_FNAME];
 char c;
 cin.get(c); // eat the crlf from previous cin

 cout << "Enter the filename on which to display the report\n";
 cout << "If there are blanks in the filename,\n"
      << "place double quotemarks around the whole filename.\n"
      << "for example, \"My Phone Book.txt\" \n";
 cin.get (filename, sizeof(filename));

 // check for long filename with quotemarks
 if (filename[0] == '\"') {// doesn't check for required ending "
  int len = (int) strlen (filename) - 2;
  strncpy_s (filename, sizeof(filename), &filename[1], len);
  filename[len] = 0;
 }
```

```

 // attempt to open the file
 ofstream outfile (filename);
 if (!outfile) {
  cerr << "Error: cannot open output file: " << filename << endl;
  return;
 }

 // now display the fancy report to this file
 DisplayPhoneListing (pb, outfile);
 outfile.close();
 cout << endl << "Report written to: " << filename << endl;
}

/***********************************************************/
/*                                                         */
/* SavePhoneBook: saves the list to a new phone book file */
/*                Note: it allows long filenames with      */
/*                blanks as part of the filename           */
/*                                                         */
/***********************************************************/

void SavePhoneBook (DoubleLL& pb, bool& needToSavePb) {
 char filename[_MAX_FNAME];
 char c;
 cin.get(c); // eat crlf from previous cin

 cout << "Enter the new filename to use\n";
 cout << "If there are blanks in the filename,\n"
      << "place double quotemarks around the whole filename.\n"
      << "for example, \"My Phone Book.txt\" \n";
 cin.get (filename, sizeof(filename));

 // check for leading "
 if (filename[0] == '\"') {        // this code doesn't check for
  int len = (int) strlen (filename) - 2; // required trailing "
  strncpy_s (filename, sizeof(filename), &filename[1], len);
  filename[len] = 0;
 }

 // attempt to open the file
 ofstream outfile (filename);
 if (!outfile) { // here we cannot, bad name or possibly bad path
  cerr << "Error: cannot open output file: " << filename << endl;
  return;
 }

 // now save all data, but do not save the record Id number
 pb.ResetToHead ();
 PhoneDirectory* ptrpd = pb.GetCurrentNode ();
 while (ptrpd) {
  outfile << "\"" << ptrpd->GetFirstName() << "\" "
          << "\"" << ptrpd->GetLastName()  << "\" "
          << ptrpd->GetAreaCode() << " "
          << ptrpd->GetPhoneNumber() << endl;
```

```
  pb.Next ();
  ptrpd = pb.GetCurrentNode ();
 }

 pb.ResetToHead ();     // leave list at a valid location
 outfile.close ();
 needToSavePb = false;  // turn off any need to save the data
 cout << "File Saved\n";
}

/***************************************************************/
/*                                                             */
/* SaveCheck: query the user - saving the data on exit         */
/*                                                             */
/***************************************************************/

bool SaveCheck (DoubleLL& pb, bool needToSavePb) {
 if (needToSavePb) { // has the data been modified and not saved?
  char yn = ' ';     // yes, so ask user if they want to quit
  while (yn != 'Y' && yn != 'N') {
   cout << "Note: you have made changes to the phone database\n"
        << "and have not yet saved those changes\n"
        << "Do you want to quit and discard those changes?\n"
        << "Enter Y or N: ";
   cin >> yn;
   yn = toupper (yn);
  }
  return yn == 'Y' ? true : false;
 }
 else // here it has not changed, so it is safe to quit
  return true;
}
```

If you are interested in further studies of templates, examine the Standard Template Library (STL) that comes with the Microsoft VC compiler as well as examine the New Style I/O stream classes.

Review Questions

1. What are the potential benefits of using one or more template functions in a program?

2. What are the potential benefits of using a template class in a program?

3. Why must a statement like

```
template<class T>
```

appear before each template function header and body?

4. Why must all of the member functions of a template class also be in the header file and not in a cpp file included in the project?

5. How can a client program specify which version of a template function the compiler is to use in a specific case? When would the client program desire to do so?

6. Why must some versions of a template function be specialized and hard coded in the header file?

7. Discuss the pro's and con's of storing the client's data as type T versus storing a pointer to type T in a container class. Be specific about these.

Stop! Do These Exercises Before Programming

1. Write a template **ReciprocalSum** function that is passed one type T parameter representing the upper limit to which to sum. Thus, if the function is called and passed an integer of 5, then it returns the sum of 1/1 + 1/2 + 1/3 + 1/4 + 1/5 as a double. It always does the division and summation using doubles. Show how the client program can use it with the parameter being an int, a long and a double.

2. Write a **FindMin** template function that is passed an array of type **T** and the maximum number of elements in use in the array. The function returns the smallest value in the array. Show how a client could use it to find the smallest element in the following arrays.

```
double array1[100];
int count1;

long array2[100];
int count2;

double* array3[100];
int count3;
```

3. Add insertion and extraction operators for the **ComplexNumber<T>** class presented in this chapter. The output should appear in the form of x + yi. The input consists of numbers in one of two formats: either 2.5 + 6.5i or (4.4, 2.2). Of course, they could also be x - yi as well.

Programming Problems

Problem Pgm08-1—A Template Growable Array Container Class

In chapter 7, we reviewed the **Array** container class. It achieved the ability to grow and be reusable by storing void pointers to the client's data. Redesign this class to be a template class storing the client's data as a pointer to type **T**. Further, the new class should perform a deep copy not a shallow copy and the client program should not have to use typecasting to get pointers back nor should it have to manually delete all items being stored before the destructor of the class is called. Thoroughly test your new class.

Problem Pgm08-2—A Template Stack Container Class

In chapter 7, we reviewed the **Stack** container class. It achieved the ability to grow and be reusable by storing void pointers to the client's data. Redesign this class to be a template class storing the client's data as a pointer to type **T**. Further, the new class should perform a deep copy not a shallow copy and the client program should not have to use typecasting to get pointers back nor should it have to manually delete all items being stored before the destructor of the class is called. Thoroughly test your new class.

Problem Pgm08-3—A Template Queue Container Class

In chapter 7, we reviewed the **Queue** container class. It achieved the ability to grow and be reusable by storing void pointers to the client's data. Redesign this class to be a template class storing the client's data as a pointer to type **T**. Further, the new class should perform a deep copy not a shallow copy and the client program should not have to use typecasting to get pointers back nor should it have to manually delete all items being stored before the destructor of the class is called. Thoroughly test your new class.

Chapter 9—Binary Files and Hashing Techniques

Introduction

A **binary file** is a file of data which are stored in internal numeric format rather than in the ASCII text format. Traditionally, the concepts and usage of binary files either are not presented or are not well covered in traditional beginning programming courses. However, virtually all company master files are in the binary format; very few, if any, data files contain text that can be streamed in using the usual extraction operator. This chapter is an attempt to remedy this situation. This chapter begins with a thorough discussion of what binary files are, how they are commonly used and finally some significant processing methods employed with binary files.

Dealing with Binary Files

Normal files are text files usually with the .txt file extension. Other names used for text files are ASCII files and DOS text files. These files contain only ASCII displayable or printable characters and are fully visible using Notepad, for instance. The end of the file is marked by a single byte that contains a ^Z (Ctrl-Z). This EOF byte is normally never visibly displayed by editors. Text files can be displayed on the screen or printed exactly as is.

For example, if a text file contained the line

```
ABC 1234<cr>
```

Then the file would contain ten bytes with the following ASCII decimal values.

```
65, 66, 67, 32, 49, 50, 51, 52, 13, 10 <— ASCII values
 A   B   C   b̸   1   2   3   4  CR  LF <- the text line
```

To input this line, we must define two variables as follows.

```
char name[10];
int qty;
```

Then, we can use **cin** to input the line.

```
cin >> name >> qty;
```

The **istream** must therefore perform internal data conversion to convert this line into the way the data is to be stored in these variables in memory as shown in Figure 9.1.

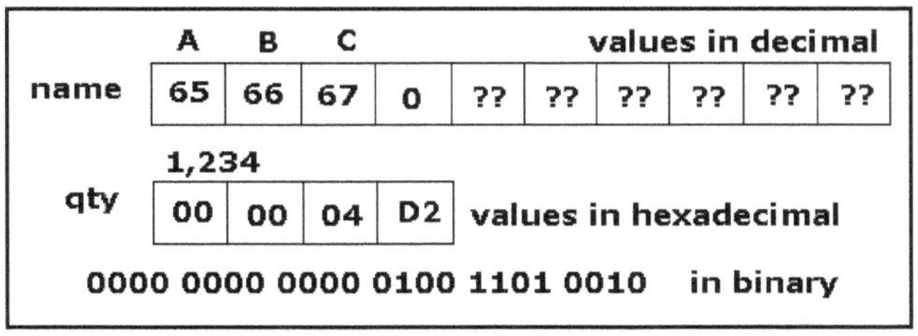

Figure 9.1 Internal Form of name and qty

In the above figure, the character string's contents are shown using the decimal values of the corresponding ASCII codes. The byte that contains the 0 is the null terminator. The integer **qty** occupies four bytes on a Win32 platform. I have shown the contents of each byte in the hexadecimal format which is usually used to show binary values. I also gave the contents of **qty** in binary. The leftmost 0 bit is the sign: 0 indicates a positive number. The 1 bit represents corresponding powers of 2. Or

$1x2^1 + 1x2^4 + 1x2^6 + 1x2^7 + 1x2^{10} = 2 + 16 + 64 + 128 + 1024 = 1234$

Notice then, that the **istream** must convert the ASCII digits into the binary number form before it can store the value into the integer. Likewise, on output, the internal forms must be converted back into a series of ASCII values. This data conversion is slow, particularly so for floating point types.

A binary file consists of data stored as a memory image of that data. Thus, if an **int** occupies four bytes and contains 00 00 04 D2 in hex, then, when written to a binary file, the binary file contains four bytes containing 00 00 04 D2 in hex.

Rule: No data conversion of any kind is ever done to binary files.

With binary files, data is transferred to and from memory precisely as it is/or will be in memory. The result is a tremendous increase in the speed of I/O operations.

Also, the end of file in a binary file is really tracked by the system and occurs when the file size number of bytes has been read into the computer.

Most all production data files will be binary files! Why? I/O speed is dramatically faster.

C++ Mechanics of Binary File Operations

When you open a binary file, you MUST tell the **iostreams** that this is a binary file. The **iostreams** default to a text file. All manner of ills will befall I/O operations if the binary file is opened as text and vice-versa. To tell the streams that this file is a binary file, OR in the **ios::binary** flag:

```
istream infile ("myfile.dat",
                ios::input | ios::nocreate | ios::binary);
ostream outfile ("newfile.dat", ios::output | ios::binary);
```

The input and output operations are much simpler. The **read** and **write** functions are used.

```
istream& read (char* inputarea,
               int number of bytes to input);
ostream& write (char* outputarea,
                int number of bytes to output);
```

If we are inputting or outputting something other than a string, we must use a typecast of the pointers.

```
infile.read ( (char*) &qty, sizeof (qty));
outfile.write ( (char*) &qty, sizeof (int));
```

Note that **sizeof (qty)** is better than **sizeof (int)** because, if you change its data type, it automatically gets the correct new size.

Here are some examples of their use. Suppose that we had an array of bounds 1000 which contained 950 elements and we wished to save that data to a binary file. The following writes all 950 elements in one write operation.

```
long array[1000];
int   count;
outfile.write ( (char*) array, sizeof (long) * count);
```

Character strings in a binary file are a bit peculiar. The binary file is a memory copy of the variable. So if **name** is defined to contain a maximum of 10 characters (including the null) and if it contains "Sam" (S, a, m, 0) at the moment, then, when written to a binary file, all ten bytes are written. When read in from a binary file, all ten bytes are input. However, C++ knows that the real contents of the string end at the null terminator.

Structures are commonly read or written to or from binary files. Suppose that we use the **CostRec** structure.

```
struct CostRec {
 int itemno;
 short qty;
 char descr[21];
 double cost;
};
```

```
...
CostRec crec;
...
outfile.write ((char*) &crec, sizeof (crec));
                           // or sizeof (CostRec)
...
infile.read ((char*) &crec, sizeof (crec));
```

In this example, an array of cost records is loaded from a binary file.

```
int LoadArray (CostRec arec[], int limit) {
 ifstream infile("master.dat",
                 ios::in | ios::nocreate | ios::binary);
 if (!infile) {
  cerr << "Error: Unable to open the input file!\n"
  exit (1);
 }
 int j = 0;
 while (j < limit &&
       infile.read ((char*) &arec[j], sizeof (CostRec))) {
  j++;
 }
 infile.close ();
 return j;
}
```

Physical I/O Versus Logical I/O Operations

The above examples have been logical I/O operations. That is, a program asks for the next cost record and the system "inputs" it into our designated input structure instance. However, in order to understand other I/O operations a program needs to make, the concepts of how the Windows/DOS system handles the physical I/O operations must be understood.

The smallest amount of data that the system will actually input or output to disk is called a **cluster**. The size of a cluster varies widely depending upon the size of the drive and the file system in use on that drive. Specifically, a cluster is **n** adjacent sectors of 512 bytes each. The number **n** varies depending upon the drive. For example, on the old 5¼ floppy disks, that held 360K of data, a cluster consisted of 2 adjacent sectors of data. Figure 9.2 shows the terminology of a track (a concentric circle of magnetic material that stores data) and a sector (a pie shaped section of a track).

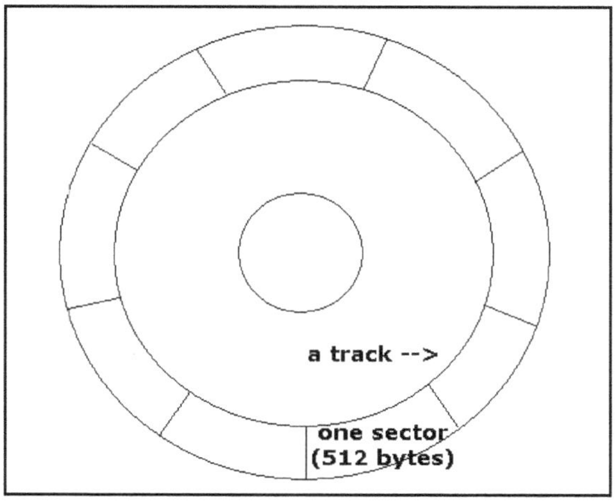

Figure 9.2 A Track and Sector of a 360k Floppy Disk

When running the FAT16 file system, Windows/DOS stores the number of clusters in an unsigned integer which is therefore limited to 65,536 clusters. The system identifies each cluster on the drive starting with cluster 0 and increases successive cluster numbers by one. On larger capacity drives, DOS must increase the number of sectors in a cluster to reduce the number of clusters to get their numbers to fit in range of the unsigned integer. Table 9.1 shows some cluster sizes for various disk drives or partitions.

Table 9.1 Cluster Sizes for Various Sized Partitions

Partition Size in MB	Type	Sectors Per Cluster	Cluster Size
16-127	FAT16	4	2K
128-255	FAT16	8	4K
256-511	FAT16	16	8K
512-1023	FAT16	32	16K
1024-2047	FAT16	64	32k
2048-4096	FAT16	128	64K
.256-8.01	FAT32	8	4K
8.02-16.02	FAT32	16	8K
16.03-32.04	FAT32	32	16K
>32.04	FAT32	64	32K

The cluster size is important. The significance is given by the following rule.

Rule: Windows/DOS physically inputs and outputs only clusters at a time.

In other words, DOS really only actually physically inputs or outputs a cluster. This is the smallest unit of I/O. Smaller requests are accumulated in a **buffer** staging area which is the size of a cluster. A buffer is a staging area for I/O operations. DOS stores smaller sized output requests in this buffer until it becomes full. When the buffer is full, DOS now actually writes that cluster. (When the file is closed, any partially filled buffers are also written. Also, there is a flush buffer instruction that a program may request.)

Suppose that you are running the FAT16 file system and have a 2G drive. The cluster size is 32K. Now suppose that you start writing a letter to me and get as far as entering the “D” (for Dear Vic) and then save the file. DOS reports that the file size is one byte. However, DOS can only write a cluster. So in fact this 1-byte file really occupies 32K of disk space!

I remember when I first got a large capacity drive and proceeded to copy all my data that was stored on several smaller drives onto this new big drive. The copy operation failed. The drive reported that there was 640M stored on a 1G drive! Most of the files were small C++ source files. I had wasted 360M of disk space because of the large cluster size.

Large cluster size also has a benefit—faster loading of data. For example, if Windows needed to load a system DLL file that was 64K in size, then only 2 physical I/O operations are required to input it if the cluster size is 32K. If I had a cluster size of say 4K instead of the 32K cluster size, then Windows would have to issue 16 I/O requests to load that same DLL file.

The vitally important fact is that a cluster is the smallest unit of information that Windows/DOS can physically I/O. Let’s see how this physical I/O buffering operation works by following how the program that loads in cost records from a binary file on disk works. The main loop in **LoadArray** was

```
int j = 0;
while (j < limit &&
       infile.read ((char*) &arec[j], sizeof (CostRec))) {
 j++;
}
```

Further, let's assume that the size of the **CostRec** structure is 100 bytes and that the cluster size of the drive holding the file is 2K or 2048 bytes. When the program issues its first read for the very first record, DOS must input the first cluster of data into its buffer and then copy the first 100 bytes into **arec[0]** as shown in Figure 9.3.

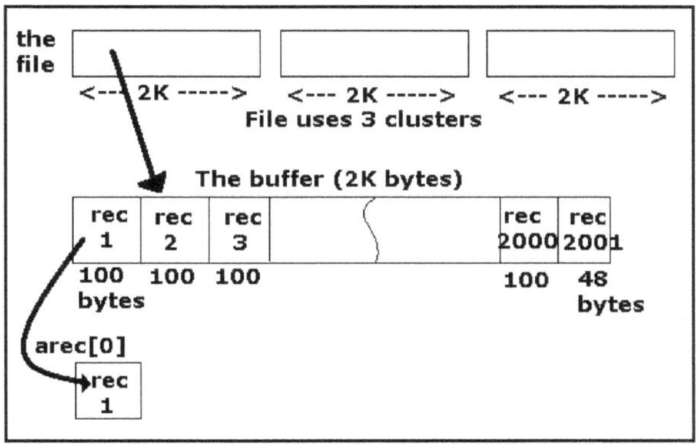

Figure 9.3 Input of the First Record

In order to input our first record, Windows/DOS inputs the first cluster into its internal buffer. Notice that there are 2000 complete 100 byte records and a partial last one of only 48 bytes. The remaining 52 bytes of the record 2001 are the first bytes in cluster 2. Next, the system copies the required 100 bytes from its buffer into our designated input area, here **arec[0]**.

However, when our program requests the next 1,999 records, Windows/DOS merely has to copy the required bytes from its buffer into our array elements. No physical I/O operations occur. However, when the program requests the 2001st record, after copying in the first 48 bytes of the data from its buffer, the system must again issue a physical I/O request to input the next cluster of data into its buffer. When that operation is complete, it can then move the remaining 52 bytes into our input area.

Note that smart disk cache controllers are highly likely to have (during some background processing time) already inputted the remaining clusters of the file and stored the data in cache memory. Thus, a real physical I/O operation might not need to be done. Instead, only a copy from cache memory is required in this case, speeding up the operation significantly.

As the system works its way through the buffer giving us our successive 100 byte records, DOS needs a pointer to keep track of where it is at in the buffer and file. This is called the **DOS File Offset Pointer** and is encapsulated by the **iostream** classes. The meaning of the DOS File Offset Pointer is this: the next input or output operation begins at this offset from the beginning of the file. And it is this DOS File Offset Pointer that we are vitally interested in understanding and using.

Figure 9.4 shows the DOS File Offset Pointer in operation during a series of successive input operations. Initially, when the file is first opened, the offset pointer is set to 0. In Figure 9.4, the first record has been input and stored in **arec[j]** and the file offset pointer has been incremented by the number of bytes just input. Figure 9.5 shows the situation after we input the second record.

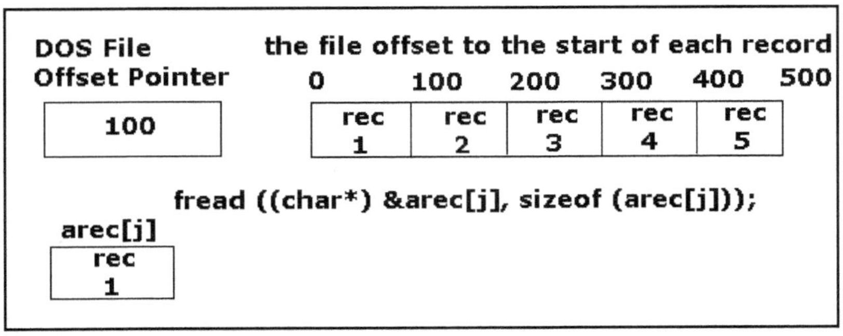

Figure 9.4 The File Offset Pointer After the First Read

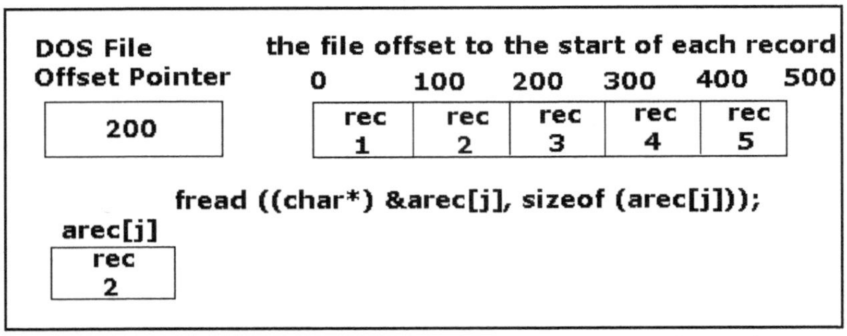

Figure 9.5 The File Offset Pointer after the Second Read

Now consider what would happen if somehow we placed 400 into the DOS file offset pointer and then issued another read instruction? Remember that the next file I/O operation will occur at this offset from the start of the file. We input record number 5. Further, what is the significance of the offset 500 in this example? It is the true DOS file size!

By adjusting the contents of the DOS file offset pointer, we can control which record in input by the next read instruction! Further, we can easily get the true file size of the file on disk. Finally, what results if we divide the file size by the size of the input record? This would be the number of records in the file! So this DOS file offset pointer is of vital importance when dealing with binary files.

Input streams have a pair of functions to read the contents of the DOS file offset pointer and to alter it. Output streams have a different pair of functions to read its contents and to alter it.

Input Streams:

```
pos_type tellg (); pos_type can be a long if filesize < 2G
istream& seekg (int offsetAmount, seekdir flag);
```

where the flag is

```
ios::beg - this offset from the beginning of the file
ios::cur - this offset from the current position in the file
ios::end - this offset from the end of the file
```

Output Streams:

```
pos_type tellp (); pos_type can be a long if filesize < 2G
istream& seekp (int offsetAmount, seekdir flag);
```

where the flag is the same as for input streams

The next series of examples illustrates some of the things we can do using binary files and the DOS file offset pointer.

Example 1: Reading and Writing Several Arrays to/from One Binary File

When the binary file contains several unrelated members, such as the contents of two different arrays that can contain differing number of elements, the current number in each array can be written first followed by that many elements of the corresponding array. Next, the number of elements in the second array is written followed by the second array.

```
long array1[1000];
int   count1;
double array2[2000];
int   count2;
...
outfile.write ((char*) &count1, sizeof (count1));
outfile.write ((char*) array1,  sizeof (long) * count1);
outfile.write ((char*) &count2, sizeof (count2));
outfile.write ((char*) array2,  sizeof (double) * count2);
```

To input the data, we code

```
infile.read ((char*) &count1, sizeof (count1));
infile.read ((char*) array1,  sizeof (long) * count1);
infile.read ((char*) &count2, sizeof (count2));
infile.read ((char*) array2,  sizeof (double) * count2);
```

Example 2: Processing an Array of Cost Records Blazingly Fast

Hard disks transfer data at very high rates. Some of today's faster disks transfer something like 120M per second or better. Let's say your drive can transfer 40M per second, roughly. How much data is 40M? To give you an appreciation for that volume, consider how many characters are in a large, fat novel. I wrote one once and it had 1,250,000 characters. How long would it take to type that many characters into the computer? Suppose that you can type as fast as the keyboard can accept data, 10 characters per second which corresponds to about 150 words per minute! This yields 125,000 seconds. How long is that? Well, let's divide by 50 seconds per minute (you need a breather each minute). This yields 2500 minutes. So let's divide by 50 minutes per hour (you will need a food break). This gives 50 hours or 2 days nonstop typing at 150 words per minute just to get the large novel entered. But in one second, the drive can give us 40M. Thus, if we had to type in that amount of data by hand, it would take us over 2 months continuous typing at 150 words per minute!

We can harness this incredible speed in our programs. There is no need for message boxes to pop up saying "10 seconds remaining" on copying a 10M file. It should take only a fraction of a second.

Here, the array **arec** can contain up to 100,000 records and **count** contains the current number in the array. To output the entire array of **count** elements, we code the following.

```
CostRec arec[100000];
long    count;
outfile.write ((char*) arec, sizeof (arec[0]) * count);
```

However, to input an array of an unknown number of cost records is more complex. We must find the number of elements that are actually in the binary file. We can use the **seekg** and **tellg** functions as follows.

```
// first, position file offset ptr to eof
infile.seekg (0, ios::end);
// get that offset and divide by size to get count
// note: if infile.tellg () % sizeof (CostRec) is not 0,
// then the file is somehow corrupt as we have a partial
// record in the file somewhere...
count = infile.tellg () / sizeof (CostRec);
```

```
// vitally important: reposition file offset to beginning!
infile.seekg (0, ios::beg);
// one read request inputs entire file at blazing speed
infile.read ((char*) arec, sizeof (CostRec) * count);
```

Just how fast is this going to be? It depends on the size of the file and available memory and the state of file fragmentation. But it will be a very dramatic speed up. I once had a student who was maintaining a production program that needed to input a very large two-dimensional array of long integers. It was a drafting type of program. However, every time the program needed to load the array, it took over three minutes! Likewise, when the user chose the save option, another three minutes elapsed. After this presentation, he rewrote the load operation to use the blazing fast approach. He wrapped a **cout** pair of messages around the new loading code: Starting the load and End of load. This way, he figured he could time how long it now took to load. When he first ran it, the two messages went by almost instantaneously so he figured the data failed to load. But upon checking, it was all there! He ran it again to be sure. His three minute delay was cut down to virtually no observable time at all!

Example 3: Using Dynamic Allocation for an Array of Unknown Number of Records

Dynamic memory allocation is very often used to load arrays of unknown numbers of elements. The idea is to determine the file size and hence the number of elements actually present in the file. Then, allocate an array sufficiently large enough to hold that data. Finally, issue a single read to load the entire file in a blaze.

```
CostRec* arec;
int   count;
infile.seekg (0, ios::end);
count = infile.tellg () / sizeof (CostRec);
infile.seekg (0, ios::beg);
arec = new CostRec [count];
infile.read ((char*) arec, sizeof (CostRec) * count);
...
delete [] arec;
```

However, the above coding is mostly working. What happens if the amount of memory the program asks for is not available? What happens if the file is corrupt? We can insert a bit of error checking as follows.

```
count = infile.tellg () / sizeof (CostRec);
if (infile.tellg () % sizeof (CostRec) != 0) {
 cerr << "Error: the input file may be corrupt\n";
 infile.close();
 exit (2);
}
infile.seekg (0, ios::beg);
arec = new CostRec [count];
if (!arec) {
 cerr << "Error: insufficient memory to load the array\n";
 infile.close();
 exit (1);
}
infile.read ((char*) arec, sizeof (CostRec) * count);
```

Example 4: Binary File Processing: the StudentRoster Linked List (Pgm09a)

Suppose that we need to maintain a student roster for a course. The needed student data is stored in a **Student** structure.

```
struct Student {
 char name[NAME_LEN];
 long ssno;
 char grade;
};
```

A linked list is ideal for this application and we can reuse our template list class from the last chapter.

Initially, the input data comes from a text file. However, the administration wants to be able to build a binary master file so that future program executions can load the data faster. Thus, our application at the minimum should be able to load the student roster from either a text or binary file and should be able to save the data to either a text or binary file. To verify that it has done this correctly, the resultant list of student structures should be traversed and displayed in a nice report. For this example, the main processing consists of loading a text file into the list, displaying the contents of the list in a report, saving the list's contents as a binary file, loading the list from the newly created binary file, and displaying the contents of the list once again.

There are two approaches one can take to the design. One way is to create the needed C style functions and let main call them. The other way is to create a wrapper class around the linked list, say called **StudentRoster**. The load and save functions would become methods of this wrapper class. In either case, we create an instance of the template list this way.

```
DoubleLinkedList<Student> list;
```

If we opt to use the first approach, then main defines the list and passes it to the series of functions. Their prototypes become cumbersome.

```
void LoadAllStudentsFromTextFile (const char* filename,
                           DoubleLinkedList<Student>& list);
```

To avoid this monstrosity in all prototypes, programmers often use a **typedef** to create a better name.

```
typedef DoubleLinkedList<Student> StudentList;
void LoadAllStudentsFromTextFile (const char* filename,
                                  StudentList& list);
```

One benefit of wrapping a **StudentRoster** class around the double linked list is that the list now becomes member data available to all methods without the need of being passed about. The **typedef** is not needed. A second benefit of choosing to write a wrapper class is "the future." Assuming that all goes well with the text-to-binary process, the administration will request a fully operational program with the ability to add, find, and remove students from the roster of a class. Thus, if we build these kinds of functionality into our wrapper class initially, then we are ready for all sorts of future operations. From an academic point of view, using a wrapper class illustrates how and why wrapper classes can be built.

Of course, the real problem with binary files is that the binary master file must be built before it can be read. One cannot use a text editor to build a binary file. Rather, a program must write the binary data to the file. Usually, these are called data entry front end programs. Such programs input the text information and edit it, thereby guaranteeing only valid data is written to disk.

Pgm09a solves this problem by reading in the text file of student data and loading up the **StudentRoster** list and displaying the roster. Then, it writes the list to a binary file. Then, **Pgm09a** loads that binary file of data into the roster list and reprints the roster so we can manually compare the results.

The **StudentRoster** class has a single data member, an instance of the template double linked list class. The class provides the functions to read a text file of students or to read a binary file of student records. There is the corresponding two write functions, one for the text file version and one for the binary file version. But the wrapper class does more. It also implements the copy constructor and assignment operator.

One can make an educated prediction of what other functions would likely be desired by client programs if the administration adopts the use of the binary master file. Those would include inserting a new student record at a specific location in the list, finding a specific student given their social security number, and deleting a specific student from the list. Obviously, there could be other actions that the client programs may desire. So if we provide a mechanism for clients to traverse the entire list, that capability can handle a good many things for which we have not yet planned. Thus, the **StudentRoster** implements the **ResetToHead**, **Next**, and **GetCurrentStudent** methods; each of which simply passes on the request to the actual list itself.

Here is the **StudentRoster** class definition. Notice the template class header file is included. Notice on line 40 how our instance of the template double linked list is defined.

StudentRoster Class Definition

```
 1 #pragma once
 2 #include "DoubleLinkedList.h"
 3
 4 /*******************************************************/
 5 /*                                                     */
 6 /* StudentRoster class                                 */
 7 /*                                                     */
 8 /* Maintain a list of students who are enrolled in a  */
 9 /* course                                              */
10 /*                                                     */
11 /* Ability to read and write a binary master file added */
12 /*                                                     */
13 /*******************************************************/
14
15 const int NAME_LEN = 21;
18
19 /******************************************************/
20 /*                                                    */
21 /* Student: contains the client's student data        */
22 /*                                                    */
23 /******************************************************/
24
25 struct Student {
26  char name[NAME_LEN];
27  long ssno;
28  char grade;
29 };
30
31
32 class StudentRoster {
33
34  /*****************************************************/
35  /*                                                   */
36  /* class data                                        */
37  /*                                                   */
38  /*****************************************************/
39
40 DoubleLinkedList<Student> list;
41
42  /*****************************************************/
43  /*                                                   */
44  /* class functions                                   */
45  /*                                                   */
```

```
/*****************************************************/

public:
          StudentRoster ();  // constructs an empty roster
          StudentRoster (const StudentRoster& r);  // copy roster
StudentRoster& operator= (const StudentRoster& r); // copy roster
         ~StudentRoster ();  // deletes the roster
 void     EmptyList ();      // removes all items from the list

 // loads all students from a file - items are in reverse order
 void LoadAllStudentsFromTextFile (const char* filename);
 // loads all students from a binary file
 void LoadAllStudentsFromBinaryFile (char* filename);

 // displays all students in the list
 void PrintAllStudents (ostream& outfile);
 // displays a single student
 void PrintThisStudent (ostream& outfile, const Student& s)const;
 // outputs the whole list to a new student roster file
 void WriteNewTextFile (const char* filename);
 // outputs a new binary master file of student data
 void WriteNewBinaryFile (char* filename);

 // finds a specific student, returns 0 if ssn is not found
 Student* FindThisStudent (long ssn);

 // inserts a new student into list after this specific student
 // or inserts thenew one at the head if this ssn is not found
 bool InsertAfter (long ssn, Student* ptrs);
 // remove this student from the list, does nothing if not found
 void DeleteThisStudent (long ssn);

 // list iterator functions
 void ResetToHead ();               // set to start of the list
 void Next ();                      // moves to the next item
 Student* GetCurrentStudent () const; // gets the current student
                                      // or 0 if there is none
protected:
 istream& InputStudentData (istream& infile, Student& s);
 void CopyList (StudentRoster& r);
};
```

Here is the **StudentRoster** implementation. I have highlighted the binary file actions in bold face. Notice how streamlined the I/O coding is when using binary files!

StudentRoster Class Implementation

```
#include <iostream>
#include <iomanip>
#include <fstream>
#include "StudentRoster.h"
using namespace std;

/*****************************************************/
/*                                                   */
/* StudentRoster: constructor to set list to empty   */
```

```
/*                                                      */
/********************************************************/

StudentRoster::StudentRoster () {
}

/*********************************************************/
/*                                                       */
/* ~StudentRoster: destructor to empty the list          */
/*                                                       */
/*********************************************************/

StudentRoster::~StudentRoster () {
 EmptyList ();
}

/************************************************************/
/*                                                          */
/* LoadAllStudentsFromTextFile:                             */
/*                  input a file of students into the list */
/*                                                          */
/************************************************************/

void StudentRoster::LoadAllStudentsFromTextFile (
                                          const char* filename) {
 Student* ptrs;
 ifstream infile (filename);
 if (!infile) {
  cerr << "StudentRoster Error - cannot open file "
       << filename << endl;
  return; // assume data is correct in the file
 }
 try {
  ptrs = new Student;
 }
 catch (std::bad_alloc e) { // check for out of memory
  cerr << "Error - out of memory\n";
  exit (1);
 }

 while (InputStudentData (infile, *ptrs)) {
  if (!list.AddAtTail (ptrs))
   exit(5);
  try {
   ptrs = new Student;
  }
  catch (std::bad_alloc e) { // check for out of memory
   cerr << "Error - out of memory\n";
   exit (1);
  }
 }
 delete ptrs;
 infile.close ();
 list.ResetToHead ();        // leave currentptr stable
}

```

```
/***************************************************************/
/*                                                             */
/* InputStudentData: read in one set of student data           */
/*                                                             */
/***************************************************************/

istream& StudentRoster::InputStudentData (istream& infile,
                                          Student& s) {
 // assumes that the file contains no bad data
 infile >> ws;
 if (!infile) return infile;
 infile.get (s.name, sizeof (s.name));
 if (!infile) return infile;
 infile >> s.ssno >> s.grade;
 return infile;
}

/**************************************************************/
/*                                                            */
/* LoadAllStudentsFromBinaryFile:                             */
/*          load list from a binary master file of data       */
/*                                                            */
/**************************************************************/

void StudentRoster::LoadAllStudentsFromBinaryFile (
                                       char* filename) {
 Student* ptrs;
 ifstream infile (filename, ios::in | ios::binary);
 if (!infile) {
  cerr << "Error: cannot open input file\n";
  exit (2);
 }
 try {
  ptrs = new Student;
 }
 catch (std::bad_alloc e) { // check for out of memory
  cerr << "Error - out of memory\n";
  exit (3);
 }

 while (infile.read ((char*)ptrs, sizeof (Student))) {
  if (!list.AddAtTail (ptrs))
   exit (6);
  try {
   ptrs = new Student;
  }
  catch (std::bad_alloc e) { // check for out of memory
   cerr << "Error - out of memory\n";
   exit (3);
  }
 }
 delete ptrs;
 infile.close ();
 list.ResetToHead ();
}
```

```
/*******************************************************/
/*                                                     */
/* WriteNewBinaryFile: save list to a binary master file*/
/*                                                     */
/*******************************************************/

void StudentRoster::WriteNewBinaryFile (char* filename) {
 ofstream out (filename, ios::out | ios::binary);
 if (!out) {
  cerr << "Error: cannot open the binary output file\n";
  exit (1);
 }
 list.ResetToHead ();
 Student* ptrstudent = list.GetCurrentNode ();
 while (ptrstudent) {
  out.write ((char*) ptrstudent, sizeof (Student));
  Next ();
  ptrstudent = list.GetCurrentNode ();
 }
 out.close ();
}

/********************************************************/
/*                                                      */
/* PrintAllStudents: display all of the students in list */
/*                                                      */
/********************************************************/

void StudentRoster::PrintAllStudents (ostream& outfile) {
 list.ResetToHead ();
 Student* ptrs = list.GetCurrentNode ();
 while (ptrs) {
  PrintThisStudent (outfile, *ptrs);
  list.Next ();
  ptrs = list.GetCurrentNode ();
 }
 list.ResetToHead ();       // leave currentptr stable
}

/********************************************************/
/*                                                      */
/* PrintThisStudent: displays one set of student data   */
/*                                                      */
/********************************************************/

void StudentRoster::PrintThisStudent (ostream& outfile,
                                      const Student& s) const {
 outfile << left << "     " << setw (25) << s.name
  << right << setw (12) << s.ssno << setw (5) << s.grade << endl;
}

/********************************************************/
/*                                                      */
/* FindThisStudent: match ssn with an item in the list  */
/*                                                      */
/* returns a pointer to the matching student or 0       */
```

```
/*                                                        */
/**********************************************************/

Student*  StudentRoster::FindThisStudent (long ssn) {
 if (list.GetSize () == 0) return 0;
 list.ResetToHead ();
 Student* ptrs = list.GetCurrentNode ();
 while (ptrs) {
  if (ptrs->ssno == ssn) return ptrs;
  list.Next ();
  ptrs = list.GetCurrentNode ();
 }
 return 0;
}

/**********************************************************/
/*                                                        */
/* InsertAfter: adds this student to list after ssn Node */
/*                                                        */
/* if no match or empty list, it is added at the head    */
/* of the list                                            */
/*                                                        */
/**********************************************************/

bool StudentRoster::InsertAfter (long ssn, Student* ptrs) {
 // if list is empty, add at head
 if (list.GetSize() == 0)
  return list.AddAtHead (ptrs);
 else { // look for matching ssn
  Student* ptrmatched = FindThisStudent (ssn);
  if (ptrmatched == 0)   // no matching ssn, so
   return list.AddAtHead (ptrs); // add this one at head
  else { // here it matches, so allocate new node and fill it
   return list.InsertAfterCurrentNode (ptrs);
  }
 }
 list.ResetToHead ();       // leave currentptr stable
}

/**********************************************************/
/*                                                        */
/* DeleteThisStudent: deletes this student from the list */
/*                                                        */
/* does not return an error code if the ssn is not found */
/*                                                        */
/**********************************************************/

void StudentRoster::DeleteThisStudent (long ssn) {
 // check for an empty list and do nothing if empty
 if (list.GetSize() == 0) return;
 Student* ptrmatched = FindThisStudent (ssn);
 if (!ptrmatched) return;  // this ssn was not found
 list.DeleteCurrentNode(); // delete the list node
 list.ResetToHead ();      // leave currentptr stable
}

```

```
/***************************************************************/
/*                                                             */
/* WriteNewTextFile: writes all students in list to a file*/
/*                                                             */
/***************************************************************/

void StudentRoster::WriteNewTextFile (const char* filename) {
 ofstream os (filename);
 if (!os) {
  cerr << "StudentRoster Error: cannot open output file "
       << filename << endl;
  return;
 }
 // traverse list and write each one to the file
 list.ResetToHead ();
 Student* ptrs = list.GetCurrentNode ();
 while (ptrs) {
  os << setw (sizeof (ptrs->name))
     << ptrs->name << " "
     << ptrs->ssno << " "
     << ptrs->grade << endl;
  list.Next ();
  ptrs = list.GetCurrentNode ();
 }
 os.close ();
 list.ResetToHead ();       // leave currentptr stable
}

/**************************************************************/
/*                                                            */
/* ResetToHead: sets currentptr to the first node in list*/
/*                                                            */
/**************************************************************/

void StudentRoster::ResetToHead () {
 list.ResetToHead ();
}

/**************************************************************/
/*                                                            */
/* GetCurrentStudent: returns ptr to the current student */
/*                                                            */
/**************************************************************/

Student* StudentRoster::GetCurrentStudent () const {
 return list.GetCurrentNode ();
}

/**************************************************************/
/*                                                            */
/* Next: sets currentptr to the next node in the list    */
/*                                                            */
/**************************************************************/

void StudentRoster::Next () {
 list.Next ();
```

```
}

/***************************************************************/
/*                                                             */
/* EmptyList: removes all items from the list                  */
/*                                                             */
/***************************************************************/

void StudentRoster::EmptyList () {
 list.EmptyList ();   // delete all nodes
}

/***************************************************************/
/*                                                             */
/* StudentRoster: copy constructor - make duplicate list */
/*                                                             */
/***************************************************************/

StudentRoster::StudentRoster (const StudentRoster& r) {
 // typecast is required because its currentptr is changed
 // if we wish to use the provided iterator functions
 // if we manually track the pointers, then it can remain
 // a constant reference
 CopyList ((StudentRoster&)r);
}

/***************************************************************/
/*                                                             */
/* operator= makes a duplicate list                            */
/*                                                             */
/***************************************************************/

StudentRoster& StudentRoster::operator= (const StudentRoster& r){
 if (this == &r) return *this;
 EmptyList ();
 // typecast is required because its currentptr is changed
 // if we wish to use the provided iterator functions
 // if we manually track the pointers, then it can remain
 // a constant reference
 CopyList ((StudentRoster&)r);
 return *this;
}

/***************************************************************/
/*                                                             */
/* CopyList: helper function to shallow copy a list            */
/*                                                             */
/***************************************************************/

void StudentRoster::CopyList (StudentRoster& r) {
 list = r.list;
 list.ResetToHead ();
}
```

Pgm09a main function coding is very simple indeed. The resulting output is shown below as well.

I took the liberty to perform some elementary testing of the additional functions that the roster class provides.

Pgm09a - Load and Save Using a Binary Master File

```
#include <iostream>
#include <iomanip>
#include <crtdbg.h>
#include "StudentRoster.h"
using namespace std;
/***************************************************************/
/*                                                             */
/* Pgm09a: illustrate saving and loading a binary master       */
/*         file                                                */
/*                                                             */
/***************************************************************/

int main () {

 {
  StudentRoster roster;
  // first load from the text file of data
  roster.LoadAllStudentsFromTextFile ("Roster.txt");
  cout << "\n\n    My Class Roster - loaded from text file\n\n"
       << "    Name                        StudentID  Grade\n\n";
  roster.PrintAllStudents (cout);

  // now save to a binary file - ie. builds the binary master
  roster.WriteNewBinaryFile ("master.dat");
  roster.EmptyList ();

  // now load from a binary master file
  roster.LoadAllStudentsFromBinaryFile ("master.dat");
  cout << "\n\n    My Class Roster - loaded from binary file\n\n"
       << "    Name                        StudentID  Grade\n\n";
  roster.PrintAllStudents (cout);

  StudentRoster dupeRoster = roster;
  cout << "\n\n    My Class Roster - from copy ctor\n\n"
       << "    Name                        StudentID  Grade\n\n";
  dupeRoster.PrintAllStudents (cout);

  StudentRoster dupeRoster2;
  dupeRoster2 = roster;
  cout << "\n\n    My Class Roster - from operator =\n\n"
       << "    Name                        StudentID  Grade\n\n";
  dupeRoster.PrintAllStudents (cout);

  Student* ptrs = roster.FindThisStudent (234234333 );
  if (ptrs) {
   cout << "\n\n  Testing Find - Should Find Jennifer\n";
   roster.PrintThisStudent (cout, *ptrs);
  }
  else cout << "\n\n Error - unable to find Jennifer\n\n";

  Student* ptrss = new Student;
  *ptrss = *ptrs;
```

```
  roster.DeleteThisStudent (234234333);
  cout << "\n\n    My Class Roster - after deleting Jennifer\n\n"
       << "    Name                            StudentID  Grade\n\n";
  roster.PrintAllStudents (cout);

  roster.InsertAfter (324234234, ptrss);
  cout << "\n\n    My Class Roster - after adding Jennifer\n\n"
       << "    Name                            StudentID  Grade\n\n";
  roster.PrintAllStudents (cout);

  cout << "\n\nMy Class Roster - testing iteration functions\n\n"
       << "    Name                            StudentID  Grade\n\n";
  roster.ResetToHead ();
  ptrs = roster.GetCurrentStudent ();
  while (ptrs) {
   roster.PrintThisStudent (cout, *ptrs);
   roster.Next ();
   ptrs = roster.GetCurrentStudent ();
  }
 }

 if (_CrtDumpMemoryLeaks())
  cout << "\nOops! Memory Leaks!!\n";
 else
  cout << "\nNo Memory Leaks\n";

 return 0;
}
```

```
Output from Pgm09a


    My Class Roster - loaded from text file

    Name                            StudentID  Grade

    Betsy                           123456789    A
    Sam Spade                       234565677    B
    Annie Smith                     324233456    A
    Thomas J. Jones                 345344344    A
    Allan Adaire                    324234234    C
    Jennifer Smallville             234234333    A


    My Class Roster - loaded from binary file

    Name                            StudentID  Grade

    Betsy                           123456789    A
    Sam Spade                       234565677    B
    Annie Smith                     324233456    A
    Thomas J. Jones                 345344344    A
    Allan Adaire                    324234234    C
    Jennifer Smallville             234234333    A
```

```


    My Class Roster - from copy ctor

    Name                          StudentID  Grade

    Betsy                         123456789    A
    Sam Spade                     234565677    B
    Annie Smith                   324233456    A
    Thomas J. Jones               345344344    A
    Allan Adaire                  324234234    C
    Jennifer Smallville           234234333    A


    My Class Roster - from operator =

    Name                          StudentID  Grade

    Betsy                         123456789    A
    Sam Spade                     234565677    B
    Annie Smith                   324233456    A
    Thomas J. Jones               345344344    A
    Allan Adaire                  324234234    C
    Jennifer Smallville           234234333    A


  Testing Find - Should Find Jennifer
    Jennifer Smallville           234234333    A


    My Class Roster - after deleting Jennifer

    Name                          StudentID  Grade

    Betsy                         123456789    A
    Sam Spade                     234565677    B
    Annie Smith                   324233456    A
    Thomas J. Jones               345344344    A
    Allan Adaire                  324234234    C


    My Class Roster - after adding Jennifer

    Name                          StudentID  Grade

    Betsy                         123456789    A
    Sam Spade                     234565677    B
    Annie Smith                   324233456    A
    Thomas J. Jones               345344344    A
    Allan Adaire                  324234234    C
    Jennifer Smallville           234234333    A


    My Class Roster - testing iteration functions

    Name                          StudentID  Grade
```

```

     Betsy                        123456789    A
     Sam Spade                    234565677    B
     Annie Smith                  324233456    A
     Thomas J. Jones              345344344    A
     Allan Adaire                 324234234    C
     Jennifer Smallville          234234333    A

No Memory Leaks
Press any key to continue
```

Overview of Direct Access File Processing Operations

The ability to access the DOS file offset pointer becomes the basis for all types of direct access file processing operations. Direct access refers to the ability to input or output one specific record out of all others. In an **Inquiry** type of program, when the user enters some kind of key identification value, the program retrieves directly the record in the file that corresponds to that key. In a direct access **update** type of program, in addition to accessing a record with a specific identification key value, the program can rewrite just that corresponding record.

Direct access processing then differs from sequential access. The only way a sequential access operation could find a record that corresponded to a specific key identification value would be to input every record in turn looking for a match. With larger files, this is unworkable.

This section deals with the general theory of the more common methods that are employed.

The Relative Record Number Method

The most fundamental method of direct access is known as the relative record number method. Every record in the file must have the same length. The first record in the file is arbitrarily assigned relative record number of 0. Each successive record in the file has a relative record number that is one greater than the previous record. Figure 9.6 illustrates this with the five cost records. The key identifier value becomes the relative record number.

To access the cost record whose relative record number is 1, we must multiply the key by the size of the records, seek to that position from the beginning of the file and input that data.

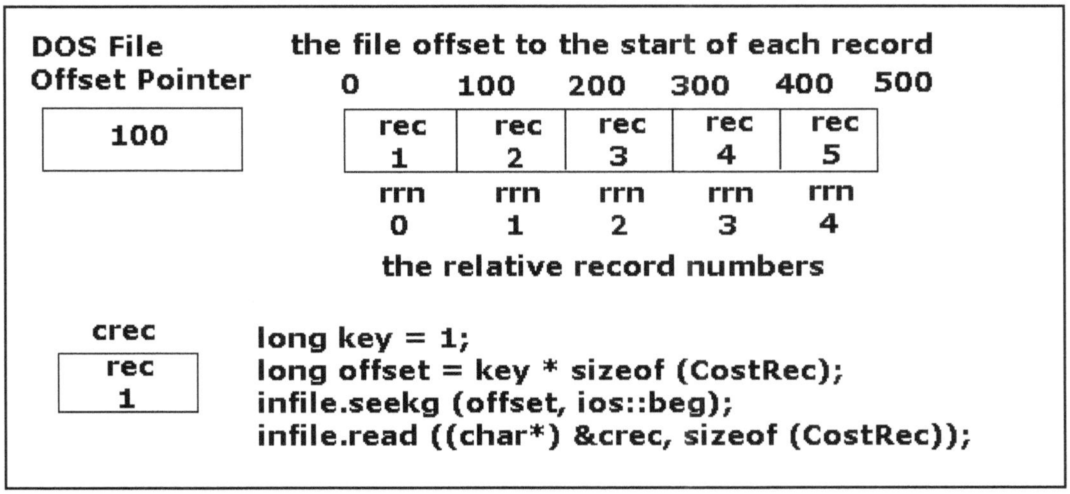

Figure 9.6 The Relative Record Number Method

Thus, given the key (which is the relative record number), one can directly access this data by the following.

```
CostRec crec;
long key;
long offset = key * sizeof (CostRec);
infile.seekg (offset, ios::beg);
infile.read ((char*) &crec, sizeof (crec);
```

The relative record number method is the fastest of all the methods for directly accessing a specific record in a binary master file. It is also the foundation of all the other more advanced methods. However, it has two serious drawbacks.

First, relative record numbers make terrible key identifier fields. Suppose your relative record number was 0. How many checks do you suppose you could cash if your account number was 0? These kinds of keys have nothing to do with real world identifiers, such as a person's social security number that is so often used as the key identifier.

Second, relative record numbers make deletion of records a total mess. Consider the following scenario as shown in Figure 9.7. Our company has five accounts. We use the relative record number as each account's id number. Now we delete Tom's account for failure to pay the balance due. What happens to the relative record numbers for those accounts that follow the deleted Tom account? They all change! Betsy's id, which was 3, now becomes 2. Fred's id, which was 4, now becomes 3. Thus, we have to issue new account numbers every time a record is deleted—reprint checks or issue a new plastic charge card and so forth.

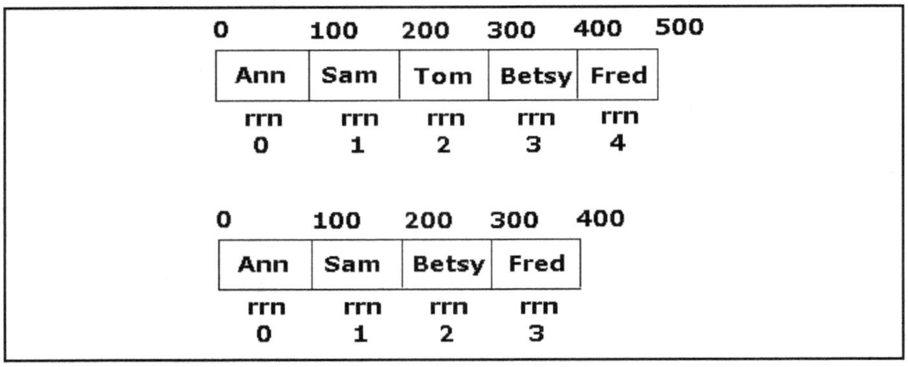

Figure 9.7 Relative Record Numbers Change After a Deletion

The Remainder Method

The remainder method is a vast improvement over the relative record number method because any numerical key can be used. Thus, one could use keys such as a person's social security number. With this method, one must know the absolute maximum number of records the binary master file is to contain. And a file containing this many records must be built. Initially all the records are dummies and contain dummy data. The procedure goes as follows.

1. Determine the maximum number of records.
2. Find the largest prime number that does not exceed this maximum number.
3. Let key equal the individual's key id number % this prime number.
4. The resulting key becomes the relative record number of that record on disk.

Suppose that we decide that our company will never have more than 3 clients. So the maximum number is three. The largest prime number that does not exceed 3 is 3. Now we decide to add Ann as a client. We assign her an id number of 1. The key becomes 1 % 3 or 1. Thus, her data goes into relative record number 1 in the file. This process is shown in Figure 9.8. In a similar manner, we add clients Tom (id = 2) and Betsy (id = 3).

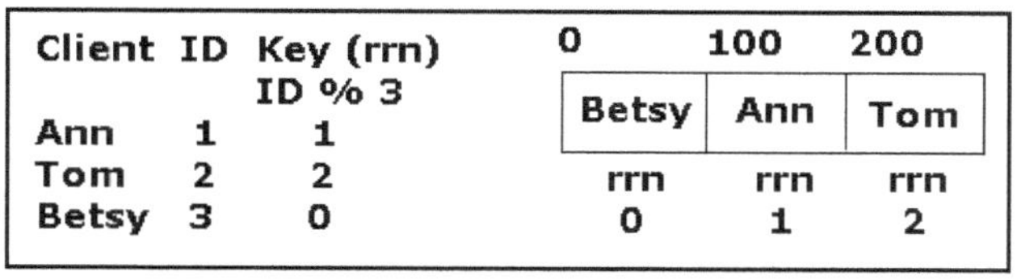
Client ID Key (rrn)
ID % 3
Ann 1 1
Tom 2 2
Betsy 3 0
0 100 200
Betsy Ann Tom
rrn rrn rrn
0 1 2

Figure 9.8 The Remainder Method in Action

So far, all is working perfectly. But what happens when we decide to expand and add another client, say Sam? We assign Sam the id number of 4. The remainder is 1 and so the relative record number is 1. However, there already is a record at that location, Ann. Oops. Now what do we do? This is the common problem of duplicate remainders. The solution is to store all duplicate remainder records sequentially in an overflow area that begins immediately after the maximum number of records. Figure 9.9 shows the situation after adding three more clients.

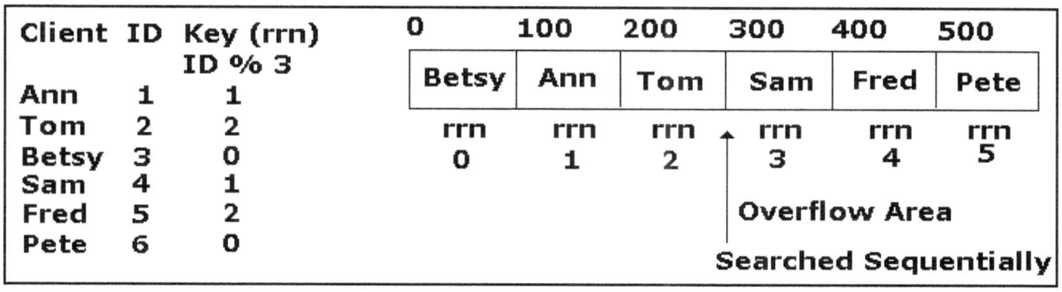
Client ID Key (rrn)
ID % 3
Ann 1 1
Tom 2 2
Betsy 3 0
Sam 4 1
Fred 5 2
Pete 6 0
0 100 200 300 400 500
Betsy Ann Tom Sam Fred Pete
rrn rrn rrn rrn rrn rrn
0 1 2 3 4 5
Overflow Area
Searched Sequentially

Figure 9.9 Three Records in the Overflow Area

The coding to access a remainder method file is as follows.

```
long idNumber;          // the person's id number just input
long key = idNumber % Max; //Max is the max number of recs
long offset = key * sizeof (CostRec);
infile.seekg (offset, ios::beg);
infile.read ((char*) &crec, sizeof (crec);
if (crec.idNumber != idNumber) {
 // oops, the record must be in the overflow area
 infile.seekg (Max * sizeof(CostRec));
 while (idNumber != crec.idNumber && infile) {
  infile.read ((char*) &crec, sizeof (crec);
 }
 if (infile) {
 // here we have the desired record
 }
 else {
  cerr << "Error: record not found in data base\n";
 }
}
else {
 // here we have the desired record
}
```

Since the overflow area must be searched sequentially, the more records that are in the overflow area, the poorer the program's performance. Consider what would have occurred if I had used these clients' social security numbers as their identification keys. We might have had the following.

```
Ann     333 33 3333
Tom     333 33 3336
Betsy   333 33 3339
Sam     666 66 6666
Fred    999 99 9999
Pete    333 66 9999
```

All of these yield the same exact relative record number of 1!

To get the best results from the remainder method, one needs a good guess of the maximum number of records ever to be needed. Secondly, one should assign id numbers beginning with 1 up to that maximum number. This would avoid as many duplicate remainders as possible.

The Indexed Sequential Access Method (ISAM)

The Indexed Sequential Access Method, or ISAM for short, permits one to have any type of key identifiers desired, including characters as well as numerical digits. The ISAM scheme then stores a table of id keys versus the relative record number assigned to that record. Figure 9.10 illustrates this approach for our three clients.

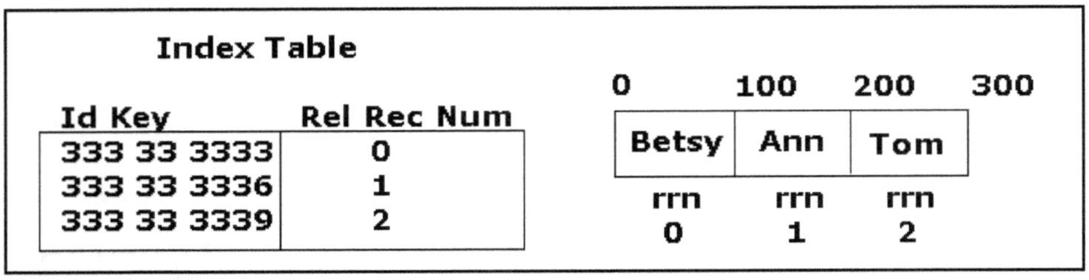

Figure 9.10 The ISAM Method with Three Clients

Notice that the key id numbers can be anything. To find any record, one searches the index table's Id Key array looking for an exact match. When found, the key to use becomes the corresponding relative record number. One would then proceed to input the data as before by finding the offset, seeking to that location and reading in the record.

Of course, one must save this index table on disk as well as the binary master file. Often the file extension .idx or .id is used. Sometimes the index file gets lost or accidentally deleted. Thus, the Id Key values must also be stored as a field within each record in the master file. Then, the index file can be recreated simply by reading in each record sequentially and adding another entry to the new index.

This method gets its name from the ability to read the file sequentially or by accessing a specific record directly. A monthly billing program certainly would access the file sequentially as it methodically printed a bill for each customer in turn.

However, of the three methods for direct access, the ISAM method is the slowest in execution because of the table lookup operation. Suppose that the Id Keys were actually character strings, such as part numbers AA-123-Z-42. How would the comparisons be done? We would have to use a **stricmp** function call for each test! To speed up the searching operation when there are large numbers of records in the index, the index is maintained in a sorted manner, usually low to high. If the Id Keys are numeric and sorted, a binary search can be used to more rapidly find the matching entry.

Further, if the index is huge, then several layers of indices can be constructed. One might have a top-level index table such as shown below.

Master Index

Id Range	Use this index file next
100 00 0000 to 199 99 9999	Index1.idx
200 00 0000 to 299 99 9999	Index2.idx

...
900 00 0000 to 999 99 9999 Index9.idx
Then in the nine additional index tables, only the indicated range of id values are present.

Handling Variable Length Records

Implicit in the entire discussion thus far is the fact that all records must be fixed in length. That is, all records contain the same number of bytes so that we can calculate the file offset by multiplying the relative record number by the constant fixed size. However, in the real world, not all records are fixed in length. How can a binary file contain variable length records and still provide direct access to them?

When a variable length record is written to disk, uniformly across all platforms, the first two or four bytes of that record contain the total length of the record. Without some idea of the length of the current record, it is impossible to effectively input it.

A trick that is often used to provide a method of direct access to a set of varying length records in a binary master file is to modify the ISAM index table. Instead of storing the relative record number, let's store the actual file offset to get to that record. It is also valuable to store the length of that record in the table as well. For example, we could have the following index table.

```
Id Number     Offset Length
111 11 1111     0       50
122 34 4444    50      100
344 43 6456   150      200
344 55 5555   350       50
555 55 5555   400      100
```

Now when a match is found, we seek to that offset and input the length number of bytes.

Handling Update Files in C++

When a program is to perform a binary file update, a record with a specific key is read into memory, changes are made to its contents, and the record rewritten back to disk at the same location in the file. This means that we need a file stream that can be both read and written. Such streams are instances of the **fstream** class.

Further, we must use **seekg** and **tellg** on the input side and **seekp** and **tellp** on the output side. However, another problem is likely to occur. Suppose we are reading records and reach the end of file. The stream goes into the end of file state. No further I/O operations are allowed because it is at the end of file. After handling any processing required because the end of file was reached, we need a way to reset the file back into the good state so that further I/O operations can be performed. The **clear** function does this for us. We pass it the flag **ios::good** as the state in which we wish the stream to be. For example,

```
file.clear (ios::good);
```

would reset all flags to the good state for the resumption of I/O operations.

Pgm09b: the Master File Update Program, Relative Record Method

Pgm09b is designed to illustrate the methods required to handle update files using **fstream** instances. Acme Credit Card Company has a master file of card holders. During the day, three types of transactions can occur. A new card holder can be added. An existing card holder can have an increase in their credit limit. An existing card holder's balance can be changed because of payments or additional charges.

Initially, the binary master file must be constructed from a text file. The file contains the person's name surrounded by double quote marks. This is followed by their balance and their credit limit. The id number of each client is the relative record number. Thus, the program begins by building the binary master file.

Next, a file of new transactions must be applied to the master file. The first character in the transaction's file determines what type of transaction this line contains. If the character is an "a," then this is an add new client request. The new client's name follows next and is surrounded by double quote marks. Then comes the balance and finally the limit for that client. If the character is a "b," then we are to modify the balance. In this case, the next number is the relative record number id field which is followed by the relative change in their balance, a positive or negative number. If the first character is an "l," then we are to change their credit limit. The client's id number again comes next followed by the relative change in their credit limit.

When the transactions have been processed, a new binary master file is written. Here is what the output from the program looks like.

```
Output from Pgm09b - Binary Master File Update Program
```

```
File initially contains 4 records


 Acme Credit Master File

Id Number   Name                   Balance   Limit

     0      Annie Jones-Smith      4500.00   5000.00
     1      Betsy Smith            3000.00   4000.00
     2      Samuel Spade           2500.42   3000.00
     3      Thomas Dunhill         3500.00   4500.00


Transaction Log

     4      Joe Smythe             4242.00   5000.00 Added
     0      Annie Jones-Smith      4750.00   5000.00 Balance +250.00
     2      Samuel Spade           2542.42   3000.00 Balance + 42.00
     1      Betsy Smith            3000.00   6000.00 Limit + 2000.00
     5      Henry P. Jones         4000.00   5000.00 Added


File now contains 6 records


 Acme Credit Master File

Id Number   Name                   Balance   Limit

     0      Annie Jones-Smith      4750.00   5000.00
     1      Betsy Smith            3000.00   6000.00
     2      Samuel Spade           2542.42   3000.00
     3      Thomas Dunhill         3500.00   4500.00
     4      Joe Smythe             4242.00   5000.00
     5      Henry P. Jones         4000.00   5000.00
```

Here are the original **Accounts.txt** input file from which the master file is constructed and the **transactions.txt** file that defines the day's operations to be performed on the master file.

```
The Original Text Accounts Input File
```

```
"Annie Jones-Smith" 4500 5000
"Betsy Smith" 3000 4000
```

```
3 "Samuel Spade" 2500.42 3000
4 "Thomas Dunhill" 3500 4500
```

```
The TransactionsText File

1 a "Joe Smythe" 4242 5000
2 b 0 250
3 b 2 42
4 L 1 2000
5 a "Henry P. Jones" 4000 5000
```

In the **main** function, notice how the update file is defined and opened.

```
fstream inout (masterfile, ios::in | ios::out | ios::binary);
```

Also, notice how the current number of records in the binary master file is obtained.

```
inout.seekg (0, ios::end);
maxCountOfRecs = inout.tellg () / sizeof (AccountRec);
cout << "File initially contains " << maxCountOfRecs
     << " records\n";
inout.seekg (0, ios::beg);
```

Remember to always keep the DOS file offset pointer at the beginning of the file. This is because **MakeReport** reads the file sequentially from beginning to end. Also notice how the update file is passed to other functions. It is a reference to a **fstream** instance.

```
void MakeReport (fstream& inout);
void ProcessTransactions (fstream& inout, int& count);
```

Notice in the **MakeReport** function, which reads the binary file sequentially until the end of file is signaled, that there must be a call to the **clear** function to reset the EOF flag. The **clear** function is passed one of the ios state flag bits: **ios::goodbit**, **ios::eofbit**, **ios::badbit**, or **ios::failbit** which indicate the file is ok, at eof, has had a physical I/O error or has encountered bad input data. If you pass **clear** no parameters, the function clears the flags as if you had passed the **ios::goodbit**.

```
in.seekg (0, ios::beg);
// and clear the eof flag so more I/O to file can occur
in.clear (ios::goodbit);
```

To add a new record to the binary master file, we must position the file offset pointer to the end of the file so that the next write is appended to the end of the file.

```
inout.seekp (0, ios::end);
// and write new data at the current end of the file
inout.write ((char*) &rec, sizeof (rec));
```

The update sequence starts with the input of the id number, that is, the relative record number. This number is multiplied by the size of the records to obtain the offset for this record in the file. The file offset pointer is then set and the original data read. Once the changes have been made, the file offset pointer is repositioned back to the start of this record and the new data is written over the top of the old data in the file. If we did not reposition, then the rewrite would write over the next record after this one in the master file because the read operation adds the number of bytes just read to the file offset pointer.

```
infile >> findId >> num;
long offset = findId * sizeof (AccountRec);
inout.seekg (offset, ios::beg);
inout.read ((char*) &rec, sizeof (rec));
rec.creditBalance += num;
inout.seekp (offset, ios::beg);
inout.write ((char*) &rec, sizeof (rec));
```

Here is the complete **Pgm09b** update program.

```
Pgm09b - Master File Update Program - Relative Record Number
```

```
#include <iostream>
#include <fstream>
#include <iomanip>
using namespace std;
/***************************************************************/
/*                                                             */
/* Pgm09b: Acme Credit Update - binary file update program     */
/*                                                             */
/***************************************************************/

const int MaxNameLen = 42;

struct AccountRec {
 int    idNum;
 char   name[MaxNameLen];
 double creditBalance;
 double creditLimit;
};

void InitialBuildOfMasterFile (const char* filename);
void MakeReport (fstream& inout);
void ProcessTransactions (fstream& inout, int& count);

int main () {
 // setup floating point output for dollars and cents
 cout << fixed << setprecision (2);

 int maxCountOfRecs;
 const char* masterfile = "AcmeCredit.dat";

 // one time only, build the binary master file from a text file
 InitialBuildOfMasterFile (masterfile);

 // open the binary master file as an update file
 fstream inout (masterfile, ios::in | ios::out | ios::binary);
 // calculate the number of records in the master file
 inout.seekg (0, ios::end);
 maxCountOfRecs = inout.tellg () / sizeof (AccountRec);
 cout << "File initially contains " << maxCountOfRecs
      << " records\n";
 inout.seekg (0, ios::beg);

 // display a report of all clients - read the binary master file
 MakeReport (inout);

 // handle all additions and updates to master file
 ProcessTransactions (inout, maxCountOfRecs);

 // now recalculate the number of records in the file
 inout.seekg (0, ios::end);
 maxCountOfRecs = inout.tellg () / sizeof (AccountRec);
 inout.seekg (0, ios::beg);
 cout << "\n\nFile now contains " << maxCountOfRecs
      << " records\n";
```

```

 // display a report of all clients after the update process
 MakeReport (inout);
 inout.close ();
 return 0;
}

/***************************************************************/
/*                                                             */
/* InitialBuildOfMasterFile: make binary master from txt file  */
/*                                                             */
/***************************************************************/

void InitialBuildOfMasterFile (const char* filename) {
 AccountRec rec;
 // open text and the binary file
 ofstream outfile (filename, ios::out | ios::binary);
 ifstream infile ("accounts.txt");
 if (!infile || !outfile) {
  cerr << "Error: cannot open files\n";
  exit (1);
 }

 char c;
 int i = 0;

 while (infile >> c && c == '\"') {
  infile.getline (rec.name, sizeof (rec.name), '\"');
  infile >> rec.creditBalance >> rec.creditLimit;
  rec.idNum = i++;
  if (infile)
   outfile.write ((char*) &rec, sizeof (rec));
 }

 if (infile.good ()) {
  cerr << "Error inputting initial data\n";
  exit (2);
 }

 infile.close ();
 outfile.close ();
}

/***************************************************************/
/*                                                             */
/* MakeReport: read binary file sequentially to eof            */
/*                                                             */
/***************************************************************/

void MakeReport (fstream& in) {
 AccountRec rec;
 int count = 0;
 cout << "\n\n Acme Credit Master File\n\n"
      << "Id Number  Name                           Balance"
         "  Limit\n\n";

```

```
 while (in.read ((char*) &rec, sizeof (rec))) {
  cout << setw (5) << rec.idNum << "      "
       << left << setw (30) << rec.name << right
       << setw (9) << rec.creditBalance << setw (9)
       << rec.creditLimit << endl;
 }

 // here it is eof, so reset file offset pointer back to start
 in.seekg (0, ios::beg);
 // and clear the eof flag so more I/O to file can occur
 in.clear (ios::goodbit);
}

/***************************************************************/
/*                                                             */
/* ProcessTransactions: add, update limit or update balance    */
/*                                                             */
/***************************************************************/

void ProcessTransactions (fstream& inout, int& count) {
 AccountRec rec;
 char transType;
 char c;
 double num;
 int findId;

 cout << "\n\nTransaction Log\n\n";

 ifstream infile ("transactions.txt");
 if (!infile) {
  cerr << "Error: cannot open transactions file\n";
  exit (3);
 }

 // handle all transactions in the file
 while (infile >> transType) {
  transType = toupper (transType);  // change code to upper case

  if (transType == 'A') { // add a new record to master file
   rec.idNum = count;
   infile >> c;
   infile.getline (rec.name, sizeof (rec.name), '\"');
   infile >> rec.creditBalance >> rec.creditLimit;
   // first point file offset pointer to eof mark
   inout.seekp (0, ios::end);
   // and write new data at the current end of the file
   inout.write ((char*) &rec, sizeof (rec));
   // display results of addition
   cout << setw (5) << rec.idNum << "      " <<
        << left << setw (30) << rec.name << right
        << setw (9) << rec.creditBalance << setw (9)
        << rec.creditLimit << " Added\n";
   count++;
  }
  else if (transType == 'B') { // do a balance update
   infile >> findId >> num;
```

```
    // calculate the file offset of this id
    long offset = findId * sizeof (AccountRec);
    // position file offset pointer to this record's location
    inout.seekg (offset, ios::beg);
    // and input the record with this id
    inout.read ((char*) &rec, sizeof (rec));
    // update its balance
    rec.creditBalance += num;
    // reposition to this record in the master file
    inout.seekp (offset, ios::beg);
    // and rewrite this updated record
    inout.write ((char*) &rec, sizeof (rec));
    // display results
    cout << setw (5) << rec.idNum << "      " << left
         << setw (30) << rec.name << right
         << setw (9) << rec.creditBalance << setw (9)
         << rec.creditLimit << " Balance + " << num << endl;
   }
   else if (transType == 'L') { // here update credit limit
    infile >> findId >> num;
    // calculate the file offset for this id
    long offset = findId * sizeof (AccountRec);
    // position file offset to point to this record
    inout.seekg (offset, ios::beg);
    // input the record with this id
    inout.read ((char*) &rec, sizeof (rec));
    // update its credit limit
    rec.creditLimit += num;
    // reposition to this record in the master file
    inout.seekp (offset, ios::beg);
    // and rewrite this record in the master file
    inout.write ((char*) &rec, sizeof (rec));
    // display the results
    cout << setw (5) << rec.idNum << "      " << left
         << setw (30) << rec.name << right
         << setw (9) << rec.creditBalance << setw (9)
         << rec.creditLimit << " Limit + " << num << endl;
   }
   else {
    cerr << "Error: invalid transaction code: " << transType
         << endl;
    exit (4);
   }
  }
 }
```

Structure Alignment

When dealing with binary files, there is another architectural concern that must be understood and used. This is the principle of structure or data alignment in memory. Applications should align structure members and data values at addresses that are "natural" for the data type. A 4-byte type should be aligned on an address evenly divisible by 4. An 8-byte type should be aligned on an address evenly divisible by 8. The reason for this is how the circuitry fetches data from memory. No matter how you have the data stored in memory, the circuitry will retrieve that data. It is a matter of how efficiently it gets that data.

When inputting data from disk, remember that DOS first inputs an entire cluster of data into its internal buffer in memory. Then, it extracts what has been requested from the buffer and moves it into the destination variable. Thus, binary files on disk mirror this structure alignment.

Suppose that we wished to access a **long** whose 4-byte value began at memory location 2 in the DOS buffer, which is an address not evenly divisible by 4. The circuitry must fetch 2 4-byte memory locations and then extract the desired 4-byte long from the two 4-byte locations. This is shown in Figure 9.11. This is action causes a hardware fetch fault to occur. The hardware proceeds to get the two pieces from memory and join them into the 4-byte resulting **long** value. This faulting operation slows the memory accessing down significantly. But it guarantees that the requested data is retrieved. If the data is properly aligned, no fault occurs and the data is fetched normally and quickly.

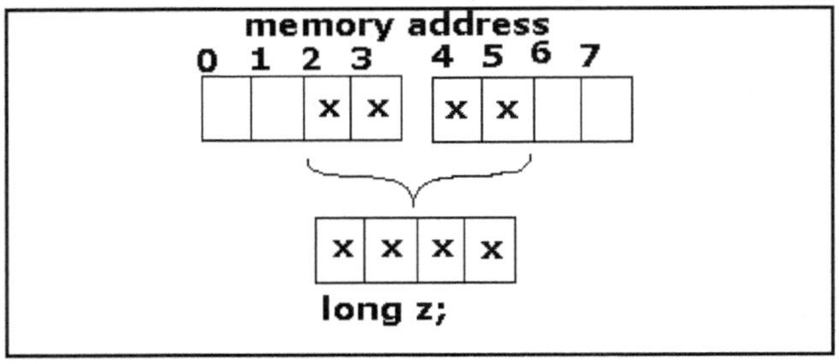

Figure 9.11 Fetching Unaligned Data

When you make a new project, Visual Studio sets the structure alignment to 8 bytes by default. The guideline is "a structure should begin on address boundaries of the worst type of data in the structure." In our case of **AccountRec** structure, the **double** is the worst type. Thus, each instance of the structure in memory should be aligned on 8-byte addresses.

However, how many bytes does our structure contain? It is 4 + 42 + 8 + 8 bytes or 62 bytes long. And this value is NOT evenly divisible by 8. If we look into the data file or the DOS internal buffer when that cluster containing the data has been input, successive records are not back to back in memory since 62 is not an even multiple of 8. If the structure alignment is 8 bytes, then the compiler adds some additional **gas** or **slack** or **pad** bytes to each structure instance so that the total size ends up a multiple of 8 bytes. That is, gas, pad, or slack bytes are added by the compiler to enforce the alignment.

On a computer with only 32-bit or 4-byte high speed registers, then the computer cannot fetch a 64-bit or 8-byte value directly from memory with one fetch: its registers are too small. In this case, 8-byte alignment becomes really 4-byte alignment. If however, you do have one of the new 64-bit PCs which has a 64-bit memory bus access, then the data will be aligned on an 8-byte boundary because the high speed work registers are indeed 8 bytes in size and can handle it.

I am running a 32-bit computer. Thus, the binary master file **Pgm09b** wrote is aligned on 4-byte addresses. Since each structure instance that was written to disk contained only 62 bytes, the compiler automatically inserts two additional gas fill bytes. When you ask for the size of the **AccountRec**, the compiler returns 64 bytes not 62 bytes! When one looks at the actual data stored in the binary file, each record has an additional 2 bytes appended to it containing garbage.

When you are going to input a binary file, you **must** know what the structure alignment was in the program that wrote the binary file in the first place. Your program must match that structure alignment. If the original data was aligned on a byte boundary and your program inputs it aligned on a 4-byte boundary, then your program will input scrambled data! In the case of the **AccountRec** structure, each input would result in 64 bytes being input while the actual byte aligned data on disk had only 62 bytes.

Structure alignment is set through the project settings—Project Settings—C++ tab—Code Generation Category combo box choice—struct member alignment combo box—make your choice.

Rule: if the data was created with older DOS programs, the data is very likely to have

been only byte aligned.

Corollary: if an older DOS program will be reading the data your program creates, then make sure that your project uses 1-byte alignment or the older DOS program will be inputting scrambled data.

To view a binary file, one needs an editor that can display the bytes in hex. Figure 9.12 shows the binary master file made by **Pgm09b** using 8-byte structure alignment.

```
  0: 00000000 416E6E69 65204A6F 6E65732D ■■■■Annie Jones-
 10: 536D6974 6800CCCC CCCCCCCC CCCCCCCC Smith■ÌÌÌÌÌÌÌÌÌÌ
 20: CCCCCCCC CCCCCCCC CCCCCCCC CCCCCCCC ÌÌÌÌÌÌÌÌÌÌÌÌÌÌÌÌ
 30: 00000000 008EB240 00000000 0088B340 ■■■■■■²@■■■■■■³@
 40: 01000000 42657473 7920536D 69746800 ■■■■Betsy Smith■
 50: 536D6974 6800CCCC CCCCCCCC CCCCCCCC Smith■ÌÌÌÌÌÌÌÌÌÌ
 60: CCCCCCCC CCCCCCCC CCCCCCCC CCCCCCCC ÌÌÌÌÌÌÌÌÌÌÌÌÌÌÌÌ
 70: 00000000 0070A740 00000000 0070B740 ■■■■■p§@■■■■■p·@
 80: 02000000 53616D75 656C2053 70616465 ■■■■Samuel Spade
 90: 006D6974 6800CCCC CCCCCCCC CCCCCCCC ■mith■ÌÌÌÌÌÌÌÌÌÌ
 A0: CCCCCCCC CCCCCCCC CCCCCCCC CCCCCCCC ÌÌÌÌÌÌÌÌÌÌÌÌÌÌÌÌ
 B0: A4703D0A D7DCA340 00000000 0070A740 ¤p=■×Ü£@■■■■■p§@
 C0: 03000000 54686F6D 61732044 756E6869 ■■■■Thomas Dunhi
 D0: 6C6C0074 6800CCCC CCCCCCCC CCCCCCCC ll■th■ÌÌÌÌÌÌÌÌÌÌ
 E0: CCCCCCCC CCCCCCCC CCCCCCCC CCCCCCCC ÌÌÌÌÌÌÌÌÌÌÌÌÌÌÌÌ
 F0: 00000000 0058AB40 00000000 0094B140 ■■■■■X«@■■■■■■±@
100: 04000000 5A6F6520 536D7974 686500CC ■■■■Zoe Smythe■Ì
110: CCCCCCCC CCCCCCCC CCCCCCCC CCCCCCCC ÌÌÌÌÌÌÌÌÌÌÌÌÌÌÌÌ
120: CCCCCCCC CCCCCCCC CCCCCCCC CCCCCCCC ÌÌÌÌÌÌÌÌÌÌÌÌÌÌÌÌ
130: 00000000 0092B040 00000000 0088B340 ■■■■■'°@■■■■■■³@
140: 05000000 5A61646C 656E6B61 204A6F6E ■■■■Zadlenka Jon
150: 65730074 6800CCCC CCCCCCCC CCCCCCCC es■th■ÌÌÌÌÌÌÌÌÌÌ
160: CCCCCCCC CCCCCCCC CCCCCCCC CCCCCCCC ÌÌÌÌÌÌÌÌÌÌÌÌÌÌÌÌ
170: 00000000 0040AF40 00000000 0088B340 ■■■■■@¯@■■■■■■³@
```

The 1st record 64 bytes

2 pad bytes added to the end of the char string

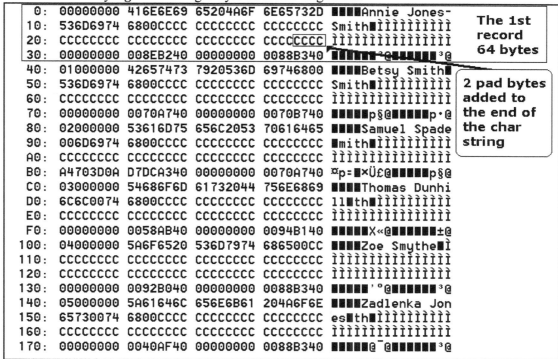

Figure 9.12 The Binary File (values in hex) Using 8-Byte Structure Alignment

Each line in Figure 9.12 shows the precise contents of 16 bytes or 10 in hexadecimal. Each byte consists of two hexadecimal nibbles. Each line shows groups of 4 bytes separated by a blank column. On the far right side of each line are the corresponding ASCII equivalent characters if there are any. Notice that on the right side we can read the contents of the string name because those are ASCII characters. I also noted where the compiler inserted the two gas bytes, right after the end of the string in the structure. It added the gas bytes here so that the next two doubles would be aligned on an 8-byte boundary. I boxed in one record which occupies 64 bytes on disk.

In Figure 9.13, I rebuilt the project and binary master file using 1-byte alignment. Now each record is only 62 bytes long.

```
  0: 00000000 416E6E69 65204A6F 6E65732D ■■■■Annie Jones-   The 1st
 10: 536D6974 6800CCCC CCCCCCCC CCCCCCCC Smith■ÌÌÌÌÌÌÌÌÌÌ   62-byte
 20: CCCCCCCC CCCCCCCC CCCCCCCC CCCC0000 ÌÌÌÌÌÌÌÌÌÌÌÌÌÌ■■   record
 30: 0000008E B2400000 00000088 B3400100 ■■■■²@■■■■■■³@■■
 40: 00004265 74737920 536D6974 6800536D ■■Betsy Smith■Sm
 50: 69746800 CCCCCCCC CCCCCCCC CCCCCCCC ith■ÌÌÌÌÌÌÌÌÌÌÌÌ
 60: CCCCCCCC CCCCCCCC CCCCCCCC 00000000 ÌÌÌÌÌÌÌÌÌÌÌÌ■■■■
 70: 0070A740 00000000 0070B740 02000000 ■p§@■■■■■p·@■■■■
 80: 53616D75 656C2053 70616465 006D6974 Samuel Spade■mit
 90: 6800CCCC CCCCCCCC CCCCCCCC CCCCCCCC h■ÌÌÌÌÌÌÌÌÌÌÌÌÌÌ
 A0: CCCCCCCC CCCCCCCC CCCCA470 3D0AD7DC ÌÌÌÌÌÌÌÌÌÌ¤p=■×Ü
 B0: A3400000 00000070 A7400300 00005468 £@■■■■■p§@■■■■Th
 C0: 6F6D6173 2044756E 68696C6C 00746800 omas Dunhill■th■
 D0: CCCCCCCC CCCCCCCC CCCCCCCC CCCCCCCC ÌÌÌÌÌÌÌÌÌÌÌÌÌÌÌÌ
 E0: CCCCCCCC CCCCCCCC 00000000 0058AB40 ÌÌÌÌÌÌÌÌ■■■■■X«@
 F0: 00000000 0094B140 04000000 5A6F6520 ■■■■■■±@■■■■Zoe 
100: 536D7974 686500CC CCCCCCCC CCCCCCCC Smythe■ÌÌÌÌÌÌÌÌÌ
110: CCCCCCCC CCCCCCCC CCCCCCCC CCCCCCCC ÌÌÌÌÌÌÌÌÌÌÌÌÌÌÌÌ
120: CCCCCCCC CCCC0000 00000092 B0400000 ÌÌÌÌÌÌ■■■■■'°@■■
130: 00000088 B3400500 00005A61 646C656E ■■■■³@■■■■Zadlen
140: 6B61204A 6F6E6573 00746800 CCCCCCCC ka Jones■th■ÌÌÌÌ
150: CCCCCCCC CCCCCCCC CCCCCCCC CCCCCCCC ÌÌÌÌÌÌÌÌÌÌÌÌÌÌÌÌ
160: CCCCCCCC 00000000 0040AF40 00000000 ÌÌÌÌ■■■■■@¯@■■■■
170: 0088B340                            ■■³@
```

Figure 9.13 The Binary Master File Using 1-Byte Structure Alignment

Here is one final detail about structure alignment. Suppose that your structure was 9 bytes long and you saved the data to a binary file. Suppose further that there were 100,000 records in that file. If we used 1-byte structure alignment, how many bytes would the file occupy on disk? 900,000. However, if we used 8-byte alignment on a computer that could handle 8-byte aligned data, how many bytes would the file size report? Since 9 is not evenly divisible by 8, the compiler would add an additional 7 gas bytes to each structure instance. Now the file size on disk would be 1,600,000 bytes. This is a substantial difference in file size.

Hence, because of larger file sizes, many production applications that utilize large binary master files use 1-byte alignment to conserve disk space.

Implementing the Remainder Method of Direct File Processing—Hashing Theory

This last example, **Pgm09c**, illustrates how to create and use a direct file based upon the remainder method. With the remainder method, the key identifiers can be any numerical value. Here, I use the social security number as the key id field required to directly access the data.

Methods of performing a direct access to data are crucial to inquiry and update type programs. This applies not only to arrays of things but also to binary files on disk. Given an identifier, such as student id, a program needs to be able to directly access that student's data whether it is currently contained in an array or in a binary file on disk.

Consider the basic problem. Suppose we have an array of student records stored in memory and we need to find the information for a given student. The program is given the student id to match. We can make a simple **MatchId** function as follows.

```
const int NoMatch = -1;
struct Student {
 int id;
 char name[21];
```

```
 char grade;
};
...
Student array[1000];
int numStudents;
int findId;
int matchIdx;
cin >> findId;
matchIdx = MatchId (array, numStudents, findId);
...
int MatchId (Student array[], int num, int findId) {
 for (j=0; j<num; j++) {
   if (findId == array[j].id) return j;
 }
 return NoMatch;
}
```

If there are only a few elements in the array or records on disk, there is not a problem with sequential searching. However, if there are thousands of elements or records and if the **findId** happens to contain the id for the last student in the array, then the program experiences a severe performance degradation.

The next improvement we can do is to have the array sorted into increasing **studentId** order. When the file or array is sorted into alphabetic order on the search key, a **binary search** can be performed. The idea is to first check the element in the middle. If you are lucky to have an exact match, you are done. If not, then decide if the **findId** lies in the upper or lower half. Now divide that half into half and search the middle once again, and so on.

```
bool  BinarySearch (Student array[], int num,
                    long findId, long& foundIdx) {
 int firstidx = 0;
 int lastidx = num - 1;
 int middleidx;
 bool foundMatch = false;
 while (lastidx >= firstidx && !foundMatch) {
  middleidx = (firstidx + lastidx) / 2;
  if (findId < id[middleidx].studentId)
    lastidx = middleidx - 1;
  else if (findId > id[middleidx].studentId)
    firstidx = middleidx + 1;
  else foundMatch = true;
 }
 foundIdx = middleidx
 return foundMatch;
}
```

The **main** program calls it as follows.

```
if (BinarySearch (array, num, findId, matchIdx)) {
 // use array[matchIdx]
}
```

How effective is the binary search? Table 9.1 shows the array size and the number of number of loop iterations required to find it in the worst case.

Table 9.1 Binary Search Effectiveness

Array Size	# iterations
1	1
3	2

7	3
15	4
31	5
63	6
127	7
255	8

Notice that the number of loop iterations to find the data varies as the $\log_2$ of array size. There is a substantial difference between 255 loop iterations versus 8 iterations for the binary search. However, with large arrays or large binary files, even this is too many iterations. We need an even faster method to quickly find a specific element in the array or in the binary master file.

Thus, the concepts of hashing are needed.

Hashing

(**Hash**: the word has several meanings from a dinner food, to chopping into small bits.) In computer terminology, **hashing** means to take a user-friendly key or id number and perform some transformations to it to yield the subscript or index of that data in the array or on disk.

Microsoft defines hash as "To be mapped to a numerical value by a transformation known as a hashing function."

Hashing is used to convert an identifier or key into a value for the location of the corresponding data in a structure, such as a table. For example, given the key MOUSE and a hashing function that 1.) added up the ASCII values of the characters, 2.) then divided the total by 127 and 3.) took the remainder as the final key value, MOUSE would hash to 12. The data identified by MOUSE would be found at entry 12 in the table.

The ultimate goal is, of course, a **perfect hash function** which is one that maps each potential search key to the unique position in the file or array.

If you have total control over what the keys' numeric values are to be and total control over the hashing algorithm, a perfect hash function can usually be made. Consider the remainder method of dividing the key by the largest prime number that does not exceed the largest key. In my earlier example above, the Id keys values were 1, 2 and 3. The corresponding hash function says that the key on disk is given by taking the Id key % 3. That is, the remainders are the indexes or relative record numbers. In this case, the indexes are 1, 2 and 0. And this is then a perfect hash function for this very tiny range of Id values. We also saw that as soon as we add even one more Id value, the perfect hash function breaks down. For example, if we add an Id of 4, then the hash function returns a key or relative record number of 1 which is already in use.

However, suppose that the hashing function remained the same but that the keys were social security numbers: 333-33-3333, 333-33-3336 and 333-33-3339. This hashing function would yield the indexes 0, 0, 0. These duplicates are called **collisions** or **synonyms**.

Collisions are usually unavoidable. Normally, the number of entries in the table or binary file is less than the number of possible key values. If we wanted to support all social security numbers, then the array size would contain 999,999,999 entries! If we only intended to have 1,000 actual customers, the amount of wasted array or disk space is gargantuan! On the other hand, if we expect to use social security numbers as the key and allocate only space for 1,000 customers, we can expect collisions to occur.

How are collisions resolved? There are many ways, but none are great.

First of all, when you are going to store a set of data with a specific key and you discover that the hashed index is already occupied by a synonym, where do you put that new one?

Linear Probing is one answer. The idea is to search the array from that point where the data should have been found on down for the first empty, unoccupied slot. If you reach the end of the array, start back over at element 0 until an empty available location is found and store the data there. Then, to look up this record, when you hash the key, look up the data at that key and discover that the data there is not the correct one, you then begin to search the array linearly down looking for it. Again, if you reach the last element in the array, begin with element 0 and continue looking until you arrive back at the original subscript. If you arrive back at the original subscript without having found the required item, it is not in the table or file. This process is called linear probing and is quite slow as you might expect.

Linear probing is highly susceptible to a phenomenon called **clustering of synonyms**. As the table is initially built, what happens frequently is that a large batch of synonyms ends up in a bunch of successive indexes somewhere beyond the index of the intended index. This of course then messes up all of those records that hash to these already occupied locations forcing them downward as well. To see this in operation, assume the hashing function to turn an Id number into the relative record number is % 3. When the file is built with the data below, notice the clustering effect.

```
Name   Id  Relative Stored in
           Record   Array Element
           Number   of Subscript
Ann     1    1        [1]
Tom     4    1        [2]<-[1] is occupied, use the next available
Pete    7    1        [3]<-[1],[2] occupied, this is next free one
Betsy 10     1        [4]<-[1],[2],[3] occupied
Fred   11    2        [5]<-should be [2] but it is occupied by
                           clustering from [1] items
```

A grandiose scheme to handle synonyms and clustering is called **chained hash tables**. Here, we add one new data member to the structure instances that are being stored, a **fwdptr**. We link list all the synonyms together into a chain based on this common subscript or relative record number. Suppose that 10 keys yield the same hash index. The first one actually stored at that location contains a pointer to the second one, which points to the third and so on in a single linked list fashion.

When the data is on disk, another possibility to handle collisions is to add all the collision records into an overflow area located at the end of the theoretical end of the table as given by the hash keys. The direct file's remainder method does just this, using linear probing to find any record in the overflow area. If you do not have a large number of records in the overflow area, this is fine. But if there are a lot of records in the overflow area, performance suffers greatly on those records.

How do hashing keys apply to a binary file? Clearly, the resulting hash key is the index into the array when it is in memory. But how do we translate that subscript into something meaningful when the array is really a binary file? It is usually done by computing the file offset of where the record begins. That is, consider the subscript or hash key to be the relative record number and multiply the hash key by the size of the record and setting the DOS file offset pointer to that value.

However, when dealing with binary files and hash keys, all potential entries **must** be in the binary file. That is, suppose that your hashing algorithm always results in a hash key between 0 and 255. Then, in the binary file, there must be 256 records actually in the file, even if there are no actual records stored in the file as yet! In other words, an empty file of 256 **dummy** records must be **pre-built**. These dummy records or place holders for the real data records have a dummy key id field set to –1 to indicate it is not yet in use. When adding a record to the file, one computes the hash key and then the file offset and retrieves the record currently stored there. If that record's id key is –1, then it is empty and you can store this new one there. If that id key is greater than or equal to 0, then you have a collision and must seek to the end of the file and add the new record there.

When doing an inquiry or update, you must first compute the hash key and then retrieve the record that corresponds to that relative record number. If that record's id matches the one you are looking for, you have found it; process it. However, if it does not match, then you must seek to the overflow area and begin a sequential search of all the records in the overflow area looking for a matching id.

Pgm09c: Direct File Processing in Action

To see this all in action, let's return to the previous example using the **AccountRec** binary file. Let's redo that program using hashing and make the master file be a direct access type of file. Initially, the file must be constructed with a known number of empty records. I call it the **InitialSize**. This value is also used to compute the offset of the overflow area.

Here are the input pair of files. I have now added lengthy id fields for each record.

The Revised Input Data to Build the Binary Direct Master File

```
12312341 "Annie Jones-Smith" 4500 5000
34234243 "Betsy Smith" 3000 4000
45435345 "Samuel Spade" 2500.42 3000
23442344 "Thomas Dunhill" 3500 4500
```

The Revised Transactions File

```
a 33453457 "Joe Smythe" 4242 5000
b 12312341 250
b 45435345 42
L 34234243 2000
a 33453453 "Henry P. Jones" 4000 5000
```

When we run the previous version of the program, recall that it printed a report of all the records in the master file. The same holds true in **Pgm09c**, however, now there are at least 100 records in the initial master file. The ones not yet in use are denoted as "empty." The next listing shows the output from the program when a bad hashing algorithm is used. The particular one I chose ends up generating duplicate has keys for all of the records!

The Output of Pgm09c with a Bad Hashing Algorithm

```
Built empty master file of 100 records
Hash for 12312341 is 0
Hash for 34234243 is 0
Hash for 45435345 is 0
Hash for 23442344 is 0
The number of records in the overflow area: 3
File initially contains 103 records


 Acme Credit Master File

Id Number  Name                      Balance  Limit

 12312341      Annie Jones-Smith    4500.00  5000.00
        0      empty                   0.00     0.00
        0      empty                   0.00     0.00
...
        0      empty                   0.00     0.00
 34234243      Betsy Smith          3000.00  4000.00
 45435345      Samuel Spade         2500.42  3000.00
 23442344      Thomas Dunhill       3500.00  4500.00

```

```

Transaction Log

Hash for 33453457 is 0
33453457       Joe Smythe              4242.00   5000.00 Added
Hash for 12312341 is 0
12312341       Annie Jones-Smith       4750.00  5000.00 Balance+250.00
Hash for 45435345 is 0
45435345       Samuel Spade            2542.42   3000.00 Balance+42.00
Hash for 34234243 is 0
34234243       Betsy Smith             3000.00   6000.00 Limit+2000.00
Hash for 33453453 is 0
33453453       Henry P. Jones          4000.00   5000.00 Added


File now contains 105 records


 Acme Credit Master File

Id Number  Name                      Balance  Limit

 12312341      Annie Jones-Smith      4750.00  5000.00
        0      empty                     0.00     0.00
        0      empty                     0.00     0.00
        0      empty                     0.00     0.00
...
        0      empty                     0.00     0.00
 34234243      Betsy Smith            3000.00  6000.00
 45435345      Samuel Spade           2542.42  3000.00
 23442344      Thomas Dunhill         3500.00  4500.00
 33453457      Joe Smythe             4242.00  5000.00
 33453453      Henry P. Jones         4000.00  5000.0
```

Notice that all the records but one are in the overflow area. This atrocious algorithm consists of adding the ASCII values of all digits in the id key and then **% 1** to get the relative record number.

```
char string[30];
ostrstream os (string, sizeof (string));
os << id << ends;
int i;
int sum = 0;
for (i=0; i<(int)strlen(string); i++) {
 sum += string[i];
}
int hash = sum % 1;
```

This coding is commented out in **Pgm09c** so that you can experiment. If you use **% 127**, then this becomes a more viable hashing algorithm

The good hashing algorithm I used consists of finding the largest prime number that does not exceed 100, the number of records in the direct file.

```
int hash = id % 97;
```

Here are the results from a good hashing algorithm.

```
The Output of Pgm09c with a Good Hashing Algorithm
```

```
Built empty master file of 100 records
```

```
Hash for 12312341 is 34
Hash for 34234243 is 33
Hash for 45435345 is 60
Hash for 23442344 is 63
The number of records in the overflow area: 0
File initially contains 100 records
 Acme Credit Master File
Id Number  Name                    Balance  Limit
         0      empty                   0.00     0.00
...
         0      empty                   0.00     0.00
  34234243      Betsy Smith          3000.00  4000.00
  12312341      Annie Jones-Smith    4500.00  5000.00
         0      empty                   0.00     0.00
...
         0      empty                   0.00     0.00
  45435345      Samuel Spade         2500.42  3000.00
         0      empty                   0.00     0.00
         0      empty                   0.00     0.00
  23442344      Thomas Dunhill       3500.00  4500.00
         0      empty                   0.00     0.00
...
         0      empty                   0.00     0.00
Transaction Log
Hash for 33453457 is 0
33453457      Joe Smythe            4242.00  5000.00 Added
Hash for 12312341 is 34
12312341      Annie Jones-Smith     4750.00 5000.00 Balance+250.00
Hash for 45435345 is 60
45435345      Samuel Spade          2542.42  3000.00 Balance+42.00
Hash for 34234243 is 33
34234243      Betsy Smith           3000.00  6000.00 Limit+2000.00
Hash for 33453453 is 93
33453453      Henry P. Jones        4000.00  5000.00 Added
File now contains 100 records
 Acme Credit Master File
Id Number  Name                    Balance  Limit
  33453457      Joe Smythe           4242.00  5000.00
         0      empty                   0.00     0.00
...
         0      empty                   0.00     0.00
  34234243      Betsy Smith          3000.00  6000.00
  12312341      Annie Jones-Smith    4750.00  5000.00
```

```
172          0       empty                   0.00      0.00
...
196          0       empty                   0.00      0.00
197   45435345       Samuel Spade         2542.42   3000.00
198          0       empty                   0.00      0.00
199          0       empty                   0.00      0.00
200   23442344       Thomas Dunhill       3500.00   4500.00
201          0       empty                   0.00      0.00
...
229          0       empty                   0.00      0.00
230   33453453       Henry P. Jones       4000.00   5000.00
231          0       empty                   0.00      0.00
...
236          0       empty                   0.00      0.00
```

Now let's examine a few details of **Pgm09c**. With a direct access type of binary master file, space must be reserved for the maximum number of records the data base is being designed to hold. The overflow area then comes after this number of records. In this example, I have set that maximum number to 100 account records. Since the records in the overflow area must be searched for matching ids and since we must detect collisions in the main portion of the file, the id number must be a part of the account record. It is now defined as follows.

```
struct AccountRec {
 int    idNum;
 char   name[MaxNameLen];
 double creditBalance;
 double creditLimit;
};
```

In the dummy place holder records, I used 0 for the **idNum** members because no social security number has that value. If 0 would be a valid id number, then one could use any negative number to indicate this is an empty, unused dummy record.

In the **InitialBuildOfMasterFile** function, one merely writes the maximum number of these dummy records to the file.

```
for (i=0; i<initSize; i++) {
 outfile.write ((char*) &rec, sizeof (rec));
}
```

Next, the real account records can be input one by one from the text file. As each one is input, the **AddRecord** function is called to add in this record.

AddRecord begins by finding what the theoretical hash number or relative record number should be for this Id number. **GetHashKey** returns the id number % 97 where 97 is the largest prime number less than or equal to 100, the maximum number of records. Next, given this proposed relative record number, one then inputs the account record at that location in the file.

```
int hash = GetHashKey (rec.idNum);
long offset = hash * sizeof (rec);
AccountRec frec;
inout.seekg (offset, ios::beg);
inout.read ((char*) &frec, sizeof (frec));
```

If this inputted record is indeed a dummy record, the new record is added at this relative record number here in the main section of the file.

```
if (frec.idNum == 0) {
 inout.seekp (offset, ios::beg);
 inout.write ((char*) &rec, sizeof (rec));
}
```

However, if there is already another real record in this location, a collision has occurred. We must then add the new record to the end of the overflow area or append this new record to the end of the file.

```
else {
 inout.seekp (0, ios::end);
 inout.write ((char*) &rec, sizeof (rec));
}
```

When processing the update transactions, either a change in limit or balance, we are given the id number. The first step is to find the relative record number of this record in the file. **FindThisRecord** first calls **GetHashKey** to get the proposed relative record number, assuming that no collisions have occurred. The record stored at this location is retrieved and its Id number is compared to the one for which we are looking. If they match, then we have the correct relative record number to use.

```
int hash = GetHashKey (findid);
AccountRec rec;
long offset = hash * sizeof (rec);
inout.seekg (offset, ios::beg);
inout.read ((char*) &rec, sizeof (rec));
if (rec.idNum == findid)
 return hash;
```

However, if the Id numbers do not match, then the record we are looking for lies in the overflow area. To begin searching the overflow area, we must first position the file offset pointer to the beginning of that area.

```
offset = initialSize * sizeof (rec);
hash = initialSize;
inout.seekg (offset, ios::beg);
while (inout.read ((char*) &rec, sizeof (rec))) {
 if (rec.idNum == findid)
  return hash; // yes, so return this rel rec num
 else hash++;
 }
return NotFound;
```

Once the relative record number is found and returned, then the update can proceed as before by positioning to the record and inputting it, modifying the data and rewriting this record. Here is the complete **Pgm09c**.

Pgm09c Accounts Update Program - Using a Direct Access File

```
#include <iostream>
#include <fstream>
#include <strstream>
#include <iomanip>
using namespace std;
/***************************************************************/
/*                                                             */
/* Pgm09c: Acme Credit Update - Using a Direct File with       */
/*         the Remainder Method                                */
/*                                                             */
/***************************************************************/

const int MaxNameLen = 42;
const int NotFound = -1;
const int InitialSize = 100;

struct AccountRec {
 int    idNum;
 char   name[MaxNameLen];
 double creditBalance;
 double creditLimit;
```

```
};


void InitialBuildOfMasterFile (const char* filename,
                               int initialSize);
void AddRecord (fstream& inout, AccountRec& rec,
                int& countCollisions);
int  GetHashKey (int id);
void MakeReport (fstream& inout);
void ProcessTransactions (fstream& inout, int& count,
                          int initialSize);
int  FindThisRecord (fstream& inout, int findid,
                     int initialSize);


int main () {
 // setup floating point for dollars and cents
 cout << fixed << setprecision (2);

 int maxCountOfRecs;
 const char* masterfile = "AcmeCredit.dat";

 InitialBuildOfMasterFile (masterfile, InitialSize);

 fstream inout (masterfile, ios::in | ios::out | ios::binary);
 inout.seekg (0, ios::end);
 maxCountOfRecs = inout.tellg () / sizeof (AccountRec);
 cout << "File initially contains " << maxCountOfRecs
      << " records\n";
 inout.seekg (0, ios::beg);

 MakeReport (inout);

 ProcessTransactions (inout, maxCountOfRecs, InitialSize);

 inout.seekg (0, ios::end);
 maxCountOfRecs = inout.tellg () / sizeof (AccountRec);
 inout.seekg (0, ios::beg);
 cout << "\n\nFile now contains " << maxCountOfRecs
      << " records\n";

 MakeReport (inout);
 inout.close ();
 return 0;
}

/***************************************************************/
/*                                                             */
/* InitialBuildOfMasterFile: build a Direct Access file with   */
/*         initSize dummy records and input the accounts file  */
/*         into the binary master file                         */
/*                                                             */
/***************************************************************/

void InitialBuildOfMasterFile (const char* filename,
                               int initSize) {
```

```
 // Step 1: setup empty file of initSize number of records
 int i;
 AccountRec rec;
 rec.idNum = 0; // we could use -1 if any id could be 0
 strcpy_s (rec.name, sizeof(rec.name), "empty");
 rec.creditBalance = rec.creditLimit = 0;

 ofstream outfile (filename, ios::out | ios::binary);
 if (!outfile) {
  cerr << "Error: could not open the output file: "
       << filename << endl;
  exit (1);
 }

 for (i=0; i<initSize; i++) {
  outfile.write ((char*) &rec, sizeof (rec));
 }
 outfile.close ();

 cout << "Built empty master file of " << initSize
      << " records\n";

 // now load in the accounts file into the empty master file
 ifstream infile ("accounts.txt");
 fstream inout (filename, ios::in | ios::out | ios::binary);

 if (!infile || !inout) {
  cerr << "Error: cannot open accounts file and/or the master\n";
  exit (2);
 }

 char c;
 int countCollisions = 0; // tracks the number of collisions
 // input each set of account data and add to master file
 while (infile >> rec.idNum >> c && c == '\"') {
  infile.getline (rec.name, sizeof (rec.name), '\"');
  infile >> rec.creditBalance >> rec.creditLimit;
  if (infile) AddRecord (inout, rec, countCollisions);
 }
 // if still in good state, something is wrong...
 if (!infile.eof ()) {
  cerr << "Error inputting initial data\n";
  exit (3);
 }
 // here all is ok
 infile.close ();
 inout.close ();
 cout << "The number of records in the overflow area: "
      << countCollisions << endl;
}

/***************************************************************/
/*                                                             */
/* GetHashKey: given the account Id, returns the hash key or   */
/*             the relative record number proposed for this    */
/*             set of data                                     */
```

```
/*                                                              */
/****************************************************************/

int GetHashKey (int id) {
 int hash = id % 97;  // mod by largest prime number <= 100

 // comment out the above line and uncomment out the following
 // block to generate a bad hashing algorithm to see its effect
/* char string[30];
 ostrstream os (string, sizeof (string));
 os << id << ends;
 int i;
 int sum = 0;
 for (i=0; i<(int)strlen(string); i++) {
  sum += string[i];
 }
 int hash = sum % 1;
 */
 cout << "Hash for " << id << " is " << hash <<endl;
 return hash;
}

/****************************************************************/
/*                                                              */
/* AddRecord: adds a new record to the Direct Access file       */
/*            by finding the proposed hash key, reading in      */
/*            record and if empty, rewriting that one           */
/*            If collision occurs, add to overflow area         */
/*                                                              */
/****************************************************************/

void AddRecord (fstream& inout, AccountRec& rec,
                int& countCollisions) {
 // get the hash key equivalent of this Id number
 int hash = GetHashKey (rec.idNum);
 // calculate the file offset for this record
 long offset = hash * sizeof (rec);
 AccountRec frec;
 // position the file to this offset
 inout.seekg (offset, ios::beg);
 // and input the record that's there
 inout.read ((char*) &frec, sizeof (frec));
 // see if this record is then an empty record
 if (frec.idNum == 0) {
  // yes, is empty, so rewrite it with the new record to be added
  inout.seekp (offset, ios::beg);
  inout.write ((char*) &rec, sizeof (rec));
 }
 else { // here, that spot is occupied - so append to overflow
  countCollisions++;
  // position to eof
  inout.seekp (0, ios::end);
  // and write this new record at the end of the file
  inout.write ((char*) &rec, sizeof (rec));
 }
}
```

```

/***************************************************************/
/*                                                             */
/* MakeReport: display a report of the contents of every       */
/*             record in the file                              */
/*                                                             */
/***************************************************************/

void MakeReport (fstream& in) {
 AccountRec rec;
 int count = 0;
 cout << "\n\n Acme Credit Master File\n\n"
  << "Id Number  Name                     Balance  Limit\n\n";
 while (in.read ((char*) &rec, sizeof (rec))) {
  cout << setw (9) << rec.idNum << "      " << left
       << setw (19) << rec.name << right
       << setw (9) << rec.creditBalance << setw (9)
       << rec.creditLimit << endl;
 }
 in.seekg (0, ios::beg);  // reset to beginning of the file
 in.clear (ios::goodbit); // clear the eof flag
}

/***************************************************************/
/*                                                             */
/* ProcessTransactions: process the additions, limit and       */
/*                      balance updates                        */
/*                                                             */
/***************************************************************/

void ProcessTransactions (fstream& inout, int& count,
                          int initialSize) {
 AccountRec rec;
 char transType;
 char c;
 double num;
 int findId;
 int countCollisions = 0;

 cout << "\n\nTransaction Log\n\n";

 ifstream infile ("transactions.txt");
 if (!infile) {
  cerr << "Error: cannot open transactions file\n";
  exit (3);
 }
 while (infile >> transType) {
  transType = toupper (transType);
  if (transType == 'A') { // here it is an addition
   // get the new data
   infile >> rec.idNum >> c;
   infile.getline (rec.name, sizeof (rec.name), '\"');
   infile >> rec.creditBalance >> rec.creditLimit;
   // and add this record to the file
   AddRecord (inout, rec, countCollisions);
   cout << setw (5) << rec.idNum << "      " << left
```

```
        << setw (19) << rec.name << right
        << setw (9) << rec.creditBalance << setw (9)
        << rec.creditLimit << " Added\n";
   count++;
  }
  else if (transType == 'B') { // here it is a balance change
   infile >> findId >> num;
   // find the relative record number of this record
   int id = FindThisRecord (inout, findId, initialSize);
   if (id == NotFound) {
    // if it is not found, display an error msg and ignore it
    cerr << "Error: cannot find id " << findId << endl;
   }
   else {
    // here it is present so input the desired record
    long offset = id * sizeof (AccountRec);
    inout.seekg (offset, ios::beg);
    inout.read ((char*) &rec, sizeof (rec));
    // update the balance
    rec.creditBalance += num;
    // rewrite the record
    inout.seekp (offset, ios::beg);
    inout.write ((char*) &rec, sizeof (rec));
    cout << setw (5) << rec.idNum << "      " << left
         << setw (19) << rec.name << right
         << setw (9) << rec.creditBalance << setw (9)
         << rec.creditLimit << " Balance + " << num << endl;
   }
  }
  else if (transType == 'L') { // here it is a limit update
   infile >> findId >> num;
   // find the relative record number of this record
   int id = FindThisRecord (inout, findId, initialSize);
   if (id == NotFound) {
    // if it is not found, display an error msg and ignore it
    cerr << "Error: cannot find id " << findId << endl;
   }
   else {
    // here it is present so input the desired record
    long offset = id * sizeof (AccountRec);
    inout.seekg (offset, ios::beg);
    inout.read ((char*) &rec, sizeof (rec));
    // change the limit
    rec.creditLimit += num;
    // and rewrite the record
    inout.seekp (offset, ios::beg);
    inout.write ((char*) &rec, sizeof (rec));
    cout << setw (5) << rec.idNum << "      " << left
         << setw (19) << rec.name << right
         << setw (9) << rec.creditBalance << setw (9)
         << rec.creditLimit << " Limit + " << num << endl;
   }
  }
  else {
   cerr << "Error: invalid transaction code: " << transType
        << endl;
```

```
    exit (4);
   }
  }
 }

/***************************************************************/
/*                                                             */
/* FindThisRecord: Given the Id to find and the max number of */
/*                 records (which pin points the start of the */
/*                 overflow area, find the relative record    */
/*                 number of this record                       */
/*                                                             */
/*  returns the rrn or NoMatch if not found                    */
/*                                                             */
/***************************************************************/

int FindThisRecord (fstream& inout, int findid, int initialSize){
 // get the proposed hash key (rel rec num)
 int hash = GetHashKey (findid);
 AccountRec rec;
 // position to this proposed record
 long offset = hash * sizeof (rec);
 inout.seekg (offset, ios::beg);
 // and input the record at the proposed rel rec num
 inout.read ((char*) &rec, sizeof (rec));
 // is this the correct record with this Id?
 if (rec.idNum == findid)
  return hash; // yes, so return this rel rec num

 // no, so now we must search the overflow area sequentially
 // position to start of the overflow area
 offset = initialSize * sizeof (rec);
 hash = initialSize; // hash will hold the rel rec num, if
                     // we find this record in the overflow
 inout.seekg (offset, ios::beg);
 // search all records in the overflow area
 while (inout.read ((char*) &rec, sizeof (rec))) {
  // is this record the correct one with the right Id number?
  if (rec.idNum == findid)
   return hash; // yes, so return this rel rec num
  else hash++;
 }
 return NotFound; // here no record matches this Id num
}
```

A Final Thought on Direct File Processing

In my *Windows MFC Programming I* ebook, I will introduce you to the Windows File Mapping approach. This method of I/O treats the binary file as if it were the Windows Swap File. The result is at least a five-fold increase in speed of access over the approaches given in this chapter! Thus, if speed was a significant design factor, there are some tricks that you can use to make this process even faster.

Review Questions

1. Explain the concept of a binary file. How does the storage of a **double** differ between a text file and a binary file? What would happen if you attempted to extract a **double** from a binary file? What would happen if you attempted to read in a **double** from a text file?

2. Under what circumstances is data conversion performed on data in a binary file?

3. How is a binary file opened in C++?

4. What functions can be used to I/O to or from a binary file? Under what circumstances can the insertion and extraction operator be used with a binary file?

5. How would an inventory structure be written to a binary file? How would it be read back in?

6. What is the most significant difference between the following two methods for outputting an array of **doubles**? What will be in the file in both cases? Is there any significant benefit for using one of these in preference to another?

```
double array[10000];
for (i=0; i<10000; i++)
 outfile.write ((char*) array[i], sizeof (double));
```

and

```
outfile.write ((char*) array, sizeof (array));
```

7. What is a cluster? On a Windows/DOS platform, what is the significance of a cluster?

8. Explain what is meant by Physical I/O. Explain what is meant by Logical I/O.

9. What is the purpose of the DOS file offset pointer? How can a program make use of this pointer? What functions provide access to it?

10. Explain the instruction sequence required to obtain the DOS file size of a binary file.

11. Would there be any real benefit to inputting an entire text file in one I/O operation into an array of characters which is the same size as the binary file?

12. What is wrong with the following sequence to input a file of data?

```
infile.seekg (0, ios::end);
long sz = infile.tellg ();
char* buf = new char [sz];
infile.read (buf, sz);
```

13. Explain how the relative record number method for direct access of a specific record in a binary master file works. Why is this approach exceedingly fast at data retrieval?

14. Why do relative record numbers make poor values for client Id numbers?

15. A binary file is supposed to contain a series of **InventoryRec** structures. How can a program tell if the file either is corrupt or may contain other items besides these structure instances?

16. A direct access file uses the remainder method for locating where a record with a specific key id is located. Explain how this method works. Why does the file have to be pre-built with enough dummy records to equal the maximum number of records the file is designed to hold?

17. What kind of user id key fields can be used with a direct access type of file?

18. Explain how the ISAM method works. What kind of user id key fields can be used?

19. Why is the ISAM method slower at retrieving a specific record on disk?

20. What **iostream** class is used to create an update file—that is, a file instance that can be both read and written?

21. What is meant by structure alignment? How does it work? What is the impact of structure alignment on a program?

22. Program 1 writes a binary master file and uses 1-byte structure alignment. Program 2 inputs the data from that binary master file but uses 8-byte structure alignment. Explain what occurs at run time with Program 2 and why.

23. What is meant by a hashing algorithm? What is the purpose of a hash number?

24. Explain how a hash number can be used to access a specific record or element of an array?

25. How can collisions of hash numbers be handled?

26. What is meant by linear probing?

27. What is a chained hash table? How does such work?

Stop! Do These Exercises Before Programming

1. Our programmer has been asked to write an inventory update program for Acme Manufacturing Corporation. The binary master file is an ISAM type of file that contains inventory records that are defined as follows.

```
const int PARTNO_LEN = 16;
const int DESCR_LEN = 46;
const int LOC_LEN = 11;
struct InvRec {
 char   partNo[PARTNO_LEN];
 char   description[DESCR_LEN];
 int    qtyOnHand;
 double unitCost;
 char   locationBin[LOC_LEN];
};
```

The key id field is the **partNo**. The master file itself is called **parts.dat** and was built using 8-byte structure alignment. The index file is called **parts.idx** and consists of instances of the structure **Index**.

```
struct Index {
 char partNo[PARTNO_LEN];
 long relRecNum;
};
```

The index records are stored in increasing ASCII sequence on the **partNo** field.

The programmer decided to implement the **FindRecord** function whose purpose is to find the relative record number of the inventory record that corresponds to a given part number. Of course, he also had to write a **LoadIndex** function to load the index file into an array. He also wrote a small driver program to test his new function. It fails completely. He has asked you for your assistance. Find his errors so that both the new function and driver work as expected. Is there anything grossly inefficient about his **FindRecord** function?

```
const int NoMatch = -1;
int main () {
 InvRec rec;
 char partNo[PARTNO_LEN];
 fstream masterfile ("parts.dat", ios::in | ios::out);
 fstream indexfile ("parts.idx", ios::in | ios::out);
 long count;
 Index* index = LoadIndex (indexfile, count);
 while (cin >> partNo) {
  long relRecNum = FindRecord (index, count, partNo);
  if (relRecNum == NoMatch)
   cout << "Record not found - part number: " << partNo << endl;
  else {
   masterfile.seekg (relRecNum * sizeof (InvRec), ios::beg);
   masterfile.read ((char*) &rec, sizeof (rec));
   cout << "Found part number: " << rec.partNo << endl;
  }
 }
 ...
}

Index* LoadIndex (fstream& file, long& count) {
 file.seekg (0, ios::end);
 long size = file.tellg ();
 count = size / sizeof (Index);
 Index* index = new Index [count];
 file.read ((char*) index, count * sizeof (index));
 return index;
}

long FindRecord (Index index[], long count,
                 const char* findThis) {
 for (long j=0; j<count; j++) {
  if (findThis == index[j].partNo)
   return j;
 }
 return NoMatch;
}
```

2. The programmer, after singing praises to you for your assistance, embarks on a total rewrite of the **FindRecord** function. He has decided to implement a binary search for the id value.

```
bool FindRecord (Index id[], long num,
                 const char* findId, long& foundIndex) {
 int firstidx = 0;
 int lastidx = num - 1;
 int middleidx;
 bool foundMatch = false;
 while (lastidx >= firstidx && !foundMatch) {
  middleidx = (firstidx + lastidx) / 2;
  if (findId < id[middleidx])
    lastidx = middleidx - 1;
  else if (findId > id[middleidx])
```

```
    firstidx = middleidx + 1;
  else foundMatch = true;
 }
 foundIndex = middleidx;
 return foundMatch;
}
```

He changed the call in **main** to the following.

```
 long relRecNum;
 if (FindRecord (index, count, partNo, relRecNum)) {
```

When it runs, the program does not find any records. After spending hours debugging it, he humbly begs you for your assistance. Fix his function so that it correctly finds matching records.

3. His enthusiasm returns when you point out his errors; his find function is working properly. So next he embarks on writing the code to perform the updates of specific inventory records. The relevant parts of his tester program now appear as follows.

```
 ... performing an update of partNo record
 ... the needed new values have been input
 long relRecNum;
 if (FindRecord (index, count, partNo, relRecNum)) {
  masterfile.seekg (relRecNum * sizeof (InvRec), ios::beg);
  masterfile.read (&rec, sizeof (rec));
  // ... made changes to rec fields
  masterfile.write (&rec, sizeof (rec));
 }
 else
  cerr << "Error: unable to find part: " << partNo << endl;
```

Unfortunately, the above coding does not compile or work properly. Find his errors in syntax and the two major logic blunders.

4. After profusely apologizing for making such a stupid blunder, he then begins the design for the addition of new records to the master file. Now he encounters a new problem. While it will be easy to add the new record to the master file, the index is another matter entirely. The new part number must be inserted into the index table in sorted order. He decides that he must add the new record to the master file first so that he knows the new relative record number of that new record. This time, he writes only the couple of lines needed to store the new record in the master file. But when he tests it, he discovers that the new record is not where it should be located and has indeed wiped other data out!

```
 // rec contains the new data, so write it at the end of the file
 masterfile.seekg (0, ios::end);
 masterfile.write ((char*) &rec, sizeof (rec));
```

After spending hours playing with this error, he comes to you once more stating the computer must be broken because these two simple lines of coding do not work! The record is not added at the end of the file! Point out his error and fix this error for him.

5. Humbled and in awe of your programming prowess, the programmer now attempts to update the index file. He is absolutely certain that he will bungle this one too. And his postulate holds. His coding does not work. Rescue the programmer once more, please. Fix this coding so that it properly adds a new entry to the index in the proper location.

```
 long newRelRecNum; // contains the new relative record number
 // for the added record while partNo contains its Id value
 long newIndex; // the location in the index
 if (!FindRecord (index, count, partNo, newIndex)) {
```

```
  // here, newIndex contains the location in index where this
  // partNo should be located. so move all entries from here
  // down one slot and insert this new one
  long j, k;
  for (j=count-1; j>=newIndex; j--) {
   index[j] = index[j-1];
  }
  index[newIndex].partNo = partNo;
  index[newIndex].relRecNum = newRelRecNum;
  count++;
  indexfile.write ((char*) index, sizeof (Index) * count);
 }
```

In fact, just before he came to you this last time, his computer started doing funny things after he had run the program, forcing him to reboot.

Programming Problems

Problem Pgm09-1 The Duplicate File Finder Program

You have been collecting some terrific scenery jpg images from the Internet. However, you notice that there are what appears to be duplicate files in your collection. That is, different filenames, but what appears to be the same images. The objective is to find out if two specific files are identical or not.

Write a function called **IsDuplicate** that takes two constant character string filenames and returns a **bool**, **true** if the two files are precisely identical. You do not need to know what the contents of the image file actually contain, just that they are identical byte for byte. The approach to take is to open each file as a binary file and get the DOS file size of each. If the file sizes do not match, return **false** as they cannot be byte-by-byte duplicates.

Next, dynamically allocate memory to hold each file's contents. Use arrays of **unsigned char**. Input both files into these two arrays. Make sure you are using binary I/O. Now compare the two arrays, byte-by-byte. At the first unequal byte result, return **false** as they do not match. Return **true** if the end of the two equal length arrays occurs as they are the same.

Verify that you have not leaked any memory. Be sure to close all opened files. Write a simple driver program to thoroughly test the function.

Problem Pgm09-2 The CD Stock Update Program

Acme Music Store wants a program written that they can use to maintain their stock inventory of CDs. The main menu consists of the following.

```
Acme CD Inventory Program

1. Display CD Inventory
2. Update CD Inventory
3. Add a New CD
4. Exit the Program

Enter the number of your choice: _
```

The file **CDinventory.dat** is located in the **Pgm09-2** folder of **TestDataForAssignments**. It is a binary file of the current inventory and was built using 8-byte structure alignment. The inventory record consists of

```
struct Inventory {
```

```
 char cdNum[11];
 char cdTitle[41];
 long qtyOnHand;
 double cost;
};
```

Initially, open this file using a **fstream** instance and open it for update operations. Before the main menu is displayed, construct an instance of a growable array container to store an array of **CD_to_RRN** structure instances. This structure stores the **cdNum** and its corresponding relative record number. So read each record in the master file and build this conversion array. When updates are done, the user provides the **cdNum** and you look it up in the **CD_to_RRN** array to obtain the relative record number of the data in the master file.

When Display CD Inventory is chosen, read the file sequentially displaying each item nicely formatted on the screen.

When Update a CD Inventory is chosen, prompt the user for the cd number. Then look it up in the **CD_to_RRN** to obtain the relative record number on disk. If that cd is not in the file, display an error message to the user. If it is, read in that cd's inventory data and display it onscreen. Prompt the user for any changes in quantity or cost. Then rewrite that record on disk.

When Add a New Cd is chosen, prompt the user for the relevant information. Then, verify that the cd number is not already in the data base. If it is, display an error message to the user. If it is not in the file, then add this record to the master file and add a new entry to the **CD_to_RRN** array. Thoroughly test your program.

Problem Pgm09-3 Modify Pgm09c to use an ISAM Master File

Revise **Pgm09c** to build and then use an ISAM master file instead of the Direct Access file. Store the index in a separate file with the .idx extension. Since the original data are not in any particular social security number order, make the searching of the index table be a simple sequential search. Test the program using the same data as was used in **Pgm09c**.

Problem Pgm09-4 Building and Reading a Binary File

Write a program that inputs the text file **cd.txt** located in the **Pgm09-4** folder of **TestDataForAssignments**. It contains cd inventory records. Make a structure called **CD** as follows.

```
struct CD {
 char cdNum[11];
 char cdTitle[41];
 long qtyOnHand;
 double cost;
};
```

Input each record from the text file into a **CD** record and then write that record to a binary output file.

Then, open the binary output file and input each record and display all four fields onscreen in a nicely formatted report.

Chapter 10—Trees

Introduction

The data structures we have examined up to this point have been **linear** in nature. That is, the structures had unique first and last elements with each element having a unique element both preceding and following it (except for the very first and last elements). However, not all data are best presented in such a linear fashion. Consider the Explorer's tree view of the folders on a disk drive. Here the data is better presented in a **hierarchical** format commonly called a **tree**.

A tree is nonlinear in nature because each element may have more than one successor. The organizational chart of a company begins with the leader or CEO or president and below him/her are several vice presidents. Below each VP are several managers and so on. The Executive Branch of our government can be viewed as a tree structure with the President at the top and the numerous department heads below him/her and so on down. Genealogy makes extensive use of tree structure showing the parents at the top, their children below them and so on down the line.

In general, a tree is a structure in which each element in below only one other element but may have none or many elements immediately below it. That is, a node of a tree has only one predecessor but many successors. Only the top node has no predecessors.

Tree Notation

The notation or terminology of tree structures borrows from the real world of trees, such as oak or maple trees. The topmost node is called the **root** of a tree. It is the single element at the top or beginning of the hierarchical structure. For example, the president of a company would be at the root of the company's organizational chart. Elements with no successors are called **leaves**. In the company analogy, the individual employees would form the leaves below their boss or manager. A tree must have only one root and should branch out into many leaves which gives the appearance of an upside down tree.

Each of the elements of a tree are called **nodes** similar to linked lists. Each node has only one predecessor called its **parent**. The potentially many nodes that succeed it are called its **children**. And two nodes with the same parent are called **siblings**. In the company organizational chart analogy, all of the vice presidents are siblings and are the children of the parent, the president. The terms **ancestor** and **descendant** also can be applied to nodes. The vice presidents are the descendants of the president's node and the president is the ancestor of the vice presidents.

How can a tree be defined? We define a general tree using the following recursive definition.

A. An empty tree, without any nodes, is a tree.
B. A single node all by itself is a tree—this is the root.
C. The structure formed by taking a node N and one or more existing trees and making node N be the parent of all the other existing tree roots is a tree.

Figure 10.1 shows three different trees.

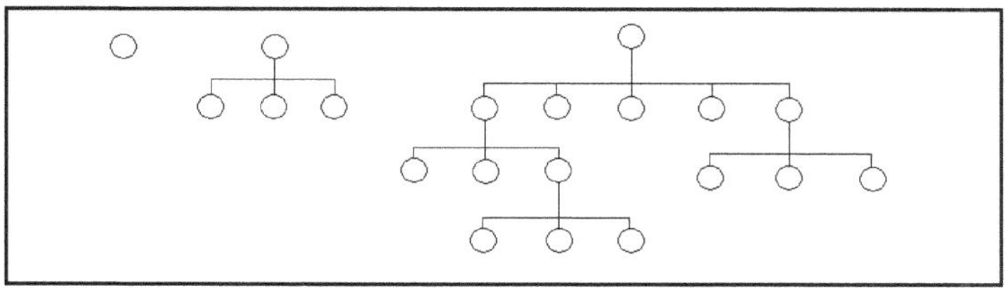

Figure 10.1 Three Trees

A subtree is a tree itself but is also part of a larger tree. Indeed, rule C above can be used to construct trees from existing trees. After the construction is done, the original trees are now subtrees of the larger tree. Figure 10.2 shows many of the subtrees of the more complex tree of Figure 10.1.

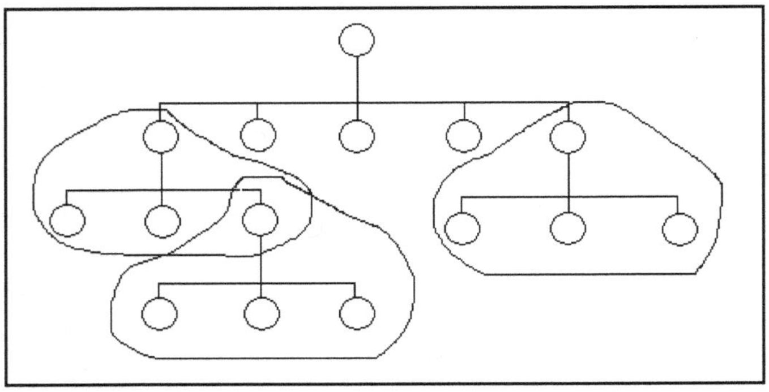

Figure 10.2 Three of the Subtrees of the Larger Tree

The term **level of a node** is often used to pin down the vertical location of that node within the entire tree. The level of the root node is defined to be 1.

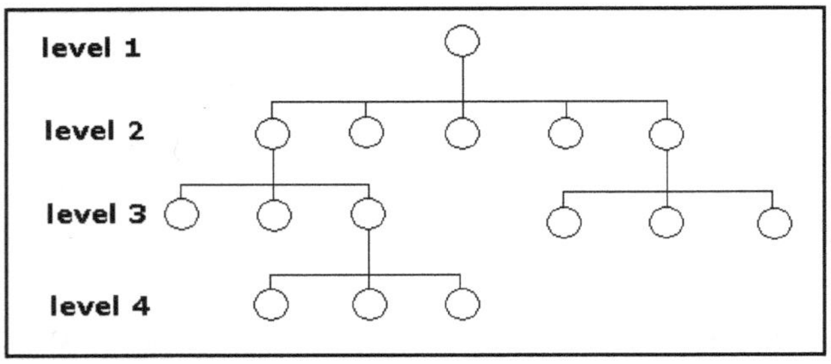

Figure 10.3 The Levels of a Tree

Its immediate children are at level 2. In Figure 10.2, the level of the lowest children on the left side is 4. This is shown in Figure 10.3.

The term **degree** of a node refers to the number of subtrees associated with that node. A leaf of a tree has degree zero since there are no subtrees below it.

The term **height (or depth) of a tree** is defined to be the maximum level of the tree's leaves. The depth of the tree shown in Figure 10.3 above is 4. In Figure 10.1 above, the middle tree's height is 2 and the leftmost tree's depth is 1.

The term **path** is defined as the non-empty sequence of nodes from the root to the desired location. In Figure 10.3, there are 15 separate paths. The topmost path is of length 0 containing only the root node. Then there are five paths to each of the nodes on level 2. Imagine the Figure 10.3 is defining the folder structure with the root node containing C:\. Each lower circle represents another folder. The 15 separate paths would represent all the possible file specification paths on that drive. In Figure 10.4, I have arbitrarily assigned a letter to each element.

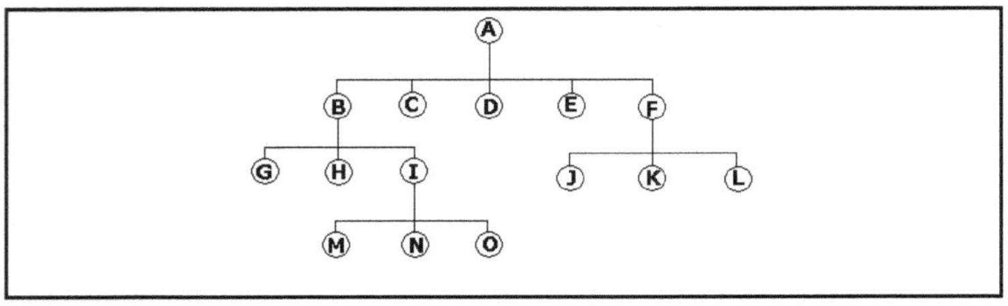

Figure 10.4 A Tree with Letter Elements

An alternate graphical representation of this same tree (Figure 10.4) is called a **Venn** diagram, which represents the tree as a series of nested regions in a plane as a series of sets. This is shown in Figure 10.5. In this form, it appears much like an outline of a chapter of a book.

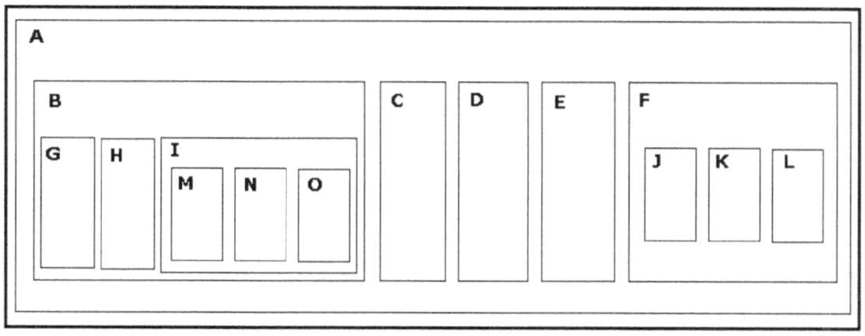

Figure 10.5 The Tree as a Venn Diagram

This same tree could be represented as a block of C++ coding as shown below!

```
A:  {
       B: {
              G: statement;
              H: statement;
              I: {
                     M: statement;
                     N: statement;
                     O: statement;
              }
       }
       C: statement;
       D: statement;
       E: statement;
       F: {
              J: statement;
              K: statement;
              L: statement;
       }
}
```

Therefore, it is not surprising that tree structures play an important role in the compiler writing, word processing and many other computer applications other than searching for matching key applications.

Trees can come in many different forms. In the general tree case, each node can have a different number of subtrees or each node can be of a different degree. The tree shown in the above series of figures is a general tree. The root node has five subtrees while each of the others has three or none. However, there are many kinds of more specialized trees.

An **N-ary tree** is a tree in which all of its nodes have the same degree. That is, every node that has children has the same number of children. In Figure 10.4, if we deleted nodes C and D, then the resulting tree would be an N-ary tree.

Binary Trees

An especially important N-ary tree is one that has degree 2, or N is 2. This is called a **binary tree**. Each node has at most two subtrees below it. They are called the **left child** and the **right child**. Thus, every node of a binary tree has zero, one, or two children. Or a parent can have at most two children. Sometimes only the left child is present; others, only the right child is present. Figure 10.6 shows five binary trees. Note that the two trees with only nodes A and B are different binary trees. One has only a left child; the other has only a right child. However, if these were defined to be general trees, these two would be the same tree.

Suppose that we wished to create a **BinaryTree** class or ADT. How can we implement it? There are many ways, but in keeping with the concept of code reusability, let's store the user data for each node as a **void***. This way, we can write the class one time and reuse it for many applications. Each node should be dynamically allocated so that there is no arbitrary maximum number of nodes in the tree.

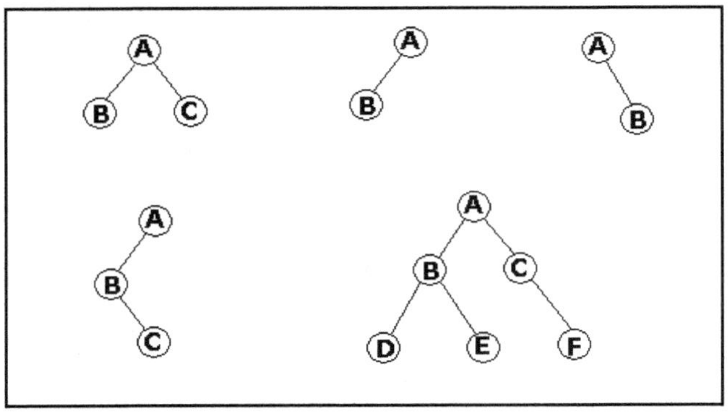

Figure 10.6 Five Binary Trees

The tree node structure could be defined then as follows.

```
struct TreeNode {
 void*     ptrData;
 TreeNode* ptrLeftChild;
 TreeNode* ptrRightChild;
};
```

What data members are needed? The only required data member is a pointer to the root node, **ptrRoot**. Here is the start of a relatively simple **BinaryTree** class definition.

```
struct TreeNode {
 void*     ptrData;
 TreeNode* ptrLeftChild;
 TreeNode* ptrRightChild;
};
class BinaryTree {
protected:
 TreeNode* ptrRoot;
public:
           BinaryTree ();
          ~BinaryTree ();
 bool      IsEmpty () const;
 void      BuildRoot (void* dataptr);
 TreeNode* GetRootNode () const;
 void AppendLeftChild (TreeNode* ptrParent, void* dataptr);
 void AppendRightChild (TreeNode* ptrParent, void* dataptr);
 void*     GetNodeData (TreeNode* ptrNode) const;
 void      SetNodeData (TreeNode* ptrNode, void* dataptr);
 TreeNode* GetLeftChild (TreeNode* ptrNode) const;
 TreeNode* GetRightChild (TreeNode* ptrNode) const;
 bool      IsLeaf (TreeNode* ptrNode) const;
 void      DeleteLeaf (TreeNode*& ptrNode);
};
```

The **BinaryTree** constructor sets **ptrRoot** to 0. **IsEmpty** returns **true** if **ptrRoot** is 0. **BuildRoot** allocates a new **TreeNode** and sets the **ptrdata** member to the user's data pointer and sets the two child pointers to 0. The two append functions perform basically the same operations. First, each function allocates a new **TreeNode** and copies in the user's data pointer to be stored in this node. Then each function sets the two child pointers to 0. Finally, each function stores the address of this new node in the passed **TreeNode** pointer's left or right child pointer. The access functions, **Get/SetNodeData** returns or changes the data that this node is storing for the user. The pair **GetLeftChild** and **GetRightChild** return the child pointer of the passed **TreeNode** pointer. The **IsLeaf** function returns **true** if both of the child pointers of the passed **TreeNode** are 0. **DeleteLeaf** deletes the passed node, setting the reference pointer to 0.

However, there are some basic problems with this design. First, if **DeleteLeaf** removes this leaf, how do we guarantee that the parent **TreeNode**'s appropriate child pointer is reset to 0? And how do we implement the destructor? The destructor some how must traverse the entire tree deleting all **TreeNodes**?

Methods of Binary Tree Traversal

Traversal means to visit each node of the binary tree. Binary trees can be traversed in several manners depending upon the requirements of the task. With a double linked list, traversal could be from the head sequentially to the end of the list or from the tail to the beginning of the list. However, a binary tree presents several different possibilities. Should ancestors be visited before the descendants or vice versa? Should siblings be visited from the right to the left or from the left to the right? There are three common traversal algorithms for binary trees.

Inorder Traversal

The **inorder** traversal method visits each node by first visiting all nodes in the left subtree of the root, then visit the root, and then visit all nodes in the right subtree. Of course, each subtree can be either nonexistent, a leaf or a subtree itself. Thus, the definition is actually a recursive one. One could define the recursive function as follows.

```
void BinaryTree::InorderTraversal (TreeNode* ptrNode) {
  if (ptrNode) {
    InorderTraversal (ptrNode->ptrLeftChild);
    Visit (ptrNode);
    InorderTraversal (ptrNode->ptrRightChild);
  }
}
```

The **Visit** function would perform whatever action was needed. Examine Figure 10.6 again and find the bottom right tree with nodes labeled A to F. What would the inorder traversal produce? Assuming that **Visit** displayed the letter of the node visited, the following represents the sequence followed.

D, B, E, A, F, C

The Preorder Traversal

The **preorder** traversal visits the node itself before visiting the left and then the right subtrees.
One could define the recursive preorder traversal function as follows.

```
void BinaryTree::PreorderTraversal (TreeNode* ptrNode) {
  if (ptrNode) {
    Visit (ptrNode);
    PreorderTraversal (ptrNode->ptrLeftChild);
    PreorderTraversal (ptrNode->ptrRightChild);
  }
}
```

Look at the tree with nodes A-F in Figure 10.6 once more. Here is the preorder traversal order.

A, B, D, E, C, F

The Postorder Traversal

The **postorder** traversal visits the node itself after visiting both the left and then the right subtrees. One could define the recursive postorder traversal function as follows.

```
void BinaryTree::PostorderTraversal (TreeNode* ptrNode) {
  if (ptrNode) {
    PostorderTraversal (ptrNode->ptrLeftChild);
    PostorderTraversal (ptrNode->ptrRightChild);
    Visit (ptrNode);
  }
}
```

Look at the tree with nodes A-F in Figure 10.6 once more. Here is the postorder traversal order.

D, E, B, F, C, A

The ~BinaryTree Function

Ok. So which of these traversal methods do we need to implement the class destructor whose task is to delete all of the dynamically allocated **TreeNode**s? A postorder traversal is needed because it guarantees that the actual node itself is visited last so that it is then safe to delete that node at that point. Here is how the destructor could be implemented.

```
BinaryTree::~BinaryTree () {
 DeleteAllNodes (ptrRoot);
}
void BinaryTree::DeleteAllNodes (TreeNode* ptrNode) {
 DeleteAllNodes (ptrNode->ptrLeftChild);
 DeleteAllNodes (ptrNode->ptrRightChild);
 delete ptrNode;
}
```

Binary Search Trees

A **binary search tree** is a specialized binary tree in which three additional properties hold true.

A. No two nodes can contain the same user data value.

B. The user data values have a means of determining the relations greater than and less than. This often means numeric data, but could also apply to string comparisons as well.

C. The data value in every node in the tree is both greater than every data value in its left child subtree and less than every data value in its right side subtree.

With these criteria met, such binary trees are very useful for searching and for sorting operations. Because there are no duplicates, when a match is found, we can be certain we have the correct user data. Also, the actual matching algorithm can take advantage of the third rule. If we have a user value to find, we can compare it to that stored in the root of the tree. If the value we are to find is greater than that value in the root node, we know for certain that it lies only in the right child subtree, if it is there at all. Thus, we can rapidly traverse the tree to find the matching node.

For example, suppose that **TreeNode** was not storing **void** pointers to the client's data but rather was storing a **long** id number and the corresponding relative record number of that data in a direct access file. That is, suppose that it had been defined as follows.

```
struct TreeNode {
 long      id; // user key
 long      userRelativeRecordNumber;
 TreeNode* ptrLeftChild;
```

```
 TreeNode* ptrRightChild;
};
```

We could then implement a fast binary search of the tree for the matching item's relative record number as follows.

```
const int NoMatch = -1;
long BinaryTree::FindId (long matchKey) {
 TreeNode* ptrNode = ptrRoot;
 while (ptrNode && ptrNode->id != matchKey) {
 if (matchKey < ptrNode->id)
   ptrNode = ptrNode->ptrLeftChild;
 else
   ptrNode = ptrNode->ptrRightChild;
 }
 return ptrNode ? ptrNode->userRelativeRecordNumber : NoMatch;
}
```

The maximum number of iterations in the worst case would be the height of the binary tree. The worst case would occur when all nodes except a single bottom level leaf node contained only one child node. This is known as a **degenerate binary tree**. A search of a degenerate binary tree cannot ignore any nodes and thus must search all nodes. Similarly a binary tree with all nodes present is called a **full binary tree**. That is, if a tree has a height of N, then it has 2^N-1 nodes. It is a full binary tree. A **complete binary tree** is either full or full down to the next-to-the-last level with all of the leaves of the last level as far to the left as possible. Finally, a **balanced tree** (sometimes called a **b-tree**) is nearly a full binary tree but does have a few scattered nodes that do not have two children. Many algorithms have been developed for b-tree processing. It is an extremely important type of tree widely used with data base processing. Figure 10.7 shows three binary search trees.

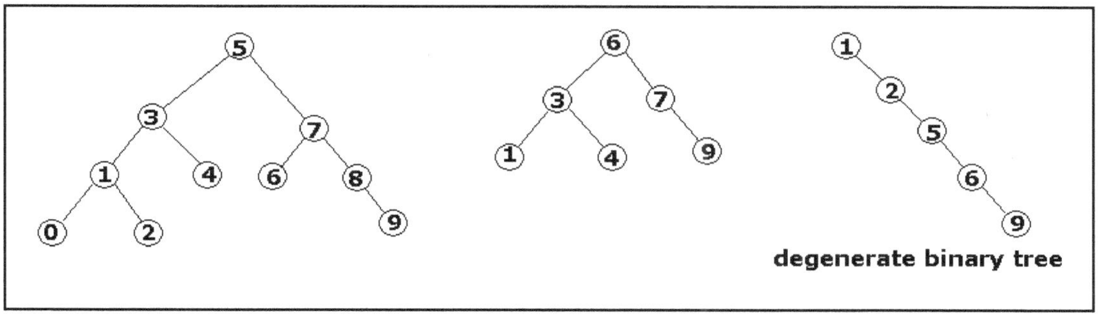

Figure 10.7 Three Binary Search Trees

However, inserting a new node into a full binary tree or a balanced tree requires some analysis. Before we tackle this more difficult problem, let's examine one last type of tree.

The Heap Tree

The C++ heap is that region of unused memory from which dynamic memory can allocate space. With trees, there is a specialized meaning. A **heap tree** is a complete binary tree in which the data stored in its nodes is arranged such that no child has a larger value than its parent. Figure 10.8 shows a heap tree. Notice that it is a binary tree but not a searchable binary tree since all of the right child nodes are not less than the parent node and all of the left child nodes are not greater than the parent.

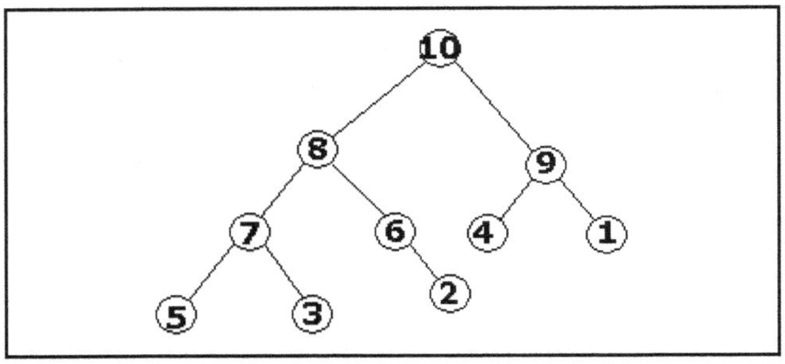

Figure 10.8 A Heap Tree

The heap type of tree can be used in sorting an array of items very quickly. In the above figure, the largest value of the integers is currently in the root node. If one saved that value in a temporary area and removed the value from the root node, one gets the situation shown in Figure 10.9.

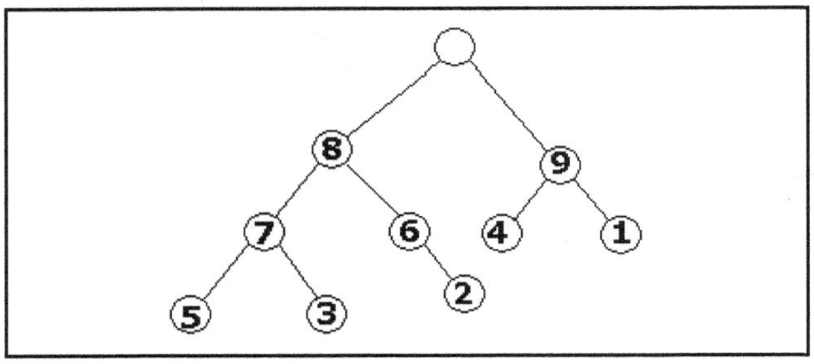

Figure 10.9 The Heap Tree with No Root Node

Next, the heap must be restructured as a binary tree. To replace the value in the empty root node, remove and use the value in the rightmost node at the lowest depth or height of the tree. In this case, it is the node containing the value of 2 since it is the rightmost node of nodes 5, 3, and 2. This yields the tree shown in Figure 10.10.

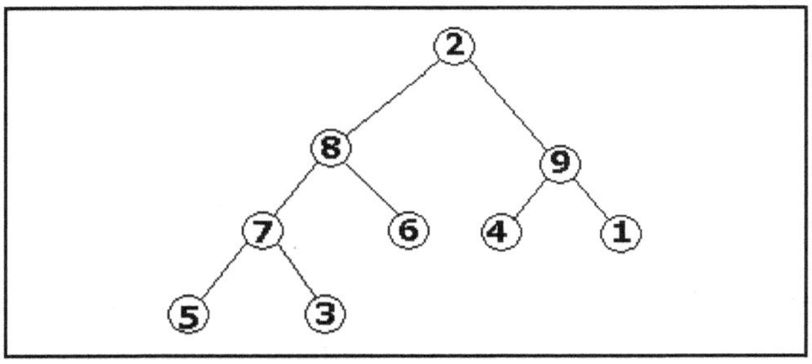

Figure 10.10 The Heap Tree with the New Root

Of course, the tree now does not satisfy the requirement that no child has a value greater than its parent. Obviously the two nodes containing the 8 and 9 are greater than the parent root node. Now a process called **Reheapify** or **RebuildHeapDownwards** must be done. This process consists of starting at the root and repeatedly exchanging its value with the larger value of its children until no more exchanges are possible. The reheapify process first compares the 2 to its two children, the 8 and 9, choosing the larger value, the 9. The 9 replaces the 2 and we get the results shown in Figure 10.11

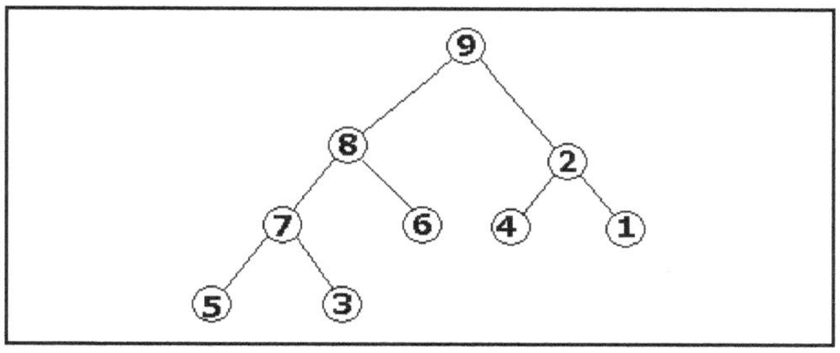

Figure 10.11 The Heap Tree After One Swap

The process must be recursive since now the node containing the value of 2 is not proper for a heap. So beginning with the new node containing the value 2, we find which of its children contain the larger value and swap once more. This yields the final reheapified tree shown in Figure 10.12.

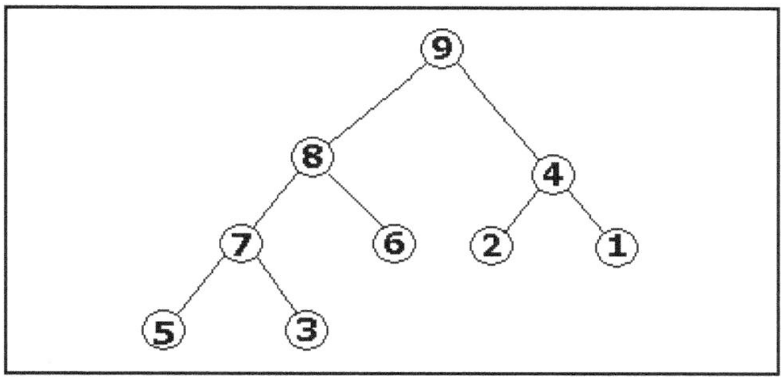

Figure 10.12 The Heap Tree After Reheapify

This process is implemented in the next chapter as a part of the fast executing sort known as the Heapsort. (See the function in **Pgm11a** called **RebuildHeapDownwards**.) However, the ideas presented here for the heap tree can be utilized to solve the problem we are facing—how to actually build a binary search tree.

Building a Binary Search Tree

The real problem we must solve in order to make use of a binary search tree is how to load it in the first place. With a double linked list, we could call the **AddAtHead**, **AddAtTail**, **InsertBefore**, or **InsertAfter** functions to initially build the list say from a file of data. We need a similar mechanism to load the binary search tree. Suppose we call it the **InsertAnItem** function. It can be implemented simply as follows.

```
bool BinaryTree::InsertAnItem (void* dataptr) {
 if (IsEmpty () ) {
  BuildRoot (dataptr);
  return true;
 }
 return Insert (ptrRoot, dataptr);
}
```

If the tree is empty, build the root node with this user item and return true, the insertion was successful. If there are items in the tree, we must find the location within the tree in which to store the new data. The **Insert** function is a recursive function that locates where within the tree this item should be located and so places it there.

However, if this item is already in the tree, placing this new one, a duplicate, would violate the criteria for a binary search tree. Should this happen, **Insert** must not add it but return **false** instead. Thus, one of the first actions of **Insert** must be to compare this node's data with the data to be inserted. However, since the data is stored as a **void** pointer, a user call back function must be used, here called **Compare**. Its prototype is

```
int Compare (const void* ptrnodedata, const void* ptrnewdata);
```

If the two user data are equal, the function returns 0. If the node data is less than the new data, it should return a negative number. If the node data is larger than the new data, it should return a positive number.

So if the node pointer exists, then **Compare** is called to determine the situation. If the new data is the same as an existing set, then the **Insert** function returns **false**, ending the entire process. Otherwise, the **Insert** function is recursively invoked passing this node's right or left child. If, however, the node is null, then this is the location for this entry. A new **TreeNode** is allocated and filled with the user data. Finally, notice that in order for us to be able to set the caller's right or left child pointer, the **Insert** function must be passed a reference to that pointer. This is a crucial point. **ptrNode** is null, it is the contents of some node's left or right child pointer and that pointer must be set to point to the new node. It must be passed by reference.

```
bool BinaryTree::Insert (TreeNode*& ptrNode, void* dataptr) {
 if (ptrNode) {
  int retcd = Compare (ptrNode->ptrdata, dataptr);
  if (retcd == 0)
   return false;
  else if (retcd < 0)
   return Insert (ptrNode->ptrLeftChild, dataptr);
  else
   return Insert (ptrNode->ptrRightChild, dataptr);
 }
 else {
  ptrNode = new TreeNode;
  ptrNode->ptrData = dataptr;
  ptrNode->ptrRightChild = ptrNode->ptrLeftChild = 0;
  return true;
 }
}
```

Let's examine just how the **Insert** function would insert data and build the tree, given several sets of input data. This is shown in Figure 10.13.

The left two trees in Figure 10.13 look very nicely built. However, the tree shape is totally determined by the order of the input values. The rightmost tree in the figure shows what happens if the data is not input in the correct order to build a tree properly—it ends up a degenerate tree! Oops indeed. So the **Insert** function works just fine if the data is already in the right order to build a proper tree. So we just have to educate the users to know how to determine the proper order to enter their data. Oh no! That would never do for at the very least, he/she would immediately ask you to write some kind of sorting program to get his/her data into the "proper" order **Insert** requires.

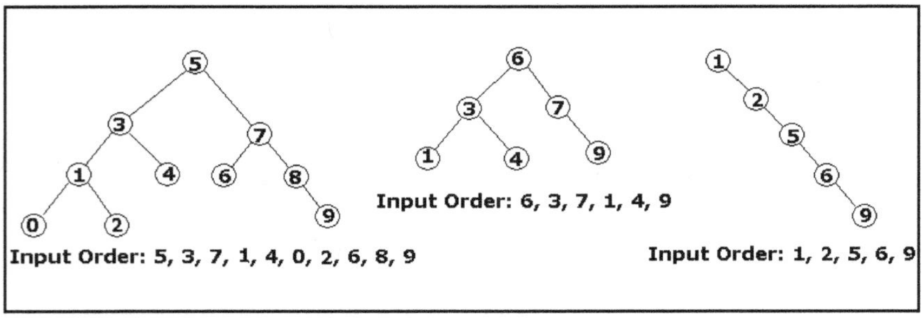

Figure 10.13 Insertion Order of Three Trees

If, however, the data values to be added to the tree are in random order, then very often the resulting tree built using the **Insert** function is acceptable. Only if the data values are sorted into order does a degenerate tree result. In practice, the **Insert** is reasonably acceptable practice. An advanced data structures course should continue from here and present methods for balancing the tree.

Determine the Height and the Number of Nodes in a Tree

To calculate the number of nodes in a tree, a recursive **CountNodes** function can be used. Again, begin with a definition of the function. Assume the function is passed a **TreeNode** pointer.

A. If the **TreeNode** pointer is null, return 0 as the number of nodes.

B. Otherwise, return the sum of the number of nodes in the left child plus the number of nodes in the right child plus one for this node.

The recursive **CountNodes** is called from the **GetNumberOfNodes** function which passes it the root node with which to begin operations. Here is the simple coding.

```
long BinaryTree::GetNumberOfNodes () const {
 return CountNodes (ptrRoot);
}
long BinaryTree::CountNodes (TreeNode* ptrNode) const {
 return ptrNode ?
  CountNodes (ptrNode->ptrLeftChild) +
  CountNodes (ptrNode->ptrRightChild) + 1 : 0;
}
```

To find the height of a tree, we need to find the maximum height of the deepest leaves. Again, this can be done by using a recursive function. Assume the height of a null tree is 0; the height of only a root node is 1 and so on. The recursive definition of the **HeightOfNodes** recursive function that is passed a **TreeNode** pointer is as follows.

A. If the **TreeNode** pointer is null, return 0 height.

B. Otherwise, return the maximum of the number of nodes in the left child branch of the tree and the number of nodes in the right child branch and add one more for this node itself.

The **HeightOfNodes** function is called from the **GetHeightOfTree** function which passes it the root pointer with which to start.

```
long BinaryTree::GetHeightOfTree () const {
 return HeightOfNodes (ptrRoot);
}
```

However, we need to write coding to find the maximum of the pair of return values from **HeightOfNodes** of the left and right children. Rather than writing a function **max**, I chose to code a simple C macro to do this.

```
#define max(a,b) (((a) > (b)) ? (a) : (b))
long BinaryTree::HeightOfNodes (TreeNode* ptrNode) const {
 if (ptrNode == 0)
  return 0;
 else
  return max (HeightOfNodes (ptrNode->ptrLeftChild),
              HeightOfNodes (ptrNode->ptrRightChild)) + 1;
}
```

Pgm10a—The BinaryTree Class and Tester Program

All of the details of binary trees that we have examined have been implemented in the **BinaryTree** class that follows. First, here is the definition of the **BinaryTree** class followed by its implementation. Notice that as usual, I have stored the user data with **void*** making the class reusable in many applications. Also notice that by making the assignment operator and the copy constructor protected functions, then client programs cannot copy a tree.

BinaryTree Class Definition

```
#pragma once

/**************************************************************/
/*                                                            */
/* BinaryTree: a class encapsulating Binary Trees             */
/*                                                            */
/**************************************************************/

/**************************************************************/
/*                                                            */
/* TreeNode: contains the user data and two child pointers    */
/*                                                            */
/**************************************************************/

struct TreeNode {
 void*     ptrData;
 TreeNode* ptrLeftChild;
 TreeNode* ptrRightChild;
};

/**************************************************************/
/*                                                            */
/* Call back functions required by the client application     */
/*                                                            */
/**************************************************************/

typedef int (*FIND) (const void* ptrThis, const void* ptrToFind);
typedef int (*COMPARE) (const void* ptrnodedata,
                        const void* ptrnewdata);
typedef void (*VISIT) (TreeNode* ptrNode);

/**************************************************************/
/*                                                            */
/* BinaryTree class                                           */
/*                                                            */
/**************************************************************/

class BinaryTree {
    protected:
     TreeNode* ptrRoot; // pointer to the root node of the tree

    public:
               BinaryTree (); // construct the tree
              ~BinaryTree (); // remove all nodes & destroy tree
 protected:
  void      DeleteAllNodes (TreeNode* ptrNode);

 public:
     bool      IsEmpty () const;          // returns true if empty
     void      BuildRoot (void* dataptr);// builds the root node
     TreeNode* GetRootNode () const;      // returns ptr to  root

  // adds a new node at the specified location
```

```
    bool      AddNode (TreeNode*& ptrNode, void* dataptr);

 // user access functions to get and set the data of a node
    void*     GetNodeData (TreeNode* ptrNode) const;
    void      SetNodeData (TreeNode* ptrNode, void* dataptr);

 // user access functions to acquire ptrs to a node's children
    TreeNode* GetLeftChild (TreeNode* ptrNode) const;
    TreeNode* GetRightChild (TreeNode* ptrNode) const;

              // returns true if this node is a leaf
    bool      IsLeaf (TreeNode* ptrNode) const;

              // manually delete a specific node
    void      DeleteLeaf (TreeNode*& ptrNode);

              // returns the number of nodes in the entire tree
 long         GetNumberOfNodes () const;
protected:
 long         CountNodes (TreeNode* ptrNode) const;

public:       // gets the height of the binary tree
 long         GetHeightOfTree () const;
protected:
 long         HeightOfNodes (TreeNode* ptrNode) const;

public:       // search tree for this data item
              // caller must provide Find call back function
              // returns 0 if not found or the user data ptr
 void*        FindThisData (void* ptrDataToFind, FIND Find);

 // three traversal functions to traverse the tree
 // user must provide a Visit call back function
 void         InorderTraversal (TreeNode* ptrNode, VISIT Visit);
 void         PreorderTraversal (TreeNode* ptrNode, VISIT Visit);
 void         PostorderTraversal (TreeNode* ptrNode, VISIT Visit);

 // inserts a new item into tree at the proper location
 // user must provide a Compare call back function
 // error displayed if item is already in the tree
 bool         InsertAnItem (void* dataptr, COMPARE Compare);
protected:
 bool Insert(TreeNode*& ptrNode, void* dataptr,COMPARE Compare);

 // class instances cannot be duplicated
 // disallow these operations
 BinaryTree (const BinaryTree&) {} // copy ctor
 BinaryTree& operator= (const BinaryTree&) {} //assignment op
};
```

BinaryTree Class Implementation

```
#include <iostream>
#include "BinaryTree.h"
```

```
using namespace std;

// max macro to return maximum of two values
#define max(a,b) (((a) > (b)) ? (a) : (b))

/****************************************************************/
/*                                                              */
/* BinaryTree: initializes tree to null                         */
/*                                                              */
/****************************************************************/

BinaryTree::BinaryTree () {
 ptrRoot = 0;
}

/****************************************************************/
/*                                                              */
/* IsEmpty: returns true if tree has no nodes at all            */
/*                                                              */
/****************************************************************/

bool BinaryTree::IsEmpty () const {
 return ptrRoot ? false : true;
}

/****************************************************************/
/*                                                              */
/* BuildRoot: allocates the root node of the tree               */
/*                                                              */
/****************************************************************/

void BinaryTree::BuildRoot (void* dataptr) {
 AddNode (ptrRoot, dataptr);
}

/****************************************************************/
/*                                                              */
/* GetRootNode: returns a pointer to the root node of the tree */
/*                                                              */
/****************************************************************/

TreeNode* BinaryTree::GetRootNode () const {
 return ptrRoot;
}

/****************************************************************/
/*                                                              */
/* AddNode: allocates a new node storing user's data in it      */
/*                                                              */
/****************************************************************/

bool BinaryTree::AddNode (TreeNode*& ptrNode, void* dataptr) {
 try {
  ptrNode = new TreeNode;
 }
 catch (std::bad_alloc e) { // check for out of memory
```

```
59    cerr << "Error - out of memory\n";
60    return false;
61  }
62  ptrNode->ptrData = dataptr;
63  ptrNode->ptrLeftChild = ptrNode->ptrRightChild = 0;
64  return true;
65 }
66
67 /******************************************************************/
68 /*                                                                */
69 /* GetNodeData: returns a ptr to user data stored in this node */
70 /*                                                                */
71 /******************************************************************/
72
73 void* BinaryTree::GetNodeData (TreeNode* ptrNode) const {
74  return ptrNode ? ptrNode->ptrData : 0;
75 }
76
77 /******************************************************************/
78 /*                                                                */
79 /* SetNodeData: replaces the user data stored in this node      */
80 /*                                                                */
81 /******************************************************************/
82
83 void BinaryTree::SetNodeData (TreeNode* ptrNode, void* dataptr) {
84  if (ptrNode)
85    ptrNode->ptrData = dataptr;
86 }
87
88 /******************************************************************/
89 /*                                                                */
90 /* GetLeftChild: returns ptr to this node's left child node     */
91 /*                                                                */
92 /******************************************************************/
93
94 TreeNode* BinaryTree::GetLeftChild (TreeNode* ptrNode) const {
95  return ptrNode ? ptrNode->ptrLeftChild : 0;
96 }
97
98 /******************************************************************/
99 /*                                                                */
100 /* GetRightChild: returns ptr to this node's right child node   */
101 /*                                                                */
102 /******************************************************************/
103
104 TreeNode* BinaryTree::GetRightChild (TreeNode* ptrNode) const {
105  return ptrNode ? ptrNode->ptrRightChild : 0;
106 }
107
108 /******************************************************************/
109 /*                                                                */
110 /* IsLeaf: returns true if this node is a leaf - no child nodes*/
111 /*                                                                */
112 /******************************************************************/
113
114 bool BinaryTree::IsLeaf (TreeNode* ptrNode) const {
```

```
 return ptrNode ? (ptrNode->ptrLeftChild == 0 &&
  ptrNode->ptrRightChild == 0 ? true : false) : false;
}

/***************************************************************/
/*                                                             */
/* DeleteLeaf: removes this node only                          */
/*             does not delete user data                       */
/*             does not delete child nodes                     */
/*                                                             */
/***************************************************************/

void BinaryTree::DeleteLeaf (TreeNode*& ptrNode) {
 if (!ptrNode) return;
 delete ptrNode;
 ptrNode = 0;
}

/***************************************************************/
/*                                                             */
/* GetNumberOfNodes: returns the total number of nodes in tree */
/*                                                             */
/***************************************************************/

long BinaryTree::GetNumberOfNodes () const {
 return CountNodes (ptrRoot);
}

/***************************************************************/
/*                                                             */
/* CountNodes: recursive protected function to count nodes     */
/*                                                             */
/***************************************************************/

long BinaryTree::CountNodes (TreeNode* ptrNode) const {
 return ptrNode ?
  CountNodes (ptrNode->ptrLeftChild) +
  CountNodes (ptrNode->ptrRightChild) + 1 : 0;
}

/***************************************************************/
/*                                                             */
/* GetHeightOfTree: returns the total height of the tree       */
/*                                                             */
/***************************************************************/

long BinaryTree::GetHeightOfTree () const {
 return HeightOfNodes (ptrRoot);
}

/***************************************************************/
/*                                                             */
/* HeightOfNodes: recursive protected function to get node's ht*/
/*                                                             */
/***************************************************************/

```

```
long BinaryTree::HeightOfNodes (TreeNode* ptrNode) const {
 if (ptrNode == 0)
  return 0;
 else
  return max (HeightOfNodes (ptrNode->ptrLeftChild),
              HeightOfNodes (ptrNode->ptrRightChild)) + 1;
}

/***************************************************************/
/*                                                             */
/* FindThisData: search tree to find this user item            */
/*   requires Find call back user function                     */
/*   returns the user data pointer of matching item            */
/*           or 0 if not found                                 */
/*                                                             */
/***************************************************************/

void* BinaryTree::FindThisData (void* ptrDataToFind, FIND Find) {
 int retcd;
 TreeNode* ptrNode = ptrRoot;
 while (ptrNode &&
       (retcd = Find (ptrNode->ptrData, ptrDataToFind)) != 0) {
 if (retcd < 0)
   ptrNode = ptrNode->ptrLeftChild;
 else
   ptrNode = ptrNode->ptrRightChild;
 }
 return ptrNode ? ptrNode->ptrData : 0;
}

/***************************************************************/
/*                                                             */
/* ~BinaryTree: deletes all nodes and the tree                 */
/*             Note: does not delete the contained user data   */
/*                                                             */
/***************************************************************/

BinaryTree::~BinaryTree () {
       DeleteAllNodes (ptrRoot);
}

/***************************************************************/
/*                                                             */
/* DeleteAllNodes: recursive function to delete all nodes      */
/*                                                             */
/***************************************************************/

void BinaryTree::DeleteAllNodes (TreeNode* ptrNode) {
 if (!ptrNode) return;
 DeleteAllNodes (ptrNode->ptrLeftChild);
 DeleteAllNodes (ptrNode->ptrRightChild);
 delete ptrNode;
}

/***************************************************************/
```

```
/*                                                              */
/* InorderTraversal: traverses the tree inorder method          */
/*                   requires Visit user call back function     */
/*                                                              */
/****************************************************************/

void BinaryTree::InorderTraversal (TreeNode* ptrNode,
                                   VISIT Visit) {
  if (ptrNode) {
    InorderTraversal (ptrNode->ptrLeftChild, Visit);
    Visit (ptrNode);
    InorderTraversal (ptrNode->ptrRightChild, Visit);
  }
}

/****************************************************************/
/*                                                              */
/* PreorderTraversal: traverses the tree preorder method        */
/*                    requires Visit user call back function    */
/*                                                              */
/****************************************************************/

void BinaryTree::PreorderTraversal (TreeNode* ptrNode,
                                    VISIT Visit) {
  if (ptrNode) {
    Visit (ptrNode);
    PreorderTraversal (ptrNode->ptrLeftChild, Visit);
    PreorderTraversal (ptrNode->ptrRightChild, Visit);
  }
}

/****************************************************************/
/*                                                              */
/* PostorderTraversal: traverses tree postorder method          */
/*                     requires Visit user call back function   */
/*                                                              */
/****************************************************************/

void BinaryTree::PostorderTraversal (TreeNode* ptrNode,
                                     VISIT Visit) {
  if (ptrNode) {
    PostorderTraversal (ptrNode->ptrLeftChild, Visit);
    PostorderTraversal (ptrNode->ptrRightChild, Visit);
    Visit (ptrNode);
  }
}

/****************************************************************/
/*                                                              */
/* InsertAnItem: inserts user item in proper location in tree   */
/*                                                              */
/****************************************************************/

bool BinaryTree::InsertAnItem (void* dataptr, COMPARE Compare) {
 if (IsEmpty () ) {
  BuildRoot (dataptr);
```

```
  return true;
 }
 return Insert (ptrRoot, dataptr, Compare);
}

/***************************************************************/
/*                                                             */
/* Insert: recursive function to find proper location of the   */
/*         insertion and to insert this new item there         */
/*                                                             */
/***************************************************************/

bool BinaryTree::Insert (TreeNode*& ptrNode, void* dataptr,
                         COMPARE Compare) {
 if (ptrNode) {
  int retcd = Compare (ptrNode->ptrData, dataptr);
  if (retcd == 0)
   return false;
  else if (retcd < 0)
   Insert (ptrNode->ptrLeftChild, dataptr, Compare);
  else
   Insert (ptrNode->ptrRightChild, dataptr, Compare);
 }
 else {
  try {
   ptrNode = new TreeNode;
  }
  catch (std::bad_alloc e) { // check for out of memory
   cerr << "Error - out of memory\n";
   return false;
  }
  ptrNode->ptrData = dataptr;
  ptrNode->ptrRightChild = ptrNode->ptrLeftChild = 0;
 }
 return true;
}
```

Now we need a tester program to test all of these functions. **Pgm10a.cpp** defines two 10-element arrays of integers that are used to build the trees. The first set yields a uniform binary tree but the second, which is in sorted order, yields a degenerate binary tree. Most of the coding is very straight forward. The only tricky coding is that that is required to produce the graphical display of the tree. First, examine the basic coding and the output from the program. Second, examine how the graphical display appears in the output. Then, after the listings, let's examine how that graphical listing is produced and its limitations.

Pgm10a Binary Tree Tester

```
#include <iostream>
#include <strstream>
#include <iomanip>
#include <crtdbg.h>
#include "BinaryTree.h"

using namespace std;

/***************************************************************/
```

```
/*                                                                  */
/* Pgm10a: BinaryTree tester program                                */
/*                                                                  */
/********************************************************************/

// array bounds for graphical display of tree
const int ROWS = 20;
const int COLS = 61;

// needed call back functions
int  Compare (const void* ptrnodedata, const void* ptrnewdata);
void Visit (TreeNode* ptrNode);
int  Find (const void* ptrThis, const void* ptrToFind);

// functions to provide a graphical display of the tree
void InsertValue (int x, char msg[][COLS], int row, int col);
void DisplayGraphicalTree (BinaryTree& tree);
int  DisplayGraphNode (TreeNode* ptrNode, char msg[][COLS],
                       int row, int col);


int main () {
 // two arrays of integers to use to build the trees
 int testNumbers[10] = {5, 3, 7, 1, 4, 0, 2, 6, 8, 9};
 int testNumbers2[10] = {0, 1, 2, 3, 4, 5, 6, 7, 8, 9};
 int i;
 {
  BinaryTree tree;
  cout << "Number of Nodes (should be 0): "
       << tree.GetNumberOfNodes () << endl;
  cout << "Height of Empty Tree (should be 0): "
       << tree.GetHeightOfTree () << endl;

  // add 10 integers to the tree
  for (i=0; i<10; i++) {
   if (!tree.InsertAnItem (&testNumbers[i], Compare))
    exit (1);
  }
  cout << "Number of Nodes: "
       << tree.GetNumberOfNodes () << endl;
  cout << "Height of Tree: " << tree.GetHeightOfTree () << endl;
  // test the three traversals
  cout << "Inorder Traversal: ";
  tree.InorderTraversal (tree.GetRootNode(), Visit);
  cout << "\nPreorder Traversal: ";
  tree.PreorderTraversal (tree.GetRootNode(), Visit);
  cout << "\nPostorder Traversal: ";
  tree.PostorderTraversal (tree.GetRootNode(), Visit);
  cout << endl;
  // make a graphical display of the tree
  DisplayGraphicalTree (tree);
  int findThis = 2;
  void* ptrfound = tree.FindThisData (&findThis, Find);
  if (!ptrfound) {
   cout << "Find Error: should have found 2 in the tree\n";
  }
```

```
  else {
   int* ptrd = (int*) ptrfound;
   cout << "Find 2 succeeded and found " << *ptrd << endl;
  }
  findThis = 42;
  ptrfound = tree.FindThisData (&findThis, Find);
  if (!ptrfound) {
   cout << "Find: correct - could not find 42 in the tree\n";
  }
  else {
   int* ptrd = (int*) ptrfound;
   cout << "Find Error looking for 42 and found "
        << *ptrd << endl;
  }


  cout << endl << endl;
  // make the second tree from the sorted integer array
  BinaryTree tree2;
  for (i=0; i<10; i++) {
   if (!tree2.InsertAnItem (&testNumbers2[i], Compare))
    exit (2);
  }
  cout << "Number of Nodes: "
       << tree2.GetNumberOfNodes () << endl;
  cout << "Height of Tree: " << tree2.GetHeightOfTree () << endl;
  cout << "Inorder Traversal: ";
  tree2.InorderTraversal (tree2.GetRootNode(), Visit);
  cout << "\nPreorder Traversal: ";
  tree2.PreorderTraversal (tree2.GetRootNode(), Visit);
  cout << "\nPostorder Traversal: ";
  tree2.PostorderTraversal (tree2.GetRootNode(), Visit);
  cout << endl;
  DisplayGraphicalTree (tree2);
 }

 if (_CrtDumpMemoryLeaks())
  cout << "\nOops! Memory Leaks!!\n";
 else
  cout << "\nNo Memory Leaks\n";
 return 0;
}

/***************************************************************/
/*                                                             */
/* Compare: call back function to compare this node's data to  */
/*          the new data being inserted into the tree          */
/*                                                             */
/***************************************************************/

int Compare (const void* ptrnodedata, const void* ptrnewdata) {
 // build intelligent pointers from the void pointers
 int* ptrNodeData = (int*) ptrnodedata;
 int* ptrNewData = (int*) ptrnewdata;
 // check the three cases
 if (*ptrNodeData == *ptrNewData)
```

```
  return 0;
 if (*ptrNodeData > *ptrNewData)
  return -1;
 else
  return 1;
}

/***************************************************************/
/*                                                             */
/* Visit: call back function displays user data from traversal */
/*                                                             */
/***************************************************************/

void Visit (TreeNode* ptrNode) {
 // display the integer being stored in this node
 int* ptrx = (int*) ptrNode->ptrData;
 cout << *ptrx << "  ";
}

/***************************************************************/
/*                                                             */
/* Find: call back function to see if this node is a match     */
/*                                                             */
/***************************************************************/

int  Find (const void* ptrThis, const void* ptrToFind) {
 int* ptrthis = (int*) ptrThis;
 int* ptrfind = (int*) ptrToFind;
 if (*ptrthis == *ptrfind)
  return 0;
 else if (*ptrfind < *ptrthis)
  return -1;
 return 1;
}

/***************************************************************/
/*                                                             */
/* DisplayGraphicalTree: make a graphical display of the tree  */
/*                                                             */
/***************************************************************/

void DisplayGraphicalTree (BinaryTree& tree) {
 int numRows = tree.GetNumberOfNodes();
 if (numRows > ROWS) {
  cerr << "DisplayGraphicalTree: Increase the number"
       << " of ROWS in the display strings from "
       << ROWS << " to " << numRows << endl;
  return;
 }
 // simple array of strings - one node per line - init to blanks
 char msg[ROWS][COLS];
 int i, j;
 for (i=0; i<ROWS; i++) {
  for (j=0; j<COLS-1; j++)
   msg[i][j] = ' ';
  msg[i][COLS-1] = 0;
```

```
 }

 TreeNode* ptrNode = tree.GetRootNode();
 if (!ptrNode) return;
 i = 0;
 j = 1;
 DisplayGraphNode (ptrNode, msg, i, j);

 // now display all the filled up lines
 for (i=0; i<numRows; i++) {
  cout << msg[i] << endl;
 }
}

/***************************************************************/
/*                                                             */
/* DisplayGraphNode: displays one node's worth of info         */
/*                                                             */
/***************************************************************/

int DisplayGraphNode (TreeNode* ptrNode, char msg[][COLS],
                      int row, int col) {
 int ct = 0;
 if (!ptrNode) return 0;
 int i = row;
 int j = col;
 int* ptrd = (int*) ptrNode->ptrData;
 // display this node's integer
 InsertValue (*ptrd, msg, i, j);
 ct++;
 i++;
 unsigned char c;
 // display all left children
 if (ptrNode->ptrLeftChild) {
  // insert proper graphic depending on whether or not there is a
  // right child
  c = ptrNode->ptrRightChild ? 195 : 192;
  msg[i][j] = c;
  msg[i][j+1] = (char) 196;
  msg[i][j+2] = (char) 196;
  msg[i][j+3] = (char) 196;
  int num =DisplayGraphNode(ptrNode->ptrLeftChild, msg, i, j+4);
  ct += num;
  // insert needed number of | lines
  for (int k=0; k<num; k++) {
   i++;
   msg[i][j] = (char) 179;
  }
 }
 // display all right children
 if (ptrNode->ptrRightChild) {
  c = 192;
  msg[i][j] = c;
  msg[i][j+1] = (char) 196;
  msg[i][j+2] = (char) 196;
  msg[i][j+3] = (char) 196;
```

```
  int num =DisplayGraphNode(ptrNode->ptrRightChild, msg, i, j+4);
  ct += num;
 }
 return ct;
}

/***************************************************************/
/*                                                             */
/* InsertValue: stores the integer into the mgs string         */
/*                                                             */
/***************************************************************/

void InsertValue (int x, char msg[][COLS], int row, int col) {
 char val[10];
 ostrstream os (val, sizeof (val));
 os << setw(2) << x << ends;
 msg[row][col] = val[1];
 msg[row][col-1] = val[0];
}
```

```
Output of Pgm12a - Tester of BinaryTree Class
```

```
Number of Nodes (should be 0): 0
Height of Empty Tree (should be 0): 0
Number of Nodes: 10
Height of Tree: 4
Inorder Traversal: 0  1  2  3  4  5  6  7  8  9
Preorder Traversal: 5  3  1  0  2  4  7  6  8  9
Postorder Traversal: 0  2  1  4  3  6  9  8  7  5
 5
 ├── 3
 │   ├── 1
 │   │   ├── 0
 │   │   └── 2
 │   └── 4
 └── 7
     ├── 6
     └── 8
         └── 9
Find 2 succeeded and found 2
Find: correct - could not find 42 in the tree


Number of Nodes: 10
Height of Tree: 10
Inorder Traversal: 0  1  2  3  4  5  6  7  8  9
Preorder Traversal: 0  1  2  3  4  5  6  7  8  9
Postorder Traversal: 9  8  7  6  5  4  3  2  1  0
 0
 └── 1
     └── 2
         └── 3
             └── 4
                 └── 5
                     └── 6
```

```
                              └── 7
                                  └── 8
                                      └── 9

No Memory Leaks
```

The graphical display of the tree is just a quick and dirty approach to showing the nodes. I needed a fast way to visually verify that the nodes I had intended to be built were in fact being built. There is nothing rigorous about the solution and it is limited. (A better solution is shown in chapter 12.) The approach is to define an array of strings sufficiently large enough to hold all of the needed lines. Since one node's value is placed on one line, the number of lines is actually given by the number of nodes in the tree. Rather than dynamically allocating an array of strings, I chose to use a fixed sized array:

```
char msg[ROWS][COLS];
```

where ROWS is 20 and COLS is 61. I do display an error message if more than 20 rows are needed.

The lowest level function, **InsertValue** is given the integer to display, the array of strings, and the row and column subscripts of the destination location within the array. It inserts the two-digit number into the correct two characters of the array of strings.

DisplayGraphicalTree gets the number of rows needed, in other words, the number of nodes and aborts if it exceeds 20. Next it fills the 20 strings with blanks and inserts the null terminator. It calls the recursive function **DisplayGraphNode** passing it the root node and the coordinates for the first node's integer, row 0, column 1. When the recursive function has finished, the proper number of strings or lines are then displayed to **cout**.

DisplayGraphNode does nothing if this is a null node. Otherwise, it begins by displaying the integer value it is storing. Next, it must determine if there are any left child nodes. If so, it must figure out which graphic character to display: a "tee" or an "L" depending on whether or not there is also a right child node present or not. It then inserts into the correct line the "tee" or "L" character and three "-" characters. Then, it can call itself passing the left child node pointer. Notice that it increases the column subscript by 4 to account for the graphics already inserted.

```
int num =DisplayGraphNode(ptrNode->ptrLeftChild, msg, i, j+4);
```

The **DisplayGraphNode** function returns the number of rows in which it has inserted data. This number is then used to control how many vertical "|" characters are also inserted in those lines, forming the connector from the parent node. Finally, if the right child node exists, the four graphics characters are inserted, an "L" and three "-" and the function calls itself passing the right child node. When everything is done, it returns the total number of lines in which insertions are made. The previous invocation then uses this number to insert the outer graphics characters providing the connections between nodes.

While the method is crude, it makes it easy to verify that the correct node structure has been created. Next, we need to utilize the **BinaryTree** class in an application.

Pgm10b – the Account Inquiry Application
Loading a Binary Search Tree from a Sorted ISAM Index File

One usage of binary search trees is to find records in a database or master file. In this example, I reuse the simple accounting record example we utilized in the binary files chapter. Acme Credit Corporation stores their account records in a binary master file. The key id field that is used to directly access a specific record is the client's social security number. An ISAM index, whose entries contain the client's key and the relative record number, has been created to allow direct access to the records. Here is the definition of both the master records and the index records.

Accounts.h Definition File

```
#pragma once
```

```

const int NAMELEN = 31;

// the data base records
struct AccountRec {
 long   ssno;            // social security number = key id field
 char   name[NAMELEN]; // customer name
 double creditLimit;    // limit of credit on this account
 double balance;        // current account balance
};

// the index records to allow direct access to accounts
struct IndexRec {
 long ssno;      // social security number = key id field
 long relRecNum; // corresponding relative record number on disk
};
```

The objective is to write an inquiry program—that is, given a client's social security number, the program displays that client's account information. Realistically, this program would display a menu prompting the operator to enter a client's social security number. Then, it would display the corresponding accounting data for that person or an error message and then wait for another look up request. However, because our emphasis is on how to build and use a binary search tree to find the records, I have made a batch file of these requests and will just have the program display the results in a columnarly aligned report.

For best results, the binary search tree should be as balanced as possible among its nodes. The incoming index records are sorted into increasing social security number order. If we just add each entry to the binary tree as it is input from the index file, the resulting tree would be degenerate, each key is larger than the previous and would be added to the right side of the node above it. In this case, any tree search would degenerate into a sequential search of keys. So the real problem we face is how to easily and quickly load a sorted set of values into a binary search tree such that it is fairly well balanced. In the actual index data file, I have 32 entries.

Suppose that I sequentially number each node and leaf beginning with 1, where 1 represents the first index record in the index file. Our desired tree should look like figure 10.14.

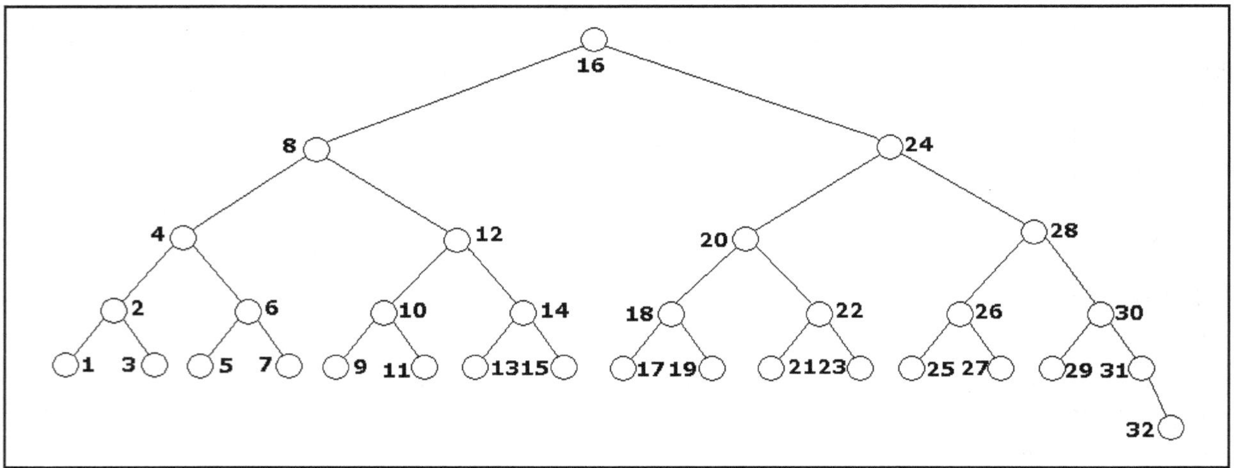

Figure 10.14 The Desired Binary Tree of 32 Index Records

This is our ideal binary search tree whose data values are **void** pointers to **IndexRec** instances containing the social security numbers and corresponding relative record numbers. There are several interesting points to note about this tree structure, given the numbering scheme I used. Notice that all nodes immediately above the bottom leaves have a number that is evenly divisible by two, ignoring leaf 32. Further, the nodes directly above those are also evenly divisible by 4. The two nodes above them are also evenly divisible by 8. This yields a crucial principle that we can exploit.

Rule: in a complete binary search tree whose nodes are numbered in sequence beginning with 1, each node is exactly as many levels above the leaves as the highest power of two that divides its number.

Since we must input the actual index data file, assume that the entire array of index records has been input into an array in memory and that we also know the exact number of items in the array with which to populate the tree. Further, theses index records are sorted into increasing social security number order. Given these facts and the rule above, a really simple algorithm immediately appears. Suppose that we choose the element in the middle of the array and use that item as the root of the tree. Numbering the elements beginning at 1 instead of 0, let **N** be the one in the middle. Now which elements should become the left and right children of this first node? If we let **factor** represent **N/2**, then the left child would be **N–factor** while the right child is given by **N+factor**. (The actual index of these is always 1 less, of course.)

Ok. Once these two children have been added, what would be the left and right children of the root's left node at **N/2–factor**? This new **factor** would be the previous **factor/2** or **(N/2)/2**. For example, if there were 31 index records, numbered from 1 to 32, then the root would be 16 and its left and right children would be 8 and 24. The left and right children of 8 would be 4 and 12, while the left and right children of 24 would be 20 and 28. What would the left and right children of the node at 4 be? 2 and 6. And finally, what would they be for the node at 2? 1 and 3. This is ideal for a recursive function, **Add**.

The recursive **Add** function is given the array of index records and the maximum number in that array along with the current node, and the values for **N** and **factor**. It calculates the numbers for the left and right child nodes—**N–factor** and **N+factor**. It then adds those two new nodes into the tree. Finally, the function would call itself twice, once to fill its left node and once to fill its right node. For the left node call, it passes **(N–factor)** as the new left **N** and **factor/2** as the new factor. For the right node call, it passes **(N+factor)** and **factor/2**.

Of course, the actual subscripts are always one less than these **N** values. Certainly we must guard against a subscript becoming less than zero and greater than or equal to the maximum number of elements. But what about the recursion ending condition? When we are adding the left and right children of node number 2, **factor** is 1, yielding node 1 and 3. The new **factor** is now 0, or 1/2. This is the ending condition, when **factor** is less than 1.

Of course, this process is not going to add every element if the number of elements in the array does not form a perfectly balanced binary tree. We cannot force every tree to have 3, 7, 15, 31 and so on number of elements. So we also need some final addition method for the extra leaves.

The problem of the extra leaves is not trivial or easily solved with our basic data structure's theory. In advanced data structures, there are other forms of trees that handle just such situations. These routines are often called "balancing the tree." Here we need something fool proof and very easy to implement. Remember that the tree nodes are storing **void** pointers to the index records.

To add a new node, I allocate a new **IndexRec** structure and copy the correct index array structure element into this new instance and link the new instance into the tree. Thus, once the data has been copied from the index array into the new node instance, I no longer need that array instance. So I chose to replace the social security number in that used array instance with a unique value, a –1. When the node addition process is finished, we only need to loop through the index array looking for social security numbers that are not –1. Those few that are found can be added to the tree using the normal **AddNode** function which places them into the correct position in the tree. There will only be a few of these to add in any case so the process is not going to be time-consuming at all.

Here is the output of **Pgm10b** which reads a transactions file of clients to find and display. I actually requested that each client in the file to be found for debugging purposes. Also, I adapted the graphic display to also show us the resultant tree. Notice the location of the 32nd node on the bottom right of the far right node. I also requested the program find three clients that are not in the data base—one that would appear before the very first social security number, one that would be after the last one in the file, and one number that would be located somewhere in the middle of the tree if it were present.

```
Output from Pgm10b Accounts Inquiry Program

345567566
├───234234234
│   ├───147360728
│   │   ├───120834844
│   │   │   ├───120487632
│   │   │   └───132323848
│   │   └───193234393
│   │       ├───173763483
│   │       └───193293934
│   └───289784744
│       ├───280482793
│       │   ├───237473650
│       │   └───289573072
│       └───333937457
│           ├───333333333
│           └───343455545
└───645343545
    ├───376360873
    │   ├───348893489
    │   │   ├───345994595
    │   │   └───349672503
    │   └───482874743
    │       ├───384720984
    │       └───545564665
    └───894378238
        ├───838747653
        │   ├───745645534
        │   └───892893298
        └───934887474
            ├───898932833
            └───943847344
                └───958274873

                         Acme Credit Inquiry

ID Number  Customer Name                     Limit    Balance

333333333  Annie Jones                     5000.00    2500.00
343455545  Tom Jones                       9000.00    5000.00
345567566  Betsy Smyth                    10500.00    6700.00
545564665  Henry Jasper                    6700.00    5344.50
645343545  William Smith                   7500.00    5555.55
745645534  Thomas Albert                   4500.00    4300.00
234234234  Lola L. Lorraine                5500.00    5000.00
193234393  Jeremie Jones                   4500.00    4242.42
943847344  Sam Spade                       5500.00    5432.11
345994595  Larime Smith                    6500.00    4500.00
934887474  Jerome Jones                    7000.00    6500.00
173763483  Ally Shows                      4500.00    4000.00
```

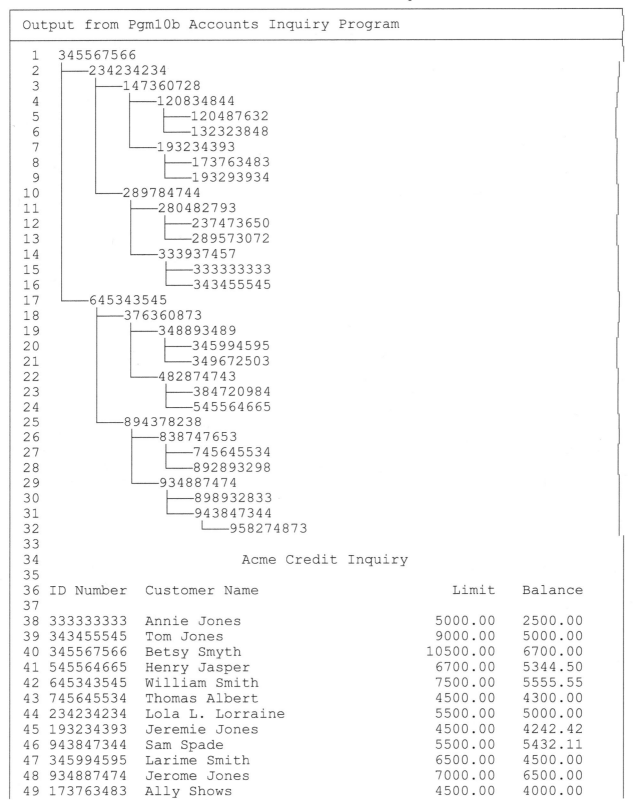

```
894378238  B. B. Jones                            5500.00    5323.50
120834844  DJ Smith                               6000.00    5400.00
898932833  Lou Anne Jones                         8000.00    7400.00
193293934  Albert Smith                           6800.00    4500.00
348893489  Thomas Thoms                           1500.00    1000.00
838747653  Bertha Bottles                         3500.00    2500.00
958274873  Ruth Smithe                            5500.00    4368.55
132323848  Lenard Jones                           8000.00    4568.47
892893298  Louis Louie                            9000.00    8888.88
333937457  Nancy Smith                           10500.00    9999.99
237473650  Mertle Jones                          11000.00   10000.00
280482793  Frodo Backwater                        9500.00    8888.50
482874743  Hank Albert                            5800.00    4800.00
147360728  Cecil Smith                            8700.00    7777.77
349672503  Larime Jones                           9700.00    8877.55
289573072  Herbert Smith                          7800.00    7788.99
384720984  Frank Jones                            5600.00    5555.55
120487632  Sammy Smith                            6500.00    5600.00
289784744  Doc Smith                              7800.00    7744.11
376360873  Lea Ann Jones                          8900.00    8765.42
Error: 444444444 is not in the master file
Error: 1111 is not in the master file
Error: 999999999 is not in the master file

No Memory Leaks
Press any key to continue
```

Here is the coding for the **Pgm10b**. The **BinaryTree** class is identical to that in **Pgm10a**. Please study the coding to build the binary tree.

Pgm10b - Accounts ISAM File Inquiry Program Using Binary Search Tree

```
#include <iostream>
#include <iomanip>
#include <fstream>
#include <strstream>
#include <crtdbg.h>
#include "Account.h"
#include "BinaryTree.h"
using namespace std;

const int ROWS = 50;
const int COLS = 79;

// functions to build the index tree
void BuildTree (BinaryTree& tree);
void Add (IndexRec* irec, long maxRecs, TreeNode*& ptrParent,
          long N, long factor);
int  Compare (const void* ptrnodedata, const void* ptrnewdata);

// cleanup action
void DeleteVisit (TreeNode* ptrNode);

// perform the set of inquiries
void ProcessInquiries (BinaryTree& tree);
```

```
int  Find (const void* ptrThis, const void* ptrToFind);

// functions to provide a graphical display of the tree
void InsertValue (long x, char msg[][COLS], int row, int col);
void DisplayGraphicalTree (BinaryTree& tree);
int  DisplayGraphNode (TreeNode* ptrNode, char msg[][COLS],
                       int row, int col);

/***************************************************************/
/*                                                             */
/* Pgm10b: Accounts data base Inquiry with ISAM and binary tree*/
/*                                                             */
/***************************************************************/

int main () {
 {
 BinaryTree index;

 BuildTree (index); // load index into a binary search tree

 DisplayGraphicalTree (index); // debug display the tree

 ProcessInquiries (index); // process all inquiries

 // remove all user data from tree prior to destruction
 index.InorderTraversal (index.GetRootNode(), DeleteVisit);
 }

 if (_CrtDumpMemoryLeaks())
  cout << "\nOops! Memory Leaks!!\n";
 else
  cout << "\nNo Memory Leaks\n";

 return 0;
}

/***************************************************************/
/*                                                             */
/* BuildTree: convert an IndexRec array into a binary tree     */
/*            the array is sorted into increasing ssno (key)   */
/*            order                                            */
/*                                                             */
/***************************************************************/

void BuildTree (BinaryTree& tree) {
 // open the Index file
 ifstream index ("Accounts.idx", ios::in | ios::binary);
 if (!index) {
  cerr << "Error: cannot open Accounts.idx file\n";
  exit (1);
 }

 // get the total file size and thus the number of records in it
 index.seekg (0, ios::end);
 long maxRecs = index.tellg () / sizeof (IndexRec);
 index.seekg (0, ios::beg);
```

```

 if (maxRecs < 1) { // if no records, quit, nothing to do
  index.close();
  return;
 }

 // allocate an array of Index records to hold them
 IndexRec* irec;
 try {
  irec = new IndexRec [maxRecs];
 }
 catch (std::bad_alloc e) { // check for out of memory
  cerr << "Error - out of memory\n";
  exit (2);
 }

 // input the entire sorted ISAM index
 index.read ((char*) irec, maxRecs * sizeof (IndexRec));
 index.close ();

 // get the middle element as the root node
 long N = (maxRecs + 1) / 2;
 long rootIdx = N - 1;          // the subscript of root node
 IndexRec* ptri;
 try {
  ptri = new IndexRec; // create a new Index rec
 }
 catch (std::bad_alloc e) { // check for out of memory
  cerr << "Error - out of memory\n";
  exit (3);
 }
 *ptri = irec[rootIdx];         // copy this one into new one
 irec[rootIdx].ssno = -1;       // mark this one as used
 tree.BuildRoot (ptri);         // set this one as the root node

 TreeNode* ptrNode = tree.GetRootNode ();

 long factor = N / 2; // calc the +- factor to get to next nodes

 // add in both left and right children recursively
 Add (irec, maxRecs, ptrNode, N, factor);

 // now manually add in all those entries not yet in nodes
 for (long i=0; i<maxRecs; i++) {
  if (irec[i].ssno != -1) {
   IndexRec* ptri;
   try {
    ptri = new IndexRec;
   }
   catch (std::bad_alloc e) { // check for out of memory
    cerr << "Error - out of memory\n";
    exit (4);
   }
   *ptri = irec[i];
   tree.InsertAnItem (ptri, Compare);
  }
```

```
  }

  delete [] irec; // and remove the index array
}

/***************************************************************/
/*                                                             */
/* Add: add the left and right nodes to this node              */
/*                                                             */
/***************************************************************/

void Add (IndexRec* irec, long maxRecs, TreeNode*& ptrParent,
          long N, long factor) {
 long lIdx = N - factor - 1; // index of the left irec to add
 long rIdx = N + factor - 1; // index of the right irec to add
 TreeNode* ptrNode;
 IndexRec* ptri;
 // add the left index record at iLdx if it is 0 or above
 if (lIdx >= 0) {
  try {
   ptrNode = new TreeNode;
  }
  catch (std::bad_alloc e) { // check for out of memory
   cerr << "Error - out of memory\n";
   exit (6);
  }
  ptrParent->ptrLeftChild = ptrNode;
  try {
   ptri = new IndexRec;
  }
  catch (std::bad_alloc e) { // check for out of memory
   cerr << "Error - out of memory\n";
   exit (6);
  }
  *ptri = irec[lIdx];
  irec[lIdx].ssno = -1;    // mark this index record as used
  ptrNode->ptrData = ptri;
  ptrNode->ptrLeftChild = ptrNode->ptrRightChild = 0;
 }
 // add the right index record at rIdx if it is < max in array
 if (rIdx < maxRecs) {
  try {
   ptrNode = new TreeNode;
  }
  catch (std::bad_alloc e) { // check for out of memory
   cerr << "Error - out of memory\n";
   exit (6);
  }
  ptrParent->ptrRightChild = ptrNode;
  try {
   ptri = new IndexRec;
  }
  catch (std::bad_alloc e) { // check for out of memory
   cerr << "Error - out of memory\n";
   exit (6);
  }
```

```
  *ptri = irec[rIdx];
  irec[rIdx].ssno = -1;    // mark this index record as used
  ptrNode->ptrData = ptri;
  ptrNode->ptrLeftChild = ptrNode->ptrRightChild = 0;
 }
 // calculate next left and right node locations
 long newLN = N - factor;
 long newRN = N + factor;
 // calculate the reduced gap size for the next pair of nodes
 long newfactor = factor / 2;
 if (newfactor == 0)
  return; // no more nodes left
 // recurively add left and right children of this node
 if (newLN >= 0)
  Add (irec, maxRecs, ptrParent->ptrLeftChild, newLN, newfactor);
 if (newRN < maxRecs)
  Add (irec, maxRecs, ptrParent->ptrRightChild, newRN,newfactor);
}

/***************************************************************/
/*                                                             */
/* Compare: call back function to match this ssno with that in */
/*          the passed tree node in order to find correct      */
/*          location in the tree at which to add this one      */
/*                                                             */
/***************************************************************/

int Compare (const void* ptrnodedata, const void* ptrnewdata) {
 // build intelligent pointers from the void pointers
 IndexRec* ptrNodeData = (IndexRec*) ptrnodedata;
 IndexRec* ptrNewData = (IndexRec*) ptrnewdata;
 // check the three cases
 if (ptrNodeData->ssno == ptrNewData->ssno)
  return 0;
 if (ptrNodeData->ssno > ptrNewData->ssno)
  return -1;
 else
  return 1;
}

/***************************************************************/
/*                                                             */
/* DeleteVisit: remove this tree node's index data             */
/*                                                             */
/***************************************************************/

void DeleteVisit (TreeNode* ptrNode) {
 IndexRec* ptri = (IndexRec*) ptrNode->ptrData;
 delete ptri;
}

/***************************************************************/
/*                                                             */
/* ProcessInquiries: Display account info for customer requests*/
/*                                                             */
/***************************************************************/
```

```

void ProcessInquiries (BinaryTree& tree) {
 // open master data base binary file
 ifstream master ("Accounts.dat", ios::in | ios::binary);
 if (!master) {
  cerr << "Error: cannot open Accounts.dat\n";
  exit (3);
 }

 // open the inquiries transactions file
 // normally, this would really be some kind of real time menu
 // driven process
 ifstream trans ("Inquiries.txt");
 if (!trans) {
  cerr << "Error: cannot open Inquiries.txt\n";
  master.close ();
  exit (4);
 }

 // set up for dollars and cents and display headings
 cout.setf (ios::fixed, ios::floatfield);
 cout << setprecision (2);
 cout << endl << "                      Acme Credit Inquiry\n\n"
      << "ID Number  Customer Name                      Limit"
      << "   Balance\n\n";

 IndexRec* ptrirec;
 AccountRec arec;
 long findId;
 while (trans >> findId) { // for all requests,
  // find their relative record number from the Index tree
  ptrirec = (IndexRec*) (tree.FindThisData (&findId, Find));

  if (!ptrirec) { // invalid ssno
   cout << "Error: " << findId << " is not in the master file\n";
  }
  else {
   // find the file offset of this account
   long offset = sizeof (AccountRec) * ptrirec->relRecNum;
   master.seekg (offset, ios::beg);
   // input this account
   master.read ((char*) &arec, sizeof (arec));
   // display this account
   cout << setw (9) << arec.ssno << "  " << left
        << setw (30) << arec.name << right
        << "  " << setw (8) << arec.creditLimit
        << "  " << setw (8) << arec.balance << endl;
  }
 }
 trans.close ();
 master.close ();
}

/***************************************************************/
/*                                                             */
/* Find: call back function to match ssno to index in tree     */
```

```
/*                                                                  */
/********************************************************************/

int  Find (const void* ptrThis, const void* ptrToFind) {
 long* ptrthis = (long*) ptrToFind;
 IndexRec* ptri = (IndexRec*) ptrThis;
 if (ptri->ssno == *ptrthis)
  return 0;
 if (ptri->ssno > *ptrthis)
  return -1;
 return 1;
}

/********************************************************************/
/*                                                                  */
/* DisplayGraphicalTree: make a graphical display of the tree       */
/*                                                                  */
/********************************************************************/

void DisplayGraphicalTree (BinaryTree& tree) {
 int numRows = tree.GetNumberOfNodes();
 if (numRows > ROWS) {
  cerr << "DisplayGraphicalTree: Increase the number"
       << " of ROWS in the display strings from "
       << ROWS << " to " << numRows << endl;
  return;
 }
 // simple array of strings - one node per line - init to blanks
 char msg[ROWS][COLS];
 int i, j;
 for (i=0; i<ROWS; i++) {
  for (j=0; j<COLS-1; j++)
   msg[i][j] = ' ';
  msg[i][COLS-1] = 0;
 }

 TreeNode* ptrNode = tree.GetRootNode();
 if (!ptrNode) return;
 i = 0;
 j = 1;
 DisplayGraphNode (ptrNode, msg, i, j);

 // now display all the filled up lines
 for (i=0; i<numRows; i++) {
  cout << msg[i] << endl;
 }
}

/********************************************************************/
/*                                                                  */
/* DisplayGraphNode: displays one node's worth of info              */
/*                                                                  */
/********************************************************************/

int DisplayGraphNode (TreeNode* ptrNode, char msg[][COLS],
                      int row, int col) {
```

```
365  int ct = 0;
366  if (!ptrNode) return 0;
367  int i = row;
368  int j = col;
369  IndexRec* ptrd = (IndexRec*) ptrNode->ptrData;
370  // display this node's integer
371  InsertValue (ptrd->ssno, msg, i, j);
372  ct++;
373  i++;
374  unsigned char c;
375  // display all left children
376  if (ptrNode->ptrLeftChild) {
377   // insert proper graphic depending on whether or not there is a
378   // right child
379   c = ptrNode->ptrRightChild ? 195 : 192;
380   msg[i][j] = c;
381   msg[i][j+1] = (char) 196;
382   msg[i][j+2] = (char) 196;
383   msg[i][j+3] = (char) 196;
384   int num =DisplayGraphNode(ptrNode->ptrLeftChild, msg, i, j+4);
385   ct += num;
386   // insert needed number of | lines
387   for (int k=0; k<num; k++) {
388    i++;
389    msg[i][j] = (char) 179;
390   }
391  }
392  // display all right children
393  if (ptrNode->ptrRightChild) {
394   c = 192;
395   msg[i][j] = c;
396   msg[i][j+1] = (char) 196;
397   msg[i][j+2] = (char) 196;
398   msg[i][j+3] = (char) 196;
399   int num =DisplayGraphNode(ptrNode->ptrRightChild, msg, i, j+4);
400   ct += num;
401  }
402  return ct;
403 }
404
405 /***************************************************************/
406 /*                                                             */
407 /* InsertValue: stores the integer into the mgs string         */
408 /*                                                             */
409 /***************************************************************/
410
411 void InsertValue (long x, char msg[][COLS], int row, int col) {
412  ostrstream os (&msg[row][col], 9);
413  os << setw(9) << x;
414 }
```

Once you are satisfied that you understand the build tree coding, examine how the tree is deleted. Remember that it is storing **void** pointers to index records. When the class destructor is called, all of the tree nodes are deleted. But how do we get the index records that we allocated deleted? Before the destructor **~BinaryTree** is called at line 51, the end block, I called one of the traversal methods. Each node is then visited with our call back function, **DeleteVisit,** being passed each instance found. Here is where I delete them.

Multiple Projects in the Same Workspace

How did the original ISAM master file and index get created in the first place? I had to write a short program to input a text file of client data and write it to the binary master file. I had to create the corresponding index records and sort them and write the index file. Since the initial build program and **Pgm10b** are so closely related, I chose to have them in the same workspace.

To add additional projects to the same workspace, with the solution selected in the Solution Explorer window, right click and choose Add New Project. Proceed as normal to make the project. I chose to make it below the Pgm10b folder. I manually copied the two master binary files that were built from the subfolder to the main **Pgm10b** folder. Likewise, I copied the Account.h header file as well. The project workspace appears as shown in Figure 10.15.

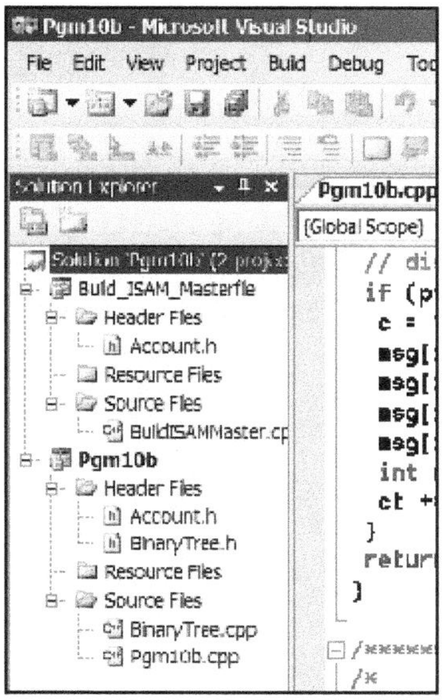

Figure 10.15

To switch between running the two programs, select one and right click and chose "Set as start up project."

Review Questions

1. Why is a tree a nonlinear data structure?

2. Give an example of a tree structure not mentioned in the text.

3. What is the difference between the root of a tree and a node of a tree and a leaf of a tree?

4. In Figure 10.4, what letter does the root node contain? What letters do the siblings of node B contain? What are the children of node I? What node is the parent of K?

5. What are the heights of the three trees shown in Figure 10.1?

6. Draw a Venn diagram of the bottom right tree shown in Figure 10.6 which contains nodes A through F.

7. What is meant by an N-ary tree?

8. What is a binary tree? How is it different from a general tree?

9. Describe the difference between an inorder, postorder, and preorder tree traversals?

10. What is a binary search tree? How is it different from a binary tree? What is the difference between a full binary tree and a balanced tree? What is a degenerate binary tree?

11. What is a heap tree? How is it different from a binary search tree?

12. Describe how a new node is added to a binary tree?

Stop! Do These Exercises Before Programming

1. The Acme Corporation programmer has been given a new programming assignment—the team leader of the Folder Tree Project. You, of course, have been assigned to his team of programmers. The task is to create a **FolderTree** class to encapsulate the directory tree structure of a disk drive. The root node contains the Drive's root folder. For example, it might be the string "D:\" or "C:\". There can be zero, one or more folders beneath the root folder and each of these can have any number of child folders as well. Thus, a general tree form is to be used.

Assume the following directory layout.

```
D:\
        Testing
                GroupA
                GroupB
        Production
                Daily
                Weekly
                Monthly
```

Then the tree contains the root folder with two children and the first child node also contains two children while the other child of the root contains three of its own. The data to be stored in a node is the character string folder name. When allocating a new tree node, dynamically allocate memory for the string and copy the passed folder name into the new string. The destructor and any node deletion functions should delete the node's character string. In other words, the nodes are not storing **void** pointers but character strings.

Our programmer has decided that to handle the varying number of child nodes beneath any given node a single linked list should be used. Here is his start of the **FolderTree** class definition.

```
#pragma once

struct TreeNode {
 char*     folder;
 TreeNode* fwdptr;    // points fwd to next child in linst
 TreeNode* ptrChild; // head pointer of a linked list of children
};

/***************************************************************/
/*                                                             */
/* Call back functions required by the client application      */
/*                                                             */
```

```
/***************************************************************/

typedef int (*FIND) (const char* string, const char* findString);
typedef int (*COMPARE) (const char* nodeString,
                        const char* newString);
typedef void (*VISIT) (TreeNode* ptrNode);

class FolderTree {
     protected:
      TreeNode* ptrRoot; // pointer to the root node of the tree

 public:
               FolderTree (); // construct the tree
              ~FolderTree (); // destroy tree
 protected:
     void      DeleteAllNodes (TreeNode* ptrNode);

 public:
      bool      IsEmpty () const;
      void      BuildRoot (const char* string);
      TreeNode* GetRootNode () const;

     // adds a new node at the specified location
      void      AddNode (TreeNode*& ptrNode,
                         const char* newString);

     // user access functions to get a node's folder string
      char*     GetNodeData (TreeNode* ptrNode) const;

      void      DeleteLeaf (TreeNode*& ptrNode);

 public:    // search tree for this data item
            // caller must provide Find call back function
            // returns 0 if not found or the user folder string
 const char* FindThisFolder (const char* findString, FIND Find);

  // three traversal functions to traverse the tree
  // user must provide a Visit call back function
  void      InorderTraversal (TreeNode* ptrNode, VISIT Visit);
  void      PreorderTraversal (TreeNode* ptrNode, VISIT Visit);
  void      PostorderTraversal (TreeNode* ptrNode, VISIT Visit);

  // class instances cannot be duplicated
  // disallow these operations
  FolderTree (const FolderTree&) {} // copy ctor
  FolderTree& operator= (const FolderTree&) {} //assignment op
};
```

Our programmer has implemented the easy functions as follows.

```
FolderTree::FolderTree () {
 ptrRoot = 0;
}

FolderTree::~FolderTree () {
 DeleteAllNodes (ptrRoot);
```

```
}

bool FolderTree::IsEmpty () const {
 return ptrRoot ? false : true;
}

void FolderTree::BuildRoot (const char* string) {
 ptrRoot = new TreeNode;
 ptrRoot->folder = new char [strlen(string)];
 strcpy (ptrRoot->folder, string);
 ptrRoot->ptrChild = ptrRoot->fwdptr = 0;
}

TreeNode* FolderTree::GetRootNode () const {
 return ptrRoot;
}

void FolderTree::AddNode (TreeNode*& ptrNode,
                          const char* newString) {
 ptrNode = new TreeNode;
 ptrNode->folder = new char [strlen(newString)];
 strcpy (ptrNode->folder, newString);
 ptrNode->ptrChild = ptrNode->fwdptr = 0;
}

char* FolderTree::GetNodeData (TreeNode* ptrNode) const {
 return ptrNode->folder;
}

void FolderTree::DeleteLeaf (TreeNode*& ptrNode) {
 delete folder;
 delete ptrNode;
 ptrNode = 0;
}
```

As usual, the coding has many problems with it. Correct the syntax and logical errors thus far. He explains that at the root node, the **ptrChild** points to the first child folder of the root and **fwdptr** is 0. Following that pointer chain to the child of the root, the **fwdptr** points to the next child of the root or is 0 if there are no more. If this child of the root has children in turn, then its **ptrChild** points to the first of its children.

2. Since you have been instrumental in fixing the beginning coding, our programmer assigns you the task of implementing the **FindThisFolder** function.

```
// search tree for this data item
// caller must provide Find call back function
// returns 0 if not found or the user folder string
const char* FolderTree::FindThisFolder (const char* findString,
                                        FIND Find) {

}
```

3. Next, you are assigned to write the **DeleteAllNodes** function.

```
void FolderTree::DeleteAllNodes (TreeNode* ptrNode) {

}
```

4. Next, you are assigned to write the **InorderTraversal** function. Our programmer has decided that means you should traverse the siblings first and then their children and then this node.

```
void FolderTree::InorderTraversal (TreeNode* ptrNode,
                                   VISIT Visit) {

}
```

5. With your excellent work on the first of the traversal functions completed, our programmer assigns the other traversal functions to the junior programmer on the team, asking him to emulate your implementation. He then embarks on the far more important function to build the tree from the folder structure on a given disk drive. He sketches out the coding to visit all folders on the drive, indicating where new nodes must be allocated. You are assigned to implement the tree portion where indicated in the following coding.

```
void FolderTree::BuildTreeFromDisk (const char* driveString) {
 if (strlen (driveString) == 0) {
  cerr << "Error: no folder to remove\n";
  return 0;
 }
 BuildRoot (driveString);
 AddChildren (ptrRoot, driveString);
}

void FolderTree::AddChildren (TreeNode*& ptrNode,
                              const char* folderString) {
 char mdir[_MAX_PATH];
 strcpy (mdir, folderString);
 // guatantee no trailing backslash
 if (mdir[strlen(mdir)-1] == '\\') mdir[strlen(mdir)-1] = 0;

 long hFind;             // used by _findxxx functions
 _finddata_t fd;         // filled in by _findxxx functions
 char idir[_MAX_PATH]; // the search string with *.* appended
 strcpy (idir, mdir);
 strcat (idir, "\\*.*");
 // attempt to find the first entry in this folder
 if ((hFind = _findfirst (idir, &fd)) == -1L )
  return ct; // failed, so abort
 // for each file found in this folder,
 // check its file attributes - is it a subdir
 // then if so, bypass . and .. system entries
 do {
  if (fd.attrib & _A_SUBDIR) { // is it a subdir?
   if (fd.name[0] != '.') {    // yes, is it not . or ..
    // here add a new child to the ptrNode
    // whose name is fd.name);

    char xdir[_MAX_PATH];      // yes, so remove
    strcpy (xdir, mdir);       // anything under it
    strcat (xdir, "\\");
    strcat (xdir, fd.name);

    // now add all children of this folder to the new folder
    AddChildren (ptrNode->????, xdir);
   }
  }
 } while (_findnext (hFind, &fd) == 0);
```

```
 // repeat for all files in the folder

 // now close the find operation
 _findclose (hFind);
}
```

Programming Problems

Problem Pgm10-1 The Binary Formula Evaluator Program

The add, subtract, multiply, and divide operators are binary in nature. If an expression is written like this

A + B

then a binary tree can be created with the operator+ in the root node and A and B in the left and right child nodes. Thus, the following tree represents this expression.

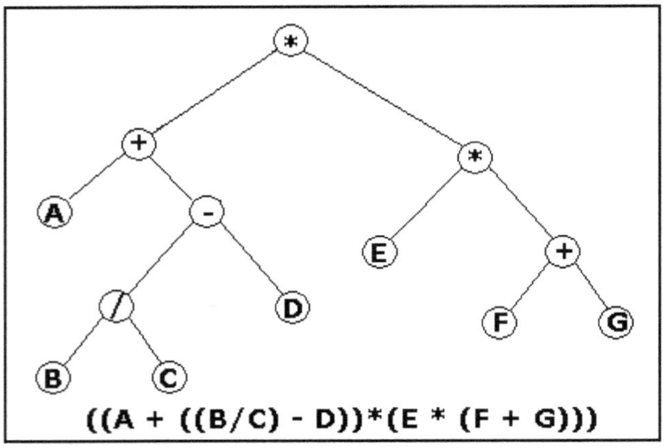

Write a program that prompts the user to input an equation in the above format using uppercase letters A through G. From that equation, construct a binary tree to store the expressions as shown in the above figure. Then prompt the user for numerical values of the doubles A through G. Then, using the binary expression tree, evaluate the formula.

The user must always use the seven variables, A-G. Thoroughly test the program. Hint: a stack can be very useful in backtracking.

Problem Pgm10-2 The Artificial Intelligence Learning Program

This program is a classic artificial intelligence program; it learns new things by asking yes/no questions. The program uses a binary tree structure as its main data structure. All nodes which are **not leaves** contain a question that can be answered yes or no. The children of this node are either subtrees or leaves. The **left child** is contains the **no** results, while the **right node** contains the **yes** result. If it is a **leaf**, then it contains the **object or answer**. If it is a **subtree**, it contains a **refining yes/no question**.

For example, the root question might be, "Is this object considered to be living or alive?" If the answer is "No", then the left node might have the question "Is this object in the animal kingdom?" However, if the answer had been yes, then the right child might contain the computer's guess, "a Rock."

Initially, construct the binary tree with the following questions and objects.

Root: Is this object considered to be living or alive?"

No-left child contains: rock

Yes-right child has a question and a subtree beneath it; its questions is: Is this object in the animal kingdom?

This right child's subtree then contains the following.

No-left child contains: tree

Yes-right child contains a question and has a subtree: Does it have legs?

This right child's subtree contains the following:

No-left child contains: fish

Yes-right child contains: person

When the program begins, display the following message to the player.

```
Welcome to the teach your computer game. I am here to learn from you. You
think of an object and I will ask you some questions that can be answered
yes or no and based on your reply, I will guess your object. Please think
of an object. When you are ready, answer my first question.

Question: Is your object considered to be living or alive? Enter y or n
__
```

The general question format is

Question: question from the tree node? enter y or n __

Suppose the user enters n for the first question. The program should display the following.

```
Is your object a/an rock? Enter y or n _
```

where the reply format is

Is your object a/an item from leaf? Enter y or n _

Now if the user replies with 'y', then display the following message.

```
Great! See how smart your computer is becoming? Do you want to continue?
If so, think of another object and enter y. If you want to quit, enter
n. Enter y or n
```

However, if the user replies with 'n' it is not a rock, then display the following message.

`What object were you thinking of?` And after inputting the object, ask `Now specify a yes/no question which if answered yes would be your object but if no would be my object.` Input the user's question. Add the question and the two answers into the binary tree at the correct position. Finally, display the following. `Do you want to continue? If so, think of another object and enter y. If you want to quit, enter n. Enter y or n __`

Accept y or n in either upper or lower case. If the yes/no entry is not valid, display an error message and get a new yes/no response.

Here is another example. Suppose in response to the first question of "Is this object considered to be living or alive?" the user responds "Yes," meaning it is alive. Now the program asks the next question: "Is this object in the animal kingdom?" If the user says "no," the program asks if the object is a "tree." If the user says "yes," then the program asks "Does it have legs?" Depending on whether no or yes is enters, the program asks if the object is either a "fish" or a "person," respectively.

Thoroughly test your program.

Problem Pgm10-3 Loading and Saving an Artificial Intelligence Tree

Familiarize yourself with the specifications of **Pgm10-2** above. In this problem, you are to design two **BinaryTree** member functions, **LoadTree** and **SaveTree**, that load the binary artificial intelligence tree as used in **Pgm10-2** or save the tree to a disk file. Devise some method to easily store the data in a text file. If you have written **Pgm10-2**, modify it to test your load and save operations. If not, modify the graphical display functions used in the sample programs **Pgm10a** and **Pgm10b** to display your resultant tree.

Problem Pgm10-4 Convert the Binary Tree Class into a Template Class

Take the **BinaryTree** class discussed in this chapter and convert it into a template class which stores user data as type **T***—that is, as a pointer to type **T**. Thoroughly test the revision.

Chapter 11—Sorting Algorithms

Introduction

Sorting refers to rearranging all elements in an array or in a set of records on disk or some unordered collection of keys into some kind of order, either ascending or descending on some value. For instance, sorting an array of cost records might be done based on the item number. Or it might be sorted into alphabetical order based on the product description. Or it might be sorted into increasing quantity purchased. Or it might be sorted into increasing total order cost. Sorting an array of phone numbers would likely be done in increasing numerical order. If one had an ISAM data base, one would need to sort the index table's keys into increasing key value order. Wherever one looks in the data processing industry, sorting can be found.

Many different algorithms exist for sorting items into order. The problem of sorting has captivated the attention of theoretical computer scientists over the years. As a result, much is now known about the efficiency of different approaches to sorting. Sometimes an approach works well on arrays in memory, but is terrible when it is used to sort large arrays stored on disk. Some methods work fast on totally unsorted data. Other methods work drastically faster when most of the data is already in sorted order and only one or a few elements are out of order - such as the problem of adding a new key into a sorted array of keys.

Within the business industry, for those companies that use main frames, sorting can be a very important and vital process. One national insurance company spends nearly 25% of all of its processing time each month sorting its insurance records in various ways in order to produce all of its needed reports. When one has 26 million records to sort, any sorting method that can do the job fast is highly desired and sought after. On the PC side, if a company's server has a large data base that must be sorted, similar considerations apply.

Indeed, various sorting packages are readily available for both the main frame and PC computer environments. And a company, which has a lot of data to sort, generally purchases just such a package. So why do we need to study sorting algorithms if, in reality, one would just purchase a package to handle it for us?

We are studying the sorting methods just to make the theoreticians at the four-year universities happy. No, just kidding. Familiarity with the performance characteristics of various sorting methods may be of value to you in selecting a sorting technique that is well-matched to your company's needs. A proficient software engineer must be able to know how to choose the best available methods to solve a problem. Additionally, one ought to have an intuitive feel for the execution speed of alternative blocks of coding that accomplish the same task.

The theoreticians have developed a complex set of mathematics to describe and discuss the relative efficiencies of the various sorting algorithms. However, my experience has shown that the average student at our junior college does not yet have a sufficient math background to understand or follow these discussions. Thus, this chapter will not be presenting the complex mathematical discussions that are often found with texts on sorting.

This chapter will present various common sorting algorithms and examine their relative efficiencies, their strengths and weaknesses. As we study these methods, let's also see if we can get an approximation of how fast the approaches will perform their task. This information can easily be applied to gaining an understanding of how other non-sorting loops and methods will perform.

The Straight Selection Sort

The straight selection sort is one of the easiest sorting methods for a beginner to remember and be able to code. It makes repeated passes through the array from top to bottom. On the initial pass, it finds the smallest element in the array and places it in the topmost element of the array. This is shown in the next two figures, Figure 11.1 and 11.2.

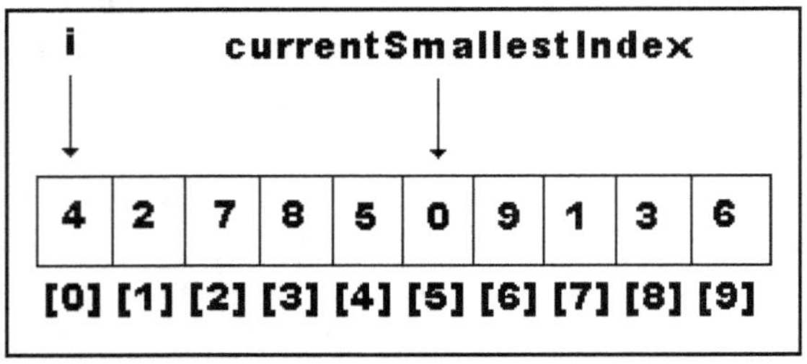

Figure 11.1 Straight Selection Sort Pass 1

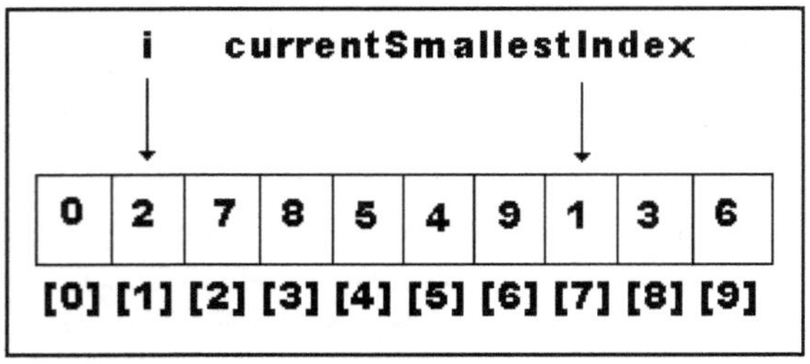

Figure 11.2 Straight Selection Sort Pass 2

On the next pass, it finds the next smallest and places it in the second element of the array and so on. It can also be done in reverse, that is, place initially the largest value in the last element of the array. Then, look through the remaining elements and place the next largest into the next to the last position and on up to the top. It gets its name from the idea that it is selecting the next largest or smallest element and placing it where it belongs. Here is the coding for the straight selection sort which is sorting an array of **count** integers.

```
void StraightSelectionSort (int array[], long count) {
 long currentSmallestIndex; // stores idx of current smallest one
 int  temp;
 long j, k;
 // outer loop traverses all elements except the last one
 for (j=0; j<count-1; j++) {
  // assume that the current j contains the smallest value
  currentSmallestIndex = j;
  // inner loop traverses all elements below j looking for the
  // next smallest one - notice we avoid swapping each time a
  // smaller one is found - just keep track of its index
  for (k=j+1; k<count; k++) {
   if (array[k] < array[currentSmallestIndex])
    currentSmallestIndex = k;
  }
  // now see if the new smallest one is in the correct position
  if (currentSmallestIndex != j) {
   // no, so one time only, swap the smallest into the correct
   // position in the array
```

```
    temp = array[j];
    array[j] = array[currentSmallestIndex];
    array[currentSmallestIndex] = temp;
   }
  }
}
```

Now let's analyze this coding and see what we can determine about its performance characteristics. How many times does the outer loop execute? It is done **count–1** times. How many times is the inner loop performed? Well, the first time, it is done **count–1** times, then **count–2**, then **count–3**. This yields the total number of inner loop iterations as approximately **count^2** times.

Sorting algorithms are often analyzed for two separate measures:

1. The number of times two array elements are compared.
2. The number of times two array elements are swapped or moved.

With the straight selection sort, the number of comparisons is about **count^2** and the maximum number of swaps is about **count**. Of course, if the array was already in sorted order, there would be no swaps at all. Notice that the number of comparisons is independent of the actual state of the data values. If the array was already mostly in the correct order, the same number of comparisons must be done, **count^2**. Thus, an important consideration with this approach is that, independent of the data values, we are always going to do **count^2** comparisons.

The Bubble Sort

The bubble sort makes repeated passes through the elements. However, each time it finds a consecutive pair of elements out of order, it swaps them into the correct order. At the end of the first traversal of the array, the largest value has been bubbled all the way to the bottom of the array. Thus, the second pass does not need to go all the way to the bottom, just to the next to the last element. This is illustrated in the next seven figures. Notice how the '9' is bubbled on down into its final resting place.

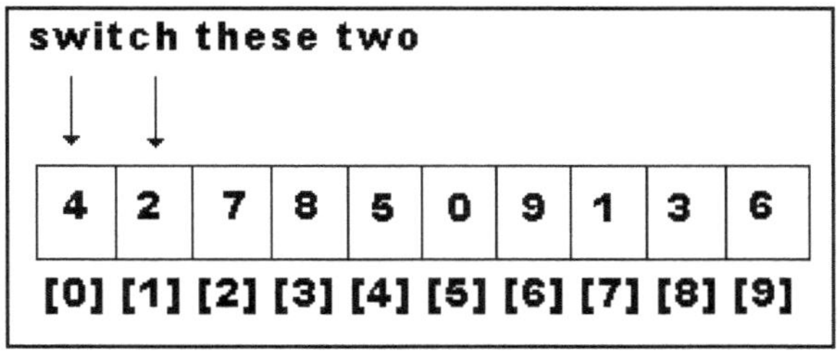

Figure 11.3 Bubble Sort — Step 1

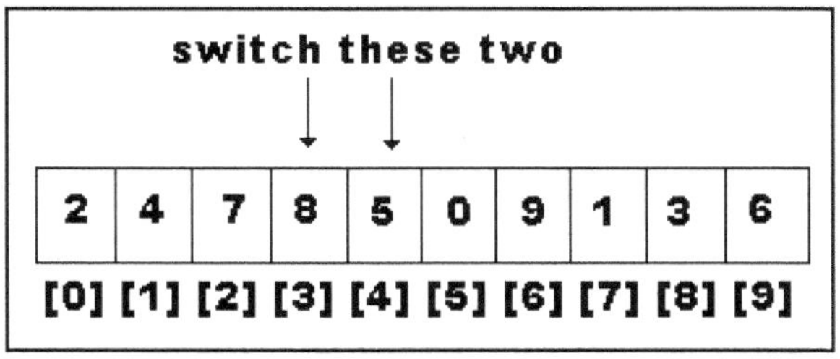

Figure 11.4 Bubble Sort — Step 2

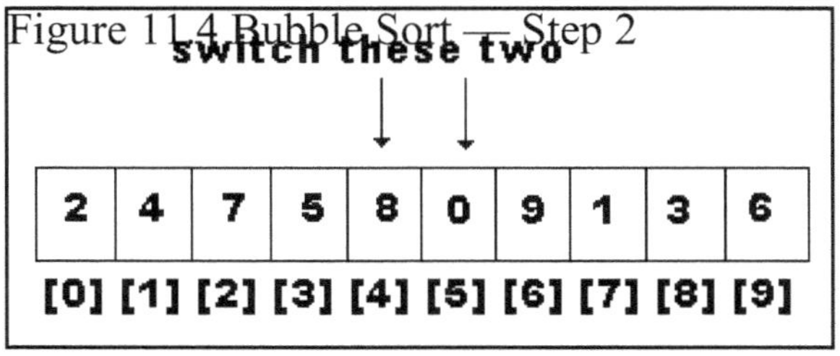

Figure 11.5 Bubble Sort — Step 3

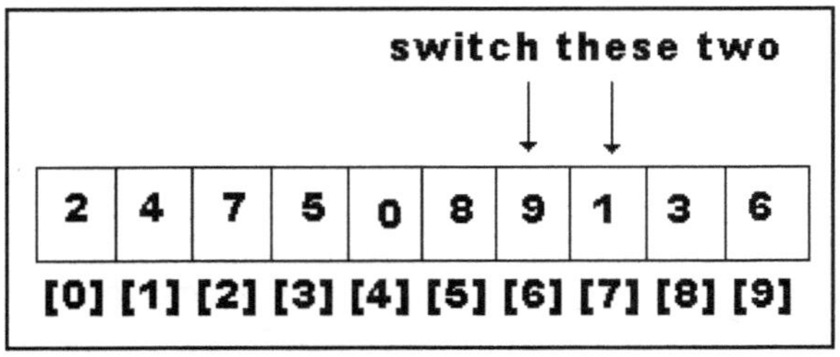

Figure 11.6 Bubble Sort — Step 4

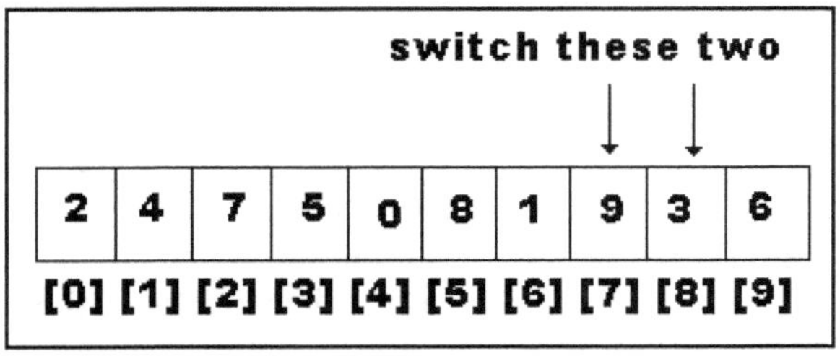

Figure 11.7 Bubble Sort — Step 5

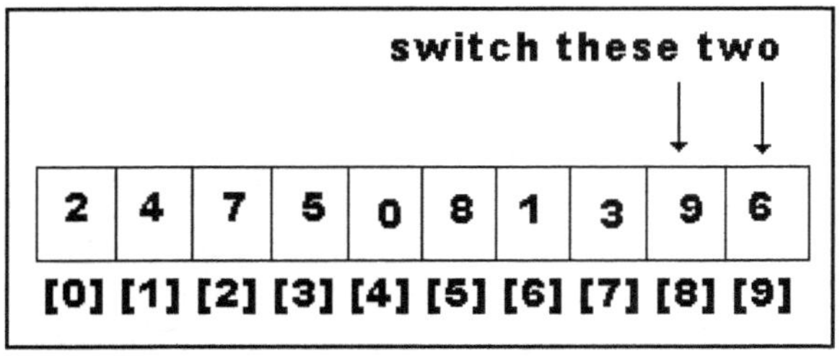

Figure 11.8 Bubble Sort — Step 6

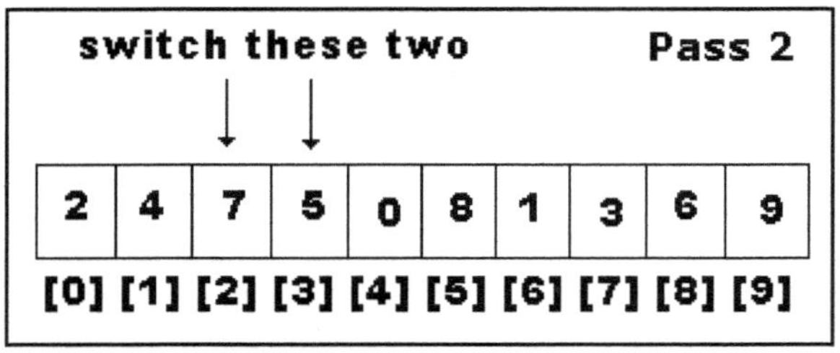

Figure 11.9 Bubble Sort — Step 7

```
void BubbleSort (int array[], int count) {
 int  temp;
 long j;
 long lastSwapIndex;          // the idx of the last one swapped
 long bottomIdx = count - 1; // the current ending idx

 while (bottomIdx > 0) { // repeat until only the top idx is left
  lastSwapIndex = 0;
  // rearrange all elements to current bottom
  for (j=0; j<bottomIdx; j++) {
   if (array[j] > array[j+1]) {
    // swap these two into increasing order
    temp = array[j];
    array[j] = array[j+1];
    array[j+1] = temp;
    lastSwapIndex = j; // reset the last idx swapped
```

```
    }
   }
   // since several lower ones might already be in increasing
   // order, we may not need to further check these - thus,
   // reposition bottom accordingly
   bottomIdx = lastSwapIndex;
  }
}
```

Notice that the bubble sort makes **count–1** total passes through the array independent of the original ordering of that data. In other words, even if the array was already in the correct order, it still makes **count–1** passes to determine this fact. In such a case, **lastSwapIndex** remains at 0 because nothing got swapped. Thus, **bottomIdx** ends up at 0 after one full pass and the while loop terminates then. So the best case scenario is if the data is already sorted into order. In this case, **count–1** comparisons are done and no swaps are done.

What would be the worst case for a bubble sort? If all the values were in descending order, then everyone would have to be swapped repeatedly to bubble the largest to the bottom and so on. Again we have the result that in the worst case, the bubble sort would need $\mathbf{count^2}$ swaps and $\mathbf{count^2}$ comparisons.

The Quicksort Method

The Quicksort algorithm was created by the British computer scientist C.A.R. Hoare. It is the method that the C built-in library **qsort** function utilizes. This method uses recursion to sort the array. Quicksort partitions the array into two sub arrays in which all elements of one sub array are greater than all the elements in the other sub array. Then it recursively calls itself to partition each sub array into two more sub arrays in which all elements in one half are greater than the other. It continues to recursively call itself on these new partitions until the array is sorted.

Since recursion is involved, we should begin by making a recursive definition of the solution. The function prototype is

```
void Quicksort (int array[], long lowIndex, long highIndex);
```

Our definition is

```
if there are no items or one item to sort, return—we are done
if there are two items to sort then
   swap them if needed and return done
else do the following
  rearrange the array so that all values in array[lowIndex through midIndex–1] are
    less than all values in array[midIndex through highIndex]
  Quicksort the array from lowIndex to midIndex–1
  Quicksort the array from midIndex to highIndex
  return done
```

The tricky part of the coding is actually the rearranging of the array into two pieces such that all values in the lower portion are less than those in the upper portion. On the initial pass, **lowIndex** is index 0 and **highIndex** is **count–1**. The method to partition into two pieces requires choosing an array value to be the **pivot** value. One portion will then contain all elements whose values are greater than this pivot value and the other portion contains all those values that are less than or equal to this **pivot** value. For best results, we should choose for the **pivot** value the element in the array that lies in the middle of the range from **lowIndex** to **highIndex**. And we then swap that **pivot** value into the array at **lowIndex**. This is shown in Figure 11.10.

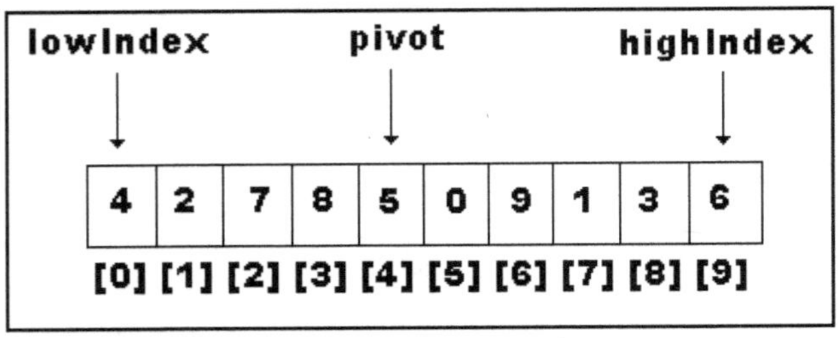

Figure 11.10 Quicksort — Initial Setup

Given this starting point, here is the coding down to this point.

```
void QuickSort (int array[], long count, long lowIndex,
                long highIndex) {
 int  pivot;
 int  temp;
 long lowSwapIndex;
 long highSwapIndex;

 if (lowIndex >= highIndex) // 0 or 1 item to sort, we are done
  return;

 if ((highIndex - lowIndex) == 1) { // only two items to sort
  if (array[lowIndex] > array[highIndex]) { // we must swap them
   temp = array[lowIndex];
   array[lowIndex] = array[highIndex];
   array[highIndex] = temp;
  }
  return;
 }

 // here we have 3 or more items to swap
 // pick the value in the middle to be the pivot value for the
 // dividing vlaue between the two portions
 long mid = (lowIndex + highIndex) / 2;
 pivot = array[mid];
 // and swap this value into lowIndex postion
 array[mid] = array[lowIndex];
 array[lowIndex] = pivot;
```

The next figure, 11.11, shows the situation after we have placed the '5' into element 0.

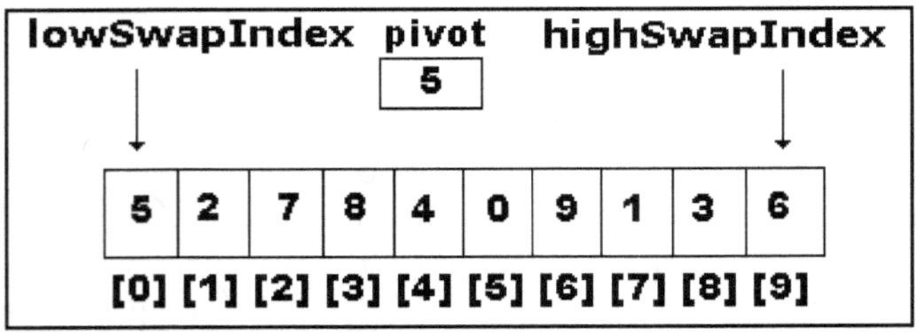

Figure 11.1 Quicksort — Ready for the First Loop

Now we set up a **lowSwapIndex** to point to the next element at index 1, and a **highSwapIndex** set to the right bounds, index 9. The first half pass, we continue checking until the **lowSwapIndex** increases to beyond the **highSwapIndex** and as long as each element pointed to by **lowSwapIndex** belongs in this half, that is, is less than or equal to the **pivot** value. At index 1, 2 is smaller than 5, so we continue. At index 2, the 7 is not, so the first loop ends with **lowSwapIndex** pointing to index 2; this element does not belong in the lower half partition.

The next loop begins at a **highSwapIndex** of 9 and continues as long as the value there is greater than the pivot element of 5. When **highSwapIndex** id decremented to 9, the array element of 3 is not greater than the **pivot** element and thus this element does not belong in the higher portion. This is shown in Figure 11.12.

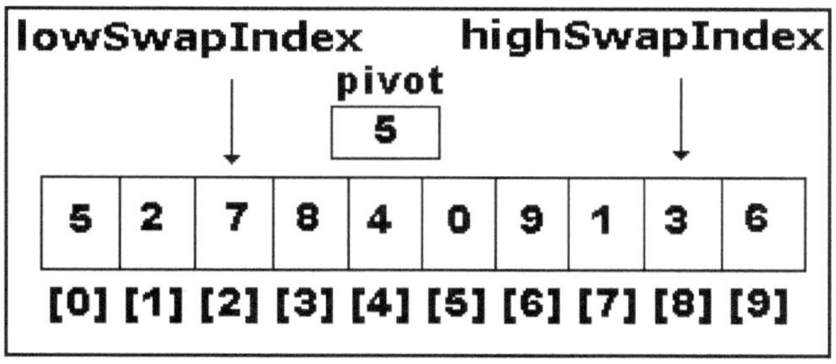

Figure 11.12 Quicksort — End of Inner Loops

```
 // divide into two portions in which one portion's array values
 // are all greater than the pivot value and the other one's
 // values are all <= to it
 lowSwapIndex = lowIndex + 1;
 highSwapIndex = highIndex;
 do {
  while (lowSwapIndex <= highSwapIndex &&
         array[lowSwapIndex] <= pivot) {
   lowSwapIndex++;
  }
  while (array[highSwapIndex] > pivot) {
   highSwapIndex--;
  }
```

Since the two swap indexes have not yet crossed, we need to swap the two array elements to get them into their correct portions of the two halves of the array.

```
  if (lowSwapIndex < highSwapIndex) {
   // here we have encountered an array value that belongs in the
   // other partition, so we must swap these two array values to
   // get them into the correct portions
   temp = array[lowSwapIndex];
   array[lowSwapIndex] = array[highSwapIndex];
   array[highSwapIndex] = temp;
  }
```

Here is what the array looks like once the swap is completed. We now repeat the entire loop because the two swap indexes have not yet crossed. This is shown in Figure 11.13.

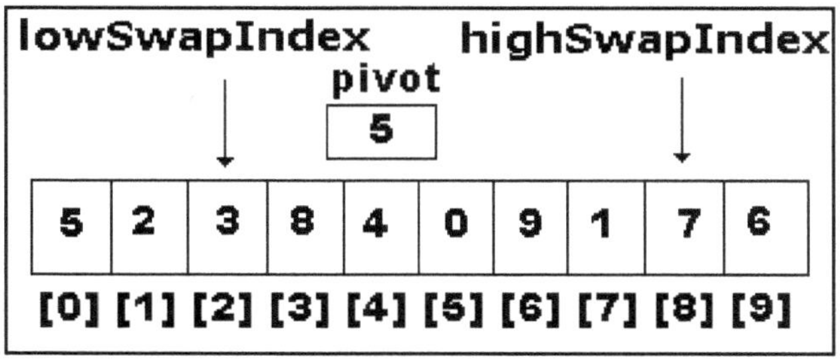

Figure 11.13 Quicksort — Swapping Values

```
  // and repeat the process until these two points cross
 } while (lowSwapIndex < highSwapIndex);
```

When the two inner loops end this time, **lowSwapIndex** is at element 3 whose value of 8 is larger than the **pivot** of 5. The **highSwapIndex** is at element 7 whose value of 1 is less than the **pivot** of 5. Once again, we swap these two array values to get them into their respective portions and is shown in Figure 11.14.

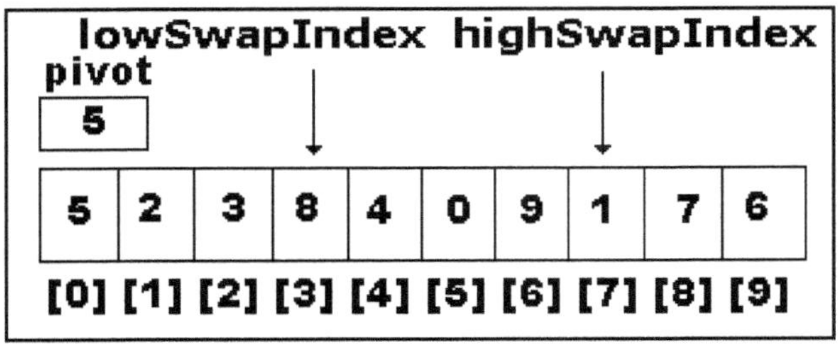

Figure 11.14 Quicksort — Second Swap

The results are shown in the next figure. Since the two swap indexes have not yet crossed, we continue the two inner loops again. This time they cross before finding their respective elements.

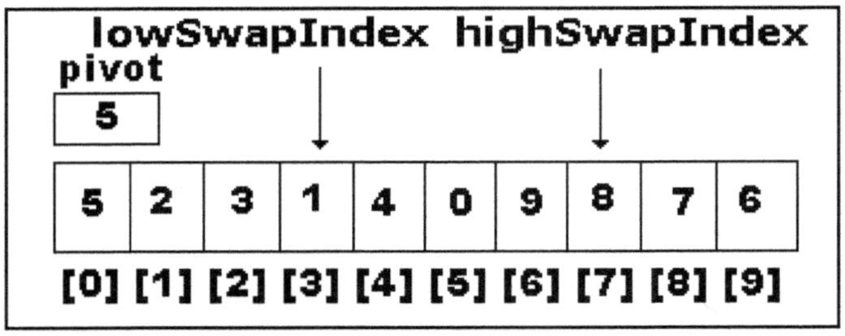

Figure 11.15 Quicksort — Next Swap Point

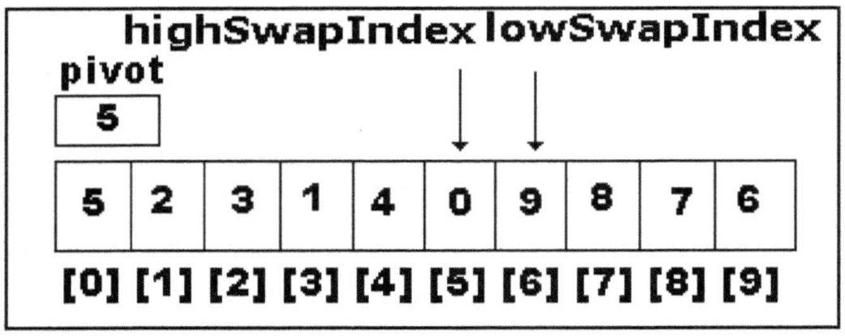

Figure 11.16 Quicksort — Indexes Have Crossed

```
 // here highSwapIndex has crossed, so all values in the
 // range of highSwapIndex through highIndex, are larger than
 // pivot. Thus, we put the value of pivot into its correct
 // position at point highSwapIndex. It is currently stored in
 // position lowIndex

 array[lowIndex] = array[highSwapIndex];
 array[highSwapIndex] = pivot;
```

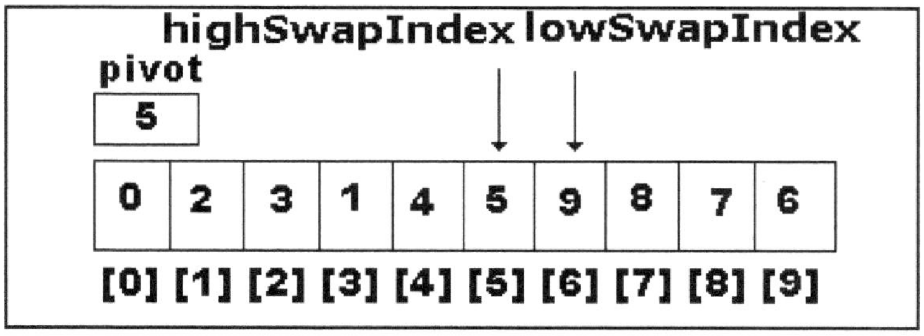

Figure 11.17 Quicksort — Placing Pivot in Destination

Now we perform the recursive call twice, once on the lower portion bounded by indexes 0 through 4 and once on the upper portion bounded by 6 through 9.

```
 QuickSort (array, count, lowIndex, highSwapIndex-1);
 QuickSort (array, count, highSwapIndex+1, highIndex);
}
```

And the process continues until the array is sorted. How can we analyze the performance of this algorithm? It certainly is more difficult. If the pivot does not divide the array evenly, the performance suffers. What happens if at the indicated pivot element we always end up finding the largest value or the smallest value? In such as case, we end up with one partition of size 0 and the rest of the array in the other partition! In this situation, we would end up with a running time proportional to **count^2** once again. The best case situation can be described by **count log count**. A major benefit of Quicksort is that it handles large arrays much more quickly than the other versions.

Shellsort

The Shellsort was discovered by Donald Shell in 1959. His idea was to avoid the large amounts of data movement. It compares elements that are far apart first and then those that are less far apart, gradually shrinking the gap toward successive elements. Thus, it is also known as the diminishing gap sort.

The outer loop begins at **count/2** or the middle. On each iteration, the gap is reduced by an arbitrary value that has been tested empirically to give good performance, 2.2. The new value of the gap is given as

```
gap = (gap==2) ? 1 : (long)(gap/2.2);
```

Next, the middle loop sweeps across all elements from gap to the end of the array. Within this middle loop, the inner loop then checks all elements separated by the gap value with the current middle loop element, swapping when necessary.

Shellsort works very fast on large arrays. It is an example of simplicity in coding but complexity in analysis. Theoreticians predict its efficiency as **count log count** as opposed to **count^2**.

```
void ShellSort (int array[], long count) {
 long gap, i, j;
 int temp;
 for (gap=count/2; gap>0;
      gap = (gap==2) ? 1 : (long)(gap/2.2)) {
  for (i=gap; i<count; i++) {
   temp = array[i];
   for (j=i; j>=gap && temp<array[j-gap]; j-=gap) {
    array[j] = array[j-gap];
   }
   array[j] = temp;
  }
 }
}
```

Heapsort

The Heapsort gets its name from pretending that the array is really a b-tree (balanced tree) with nodes or a heap or linked tree. In a b-tree, each node can contain at most two leaves below it. Often a b-tree is used to rapidly find a specific key. Figure 11.18 shows what one would normally consider to be a b-tree to rapidly find a matching key. Notice that all values on the right side of the root node are greater than the root node's value while all values on the left side of the root node are less than the root node's value.

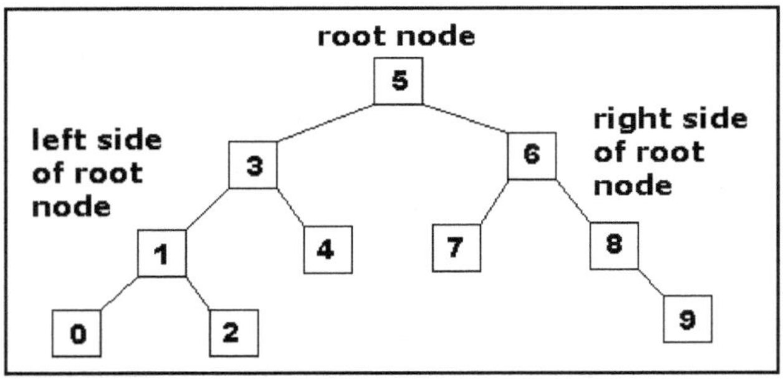

Figure 11.18 A Balanced Tree

The Heapsort pretends the original array is a b-tree that is out of order. Figure 11.19 shows the initial array that the tester program uses viewed as a b-tree.

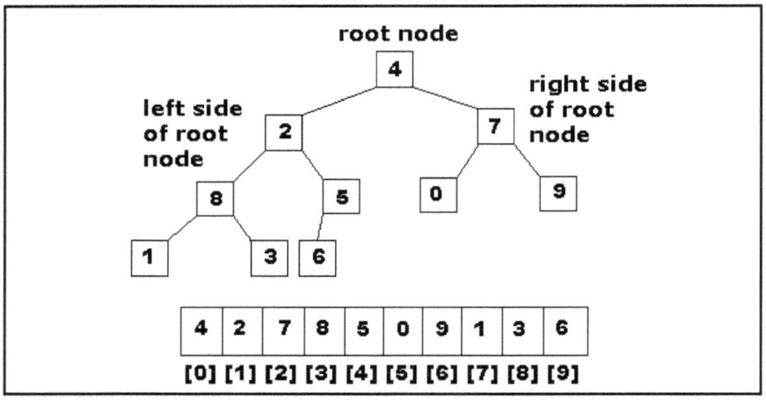

Figure 11.19 The Original Array Viewed as a b-tree

Of course, the nodes are out of order. That is, all values on the right side of a node are not all greater than that node's value while all nodes on the left side of a node are not all less than that node's value. Heapsort must then perform a "rebuild the heap downward" action to get the nodes in their proper order. The proper order is dictated by **array[node] >= array[node*2+1]** for the left side and **array[node] >= array[node*2+2]** for the right side. The action consists of going down each node and moving the elements around such that all the nodes on the right side of a given node are greater than the node and similarly with the left side. It begins at the top node and works its way to the bottom.

The **RebuildHeapDownwards** function is passed the current root node. It compares the two leaves below it to find which one is the greater value and whose index is then stored in **maxChild**. If that found largest value is greater than the root's value, it swaps that **maxChild**'s value with the root's value. Then, it recursively calls itself using the index of **maxChild** as the next downward node.

```
void RebuildHeapDownward (int array[], long root, long bottom) {
 int temp;
 long maxChild;
 long leftChild   = root * 2 + 1;
```

```
 long rightChild = root * 2 + 2;
 if (leftChild <= bottom) {
  if (leftChild == bottom)
   maxChild = leftChild;
  else {
   if (array[leftChild] <= array[rightChild])
    maxChild = rightChild;
   else
    maxChild = leftChild;
  }
  if (array[root] < array[maxChild]) {
   temp = array[root];
   array[root] = array[maxChild];
   array[maxChild] = temp;
   RebuildHeapDownward (array, maxChild, bottom);
  }
 }
}
```

The Heapsort itself begins by choosing as the root node that node located in the middle of the array, **count/2**. It calls **RebuildHeapDownward** from this point to the end of the array. When those are finished, it decrements the index of the root node and repeats the process. When the first loop is finished, here is what the original array has become. The original array is on the first line, the rebuilt one on the second line.

```
 4 2 7 8 5 0 9 1 3 6
 9 8 7 3 6 0 4 1 2 5
```

The second loop first stores the largest value which is at index 0 into its proper slot, index 9 and then rebuilds the heap downward again. Here is a consecutive display after each rebuild is completed.

```
 8 6 7 3 5 0 4 1 2 9
 7 6 4 3 5 0 2 1 8 9
 6 5 4 3 1 0 2 7 8 9
 5 3 4 2 1 0 6 7 8 9
 4 3 0 2 1 5 6 7 8 9
 3 2 0 1 4 5 6 7 8 9
 2 1 0 3 4 5 6 7 8 9
 1 0 2 3 4 5 6 7 8 9
 0 1 2 3 4 5 6 7 8 9
```

```
void HeapSort (int array[], long count) {
 int temp;
 long i;
 for (i=count/2 - 1; i>=0; i--) {
  RebuildHeapDownward (array, i, count-1);
 }
 for (i=count-1; i>=1; i--) {
  temp = array[0];
  array[0] = array[i];
  array[i] = temp;
  RebuildHeapDownward (array, 0, i-1);
 }
}
```

With such a complex algorithm, does it actually execute with speed? The answer is yes, it does indeed run significantly faster than the straight selection and bubble sorts. Theoreticians predict its efficiency as **count log count**, similar to the Quicksort and Shellsort methods.

Pgm11a—Tester Program for the Different Sorting Methods

To test these sorting functions, **Pgm11a** has an array of **COUNT** integers initialized to some non-sorted order. Before each sorting function is called, it copies the unsorted array into a new array and passes the new array to the sorting function. When the sorting function returns, it displays the contents of the sorted array.

Pgm11a - Sort Methods Tester Program

```
#include <iostream>
#include <iomanip>
using namespace std;

void CopyArray (int src[], int des[], long count);
ostream& PrintArray (ostream& os, int array[], long count);

void StraightSelectionSort (int array[], long count);
void BubbleSort (int array[], int count);
void QuickSort (int array[], long count, long lowIndex,
                long highIndex);
void HeapSort (int array[], long count);
void RebuildHeapDownward (int array[], long i, long num);
void ShellSort (int array[], long count);

/***************************************************************/
/*                                                             */
/* Pgm11a - Tester Program to Test the Sorting Functions       */
/*                                                             */
/***************************************************************/

const int COUNT = 10;

int main () {
 int x[COUNT] = {4, 2, 7, 8, 5, 0, 9, 1, 3, 6};
 int xx[COUNT];
 CopyArray (x, xx, COUNT);
 cout << "Original Array: ";
 PrintArray (cout, x, COUNT);

 StraightSelectionSort (xx, COUNT);
 cout << "St. Selection:  ";
 PrintArray (cout, xx, COUNT);
 CopyArray (x, xx, COUNT);

 BubbleSort (xx, COUNT);
 cout << "Bubble Sort:    ";
 PrintArray (cout, xx, COUNT);
 CopyArray (x, xx, COUNT);

 QuickSort (xx, COUNT, 0, COUNT-1);
 cout << "Quicksort:      ";
 PrintArray (cout, xx, COUNT);
 CopyArray (x, xx, COUNT);

 HeapSort (xx, COUNT);
```

```
 cout << "Heap Sort:      ";
 PrintArray (cout, xx, COUNT);
 CopyArray (x, xx, COUNT);

 ShellSort (xx, COUNT);
 cout << "Shell Sort:     ";
 PrintArray (cout, xx, COUNT);

 return 0;
}

/***************************************************************/
/*                                                             */
/* CopyArray: Helper function to make a duplicate array copy   */
/*                                                             */
/***************************************************************/

void CopyArray (int src[], int des[], long count) {
 for (long i=0; i<count; i++)
  des[i] = src[i];
}

/***************************************************************/
/*                                                             */
/* PrintArray: Helper function to display the array's contents */
/*                                                             */
/***************************************************************/

ostream& PrintArray (ostream& os, int array[], long count) {
 for (long i=0; i<count; i++) {
  os << setw(4) << array[i];
  if ((i % 60) == 0 && i != 0)
   os << endl;
 }
 os << endl;
 return os;
}

/***************************************************************/
/*                                                             */
/* StraightSelectionSort:                                      */
/*                                                             */
/***************************************************************/

void StraightSelectionSort (int array[], long count) {
 long currentSmallestIndex; // stores idx of current smallest one
 int  temp;
 long j, k;
 // outer loop traverses all elements except the last one
 for (j=0; j<count-1; j++) {
  // assume that the current j contains the smallest value
  currentSmallestIndex = j;
  // inner loop traverses all elements below j looking for the
  // next smallest one - notice we avoid swapping each time a
  // smaller one is found - just keep track of its index
  for (k=j+1; k<count; k++) {
```

```
    if (array[k] < array[currentSmallestIndex])
     currentSmallestIndex = k;
   }
   // now see if the new smallest one is in the correct position
   if (currentSmallestIndex != j) {
    // no, so one time only, swap the smallest into the correct
    // position in the array
    temp = array[j];
    array[j] = array[currentSmallestIndex];
    array[currentSmallestIndex] = temp;
   }
  }
}

/***************************************************************/
/*                                                             */
/* BubbleSort:                                                 */
/*                                                             */
/***************************************************************/

void BubbleSort (int array[], int count) {
 int  temp;
 long j;
 long lastSwapIndex;          // the idx of the last one swapped
 long bottomIdx = count - 1; // the current ending idx

 while (bottomIdx > 0) { // repeat until only the top idx is left
  lastSwapIndex = 0;
  // rearrange all elements to current bottom
  for (j=0; j<bottomIdx; j++) {
   if (array[j] > array[j+1]) {
    // swap these two into increasing order
    temp = array[j];
    array[j] = array[j+1];
    array[j+1] = temp;
    lastSwapIndex = j; // reset the last idx swapped
   }
  }
  // since several lower ones might already be in increasing
  // order, we may not need to further check these - thus,
  // reposition bottom accordingly
  bottomIdx = lastSwapIndex;
 }
}

/***************************************************************/
/*                                                             */
/* QuickSort:                                                  */
/*                                                             */
/***************************************************************/

void QuickSort (int array[], long count, long lowIndex,
                long highIndex) {
 int  pivot;
 int  temp;
 long lowSwapIndex;
```

```
long highSwapIndex;

if (lowIndex >= highIndex)// 0 or 1 item to sort, so we are done
 return;

if ((highIndex - lowIndex) == 1) { // only two items to sort
 if (array[lowIndex] > array[highIndex]) { // we must swap them
  temp = array[lowIndex];
  array[lowIndex] = array[highIndex];
  array[highIndex] = temp;
 }
 return;
}

// here we have 3 or more items to swap
// pick the value in the middle to be the pivot value for the
// dividing vlaue between the two portions
long mid = (lowIndex + highIndex) / 2;
pivot = array[mid];
// and swap this value into lowIndex postion
array[mid] = array[lowIndex];
array[lowIndex] = pivot;
// now divide into two portions in which one portion's array
// values are all greater than the pivot value and
// the other's is <= to it
lowSwapIndex = lowIndex + 1;
highSwapIndex = highIndex;
do {
 while (lowSwapIndex <= highSwapIndex &&
        array[lowSwapIndex] <= pivot) {
  lowSwapIndex++;
 }
 while (array[highSwapIndex] > pivot) {
  highSwapIndex--;
 }
 if (lowSwapIndex < highSwapIndex) {
  // here we have encountered an array value that belongs in the
  // other partition, so we must swap these two array values to
  // get them into the correct portions
  temp = array[lowSwapIndex];
  array[lowSwapIndex] = array[highSwapIndex];
  array[highSwapIndex] = temp;
 }
 // and repeat the process until these two points cross
} while (lowSwapIndex < highSwapIndex);

// here highSwapIndex has crossed, so all values in the
// range of highSwapIndex through highIndex, are larger than
// pivot. Thus, we put the value of pivot into its correct
// position at point highSwapIndex. It is currently stored in
// position lowIndex

array[lowIndex] = array[highSwapIndex];
array[highSwapIndex] = pivot;

// now we repeat the process on each half - note that
```

```
 // array[highSwapIndex] is in its correct final position and
 // does not need to be further used

 QuickSort (array, count, lowIndex, highSwapIndex-1);
 QuickSort (array, count, highSwapIndex+1, highIndex);
}

/***************************************************************/
/*                                                             */
/* HeapSort:                                                   */
/*                                                             */
/***************************************************************/

void HeapSort (int array[], long count) {
 int temp;
 long i;

 for (i=count/2 - 1; i>=0; i--) {
  RebuildHeapDownward (array, i, count-1);
 }

 for (i=count-1; i>=1; i--) {
  temp = array[0];
  array[0] = array[i];
  array[i] = temp;
  RebuildHeapDownward (array, 0, i-1);
 }
}

/***************************************************************/
/*                                                             */
/* RebuildHeapDownward: used by HeapSort                       */
/*                                                             */
/***************************************************************/

void RebuildHeapDownward (int array[], long root, long bottom) {
 int temp;
 long maxChild;
 long leftChild  = root * 2 + 1;
 long rightChild = root * 2 + 2;

 // find which leaf is larger
 if (leftChild <= bottom) {
  if (leftChild == bottom)
   maxChild = leftChild;
  else {
   if (array[leftChild] <= array[rightChild])
    maxChild = rightChild;
   else
    maxChild = leftChild;
  }

  // replace root element with the larger and rebuild the heap
  if (array[root] < array[maxChild]) {
   temp = array[root];
   array[root] = array[maxChild];
```

```
   array[maxChild] = temp;
   RebuildHeapDownward (array, maxChild, bottom);
  }
 }
}

/***************************************************************/
/*                                                             */
/* ShellSort:                                                  */
/*                                                             */
/***************************************************************/

void ShellSort (int array[], long count) {
 long gap, i, j;
 int temp;
 for (gap=count/2; gap>0;
      gap = (gap==2) ? 1 : (long)(gap/2.2)) {
  for (i=gap; i<count; i++) {
   temp = array[i];
   for (j=i; j>=gap && temp<array[j-gap]; j-=gap) {
    array[j] = array[j-gap];
   }
   array[j] = temp;
  }
 }
}
```

Here is the output from the tester program.

```
Output from Pgm15a - Sort Methods Tester Program

 1 Original Array:    4   2   7   8   5   0   9   1   3   6
 2 St. Selection:     0   1   2   3   4   5   6   7   8   9
 3 Bubble Sort:       0   1   2   3   4   5   6   7   8   9
 4 Quicksort:         0   1   2   3   4   5   6   7   8   9
 5 Heap Sort:         0   1   2   3   4   5   6   7   8   9
 6 Shell Sort:        0   1   2   3   4   5   6   7   8   9
```

Benchmarks

In order to properly evaluate these sorting algorithms, one must time how long each takes to sort the same array. By varying the array size and the degree that the initial array is already sorted, we can get a good feel for their performance.

The starting point is how to create a large array of "random" values. I would not want to build a file of 100,000 numbers by hand. Instead, C++ had a random number generator function that can be used to provide as many "random" numbers as we require. The built-in random number generator requires the use of a "seed" value. For any given seed value, the random number function returns the same sequence of "random" numbers. Thus, it really is not creating true random numbers. This is actually a useful property. If you are creating a game program based upon random events, by using the same seed and thus obtaining the same series of random numbers, you can debug the program. If each run created a truly different set of numbers, debugging would become much more difficult since it would be hard to reproduce the error situations.

The C++ function is called **rand**. I wrote a small helper function, **GetRandom** that is passed the maximum value of the generated numbers. The function then returns a random number between zero and that maximum.

```
unsigned  GetRandom (int maxVal) {
 return rand () % maxVal;
}
```

For a seed value, game programmers often use the current time as a seed because from one execution of the program to another, it is nearly impossible to launch the program at the same exact instant. The C++ **time** function returns the number of seconds elapsed since midnight (00:00:00), January 1, 1970, coordinated universal time, according to the system clock. (The function is passed a zero for the pointer to the time location to set to the current time; we just need the return value.) The C++ function to set the initial seed value of the random number generator is called **srand**. I invoke it this way.

```
srand ((unsigned) time (0));
```

To use these, include the **ctime** header file. Here is the start of the program. It defines two arrays of 100,000 integers and fills the first with the random numbers and then copies that array into the working array **xx**. It is array **xx** that will be sorted by the various methods.

```
const int MAX = 100000;
int main () {
 srand ((unsigned) time (0));

 int x[MAX];
 int i;
 for (i=0; i<MAX; i++)
  x[i] = GetRandom (MAX);

 int xx[MAX];
 CopyArray (x, xx, MAX);
```

How do we know how long it takes for any sorting method to execute? The C++ function **clock** returns the number of clock ticks that has elapsed since the machine was turned on. If you divide by the constant, **CLOCKS_PER_SEC**, the number is converted into seconds. Thus, if we call **clock** before calling the sort function and then immediately after the function returns, we can subtract the two values and divide by the constant to determine the total elapsed time that sort function executed. The return value of **clock** is really a long but has been type defined as a **clock_t** data type.

This gives us the basic logic behind all of the timings.

```
clock_t timeStart, timeEnd;
timeStart = clock ();
StraightSelectionSort (xx, max);
timeEnd = clock ();
cout << setw (10)
     << ((double)(timeEnd-timeStart))/CLOCKS_PER_SEC;
```

I want to benchmark how long it takes these five sorting functions to execute as a function of the number of elements in the array. Thus, I created another array that provided the number of elements to sort.

```
const long amts[NUM] = {100, 200, 500, 1000, 2000, 5000, 10000,
                        20000, 50000, 100000};
```

So the program then times each of the sorting functions for each of these array sizes.

For variation, I also performed the whole series on an array that was already in sorted order, but in high to low or backwards order. Then, I performed the whole series on an array in which all elements were already in their proper order except the last element. This might be the situation facing an update program which must add a new record to the array in its proper position.

Here are the output benchmark timings I obtained from a Release Build of **Pgm11b**.

```
Output of Pgm11b - Sort Efficiencies - Results From Two Machines
```

Processor p6-II at 333MHz with 348M Memory

Times in seconds for a random order array

Count	Straight Selection	Bubble Sort	Quick Sort	Heap Sort	Shell Sort
100	0.000	0.000	0.000	0.000	0.000
200	0.000	0.000	0.000	0.000	0.000
500	0.000	0.000	0.010	0.000	0.000
1000	0.000	0.020	0.000	0.000	0.000
2000	0.030	0.070	0.000	0.000	0.000
5000	0.200	0.371	0.000	0.000	0.010
10000	0.761	1.512	0.000	0.010	0.010
20000	3.405	6.349	0.010	0.020	0.020
50000	36.042	63.231	0.030	0.060	0.070
100000	162.644	299.541	0.080	0.140	0.170

Times for an already sorted array - last element new

Count	Straight Selection	Bubble Sort	Quick Sort	Heap Sort	Shell Sort
100	0.000	0.000	0.000	0.000	0.000
200	0.000	0.000	0.000	0.000	0.000
500	0.010	0.000	0.000	0.000	0.000
1000	0.010	0.000	0.000	0.000	0.000
2000	0.030	0.000	0.000	0.000	0.000
5000	0.191	0.000	0.000	0.010	0.000
10000	0.761	0.000	0.010	0.000	0.010
20000	3.455	0.000	0.010	0.010	0.010
50000	37.263	0.000	0.010	0.060	0.041
100000	163.855	163.155	0.030	0.080	0.090

Times in seconds for backwards sorted array

Count	Straight Selection	Bubble Sort	Quick Sort	Heap Sort	Shell Sort
100	0.000	0.000	0.000	0.000	0.000
200	0.000	0.000	0.000	0.000	0.000
500	0.010	0.000	0.000	0.000	0.000
1000	0.020	0.010	0.000	0.000	0.000
2000	0.050	0.030	0.000	0.000	0.000
5000	0.281	0.240	0.000	0.000	0.010
10000	1.172	0.911	0.000	0.000	0.010
20000	5.118	3.965	0.000	0.020	0.010
50000	44.865	51.814	0.020	0.040	0.050
100000	219.296	293.282	0.040	0.080	0.090

```
Processor P6-IV at 1.6GHz with 512M Memory


Times in seconds for a random order array

  Count  Straight     Bubble      Quick       Heap      Shell
         Selection      Sort       Sort       Sort       Sort

    100     0.000      0.000      0.000      0.000      0.000
    200     0.000      0.000      0.000      0.000      0.000
    500     0.000      0.000      0.000      0.000      0.000
   1000     0.000      0.000      0.000      0.000      0.000
   2000     0.010      0.020      0.000      0.000      0.000
   5000     0.040      0.100      0.000      0.000      0.000
  10000     0.160      0.401      0.000      0.000      0.000
  20000     0.661      1.602      0.010      0.000      0.010
  50000     3.986     10.094      0.010      0.010      0.020
 100000    18.787     47.368      0.020      0.040      0.030



Times for an already sorted array - last element new
  Count  Straight     Bubble      Quick       Heap      Shell
         Selection      Sort       Sort       Sort       Sort

    100     0.000      0.000      0.000      0.000      0.000
    200     0.000      0.000      0.000      0.000      0.000
    500     0.000      0.000      0.000      0.000      0.000
   1000     0.000      0.000      0.000      0.000      0.000
   2000     0.010      0.000      0.000      0.000      0.000
   5000     0.031      0.000      0.000      0.000      0.000
  10000     0.170      0.000      0.000      0.000      0.000
  20000     0.611      0.000      0.000      0.010      0.000
  50000     4.005      0.000      0.010      0.010      0.000
 100000    18.828     16.083      0.000      0.020      0.020



Times in seconds for backwards sorted array
  Count  Straight     Bubble      Quick       Heap      Shell
         Selection      Sort       Sort       Sort       Sort

    100     0.000      0.000      0.000      0.000      0.000
    200     0.000      0.000      0.000      0.000      0.000
    500     0.000      0.000      0.000      0.000      0.000
   1000     0.010      0.000      0.000      0.000      0.000
   2000     0.010      0.010      0.000      0.000      0.000
   5000     0.080      0.060      0.000      0.000      0.000
  10000     0.340      0.251      0.000      0.000      0.000
  20000     1.312      1.021      0.000      0.010      0.000
  50000     8.232      6.640      0.000      0.000      0.000
 100000    34.439     40.098      0.010      0.020      0.020
```

As you examine these results, notice how dramatic the time variations between the first two methods (straight selection and bubble) and the last three (Quicksort, Heapsort, and Shellsort) are. Then, compare the times for the straight selection and bubble sorts in the three different circumstances; there is quite a difference in speed depending upon the initial state of the data to be sorted. This is also true with Quicksort. However, the Heapsort and Shellsort show much less of a dependency on this effect.

Here is the benchmark program, **Pgm11b**.

Pgm11b - Sort Efficiencies Program

```
#include <iostream>
#include <iomanip>
#include <ctime>
using namespace std;
unsigned GetRandom (int maxVal);

void CopyArray (int src[], int des[], long count);
ostream& PrintArray (ostream& os, int array[], long count);

void StraightSelectionSort (int array[], long count);
void BubbleSort (int array[], int count);
void QuickSort (int array[], long count, long lowIndex,
                long highIndex);
void HeapSort (int array[], long count);
void RebuildHeapDownward (int array[], long root, long bottom);
void ShellSort (int array[], long count);

const int MAX = 100000;
const int NUM = 10;

/***************************************************************/
/*                                                             */
/* Pgm11b - Tester Program to Test the Sorting Functions       */
/*                                                             */
/***************************************************************/

int main () {
 cout.setf (ios::fixed, ios::floatfield);
 cout << setprecision (3);

 srand ((unsigned) time (0));

 int x[MAX];
 int i;
 for (i=0; i<MAX; i++)
  x[i] = GetRandom (MAX);

 int xx[MAX];
 CopyArray (x, xx, MAX);

 clock_t timeStart, timeEnd;

 long max;
 const long amts[NUM] = {100, 200, 500, 1000, 2000, 5000, 10000,
                         20000, 50000, 100000};

 cout << "Times in seconds for a random order array\n\n"
   << "  Count  Straight    Bubble     Quick      Heap     Shell"
```

```
   << "\n"
   << "        Selection      Sort       Sort       Sort        Sort"
   << "\n\n";
 for (i=0; i<NUM; i++) {
  max=amts[i];
  cout << setw(7) << max;
  timeStart = clock ();
  StraightSelectionSort (xx, max);
  timeEnd = clock ();
  cout << setw (10)
       << ((double)(timeEnd-timeStart))/CLOCKS_PER_SEC;
  CopyArray (x, xx, max);

  timeStart = clock ();
  BubbleSort (xx, max);
  timeEnd = clock ();
  cout << setw (10)
       << ((double)(timeEnd-timeStart))/CLOCKS_PER_SEC;
  CopyArray (x, xx, max);

  timeStart = clock ();
  QuickSort (xx, max, 0, max-1);
  timeEnd = clock ();
  cout << setw (10)
       << ((double)(timeEnd-timeStart))/CLOCKS_PER_SEC;
  CopyArray (x, xx, max);

  timeStart = clock ();
  HeapSort (xx, max);
  timeEnd = clock ();
  cout << setw (10)
       << ((double)(timeEnd-timeStart))/CLOCKS_PER_SEC;
  CopyArray (x, xx, max);

  timeStart = clock ();
  ShellSort (xx, max);
  timeEnd = clock ();
  cout << setw (10)
       << ((double)(timeEnd-timeStart))/CLOCKS_PER_SEC;
  CopyArray (x, xx, max);

  cout << endl;
 }

 cout << endl << endl << endl;
 cout <<"Times for an already sorted array -last element new\n"
   << "  Count  Straight    Bubble     Quick      Heap      Shell"
   << "\n"
   << "        Selection      Sort       Sort       Sort        Sort"
   << "\n\n";
 QuickSort (xx, MAX, 0, MAX-1);
 for (i=0; i<MAX-1; i++) {
  x[i] = xx[i+1];
 }
 x[MAX-1] = 42;
 CopyArray (x, xx, max);
```

```

 for (i=0; i<NUM; i++) {
  max=amts[i];
  cout << setw(7) << max;
  timeStart = clock ();
  StraightSelectionSort (xx, max);
  timeEnd = clock ();
  cout << setw (10)
       << ((double)(timeEnd-timeStart))/CLOCKS_PER_SEC;
  CopyArray (x, xx, max);

  timeStart = clock ();
  BubbleSort (xx, max);
  timeEnd = clock ();
  cout << setw (10)
       << ((double)(timeEnd-timeStart))/CLOCKS_PER_SEC;
  CopyArray (x, xx, max);

  timeStart = clock ();
  QuickSort (xx, max, 0, max-1);
  timeEnd = clock ();
  cout << setw (10)
       << ((double)(timeEnd-timeStart))/CLOCKS_PER_SEC;
  CopyArray (x, xx, max);

  timeStart = clock ();
  HeapSort (xx, max);
  timeEnd = clock ();
  cout << setw (10)
       << ((double)(timeEnd-timeStart))/CLOCKS_PER_SEC;
  CopyArray (x, xx, max);

  timeStart = clock ();
  ShellSort (xx, max);
  timeEnd = clock ();
  cout << setw (10)
       << ((double)(timeEnd-timeStart))/CLOCKS_PER_SEC;
  CopyArray (x, xx, max);

  cout << endl;
 }


 cout << endl << endl << endl;
 cout << "Times in seconds for backwards sorted array\n"
   << "  Count  Straight    Bubble     Quick      Heap      Shell"
   << "\n"
   << "         Selection      Sort      Sort      Sort      Sort"
   << "\n\n";
 QuickSort (xx, MAX, 0, MAX-1);
 for (i=0; i<MAX-1; i++) {
  x[i] = xx[MAX-1-i];
 }
 CopyArray (x, xx, max);

 for (i=0; i<NUM; i++) {
```

```
   max=amts[i];
   cout << setw(7) << max;
   timeStart = clock ();
   StraightSelectionSort (xx, max);
   timeEnd = clock ();
   cout << setw (10)
        << ((double)(timeEnd-timeStart))/CLOCKS_PER_SEC;
   CopyArray (x, xx, max);

   timeStart = clock ();
   BubbleSort (xx, max);
   timeEnd = clock ();
   cout << setw (10)
        << ((double)(timeEnd-timeStart))/CLOCKS_PER_SEC;
   CopyArray (x, xx, max);

   timeStart = clock ();
   QuickSort (xx, max, 0, max-1);
   timeEnd = clock ();
   cout << setw (10)
        << ((double)(timeEnd-timeStart))/CLOCKS_PER_SEC;
   CopyArray (x, xx, max);

   timeStart = clock ();
   HeapSort (xx, max);
   timeEnd = clock ();
   cout << setw (10)
        << ((double)(timeEnd-timeStart))/CLOCKS_PER_SEC;
   CopyArray (x, xx, max);

   timeStart = clock ();
   ShellSort (xx, max);
   timeEnd = clock ();
   cout << setw (10)
        << ((double)(timeEnd-timeStart))/CLOCKS_PER_SEC;
   CopyArray (x, xx, max);

   cout << endl;
  }

 return 0;
}

/***************************************************************/
/*                                                             */
/* GetRandom: gets a random number from 0 to maxVal            */
/*                                                             */
/***************************************************************/

unsigned  GetRandom (int maxVal) {
 return rand () % maxVal;
}
... the actual sorting functions are unchanged from Pgm15a
}
```

Review Questions

1. Explain in your own words how the straight selection sort works.

2. Explain in your own words how the bubble sort works.

3. Explain in your own words how the Quicksort works.

4. Explain in your own words how the Heapsort works.

5. Explain in your own words how the Shellsort works.

6. In the benchmark runs, the straight selection sort ran twice as fast as the bubble sort when the data was in random order. Yet, when the array was already in sorted order except for the last element, the two methods took about the same amount of time to sort the array. How do you explain this difference?

7. In the benchmark runs, why should the straight selection sort run times be nearly identical for the random order array and the array in which the data is already in order except for the last element?

8. In the benchmark runs, the Heapsort times for the backwards sorted array and the array that was already in sorted order except for the last element were nearly identical. Why should this be the case? Why is the random order case running slower?

9. Using the benchmark runs as a guideline, suppose that your company needed to sort an array of 6,000,000 cost records. Which sort method would you recommend? Why? What is the impact of recursion when the array size becomes huge?

Stop! Do These Exercises Before Programming

1. Our programmer has had his ISAM inventory update program for Acme Consolidated accepted and put into production. While it was running in the production environment, a speed issue has arisen. The company has in excess of 500,000 parts to track in the ISAM data base. They are constantly adding new parts. It was discovered that the add new part function and the find this record functions were consuming huge amounts of execution time. Management has asked our programmer to speed these operations up significantly.

The index file is called **parts.idx** and consists of instances of the structure **Index**.

```
struct Index {
 char partNo[PARTNO_LEN];
 long relRecNum;
};
```

The index records are stored in increasing ASCII sequence on the **partNo** field.

The **FindRecord** function he currently has does a binary search to find the matching item in the index array. Its prototype is

```
bool FindRecord (Index id[], long num,
                 const char* findId, long& foundIndex);
```

It returns **true** if it finds a match and **false** if not. Of course, with a binary search, if there was no match, the **foundIndex** contained the subscript of where this item should have been located. That meant the programmer could also use this routine when adding new items to the index as well as matching existing ones.

The programmer has decided that a better way to handle the addition problem is to just add the new index element to the end of the already sorted index array and call a sort function to properly resort the index. Since your prowess as a programmer is now widely known, our programmer has gotten management approval to have you assist him in this project.

Write a **Quicksort** function to sort the array of index elements. Its prototype should be

```
void QuickSort (Index array[], long count, long lowIndex,
                long highIndex);
```

2. Write a **Shellsort** function to sort the array of index elements. Its prototype should be

```
void ShellSort (Index array[], long count);
```

3. With these new changes for sorting the Index array, the speed of the add new parts operation has improved. Why does this not affect the speed of the other operations, update this part and delete this part?

4. Look back over the implementation of the **FindRecord** binary search function presented in the Stop! Exercises for chapter 9. What is the real reason the **FindRecord** function is running slowly with this many records in the index? What would you recommend to management for drastically speeding up this matching operation?

Programming Problems

Problem Pgm11-1 The Benchmark Program Revised

When a program has a huge amount of automatic storage defined in **main** or another function, to avoid a runtime stack overflow, there is a project setting that can be made. Project Settings—Link tab—Output choice in the Category combobox—Stack Allocations edit control—enter the basic amount needed, such as 4000000 for close to 4M of memory.

Revise the benchmark program, **Pgm11b**, as follows. Remove the Straight Selection and Bubble sorts completely. Set the total array size to 4000000. Run a series of speed tests on random data for the Quicksort, Heapsort, and Shellsort. Test with 100,000 elements, 500,000 elements, 1,000,000 elements.

Problem Pgm11-2 Write a Shellsort Function to Sort Inventory Records

An **InventoryRec** structure is defined as follows. The **itemNumber** consists of two letters, a dash, and three numerical digits.

```
const int DESCRLEN = 21;
const int ITEMLEN = 7;

struct InventoryRec {
 char   itemNumber[ITEMLEN]; // format aa-nnn
 char   descr[DESCRLEN];
 short  quantity;
 double cost;
};
```

The DOS command line provides two filenames for the program. The first filename is the name of the input file to use. The input file is a binary file of inventory records that was built using **1-byte** structure alignment. The output file should also be a binary file.

The program loads the binary file into an array, sorts them into increasing order on **itemNumber**, and writes a new sorted binary file. Since the number of elements in the array is not known, use dynamic memory methods to allocate the array. That is, determine the input file size and divide by the size of an **InventoryRec** to get the number of elements. Then, dynamically allocate the array. Next, invoke a **LoadArray** function followed by **ShellSort** function followed by **WriteArray** function. Also, make a printed report of the first 20 and the last 20 records in the sorted array. However, if the array is smaller than 40 elements, display all the sorted elements.

Use the **invmast.dat** file provided in the **Pgm11-2** folder under **TestDataForAssignments** for your input file.

Problem Pgm11-3 Write a Quicksort Function to Sort Inventory Records

An **InventoryRec** structure is defined as follows. The **itemNumber** consists of two letters, a dash, and three numerical digits.

```
const int DESCRLEN = 21;
const int ITEMLEN = 7;

struct InventoryRec {
 char   itemNumber[ITEMLEN]; // format aa-nnn
 char   descr[DESCRLEN];
 short  quantity;
 double cost;
};
```

The DOS command line provides two filenames for the program. The first filename is the name of the input file to use. The input file is a binary file of inventory records that was built using **1-byte** structure alignment. The output file should also be a binary file.

The program loads the binary file into an array, sorts them into increasing order on **itemNumber**, and writes a new sorted binary file. Since the number of elements in the array is not known, use dynamic memory methods to allocate the array. That is, determine the input file size and divide by the size of an **InventoryRec** to get the number of elements. Then, dynamically allocate the array. Next, invoke a **LoadArray** function followed by **QuickSort** function followed by **WriteArray** function. Also, make a printed report of the first 20 and the last 20 records in the sorted array. However, if the array is smaller than 40 elements, display all the sorted elements.

Use the **invmast.dat** file provided in the **Pgm11-2** folder under **TestDataForAssignments** for your input file.

Chapter 12—B-trees and AVL Trees

Introduction

In chapter 10, the general theory of the tree data structure and the binary search tree were presented. Now it's time to extend those principles to more complex situations, databases which reside on disk. Historically, methods of direct access of a specific database record have been widely explored.

Note, the data structures presented in this chapter are among the most difficult to implement. Rather than tackling rather complex coding for these, I am presenting a broad overview. Your instructor will give you a presentation in class of specific coding techniques for one of these trees or one of the variations. I am only showing the coding for the AVL tree class.

The problem with disk databases centers on application speed of execution. When a block of data needs to be read from disk, the drive must reposition the read-write heads to the correct location that contains the track on which the data resides. Next, it must pause a moment until the home address of the circular spinning track is detected. Then, it must find the desired sector on that track relative to the beginning of the track. Once found, then the sector of data can be input. This is represented by the following disk access formula.

Access Time = Seek Time + Rotational Delay (latency) + Transfer Rate

Using my C: drive as an example, it has a seek time of 9 ms, 4 ms latency, and a transfer rate of 34 MB/sec. Thus, for any disk read, 13 milliseconds are required in the worst case before including the time it takes to actually transfer the data. By comparison, the CPU can perform an addition in about 6 nanoseconds. Thus, the ratio is about 2,000,000 to 1! Disk I/O is slow by comparison.

Thus, anything we can do programming-wise to reduce the number of disk accesses to obtain the desired information greatly aids application performance with large databases. In chapter 10, we saw that a binary search tree is a very effective method of directly retrieving a specific record with a specific key. However, if that binary tree is not loaded into memory, but rather utilized directly on disk by reading in each node as needed, performance greatly suffers. Insertion of new keys and deletion of keys often require a great deal of tree node shuffling which also slows down the operations. With large databases, we may not be able to store the entire index in memory to avoid direct disk accessing while searching the tree.

Another design consideration is the amount of data requested per I/O operation. From our discussion in chapter 9, the system actually I/O's a cluster of data at one time. On my C: drive, a cluster is 4K in size. Compute the access time required for 4K blocks and then for a 16 256 byte blocks. We get the following worst case times.

1-4K block = 9 + 4 + .1 ms = 13.1 ms
16-256 byte blocks = 16 (9 + 4 + .007) ms = 208.1 ms

Thus, it is better to input single 4K blocks than to input 16 smaller portions.

Historically, the b-tree (balanced tree) offers a significant improvement in disk database operations. It has been widely implemented with many specialized refinements to aid performance in certain situations.

The B-Tree

Perfect balance in a binary search tree yields the shortest average search paths. If the database operations expect to insert and delete numerous keys, then costly rebalancing of the tree can occur. This is particularly true if many nodes must be rearranged in the process. A compromise is to maintain th perfect balance only in the tree's height and let the number of search keys stored in a node vary.

In other words, any given tree node contains up to M search keys. This is a **b-tree,** a multi way tree in which the height is balanced but any node can contain up to M keys. The number M is called the **branching factor** of the b-tree. The root node can either be a leaf (empty tree) or can have up to M children. All leaves lie on the bottommost level. Typically, M is adjusted for optimum performance so that the size of the node with M keys occupies a disk's cluster.

What does this imply for database capacity? Suppose that we have a tree with M set at 256. Further, let's only allow 3 levels. There is one node at the root level 0, M nodes on level 1, M^2 nodes on level 2, and M^3 on level 3. Thus, about 16 million records could be stored in this database with only the three levels! More importantly for disk accessing, it only requires searching a maximum of 3 nodes to find the record. In contrast, if we used a binary search tree, 24 levels are required to store 16 million records and a search could require 24 nodes to find the desired record.

However, before we tackle the b-tree design and implementation, let's examine a simpler case from which we can extend to obtain the b-tree.

The 2-3 Tree as a Simplification of the B-tree Process

A simpler, yet similar tree, is called the **2-3 tree** which is a multi way tree in which the height is balanced. Each node can contain 1 or 2 search keys and may have 2 or 3 descendants. All leaves are empty trees that lie on the bottom level. in Figure 12.1 below, each yellow box represents an item number key and a pointer to its location on disk or in memory. Each node can hold one or two keys. However, each node can have up to three descendants. Notice that the tree is balanced in height always.

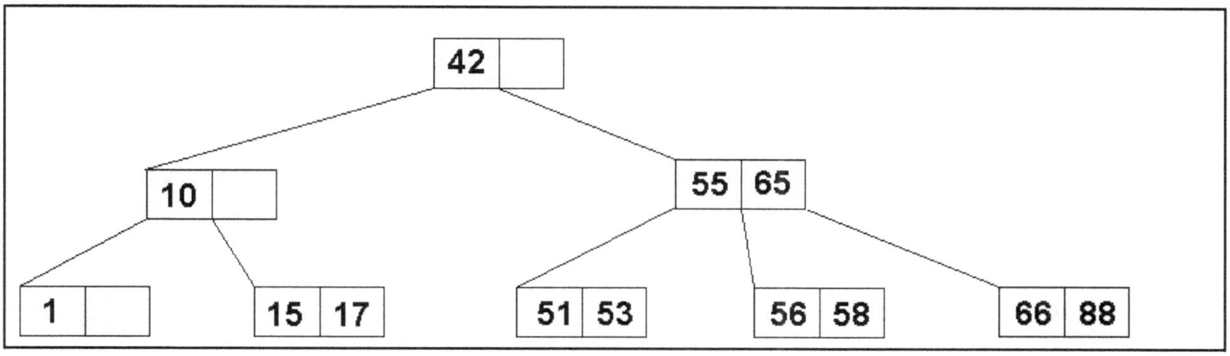

Figure 12.1 The 2-3 Tree

Suppose that the program needed to find the item whose id number was 58. Begin at the root. 58 is larger than the item stored in the root, 42, so we go to the right subtree. This node has two keys. So we compare 58 to the ids present and find that it lies between 55 and 65. Thus, we take the middle subtree branch. And finally, we find a match on 58. From here, we obtain the pointer to where this item is located. If it is in memory, it is an actual pointer. If it is on disk, it is likely the file offset to the record.

Addition of a new item number into the 2-3 tree is more complex than a simple binary tree. There are several possibilities. The simplest situation arises when we need to add item number 6. First, we find that 6 is less than the root 42 entry and so take the left subtree branch. Next, 6 is less than the 10 entry and again take the left branch. Having reached the bottom level, we see that there is an available location in this node in which to store the new item number 6. Figure 12.2 shows what the 2-3 tree looks like after we have inserted the new item 6.

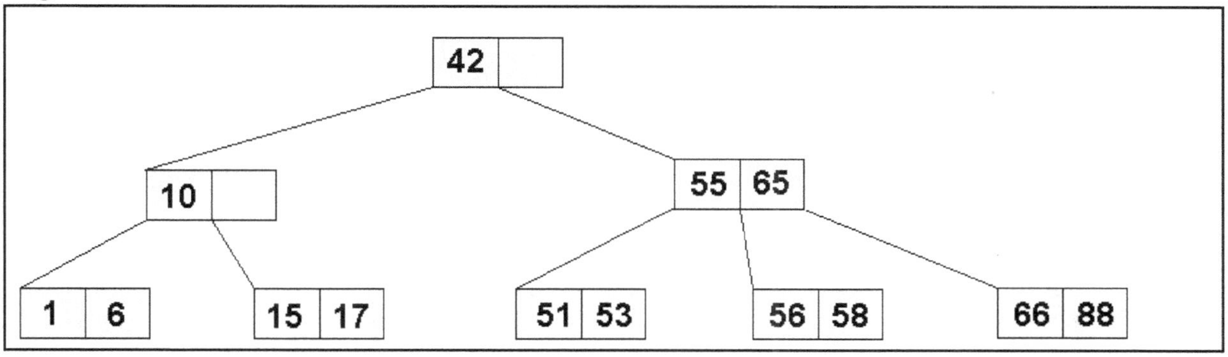

Figure 12.2 The 2-3 Tree After Insertion of Key 6

If we try to insert a key into a node that already has two keys in it, that node would overflow. The overflow algorithm is to split that node into two parts and pass the middle key on up to the parent node. Of course, when we attempt to add that middle node to the parent, the parent may also be full and similarly must be split. Eventually, we may even need to split the root node as well, if the overflow continues all the way to the root.

To see how this works, let's add a new key of 57. It fits in the node that already contains keys 56 and 58. Since that node is full, it must be overflowed. We split that node into two portions, one contains 56 and the other contains 58 with key 57 being passed on up to the parent. The results are shown in Figure 12.3.

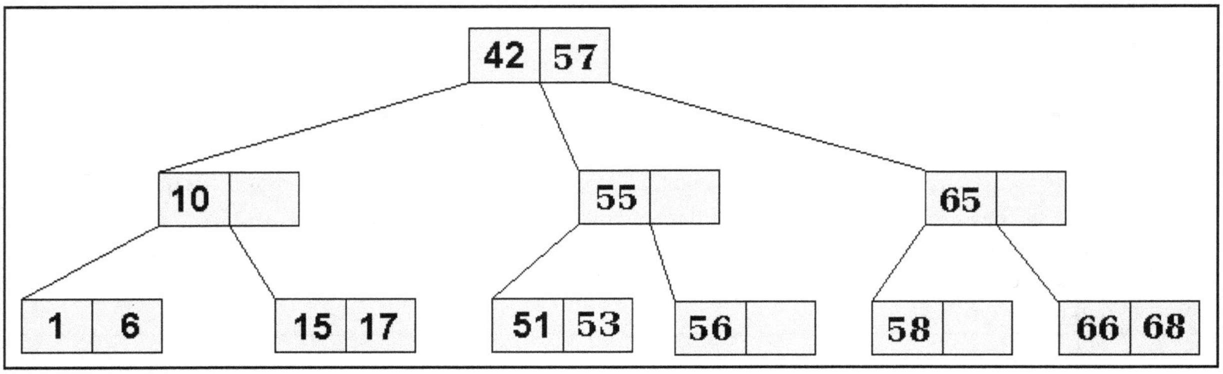

Figure 13.3 The 2-3 Tree After Adding Node 57

The 2-3 tree illustrates in a simple way how a node can hold two keys and have three children. We would not use the 2-3 tree to provide direct access to a large disk file because the number of nodes would be rather large. Instead, we generalize this approach to the b-tree, in which a node's actual size in bytes closely approaches the size of a cluster. A b-tree may contain hundreds of keys. But the insertion of a new key parallels that of the 2-3 tree we have just seen.

The B-tree Algorithm

The rules for the b-tree closely parallel those of the 23 tree. First, the root has at least two subtrees unless it is a leaf. Second, each non-root and each non-leaf node holds k-1 keys and k pointers to subtrees where (m/2) <= k <= m. That is, we try to keep a node at least half full of entries. Third, each leaf node contains k-1 keys where (m/2) <= k <= m. Fourth, all leaves are on the same level, the bottom.

The order of the b-tree is given by m which is often large so that the complete node fills a cluster on the disk drive. What does the node definition look like? That depends upon how one wishes to implement the b-tree itself. First, the light green boxes in the above figures containing the keys actually is either a class or a structure that contains at least two members, the key and its corresponding location on disk, that is, that record's file offset pointer. A simple structure would suffice here. Assume that the keys are numerical in nature. The following could be a reasonable definition for the key and data portion.

```
struct KeyData {
 long idNumber;
 long fileOffset;
};
```

Assume that we wish to make the b-tree implementation a template container class. Then, we could begin by defining the following for the nodes.

```
template<class T, int M>
struct BTreeNode {
 int          isLeaf;
 int          numItems;
 T            keys[M-1];
 BTreeNode*  ptrnodes[M];
};
```

How much space will this structure occupy? Assume that the program uses 1-byte alignment. Each int occupies four bytes. Each instance of **KeyData** occupies eight bytes. Each pointer, four bytes. We can write the following formula for its size, depending on M.

```
Total bytes = 8 + (M - 1) * 8 + M * 4
```

or

```
Total bytes = 12 * M
```

Okay. If we know the cluster size is 4K, then solving for M yields a value of 341. The b-tree for my system's drive should be of order 341. If the cluster size was say 32K, then the value of M would be 2730. Yes, for optimum disk performance, the order of the b-tree is large!

The two key algorithms that we must implement at once are **InsertNode** and **DeleteNode**. Given these two, we can build the b-tree. Let's begin with the process to insert a new node. I am not going to try to draw nodes with 100 plus keys in them. Instead, let's use an M of say 4 in the figures.

Inserting a Node

As we saw with the 2-3 tree, there are three situations that can arise when a new key is inserted into the b-tree. Assume that our b-tree currently looks like this, Figure 12.4.

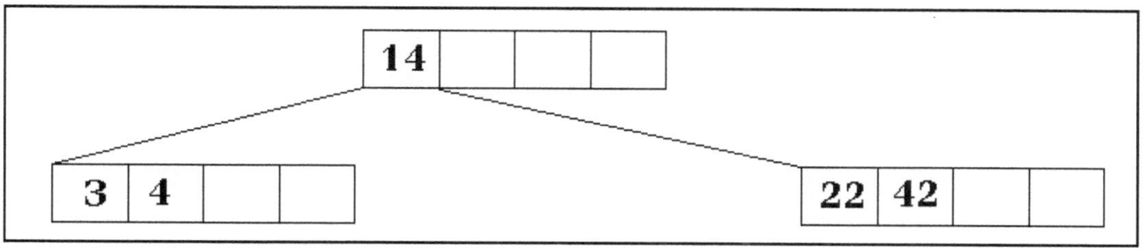

Figure 12.4 The Initial State of the B-tree

Suppose that a key of 1 is to be added. We always try to add the key to the node in which it belongs. In this case, it belongs in the node containing 3 and 4. This is the first situation that arises; there is room for that key, so we must move the 3 and 4 keys down one slot, making room for the key of 1 entry. Then, we can add the key of 1. Figure 12.5 shows the results.

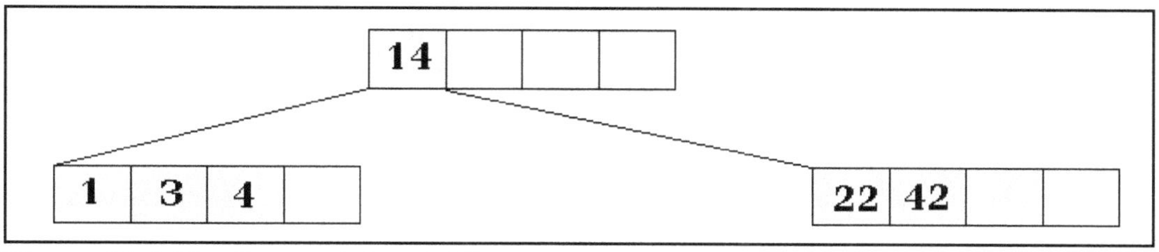

Figure 12.5 The B-tree After Adding Key 1

Now let's continue and add a key of 8. Figure 12.6 shows the tree with 8 added.

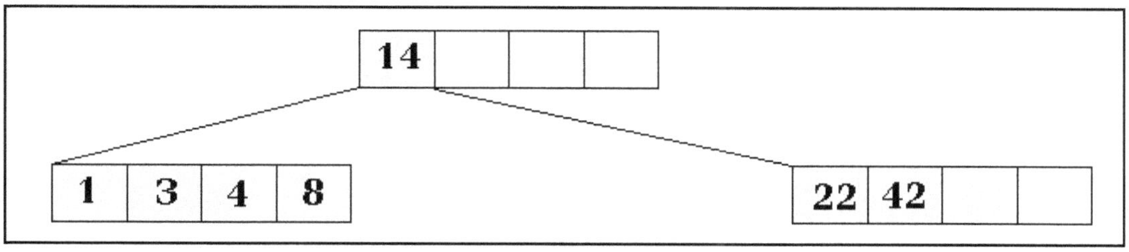

Figure 12.6 The B-tree After Adding Key 8

Next, let's add in a key of 5. It belongs in the same node as the 1 3 4 8 keys, but adding it causes an overflow of the array. This is the second situation of the three that can arise. Thus, we must split this overflowing node into two nodes, placing the left half of the keys in the new left node and the right half into the new right node. Note that we only need to create one new node. We can retain the existing overflowing node as the new left node, moving the right half of its keys into a new right node. The key that is in the middle must be moved up into the next higher node. If the number of keys is even, then pick one of the two in the middle. Figure 12.7 shows this process partially completed.

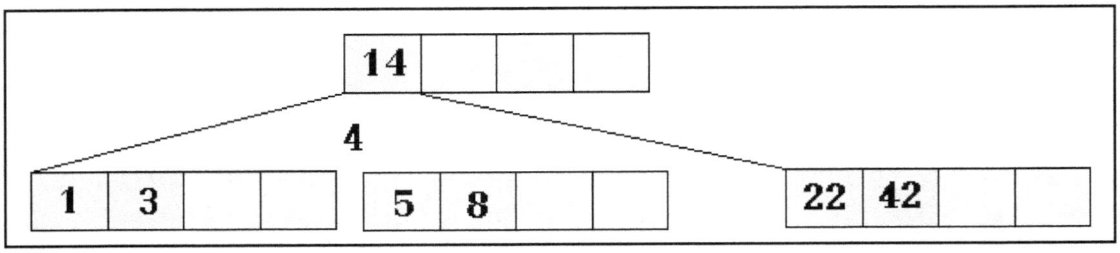

Figure 12.7 The B-tree Partially Done After Adding a Key of 5 and Splitting the Node

The 4 key, the one in the middle, is moved upward into the next higher level. In this case, it is the root node. The 14 key must be moved down to make room for it and the pointers adjusted. Figure 12.8 shows the finished addition. Remember, that when we speak of adding a new key, we are really adding a new instance of the **KeyData** structure. Further, realize that in this root node, we also needed to modify the pointers to the child nodes as well. Notice also in Figure 12.8 that each node is half filled. That is a property of a b-tree, the nodes tend to be half filled.

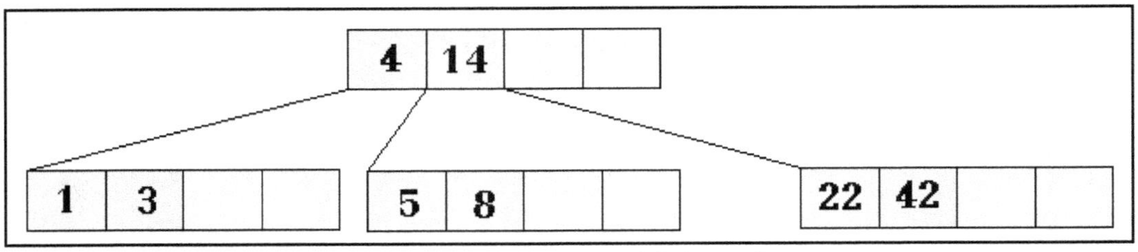

Figure 12.8 The B-tree After the Complete Addition of Key 5

The third situation that can occur is when the root itself overflows. Obviously we must add a number of additional keys before this can occur in the above figure. Figure 12.9 shows the b-tree nearly filled up. Consider what happens next if we need to add key 20 to the b-tree.

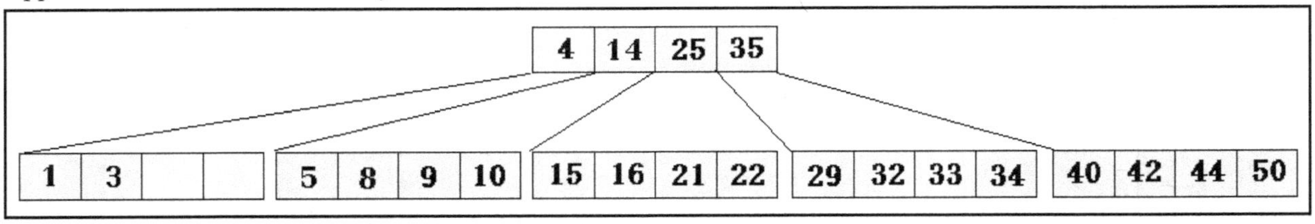

Figure 12.9 The B-tree Prior to Root Overflow

If we follow the procedure, the new key of 20 causes the middle node to be split into two new nodes, the left one containing 15 and 16, while the right new node contains 21 and 22. The key in the middle is 20 which is moved up to the next higher level. But the root is full. So the root node is similarly split into two nodes using the same process. The left node would contain 1 and 14 while the right new node contains 25 and 35. The one in the middle is promoted up to the next level which does not exist. So we allocate a new root node in which to store the key of 20. This yields the b-tree shown in Figure 12.10. Note also that the splitting of the root node increased the total depth of the tree.

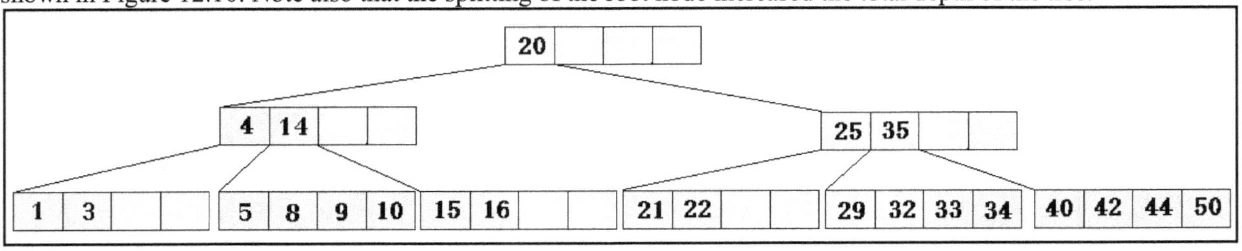

Figure 12.10 The B-tree After the Root Node Split

The following summarizes b-tree insertion.
1. Find the leaf node in which it belongs.
2. Insert the new key into that node, if it fits.
3. If the node overflows, then
   Allocate a new node and copy one half of the keys into the new right node.
   The key in the middle of these two halves is promoted upwards into the original parent node.
4. If the parent node overflows, repeat the process on the parent, splitting it into two halves and promoting the key in the middle up to the parent node.
5. If there is no parent, then make a new root node with this newly promoted node as the sole occupant.

The Process of Deleting a Key

Deletion of a key is largely the reverse of an insertion. The prime consideration is to avoid having a node end up with less than half of its entries present. That is, we wish to maintain the concept that any node should be at least half full if possible. To do so, we may have to merge some nodes during the removal process. There are two main cases to examine: deleting a key from a leaf and deleting a key from a non-leaf.

Deleting a Key from a Leaf

Deleting a key from a leaf begins by finding the node that contains the key. Then, we must determine if that leaf will contain sufficient keys after we remove the desired key.

1. If that leaf would still be at least half full, we merely copy all of the higher keys and pointers down one slot in the arrays to replace the deleted key's vacated location. This is shown in Figure 12.11 and Figure 12.12. We wish to delete key 8.

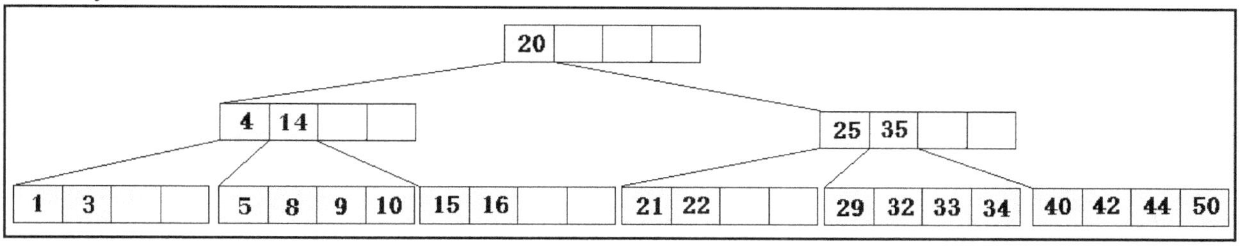

Figure 12.11 The B-tree Before Deletion of Key 8

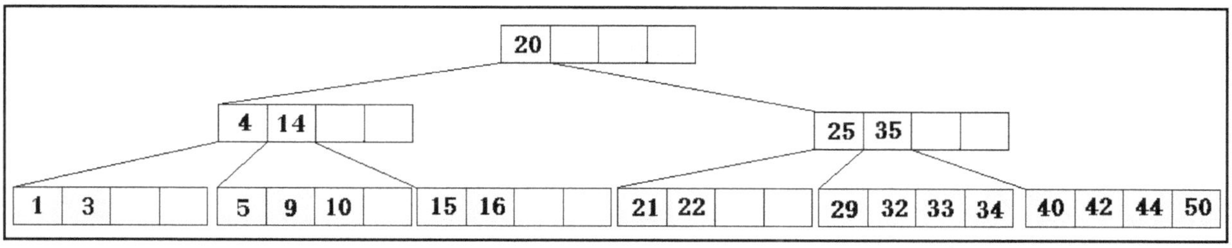

Figure 12.12 The B-tree After the Deletion of Key 8 Using Rule 1

2. If the leaf would contain too few keys, that is less than M/2, check to see if there is a right or left sibling node whose keys exceed M/2. That is we look at all of the children of the parent node of the node which is now too small. If we find one of the other child nodes is more than half full, we redistribute the keys between the node which has the deleted key and the sibling which has too many. Often, this results in a replacement of the separator key in the parent node between these two siblings. Using Figure 12.12 as the base, let's delete key 16. Figure 12.13 shows the result of this rule.

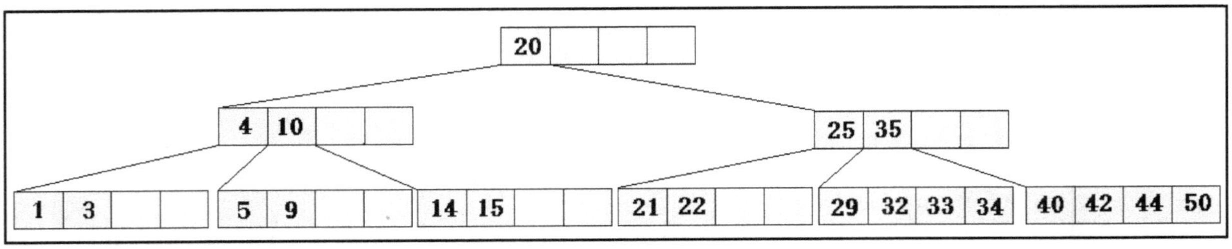

Figure 12.13 The B-tree After Deletion of Key 16 Using Rule 2

3. Worse still is the situation in which none of the siblings of the node in which the key is deleted is too full. Now we must merge nodes. We take all of the keys in the node in which we have just deleted the key and merge them with its sibling and the key of the parent which points to the two nodes. Discard the now empty sibling node. Removing the key in the parent may create a hole in the parent's arrays, so the keys and pointers of the parent must be moved down one element.

Using Figure 12.13 as the base, let's delete key 14. This means we must merge the node with 5 and 9 with the parent's 10 and the remaining key of 14, leaving the original node with key 15 now empty and can be deleted. This first portion is shown in Figure 12.14.

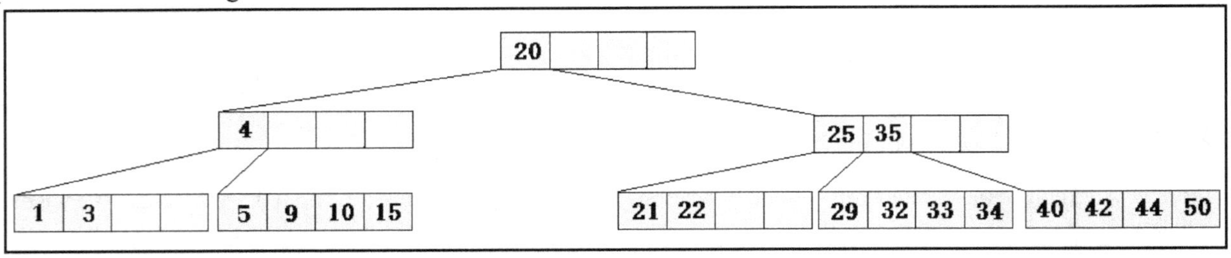

Figure 12.14 The B-tree After Deleting Key 14 and Merging But Before Merging Parent Node

Notice that now the parent node with key 4 has too few keys in it. So we must continue the process.

4. If the parent is now less than one half full, we treat the parent as if it is the bottom leaf and repeat step 3 until step 2 is reached creating balanced nodes or until we encounter the root.

5. When merging a node with its sibling, if their parent is the root which has only one key in it, then all of the keys are merged into one new root node and the two child nodes are deleted. This is the only time that we delete two nodes at one time and it decreases the height of the tree.

In Figure 12.14 above, this is just what has happened. The parent node with key 4 is too small. So we must merge it and its sibling node with keys 25 and 35 plus its parent with key 20 into a new node. The result of the merger and deletion of two empty nodes is shown in Figure 12.15.

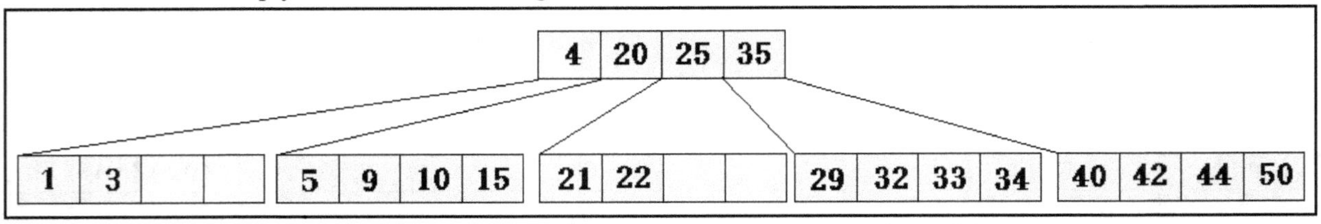

Figure 12.15 The B-tree After Merging and Deleting Empty Nodes of Parent

Deleting a Key from a Non-leaf

When the key to be deleted is located in a non-leaf, that is in a node that has children, additional problems arise. Deleting that key can completely mess up the tree organization. So that key must be replaced by its immediate successor or predecessor in the child nodes below this node, but always going all the way down to a leaf node to find that new key. Once that replacement key is found, it is deleted from the bottom leaf by using the above process for a leaf case.

The Complete Algorithm for Key Deletion

Here is the pseudocode for the entire deletion process.

```
node = find the node with key K
if the node is 0, there the key is not found so quit.
if the node is not a leaf, then
        find a leaf with the closest successor S of this key K
        copy S over the top of K in the node
        node now equals the leaf with S in it.
        delete S from node
else delete K from node
while (true) do the following to balance the tree
        if the node is half full or more, we are done, return
        if there is a sibling of node with enough keys
                redistribute keys between node and its sibling and return
        if node's parent is the root
                if parent has only one key
                        merge node, its sibling and parent to form a new root and return
                else
                        merge node and its sibling and return
        else
                merge node and its sibling
                node = its parent
```

Summary of B-trees

The b-tree is a good method to handle direct access of very large disk files. Each node can contain a rather large number of keys, minimizing disk access time when in search of a specific key. However, the process of insertion and deletion, while complex, tends to keep any specific node only half full, wasting the remainder of the available potential keys.

A number of variations of a b-tree have been created in an attempt to eliminate this wasted space in the nodes. One of these, the **b*-tree,** was introduced by Donald Knuth. In this variation, nodes are maintained two-thirds full. When a node must be split, it is split into thirds not halves. Further, when a node overflow, before considering a split, an attempt is made to redistribute keys among the existing sibling nodes. Only if the sibling is also full do we split the node into thirds.

AVL Trees

The AVL tree was created by two Russian mathematicians, Adelson-Velskii and Landis. The AVL tree is a height-balanced binary tree structure. The heights of the subtrees differ by no more than one. Hence, it is a balanced binary tree which provides a uniformly fast direct access of any specific key. And that is its objective, to guarantee that for any specific key, we get a uniformly fast look up process. Figure 12.16 shows several AVL trees.

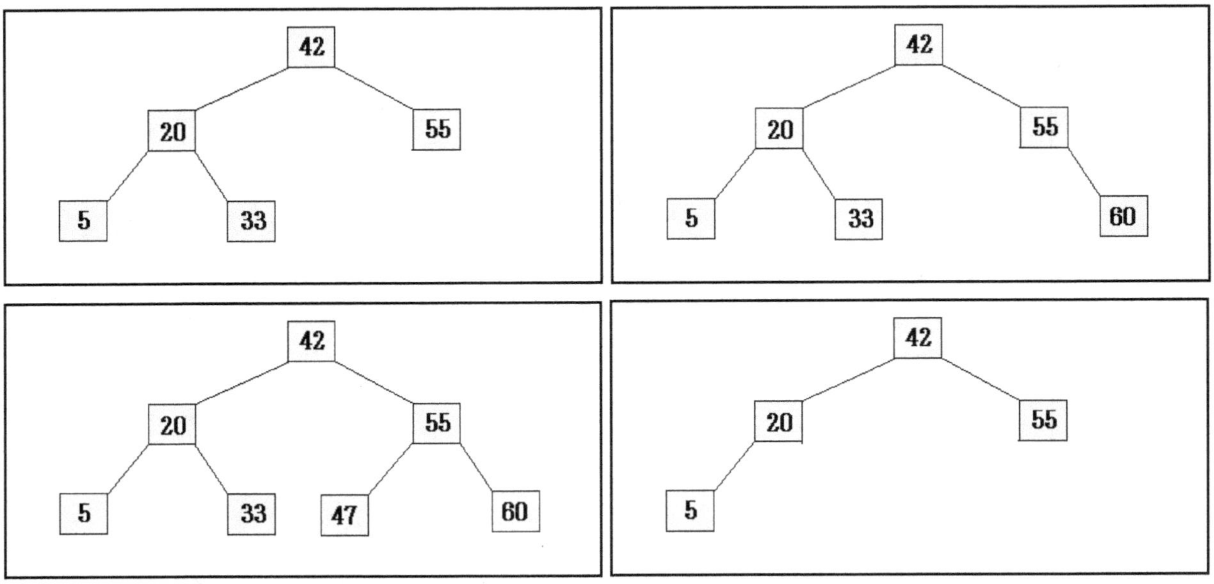

Figure 12.16 Several AVL Trees

Recall that the balance factor of a tree is the height of the left subtree minus the height of the right subtree. The AVL tree forces the balance factor to be +1, 0, or –1 only. As you might have guessed, this new requirement impacts adding a new node which can force the tree to become unbalanced in its height requirements. An AVL tree can become out of balance in four ways and there are four methods we must implement to bring the tree back into height balance. The four ways the tree can become unbalanced during the insertion of a new node is shown in Figure 12.17.

In Figure 12.17a, by adding a node with a key of 2, the already left heavy side of the node at 42 has now become out of balance on its left side. This is called LL or left-left out of balance

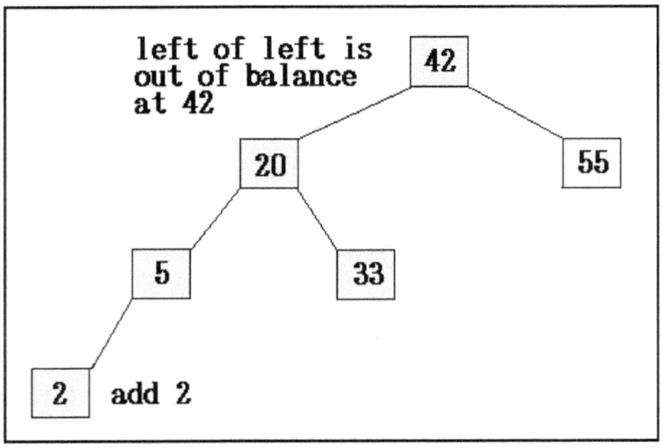

Figure 12.17a Left - Left Out of Balance

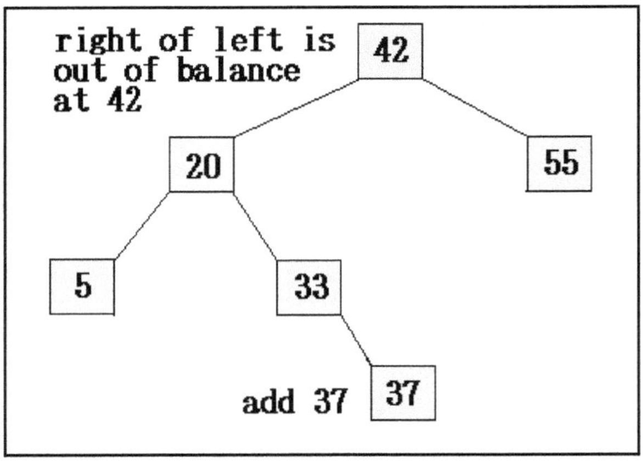

Figure 12.17b Right of Left Out of Balance

In Figure 12.17b, by adding a node with a key of 37, the left heavy side of node 42 now has its right portion out of balance. This is called RL or right of left out of balance.

In Figure 12.17c, adding a node with a key of 47 has made the left portion of the right heavy node 42 now out of balance. This is called LR or left of right out of balance.

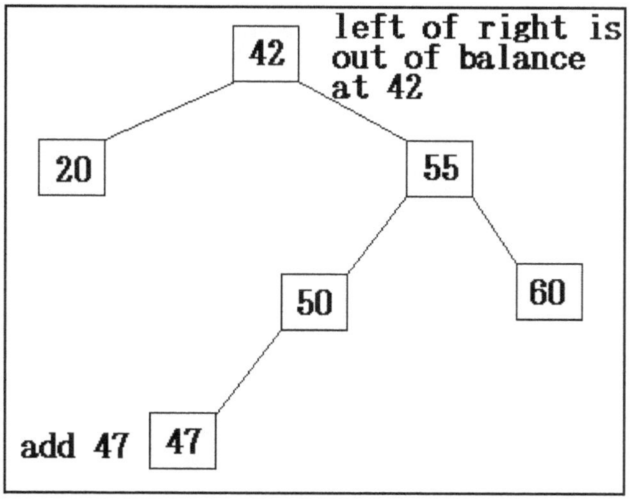

Figure 12.17c Left of Right Out of Balance

In Figure 12.17d, adding a node with a key of 70 has made the right portion of the already right side of node 42 now out of balance. This is called RR or right of right out of balance.

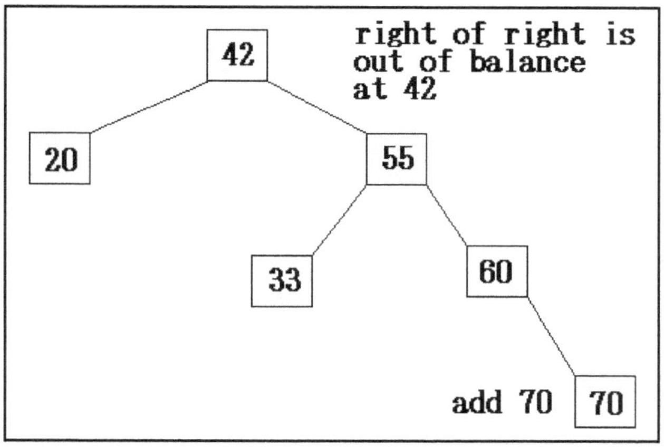

Figure 12.17d Right of Right Out of Balance

When an AVL tree becomes out of balance, nodes are rotated left or right to being the tree back into balance and preserve the binary search nature in which all nodes to the left of a node are less than that parent node and those to the right are larger. There are several possibilities. Let's examine them one by one.

In Figure 12.18a, by adding node 47, the tree becomes LL out of balance at the root. So we rotate the 55 root node to the right. Node 50 becomes the new parent.

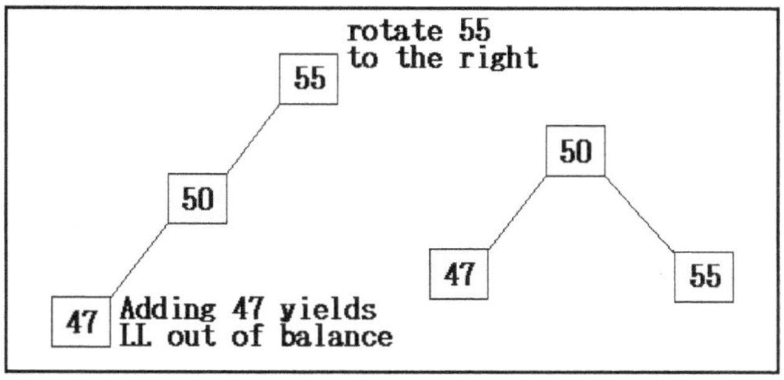

Figure 12.18a A Simple LL Rotation

The right rotation can be more complex. Consider the actions needed to rotate right in the following tree, Figure 12.18b. When node 2 is added, node 42 is LL out of balance. So we rotate node 42 to the right bringing node 20 up as the new parent. However, node 20 already has a right node of 33. So the node 33 is attached to the unused left node of the rotated 42 node.

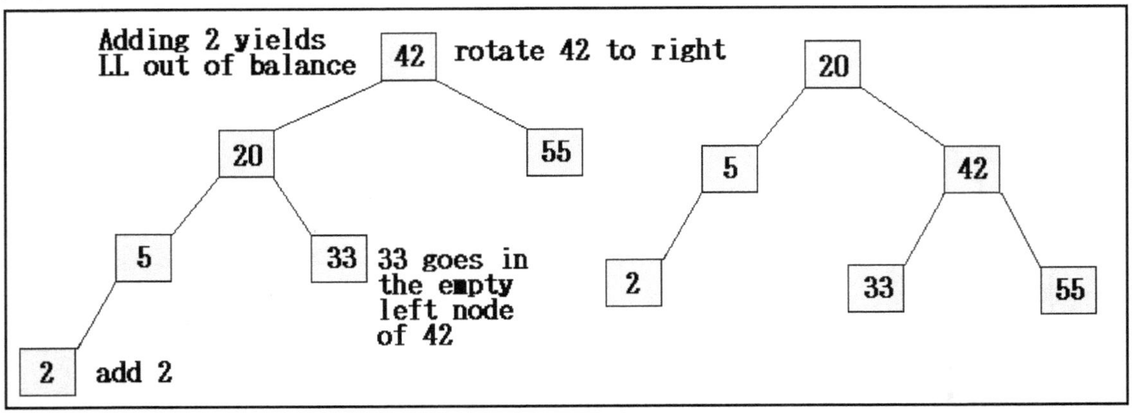

Figure 12.18b A More Complex LL Rotation

RR rotation is the mirror image of LL rotation. In Figure 12.19, after adding node 60, the tree is RR out of balance. So we rotate node 20 to the left side, bringing node 42 as its parent. However, node 43 already has a left subnode, 33, so it is placed in the vacated node 20's right side.

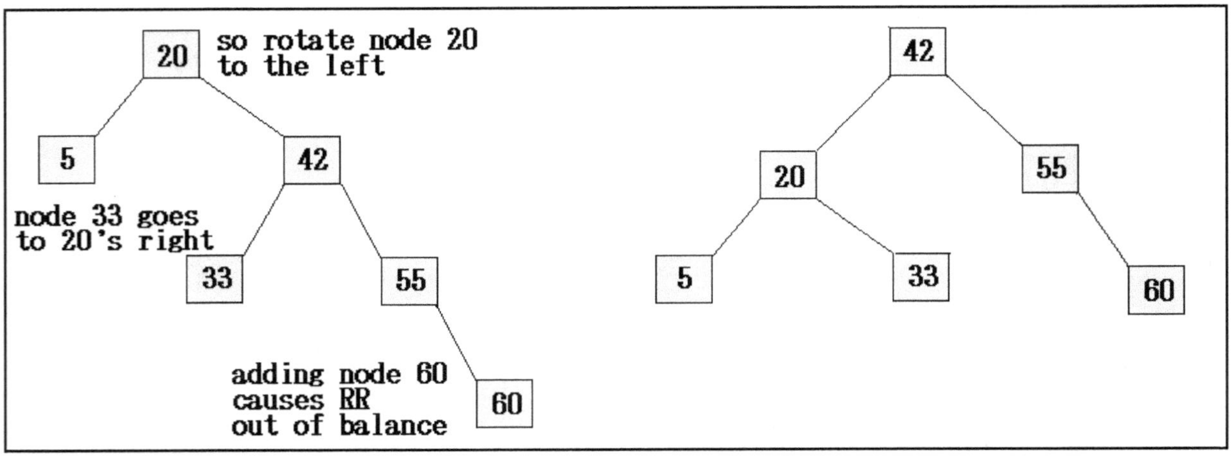

Figure 12.19 A Complex RR Rotation

Thus, to handle either RR or LL out of balance conditions, it is only necessary to rotate either to the left or right. However, the RL and LR cases are more complex and require two separate rotations to correct the balance. In Figure 12.20, after adding node 37, the tree is RL out of balance. So we first rotate node 20 to the left making node 33 its parent and then we rotate node 42 to the right.

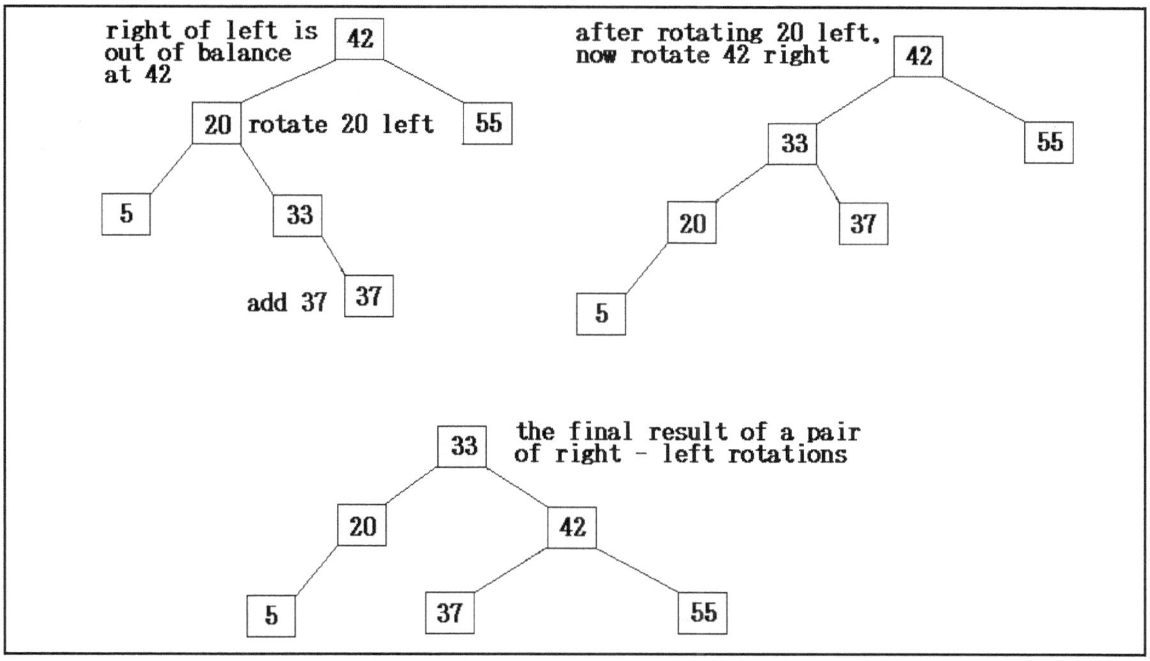

Figure 12.20 Handling RL by a Rotate Left and then a Rotate Right

Finally, consider how we can fix a LR out of balance situation. Suppose that we add key 47. First, we rotate key 55 right. Then, we rotate key 42 left to bring the tree back into balance.

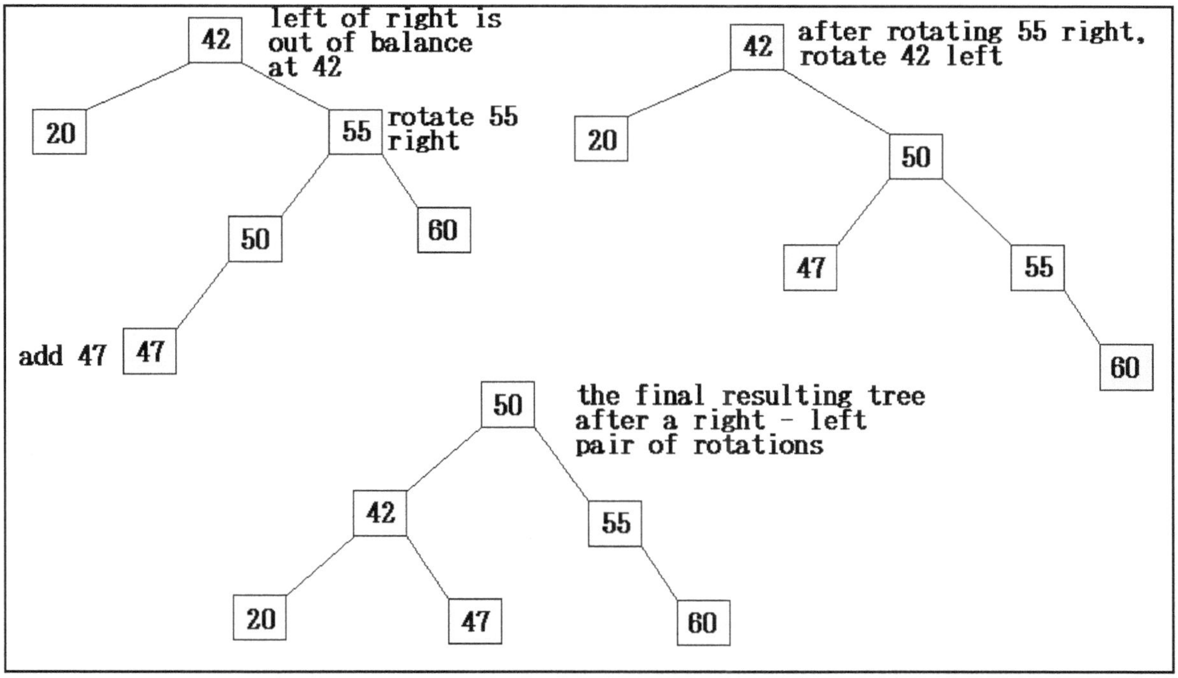

Figure 12.21 Handling a LR Out of Balance Tree with a Right - Left Rotation

Designing an AVL Tree

The design of an AVL tree parallels that of a binary tree. The node must store a pointer to the left and right child nodes as well as the key and data information for the node.

Because of the balancing that must be done, the node structure must also store a integer balance. The usual notation of the balance factor is Left High, Even High, and Right High. This is an ideal situation for an enumerated data type to make the coding more readable. Thus, the start of the **AVLTree** template class is thus.

```
#pragma once

enum Balance {LeftHigh = 1, EvenHigh = 0, RightHigh = -1};
// these represent the error codes some functions may enum ReturnCode
{Ok, DuplicateKey, OutOfMemory,
                  KeyNotFound};

template <class T>
struct TreeNode {
     T             keyData;        // user's data
     Balance       balanceFactor;  // the balance factor
     TreeNode<T>*  ptrLeftChild;   // ptr to left child node
     TreeNode<T>*  ptrRightChild;  // ptr to right child node
};

template <class T>
class AVLTree {
public:
 TreeNode<T>* root;
```

Notice that I also added an enum, **ReturnCode**. Many of the member functions return error indicators back to the client program. Here is another good usage of class enumerated data type.

Using an INL Header File

Since this class is going to be a rather lengthy one and since it is also a template class, we know that the entire implementation must be known at compile time when the header is included. This does not mean that we are limited to inserting all of the class member function implementations in this single header file. Since a header file can include other files, I show the common Microsoft approach. Place the implementation portion in a file called .INL for inline, and include it in the header after the class definition is complete.

The AVLTree Class Definition

Here is the AVLTree class definition. Much of it is quite obvious, such as the ctor, copy ctor and assignment operator. Certainly the various methods of tree traversal must be implemented. And of course, Insert and Delete functions allow the client to add and remove nodes. Notice the next to the last line of the header file. Here is where the inl file is included. The first 64 lines represent the client interface. I have collected the private functions together at the end of the class listing.

AVL Tree Class Definition

```
 1 #pragma once
 2 #include <iostream>
 3 using namespace std;
 4
 5 enum Balance {LeftHigh = 1, EvenHigh = 0, RightHigh = -1};
 6 // these represent the error codes some functions may return
 7 enum ReturnCode {Ok, DuplicateKey, OutOfMemory, KeyNotFound};
```

```

template <class T>
struct TreeNode {
 T            keyData;       // user's data
 Balance      balanceFactor; // the balance factor
 TreeNode<T>* ptrLeftChild;  // ptr to left child node
 TreeNode<T>* ptrRightChild; // ptr to right child node
};

template <class T>
class AVLTree {
public:
 TreeNode<T>* root;

public:

 AVLTree ();                                      // makes a new tree
 AVLTree (const AVLTree& tree);                   // copies a tree
 AVLTree& operator= (const AVLTree& tree); // assigns a tree
~AVLTree ();                                      // removes all nodes

 void EmptyTree (); // removes all nodes - instance can be reused
 bool IsEmpty () const;         // returns true if tree is empty

 long GetNumberOfNodes() const; // returns count of nodes in tree

 long GetTreeHeight() const; // returns height of tree

 ostream& DisplayTree (ostream& os);

 // Traverses the tree by Visit, Left, Right
 ostream& PreOrderTraversal (ostream& os);

 // Traverses the tree in inorder by Left, Visit, Right
 ostream& InOrderTraversal (ostream& os);

 // Traverses the tree by Left, Right, Visit
 ostream& PostOrderTraversal (ostream& os);

 // Traverses the tree by level. Displays all the nodes
 ostream& LevelOrderTraversal (ostream& os);

 // Insert a new item into the tree
 // returns Ok if item is inserted into its proper postion
 //         and the tree is rebalanced as needed
 // returns DuplicateKey if the key is already in the tree
 // returns OutOfMemory if allocations fail
 ReturnCode Insert (const T& newkeydata);

 // Delete removes the node with the findKey value
 // returns Ok if the deletion was successful
 //         and the tree is rebalanced as needed
 // returns KeyNotFound if the item is not in the tree
 ReturnCode Delete (const T& findKey);

private:
```

```
 void RecursiveDestroyTree (TreeNode<T>*& ptrnode);

 void RecursiveCopyTree (TreeNode<T>* treeptr,
                         TreeNode<T>*& newTreeptr);

 long RecursiveCountNodes(TreeNode<T>* treeptr) const;

 TreeNode<T>* MakeNewNode (const T& newitem);
 TreeNode<T>* RecursiveInsert (TreeNode<T>* ptrroot,
                               TreeNode<T>*  ptrnewnode,
                               bool& taller,
                               ReturnCode& rc);
 TreeNode<T>* LeftBalanceOnInsert (TreeNode<T>* ptrroot,
                                   bool& taller);
 TreeNode<T>* RightBalanceOnInsert (TreeNode<T>* ptrroot,
                                    bool& taller);
 TreeNode<T>* RotateRight (TreeNode<T>* ptrroot);
 TreeNode<T>* RotateLeft (TreeNode<T>* ptrroot);

 TreeNode<T>* RecursiveDelete (TreeNode<T>* ptrroot,
                               const T& findKey, bool& smaller,
                               ReturnCode& retcd);
 TreeNode<T>* RightBalanceOnDelete (TreeNode<T>* ptrroot,
                                    bool& smaller);
 TreeNode<T>* LeftBalanceOnDelete (TreeNode<T>* ptrroot,
                                   bool& smaller);

 ostream& RecursivePreOrder(TreeNode<T>* r, ostream& os) const;
 ostream& RecursiveInOrder(TreeNode<T>* r, ostream& os) const;
 ostream& RecursivePostOrder(TreeNode<T>* r, ostream& os) const;

 long RecursiveHeightOfNodes(TreeNode<T>* ptrroot) const;

 void RecursiveDisplayTree (TreeNode<T>* ptrroot, int depth,
                            ostream& os);
};

#include "AVLTree.inl"
```

From just a quick glance at the **AVLTree** definition, you can see that there are going to be many recursive functions to implement this data structure. I added one for debugging, **DisplayTree** what outputs the tree in a fashion we can easily use to verify that the tree is built correctly.

Because I added a **LevelOrderTraversal** function, I need a **Queue** template class to implement it. This is a very simple class with nothing fancy in it.

The implementation is fairly straightforward, until you encounter the **Insert** and **Delete** functions. So let's examine the other functions first and save the hardest for last.

AVL Tree Class Inl Implementation

```
// implementation of AVLTree class

#include "Queue.h"

/***************************************************************/
/*                                                             */
/* AVLTree: makes an empty tree                                */
```

```
/*                                                                  */
/********************************************************************/
template <class T>
AVLTree<T>::AVLTree () {
 root = 0;
}

/********************************************************************/
/*                                                                  */
/* ~AVLTree: removes all nodes                                      */
/*                                                                  */
/********************************************************************/
template <class T>
AVLTree<T>::~AVLTree () {
 EmptyTree ();
}

/********************************************************************/
/*                                                                  */
/* EmptyTree: removes all nodes so tree can be reused               */
/*                                                                  */
/********************************************************************/
template <class T>
void AVLTree<T>::EmptyTree () {
 RecursiveDestroyTree (root);
}

/********************************************************************/
/*                                                                  */
/* RecursiveDestroyTree: recursively visits all children and        */
/*      and deletes those before deleting parent                    */
/*                                                                  */
/********************************************************************/
template <class T>
void AVLTree<T>::RecursiveDestroyTree (TreeNode<T>*& ptrnode) {
 if (!ptrnode) return;
 RecursiveDestroyTree(ptrnode->ptrLeftChild);
 RecursiveDestroyTree(ptrnode->ptrRightChild);
 delete ptrnode;
 ptrnode = 0;
}

/********************************************************************/
/*                                                                  */
/* IsEmpty: returns true if tree has no nodes                       */
/*                                                                  */
/********************************************************************/
template <class T>
bool AVLTree<T>::IsEmpty () const {
 return root ? false : true;
}

/********************************************************************/
/*                                                                  */
/* GetNumberOfNodes: returns the number of nodes in tree            */
/*                                                                  */
```

```
/**************************************************************/
template <class T>
long AVLTree<T>::GetNumberOfNodes() const {
 return RecursiveCountNodes(root);
}

/**************************************************************/
/*                                                            */
/* RecursiveCountNodes: returns the number of nodes           */
/*                                                            */
/**************************************************************/
template <class T>
long AVLTree<T>::RecursiveCountNodes (TreeNode<T>* treeptr)
                                                     const {
 return treeptr ? RecursiveCountNodes(treeptr->ptrLeftChild) +
  RecursiveCountNodes(treeptr->ptrRightChild) + 1 : 0;
}

/**************************************************************/
/*                                                            */
/* PreOrderTraversal: uses recursion: visit parent, left, right*/
/*                                                            */
/**************************************************************/
template <class T>
ostream& AVLTree<T>::PreOrderTraversal (ostream& os) {
 return RecursivePreOrder(root, os);
}

/**************************************************************/
/*                                                            */
/* RecursivePreOrder: visits parent then left and right childs */
/*                                                            */
/**************************************************************/
template <class T>
ostream& AVLTree<T>::RecursivePreOrder (TreeNode<T>* ptrroot,
                                        ostream& os) const {
 if (r)  {
  os << r->keyData << " ";        // visit
  PreOrder(r->ptrLeftChild, os);  // left subtree
  PreOrder(r->ptrRightChild, os); // right subtree
 }
 return os;
}

/**************************************************************/
/*                                                            */
/* InOrderTraversal: uses recursion to visit left, this, right */
/*                                                            */
/**************************************************************/
template <class T>
ostream& AVLTree<T>::InOrderTraversal (ostream& os) {
 return RecursiveInOrder(root, os);
}

/**************************************************************/
/*                                                            */
```

```
/* RecursiveInOrder: visits left, parent, right nodes           */
/*                                                              */
/****************************************************************/
template <class T>
ostream& AVLTree<T>::RecursiveInOrder (TreeNode<T>* ptrroot,
                                        ostream& os) const {
 if (ptrroot)  {
  RecursiveInOrder(ptrroot->ptrLeftChild, os);   // left subtree
  os << ptrroot->keyData << " ";                  // visit
  RecursiveInOrder(ptrroot->ptrRightChild, os);  // right subtree
 }
 return os;
}

/****************************************************************/
/*                                                              */
/* PostOrderTraveral: uses recursion to visit left, right, this*/
/*                                                              */
/****************************************************************/
template <class T>
ostream& AVLTree<T>::PostOrderTraversal (ostream& os) {
 return RecursivePostOrder (root, os);
}

/****************************************************************/
/*                                                              */
/* RecursivePostOrder: visits left, right, parent nodes        */
/*                                                              */
/****************************************************************/
template <class T>
ostream& AVLTree<T>::RecursivePostOrder (TreeNode<T>* ptrroot,
                                          ostream& os) const {
 if (ptrroot) {
  RecursivePostOrder(ptrroot->ptrLeftChild, os); // left subtree
  RecursivePostOrder(ptrroot->ptrRightChild, os);// right subtree
  os << ptrroot->keyData << " ";                  // visit
 }
 return os;
}

/****************************************************************/
/*                                                              */
/* LevelOrderTraversal: visits nodes at same level before child*/
/*                                                              */
/****************************************************************/
template <class T>
ostream& AVLTree<T>::LevelOrderTraversal (ostream& os) {
 Queue<TreeNode<T>*> q;
 TreeNode<T>* workptr = root;
 while (workptr != NULL)  {
  os << workptr->keyData << " ";        // visit
  if (workptr->ptrLeftChild)
   q.Enqueue (workptr->ptrLeftChild);   // add left subtree
  if (workptr->ptrRightChild)
   q.Enqueue (workptr->ptrRightChild); // add right subtree
  if (!q.IsEmpty() ) {
```

```
   workptr = q.GetFront();    // get next level, starting at left
   q.Dequeue ();              // remove this node from the queue
  }
  else
   break;
 }
 return os;
}

/***************************************************************/
/*                                                             */
/* operator=: copies a tree                                    */
/*                                                             */
/***************************************************************/
template <class T>
AVLTree<T>& AVLTree<T>::operator= (const AVLTree<T>& tree) {
 if (this == &tree)
  return *this;
 EmptyTree ();
 RecursiveCopyTree (tree.root, root);
 return *this;
}

/***************************************************************/
/*                                                             */
/* AVLTree: copy ctor copies a tree                            */
/*                                                             */
/***************************************************************/
template <class T>
AVLTree<T>::AVLTree (const AVLTree<T>& tree) {
 RecursiveCopyTree (tree.root, root);
}

/***************************************************************/
/*                                                             */
/* RecursiveCopyTree: makes this a duplicate of passed tree    */
/*                                                             */
/***************************************************************/
template <class T>
void AVLTree<T>::RecursiveCopyTree (TreeNode<T>* ptrOldTree,
                          TreeNode<T>*& ptrNewTree) {
 // preorder traversal logic, Visit (copy node), Left, Right
 if (ptrOldTree) {
  ptrNewTree = MakeNewNode (ptrOldTree->keyData);
  if (!ptrNewTree) {

  }
  ptrNewTree->balanceFactor = ptrOldTree->balanceFactor;
  ptrNewTree->ptrLeftChild = ptrOldTree->ptrLeftChild;
  ptrNewTree->ptrRightChild = ptrOldTree->ptrRightChild;

  // recursively traverse through nodes
  RecursiveCopyTree (ptrOldTree->ptrLeftChild,
                     ptrNewTree->ptrLeftChild);
  RecursiveCopyTree (ptrOldTree->ptrRightChild,
                     ptrNewTree->ptrRightChild);
```

```
 }
 else
  ptrNewTree = 0;
}

/***************************************************************/
/*                                                             */
/* GetTreeHeight: returns height of the tree using recursion   */
/*                                                             */
/***************************************************************/
template <class T>
long AVLTree<T>::GetTreeHeight() const {
 return RecursiveHeightOfNodes (root);
}

/***************************************************************/
/*                                                             */
/* RecursiveHeightOfNodes: returns the height of all nodes     */
/*                                                             */
/***************************************************************/
template <class T>
long AVLTree<T>::RecursiveHeightOfNodes (TreeNode<T>* ptrroot)
                                                       const {
 if (!ptrroot) return 0;
 long leftHeight = RecursiveHeightOfNodes(ptrroot->ptrLeftChild);
 long rightHeight=RecursiveHeightOfNodes(ptrroot->ptrRightChild);
 return (leftHeight > rightHeight) ?
        leftHeight + 1 : rightHeight + 1;
}

/***************************************************************/
/*                                                             */
/* DisplayTree: simple display of the tree structure           */
/*                                                             */
/***************************************************************/
template <class T>
ostream& AVLTree<T>::DisplayTree (ostream& os) {
 os << "Depth (0 is root node)\n\n";
 RecursiveDisplayTree (root, 0, os);
 return os;
}

/***************************************************************/
/*                                                             */
/* RecursiveDisplayTree: shows all left, parent, all right     */
/*                                                             */
/***************************************************************/
template <class T>
void  AVLTree<T>::RecursiveDisplayTree (TreeNode<T>* ptrroot,
                                        int depth, ostream& os) {
 if (!ptrroot) return;
 RecursiveDisplayTree (ptrroot->ptrRightChild, depth + 1, os);
 os << setw(3) << depth;
 for (int i=0; i<=depth; i++) os << "....";
 os << setw(3) << ptrroot->keyData;
 if (ptrroot->balanceFactor == LeftHigh) os << " (LH)\n";
```

```
 else if (ptrroot->balanceFactor == RightHigh) os << " (RH)\n";
 else os << " (EH)\n";
 RecursiveDisplayTree (ptrroot->ptrLeftChild, depth + 1, os);
}

/***************************************************************/
/*                                                             */
/* MakeNewNode: allocates a new node; returns 0 if out of mem  */
/*                                                             */
/***************************************************************/
template <class T>
TreeNode<T>* AVLTree<T>::MakeNewNode (const T& newitem) {
 TreeNode<T>* ptrnewnode;
 try {
  ptrnewnode = new TreeNode<T>;
 }
 catch (std::bad_alloc e) {
  cerr << "Error: out of memory in MakeNewNode of AVLTree\n";
  return 0;
 }
 ptrnewnode->keyData = newitem; // store user's data in node
 ptrnewnode->balanceFactor = EvenHigh;// set balance factor to EH
 ptrnewnode->ptrLeftChild  = 0; // set left child to 0
 ptrnewnode->ptrRightChild = 0; // set right child to 0
 return ptrnewnode;
}

/***************************************************************/
/*                                                             */
/* Insert: adds a new node to the tree                         */
/*         returns Ok, OutOfMemory, DuplicateKey               */
/*         does not add duplicate keys to tree                 */
/*                                                             */
/***************************************************************/
template <class T>
ReturnCode AVLTree<T>::Insert (const T& newkeydata) {
 TreeNode<T>* ptrnewnode = MakeNewNode (newkeydata);
 if (!ptrnewnode) return OutOfMemory;
 bool taller = true;
 ReturnCode retcd = Ok;
 root = RecursiveInsert (root, ptrnewnode, taller, retcd);
 return retcd;
}

/***************************************************************/
/*                                                             */
/* RecursiveInsert: uses recursion to find the insertion point */
/*                                                             */
/***************************************************************/
template <class T>
TreeNode<T>* AVLTree<T>::RecursiveInsert (TreeNode<T>* ptrroot,
                                TreeNode<T>*  ptrnewnode,
                                bool& taller,
                                ReturnCode& retcd) {
 if (!ptrroot) {
  ptrroot = ptrnewnode;
```

```
  taller = true;
  return ptrroot;
 }
 if (ptrnewnode->keyData == ptrroot->keyData) {
  retcd = DuplicateKey;
  return ptrroot;
 }
 if (ptrnewnode->keyData < ptrroot->keyData) {
  ptrroot->ptrLeftChild = RecursiveInsert (ptrroot->ptrLeftChild,
                                           ptrnewnode, taller, retcd);
  if (taller) {
   if (ptrroot->balanceFactor == LeftHigh) {
    ptrroot = LeftBalanceOnInsert (ptrroot, taller);
   }
   else if (ptrroot->balanceFactor == EvenHigh) {
    ptrroot->balanceFactor = LeftHigh;
   }
   else {
    ptrroot->balanceFactor = EvenHigh;
    taller = false;
   }
  }
 }
 else {
  ptrroot->ptrRightChild = RecursiveInsert (
             ptrroot->ptrRightChild, ptrnewnode, taller, retcd);
  if (taller) {
   if (ptrroot->balanceFactor == LeftHigh) {
    ptrroot->balanceFactor = EvenHigh;
    taller = false;
   }
   else if (ptrroot->balanceFactor == EvenHigh) {
    ptrroot->balanceFactor = RightHigh;
   }
   else {
    ptrroot = RightBalanceOnInsert (ptrroot, taller);
   }
  }
 }
 return ptrroot;
}

/***************************************************************/
/*                                                             */
/* LeftBalanceOnInsert:                                        */
/*                                                             */
/***************************************************************/
template <class T>
TreeNode<T>* AVLTree<T>::LeftBalanceOnInsert (
                            TreeNode<T>* ptrroot, bool& taller) {
 TreeNode<T>* ptrLeftChildTree = ptrroot->ptrLeftChild;
 if (ptrLeftChildTree->balanceFactor == LeftHigh) {
  ptrroot->balanceFactor = EvenHigh;
  ptrLeftChildTree->balanceFactor = EvenHigh;
  ptrroot = RotateRight (ptrroot);
  taller = false;
```

```
  return ptrroot;
 }
 else if (ptrLeftChildTree->balanceFactor == EvenHigh) {
  cerr << "Error: Opps\n";
  exit (1);
 }
 TreeNode<T>* ptrRightChildTree =ptrLeftChildTree->ptrRightChild;
 if (ptrRightChildTree->balanceFactor == LeftHigh) {
  ptrroot->balanceFactor = RightHigh;
  ptrLeftChildTree->balanceFactor = EvenHigh;
 }
 else if (ptrRightChildTree->balanceFactor == EvenHigh) {
  ptrLeftChildTree->balanceFactor = EvenHigh;
  ptrroot->balanceFactor = EvenHigh;
 }
 else {
  ptrroot->balanceFactor = EvenHigh;
  ptrLeftChildTree->balanceFactor = LeftHigh;
 }
 ptrRightChildTree->balanceFactor = EvenHigh;
 ptrroot->ptrLeftChild = RotateLeft (ptrLeftChildTree);
 ptrroot = RotateRight (ptrroot);
 taller = false;
 return ptrroot;
}

/***************************************************************/
/*                                                             */
/* RightBalanceOnInsert:                                       */
/*                                                             */
/***************************************************************/
template <class T>
TreeNode<T>* AVLTree<T>::RightBalanceOnInsert (
                            TreeNode<T>* ptrroot, bool& taller) {
 TreeNode<T>* ptrLeftChildTree;
 TreeNode<T>* ptrRightChildTree = ptrroot->ptrRightChild;
 if (ptrRightChildTree->balanceFactor == LeftHigh) {
  ptrLeftChildTree = ptrRightChildTree->ptrLeftChild;
  if (ptrLeftChildTree->balanceFactor == LeftHigh) {
   ptrRightChildTree->balanceFactor = RightHigh;
   ptrroot->balanceFactor = EvenHigh;
  }
  else if (ptrLeftChildTree->balanceFactor == EvenHigh) {
   ptrroot->balanceFactor = EvenHigh;
   ptrRightChildTree->balanceFactor = EvenHigh;
  }
  else {
   ptrroot->balanceFactor = LeftHigh;
   ptrRightChildTree->balanceFactor = EvenHigh;
  }
  ptrLeftChildTree->balanceFactor = EvenHigh;
  ptrroot->ptrRightChild = RotateRight (ptrRightChildTree);
  ptrroot = RotateLeft (ptrroot);
  taller = false;
 }
 else if (ptrRightChildTree->balanceFactor == EvenHigh) {
```

```
   ptrroot->balanceFactor = EvenHigh;
   taller = false;
  }
 else {
   ptrroot->balanceFactor = EvenHigh;
   ptrRightChildTree->balanceFactor = EvenHigh;
   ptrroot = RotateLeft (ptrroot);
   taller = false;
  }
 return ptrroot;
}

/***************************************************************/
/*                                                             */
/* RotateRight:                                                */
/*                                                             */
/***************************************************************/
template <class T>
TreeNode<T>* AVLTree<T>::RotateRight (TreeNode<T>* ptrroot) {
 TreeNode<T>* ptrswap = ptrroot->ptrLeftChild;
 ptrroot->ptrLeftChild = ptrswap->ptrRightChild;
 ptrswap->ptrRightChild = ptrroot;
 return ptrswap;
}

/***************************************************************/
/*                                                             */
/* RotateLeft:                                                 */
/*                                                             */
/***************************************************************/
template <class T>
TreeNode<T>* AVLTree<T>::RotateLeft (TreeNode<T>* ptrroot) {
 TreeNode<T>* ptrswap = ptrroot->ptrRightChild;
 ptrroot->ptrRightChild = ptrswap->ptrLeftChild;
 ptrswap->ptrLeftChild = ptrroot;
 return ptrswap;
}

/***************************************************************/
/*                                                             */
/* Delete: removes node with matching key                      */
/*         returns Ok or KeyNotFound                           */
/*                                                             */
/***************************************************************/
template <class T>
ReturnCode AVLTree<T>::Delete (const T& findKey) {
 ReturnCode retcd;
 bool       smaller = true;
 TreeNode<T>* ptrnewroot = RecursiveDelete (root, findKey,
                                      smaller, retcd);
 if (retcd == Ok)
  root = ptrnewroot;
 return retcd;
}

/***************************************************************/
```

```
/*                                                              */
/* RecursiveDelete: uses recursion to find the node to delete   */
/*                                                              */
/***************************************************************/
template <class T>
TreeNode<T>* AVLTree<T>::RecursiveDelete (TreeNode<T>* ptrroot,
                             const T& findKey, bool& smaller,
                             ReturnCode& retcd) {
 if (!ptrroot) {
  smaller = false;
  retcd = KeyNotFound;
  return 0;
 }
 if (findKey < ptrroot->keyData) {
  ptrroot->ptrLeftChild = RecursiveDelete (ptrroot->ptrLeftChild,
                                       findKey, smaller, retcd);
  if (smaller)
   ptrroot = RightBalanceOnDelete (ptrroot, smaller);
  return ptrroot;
 }
 else if (findKey > ptrroot->keyData) {
  ptrroot->ptrRightChild = RecursiveDelete (
                ptrroot->ptrRightChild, findKey, smaller, retcd);
  if (smaller)
   ptrroot = LeftBalanceOnDelete (ptrroot, smaller);
  return ptrroot;
 }
 if (!ptrroot->ptrRightChild) {
  TreeNode<T>* ptrnewroot = ptrroot->ptrLeftChild;
  delete ptrroot;
  smaller = true;
  retcd = Ok;
  return ptrnewroot;
 }
 else if (!ptrroot->ptrLeftChild) {
  TreeNode<T>* ptrnewroot = ptrroot->ptrRightChild;
  delete ptrroot;
  smaller = true;
  retcd = Ok;
  return ptrnewroot;
 }
 else {
  TreeNode<T>* ptrswap = ptrroot->ptrLeftChild;
  while (ptrswap->ptrRightChild)
   ptrswap = ptrswap->ptrRightChild;
  ptrroot->keyData = ptrswap->keyData;
  ptrroot->ptrLeftChild = RecursiveDelete (ptrroot->ptrLeftChild,
   ptrswap->keyData, smaller, retcd);
  if (smaller)
   ptrroot = RightBalanceOnDelete (ptrroot, smaller);
  return ptrroot;
 }
}

/***************************************************************/
/*                                                              */
```

```
/* LeftBalanceOnDelete:                                         */
/*                                                              */
/***************************************************************/
template <class T>
TreeNode<T>* AVLTree<T>::LeftBalanceOnDelete (
                           TreeNode<T>* ptrroot, bool& smaller) {
 if (ptrroot->balanceFactor == RightHigh) {
  ptrroot->balanceFactor = EvenHigh;
  return ptrroot;
 }
 else if (ptrroot->balanceFactor == EvenHigh) {
  ptrroot->balanceFactor = LeftHigh;
  smaller = false;
  return ptrroot;
 }
 TreeNode<T>* ptrLeftChild = ptrroot->ptrLeftChild;
 if (ptrLeftChild->balanceFactor == LeftHigh) {
  ptrroot->balanceFactor = ptrLeftChild->balanceFactor =EvenHigh;
  ptrroot = RotateRight (ptrroot);
  return ptrroot;
 }
 else if (ptrLeftChild->balanceFactor == EvenHigh) {
  ptrroot->balanceFactor = LeftHigh;
  ptrLeftChild->balanceFactor = RightHigh;
  smaller = false;
  ptrroot = RotateRight (ptrroot);
  return ptrroot;
 }
 TreeNode<T>* ptrRightChild = ptrLeftChild->ptrRightChild;
 if (ptrRightChild->balanceFactor == LeftHigh) {
  ptrroot->balanceFactor = RightHigh;
  ptrLeftChild->balanceFactor = EvenHigh;
 }
 else if (ptrRightChild->balanceFactor == EvenHigh) {
  ptrroot->balanceFactor = ptrLeftChild->balanceFactor =EvenHigh;
 }
 else {
  ptrroot->balanceFactor = EvenHigh;
  ptrLeftChild->balanceFactor = LeftHigh;
 }
 ptrRightChild->balanceFactor = EvenHigh;
 ptrroot->ptrLeftChild = RotateLeft (ptrLeftChild);
 ptrroot = RotateRight (ptrroot);
 return ptrroot;
}

/***************************************************************/
/*                                                              */
/* RightBalanceOnDelete:                                        */
/*                                                              */
/***************************************************************/
template <class T>
TreeNode<T>* AVLTree<T>::RightBalanceOnDelete (
                           TreeNode<T>* ptrroot, bool& smaller) {
 if (ptrroot->balanceFactor == LeftHigh) {
  ptrroot->balanceFactor = EvenHigh;
```

```
  return ptrroot;
 }
 else if (ptrroot->balanceFactor == EvenHigh) {
  ptrroot->balanceFactor = RightHigh;
  smaller = false;
  return ptrroot;
 }
 TreeNode<T>* ptrRightChild = ptrroot->ptrRightChild;
 if (ptrRightChild->balanceFactor == LeftHigh) {
  TreeNode<T>* ptrLeftChild = ptrRightChild->ptrLeftChild;
  if (ptrLeftChild->balanceFactor == LeftHigh) {
   ptrRightChild->balanceFactor = RightHigh;
   ptrroot->balanceFactor = EvenHigh;
  }
  else if (ptrLeftChild->balanceFactor == EvenHigh) {
   ptrroot->balanceFactor = EvenHigh;
   ptrRightChild->balanceFactor = EvenHigh;
  }
  else {
   ptrroot->balanceFactor = LeftHigh;
   ptrRightChild->balanceFactor = EvenHigh;
  }
  ptrLeftChild->balanceFactor = EvenHigh;
  ptrroot->ptrRightChild = RotateRight (ptrRightChild);
  ptrroot = RotateLeft (ptrroot);
 }
 else {
  if (ptrRightChild->balanceFactor != EvenHigh) {
   ptrroot->balanceFactor = EvenHigh;
   ptrRightChild->balanceFactor = EvenHigh;
  }
  else {
   ptrroot->balanceFactor = RightHigh;
   ptrRightChild->balanceFactor = LeftHigh;
   smaller = false;
  }
  ptrroot = RotateLeft (ptrroot);
 }
 return ptrroot;
}
```

As you look over the implementation, most of the simpler functions are directly extracted from the earlier Tree class or are very simple one-liners. However, the **DisplayTree** function is a bit abstract without seeing what it produces. Here is a sample of what it produces.

```
Depth (0 is root node)

  3................400 (EH)
  2............350 (EH)
  3................300 (EH)
  1........200 (RH)
  2............100 (EH)
  0.... 50 (RH)
  2............ 40 (EH)
  1........ 10 (EH)
  2............  5 (EH)
```

It is the tree turned onto its side. We can see the key values and the balance factor abbreviations along with the node depth or level, 0 being the root of the AVL tree.

The Value of Instruction Comments

Have you noticed the total lack of instruction comments on the **Insert** and **Delete** and related recursive functions? It is intentional on my part. All through my various textbooks and ebooks, I always have tried to thoroughly document the sample programs so that you, the reader, could more easily understand and follow the coding sequences. However, I know for a fact that only a tiny percentage of my students actually well document their own student programming assignments. So this time I am going to attempt one last time to drive home the value of a well documented program. As you study these functions' implementations, see how much harder it is to actually read and understand what is going on. These are **not** easy functions to understand, particularly without any documentation.

Insertions are done at a leaf node just as in a binary tree. After allocating a new node to be inserted and placing the client's data in it, the next step is to find where the new node should be placed. This is done by recursively hunting down the tree, checking whether a node's key is greater than or less than the new key to be inserted, until at last we arrive at the bottom, where **ptrroot** is now null or 0. Here is where we then insert the new node.

However, the insertion of a new node is likely to cause the depth to grow, so taller is set to true. Now on the recursive back out return portion, the balance factors are adjusted and any needed rotations done to maintain the AVL tree properties.

Notice that I do not allow a duplicate key to be added to the tree. And out of memory checks are also trapped. So this class should be fairly bullet-proof.

Your instructor will very likely at this point use a set of Power Point slides to illustrate the actions occurring during the insertion and deletion operations. Also, since one of the Stop Exercises is to fully document the instructions in the **Insert** and **Delete** and related recursive functions, I will leave the discussion at this point.

Let's examine a Tester program, **Pgm12a**. A good tester program should thoroughly test the program. I purposely have not done that. There are some combinations that I left out of the testing phase. These are also the subject of a Stop Exercise. First, let's see what the output of **Pgm12a** looks like.

Output from Pgm12a

```
Starting with this tree
100 200

200 100 300

Depth (0 is root node)

  1........300 (EH)
  0....200 (EH)
  1........100 (EH)

Press any key to continue...


After 300 insert
increases height of right subtree of right subtree
Tree should be
200 100 300.
 200 100 300

After 50 insert,
tree should be
200 100 300 50.
200 100 300 50

```

```
After 10 insert
increase height of left subtree of a left subtree
a left child. Tree should be
200 50 300 10 100.
200 50 300 10 100

Depth (0 is root node)

  1........300 (EH)
  0....200 (LH)
  2............100 (EH)
  1........ 50 (EH)
  2............ 10 (EH)

Press any key to continue...


After 40 insert
increase height of left subtree of left subtree
a right child  tree should be
50 10 200 40 100 300
50 10 200 40 100 300

Inserting 5, then inserting 400,
tree should be
50 10 200 5 40 100 300 400.
50 10 200 5 40 100 300 400

After 350 insert
increase height of right tree by adding left child
tree should be
50 10 200 5 40 100 350 300 400
50 10 200 5 40 100 350 300 400

Depth (0 is root node)

  3................400 (EH)
  2............350 (EH)
  3................300 (EH)
  1........200 (RH)
  2............100 (EH)
  0.... 50 (RH)
  2............ 40 (EH)
  1........ 10 (EH)
  2............  5 (EH)

Press any key to continue...


After 225 insert
tree should be
50 10 300 5 40 200 350 100 225 400
50 10 300 5 40 200 350 100 225 400

After 250 insert
tree should be
```

```
200 50 300 10 100 225 350 5 40 250 400
200 50 300 10 100 225 350 5 40 250 400

After 35 insert
Tree should be
200 40 300 10 50 225 350 5 35 100 250 400
200 40 300 10 50 225 350 5 35 100 250 400

Depth (0 is root node)

  3................400 (EH)
  2............350 (RH)
  1........300 (EH)
  3................250 (EH)
  2............225 (RH)
  0....200 (EH)
  3................100 (EH)
  2............ 50 (RH)
  1........ 40 (EH)
  3................ 35 (EH)
  2............ 10 (EH)
  3................  5 (EH)

Press any key to continue...


There should be 12 nodes in the tree. Calling GetNumberNodes().
There are 12 nodes in the tree.

Press any key to continue...

now deleting all nodes.
There are 0 nodes in the tree.


Press any key to continue...


Rebuilding tree, insert 500, 300, then 400.

After 400 insert
tree should be
400 300 500.
400 300 500

400 300 500 200

400 300 500 200 600

400 300 500 200 350 600

400 300 500 200 350 600 310

400 300 500 200 350 600 310 380

Now insert 200, 600, 350, 310, 380, 100
```

```
tree should be
400 300 500 200 350 600 100 310 380
400 300 500 200 350 600 100 310 380

After 370 insert, (LR rotation, case -1)
tree should be
350 300 400 200 310 380 500 100 370 600
350 300 400 200 310 380 500 100 370 600

Depth (0 is root node)

  3................600 (EH)
  2............500 (RH)
  1........400 (EH)
  2............380 (LH)
  3................370 (EH)
  0....350 (EH)
  2............310 (EH)
  1........300 (LH)
  2............200 (LH)
  3................100 (EH)

Press any key to continue...


Testing copy constructor
avltree 350 300 400 200 310 380 500 100 370 600
btree   350 300 400 200 310 380 500 100 370 600


Testing op=
treeb 350 300 400 200 310 380 500 100 370 600
treec 350 300 400 200 310 380 500 100 370 600

calling treec destructor, then treeb destructor...

Original avltree should still exist...
350 300 400 200 310 380 500 100 370 600


Press any key to continue...


Deleting all nodes and building new tree...

Delete 400
Tree before deletion:
300 200 400 100

after deleting 400, tree should be
200 100 300
200 100 300

Depth (0 is root node)

  1........300 (EH)
```

```
  0....200 (EH)
  1........100 (EH)

Press any key to continue...

Deleted all nodes and built this tree...
300 200 400 100 250

Delete 400
After deleting 400, tree should be
200 100 300 250
200 100 300 250

Depth (0 is root node)

  1........300 (LH)
  2............250 (EH)
  0....200 (RH)
  1........100 (EH)

Press any key to continue...


New tree should be
1000 500 2500 300 600 2000 3000 200 400 700 4000 100 250
1000 500 2500 300 600 2000 3000 200 400 700 4000 100 250

Delete 400
After deleting 400, tree should be
1000 500 2500 200 600 2000 3000 100 300 700 4000 250
1000 500 2500 200 600 2000 3000 100 300 700 4000 250

Depth (0 is root node)

  3................4000 (EH)
  2............3000 (RH)
  1........2500 (RH)
  2............2000 (EH)
  0....1000 (LH)
  3................700 (EH)
  2............600 (RH)
  1........500 (LH)
  3................300 (LH)
  4....................250 (EH)
  2............200 (RH)
  3................100 (EH)

Press any key to continue...


New tree:
1000 500 2500 300 600 2000 3000 200 400 700 4000 100 250

Delete 600After deleting 600, tree should be
1000 300 2500 200 500 2000 3000 100 250 400 700 4000
1000 300 2500 200 500 2000 3000 100 250 400 700 4000
```

```

Depth (0 is root node)

  3................4000 (EH)
  2............3000 (RH)
  1........2500 (RH)
  2............2000 (EH)
  0....1000 (EH)
  3................700 (EH)
  2............500 (EH)
  3................400 (EH)
  1........300 (EH)
  3................250 (EH)
  2............200 (EH)
  3................100 (EH)

Press any key to continue...


New tree:
1000 500 2500 300 600 3000 400

Delete 600

After deleting 600, tree should be
1000 400 2500 300 500 3000
1000 400 2500 300 500 3000

Depth (0 is root node)

  2............3000 (EH)
  1........2500 (RH)
  0....1000 (EH)
  2............500 (EH)
  1........400 (EH)
  2............300 (EH)

Press any key to continue...


tree should be
500 300 600 400
500 300 600 400

Delete 600
After deleting 600, tree should be
400 300 500
400 300 500

Depth (0 is root node)

  1........500 (EH)
  0....400 (EH)
  1........300 (EH)

Press any key to continue...
```

```
tree should be
1000 500 2000 400 600 1500 3000 300 550 700 1700 2500 4000 525 28
1000 500 2000 400 600 1500 3000 300 550 700 1700 2500 4000 525 28
Delete 2000
2500 will be the replacement node.
After deleting 2000, tree should be
1000 500 2500 400 600 1500 3000 300 550 700 1700 2800 4000 525
1000 500 2500 400 600 1700 3000 300 550 700 1500 2800 4000 525
Depth (0 is root node)
  3................4000 (EH)
  2............3000 (EH)
  3................2800 (EH)
  1........2500 (EH)
  2............1700 (LH)
  3................1500 (EH)
  0....1000 (LH)
  3................700 (EH)
  2............600 (LH)
  3................550 (LH)
  4....................525 (EH)
  1........500 (RH)
  2............400 (LH)
  3................300 (EH)
Press any key to continue...
New tree with only a root and right child
2000 3000
After deleting root 2000, tree is
3000
No Memory Leaks
```

Since there is a lot of output, even more lines if it were thoroughly tested, I decided to break it up into screen shots or about 24 lines at a time so one can see what is going on as the program is running. This is very useful when debugging. So we need a way to implement the famous "Press any key to continue..." situation.

There are a wide variety of ways to incorrectly implement this and only one correct one. You cannot just say extract a junk char instance. Why? Extraction skips over whitespace. Thus, the user would have to actually enter a letter and then press the enter key. Okay. How about using the **cin.get** function? Well, it comes closer. But the message does say **any** key. What happens if the user presses an arrow key or Alt-F1?

In the header file, **conio.h**, are the console and keyboard specific functions. One of these is called **_getch** for get a character from the keyboard. This is a DOS function, and does not correspond to the way C++ get function operates. Under DOS, when any function to acquire a keystroke is made, DOS has a major problem with the ASCII codes and the 101-Special keys. Since all of the ASCII codes are filled, DOS must use special codes for the extra keys on the keyboard, such as the arrow keys and Function keys. DOS handles this by returning the ASCII code if the user has pressed one of the normal keys. However, if the user has pressed any of the 101-Special keys, then DOS returns 0 and then will return that special key code as the next character to whomever requests the next keystroke from DOS!

So when you call **_getch**, this gets the next keystroke and returns it as a char. However, if it returns 0 or a 0xE0, then you must call **_getch** a second time to get the special key code that the user specified. Hence, the only correct way to implement the "Press any key to continue" operation is

```
int c = _getch();
if (!c || c == 0xE0) c = _getch();
```

This assumes that you do not want to save that keystroke. I encapsulated this whole operation in the **Pause** function in **Pgm12a**.

Here is the **Pgm12a** coding.

Pgm12a Tester Program for AVLTree

```
#include <iostream>
#include <iomanip>
#include <strstream>
#include <crtdbg.h>
#include <conio.h>

using namespace std;

#include "AVLTree.h"

struct KeyData {
 long key;
 char data[10];
 bool operator< (const KeyData& k) const;
 bool operator> (const KeyData& k) const;
 bool operator== (const KeyData& k) const;
 friend ostream& operator<< (ostream& os, const KeyData& k);
};
bool KeyData::operator< (const KeyData& k) const {
 return key < k.key;
}

bool KeyData::operator> (const KeyData& k) const {
 return key>k.key;
}

bool KeyData::operator== (const KeyData& k) const {
 return key==k.key;
}

ostream& operator<< (ostream& os, const KeyData& k) {
 return os << k.key;
}


void Pause ();

int main () {
 {
 AVLTree<KeyData> tree;
 KeyData k;

 k.key = 100;
 tree.Insert(k);
 k.key = 200;
```

```
tree.Insert(k);
cout << "Starting with this tree\n";
tree.LevelOrderTraversal(cout) << endl << endl;
k.key = 300;
tree.Insert(k);
tree.LevelOrderTraversal (cout) << endl << endl;
tree.DisplayTree (cout);
Pause ();

cout << "After 300 insert\n";
cout << "increases height of right subtree of right subtree\n";
cout << "Tree should be\n200 100 300.\n ";
tree.LevelOrderTraversal(cout) << endl << endl;
k.key = 50;
tree.Insert(k);
cout << "After 50 insert, \ntree should be \n200 100 300 50.\n";
tree.LevelOrderTraversal(cout) << endl << endl;
k.key = 10;
tree.Insert(k);

cout << "After 10 insert\n";
cout << "increase height of left subtree of a left subtree\n";
cout << "a left child. Tree should be\n200 50 300 10 100.\n";
tree.LevelOrderTraversal(cout) << endl << endl;
tree.DisplayTree (cout);
Pause();

k.key = 40;
tree.Insert(k);
cout << "After 40 insert\n";
cout << "increase height of left subtree of left subtree\n";
cout << "a right child  tree should be\n50 10 200 40 100 300\n";
tree.LevelOrderTraversal(cout) << endl << endl;

k.key = 5;
tree.Insert(k);
k.key = 400;
tree.Insert(k);
cout << "Inserting 5, then inserting 400, \n";
cout << "tree should be \n50 10 200 5 40 100 300 400.\n";
tree.LevelOrderTraversal(cout) << endl << endl;

k.key = 350;
tree.Insert(k);
cout << "After 350 insert\n";
cout << "increase height of right tree by adding left child\n";
cout << "tree should be \n50 10 200 5 40 100 350 300 400\n";
tree.LevelOrderTraversal(cout)<< endl << endl;
tree.DisplayTree (cout);
Pause();

k.key = 225;
tree.Insert(k);
cout << "After 225 insert\n";
cout << "tree should be \n50 10 300 5 40 200 350 100 225 400\n";
tree.LevelOrderTraversal(cout) << endl << endl;
```

```

k.key = 250;
tree.Insert(k);
cout << "After 250 insert\n";
cout <<
     "tree should be\n200 50 300 10 100 225 350 5 40 250 400\n";
tree.LevelOrderTraversal(cout) << endl << endl;

k.key = 35;
tree.Insert(k);
cout << "After 35 insert\n";
cout <<
   "Tree should be\n200 40 300 10 50 225 350 5 35 100 250 400\n";
tree.LevelOrderTraversal(cout) << endl << endl;
tree.DisplayTree (cout);
Pause ();

cout << "\nThere should be 12 nodes in the tree."
     << " Calling GetNumberNodes().\n";
cout << "There are " << tree.GetNumberOfNodes()
     << " nodes in the tree.\n";
Pause();

cout << "now deleting all nodes.\n";
tree.EmptyTree();
cout << "There are " << tree.GetNumberOfNodes()
     << " nodes in the tree.\n\n";
Pause();

cout << "Rebuilding tree, insert 500, 300, then 400.\n\n";
k.key = 500;
tree.Insert(k);
k.key = 300;
tree.Insert(k);
k.key = 400;
tree.Insert(k);
cout << "After 400 insert\n";
cout << "tree should be \n400 300 500.\n";
tree.LevelOrderTraversal(cout) << endl << endl;

k.key = 200;
tree.Insert(k);
tree.LevelOrderTraversal(cout) << endl << endl;
k.key = 600;
tree.Insert(k);
tree.LevelOrderTraversal(cout) << endl << endl;
k.key = 350;
tree.Insert(k);
tree.LevelOrderTraversal(cout) << endl << endl;
k.key = 310;
tree.Insert(k);
tree.LevelOrderTraversal(cout) << endl << endl;
k.key = 380;
tree.Insert(k);
tree.LevelOrderTraversal(cout) << endl << endl;
k.key = 100;
```

```
tree.Insert(k);
cout << "Now insert 200, 600, 350, 310, 380, 100\n";
cout << "tree should be\n400 300 500 200 350 600 100 310 380\n";
tree.LevelOrderTraversal(cout) << endl << endl;
k.key = 370;
tree.Insert(k);
cout << "After 370 insert, (LR rotation, case -1)\n";
cout <<
    "tree should be\n350 300 400 200 310 380 500 100 370 600\n";
tree.LevelOrderTraversal(cout) << endl << endl;
tree.DisplayTree (cout);
Pause();

// test copy constructor
{  // begin block of code for treeb
 AVLTree<KeyData> treeb(tree);
 cout << "\nTesting copy constructor\n";
 cout << "avltree ";
 tree.LevelOrderTraversal(cout);
 cout << "\nbtree   ";
 tree.LevelOrderTraversal(cout) << endl;

 // testing op=
 AVLTree<KeyData> treec;
 treec = treeb;
 cout << "\n\nTesting op=\n";
 cout << "treeb ";
 treeb.LevelOrderTraversal(cout) << endl;
 cout << "treec ";
 treec.LevelOrderTraversal(cout) << endl << endl;
 cout << "calling treec destructor, then treeb destructor...\n";
}  // end block of code for treeb and treec

cout << "\nOriginal avltree should still exist...\n";
tree.LevelOrderTraversal(cout) << endl << endl;
Pause();

tree.EmptyTree();
cout << "Deleting all nodes and building new tree...\n\n";
k.key = 300;
tree.Insert(k);
k.key = 200;
tree.Insert(k);
k.key = 400;
tree.Insert(k);
k.key = 100;
tree.Insert(k);
cout << "Delete 400\nTree before deletion:\n";
tree.LevelOrderTraversal(cout) << endl << endl;
k.key = 400;
tree.Delete(k);
cout << "after deleting 400, tree should be\n200 100 300\n";
tree.LevelOrderTraversal(cout) << endl << endl;
tree.DisplayTree (cout);
tree.EmptyTree();
Pause();
```

```
 // rebuild tree
 k.key = 300;
 tree.Insert(k);
 k.key = 200;
 tree.Insert(k);
 k.key = 400;
 tree.Insert(k);
 k.key = 100;
 tree.Insert(k);
 k.key = 250;
 tree.Insert(k);
 cout << "Deleted all nodes and built this tree...\n";
 tree.LevelOrderTraversal(cout) << endl << endl;
 cout << "Delete 400\n";
 k.key = 400;
 tree.Delete(k);
 cout << "After deleting 400, tree should be\n200 100 300 250\n";
 tree.LevelOrderTraversal(cout) << endl << endl;
 tree.DisplayTree (cout);
 tree.EmptyTree();
 Pause();

 // rebuild tree
 k.key = 1000;
 tree.Insert(k);
 k.key = 500;
 tree.Insert(k);
 k.key = 2000;
 tree.Insert(k);
 k.key = 300;
 tree.Insert(k);
 k.key = 600;
 tree.Insert(k);
 k.key = 3000;
 tree.Insert(k);
 k.key = 2500;
 tree.Insert(k);
 k.key = 200;
 tree.Insert(k);
 k.key = 400;
 tree.Insert(k);
 k.key = 700;
 tree.Insert(k);
 k.key = 4000;
 tree.Insert(k);
 k.key = 100;
 tree.Insert(k);
 k.key = 250;
 tree.Insert(k);
 cout << "New tree should be\n"
 << "1000 500 2500 300 600 2000 3000 200 400 700 4000 100 250\n";
 tree.LevelOrderTraversal(cout) << endl << endl;
 cout << "Delete 400\n";
 k.key = 400;
 tree.Delete(k);
```

```
cout << "After deleting 400, tree should be\n";
cout <<"1000 500 2500 200 600 2000 3000 100 300 700 4000 250\n";
tree.LevelOrderTraversal(cout) << endl << endl;
tree.DisplayTree (cout);
tree.EmptyTree();
Pause();

// rebuild tree
k.key = 1000;
tree.Insert(k);
k.key = 500;
tree.Insert(k);
k.key = 2000;
tree.Insert(k);
k.key = 300;
tree.Insert(k);
k.key = 600;
tree.Insert(k);
k.key = 3000;
tree.Insert(k);
k.key = 2500;
tree.Insert(k);
k.key = 200;
tree.Insert(k);
k.key = 400;
tree.Insert(k);
k.key = 700;
tree.Insert(k);
k.key = 4000;
tree.Insert(k);
k.key = 100;
tree.Insert(k);
k.key = 250;
tree.Insert(k);
cout << "New tree:\n";
tree.LevelOrderTraversal(cout) << endl << endl;
cout << "Delete 600";
k.key = 600;
tree.Delete(k);
cout << "After deleting 600, tree should be\n";
cout <<"1000 300 2500 200 500 2000 3000 100 250 400 700 4000\n";
tree.LevelOrderTraversal(cout) << endl << endl;
tree.DisplayTree (cout);
tree.EmptyTree();
Pause();

k.key = 1000;
tree.Insert(k);
k.key = 500;
tree.Insert(k);
k.key = 2500;
tree.Insert(k);
k.key = 300;
tree.Insert(k);
k.key = 600;
tree.Insert(k);
```

```
k.key = 3000;
tree.Insert(k);
k.key = 400;
tree.Insert(k);
cout << "New tree:\n";
tree.LevelOrderTraversal(cout) << endl << endl;
cout << "Delete 600\n\n";
k.key = 600;
tree.Delete(k);
cout << "After deleting 600, tree should be\n";
cout << "1000 400 2500 300 500 3000\n";
tree.LevelOrderTraversal(cout) << endl << endl;
tree.DisplayTree (cout);
tree.EmptyTree();
Pause();

k.key = 500;
tree.Insert(k);
k.key = 300;
tree.Insert(k);
k.key = 600;
tree.Insert(k);
k.key = 400;
tree.Insert(k);
cout << "tree should be\n500 300 600 400\n";
tree.LevelOrderTraversal(cout) << endl << endl;
cout << "Delete 600\n";
k.key = 600;
tree.Delete(k);
cout << "After deleting 600, tree should be\n";
cout << "400 300 500\n";
tree.LevelOrderTraversal(cout) << endl << endl;
tree.DisplayTree (cout);
tree.EmptyTree();
Pause();

// rebuild tree
k.key = 1000;
tree.Insert(k);
k.key = 500;
tree.Insert(k);
k.key = 2000;
tree.Insert(k);
k.key = 400;
tree.Insert(k);
k.key = 600;
tree.Insert(k);
k.key = 1500;
tree.Insert(k);
k.key = 3000;
tree.Insert(k);
k.key = 300;
tree.Insert(k);
k.key = 550;
tree.Insert(k);
k.key = 700;
```

```
 tree.Insert(k);
 k.key = 4000;
 tree.Insert(k);
 k.key = 525;
 tree.Insert(k);
 k.key = 2500;
 tree.Insert(k);
 k.key = 1700;
 tree.Insert(k);
 k.key = 2800;
 tree.Insert(k);
 cout << "tree should be\n"
      << "1000 500 2000 400 600 1500 3000 300 550 700 "
      << "1700 2500 4000 525 2800\n";
 tree.LevelOrderTraversal(cout) << endl << endl;
 cout << "Delete 2000\n";
 cout << "2500 will be the replacement node.\n\n";
 k.key = 2000;
 tree.Delete(k);
 cout << "After deleting 2000, tree should be\n";
 cout << "1000 500 2500 400 600 1500 3000 300 550 700"
      << " 1700 2800 4000 525\n";
 tree.LevelOrderTraversal(cout) << endl << endl;
 tree.DisplayTree (cout);
 tree.EmptyTree();
 Pause();

 // rebuild tree
 k.key = 2000;
 tree.Insert(k);
 k.key = 3000;
 tree.Insert(k);
 cout << "New tree with only a root and right child\n";
 tree.LevelOrderTraversal(cout) << endl << endl;
 k.key = 2000;
 tree.Delete(k);
 cout << "After deleting root 2000, tree is\n";
 tree.LevelOrderTraversal(cout) << endl << endl;
 k.key = 3000;
 tree.Delete(k);
 tree.EmptyTree();
 }

 if (_CrtDumpMemoryLeaks())
  cout << "\nOops! Memory Leaks!!\n";
 else
  cout << "\nNo Memory Leaks\n";

 return 0;
}

/***************************************************************/
/*                                                             */
/* Pause: press any key to continue helper function            */
/*                                                             */
/***************************************************************/
```

```

void Pause() {
 cout << "\nPress any key to continue..." << endl;
 int c = _getch();
 if (!c || c == 0xE0) c = _getch();
 system("cls");
}
```

You now have a generic AVL tree class on which you can base your future needs.

Review Questions

1. What is a b-tree?

2. Why do we need b-trees in the first place? What benefits do they offer?

3. What is the purpose of having more than one set of user key-data in a single tree node?

4. Explain how the 2-3 tree works. Use appropriate drawings not shown in the ebook.

5. Explain how a new user key-data item is added to an M-way tree.

6. Explain how a key is deleted from an M-way tree.

7. What is an AVL tree? How does it differ from a b-tree and an M-way tree?

8. What is meant by the balance factor of an AVL tree? What is meant my Left High, Equal High, and Right High?

9. Why are rotations necessary in an AVL tree during insertions and deletions?

10. Under what circumstances is a double rotation needed when inserting into an AVL tree? Would a double rotation ever be needed when a key is deleted?

11. What purpose does using an .inl file have in programming?

Stop! Do These Exercises Before Programming

Because both of these questions are rather time-consuming, I am limiting the number of Stop Exercises for this chapter to these two.

1. To ensure that you understand the logic behind the AVL tree insertions and deletions, add any needed comments to the instructions of the **Insert**, **Delete**, and the recursive functions these two call in the AVLTree.inl file.

2. Now examine the **Pgm12a** tester program. It does not fully test all of the rotations and node possibilities. Work out a testing oracle that would indeed fully test this **AVLTree** class. This is a rather extensive question, but well worth your time. It develops your skill in proving programs correct or not.

Programming Problems

Problem Pgm12-1 The Friend's Phone Directory

Create a data file containing at least 20 friend's names and their phone numbers. The format should be as follows.
"firstname" "lastname" areacode phonenumber
"Sam" "Spade" 309 699-9999
The first and last names can be a maximum of 20 characters long. Both phone numbers should be stored as integers.

Now write a client program that begins by loading your file of friends into an AVL tree. Use the AVL tree given in this chapter. You are writing a client program that uses it.

Next, present the user with a menu to list all friends, add a new friend, update a friend, save the data to a new file, and to quit. The key for the AVL tree is a dual one, that is, it is last name but if the last names are the same, the first name is used as well to differentiate them.

Fully test the client program.

Problem 12-2 The Indexer Program

Look over this chapter and make a list of the main keywords used in this chapter, words that you would expect to find in the index of the book. Then, enter them into a file, one on a line.

Write a client program that inputs that index file into an AVL tree, using the implementation given in this chapter.

The client program then inputs the text version of a portion of this chapter, **Pgm12a-chapter.txt**, that I have provided. Perform the indexing operation. For the key data in the tree, no duplicates are allowed. This means that should you find more than one occurrence of a specific index word on a page, that page is only included one time in the index.

For your node structure, and to keep the problem somewhat simplified, use the following.

```
struct Index {
 char keyword[21];
 int pageOccurrence[100];
 int numPageOccurrences;
};
```

Here **numPageOccurrences** is the number of elements in the **pageOccurrence** array which stores which pages this keyword occurs. Initialize them to 0.

With the index loaded and all nodes initialized to zero, begin inputting the text file and looking for words that match. For simplicity, a word is defined as any consecutive series of letters and the dash. Thus, twenty-one would be considered a single word. If a given word from the page is contained in the index AVL tree, store the page number in the next slot in the array and increment the number in that word's array.

The first line of each new page begins:
Page nnn
That is, the keyword "Page" followed by one blank and then the number. There is no other text on these page number lines.

When you have processed the text file and built the index, then print the index out in the following format.

Word...3, 4, 5, 6, 7

This is saying that the word "Word" may be found on pages 3, 4, 5, 6, and 7.

There must be at least twenty words actually contained in your final index printout.

Chapter 13—Heaps, Priority Queues, and Graphs

Introduction

We have just explored the idea of a heap and how a heap can be used to create a fast sorting algorithm, the Heapsort. Heaps have many other uses, so next let's formalize the heap methods and utilize them to create a priority queue. In Beginning Data Structures, you may have designed a priority queue while doing one of the Stop Exercises. In a priority queue, the client's items are stored with some kind of retrieval priority. For example, a veterinarian could use a queue to schedule incoming patients normally on a first come-first handled basis. However, emergency cases can arrive which require immediate care—a "go to the head of the queue" type operation. Thus, when a new patient arrives at the veterinarian's clinic, they are added to a priority queue based upon their level of urgency. We will implement a priority queue class by using a heap approach.

The last, and most important topic of this chapter are that of graphs. Probably, when you hear the word "graphs" you immediately think of a two-dimensional graph with an x and y axis showing a plot of some kind. In data structures, a graph has a different meaning. Recall that in a binary tree, any given node has only one other node pointing to it, its parent. Further, any given node can point to, at most, two child nodes below it. However, we have seen that the general tree removes this last requirement; in a general tree, a node can have as many children as needed. Finally, if we also remove the idea that any given node can have only one parent pointing to it, we have the **graph data structure**.

In a graph, the nodes are called **vertices**. And the lines that connect the vertices (nodes) are called either **edges** or **arcs**. Further, the edges or lines connecting the vertices (nodes) can have some kind of weight or importance or significance attached to them. Additionally, each edge can have a direction associated with it. For example, examine an airline's flying schedule between cities. Between any given two cities, flights may go in both directions or maybe only from city A to city B and not from city B back to city A. This shows the idea of direction associated with the edges. The weight is likely the air distance between the connected cities (vertices). And this gets us to the importance of the graph data structure. Now we can answer questions such as "Can I fly from city A to city B?" "Among all the flights, what is the shortest route to take to get from city A to city B?"

Here is another example. Suppose that you want to plan a vacation from Peoria. You've decided to visit ten parks scattered around the country. In what order do you visit the parks? If you just travel from park to park in a random fashion, you may end up spending the whole vacation driving from place to place, from one side of the country to the other, back and forth. So you might wish to determine the order of visiting based on the least amount of driving time. Here the parks and Peoria represent the vertices (nodes), the routes between them are the edges, and the weight of each edge is the number of miles separating the two places. This is a graph. And we can write a simple program that outputs the order that we need to take to visit the park that involves the least number of miles driven.

Heaps

Let's review what we know about heaps from the Trees chapter and last chapter's Heapsort discussion. A **heap** is a complete binary tree in which the data stored in its nodes is arranged such that no child has a larger value than its parent. A complete binary tree is either full or full down to the next-to-the-last level with all of the leaves of the last level as far to the left as possible. Figure 13.1 shows a heap tree. Notice that it is a binary tree but not a searchable binary tree since all of the right child nodes are not less than the parent node and all of the left child nodes are not greater than the parent.

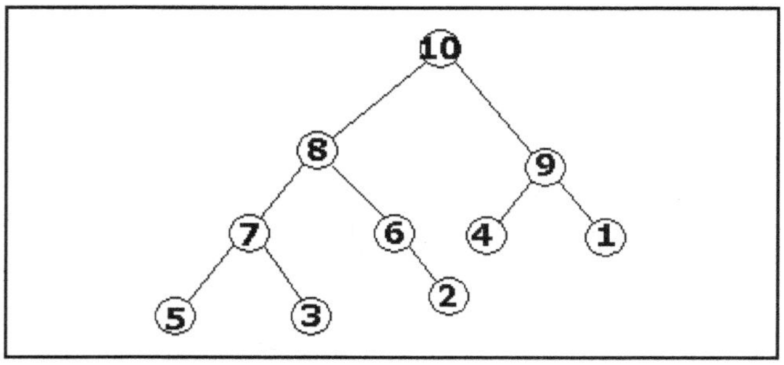

Figure 13.1 A Heap

Technically, a heap is a binary tree which is a complete binary tree and for every node in the heap, the value stored in that node is greater than or equal to the values stored in its children. This gives us the very useful property that the largest value is always stored in the root node!

Very often, an algorithm desires the maximum value. Here it is at a known location, the root node. So if we remove that maximum value, we are then left with a hole at the top of the tree. And the heap must be rebuilt. We have already seen how that can be done with Heapsort.

Recall that the Heapsort pretends the original array is a b-tree that is out of order. Figure 13.2 shows the initial array as if it were a heap tree. Of course, in the unsorted array, the nodes are out of order. That is, all values on the right side of a node are not all greater than that node's value while all nodes on the left side of a node are not all less than that node's value. Heapsort must then perform a "rebuild the heap downward" action to get the nodes in their proper order. The proper order is dictated by **array[node] >= array[node*2+1]** for the left side and **array[node] >= array[node*2+2]** for the right side. The action consists of going down each node and moving the elements around such that all the nodes on the right side of a given node are greater than the node and similarly with the left side. It begins at the top node and works its way to the bottom.

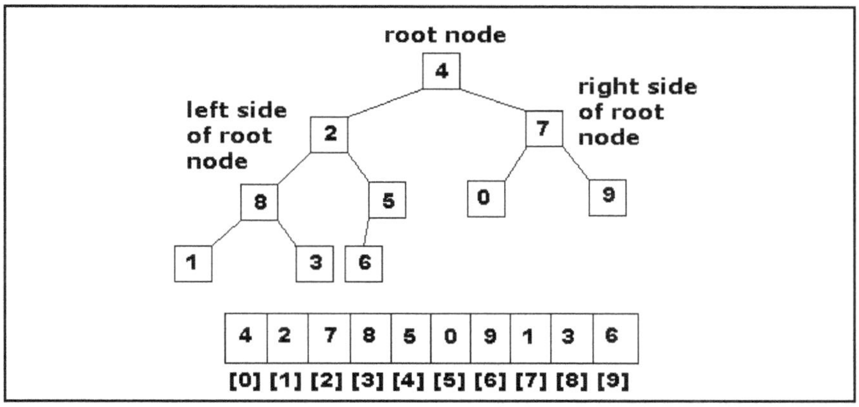

Figure 13.2 The Original Array to Be Sorted Viewed as a b-tree

Returning to the situation when the application has removed the maximum value, which is the root, we have a hole at the top as shown in Figure 13.3.

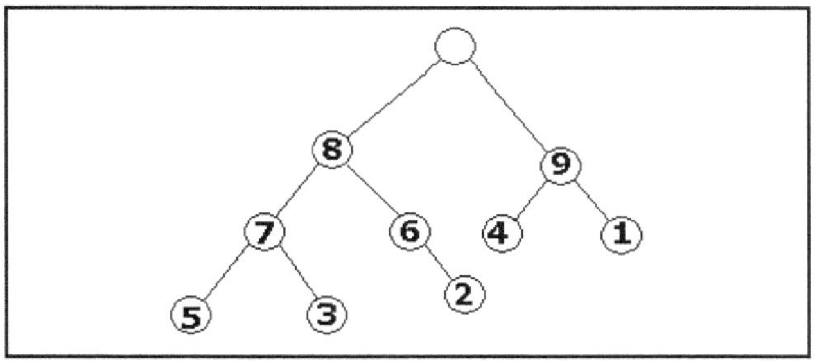

Figure 13.3 The Heap with Root Node Removed

Next, the heap must be restructured as a binary tree. To replace the value in the empty root node, remove and use the value in the rightmost node at the lowest depth or height of the tree. In this case, it is the node containing the value of 2 since it is the rightmost node of nodes 5, 3, and 2. This yields the tree shown in Figure 13.4.

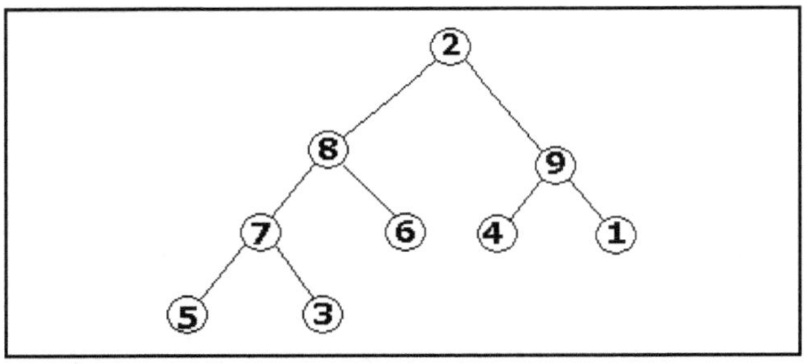

Figure 13.4 The Heap Tree with the New Root

Of course, the tree now does not satisfy the requirement that no child has a value greater than its parent. Obviously the two nodes containing the 8 and 9 are greater than the parent root node. Now a process called **Reheapify** or **RebuildHeapDownwards** must be done. This process consists of starting at the root and repeatedly exchanging its value with the larger value of its children until no more exchanges are possible. The reheapify process first compares the 2 to its two children, the 8 and 9, choosing the larger value, the 9. The 9 replaces the 2 and we get the results shown in Figure 13.5

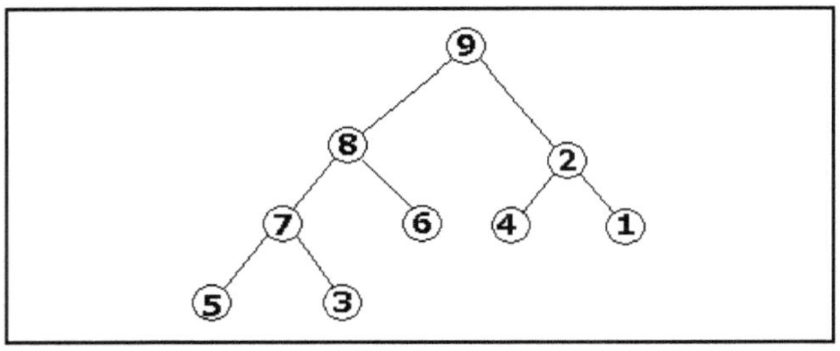

Figure 13.5 The Heap Tree After One Swap

We saw that the process must be recursive since now the node containing the value of 2 is not proper for a heap. So beginning with the new node containing the value 2, we find which of its children contain the larger value and swap once more. This yields the final reheapified tree shown in Figure 13.6.

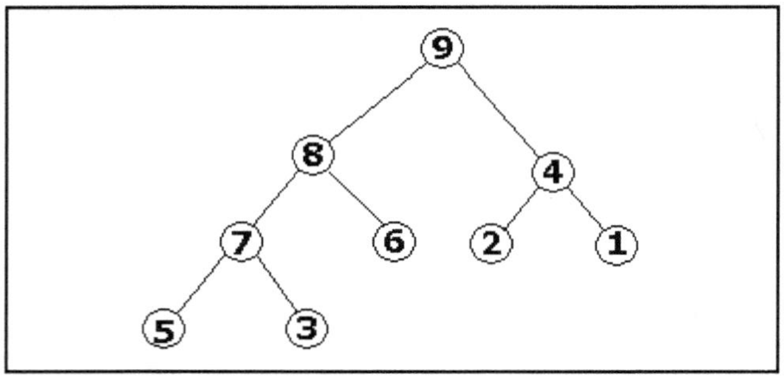

Figure 13.6 The Heap Tree After Reheapify

The **RebuildHeapDownwards** function from the Heapsort is passed the current root node. It compares the two leaves below it to find which one is the greater value and whose index is then stored in **maxChild**. If that found largest value is greater than the root's value, it swaps that **maxChild**'s value with the root's value. Then, it recursively calls itself using the index of **maxChild** as the next downward node.

```
void RebuildHeapDownward (int array[], long root, long bottom) {
 int temp;
 long maxChild;
 long leftChild  = root * 2 + 1;
 long rightChild = root * 2 + 2;
 if (leftChild <= bottom) {
  if (leftChild == bottom)
```

```
    maxChild = leftChild;
   else {
    if (array[leftChild] <= array[rightChild])
     maxChild = rightChild;
    else
     maxChild = leftChild;
   }
   if (array[root] < array[maxChild]) {
    temp = array[root];
    array[root] = array[maxChild];
    array[maxChild] = temp;
    RebuildHeapDownward (array, maxChild, bottom);
   }
  }
}
```

However, rebuilding the heap downward is only one half of the general problem. The other situation we must handle is how to insert a new item into the heap. Of course, this does not occur when sorting. If we want to add a new item to the heap, where do we place it? Because the tree must be a complete tree, we have no choice but to add that item at the bottom rightmost location in the tree. Remember that a complete binary tree is either full or full down to the next-to-the-last level with all of the leaves of the last level as far to the left as possible.

Suppose that we wish to add item 10 back into the heap. Figure 13.7 shows where we must insert it.

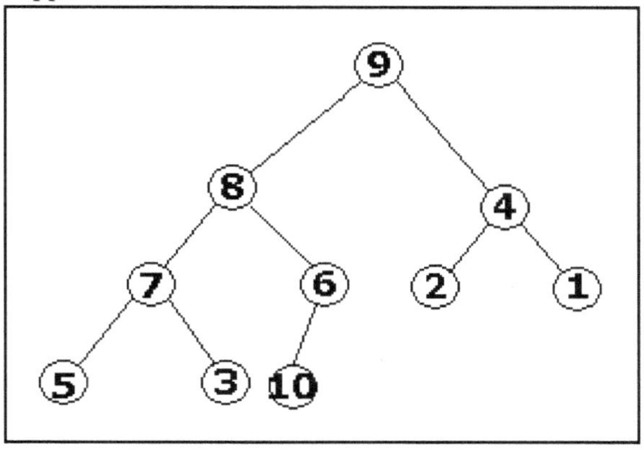

Figure 13.7 Inserting Item 10 into the Heap

Now the heap meets the first criteria, a complete binary tree, but it fails the second: for every node in the heap, the value stored in that node is greater than or equal to the values stored in its children. The 6 is not greater than the 10. Now we must rebuild the heap upwards to get the 10 where it belongs, at the root. The function is much simpler than the downward operation. First, for the node we are at, we must find our parent in order to compare our value to our parents and swap them if needed. Again the function is passed the root and the bottom indexes. The parent is given by (bottom – 1) /2.

```
void RebuildHeapUpward (int array[], long root, long bottom) {
 int temp;
 long parentNode;
 if (bottom <= root) return;
 parent = (bottom - 1) / 2;
 if (array[parent] < array[bottom]) {
  temp = array[parent];
  array[parent] = array[bottom];
  array[bottom] = temp;
  RebuildHeapUpward (array, root, parent);
 }
}
```

Implementation of a Heap

Thus, a heap has these two basic operations, rebuilding upwards or downwards. Now the question becomes how do we implement a heap in general? Do we make it a class or leave it as stand alone functions? How do we deal with the array of items? The last question is more readily answered. In the Heapsort, we just passed the array of integers to be sorted and the number in that array. Certainly, we must generalize this approach.

Could we pass a **void*** array of items? Yes, we could, but if we did so, we would force users to have to provide a callback function to perform the comparisons. Further, we must swap items in the array. Thus, we must also be passing the total size of the items so that we could dynamically allocate the temp area and use the **memcopy** function to perform the actual movement of data. If this is beginning to sound complicated to you, it should. We have reached a threshold of complexity at which storing generic **void*** to the user's data is no longer viable. The heap coding must know the data type of the user's data. Here is the first time that using templates really offers us great value. Our heap solution must be a template operation.

Do we make this a class or leave it as stand alone functions, perhaps as part of a structure? If we make it into a class, then other ADTs can derive from us and inherit our methods. However, if we do so, we must consider what additional operations a user might desire in their derived classes and provide virtual functions for them. If we fail to do so, then the client programs cannot use a base class pointer to invoke derived class functions. These considerations are best summarized by saying that the heap is really a fundamental building block for other ADTs and not really a stand-alone entity in and of itself. Thus, some designers choose to implement the heap as a structure which contains the dynamically allocated array of user items and the number of elements in that array along with the two heap operation functions. Functions can be members of a structure. All structure member functions have public access to all other structure members. And all members, whether data or methods, have public access to clients.

Thus, there is a strong argument for implementing our heap as a structure with the two heap functions as structure member methods. Other ADTs would then create an instance of the heap structure as one of its data members and directly manipulate and invoke the heap methods.

However, from an educational viewpoint, I think that illustrating how a **Heap** template class can be written is also useful, particularly later on when other ADTs wish to make use of it by creating instances of the **Heap** class or deriving from it. So here, we will embark on the construction of a **Heap** template class.

Let's assume that the user data is to be called **type T** as is usual with templates. The **Heap** class would contain then a dynamically allocated array of **type T** and a count of the number of elements in that array. Notice that it is not containing pointers to the user's data of **type T** but an actual instance of that type. This removes the burden on the user from allocating and deleting these instances.

But normally, the heap views the items as being in an array. Thus, we can go two ways. One is to begin with an empty array and provide functions to grow the array—that is, take the growable array approach. When there are many items to be added, this can be time consuming unless we store pointers to the user's data. A more restrictive approach is to have the constructor be passed the maximum array size and pre build the array that size but set the number of items in the heap to 0. Then, let the user add items to the heap, incrementing the count until the maximum array size is reached. Let's use this more restrictive approach because it is much easier to implement.

Next, consider how the user is to access items in the heap array itself. If we make the actual array protected, then we must also provide the requisite access functions and so on. With this particular class, it is going to be more difficult to predict the demands that client programs are going to make of it. If we cannot foresee what our client's will likely need in the way of access operations, later revisions of the class are inherent. Thus, here is a situation in which giving the array of items and the number of items currently in use public access. This way, the clients can access the array directly. Our heap class will make no attempt to maintain the heap order at all times. That is, if the user adds a new item to the heap, it is their responsibility to call the reheap building functions. This "gets us off the hook" so to speak. We construct and destroy the actual array and, when called, rebuild the heap. But the clients must handle inserting and removing elements from the array, subject to their verifying that they are not exceeding the maximum array size. The Heap class is then a skeletal class only.

It should have a constructor, but I default the maximum size so that the function can serve as the default ctor as well. The destructor is virtual in case of derivations. I provide simple access functions for the number of elements and current array size strictly for the convenience of the user. We need the two rebuild functions. But then I added some extra functions.

SortHeap will sort an unsorted array. **GrowHeapBy** dynamically allocates a larger heap and copies existing items onto the new heap before deleting the original heap. And I added support for deep copies by providing the copy ctor and assignment operator.

What kind of user items can be placed in this **Heap**? Any item can be used as long as it provides support for two operators: the assignment operator and the less than relational operator. Since **Heap** is not storing pointers to the user's objects, it must have a way to assign them. Further, the rebuild heap functions require the ability for a less-than comparison operator.

Here is the **Heap** template class. Notice how simple it is to implement this template class.

Heap Template Class

```
#pragma once

/***************************************************************/
/*                                                             */
/* Heap: a class to encapsulate a heap                         */
/*                                                             */
/* user class must provide operator = and < and <=             */
/*                                                             */
/***************************************************************/

template<class UserData>
class Heap {
public:
 UserData*   array;        // the array of user items
 long numElements;  // current number of user items
 long maxSize;      // maximum size of the array

         Heap (long max = 100);
virtual ~Heap ();
bool     IsArrayFull () const;     // true if numElements=maxSize
bool     IsArrayEmpty () const;    // true if numElements=0

long     GetNumElements () const;
long     GetMaxHeapSize () const;

void     EmptyHeap ();            // sets number of elements to 0

void     RebuildHeapUpward (long root, long bottom);
void     RebuildHeapDownward (long root, long bottom);

void     SortHeap ();              // sorts the heap
bool     GrowHeapBy (long growby); // grow the array size

         Heap (const Heap<UserData>& h);
virtual Heap<UserData>& operator= (const Heap<UserData>& h);
protected:
void     Copy (const Heap<UserData>& h); // make a duplicate Heap
};

/***************************************************************/
/*                                                             */
/* Heap: allocate the empty max sized array of user items      */
/*                                                             */
/***************************************************************/

template<class UserData>
Heap<UserData>::Heap (long max) {
 numElements = 0;
```

```
 maxSize = max > 0 ? max : 100;
 try {
  array = new UserData [maxSize];
 }
 catch (std::bad_alloc e) {
  // check if out of memory
  cerr << "Error: out of memory\n";
 }
}

/***************************************************************/
/*                                                             */
/* ~Heap: delete the array of user items                       */
/*                                                             */
/***************************************************************/

template<class UserData>
Heap<UserData>::~Heap () {
 delete [] array;
}

/***************************************************************/
/*                                                             */
/* IsArrayFull: returns true if the array is full              */
/*                                                             */
/***************************************************************/

template<class UserData>
bool Heap<UserData>::IsArrayFull () const {
 return numElements == maxSize;
}

/***************************************************************/
/*                                                             */
/* IsArrayEmpty: returns true if the array is empty            */
/*                                                             */
/***************************************************************/

template<class UserData>
bool Heap<UserData>::IsArrayEmpty () const {
 return numElements == 0;
}

/***************************************************************/
/*                                                             */
/* EmptyHeap: empties heap by resetting numElements to 0       */
/*                                                             */
/***************************************************************/

template<class UserData>
void Heap<UserData>::EmptyHeap () {
 numElements = 0;
}

/***************************************************************/
/*                                                             */
```

```
/* GetNumElements: returns numElements                          */
/*                                                               */
/*****************************************************************/

template<class UserData>
long Heap<UserData>::GetNumElements () const {
 return numElements;
}

/*****************************************************************/
/*                                                               */
/* GetMaxHeapSize: returns the max array size                   */
/*                                                               */
/*****************************************************************/

template<class UserData>
long Heap<UserData>::GetMaxHeapSize () const {
 return maxSize;
}

/*****************************************************************/
/*                                                               */
/* RebuildHeapDownward: rebuilds heap when top is bad           */
/*                                                               */
/*****************************************************************/

template<class UserData>
void Heap<UserData>::RebuildHeapDownward (long root,
                                          long bottom) {
 UserData temp;
 long maxChild;
 long leftChild  = root * 2 + 1;
 long rightChild = root * 2 + 2;
 if (leftChild <= bottom) {
  if (leftChild == bottom)
   maxChild = leftChild;
  else {
   if (array[leftChild] <= array[rightChild])
    maxChild = rightChild;
   else
    maxChild = leftChild;
  }
  if (array[root] < array[maxChild]) {
   temp = array[root];
   array[root] = array[maxChild];
   array[maxChild] = temp;
   RebuildHeapDownward (maxChild, bottom);
  }
 }
}

/*****************************************************************/
/*                                                               */
/* RebuildHeapUpward: rebuilds heap when new item added at bot */
/*                                                               */
/*****************************************************************/
```

```
template<class UserData>
void Heap<UserData>::RebuildHeapUpward (long root, long bottom) {
 if (bottom <= root) return;
 UserData temp;
 long parentNode;
 parentNode = (bottom - 1) / 2;
 if (array[parentNode] < array[bottom]) {
  temp = array[parentNode];
  array[parentNode] = array[bottom];
  array[bottom] = temp;
  RebuildHeapUpward (root, parentNode);
 }
}

/***************************************************************/
/*                                                             */
/* SortHeap: sort the heap into numerical order                */
/*                                                             */
/***************************************************************/

template<class UserData>
void Heap<UserData>::SortHeap () {
 long i;
 for (i=numElements/2 - 1; i>=0; i--) {
  RebuildHeapDownward (i, numElements-1);
 }

 for (i=numElements-1; i>=1; i--) {
  UserData temp = array[0];
  array[0] = array[i];
  array[i] = temp;
  RebuildHeapDownward (0, i-1);
 }
}

/***************************************************************/
/*                                                             */
/* GrowHeapBy: enlarge max size of array,copying existing items*/
/*                                                             */
/***************************************************************/

template<class UserData>
bool Heap<UserData>::GrowHeapBy (long growby) {
 if (growby <= 0) return false;
 UserData* newarray;
 try {
  newarray = new UserData [maxSize + growby];
 }
 catch (std::bad_alloc e) {
  // check if out of memory
  cerr << "Error: out of memory\n";
  return false;
 }
 for (long i=0; i<numElements; i++) {
  newarray[i] = array[i];
```

```
 }
 delete [] array;
 array = newarray;
 maxSize += growby;
 return true;
}

/***************************************************************/
/*                                                             */
/* Heap: copy ctor - make a duplicate copy of passed Heap      */
/*                                                             */
/***************************************************************/

template<class UserData>
Heap<UserData>::Heap (const Heap<UserData>& h) {
 Copy (h);
}

/***************************************************************/
/*                                                             */
/* operator= make us a duplicate of passed Heap object         */
/*                                                             */
/***************************************************************/

template<class UserData>
Heap<UserData>& Heap<UserData>::operator= (
                                       const Heap<UserData>& h) {
 if (this == &h) return *this;
 delete [] array;
 Copy (h);
 return *this;
}

/***************************************************************/
/*                                                             */
/* Copy: make a duplicate of passed Heap object                */
/*                                                             */
/***************************************************************/

template<class UserData>
void Heap<UserData>::Copy (const Heap<UserData>& h){
 numElements = h.numElements;
 maxSize = h.maxSize;
 try {
  array = new UserData [maxSize];
 }
 catch (std::bad_alloc e) { // check if out of memory
  cerr << "Error: out of memory\n";
  array = 0;
  numElements = maxSize = 0;
  return;
 }
 for (long i=0; i<numElements; i++) {
  array[i] = h.array[i];
 }
}
```

273

A Priority Queue Based Upon a Heap

Next, let's see how we can implement a priority queue based upon our **Heap** class. Recall with a priority queue, when items are enqueued, they must be placed into order based on some kind of priority scheme. Then the dequeue operation is simple, it just gets the item at the head of the queue and rebuilds the heap downward. So all the modifications apply to the enqueue operation which must ensure that the item with the highest priority is at the front of the queue.

The implementation of **Dequeue** is simple if we maintain a heap. That is, the highest priority item is at the front of the queue in element 0. This we must remove it or rather copy it out of the array. Element 0 is then replaced by the last item in the queue and the number of elements decremented. By calling **RebuildHeapDownward** we guarantee that the next item of highest priority is now at element 0.

The **Enqueue** operation is actually even easier because of the Heap. Since the heap is maintained as a heap, the new item is added at the end of the array, which will be the lowest level and rightmost leaf. Then, by calling **RebuildHeapUpwards**, the item with the highest priority is placed at the top once again.

What restrictions are placed on user objects that can be in the priority queue? Only those required by the **Heap** class, operators = and <. Note the vital importance that operator< now takes on—what must be compared in the user items is the priority of each item!

The only remaining question is whether the **PriorityQueue** class should derive from Heap or use an instance of **Heap** as its data member? It can be done either way. However, I choose derivation to illustrate inheritance. Here is the **PriorityQueue** class as a template class derived from the **Heap** class.

Priority Queue Template Class Bases on a Heap

```
#pragma once
#include "Heap.h"

/***************************************************************/
/*                                                             */
/* PriorityQueue: a class to encapsulate a priority queue      */
/*                                                             */
/* user class must provide operator = and < and <=             */
/* operators < <= used to determine the priority of this item  */
/*                                                             */
/* Vital: if two items have the same priority, then            */
/*        if those items must remain in FIFO order, these      */
/*        operator functions must account for their order      */
/*                                                             */
/***************************************************************/

template<class UserData>
class PriorityQueue : public Heap<UserData> {
public:

     PriorityQueue (long max = 100);
    ~PriorityQueue () {}

// Dequeue returns true and fills userdata with the item
bool Dequeue (UserData& userdata);

// Enqueue a copy of the user's data
bool Enqueue (const UserData& data);
};

```

```
/***************************************************************/
/*                                                             */
/* Heap: allocate the empty max sized array of user items     */
/*                                                             */
/***************************************************************/

template<class UserData>
PriorityQueue<UserData>::PriorityQueue (long max)
                       : Heap<UserData> (max) {}

/***************************************************************/
/*                                                             */
/* Dequeue: returns userdata filled with next item and true   */
/*          or returns false is queue is empty                */
/*                                                             */
/***************************************************************/

template<class UserData>
bool PriorityQueue<UserData>::Dequeue (UserData& userdata) {
 if (IsArrayEmpty())
  return false;
 userdata = array[0];
 array[0] = array[numElements - 1];
 numElements--;
 if (numElements)
  RebuildHeapDownward (0, numElements - 1);
 return true;
}

/***************************************************************/
/*                                                             */
/* Enqueue: if no more room in array, it grows the array      */
/*          then enqueues a copy of the user's data           */
/* Note: UserData's op< is called to determine item priority  */
/*                                                             */
/***************************************************************/

template<class UserData>
bool PriorityQueue<UserData>::Enqueue (const UserData& userdata){
 if (IsArrayFull())
  if (!GrowHeapBy (100)) return false;
 array[numElements] = userdata;
 numElements++;
 RebuildHeapUpward (0, numElements - 1);
 return true;
}
```

There is only one problem with this priority queue class being based upon a heap class. If two or more user items have the same priority, then ideally a queue should keep those items in the order that they were enqueued, first in-first out. However, neither the queue nor heap rebuilding functions can recall the actual original order of the items. Thus, as it is now implemented, items with the same priority are going to lose their basic FIFO nature. However, if the items themselves can maintain an indication of their enqueue order, then the operators < and <= functions can deal with this situation, providing the correct order between items of the same priority.

Pgm13a tests both of these new classes, the **Heap** and the **PriorityQueue**. It illustrates how the user item can maintain the FIFO nature of items with the same priority. It begins by making a heap of a series of eleven integers, sorts them and displays the heap.

To show the **PriorityQueue** in operation, **Pgm13a** next simulates a veterinarian's patient queue. At a clinic, as people arrive with their pets, they are serviced in a FIFO manner. However, emergency cases can arrive and are handled ahead of the non-emergency pets. File **patients.txt** simulates a few hours of a day at the clinic.

The Patients.txt File

```
A Samuel Spade        Fido                 0
A John Jones          Rover                0
A Betsy Ann Smithville Jenny               0
H
H
A Lou Ann deVille     Kitty                1
H
A Tom Smythe          Fifi                 0
A Marie Longfellow    Jack                 1
A Alicia J. Jammissons Pretty Little Kitten 0
A Harry Thumbs        Buster Brown         1
H
H
H
H
H
```

The first character of each line contains A for the arrival of a new patient or H for handle the next patient. The remainder of the arrival lines contains the owner's name and the pet's name followed by a priority code. A code of 1 indicates an emergency case, while a code of 0 is represents a routine visit.

The output of the program is shown below. Notice the order of handling that occurs when an emergency case becomes enqueued.

Output of Pgm13a Tester Program

```
0
1
2
3
4
5
6
7
8
9


Handling the Patient Queue

Added:    Samuel Spade         Fido                 0
Added:    John Jones           Rover                0
Added:    Betsy Ann Smithville Jenny                0
Treated:  Samuel Spade         Fido                 0
Treated:  John Jones           Rover                0
Added:    Lou Ann deVille      Kitty                1
Treated:  Lou Ann deVille      Kitty                1
Added:    Tom Smythe           Fifi                 0
Added:    Marie Longfellow     Jack                 1
Added:    Alicia J. Jammissons Pretty Little Kitten 0
Added:    Harry Thumbs         Buster Brown         1
```

```
Treated: Marie Longfellow      Jack                    1
Treated: Harry Thumbs          Buster Brown            1
Treated: Betsy Ann Smithville  Jenny                   0
Treated: Tom Smythe            Fifi                    0
Treated: Alicia J. Jammissons  Pretty Little Kitten    0

File processing is complete
No memory leaks.
```

Pgm13a also illustrates some additional features of structures. A structure can have member functions, just as a class can. However, those member functions are always public in nature, as are all of the structure data members. This is vital because I am implementing the user data as a Patient structure which must therefore implement the two comparison operator functions. The syntax of structure member functions is exactly the same as that of a class.

The only tricky aspect of the program and the operator functions is the need to maintain the FIFO order for all patients with the same priority code. To do that, I added an additional member to the structure, **order**. As each new item is added into the queue, I increment the order number. Thus, each item has a different order number increasing in size with each new addition to the queue. Hence, the two operator functions can then correctly maintain the FIFO order of items whose priority values are the same.

Pgm13a Tester of Heap and PriorityQueue Classes

```
#include <iostream>
#include <iomanip>
#include <fstream>
#include <cctype>
#include <crtdbg.h>

#include "Heap.h"
#include "PriorityQueue.h"

using namespace std;

const int MAXLEN = 21;

/***************************************************************/
/*                                                             */
/* Patient: defines a patient for the priority queue operation */
/*                                                             */
/* must implement ops < and <= for Heap operations             */
/*                                                             */
/***************************************************************/

struct Patient {
 char ownerName[MAXLEN];
 char petName[MAXLEN];
 int  priority;
 int  order;
 bool operator< (const Patient& p) const;
 bool operator<= (const Patient& p) const;
};

/***************************************************************/
/*                                                             */
/* operator<: if this priority is < p's return true            */
/*            however, if they have the same priority,         */
```

```
/*             we must keep the original queue order intact,    */
/*         so check on reverse on incremental order of arrival */
/*                                                               */
/*****************************************************************/

bool Patient::operator< (const Patient& p) const {
 if (priority < p.priority)
  return true;
 else if (priority == p.priority && order > p.order)
  return true;
 return false;
}

/*****************************************************************/
/*                                                               */
/* operator<=: if this priority is < p's return true             */
/*             however, if they have the same priority,          */
/*             we must keep the original queue order intact,    */
/*         so check on reverse on incremental order of arrival */
/*                                                               */
/*****************************************************************/

bool Patient::operator<= (const Patient& p) const {
 if (priority < p.priority)
  return true;
 if (priority == p.priority && order > p.order)
  return true;
 return false;
}

/*****************************************************************/
/*                                                               */
/* Pgm12a: tests the Heap and PriorityQueue classes              */
/*                                                               */
/*****************************************************************/

int main () {
 {
  // test the Heap class by inserting & sorting some integers
  Heap<int> heap;
  int i;
  for (i=0; i<10; i++) {
   if (!heap.IsArrayFull()) {
    heap.array[i] = i;
    heap.numElements++;
   }
  }

  heap.SortHeap ();

  for (i=0; i<heap.GetNumElements(); i++) {
   cout << heap.array[i] << endl;
  }

  // now test the priority queue
```

```
 PriorityQueue<Patient> queue;
 ifstream infile ("patients.txt");
 if (!infile) {
  cerr << "Error: cannot open patients.txt\n";
  return 1;
 }
 int line = 1;
 char type;
 Patient p;
 cout << "\n\nHandling the Patient Queue\n\n";
 while (infile >> type) {
  type = (char) toupper (type);
  if (type == 'A') {
   infile.get (type);
   infile.get (p.ownerName, sizeof (p.ownerName));
   infile.get (type);
   infile.get (p.petName, sizeof (p.petName));
   infile >> p.priority;
   if (!infile) {
    cerr << "Error: bad data on line: " << line << endl;
    infile.close ();
    return 2;
   }
   p.order = line;
   if (!queue.Enqueue (p)) {
    infile.close ();
    exit (1);
   }
   cout << "Added:   " << p.ownerName << "  " << p.petName
        << setw (3) << p.priority << endl;
  }
  else if (type == 'H') {
   if (queue.Dequeue (p)) {
    cout << "Treated: " << p.ownerName << "  " << p.petName
         << setw (3) << p.priority << endl;
   }
   else {
    cout << "Error: no more patients in queue\n";
   }
  }
  else {
   cerr << "Error: bad type code in patients.txt file on line: "
        << line << endl;
   infile.close ();
   return 3;
  }
  line++;
 }
 infile.close ();
 cout << "\nFile processing is complete\n";
}

// check for memory leaks
if (_CrtDumpMemoryLeaks())
 cerr << "Memory leaks occurred!\n";
else
```

```
    cerr << "No memory leaks.\n";

  return 0;
}

```

Now that we have these two classes operational, we can turn to the more complex graph situation which will make use of these classes.

Graphs

Basic Graph Terminology

The **graph data structure** is a tree in which any given node can have more than one parent node pointing to it and it can point to many child nodes. The nodes are called **vertices**. The lines that connect the vertices (nodes) are called either **edges** or **arcs**. Further, the edges or lines connecting the vertices (nodes) often have some kind of **weight** or importance or significance attached to them. Additionally, each edge can have a **direction** associated with it. For example, examine an airline's flying schedule between cities. Between any given two cities, flights may go in both directions or maybe only from city A to city B and not from city B back to city A. The air distance between the connected cities (vertices) is often the weight.

Graphs are frequently used to solve routing type problems. Airline routes, mass transportation routes, even Internet routing can make use of graphs. Graphs are used to answer two key questions: "Can I get from A to B?" and "Among all the routes between A and B, what is the shortest route to take?"

If a graph has direction associated with its lines or edges, it is called a **directed graph** or **digraph** for short. If none of a graph's lines or edges has any direction arrows on them, it is an **undirected graph**. Figure 13.8 shows an example of each.

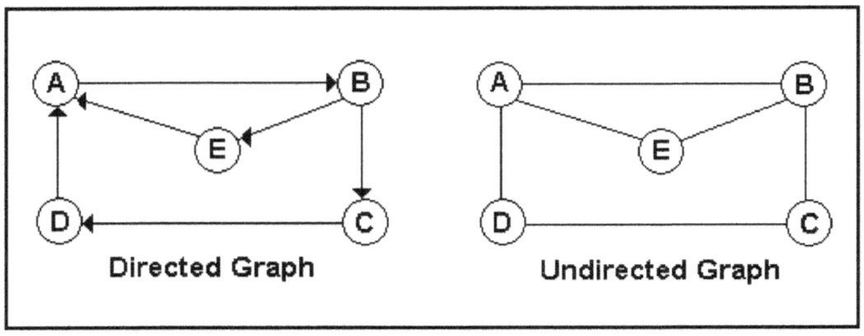

Figure 13.8 Directed and Undirected Graphs

Two vertices are said to be **adjacent vertices** if an edge or line directly connects them. Sometimes adjacent vertices are called **neighbors**. If the above Figure 13.8, A and B are adjacent vertices while A and C are not.

The sequence of vertices where each vertex is adjacent to the next one is called a **path**. A path can only follow the direction of travel along the edge or arc or line. In Figure 13.8 above, one path is {A, B, C, D} and another is {A, B, E} for example. In a digraph, travel is restricted to the direction of the arrows while in an undirected graph, travel can be in both directions.

A **cycle** is a path with at least three vertices that starts and ends on the same vertex. In the above figure and in both graphs, A, B, C, D, A is a cycle as is A, B, E, A. However, A, D, C, B, A is a cycle in the undirected graph but not in the digraph because a path must follow the direction arrows in the digraph. One special case of a cycle is known as a **loop**; in a loop there is one vertex and the line goes out from it and then back into that same vertex, rather like driving out of a city and then coming right back into that same city.

Another property known as **connected** applies to two vertices. If, ignoring direction, there is a path between two vertices, they are said to be **connected**. Further, in a digraph, there are three qualifiers to the connected property. If there is a path from each vertex to every other vertex, it is said to be **strongly connected**. However, if at least two vertices are not connected, the digraph is said to be **weakly connected**. The connected property only applies to digraphs because all undirected graphs would be strongly connected since there is no direction of travel to consider. A graph is **disjoint** is not connected in some manner. In Figure 13.8 above, the digraph is strongly connected because there is a path from every vertex to every other vertex. If the edge from E to A were removed, then the digraph would be weakly connected because there would then be no path from E to any other vertex. If we considered both of the graphs in Figure 13.8 to be one graph, it would be a disjointed graph because there is no way to get from the right portion to the left portion.

The final property of a graph is the **degree** of a vertex which is the total number of lines or edges into or out of it. The **outdegree** of a vertex is the total number of lines leaving that vertex while the **indegree** of a vertex is the total number of lines entering that vertex. In the digraph in Figure 13.8 above, the degree of vertex A is 3 while its outdegree is 1 and its indegree is 2. The degree of vertex E is 2 and its indegree and outdegree are both 1. The degree of vertex B in the digraph is also 3 but its outdegree is 2 while its indegree is 1.

A **network** is a graph whose edges or lines are weighted in some manner. For example, consider an airline's routes between cities. The weight would likely be the frequent traveler's miles between the two cities. Alternatively, the weight could be the price of the ticket or time of day travel or even the dates of travel. The nature of this weight information is unknown to a graph and it stored in an Edge structure provided by the client program. If the client program implements a few Edge structure operations, such as operator<, then the graph itself can find the minimum weighted route between two vertices.

I frequently fly out to Burbank, California (close to Los Angeles), to visit my young nephews. Figure 13.18 shows an airline's flight network from Peoria, Illinois to the Los Angeles area. I also inserted a flight from New York as well. The weight of each edge is the flight miles between those cities.

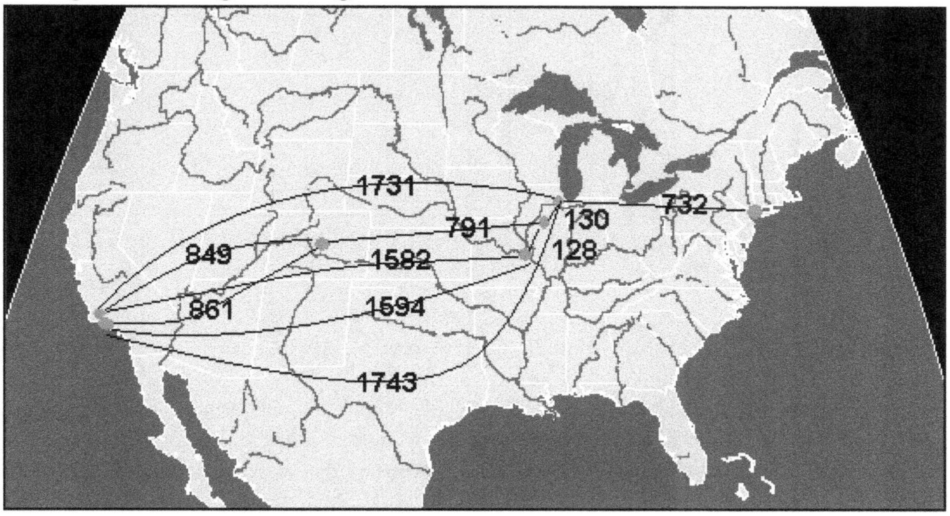

Figure 13.18 A Airline Flight Network

From a graph representing the data shown in Figure 13.18, we can as the graph if there is a flight from Peoria to Burbank. We can also ask what is the shortest path between Peoria and Burbank. "Is there a path?" and "What is the shortest path?" are two vital uses of a graph.

A **spanning tree** is a tree that contains all of the vertices in a graph. A **minimum spanning tree** of a network is a spanning tree in which the sum of its weights are the minium. So if a graph has weighted edges, then we can construct its minimum spanning tree. If the graph represented a computer network (the workstations are the vertices and the cables are the edges), then its minimum spanning tree would tell us how to connect all these computers to the network using the minimum amount of cabling. Of course, if two or more edges have the same weight, there can be more than one such minimum spanning tree.

Graph Basic Operations

Seven basic operations must be supported by a graph. These include Add a Vertex, Add an Edge, Delete a Vertex, Delete an Edge, Find a Vertex, Find an Edge, and Traverse the Graph. Then, other additional specialized processing functions can be added. Let's examine these basic functions in detail before we consider how to implement them.

Add a Vertex inserts a new vertex into the graph. It is always disjointed when it is added because no edges (lines connecting the new vertex to any other vertex) have yet been added. So normal operation usually involves a call to Add a Vertex followed by one or more calls to Add an Edge. This is shown in Figure 13.9 in which vertex E has just been added.

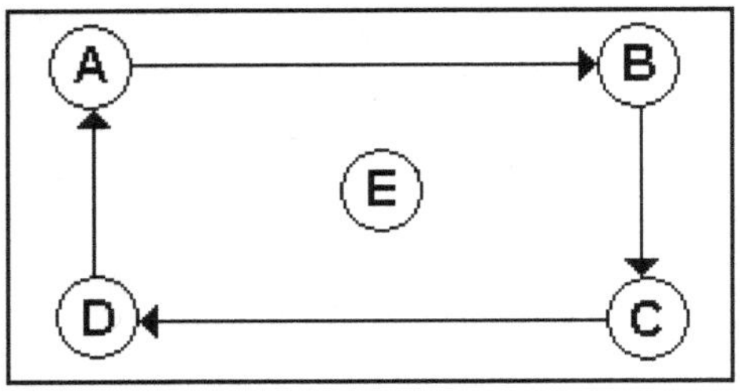

Figure 13.9 Add Vertex E

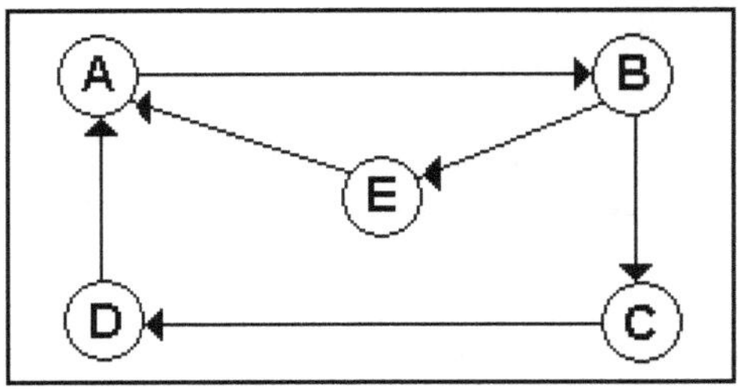

Figure 13.10 Add Edge E->A;B->E

Add an Edge connects a vertex to another vertex. In Figure 13.10, two calls to Add an Edge have been made, adding directed edge E->A and B->E. Further, if the graph is a digraph, then one vertex must be specified as the source and one is the destination.

Delete a Vertex deletes a vertex from the graph. It also deletes all edges or lines that connect to it. If we begin with the graph in Figure 13.10 and delete vertex E, then the resultant digraph is shown in Figure 13.11.

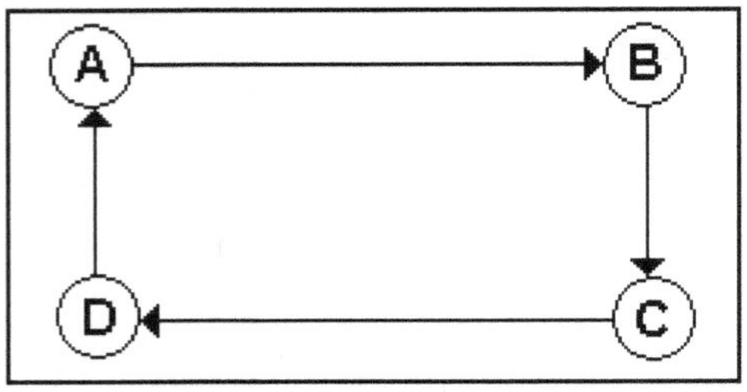

Figure 13.11 The Result of Deleting Vertex E from Figure 13.10

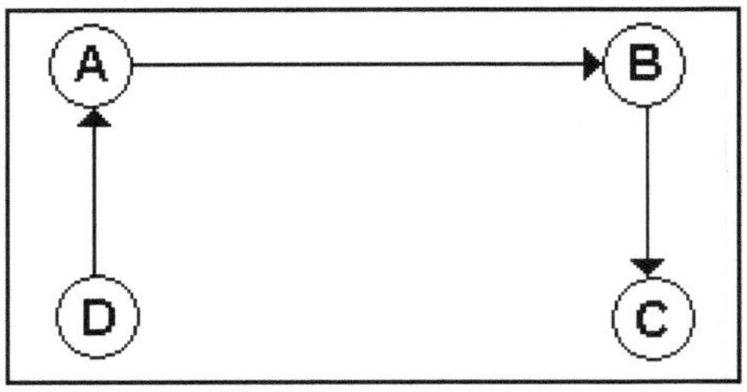

Figure 13.12 Deletion of Edge C-D

Delete an Edge removes one edge or line that connects two vertices. Figure 13.12 shows what results if we delete the edge from C to D.

Traverse Graph permits the client to visit all of the vertices in the graph. But a traversal of a graph is a bit more complex. Since any given vertex can have many different parents, there are going to be multiple ways to get to any specific vertex. How can we tell if we have already visited a given vertex? The usual method is to maintain a **visited** indicator. Initially as the traversal begins, all flags are cleared or set to **0**. Then, as a vertex is visited or processed, its **visited** indicator is set to a non-zero value.

Recall that with trees, there were several different ways the tree nodes and leaves could be visited. In what order do we visit the vertices? There are two usual methods. The first is a **depth-first traversal** in which we process all of the descendants of a node or vertex before we move to an adjacent vertex. If we were processing airline travel routes, a depth-first approach would yield the routing which had the most connections. This is usually considered undesirable by passengers. The other method is **a breath-first traversal** in which we visit all adjacent vertices before we visit descendants. In the airline travel example, a breadth-first traversal would yield the nonstop flights before those with many connections. These traversals parallel those of a tree and are more easily seen if you view the graph as a tree.

The **depth-first** process begins by visiting the first vertex. Next, we choose any one of its descendants and visit it and then one of its descendants. When we finally encounter a vertex with no more descendants (parallel to reaching a leaf in a tree), we back track to its parent and choose the next descendant and follow it down. This backtracking immediately tells us that a stack is needed to handle the processing. However, we must avoid revisiting vertices. Consider the undirected graph shown below in Figure 13.13. Let's assume that the first vertex is A.

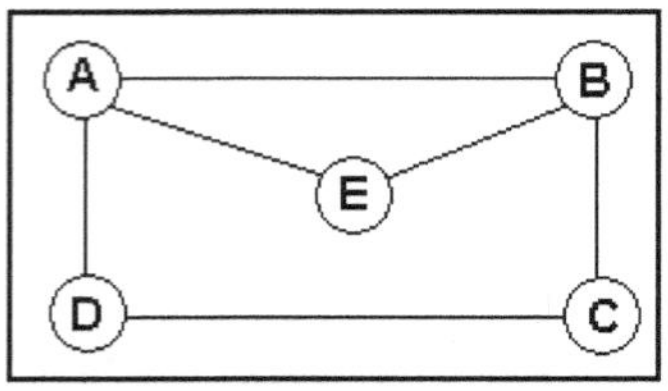

Figure 13.13 Undirected

We begin by pushing A onto the stack. The main loop then operates while there is still another vertex on the stack. We pop A off of the stack, process A, and push all of its descendant vertices onto the stack: E, D, and B in this case. Now we repeat the main loop and pop off B. We process B, but when we go to push the descendants of B, notice that those would be A and C and E. We have already processed A and E is on the stack to be done later on. Here is where we must know additional facts or we end up with an infinite loop forever pushing the same vertices onto the stack.

We actually need to know two key items: has this vertex been processed and has this vertex been pushed onto the stack? This is accomplished by creating a visited array of integers values. Initially, all are set to 0. When we push a vertex onto the stack, we mark it as having been visited by changing its indicator to 1. When we actually process a vertex, we can mark it with a 2, for example. Thus, initially A is so marked. When we push its descendants E, D and B onto the stack, we mark their visited indicators to 1. Thus, when we pop and actually process vertex B and are ready to push its descendants onto the stack, we can avoid pushing vertices A and E because A has already been visited and E is on the stack to be visited. Thus, when processing vertex B, only vertex C is pushed onto the stack. Figure 13.14 shows the sequence of vertices that are processed and the stack as its descendants are pushed.

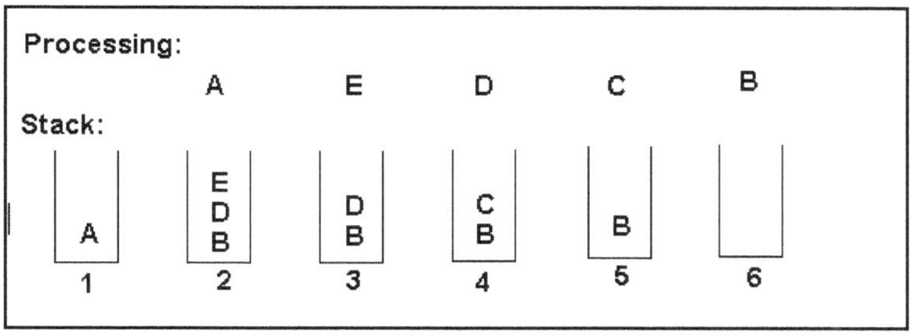

Figure 13.14 Depth Traversal Steps

In the **breath-first traversal** method, we visit all adjacent vertices before visiting any descendants. This means that we must queue up the sequence of vertices to be visited. So a queue structure is used, not a stack. Again referring to Figure 13.13 above, initially, we set our graph vertex pointer to that of the first one, vertex A. The main outer loop runs as long as there remains vertices in the graph. If this current vertex has not yet been processed or enqueued, we perform all of the following steps. If this one has not been enqueued, it is enqueued and marked as enqueued. In all cases, we must now process all items currently in the queue as these represent all of a vertex's descendants. So until the queue is empty, we dequeue a vertex and process it and mark it as having been processed. Next, we enqueue all of this vertex's descendants and mark each as having been enqueued. Finally, at the bottom of the main loop, we move onto the next vertex in the graph. As shown in Figure 13.15 below, we would process the vertices in this order: A, B, D, E, C.

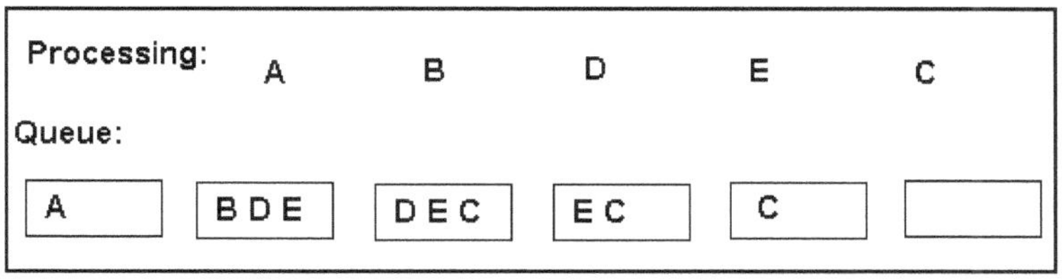

Figure 13.15 Breadth Traversal Using a Queue

Data Structures to Represent Graphs

The graph data is composed of the vertices and all of the edges. Two methods to store these data immediately suggest themselves: two arrays or two linked lists.

The array method is simpler to implement but costly in terms of wasted space, and, unless one uses growable arrays, the number of vertices and edges must be known ahead of time. The linked list method minimizes the amount of memory required; the number of vertices and edges does not need to be known before hand.

Referring again to the undirected graph in Figure 13.13 above, let's see how the data could be stored using arrays. First, one would define an array of five Vertex structures or class instances. Each element in the **Vertex** array represents one vertex in Figure 13.13. In the general case, any one vertex could be connected to all of the other vertices, the second array of **Edge** structures or classes would have to be a two-dimensional array. Figuratively, the rows represent the "from" vertices while the columns of a row represent the vertices that are connected "to" that from vertex. If no weights were needed, then this two-dimensional array could be of type **bool**, where a **true** indicates that there is a connection between this row's vertex and this column's vertex. This is illustrated in Figure 13.16 where I used 1's and 0's to indicate **true** and **false**.

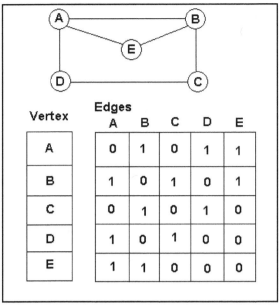

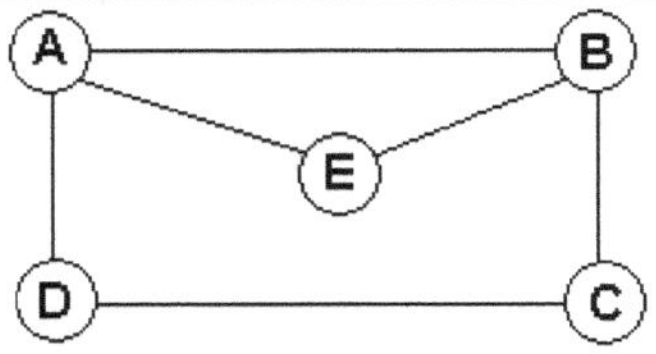

Vertex	Edges A	B	C	D	E
A	0	1	0	1	1
B	1	0	1	0	1
C	0	1	0	1	0
D	1	0	1	0	0
E	1	1	0	0	0

Figure 13.16 Using Arrays to Define an Undirected Graph Structure

For example, for vertex A, the **Edge** array says it is not connected to itself or C but vertex A is connected to B, D, and E. The **Edge** array can also indicate any direction of the connection. For example, if A was connected to B but B was not connected to A, then in the second row (the B "from" row), the A column would contain a 0 or **false**.

If we use single linked lists, we gain far more flexibility in the design. A vertex's list would hold all of the vertex data. Each of these vertex nodes would contain a head pointer to a list of edge nodes to which this vertex was connected. Then, for each vertex in the list, we build a linked list of edge nodes which can contain the weight of that edge as well as a pointer to the vertex of the connection. This is shown in Figure 13.17 below.

The **Vertex** structure or class contains basic data about the vertex itself. The **Edge** structure or class contains the weight of the edge or similar information. If there were no weight or properties associated with an edge, then this structure is not needed or can be a dummy place holder.

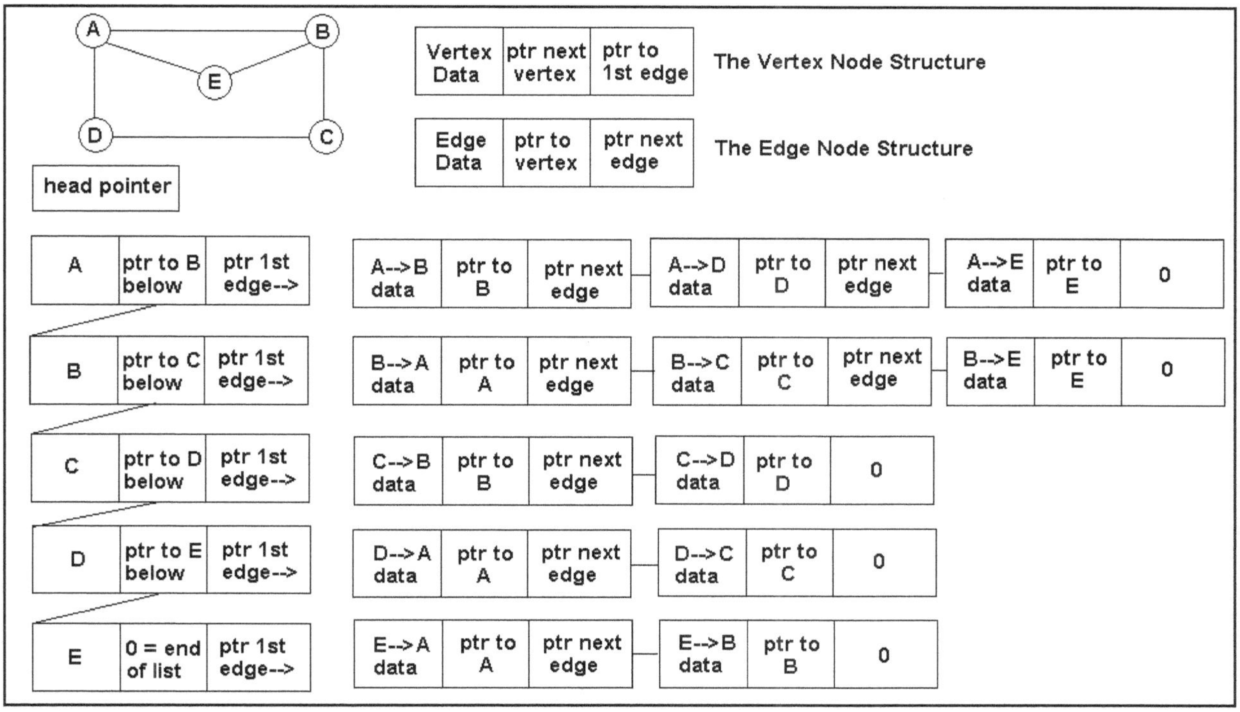

Figure 13.17 Using Lists to Define the Graph

The linked list is the method that I use implement to the graph data structure. The starting point is to implement the set of basic functions as outlined above. However, I will add one more function to that group, **DisplayTree**. The **DisplayTree** function displays each vertex in the vertex list followed by all of the vertices that are connected to it. This is useful to visually verify we have constructed the graph correctly.

Caution. The graph data structure utilizes nearly everything you have learned about data structures to this point. The complete implementation makes use of single and double linked lists, stacks, queues and priority queues.

How Do We Design a Graph Data Structure?

The first design consideration is, do we store **void** pointers to the user's data items or use a template class or perhaps use some kind of derived class? This time, the answer is nearly forced upon us.

From the above discussion and from the priority queue based upon the Heap class, the user's data must be stored in either structures or classes because those structures or classes must implement the basic comparison operators, such as < or <= or ==, for example. This tells us at once that we cannot store **void** pointers to the user's data because we would be unable to invoke these operator functions when we need them within the graph functions.

The graph structure as depicted in Figure 13.17 above is not closely related to any other data structure from which we could derive a graph structure. So using a template class might be the next suggestion as a viable method of writing a generic graph container class.

But there is a serious design consideration that must be met. We cannot know in advance exactly what the user data will be. So let's say that the user always provides his data in a pair of structures or classes called **Vertex** and **Edge**. These contain the vertex and edge **application-specific** data. Now before we get into the complexities, let's make this more real by seeing just what that means.

The sample application **Pgm13b** is airline routes across the country. Each **Vertex** is a city that the airline services. The client program can store any number of properties in this **Vertex** structure, but for simplicity, I am storing only the city name. The **Edge** contains the distance in air miles between a pair of cities. Here are the application's definition and implementation of the needed comparison operators. I call them **Vertex** and **Edge**; both are structures with public, operator overloaded member functions for the comparisons.

Here is the **VertexNode.h** application file. In the sample program, I split the function bodies off into the **VertexNode.cpp** file.

Pgm13b's Airline Travel Vertex and Edge Structures

```
#pragma once
#include <cstring>
using namespace std;


/***************************************************************/
/*                                                             */
/* Vertex: this structure contains the city name of the        */
/*         airport - it could contain other application        */
/*         specific information as needed                      */
/* It must implement the comparison operators for graph's      */
/* internal usage.                                             */
/*                                                             */
/* It can be a structure or a class                            */
/*                                                             */
/***************************************************************/

const int CITYLEN = 51;

struct Vertex {
 char city[CITYLEN]; // the city containing the airport

 bool operator> (const Vertex& v2) const;
 bool operator!= (const Vertex& v2) const;
 bool operator>= (const Vertex& v2) const;
 bool operator< (const Vertex& v2) const;
 bool operator<= (const Vertex& v2) const;
 bool operator== (const Vertex& v2) const;
};

/***************************************************************/
/*                                                             */
/* Edge: This structure contains edge specific information*/
/*       and most often is the weight assigned to this         */
/*       edge. With airplane travel, it is the distance        */
/*       between the from city and to city.                    */
/*                                                             */
/* If there is no weights needed in the graph, the Edge        */
/* still must be provided, however, it can be dummied          */
/* that is, one could store a single dummy char member so      */
/* that the structure exists as far as Graph is concerned      */
/*                                                             */
/***************************************************************/

struct Edge {
 double distance;
 bool operator< (const Edge& e2) const;
 bool operator== (const Edge& e2) const;
 Edge operator+ (const Edge& e2) const;
};

```

Pgm13b's Airline Travel Vertex and Edge Structures Implementation

```
#include "VertexEdge.h"

/***************************************************************/
/*                                                             */
/* The Edge comparison functions that are required by          */
/*        Graph - these must be provided, even if dummied */
/*                                                             */
/***************************************************************/

Edge Edge::operator+ (const Edge& e2) const {
 Edge res = *this;
 res.distance += e2.distance;
 return res;
}

bool Edge::operator< (const Edge& e2) const {
 if (distance < e2.distance) return true;
 return false;
}

bool Edge::operator== (const Edge& e2) const {
 return distance == e2.distance ? true : false;
}

/***************************************************************/
/*                                                             */
/* The Vertex comparison operators                             */
/*                                                             */
/* These must be implemented in terms of the actual data       */
/* contained in the Vertex - here the city's name              */
/*                                                             */
/***************************************************************/

bool Vertex::operator> (const Vertex& v2) const {
 return strcmp (city, v2.city) > 0 ? true : false;
}

bool Vertex::operator!= (const Vertex& v2) const {
 return strcmp (city, v2.city) != 0 ? true : false;
}

bool Vertex::operator>= (const Vertex& v2) const {
 return strcmp (city, v2.city) >= 0 ? true : false;
}

bool Vertex::operator< (const Vertex& v2) const {
 return strcmp (city, v2.city) < 0 ? true : false;
}

bool Vertex::operator<= (const Vertex& v2) const {
 return strcmp (city, v2.city) <= 0 ? true : false;
}

bool Vertex::operator== (const Vertex& v2) const {
```

```
 return strcmp (city, v2.city) == 0 ? true : false;
}
```

Notice that the **Edge** structure must also implement the **operator+** function. This feature is needed when finding the shortest path between two vertices as we will soon examine.

Next, what data does the **Graph** class need? For each vertex, we must store traversal data in addition to the user's **Vertex** instance. We should store the indegree and outdegree counts. For each edge, besides storing the user's **Edge** information, we need to store the "to" vertex pointer along with a pointer to the next edge. In other words, the **Graph** class must store some additional information for both the vertices and edges. So we wind up defining a **VertexNode** and an **EdgeNode** as follows.

```
// the Visited Enum Flag Definition for Traversal Usage
enum VisitedFlag {NotVisited, Visited, Processed};

struct VertexNode {
 Vertex      vertexData;      // the user's actual data
 VisitedFlag visitedFlag;     // used by traversals
 long        inDegree;        // num edges coming into this vertex
 long        outDegree;       // num edges going out from this one
 bool        inShortestPath;  // used by FindShortestPath
 VertexNode* ptrFwd;          // fwd ptr to next VertexNode
 EdgeNode*   ptrEdgeHead;     // head ptr for list of EdgeNodes
};

struct EdgeNode {
 Edge        edgeData;         // the user's actual weighted edge
 bool        inShortestPath;   // used by FindShortestPath
 VertexNode* ptrToVertex;      // the vertex this one goes to
 EdgeNode*   ptrFwd;           // fwd ptr to next edge in list
};
```

If we choose to go the template route, then each of these structures becomes a template.

```
template<classVertex, class Edge>
struct VertexNode {
 Vertex      vertexData;
 VisitedFlag visitedFlag;
 long        inDegree;
 long        outDegree;
 bool        inShortestPath;
 VertexNode<Vertex, Edge>* ptrFwd;
 EdgeNode<Vertex, Edge>*   ptrEdgeHead;
};
```

If we used the template definitions for the two nodes, then the **Graph** is a template also based on **Vertex** and **Edge**. And herein lies the problem. Several member functions of **Graph** are going to use the **Stack**, **Queue**, **DoubleLinkedList**, and the **PriorityQueue** classes to carry out their tasks. These four classes are now template classes. And we now cannot construct specific instances of these four containers by coding the following.

```
Stack<VertexNode<Vertex, Edge>*> stack;
```

To create instances of the **Stack** template class, we must use a known at compile-time data type.

We cannot get around this problem by rewriting the four template classes to use **void** pointers to the user's data instead of being template classes. If we did so, then we would not be able to invoke the required operator comparison functions of the user's data. A **void** pointer cannot be used to invoke a function unless it is typecast to the type of data to which it is really pointing, which is the user's data—of which we know nothing. It is rather a catch-22 situation with the **void** pointers.

We could create specific instances of the container classes by having the type of data be a **void***.

```
Stack<void*> stack;
```

However, two new problems arise. We get back **void** pointers which must be typecasted back to the type of data to which they really are pointing.

```
VertexNode<Vertex, Edge>* ptrvertex =
                          (VertexNode<Vertex, Edge>*) stack.Pop();
```

This is cumbersome at best, though doable. However, if the four container classes are storing **void** pointers, then the **PriorityQueue** is in trouble because its operation requires user operator comparison functions to determine the largest priority item during the heap rebuilding operations. Again, we cannot do so with a **void** pointer. So the approach of using templates for these **Graph** node structures is not going to work.

Does this mean that we must forsake our overall design guidelines of writing reusable container classes and write something totally specific to the air travel problem? No. There is another approach we can take that still retains a generalized nature.

Notice that in every graph situation, the user must be specifying their vertex data and edge information, even if the edge information is just a placeholder because there is no weight associated with edges. What if we **force** the user to provide a header file that must define **Vertex** and **Edge** as either structures or classes along with the required operator comparison functions? If we can include this file in **Graph.h**, then we know at compile-time what the actual items are going to be. We do not need to "template-ize" our two node structures that wrap around the user's data. Thus, **Graph** does not need to be a template class. Hence, **Graph** functions can then actually create specific instances of the template containers this way.

```
Stack<VertexNode> stack;
```

Here, the compiler knows exactly what a **VertexNode** is at compile-time.

This is the approach that I am taking. Force the user to provide a header file called **VertexEdge.h** in which they define **Vertex** and **Edge** as structures or classes and provide the implementation of the needed comparison functions.

With my design, the **Graph** can be a weighted (network) graph or not. If there is no weight to an edge, the edge structure or class must still be provided, but it can be dummied out, say containing a single char item that is never really used. The edge instance is used to indicate that there is a connection from a vertex to another vertex. If there is an actual weight to an edge, then the contents of the edge instance can be used to find the shortest path and so on. By designing the **Graph** class this way, we can write one class that can handle any **Graph** situation. Specifically, we do not need a separate class to handle a weighted or network graph. By using the linked list of connected vertices approach, the single **Graph** class can handle undirected graphs as well as digraphs. The only drawback is the user can only have one kind of **Graph** per application and they must provide the needed header file of that precise name with those precise class or structure names.

Next, let's examine the overall **Graph** class definition.

Graph Class Definition

```
#pragma once
#include "VertexEdge.h" // !!!! user must supply this file !!!!!!
#include "Stack.h"
#include "PriorityQueue.h"
#include "Queue.h"
#include "DoubleLinkedList.h"
using namespace std;

struct EdgeNode;              // forward reference

// the Visited Enum Flag Definition for Traversal Usage
enum VisitedFlag {NotVisited, Visited, Processed};


/***************************************************************/
/*                                                             */
/* VertexNode: stores user Vertex info along with Graph data   */
/*                                                             */
/***************************************************************/

struct VertexNode {
 Vertex      vertexData;      // the user's actual data
 VisitedFlag visitedFlag;     // used by traversals
 long        inDegree;        // num edges coming into this vertex
 long        outDegree;       // num edges going out from this one
 bool        inShortestPath;  // used by FindShortestPath
 VertexNode* ptrFwd;          // fwd ptr to next VertexNode
```

```
 EdgeNode*   ptrEdgeHead;    // head ptr for list of EdgeNodes
};


/***************************************************************/
/*                                                             */
/* EdgeNode: stores user's Edge info along with Graph's info   */
/*                                                             */
/***************************************************************/

struct EdgeNode {
 Edge        edgeData;        // the user's actual weighted edge
 bool        inShortestPath;  // used by FindShortestPath
 VertexNode* ptrToVertex;     // the vertex this one goes to
 EdgeNode*   ptrFwd;          // fwd ptr to next edge in list
};


/***************************************************************/
/*                                                             */
/* Graph: a class to encapsulate any kind of graph data str    */
/*                                                             */
/***************************************************************/

class Graph {
protected:
 VertexNode* ptrHead; // ptr to the list of vertices

public:
     Graph ();
    ~Graph ();
void EmptyGraph ();

bool AddVertex (const Vertex& vert);
int  AddEdge   (const Vertex& fromVert, const Vertex& toVert,
                const Edge& edge);

VertexNode* FindThisVertex (const Vertex& v) const;
VertexNode* FindThisVertex (const Vertex& v,
                            VertexNode*& ptrprev) const;
EdgeNode*   FindThisEdge   (const Vertex& from,
                            const Vertex& to) const;

bool DeleteVertex (const Vertex& hasIdToDel);
int  DeleteEdge (const Vertex& fromVert, const Vertex& toVert);

void DisplayTree (void (*ShowTree) (Vertex& v,
                                    bool isConnectedVertex));

void ClearProcessedFlags ();
void DepthFirstTraversal (void (*Process) (Vertex& v));
void BreadthFirstTraversal (void (*Process) (Vertex& v));


bool DoesPathExistBetween_DepthFirst   (const Vertex& from,
                                        const Vertex& to);
```

```
bool DoesPathExistBetween_BreadthFirst (const Vertex& from,
                                        const Vertex& to);

void ClearInShortestTreeFlags ();
void BuildMinimumSpanningTree (Edge& maxValue);
void ShowMinimumSpanningTree (
       void (*DisplayEdge) (const Vertex& from, const Vertex& to,
                            const Edge& edge));

bool FindShortestPath (const Vertex& from, const Vertex& to,
                       const Edge& minDist, bool showOnlyShortest,
                       bool smallestIsHighest,
                  void (*DisplayShortestPath) (const Vertex& from,
                         const Vertex& to, const Edge& distance));
};
```

The Graph Basic Functions' Implementation

Let's begin by examining the simpler functions. The only data member is the pointer to the head of the single linked list of vertices which is initialized to 0 in the constructor. The user would next call **AddVertex**.

AddVertex begins by allocating a new **VertexNode** and copying the user's passed vertex data into the new structure instance. After then setting the other members to zeros, this new node must be added to the linked list. There are two cases. If the list is empty, then this one goes at the head of the list. If there are vertices in the list, we must insert this one in sorted order. The sorted order is dictated by the user's **operator>** function.

```
VertexNode* ptrthis = ptrHead;
VertexNode* ptrprev = 0;
while (ptrthis && vertNew > ptrthis->vertexData) {
 ptrprev = ptrthis;
 ptrthis = ptrthis->ptrFwd;
}
```

Once we have found where this one goes (at the head or after another vertex), we use the normal list insertion coding.

Adding an edge along with some other functions are going to need a **FindThisVertex** function. One version simply returns a pointer to the found **VertexNode**. The overloaded version also fills in the passed reference to the previous **VertexNode** for ease of list insertion. To find out if this **VertexNode** matched the user's requested **Vertex**, I call the user's **operator!=** function.

```
VertexNode* Graph::FindThisVertex (const Vertex& v,
                                   VertexNode*& ptrprev) const {
 ptrprev = 0;
 VertexNode* ptrfind = ptrHead;
 while (ptrfind && v != ptrfind->vertexData) {
  ptrprev = ptrfind;
  ptrfind = ptrfind->ptrFwd;
 }
 return ptrfind;
}
```

Again, there is really nothing new in this routine either.

After adding some vertices, the user is likely to add one or more edges connecting pairs of vertices. This time, three errors are possible: out of memory, unable to find the "from" vertex, and unable to find the "to" vertex. The **AddEdge** function must therefore return an integer indicating success (0) or one of the three failures. Thus, the function begins by attempting to find the two needed vertices. If both are found, then a new **EdgeNode** is allocated and filled with the user's data and the graph members initialized. The **indegree** and **outdegree** members of the two found vertex nodes are also incremented.

```
int Graph::AddEdge (const Vertex& fromVert, const Vertex& toVert,
                    const Edge& edge) {
 VertexNode* ptrFrom = FindThisVertex (fromVert);
 if (!ptrFrom) return -2;
```

```
 VertexNode* ptrTo = FindThisVertex (toVert);
 if (!ptrTo) return -3;
 EdgeNode* ptrnew = new EdgeNode; // allcoate a new edge node
 if (!ptrnew) return -1;
 ptrnew->edgeData = edge;
 ptrnew->inShortestPath = false;
 ptrFrom->outDegree++;
 ptrTo->inDegree++;
 ptrnew->ptrToVertex = ptrTo;
```

Examine Figure 13.17 once more. Ths new **EdgeNode** must be chained into the single linked list of edges attached to the "from" **VertexNode**. If this is the first edge, then it is added at the head of the edge list in the "from" **VertexNode**. If not, the **EdgeNode** list must be searched to find the insertion point. Again, the edges are stored in sorted order. The user's **Edge operator>=** is called to determine the insertion point. Notice that as I traverse the list of **EdgeNodes**, I am saving the previous **EdgeNode**'s address to be used in the next insertion.

```
 if (!ptrFrom->ptrEdgeHead) {     // no edges from this one yet
  ptrFrom->ptrEdgeHead = ptrnew; // add at head
  ptrnew->ptrFwd = 0;
  return 0;
 }
 EdgeNode* ptrEdge = ptrFrom->ptrEdgeHead;
 EdgeNode* ptrprev = 0;
 while (ptrEdge &&
        ptrTo->vertexData >= ptrEdge->ptrToVertex->vertexData) {
  ptrprev = ptrEdge;
  ptrEdge = ptrEdge->ptrFwd;
 }
 if (!ptrprev) { // add at head
  ptrnew->ptrFwd = ptrFrom->ptrEdgeHead;
  ptrFrom->ptrEdgeHead = ptrnew;
 }
 else { // add in middle
  ptrprev->ptrFwd = ptrnew;
  ptrnew->ptrFwd = ptrEdge;
 }
 return 0;
}
```

The **DeleteVertex** and **DeleteEdge** functions are straightforward, single linked list operations once the vertex or edge is located. Don't forget to decrement the **indegree** and **outdegree** members of the vertices. The destructor calls **EmptyGraph** which is a very simple function that traverses the list of vertices and for each vertex, deletes all of its edges and then that vertex.

The **DisplayTree** function walks down the list of vertices and for each vertex, displays the edges connected to it. The user must provide a callback function that actually displays each vertex. The callback function is passed a **bool** which indicates whether or not this vertex is in the edges list of a given vertex. The user function is here called **ShowTree**.

```
void Graph::DisplayTree (
          void (*ShowTree) (Vertex& v, bool isConnectedVertex)) {
 if (!ptrHead) return;           // empty graph, so nothing to do
 VertexNode* ptrthis = ptrHead;
 while (ptrthis) {                        // for each VertexNode,
  ShowTree (ptrthis->vertexData, false); // display it
  EdgeNode* ptre = ptrthis->ptrEdgeHead;
  while (ptre) {                          // for each of its edges
   ShowTree (ptre->ptrToVertex->vertexData, true); // display it
   ptre = ptre->ptrFwd;
  }
  ptrthis = ptrthis->ptrFwd;
 }
}
```

Now examine the two traversal methods, **DepthFirstTraversal** and **BreadthFirstTraversal**. Both begin by clearing the visited flags. With the depth first form, the initial vertex is examined first. The main loop continues until all have been visited. What happens when a vertex is actually visited? That is entirely up to the user. The user provides a call-back function, **Process**, that is given each vertex to be actually processed. If a vertex has not been even visited, it is pushed onto the stack. Next, all of the other descendants of this current vertex are popped from the stack and actually processed and all of its descendants or edges that have not yet been visited are pushed onto the stack. Only then do we go on down the actual list of vertices. Thus, we are traversing depth first.

```
void Graph::DepthFirstTraversal (void (*Process) (Vertex& v)){
 if (!ptrHead) return;      // nothing to do
 ClearProcessedFlags ();    // set all flags to NotVisited yet
 Stack<VertexNode> stack;   // create a stack of VertexNode ptrs
 VertexNode* ptrthis = ptrHead;
 while (ptrthis) {
  if (ptrthis->visitedFlag < Processed) {
   if (ptrthis->visitedFlag < Visited) {
    stack.Push (ptrthis);   // push each not yet visited nodes
    ptrthis->visitedFlag = Visited; // but mark them as visited
                                    // as they are pushed
   }
  }
  // process descendants of this vertex at the top of stack
  while (!stack.IsEmpty()) {
   VertexNode* ptrnode = stack.Pop (); // get most recent Vertex
   Process (ptrnode->vertexData);      // let user process it
   ptrnode->visitedFlag = Processed;   // and mark it processed
   // now traverse all edges of this vertex
   EdgeNode* ptrthisedge = ptrnode->ptrEdgeHead;
   while (ptrthisedge) {
    VertexNode* ptrv = ptrthisedge->ptrToVertex;
    if (ptrv->visitedFlag == NotVisited) {// if this one is not
     stack.Push (ptrv);                   // yet visited, push it
     ptrv->visitedFlag = Visited;
    }
    ptrthisedge = ptrthisedge->ptrFwd;
   }
  }
  // now move on down the VertexNode list to the next Vertex
  ptrthis = ptrthis->ptrFwd;
 }
}
```

In contrast, the **BreadthFirstTraversal** uses a queue to store the **VertexNodes**, so that all of a given vertex's siblings are examined before going on down the edge chain. The coding is very parallel.

```
void Graph::BreadthFirstTraversal (void (*Process) (Vertex& v)) {
 if (!ptrHead) return;      // here, nothing to do
 ClearProcessedFlags ();    // set all flags to NotVisited yet
 Queue<VertexNode> queue;   // our queue of nodes visited FIFO
 VertexNode* ptrthis = ptrHead;
 while (ptrthis) {          // for each VertexNode,
  if (ptrthis->visitedFlag < Processed) {
   if (ptrthis->visitedFlag < Visited) {
    queue.Enqueue (ptrthis); // enqueue NotVisited Vertex and
    ptrthis->visitedFlag = Visited; // mark it as now Visited
   }
  }
  // for each remaining Vertex in the queue, process it
  while (!queue.IsEmpty()) {
   VertexNode* ptrv = queue.Dequeue (); // get next Vertex
   Process (ptrv->vertexData);          // let user process it
   ptrv->visitedFlag = Processed;       // and mark as processed
   EdgeNode* ptre = ptrv->ptrEdgeHead;
   while (ptre) {                       // for all of its edges,
    VertexNode* ptrve = ptre->ptrToVertex;
    if (ptrve->visitedFlag == NotVisited) {// if it's not visited
     queue.Enqueue (ptrve);             // enqueue this node and
```

```
      ptrve->visitedFlag = Visited;       // mark it as now Visited
     }
    ptre = ptre->ptrFwd;
   }
  }
  // move on to the next VertexNode in the list
  ptrthis = ptrthis->ptrFwd;
 }
}
```

Now we have a basic graph class. But as yet, it does not do much for the user. We need some powerhouse advanced functions to make this class fully operational. Here is the first part of the **Graph.cpp** file covering the functions so far discussed.

Graph Class Implementation

```
#include "Graph.h"

/***************************************************************/
/*                                                             */
/* Graph: set head pointer to 0                                */
/*                                                             */
/***************************************************************/

Graph::Graph () : ptrHead (0) {}

/***************************************************************/
/*                                                             */
/* AddVertex: add a new vertex to the chain of vertices        */
/*            returns false if out of memory                   */
/*  The vertices list is sorted into increasing user Vertex    */
/*  order - that is, we maintain it as a sorted list           */
/*                                                             */
/***************************************************************/

bool Graph::AddVertex (const Vertex& vertNew) {
 VertexNode* ptrnew = new VertexNode; // allocate a new node

 // fill up node with default values and the user's data
 ptrnew->vertexData = vertNew;
 ptrnew->visitedFlag = NotVisited;
 ptrnew->ptrEdgeHead = 0;
 ptrnew->inShortestPath = false;
 ptrnew->inDegree = ptrnew->outDegree = 0;

 // chain into the list of VertexNodes
 if (!ptrHead) {        // is there anything in the list yet?
  ptrnew->ptrFwd = 0;   // no, so add at head
  ptrHead = ptrnew;
  return true;
 }

 // here try to find where in the list this vertex should go
 // by calling user's operator> to find its position
 VertexNode* ptrthis = ptrHead;
 VertexNode* ptrprev = 0;
 while (ptrthis && vertNew > ptrthis->vertexData) {
  ptrprev = ptrthis;
```

```
   ptrthis = ptrthis->ptrFwd;
  }

  // sort out the two cases - at the head or after another vertex
  if (!ptrprev) {              // it goes at the very head
   ptrnew->ptrFwd = ptrHead; // us points fwd to the next node
   ptrHead = ptrnew;         // head is now us
   return true;
  }

  // here ptrprev points to the one to insert after
  ptrnew->ptrFwd = ptrprev->ptrFwd; // us points prev's fwd
  ptrprev->ptrFwd = ptrnew;  // previous one points to us
  return true;
 }

/***************************************************************/
/*                                                             */
/* FindThisVertex: Given a Vertex, find it in the list         */
/*                                                             */
/***************************************************************/

VertexNode* Graph::FindThisVertex (const Vertex& v) const {
 VertexNode* ptrfind = ptrHead;
 while (ptrfind && v != ptrfind->vertexData)
  ptrfind = ptrfind->ptrFwd;
 return ptrfind;
}

/***************************************************************/
/*                                                             */
/* FindThisVertex: Given a Vertex, find it in the list         */
/*                 but also return the previous item in the list*/
/*                                                             */
/***************************************************************/

VertexNode* Graph::FindThisVertex (const Vertex& v,
                                   VertexNode*& ptrprev) const {
 ptrprev = 0;
 VertexNode* ptrfind = ptrHead;
 while (ptrfind && v != ptrfind->vertexData) {
  ptrprev = ptrfind;
  ptrfind = ptrfind->ptrFwd;
 }
 return ptrfind;
}

/***************************************************************/
/*                                                             */
/* AddEdge: add an edge - vertices must be already added       */
/*                                                             */
/* returns 0 if added, -1 if out of memory, -2 if it cannot    */
/*         find the from vert, -3 if it cannot find to vert    */
/*                                                             */
/***************************************************************/
```

```
int Graph::AddEdge (const Vertex& fromVert, const Vertex& toVert,
                    const Edge& edge) {
 // find the from and to vertices in the VertexNode list
 VertexNode* ptrFrom = FindThisVertex (fromVert);
 if (!ptrFrom) return -2;

 VertexNode* ptrTo = FindThisVertex (toVert);
 if (!ptrTo) return -3;

 EdgeNode* ptrnew = new EdgeNode; // allocate a new edge node

 // fill with user's data and the default values
 ptrnew->edgeData = edge;
 ptrnew->inShortestPath = false;


 // increment the vertices degrees and set the EdgeNode's to vert
 ptrFrom->outDegree++;
 ptrTo->inDegree++;
 ptrnew->ptrToVertex = ptrTo;

 // see if this from node has any edges in its list as yet
 if (!ptrFrom->ptrEdgeHead) {    // no edges from this one yet
  ptrFrom->ptrEdgeHead = ptrnew; // add at head
  ptrnew->ptrFwd = 0;
  return 0;
 }

 // here from vert edges exist, so find the insertion point
 // again, calling the user's operator>= to find its location
 EdgeNode* ptrEdge = ptrFrom->ptrEdgeHead;
 EdgeNode* ptrprev = 0;
 while (ptrEdge &&
        ptrTo->vertexData >= ptrEdge->ptrToVertex->vertexData) {
  ptrprev = ptrEdge;
  ptrEdge = ptrEdge->ptrFwd;
 }

 // sort out the two cases - at head and after another EdgeNode
 if (!ptrprev) { // add at head
  ptrnew->ptrFwd = ptrFrom->ptrEdgeHead;
  ptrFrom->ptrEdgeHead = ptrnew;
 }
 else { // add in middle
  ptrprev->ptrFwd = ptrnew;
  ptrnew->ptrFwd = ptrEdge;
 }
 return 0;
}

/***************************************************************/
/*                                                             */
/* DeleteVertex: deletes the vertex requested                  */
/*               returns false if not found or still has edges */
/*                                                             */
/***************************************************************/
```

```
bool Graph::DeleteVertex (const Vertex& hasIdToDel) {
 // find the vertex which has an id key given by hasIdToDel
 VertexNode* ptrprev = 0;
 VertexNode* ptrthis = FindThisVertex (hasIdToDel, ptrprev);

 // quit if Vertex is not found or VertexNode still has Edges
 if (!ptrthis) return false;
 if (ptrthis->ptrEdgeHead) return false;

 // here it has no EdgeNodes, so it is safe to delete it
 if (!ptrprev) // this is the first one
  ptrHead = ptrthis->ptrFwd;
 else
  ptrprev->ptrFwd = ptrthis->ptrFwd;
 delete ptrthis;
 return true;
}

/***************************************************************/
/*                                                             */
/* DeleteEdge: deletes the requested EdgeNode                  */
/*             returns 0 if it is successful                   */
/*                    -1 if there are no vertices at all       */
/*                    -2 if vertex is not found                */
/*                    -3 if edge is not found                  */
/*                                                             */
/***************************************************************/

int Graph::DeleteEdge (const Vertex& fromVert,
                       const Vertex& toVert) {
 if (!ptrHead) return -1;

 // find the Edge given by the id keys in the two vertices
 VertexNode* ptrFrom = FindThisVertex (fromVert);
 if (!ptrFrom) return -2;

 // now find the to edge in this list
 EdgeNode* ptrprev = 0;
 EdgeNode* ptredge = ptrFrom->ptrEdgeHead;
 if (!ptredge) return -3; // no edges left!

 // find the required edge by using user's != operator function
 while (ptredge && ptredge->ptrToVertex->vertexData != toVert) {
  ptrprev = ptredge;
  ptredge = ptredge->ptrFwd;
 }
 if (!ptredge) return -3; // did not find the required edge

 // here we found the edge, so decrement vertices' degrees
 ptrFrom->outDegree--;
 ptredge->ptrToVertex->inDegree--;

 if (!ptrprev) // deleting the first one?
  ptrFrom->ptrEdgeHead = ptredge->ptrFwd;
 else
```

```
  ptrprev->ptrFwd = ptredge->ptrFwd;
 delete ptredge;
 return 0;     // succesful
}

/***************************************************************/
/*                                                             */
/* ~Graph: remove dynamically allocated memory                 */
/*                                                             */
/***************************************************************/

Graph::~Graph () {
 EmptyGraph ();
}

/***************************************************************/
/*                                                             */
/* EmptyGraph: delete all items so graph can be reused         */
/*                                                             */
/***************************************************************/

void Graph::EmptyGraph () {
 if (!ptrHead) return;           // nothing to do
 VertexNode* ptrthis = ptrHead;
 VertexNode* ptrnext = 0;

 // loop through all vertices
 while (ptrthis) {
  EdgeNode* ptrthisedge = ptrthis->ptrEdgeHead;
  while (ptrthisedge) {   // delete all edge nodes of this vertex
   EdgeNode* ptrnextedge = ptrthisedge->ptrFwd;
   delete ptrthisedge;
   ptrthisedge = ptrnextedge;
  }
  ptrnext = ptrthis->ptrFwd; // point to next vertex node
  delete ptrthis;            // and delete this vertex node
  ptrthis = ptrnext;
 }
}

/***************************************************************/
/*                                                             */
/* ClearProcessedFlags: set all visited flags to NotVisited    */
/*                                                             */
/***************************************************************/

void Graph::ClearProcessedFlags () {
 if (!ptrHead) return;
 VertexNode* ptrthis = ptrHead;
 while (ptrthis) {
  ptrthis->visitedFlag = NotVisited;
  ptrthis = ptrthis->ptrFwd;
 }
}

/***************************************************************/
```

```
/*                                                             */
/* ClearInShortestTreeFlags: clear all inShortestTree flags    */
/*                                                             */
/***************************************************************/

void Graph::ClearInShortestTreeFlags () {
 if (!ptrHead) return;
 VertexNode* ptrthis = ptrHead;
 while (ptrthis) {                      // for each VertexNode,
  ptrthis->inShortestPath = false;    // clear its flag
  EdgeNode* ptre = ptrthis->ptrEdgeHead;
  while (ptre) {                        // for all of its EdgeNodes
   ptre->inShortestPath = false;      // clear its flag
   ptre = ptre->ptrFwd;
  }
  ptrthis = ptrthis->ptrFwd;
 }
}

/***************************************************************/
/*                                                             */
/* DisplayTree: Display a representation of the tree for debug */
/*  requires user callback function to do actual displaying    */
/*                                                             */
/***************************************************************/

void Graph::DisplayTree (
          void (*ShowTree) (Vertex& v, bool isConnectedVertex)) {
 if (!ptrHead) return;          // empty graph, so nothing to do
 VertexNode* ptrthis = ptrHead;
 while (ptrthis) {                         // for each VertexNode,
  ShowTree (ptrthis->vertexData, false); // display it
  EdgeNode* ptre = ptrthis->ptrEdgeHead;
  while (ptre) {                           // for each of its edges
   ShowTree (ptre->ptrToVertex->vertexData, true); // display it
   ptre = ptre->ptrFwd;
  }
  ptrthis = ptrthis->ptrFwd;
 }
}

/***************************************************************/
/*                                                             */
/* DepthFirstTraversal: perfom a depth first traversal         */
/*   requires a user callback function to perform any desired  */
/*   work on each node found                                   */
/*                                                             */
/***************************************************************/

void Graph::DepthFirstTraversal (void (*Process) (Vertex& v)){
 if (!ptrHead) return;     // nothing to do
 ClearProcessedFlags ();   // set all flags to NotVisited yet

 Stack<VertexNode> stack;  // create a stack of VertexNode ptrs
 VertexNode* ptrthis = ptrHead;
 while (ptrthis) {
```

```
  if (ptrthis->visitedFlag < Processed) {
   if (ptrthis->visitedFlag < Visited) {
    stack.Push (ptrthis);  // push each not yet visited nodes
    ptrthis->visitedFlag = Visited; // but mark them as visited
                                    // as they are pushed
   }
  }

  // process descendants of this vertex at the top of stack
  while (!stack.IsEmpty()) {
   VertexNode* ptrnode = stack.Pop (); // get most recent Vertex
   Process (ptrnode->vertexData);      // let user process it
   ptrnode->visitedFlag = Processed;   // and mark it processed
   // now traverse all edges of this vertex
   EdgeNode* ptrthisedge = ptrnode->ptrEdgeHead;
   while (ptrthisedge) {
    VertexNode* ptrv = ptrthisedge->ptrToVertex;
    if (ptrv->visitedFlag == NotVisited) {// if this one is not
     stack.Push (ptrv);                   // yet visited, push it
     ptrv->visitedFlag = Visited;
    }
    ptrthisedge = ptrthisedge->ptrFwd;
   }
  }

  // now move on down the VertexNode list to the next Vertex
  ptrthis = ptrthis->ptrFwd;
 }
}

/***************************************************************/
/*                                                             */
/* BreadthFirstTraversal: perform a breadth first traversal    */
/*    requires a user callback function to process each vertex */
/*                                                             */
/***************************************************************/

void Graph::BreadthFirstTraversal (void (*Process) (Vertex& v)) {
 if (!ptrHead) return;     // here, nothing to do
 ClearProcessedFlags ();   // set all flags to NotVisited yet

 Queue<VertexNode> queue;  // our queue of nodes visited FIFO
 VertexNode* ptrthis = ptrHead;
 while (ptrthis) {         // for each VertexNode,
  if (ptrthis->visitedFlag < Processed) {
   if (ptrthis->visitedFlag < Visited) {
    queue.Enqueue (ptrthis); // enqueue NotVisited Vertex and
    ptrthis->visitedFlag = Visited; // mark it as now Visited
   }
  }

  // for each remaining Vertex in the queue, process it
  while (!queue.IsEmpty()) {
   VertexNode* ptrv = queue.Dequeue (); // get next Vertex
   Process (ptrv->vertexData);          // let user process it
   ptrv->visitedFlag = Processed;       // and mark as processed
```

```
    EdgeNode* ptre = ptrv->ptrEdgeHead;
    while (ptre) {                          // for all of its edges,
     VertexNode* ptrve = ptre->ptrToVertex;
     if (ptrve->visitedFlag == NotVisited) {// if it's not visited
      queue.Enqueue (ptrve);                // enqueue this node and
      ptrve->visitedFlag = Visited;         // mark it as now Visited
     }
     ptre = ptre->ptrFwd;
    }
   }

   // move on to the next VertexNode in the list
   ptrthis = ptrthis->ptrFwd;
  }
 }
 ...
```

Advanced Graph Functions

The first question a client program might have is, "Does a path exist between two vertices?" For illustration's sake, I implement two versions of this operation based upon the two types of **Graph** traversals. The first, **DoesPathExistBetween_DepthFirst**, uses a depth first approach.

It is given the "from" and "to" vertices and returns either **true**, a path exists, or **false**. It begins by finding the "from" vertex in the list of vertices. First, the "from" vertex is pushed onto the stack. The entire process is repeated until the stack is empty (not found) or we find the "to" vertex that is connected directly or via other vertices to the "from" vertex. The process begins by popping the next vertex to try off of the stack. Then, the user's **Vertex** structure's **operator==** is called to see if this is the "to" **Vertex**. If it is, we return **true** and are done. If not, then we check to see if this vertex has already been visited. If it has, it is, of course, skipped. If it has not yet been visited, then all of its **EdgeNode**s are enqueued into a queue. Once the queue is built, then each vertex in the queue is examined to see if it has been visited. If not, it is pushed onto the stack to be tried. And the process is repeated using the next vertex in the stack.

```
bool Graph::DoesPathExistBetween_DepthFirst
                         (const Vertex& from, const Vertex& to) {
 if (!ptrHead) return false; // an empty graph

 // try to find the from vertex
 VertexNode* ptrfrom = FindThisVertex (from);
 if (!ptrfrom) return false;

 // from Vertex is found, so now try to find a path to "to" vert.
 Stack<VertexNode> stack;     // stack of vertices to try
 ClearProcessedFlags ();      // set all flags to NotVisited
 Queue<VertexNode> queue;     // queue of vertices to try next
 bool found = false;          // found is true when a path exists
 stack.Push (ptrfrom);        // store initial from vertex
 VertexNode* ptrthis;
 do {
  ptrthis = stack.Pop ();     // pop next vertex to try
  // call user's operator= function to look for the "to" vertex
  if (ptrthis->vertexData == to) {
   found = true;              // it was found, so we are done
   break;
  }

  // this vertex is not it, so if it has not yet been visited,
  // enqueue all of its edges and try them
  if (ptrthis->visitedFlag == NotVisited) {
   ptrthis->visitedFlag = Visited;
```

```
    EdgeNode* ptre = ptrthis->ptrEdgeHead;
    while (ptre) { // enqueues all of this vertex's edges
     queue.Enqueue (ptre->ptrToVertex);
     ptre = ptre->ptrFwd;
    }
    // now try each edge. If an edge has not yet been visited,
    // push that vertex onto the stack to be tried later on
    while (!queue.IsEmpty()) {
     VertexNode* ptrv = queue.Dequeue ();
     if (ptrv->visitedFlag == NotVisited)
      stack.Push (ptrv);
    }
   }
 } while (!stack.IsEmpty() && !found); // repeat for all vertices
 return found;
}
```

In the **DoesPathExistBetween_BreathFirst** function, a queue replaces the stack, since we wish to test all of the siblings before we go deeper into the tree. Its coding is parallel to what we have seen before.

```
bool Graph::DoesPathExistBetween_BreadthFirst
                          (const Vertex& from, const Vertex& to) {
 if (!ptrHead) return false; // no vertices in the graph

 // try to find the from vertex, returning false if not found
 VertexNode* ptrfrom = FindThisVertex (from);
 if (!ptrfrom) return false;

 ClearProcessedFlags ();  // set all flags as NotVisited yet
 bool found = false;      // true when we have found the "to"

 Queue<VertexNode> queue1; // the main queue to check
 queue1.Enqueue (ptrfrom); // store the first vertex

 Queue<VertexNode> queue2; // secondary to try queue
 VertexNode* ptrthis;
 do {
  ptrthis = queue1.Dequeue (); // retrieve next vertex to try
  // call the user's operator== function to see it this is it
  if (ptrthis->vertexData == to) {
   found = true;           // we have found the "to" vertex!
   break;
  }

  // this one is not it, if this vertex has not yet been visited
  if (ptrthis->visitedFlag == NotVisited) { // then visit it
   ptrthis->visitedFlag = Visited;
   EdgeNode* ptre = ptrthis->ptrEdgeHead;

   // enqueue all of this vertex's edges
   while (ptre) {
    queue2.Enqueue (ptre->ptrToVertex);
    ptre = ptre->ptrFwd;
   }

   // now check all of this vertex's edges - if any are not yet
   // visited, then add them to the main queue to be visited
   while (!queue2.IsEmpty()) {
    VertexNode* ptrv = queue2.Dequeue ();
    if (ptrv->visitedFlag == NotVisited)
     queue1.Enqueue (ptrv);
   }
  }
 } while (!queue1.IsEmpty() && !found); // repeat for all vertex
```

```
 return found;
}
```

A client program may wish to create a minimum spanning tree. Recall that this can only be done if the edges have a weight associated with them. The minimum spanning tree is a network such that all of its edge weights are guaranteed to be the minimum value. Remember that one use for this spanning tree is to find the shortest cabling required to tie a series of networked computers together.

The general process is: from all of the vertices in the tree, select the edge with the minium distance to a vertex not currently in the tree and add it (flag it) to the minimal tree. This process is illustrated in the next series of figures. Consider the network shown in Figure 16.19 below.

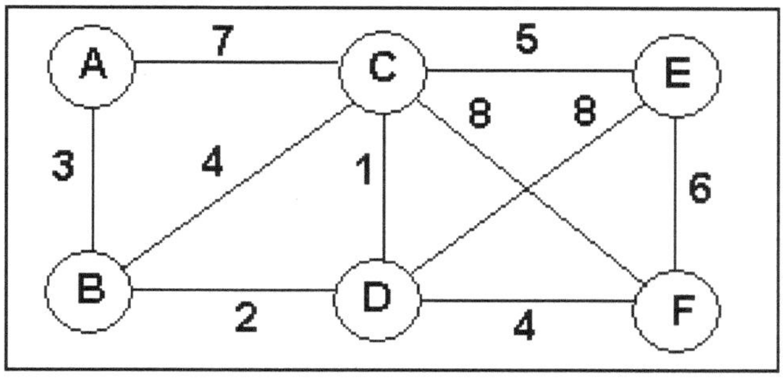

Figure 13.19 A Network with Weighted Edges

We start with the initial vertex A and find the shortest path to vertex B. Then we find the shortest path to C which goes through D. Part way through the process, we now have the following nodes added to the minimal spanning tree.

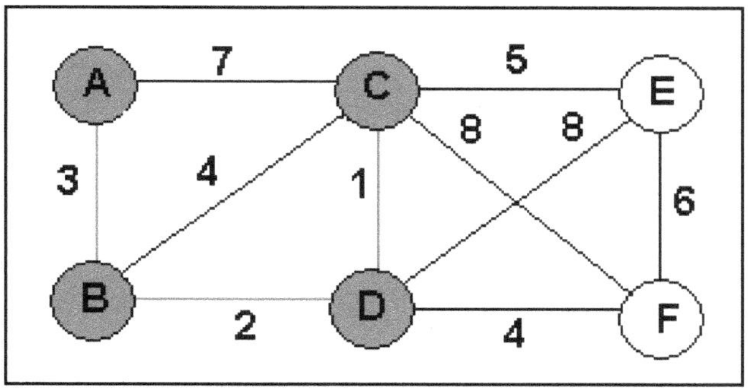

Figure 13.20 The First Four Minimum Nodes

We continue with the process. The shortest distance to vertex E is from C and to F is from D. Thus, we end up with the following minimum spanning tree shown in red below in Figure 13.21.

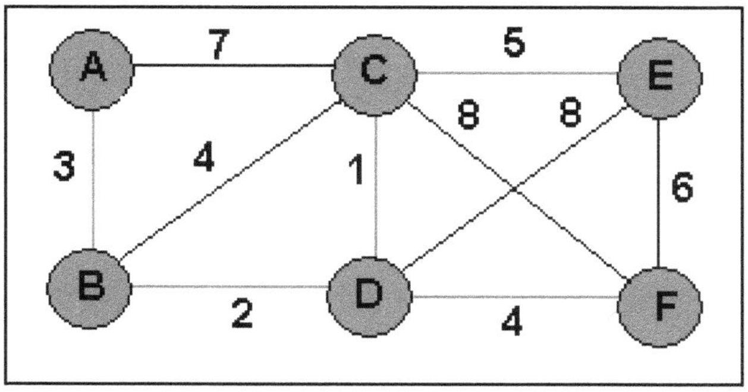

Figure 13.21 The Minimum Spanning Tree

The implementation is in two parts. The first step is to build the minimum spanning tree and the second is to display it in some manner. Have you spotted the one piece of information that the graph functions cannot possibly know? If we are to find the minimum weight, what kind of data is that weight? And what is the largest value that kind of data can have? Ok, if the distance was a **double** that represents miles, then what is the largest value it can have, since we need to find distances that are less than this? Thus, we must have the user provide the build function with an **Edge** structure that contains the largest possible weight value in this situation.

Unlike the traversal methods that need a "visited" flag for the duration of the traversal, here we need to retain the state of being in the minimum spanning tree until the user is finished using the graph. Thus, I chose to have another member of our nodes keep track of whether or not this item is in the minimum spanning tree. It is the **bool inShortestPath** found in both the **VertexNode** and **EdgeNode** structure.

The **BuildMinimumSpanningTree** function is passed an **Edge** that contains the maximum distance. The function first clears all of the **inShortestPath bool**s. The process begins with the head vertex of the list and processes all of the vertices. Within the outer loop, I define a minimum Edge instance as containing the maximum Edge value. Now, we look at all of the edges connected to this vertex and find the minimum distance edge for any one that is not already in the shortest path. If we find one that is smaller than the currently smallest one, I save a pointer to the found one and adjust the minium distance downward. If one is found, then I set both the "from" and "to" vertices' **inShortestPath** members to **true**. Notice that I must rely on the user's **Edge operator<** function.

```
void Graph::BuildMinimumSpanningTree (Edge& maxEdgeValue) {
 ClearInShortestTreeFlags ();     // clear all span flags
 if (!ptrHead) return;            // here there is nothing to do
 VertexNode* ptrthis = ptrHead;   // begin with the first vertex
 ptrthis->inShortestPath = true; // set in shortest path
 bool treeComplete = false;
 while (!treeComplete) {          // repeat until tree is done
  // assume it's done unless we find another one
  treeComplete = true;
  VertexNode* ptrcheck = ptrthis; // check this one out
  EdgeNode* ptrMinEdge = 0;
  Edge minEdge = maxEdgeValue;    // set to smallest value
  while (ptrcheck) {
   // if this one is in the shortest path and has edges, then
   if (ptrcheck->inShortestPath && ptrcheck->outDegree > 0) {
    EdgeNode* ptre = ptrcheck->ptrEdgeHead; // process all edges
    while (ptre) {
     if (!ptre->ptrToVertex->inShortestPath) { // if it is not,
      treeComplete = false;         // then we must check it out
      // call user's op< function to check if this edge is < min
      if (ptre->edgeData < minEdge) {
       minEdge = ptre->edgeData;    // it is, so update the min
       ptrMinEdge = ptre;
      }
     }
     ptre = ptre->ptrFwd;           // repeat for all edges
    }
   }
   ptrcheck = ptrcheck->ptrFwd;     // repeat for all verts
  }
  if (ptrMinEdge) {                 // if we found one,
   ptrMinEdge->inShortestPath = true; // flag being in shortest
   ptrMinEdge->ptrToVertex->inShortestPath = true; // path
  }
 }
}
```

With the minimum spanning tree build, **ShowMinimumSpanningTree** can be used to display the resultant tree. The caller provides a callback function that is passed a pair of pair of minimum spanning vertices and the distance between them.

```
void Graph::ShowMinimumSpanningTree (
      void (*DisplayEdge) (const Vertex& from, const Vertex& to,
                           const Edge& edge)) {
 if (!ptrHead) return; // an empty graph
```

```
 VertexNode* ptrthis = ptrHead; // loop through all vertices
 while (ptrthis) {
  EdgeNode* ptre = ptrthis->ptrEdgeHead; // loop thru all edges
  while (ptre) {
   if (ptre->inShortestPath)  // if in shortest path, display it
    DisplayEdge (ptrthis->vertexData,
                 ptre->ptrToVertex->vertexData, ptre->edgeData);
   ptre = ptre->ptrFwd;
  }
  ptrthis = ptrthis->ptrFwd;
 }
}
```

The next likely question we will be asked is "What is the shortest path between two vertices?" The caller passes our function a "from" and "to" **Vertex** instances; we must find the minimum path between them. Finding the minimum path between two vertices is much like the other two traversal methods. However, the stack and queue which were used before are now replaced by a priority queue. That is, when we must order the vertices to search by priority based upon the smallest weight. In other words, when we queue up vertices to try, we always want that vertex with the smallest distance from the current one to be at the front of the queue to try next.

Our priority queue is derived from the **Heap** class and this poses a new problem. When the heap is rebuilt, it places the largest value item at element 0. So if we blindly check is any item is less than another item, we will have the heap backwards! On the other hand, sometimes, the minimum value, from the user's position is actually the larger value. Rather than locking our solution into either "smallest value is largest" or "largest value is smallest," I let the user notify us of the situation via a **bool**, **smallestIsHighest**. Then, if I relay that state to all of the items, then the comparison operators can return the proper result no matter which way the user desires. Again, this makes a more generalized solution.

Typically, these shortest path algorithms, display all possible shortest paths from a given vertex. While this extra information is sometimes useful, normally, the user wants to just see that shortest path from A to B. Hence, the function is passed another **bool**, **showOnlyShortest**, which is **true** if the user only wants to see the actual shortest path from A to B.

The caller must also provide a callback function to receive pairs of **Vertex** structures and the minimum distance between them. The final item that is required is the smallest value that the user's distance item can hold. Since we do not know its data type, the caller passes an **Edge** structure that contains the smallest distance value. Notice that this is the opposite of the previous function which required the largest value.

In order to handle this process, we need a helper structure to organize the results. I call it **ItemNode**. It contains the "from" and "to" **VertexNode** pointers along with the **Edge** distance between these and the order long which the priority queue uses when two items have equal priority and the **smallestIsHighest** flag. Notice how I have implemented the two different sets of comparison operator results, depending on the setting of **smallestIsHighest**.

```
/***************************************************************/
/*                                                             */
/* ItemNode: helper struct for finding shortest distances      */
/*                                                             */
/* because of heap, the largest value is at top - so we must   */
/* reverse test results is smallest is the highest value       */
/*                                                             */
/***************************************************************/

struct ItemNode {
 VertexNode* ptrFromVertex;
 VertexNode* ptrToVertex;
 bool        smallestIsHighest;
 long        order;
 Edge        distance;
 bool operator< (const ItemNode& i2) const;
 bool operator<= (const ItemNode& i2) const;
};

bool ItemNode::operator< (const ItemNode& i2) const {
 if (smallestIsHighest) {
  if (distance < i2.distance) return false;
  if (distance == i2.distance)
```

```
   return order < i2.order ? false : true;
  return true;
 }
 else {
  if (distance < i2.distance) return true;
  if (distance == i2.distance)
   return order < i2.order ? true : false;
  return false;
 }
}

bool ItemNode::operator<= (const ItemNode& i2) const {
 if (smallestIsHighest) {
  if (distance < i2.distance) return false;
  if (distance == i2.distance)
   return order < i2.order ? false : true;
  return true;
 }
 else {
  if (distance < i2.distance) return true;
  if (distance == i2.distance)
   return order < i2.order ? true : false;
  return false;
 }
}
```

This **FindShortestPath** function is the longest function in the class. It is composed of two sections: finding all of the shortest paths from a given vertex and then finding and showing just the path desired in the correct order of vertices from the "from" vertex to the "to" vertex.

The finding the shortest path uses a **PriorityQueue** in place of the stack and uses a queue to store the ones to try next just as in the previous examples. However, when an item is found to be in the shortest path sequence, it is copied and placed into a linked list of answers for use in the second half of the function. Thus, when the first half of the processing is finished, the **answers** list contains a collection of **ItemNode** structures each with a "from" and "to" set of nodes and the accumulated distance between the original "from" vertex and the current to vertex.

FindShortestPath begins by finding the "from" vertex in the list of vertices. If it is found, then all of the visited flags are cleared. The **order long** is initialized to 1, in case there are duplicate distances to be priority enqueued.

```
bool Graph::FindShortestPath (const Vertex& from,
                               const Vertex& to,
                               const Edge& minDist,
                               bool showOnlyShortest,
                               bool smallestIsHighest,
 void (*DisplayShortestPath) (const Vertex& from,
                               const Vertex& to,
                               const Edge& distance) ) {
 if (!ptrHead) return false; // nothing to do

 // find the from vertex
 VertexNode* ptrfrom = FindThisVertex (from);
 if (!ptrfrom) return false; // nothing to do

 ClearProcessedFlags ();
 // order is required in case queue items have same priority
 long order = 1;
```

Next, an **ItemNode** instance, called **item**, is initialized to the starting node. A minimum distance Edge structure is initialized to the minimum value a user's distance can have. And an instance of the **PriorityQueue**, **Queue**, and **DoubleLinkedList** classes are created and this original **item** is priority enqueued.

```
 ItemNode item; // setup the initial beginning node
 item.smallestIsHighest = smallestIsHighest;
 item.ptrFromVertex = ptrfrom;
 item.ptrToVertex = ptrfrom;
 item.distance = minDist;
 item.order = order++;
```

```
Edge minimumDistance = minDist; // set min dist to default min
PriorityQueue<ItemNode> pqueue;
Queue<VertexNode> queue;
DoubleLinkedList<ItemNode> answers;

pqueue.Enqueue (item);// put this first item into priority queue
bool failed = false;  // set to true if we encounter an internal
                      // error
```

The main loop dequeues the highest priority item. If it is not yet visited, it is handled as follows. It is marked as visited and a new **ItemNode** structure is allocated and the current **item** instance is copied into it and it is added to the tail of the **answers** list. Note that this first answer contains a "from" and "to" vertex which are the same value, the "from" vertex and the accumulated distance is the minimum value an **Edge** can have, usually 0. With this node saved in the answer list, I now change the "from" destination of the **item** to be the "to" vertex and set the currently found **minimumDistance** to the currently found **item distance**. Since I made a copy of the original state of **item**, the answer **ItemNode** does not get altered by this process.

Next, I do a normal enqueue of all of the edges of this current vertex.

```
do {
 pqueue.Dequeue (item); // get highest priotity vertex to check
 // if it is not yet visited, handle it
 if (item.ptrToVertex->visitedFlag == NotVisited) {
  item.ptrToVertex->visitedFlag = Visited;
  ItemNode* ptrqi = new ItemNode; // copy current item node and
  *ptrqi = item;                  // add it to the answers list
  answers.AddAtTail (ptrqi);
  item.ptrFromVertex = item.ptrToVertex; // reset from vertex
  minimumDistance = item.distance;       // store new min dist
  // now queue up all of its edges
  EdgeNode* ptre = item.ptrFromVertex->ptrEdgeHead;
  while (ptre) {
   queue.Enqueue (ptre->ptrToVertex);
   ptre = ptre->ptrFwd;
  }
```

Now, we must examine all edges in turn that are queued up. If any are not yet visited, I must find that node's list of **EdgeNodes** to check. Here, I used a helper function, **FindThisEdge** which returns a pointer to the found **EdgeNode** structure. **FindThisEdge** is given the two vertices and it then finds the corresponding **EdgeNode** between them by finding the "from" vertex in the main list of vertices and then searches its list of **EdgeNode** structures looking for a match.

```
  while (!queue.IsEmpty ()) {
   VertexNode* ptrthis = queue.Dequeue ();
   if (ptrthis->visitedFlag == NotVisited) {
    item.ptrToVertex = ptrthis;
    EdgeNode* ptree = FindThisEdge (
                             item.ptrFromVertex->vertexData,
                             ptrthis->vertexData);
    if (!ptree) { // here we cannot find the requested edge
     failed = true;
     break;
    }
```

Having found the edge between these two, we add in the edge's distance into the **item**'s accumulated **distance**. After incrementing the count, this item is then priority enqueued.

```
    // add in the distance to this edge
    item.distance = minimumDistance + ptree->edgeData;
    item.order = order++;
    pqueue.Enqueue (item); // add this one to the priority queue
   }
  }
 }
} while (!failed && !pqueue.IsArrayEmpty ());
```

When all items have been processed, the **answers** list contains a series of all possible minimum distances from the original "from" vertex. To understand what is in the list of **answers**, refer to Figure 13.21 The Minimum Spanning

Tree above. The red lines represent the minimum paths. Suppose that we called **FindShortestPath** passing it vertex A and E. The list of items in the **answers** linked list for this graph would be as follows.

A A 0
A B 3
B D 5
D C 6
C E 11 <---
D F 9

Sometimes, the user wants all of this information. But usually, they desire only the shortest path, in this case from A to E.

The second half of the function either displays all of the results or finds only the shortest path and then shows it. The algorithm to find the shortest path out of this set of results is simple. Search the list of items looking for the "to" vertex in the "to" column. I indicated that one with an arrow above. Push that item onto a stack. Now, we got to E by "from" vertex C, so look from the beginning of the list for a "to" vertex of C. Push that one onto the stack. We got there using a "from"vertex of D, so look from the beginning for a "to" vertex of D and push that one onto the stack. The process is repeated until we push onto the stack an **ItemNode** whose "from" vertex is the original "from" vertex, here A. Finally, to display the path, just pop each item off in turn and display it. Using the above we would produce the following.

A B 3
B D 5
D C 6
C E 11

And this is the shortest path from A to E. And it is presented to the user in a manner that they can effectively use.

```
ItemNode* ptri;
if (!failed) {
 answers.ResetToHead ();
 ptri = answers.GetCurrentNode ();
 if (showOnlyShortest) { // if we want to show only the shortest
  Vertex findThisOne = to; // path, then begin by finding the to
  Stack<ItemNode> path;    // node and push it on the stack
  answers.ResetToHead ();  // then find how we got to it
  ptri = answers.GetCurrentNode (); // and so on til we get to
  while (ptri) {           // the from vertex
   if (ptri->ptrToVertex->vertexData == findThisOne) {
    path.Push (ptri);
    if (ptri->ptrFromVertex->vertexData == from)
     break;
    findThisOne = ptri->ptrFromVertex->vertexData;
    answers.ResetToHead ();
   }
   else
    answers.Next();
   ptri = answers.GetCurrentNode ();
  }
  // now poping off the vertices shows the path from-to
  ptri = path.Pop ();
  while (ptri) {
   DisplayShortestPath (ptri->ptrFromVertex->vertexData,
                 ptri->ptrToVertex->vertexData, ptri->distance);
   ptri = path.Pop ();
  }
 }
 // otherwise, user wants all shortest paths found
 else {
  while (ptri) {
   DisplayShortestPath (ptri->ptrFromVertex->vertexData,
                 ptri->ptrToVertex->vertexData, ptri->distance);
   answers.Next ();
   ptri = answers.GetCurrentNode ();
  }
```

```
  }
 }
 return true;
}
```

Here is the remainder of the **Graph.cpp** file with the advanced functions. For completeness, I also show the other template container classes that are used.

```
/***************************************************************/
/*                                                             */
/* DoesPathExistBetween_DepthFirst: returns true if a path     */
/*                  exists between the two indicated Vertices */
/*                                                             */
/***************************************************************/

bool Graph::DoesPathExistBetween_DepthFirst
                         (const Vertex& from, const Vertex& to) {
 if (!ptrHead) return false; // an empty graph

 // try to find the from vertex
 VertexNode* ptrfrom = FindThisVertex (from);
 if (!ptrfrom) return false;

 // from Vertex is found, so now try to find a path to "to" vert.
 Stack<VertexNode> stack;     // stack of vertices to try
 ClearProcessedFlags ();      // set all flags to NotVisited
 Queue<VertexNode> queue;     // queue of vertices to try next
 bool found = false;          // found is true when a path exists
 stack.Push (ptrfrom);        // store initial from vertex
 VertexNode* ptrthis;
 do {
  ptrthis = stack.Pop ();     // pop next vertex to try
  // call user's operator= function to look for the "to" vertex
  if (ptrthis->vertexData == to) {
   found = true;              // it was found, so we are done
   break;
  }

  // this vertex is not it, so if it has not yet been visited,
  // enqueue all of its edges and try them
  if (ptrthis->visitedFlag == NotVisited) {
   ptrthis->visitedFlag = Visited;
   EdgeNode* ptre = ptrthis->ptrEdgeHead;
   while (ptre) { // enqueues all of this vertex's edges
    queue.Enqueue (ptre->ptrToVertex);
    ptre = ptre->ptrFwd;
   }
   // now try each edge. If an edge has not yet been visited,
   // push that vertex onto the stack to be tried later on
   while (!queue.IsEmpty()) {
    VertexNode* ptrv = queue.Dequeue ();
    if (ptrv->visitedFlag == NotVisited)
     stack.Push (ptrv);
   }
  }
 } while (!stack.IsEmpty() && !found); // repeat for all vertices
 return found;
}
```

```

/***************************************************************/
/*                                                             */
/* DoesPathExistBetween_BreadthFirst: returns true if a path   */
/*                  exists between the two indicated Vertices */
/*                                                             */
/***************************************************************/

bool Graph::DoesPathExistBetween_BreadthFirst
                         (const Vertex& from, const Vertex& to) {
 if (!ptrHead) return false; // no vertices in the graph

 // try to find the from vertex, returning false if not found
 VertexNode* ptrfrom = FindThisVertex (from);
 if (!ptrfrom) return false;

 ClearProcessedFlags ();  // set all flags as NotVisited yet
 bool found = false;      // true when we have found the "to"

 Queue<VertexNode> queue1; // the main queue to check
 queue1.Enqueue (ptrfrom); // store the first vertex

 Queue<VertexNode> queue2; // secondary to try queue
 VertexNode* ptrthis;
 do {
  ptrthis = queue1.Dequeue (); // retrieve next vertex to try
  // call the user's operator== function to see it this is it
  if (ptrthis->vertexData == to) {
   found = true;            // we have found the "to" vertex!
   break;
  }

  // this one is not it, if this vertex has not yet been visited
  if (ptrthis->visitedFlag == NotVisited) { // then visit it
   ptrthis->visitedFlag = Visited;
   EdgeNode* ptre = ptrthis->ptrEdgeHead;

   // enqueue all of this vertex's edges
   while (ptre) {
    queue2.Enqueue (ptre->ptrToVertex);
    ptre = ptre->ptrFwd;
   }

   // now check all of this vertex's edges - if any are not yet
   // visited, then add them to the main queue to be visited
   while (!queue2.IsEmpty()) {
    VertexNode* ptrv = queue2.Dequeue ();
    if (ptrv->visitedFlag == NotVisited)
     queue1.Enqueue (ptrv);
   }
  }
 } while (!queue1.IsEmpty() && !found); // repeat for all vertex
 return found;
}

/***************************************************************/
```

```
/*                                                               */
/* BuildMinimumSpanningTree: construct a min span tree           */
/*                                                               */
/*****************************************************************/

void Graph::BuildMinimumSpanningTree (Edge& maxEdgeValue) {
 ClearInShortestTreeFlags ();     // clear all span flags
 if (!ptrHead) return;            // here there is nothing to do
 VertexNode* ptrthis = ptrHead;   // begin with the first vertex
 ptrthis->inShortestPath = true;  // set in shortest path
 bool treeComplete = false;
 while (!treeComplete) {          // repeat until tree is done
  // assume it's done unless we find another one
  treeComplete = true;
  VertexNode* ptrcheck = ptrthis; // check this one out
  EdgeNode* ptrMinEdge = 0;
  Edge minEdge = maxEdgeValue;    // set to smallest value
  while (ptrcheck) {
   // if this one is in the shortest path and has edges, then
   if (ptrcheck->inShortestPath && ptrcheck->outDegree > 0) {
    EdgeNode* ptre = ptrcheck->ptrEdgeHead; // process all edges
    while (ptre) {
     if (!ptre->ptrToVertex->inShortestPath) { // if it is not,
      treeComplete = false;        // then we must check it out
      // call user's op< function to check if this edge is < min
      if (ptre->edgeData < minEdge) {
       minEdge = ptre->edgeData;   // it is, so update the min
       ptrMinEdge = ptre;
      }
     }
     ptre = ptre->ptrFwd;          // repeat for all edges
    }
   }
   ptrcheck = ptrcheck->ptrFwd;    // repeat for all verts
  }
  if (ptrMinEdge) {                // if we found one,
   ptrMinEdge->inShortestPath = true; // flag being in shortest
   ptrMinEdge->ptrToVertex->inShortestPath = true; // path
  }
 }
}

/*****************************************************************/
/*                                                               */
/* ShowMinimumSpanningTree: display the resultant min span tree*/
/*                                                               */
/*****************************************************************/

void Graph::ShowMinimumSpanningTree (
       void (*DisplayEdge) (const Vertex& from, const Vertex& to,
                            const Edge& edge)) {
 if (!ptrHead) return; // an empty graph

 VertexNode* ptrthis = ptrHead; // loop through all vertices
 while (ptrthis) {
  EdgeNode* ptre = ptrthis->ptrEdgeHead; // loop thru all edges
```

```
  while (ptre) {
   if (ptre->inShortestPath)  // if in shortest path, display it
    DisplayEdge (ptrthis->vertexData,
                 ptre->ptrToVertex->vertexData, ptre->edgeData);
   ptre = ptre->ptrFwd;
  }
  ptrthis = ptrthis->ptrFwd;
 }
}

/***************************************************************/
/*                                                             */
/* ItemNode: helper struct for finding shortest distances      */
/*                                                             */
/* because of heap, the largest value is at top - so we must   */
/* reverse test results is smallest is the highest value       */
/*                                                             */
/***************************************************************/

struct ItemNode {
 VertexNode* ptrFromVertex;
 VertexNode* ptrToVertex;
 bool        smallestIsHighest;
 long        order;
 Edge        distance;
 bool operator< (const ItemNode& i2) const;
 bool operator<= (const ItemNode& i2) const;
};

bool ItemNode::operator< (const ItemNode& i2) const {
 if (smallestIsHighest) {
  if (distance < i2.distance) return false;
  if (distance == i2.distance)
   return order < i2.order ? false : true;
  return true;
 }
 else {
  if (distance < i2.distance) return true;
  if (distance == i2.distance)
   return order < i2.order ? true : false;
  return false;
 }
}

bool ItemNode::operator<= (const ItemNode& i2) const {
 if (smallestIsHighest) {
  if (distance < i2.distance) return false;
  if (distance == i2.distance)
   return order < i2.order ? false : true;
  return true;
 }
 else {
  if (distance < i2.distance) return true;
  if (distance == i2.distance)
   return order < i2.order ? true : false;
  return false;
```

```
 }
}

/***************************************************************/
/*                                                             */
/* FindShortestPath: calcs the shortest path from - to verts   */
/*                                                             */
/* Caller provides an Edge that is storing the minimum value   */
/* that that data type can hold                                */
/*                                                             */
/* if showOnlyShortest, then only display that path            */
/* otherwise, show all the shortest paths for all from "from"  */
/*                                                             */
/* if smallestIsHighest, we must reverse the comparison op's   */
/* results so that the "highest" is in heap element [0]        */
/*                                                             */
/***************************************************************/

bool Graph::FindShortestPath (const Vertex& from,
                              const Vertex& to,
                              const Edge& minDist,
                              bool showOnlyShortest,
                              bool smallestIsHighest,
 void (*DisplayShortestPath) (const Vertex& from,
                              const Vertex& to,
                              const Edge& distance) ) {
 if (!ptrHead) return false; // nothing to do

 // find the from vertex
 VertexNode* ptrfrom = FindThisVertex (from);
 if (!ptrfrom) return false; // nothing to do

 ClearProcessedFlags ();
 // order is required in case queue items have same priority
 long order = 1;

 ItemNode item; // setup the initial beginning node
 item.smallestIsHighest = smallestIsHighest;
 item.ptrFromVertex = ptrfrom;
 item.ptrToVertex = ptrfrom;
 item.distance = minDist;
 item.order = order++;
 Edge minimumDistance = minDist; // set min dist to default min
 PriorityQueue<ItemNode> pqueue;
 Queue<VertexNode> queue;
 DoubleLinkedList<ItemNode> answers;

 pqueue.Enqueue (item);// put this first item into priority queue
 bool failed = false;  // set to true if we encounter an internal
                       // error
 do {
  pqueue.Dequeue (item); // get highest priotity vertex to check
  // if it is not yet visited, handle it
  if (item.ptrToVertex->visitedFlag == NotVisited) {
   item.ptrToVertex->visitedFlag = Visited;
   ItemNode* ptrqi = new ItemNode; // copy current item node and
```

```
    *ptrqi = item;                        // add it to the answers list
    answers.AddAtTail (ptrqi);
    item.ptrFromVertex = item.ptrToVertex; // reset from vertex
    minimumDistance = item.distance;       // store new min dist
    // now queue up all of its edges
    EdgeNode* ptre = item.ptrFromVertex->ptrEdgeHead;
    while (ptre) {
     queue.Enqueue (ptre->ptrToVertex);
     ptre = ptre->ptrFwd;
    }
    // now examine all edges
    while (!queue.IsEmpty ()) {
     VertexNode* ptrthis = queue.Dequeue ();
     if (ptrthis->visitedFlag == NotVisited) {
      item.ptrToVertex = ptrthis;
      EdgeNode* ptree = FindThisEdge (
                             item.ptrFromVertex->vertexData,
                             ptrthis->vertexData);
      if (!ptree) { // here we cannot find the requested edge
       failed = true;
       break;
      }
      // add in the distance to this edge
      item.distance = minimumDistance + ptree->edgeData;
      item.order = order++;
      pqueue.Enqueue (item); // add this one to the priority queue
     }
    }
   }
  } while (!failed && !pqueue.IsArrayEmpty ());

  // now examine the answer list and display just that part of the
  // result the user requires
  ItemNode* ptri;
  if (!failed) {
   answers.ResetToHead ();
   ptri = answers.GetCurrentNode ();
   if (showOnlyShortest) { // if we want to show only the shortest
    Vertex findThisOne = to; // path, then begin by finding the to
    Stack<ItemNode> path;    // node and push it on the stack
    answers.ResetToHead (); // then find how we got to it
    ptri = answers.GetCurrentNode (); // and so on til we get to
    while (ptri) {            // the from vertex
     if (ptri->ptrToVertex->vertexData == findThisOne) {
      path.Push (ptri);
      if (ptri->ptrFromVertex->vertexData == from)
       break;
      findThisOne = ptri->ptrFromVertex->vertexData;
      answers.ResetToHead ();
     }
     else
      answers.Next();
     ptri = answers.GetCurrentNode ();
    }
    // now poping off the vertices shows the path from-to
    ptri = path.Pop ();
```

```
   while (ptri) {
    DisplayShortestPath (ptri->ptrFromVertex->vertexData,
                  ptri->ptrToVertex->vertexData, ptri->distance);
    ptri = path.Pop ();
   }
  }
  // otherwise, user wants all shortest paths found
  else {
   while (ptri) {
    DisplayShortestPath (ptri->ptrFromVertex->vertexData,
                  ptri->ptrToVertex->vertexData, ptri->distance);
    answers.Next ();
    ptri = answers.GetCurrentNode ();
   }
  }
 }
 return true;
}

/***************************************************************/
/*                                                             */
/* FindThisEdge: given two vertices, find corresponding edge   */
/*                                                             */
/***************************************************************/

EdgeNode* Graph::FindThisEdge (const Vertex& from,
                               const Vertex& to) const {
 if (!ptrHead) return 0; // nothing to find

 // find the from vertex in the vertex list
 VertexNode* ptrfrom = FindThisVertex (from);
 if (!ptrfrom) return 0; // from vertex not in the list

 // find the to vertex in the from's edge list
 EdgeNode* ptre = ptrfrom->ptrEdgeHead;
 while (ptre) {
  if (ptre->ptrToVertex->vertexData == to)
   return ptre; // found it, so return this edge
  ptre = ptre->ptrFwd;
 }

 return 0; // return not found
}
```

Stack Class Template

```
#pragma once
#include <iostream>
using namespace std;

/***************************************************************/
/*                                                             */
/* StackNode: contains the forward pointer and this item data  */
/*                                                             */
/***************************************************************/
```

```
template<class UserData>
struct StackNode {
 StackNode* fwdptr;
 UserData*  dataptr;
};

/***************************************************************/
/*                                                             */
/* Stack: a generic stack class                                */
/*                                                             */
/***************************************************************/

template<class UserData>
class Stack {
protected:
 StackNode<UserData>* headptr; // the top of the stack pointer
 long                 count;   // number of items in the stack

public:
 Stack ();                         // construct an empty stack
 Stack (const Stack<UserData>& s); // the copy constructor
 Stack& operator= (const Stack<UserData>& s); // assignment op

 ~Stack ();                        // delete the stack

 void Push (UserData* ptrdata); // store new node on the stack
 UserData* Pop ();            // removes top node from the stack
 UserData* GetCurrentData () const; // returns user's data on top
 long GetCount () const; // returns the number of nodes in stack

 bool IsEmpty () const;  // returns true if stack is empty
 void RemoveAll ();      // removes all nodes in the stack

protected:
 // helper function to duplicate the stack
 void CopyStack (const Stack& s);
};

/***************************************************************/
/*                                                             */
/* Stack: create an empty stack                                */
/*                                                             */
/***************************************************************/

template<class UserData>
Stack<UserData>::Stack () {
 headptr = 0;
 count = 0;
}

/***************************************************************/
/*                                                             */
/* ~Stack: deletes the stack                                   */
/*                                                             */
/***************************************************************/

```

```
template<class UserData>
Stack<UserData>::~Stack () {
 RemoveAll ();
}

/***************************************************************/
/*                                                             */
/* RemoveAll: deletes all nodes of the stack                   */
/*                                                             */
/***************************************************************/

template<class UserData>
void Stack<UserData>::RemoveAll () {
 while (!IsEmpty()) Pop ();
}

/***************************************************************/
/*                                                             */
/* Push: store new node on the top of the stack                */
/*                                                             */
/***************************************************************/

template<class UserData>
void Stack<UserData>::Push (UserData* ptrdata) {
 StackNode<UserData>* ptrnew = new StackNode<UserData>;
 ptrnew->dataptr = ptrdata;
 ptrnew->fwdptr = headptr;
 headptr = ptrnew;
 count++;
}

/***************************************************************/
/*                                                             */
/* Pop: remove the top item from the stack                     */
/*                                                             */
/***************************************************************/

template<class UserData>
UserData* Stack<UserData>::Pop () {
 if (!headptr) return 0;
 StackNode<UserData>* ptrtodel = headptr;
 headptr = headptr->fwdptr;
 UserData* ptrdata = ptrtodel->dataptr;
 delete ptrtodel;
 count--;
 return ptrdata;
}

/***************************************************************/
/*                                                             */
/* GetCurrentData: returns a pointer to user data on the top   */
/*                 of the stack or 0 if it is empty            */
/*                                                             */
/***************************************************************/

template<class UserData>
```

```
UserData* Stack<UserData>::GetCurrentData () const {
 return !IsEmpty () ? headptr->dataptr : 0;
}

/***************************************************************/
/*                                                             */
/* IsEmpty: returns true when there are no items on the stack  */
/*                                                             */
/***************************************************************/

template<class UserData>
bool Stack<UserData>::IsEmpty () const{
 return headptr ? false : true;
}

/***************************************************************/
/*                                                             */
/* GetCount: returns the number of nodes on the stack          */
/*                                                             */
/***************************************************************/

template<class UserData>
long Stack<UserData>::GetCount () const {
 return count;
}

/***************************************************************/
/*                                                             */
/* Stack: copy constructor - make a duplicate copy of passed s */
/*                                                             */
/***************************************************************/

template<class UserData>
Stack<UserData>::Stack (const Stack<UserData>& s) {
 CopyStack (s);
}

/***************************************************************/
/*                                                             */
/* operator=: assignment op - makes a copy of passed stack     */
/*                                                             */
/***************************************************************/

template<class UserData>
Stack<UserData>& Stack<UserData>::operator= (
                                      const Stack<UserData>& s) {
 if (this == &s) return *this; // avoid a = a; situation
 RemoveAll ();  // remove all items in this stack
 CopyStack (s);  // make a copy of stack s
 return *this;
}

/***************************************************************/
/*                                                             */
/* CopyStack: helper that makes a duplicate copy               */
/*                                                             */
```

```
/*************************************************************/

template<class UserData>
void Stack<UserData>::CopyStack (const Stack<UserData>& s) {
 if (!s.headptr) { // handle stack s being empty
  headptr = 0;
  count = 0;
  return;
 }
 count = s.count;
 StackNode<UserData>* ptrScurrent = s.headptr;
 // previousptr tracks our prior node so we can set its
 // forward pointer to the next new one
 StackNode<UserData>* previousptr = 0;
 // prime the loop so headptr can be set one time
 StackNode<UserData>* currentptr = new StackNode<UserData>;
 headptr = currentptr;  // assign this one to the headptr

// traverse s stack's nodes
 while (ptrScurrent) {
  // copy node of s into our new node
  currentptr->dataptr = ptrScurrent->dataptr;
  currentptr->fwdptr = 0;  // set our forward ptr to 0
  // if previous node exists, set its forward ptr to the new one
  if (previousptr)
   previousptr->fwdptr = currentptr;
  // save this node as the prevous node
  previousptr = currentptr;
  // and get a new node for the next iteration
  currentptr = new StackNode;
  // move to s's next node
  ptrScurrent = ptrScurrent->fwdptr;
 }
 delete currentptr; // delete the extra unneeded node
}
```

Queue Class Template

```
#pragma once
using namespace std;

/*************************************************************/
/*                                                           */
/* QueueNode: stores the double linked list's fwd/back ptrs  */
/*            and the user's data ptr                        */
/*                                                           */
/*************************************************************/

template<class UserData>
struct QueueNode {   // a double linked list
 QueueNode* fwdptr;
 QueueNode* backptr;
 UserData*  dataptr; // the user's object being stored
};

```

```
/***************************************************************/
/*                                                             */
/* Queue Container Class                                       */
/*                                                             */
/* stores void pointers to user's objects                      */
/* before deleting an instance, the user MUST traverse and     */
/* delete any objects whose pointers are being stored          */
/*                                                             */
/***************************************************************/

template<class UserData>
class Queue {

public:
 Queue ();                            // makes an empty queue
 Queue (const Queue<UserData>& q);  // copy constructor
 Queue<UserData>& operator= (const Queue<UserData>& q);
 // VITAL NOTE: when a copy is made, the copy contains the SAME
 // pointers as the original Queue - be careful not to delete
 // them twice

 ~Queue ();            // the destructor removes the queue
 void  RemoveAll (); // but not the user objects being stored!

 void  Enqueue (UserData* ptrdata);// add an object to the queue
 UserData* Dequeue ();              // ret and remove current node
 long  GetSize () const;            // returns size of the queue
 bool  IsEmpty () const;

 void  ResetToHead (); // reset current to the start of the queue
 UserData* GetNext (); // returns next user object or 0 when at
                       // the end of the queue
 // for cleanup operations, traverse the queue and delete the
 // objects the queue is saving for you before you destroy or
 // empty the queue

/***************************************************************/
/*                                                             */
/* for Queue's internal use only                               */
/* Queue uses a double linked list                             */
/*                                                             */
/***************************************************************/

private:
 QueueNode<UserData>* headptr;    // pointer to first node
 QueueNode<UserData>* tailptr;    // pointer to last node
 QueueNode<UserData>* currentptr; // current node when traversing
 long       count;      // the number of nodes

 // helper function to copy a Queue
 void  CopyQueue (const Queue<UserData>& q);
};

/***************************************************************/
/*                                                             */
/* Queue: construct an empty queue                             */
```

```
/*                                                              */
/****************************************************************/

template<class UserData>
Queue<UserData>::Queue () {
 headptr = currentptr = tailptr = 0;
 count = 0;
}

/****************************************************************/
/*                                                              */
/* ~Queue: remove all QueueNode objects - but does not delete   */
/*         any user objects                                     */
/*                                                              */
/****************************************************************/

template<class UserData>
Queue<UserData>::~Queue () {
 RemoveAll ();
}

/****************************************************************/
/*                                                              */
/* RemoveAll: removes all QueueNode Objects, leaving the queue */
/*            in an empty but valid state                       */
/*                                                              */
/****************************************************************/

template<class UserData>
void Queue<UserData>::RemoveAll () {
 if (!headptr) return;         // nothing to do case
 QueueNode<UserData>* ptrnext = headptr; // start at the front
 QueueNode<UserData>* ptrdel;
 while (ptrnext) {            // for all QueueNodes,
  ptrdel = ptrnext;           // save its pointer for later deletion
  ptrnext = ptrnext->fwdptr;// set for next node in the queue
  delete ptrdel;              // remove this node
 }
 // leave queue in a default, valid , empty state
 currentptr = tailptr = headptr = 0;
 count = 0;
}

/****************************************************************/
/*                                                              */
/* Queue Copy Constructor: duplicate the passed Queue object   */
/*                                                              */
/* VITAL: we will not duplicate the user's actual data         */
/*                                                              */
/****************************************************************/

template<class UserData>
Queue<UserData>::Queue (const Queue<UserData>& q) {
 CopyQueue (q);               // call helper function to do the work
}

```

```
/***************************************************************/
/*                                                             */
/* Operator= - Assignment operator: duplicate this Queue object*/
/*                                                             */
/* VITAL: we will not duplicate the user's actual data         */
/*                                                             */
/***************************************************************/

template<class UserData>
Queue<UserData>& Queue<UserData>::operator= (
                                      const Queue<UserData>& q) {
 if (&q == this) return *this; // avoid silly case of x = x;
 if (count != 0) RemoveAll (); // if we are not empty, empty us
 CopyQueue (q);                // call helper function to do it
 return *this;                 // return us so user can chain
}

/***************************************************************/
/*                                                             */
/* CopyQueue: make a shallow copy of the passed queue          */
/*                                                             */
/* VITAL: we will not duplicate the user's actual data         */
/*                                                             */
/***************************************************************/

template<class UserData>
void  Queue<UserData>::CopyQueue (const Queue<UserData>& q) {
 // initialize queue so that we can use Enqueue to add the nodes
 currentptr = tailptr = headptr = 0;
 count = 0;
 if (!q.count) // if there are none, queue is now initialized
  return;
 // point to their head
 QueueNode<UserData>* ptrqcurrent = q.headptr;
 while (ptrqcurrent) {                // while there's another node
  Enqueue (ptrqcurrent->dataptr);    // add it to our queue
  ptrqcurrent = ptrqcurrent->fwdptr;// point to next one to copy
 }
}

/***************************************************************/
/*                                                             */
/* IsEmpty: returns true if queue is empty                     */
/*                                                             */
/***************************************************************/

template<class UserData>
bool Queue<UserData>::IsEmpty () const {
 return count == 0 ? true : false;
}

/***************************************************************/
/*                                                             */
/* Enqueue: Add a new node to the tail of the queue            */
/*                                                             */
/***************************************************************/
```

```
template<class UserData>
void  Queue<UserData>::Enqueue (UserData* ptrdata) {
 QueueNode<UserData>* ptrnew = new QueueNode<UserData>;
 ptrnew->dataptr = ptrdata;     // insert user's object
 count++;                       // increment number of nodes
 if (tailptr) {                 // if there are other nodes,
  tailptr->fwdptr = ptrnew;     // last one now points to us
  ptrnew->backptr = tailptr;    // us points to previous last one
  ptrnew->fwdptr = 0;           // us points to none
  tailptr = currentptr = ptrnew;// reset tail to us
 }
 else { // queue is currently empty, so just add us
  headptr = tailptr = currentptr = ptrnew;
  ptrnew->fwdptr = ptrnew->backptr = 0;
 }
}

/***************************************************************/
/*                                                             */
/* Dequeue: return object at the head and delete that node     */
/*                                                             */
/***************************************************************/

template<class UserData>
UserData* Queue<UserData>::Dequeue () { // remove at head
 if (!headptr) return 0;       // we are empty, so do nothing
 currentptr = headptr;         // reset to the head object
 if (headptr->fwdptr)          // is there more than one node?
  headptr->fwdptr->backptr = 0;// yes,set next one's back to none
 headptr = headptr->fwdptr;    // reset head ptr to the next one
 count--;                      // decrement count of nodes
 if (count == 0) tailptr = 0;  // reset tailptr if queue is empty
 UserData* retval = currentptr->dataptr;// save object to be ret
 delete currentptr;            // remove previous head object
 currentptr = headptr;         // reset the current node ptr
 return retval;                // give the user their object
}

/***************************************************************/
/*                                                             */
/* GetSize: returns the number of items in the queue           */
/*                                                             */
/***************************************************************/

template<class UserData>
long  Queue<UserData>::GetSize () const {
 return count;
}

/***************************************************************/
/*                                                             */
/* ResetToHead: reset currentptr to head pointer for queue     */
/*              traversal operations                           */
/*                                                             */
/***************************************************************/
```

```
template<class UserData>
void  Queue<UserData>::ResetToHead () {
 currentptr = headptr;
}

/***************************************************************/
/*                                                             */
/* GetNext: returns next user object & sets currentptr for next*/
/*                                                             */
/***************************************************************/

template<class UserData>
UserData* Queue<UserData>::GetNext () {
 if (!currentptr) return 0;       // queue is empty, so do nothing
 UserData* retval = currentptr->dataptr;// save object to be ret
 currentptr = currentptr->fwdptr;// set currentptr to next in one
 return retval;                   // give the user the current obj
}
```

Pgm13b—A Sample Application—Airline Routes

I often spend my Christmas holidays with my two young nephews who live near Burbank, California. I am in Peoria, Illinois. Thus, I fly. But which airline and which route should I take? From Peoria, one can fly there several ways, including via Chicago, St. Louis, and Denver, for example. **Pgm13b** builds a graph of a number of airline flights around the country. The **Vertex** contains the city name. The **Edge** contains the air distance between the two cities. See Figure 13.18 once more. And then reexamine the listing for **VertexNode.h** and **VertexNode.cpp** just below that figure.

I created a **Routes.txt** file that contains a number of direct flights. Here is a sample line from the file.

```
From "Peoria, IL" To "Chicago, IL" is 130
```

Pgm13b inputs this routes file and builds a graph from the data. For each line, after inputting the "from" vertex and "to" vertex, **FindThisVertex** is called to verify each vertex is already in the graph. If a vertex is not in the graph, **AddVertex** is called. Once both vertices are present, the **AddEdge** is called to store the distance between the cities. In this manner, a graph can easily be loaded with user information.

However, in order to write a reasonable client program that utilizes these vertices, they need to be stored in an array of **Vertex** structures. I chose to make that an **Array** template class. Then, when the user needs to pick a "from" or "to" city, I can retrieve the vertices from the array and display the city names as well as pass the requested **Vertex** to the various **Graph** functions.

First, let's see what the output of this simple program looks like. After loading the file of vertices, the basic form of the graph is displayed on lines 1 through 40. Then, the two graph traversal functions are called whose output is shown on lines 42 through 59. A minimum spanning tree is built next and shown on lines 62 through 68. Finally, the remainder illustrates a simple user application of determining whether or not a flight exists between two cities and/or the shortest path.

```
Output from Pgm13b Airline Flight Picker Program

 1 A Display of the Graph Tree - Vertex with its Edges
 2
 3 From: Burbank, CA
 4   To: Chicago, IL
 5   To: Denver, CO
 6   To: St. Louis, MO
 7
 8 From: Chicago, IL
 9   To: Burbank, CA
```

```
  To: Denver, CO
  To: Los Angeles, CA
  To: New York, NY
  To: Peoria, IL

From: Denver, CO
  To: Burbank, CA
  To: Chicago, IL
  To: Los Angeles, CA
  To: Peoria, IL
  To: St. Louis, MO

From: Los Angeles, CA
  To: Chicago, IL
  To: Denver, CO
  To: St. Louis, MO

From: New York, NY
  To: Chicago, IL

From: Peoria, IL
  To: Chicago, IL
  To: Denver, CO
  To: St. Louis, MO

From: St. Louis, MO
  To: Burbank, CA
  To: Denver, CO
  To: Los Angeles, CA
  To: Peoria, IL


Depth First Traversal:
Burbank, CA
St. Louis, MO
Peoria, IL
Los Angeles, CA
Denver, CO
Chicago, IL
New York, NY


Breadth First Traversal:
Burbank, CA
Chicago, IL
Denver, CO
St. Louis, MO
Los Angeles, CA
New York, NY
Peoria, IL


The Minimum Spanning Tree
From Vertex: Burbank, CA      To Vertex: Denver, CO         849
From Vertex: Chicago, IL      To Vertex: New York, NY       732
From Vertex: Denver, CO       To Vertex: Los Angeles, CA    861
```

```
From Vertex: Denver, CO      To Vertex: Peoria, IL        791
From Vertex: Peoria, IL      To Vertex: Chicago, IL       130
From Vertex: Peoria, IL      To Vertex: St. Louis, MO     128
        Vic's Airplane Flight Checker
        1. Does a flight exist (depth first)?
        2. Does a flight exist (breadth first)?
        3. What is the shortest route? (Show only shortest)
        4. What is the shortest route? (Show all)
        5. Quit
Enter the number of your choice: 3
        Pick the "From" city
        1. Peoria, IL
        2. Chicago, IL
        3. Denver, CO
        4. St. Louis, MO
        5. Los Angeles, CA
        6. Burbank, CA
        7. New York, NY
        8. Abort this action
Enter the number of your choice: 1
        Pick the "To" city
        1. Peoria, IL
        2. Chicago, IL
        3. Denver, CO
        4. St. Louis, MO
        5. Los Angeles, CA
        6. Burbank, CA
        7. New York, NY
        8. Abort this action
Enter the number of your choice: 6
Shortest path from Peoria, IL to Burbank, CA
   From City            To City                  Total Miles
   Peoria, IL           Denver, CO                   791
   Denver, CO           Burbank, CA                 1640
Enter C to continue c
        Vic's Airplane Flight Checker
```

```

        1. Does a flight exist (depth first)?
        2. Does a flight exist (breadth first)?
        3. What is the shortest route? (Show only shortest)
        4. What is the shortest route? (Show all)
        5. Quit

Enter the number of your choice: 1



        Pick the "From" city
        1. Peoria, IL
        2. Chicago, IL
        3. Denver, CO
        4. St. Louis, MO
        5. Los Angeles, CA
        6. Burbank, CA
        7. New York, NY
        8. Abort this action


Enter the number of your choice: 1



        Pick the "To" city
        1. Peoria, IL
        2. Chicago, IL
        3. Denver, CO
        4. St. Louis, MO
        5. Los Angeles, CA
        6. Burbank, CA
        7. New York, NY
        8. Abort this action


Enter the number of your choice: 6
A path exists between Peoria, IL and Burbank, CA
Enter C to continue
c



        Vic's Airplane Flight Checker

        1. Does a flight exist (depth first)?
        2. Does a flight exist (breadth first)?
        3. What is the shortest route? (Show only shortest)
        4. What is the shortest route? (Show all)
        5. Quit

Enter the number of your choice: 2



```

```
        Pick the "From" city
        1. Peoria, IL
        2. Chicago, IL
        3. Denver, CO
        4. St. Louis, MO
        5. Los Angeles, CA
        6. Burbank, CA
        7. New York, NY
        8. Abort this action

Enter the number of your choice: 1

        Pick the "To" city
        1. Peoria, IL
        2. Chicago, IL
        3. Denver, CO
        4. St. Louis, MO
        5. Los Angeles, CA
        6. Burbank, CA
        7. New York, NY
        8. Abort this action

Enter the number of your choice: 6
A path exists between Peoria, IL and Burbank, CA
Enter C to continue c

        Vic's Airplane Flight Checker

        1. Does a flight exist (depth first)?
        2. Does a flight exist (breadth first)?
        3. What is the shortest route? (Show only shortest)
        4. What is the shortest route? (Show all)
        5. Quit

Enter the number of your choice: 4

        Pick the "From" city
        1. Peoria, IL
        2. Chicago, IL
        3. Denver, CO
        4. St. Louis, MO
        5. Los Angeles, CA
        6. Burbank, CA
        7. New York, NY
        8. Abort this action

Enter the number of your choice: 1
```

```



        Pick the "To" city
        1. Peoria, IL
        2. Chicago, IL
        3. Denver, CO
        4. St. Louis, MO
        5. Los Angeles, CA
        6. Burbank, CA
        7. New York, NY
        8. Abort this action


Enter the number of your choice: 6


Shortest path from Peoria, IL to Burbank, CA
   From City            To City                  Total Miles
   Peoria, IL           Peoria, IL                      0
   Peoria, IL           St. Louis, MO                 128
   Peoria, IL           Chicago, IL                   130
   Peoria, IL           Denver, CO                    791
   Chicago, IL          New York, NY                  862
   Denver, CO           Burbank, CA                  1640
   Denver, CO           Los Angeles, CA              1652
Enter C to continue c



        Vic's Airplane Flight Checker

        1. Does a flight exist (depth first)?
        2. Does a flight exist (breadth first)?
        3. What is the shortest route? (Show only shortest)
        4. What is the shortest route? (Show all)
        5. Quit

Enter the number of your choice: 5
No memory leaks
```

The most important aspect of **Pgm13b** is how the graph is actually built from the user's data file. Notice I separated the lower level action of inputting the line of data into a separate function, **InputLine**, which leaves **LoadGraph** to concentrate only on building the graph. The basic idea is as follows. If a vertex does not exist, then add it. Once both vertices have been added or exist, then add in the edges. In this case, I assume that one can fly both ways—a digraph. You could easily modify this procedure to implement direction as well by changing how the edges are added.

```
Vertex from;
Vertex to;
Edge edge;
while (InputLine (infile, from, to, edge)) {
 if (!g.FindThisVertex (from)) {
  g.AddVertex (from);
  array.Add (from);
 }
 if (!g.FindThisVertex (to)) {
  g.AddVertex (to);
```

```
   array.Add (to);
  }
  g.AddEdge (from, to, edge);
  g.AddEdge (to, from, edge);
 }
```

Notice that if a **Vertex** is not found in the graph, it is added to the graph and to my array of vertices.

Here is the complete **Pgm13b** coding.

Pgm13b Airline Flight Picker Program

```
#include <iostream>
#include <iomanip>
#include <cstring>
#include <crtdbg.h>
#include <fstream>
using namespace std;

/***************************************************************/
/*                                                             */
/* Pgm13b: a Simple Graph Class Tester Program                 */
/*                                                             */
/***************************************************************/

#include "Graph.h"
#include "Array.h"
#include "Heap.h"
#include "PriorityQueue.h"
#include "VertexEdge.h"

/***************************************************************/
/*                                                             */
/* Needed Graph Callback Functions                             */
/*                                                             */
/***************************************************************/

void Display (Vertex& v);
void DisplayTree (Vertex& v, bool isConnectedVertex);
void DisplayShortestPath (const Vertex& from, const Vertex& to,
                          const Edge& distance);
void DisplaySpanningTree (const Vertex& from, const Vertex& to,
                          const Edge& edge);

/***************************************************************/
/*                                                             */
/* Pgm13b: functions                                           */
/*                                                             */
/***************************************************************/

void     LoadGraph (Graph& g, Array<Vertex>& list);
istream& InputLine (istream& is, Vertex& from, Vertex& to,
                    Edge& e);

enum MainMenuChoice {ExistDepth = 1, ExistBreadth, Shortest,
                     ShortestAll, Quit};
MainMenuChoice GetValidMainMenuChoice ();
void DisplayMainMenu ();
```

```

int GetValidCityChoice (Array<Vertex>& array, const char* title);
void DisplayCityPicker (Array<Vertex>& array, const char* title);

int main () {
{
 cin.sync_with_stdio ();
 cout.setf (ios::fixed, ios::floatfield);
 Graph g;

 // illustrate how a graph can be loaded from a file
 Array<Vertex> array;
 LoadGraph (g, array);

 // a simple display to verify graph appears correctly loaded
 cout << "A Display of the Graph Tree - Vertex with its Edges\n";
 g.DisplayTree (DisplayTree);
 cout << endl << endl;

 // sample traversals
 cout << "Depth First Traversal:\n";
 g.DepthFirstTraversal (Display);

 cout << "\n\nBreadth First Traversal:\n";
 g.BreadthFirstTraversal (Display);

 // find the minimum spanning tree
 Edge max;
 max.distance = 1e10;
 g.BuildMinimumSpanningTree (max);
 cout << "\n\nThe Minimum Spanning Tree\n";
 g.ShowMinimumSpanningTree (DisplaySpanningTree);

 // illustrate using the graph to find the shortest paths
 MainMenuChoice choice = GetValidMainMenuChoice ();
 while (choice != Quit) {
  // next pick the from and to cities
  int from = GetValidCityChoice(array, "Pick the \"From\" city");
  if (from == array.GetSize() || from == -1) break;
  int to = GetValidCityChoice (array, "Pick the \"To\" city");
  if (to == array.GetSize() || from == -1) break;

  Vertex fromV = *(array.GetAt (from));
  Vertex toV = *(array.GetAt (to));
  Edge es;
  es.distance = 0;

  switch (choice) {
   case ExistDepth:
    if (g.DoesPathExistBetween_DepthFirst (fromV, toV))
     cout << "A path exists between " << array.GetAt(from)->city
          << " and " << array.GetAt(to)->city << endl;
    else
     cout << "A path does not exist between "
          << array.GetAt(from)->city
          << " and " << array.GetAt(to)->city << endl;
```

```
    break;
   case ExistBreadth:
    if (g.DoesPathExistBetween_BreadthFirst (fromV, toV))
     cout << "A path exists between " << array.GetAt(from)->city
          << " and " << array.GetAt(to)->city << endl;
    else
     cout << "A path does not exist between "
          << array.GetAt(from)->city
          << " and " << array.GetAt(to)->city << endl;
    break;
   case Shortest:
     cout << "\n\nShortest path from " << array.GetAt(from)->city
          << " to " << array.GetAt(to)->city << endl
          <<
 "   From City          To City                    Total Miles\n";
     g.FindShortestPath (fromV, toV, es, true, true,
                         DisplayShortestPath);
    break;
   case ShortestAll:
    cout << "\n\nShortest path from " << array.GetAt(from)->city
         << " to " << array.GetAt(to)->city << endl
         <<
 "   From City          To City                    Total Miles\n";
    g.FindShortestPath (fromV, toV, es, false, true,
                        DisplayShortestPath);
    break;
  }
  char c;
  cout << "Enter C to continue ";
  cin >> c;
  choice = GetValidMainMenuChoice ();
 }
}
 // check for memory leaks
 if (_CrtDumpMemoryLeaks())
  cerr << "Memory leaks occurred!\n";
 else
  cerr << "No memory leaks.\n";
 return 0;
}

/***********************************************************/
/*                                                         */
/* LoadGraph: illustrates how to load a graph from a file */
/*                                                         */
/***********************************************************/

void LoadGraph (Graph& g, Array<Vertex>& array) {
 ifstream infile ("Routes.txt");
 if (!infile) {
  cerr << "Error: cannot open Routes.txt\n";
  exit (2);
 }
 Vertex from;
 Vertex to;
 Edge edge;
```

```
 while (InputLine (infile, from, to, edge)) {
  if (!g.FindThisVertex (from)) {
   g.AddVertex (from);
   array.Add (from);
  }
  if (!g.FindThisVertex (to)) {
   g.AddVertex (to);
   array.Add (to);
  }
  g.AddEdge (from, to, edge);
  g.AddEdge (to, from, edge);
 }
 if (!infile.eof()) {
  infile.close ();
  exit (1);
 }
 infile.close ();
}

/***************************************************************/
/*                                                             */
/* InputLine: inputs a single data line                        */
/*                                                             */
/***************************************************************/

istream& InputLine (istream& is, Vertex& from, Vertex& to,
                    Edge& e) {
 char str[80];
 is >> str;
 if (!is) return is;
 if (_stricmp (str, "From") != 0) {
  cerr << "Error: bad data - expected From but found " << str
       << endl;
  is.clear (ios::failbit);
  return is;
 }
 char c;
 is >> c;
 if (c != '\"') {
  cerr << "Error: expected a \" before From city\n";
  is.clear (ios::failbit);
  return is;
 }
 is.getline (from.city, sizeof (from.city), '\"');
 is >> str;
 if (!is || _stricmp (str, "To") != 0) {
  cerr << "Error: expected To but found " << str << endl;
  is.clear (ios::failbit);
  return is;
 }
 is >> c;
 if (c != '\"') {
  cerr << "Error: expected a \" before To city\n";
  is.clear (ios::failbit);
  return is;
 }
```

```
 is.getline (to.city, sizeof (to.city), '\"');
 is >> str;
 if (!is || _stricmp (str, "is") != 0) {
  cerr << "Error: expected is but found " << str << endl;
  is.clear (ios::failbit);
  return is;
 }
 is >> e.distance;
 return is;
}

/*********************************************************/
/*                                                       */
/* Display: a callback function to display a single vert*/
/*                                                       */
/*********************************************************/

void Display (Vertex& v) {
 cout << v.city << endl;
}

/*********************************************************/
/*                                                       */
/* DisplayTree: a callback function to show a vertex     */
/*                                                       */
/*********************************************************/

void DisplayTree (Vertex& v, bool isConnectedVertex) {
 if (!isConnectedVertex)
  cout << "\nFrom: " << v.city << endl;
 else
  cout << "  To: " << v.city << endl;
}

/*********************************************************/
/*                                                       */
/* DisplayShortestPath: a callback function to show path*/
/*                                                       */
/*********************************************************/

void DisplayShortestPath (const Vertex& from, const Vertex& to,
                          const Edge& edge) {
 cout.setf (ios::left, ios::adjustfield);
 cout << "   " << setw (20) << from.city << setw(25)
      << to.city;
 cout.setf (ios::right, ios::adjustfield);
 cout << setw(8) << setprecision (0) << edge.distance << endl;
}

/*********************************************************/
/*                                                       */
/* DisplaySpanningTree: callback to display span tree    */
/*                                                       */
/*********************************************************/

void DisplaySpanningTree (const Vertex& from, const Vertex& to,
```

```
                          const Edge& edge) {
 cout.setf (ios::left, ios::adjustfield);
 cout << "From Vertex: " << setw (20) << from.city << "   "
      << "To Vertex: " << setw (20) << to.city << "   ";
 cout.setf (ios::right, ios::adjustfield);
 cout << setprecision (0) << setw (5) << edge.distance << endl;
}

/***************************************************************/
/*                                                             */
/* GetValidMainMenuChoice and DisplayMainMenu:                 */
/*                                                             */
/***************************************************************/

MainMenuChoice GetValidMainMenuChoice () {
 int choice = 6;
 while (choice < 1 || choice > 5) {
  DisplayMainMenu ();
  cin >> choice;
  if (!cin) return Quit;
 }
 return (MainMenuChoice) choice;
}

void DisplayMainMenu () {
 cout << "\n\n\n\tVic's Airplane Flight Checker\n\n"
     << "\t1. Does a flight exist (depth first)?\n"
     << "\t2. Does a flight exist (breadth first)?\n"
     << "\t3. What is the shortest route? (Show only shortest)\n"
     << "\t4. What is the shortest route? (Show all)\n"
     << "\t5. Quit\n\n"
     << "Enter the number of your choice: ";
}

/***************************************************************/
/*                                                             */
/* DisplayCityPicker and GetValidCityChoice:                   */
/*                                                             */
/***************************************************************/

void DisplayCityPicker (Array<Vertex>& array, const char* title){
 cout << "\n\n\n\t" << title << endl;
 for (int i=0; i<array.GetSize(); i++) {
  cout << "\t" << i+1 << ". " << array.GetAt(i)->city << endl;
 }
 cout << "\t" << array.GetSize()+1 << ". Abort this action\n\n";
 cout << "\nEnter the number of your choice: ";
}

int GetValidCityChoice (Array<Vertex>& array, const char* title){
 int choice = array.GetSize()+2;
 while (choice < 1 || choice > array.GetSize()+1) {
  DisplayCityPicker (array, title);
  cin >> choice;
  if (!cin) return array.GetSize();
 }
```

```
 return choice -1;
}
```

Finally, here is the coding for the **Array** class.

The Array Template Class

```
#pragma once
#include <iostream>
using namespace std;

/********************************************************/
/*                                                      */
/* Array: container for growable array of user items    */
/*        it can store a variable number of elements    */
/*                                                      */
/*        elements stored are copies of the original    */
/*                                                      */
/*  errors are logged to cerr device                    */
/*                                                      */
/********************************************************/

template<class UserData>
class Array {

 /*******************************************************/
 /*                                                     */
 /* class data                                          */
 /*                                                     */
 /*******************************************************/

protected:
 UserData* array;
 long      numElements;

 /*******************************************************/
 /*                                                     */
 /* class functions                                     */
 /*                                                     */
 /*******************************************************/

public:
 Array ();    // default constructor - makes an empty array
 ~Array ();   // deletes the array

 bool Add (const UserData& newElement); // add an element
 bool InsertAt (long i, const UserData& newElement);
      // adds this element at subscript i
      // if i < 0, it is added at the front
      // if i >= numElements, it is added at the end
      // otherwise, it is added at the ith position
      // returns true if successful

 UserData* GetAt (long i) const; // rets element at the ith pos
                   // If i is out of range, it returns 0

```

```
 bool RemoveAt (long i); // removes the element at subscript i
           // if i is out of range, an error is displayed on cerr
           // returns true if successful

 void RemoveAll (); // removes all elements

 long GetSize () const; // rets num elements in array

 // copy ctor and assignment operator
 Array (const Array<UserData>& a);
 Array<UserData>& operator= (const Array<UserData>& a);

protected:
 void Copy (const Array<UserData>& a); // performs the copy
};

/***************************************************************/
/*                                                             */
/* Array: constructs an empty array                            */
/*                                                             */
/***************************************************************/

template<class UserData>
Array<UserData>::Array () {
 numElements = 0;
 array = 0;
}

/***************************************************************/
/*                                                             */
/* ~Array: deletes dynamically allocated memory                */
/*                                                             */
/***************************************************************/

template<class UserData>
Array<UserData>::~Array () {
 RemoveAll ();
}

/***************************************************************/
/*                                                             */
/* Add: Adds this new element to the end of the array          */
/*      if out of memory, displays error message to cerr       */
/*                                                             */
/***************************************************************/

template<class UserData>
bool Array<UserData>::Add (const UserData& newElement) {
 // allocate new temporary array one element larger
 UserData* temp = new UserData [numElements + 1];

 // check for out of memory
 if (!temp) {
  cerr << "Array: Add Error - out of memory\n";
  return false;
 }
```

```

 // copy all existing elements into the new temp array
 for (long i=0; i<numElements; i++) {
  temp[i] = array[i];
 }

 // copy in the new element to be added
 temp[numElements] = newElement;

 numElements++;  // increment the number of elements in the array
 if (array) delete [] array; // delete the old array
 array = temp;    // point out array to the new array
 return true;
}

/*********************************************************/
/*                                                       */
/* InsertAt: adds the new element to the array at index i*/
/*  if i is in range, it is inserted at subscript i      */
/*  if i is negative, it is inserted at the front        */
/*  if i is greater than or equal to the number of       */
/*     elements, then it is added at the end of the array*/
/*                                                       */
/*  if there is insufficient memory, an error message    */
/*     is displayed to cerr                              */
/*                                                       */
/*********************************************************/

template<class UserData>
bool Array<UserData>::InsertAt (long i,
                                const UserData& newElement) {
 UserData* temp;
 long j;
 // allocate a new array one element larger
 temp = new UserData [numElements + 1];

 // check if out of memory
 if (!temp) {
  cerr << "Array: InsertAt - Error out of memory\n";
  return false;
 }

 // this case handles an insertion that is within range
 if (i < numElements && i >= 0) {
  for (j=0; j<i; j++) { // copy all elements below insertion
   temp[j] = array[j];  // point
  }
  temp[i] = newElement; // insert new element
  for (j=i; j<numElements; j++) { // copy remaining elements
   temp[j+1] = array[j];
  }
 }

 // this case handles an insertion when the index is too large
 else if (i >= numElements) {
  for (j=0; j<numElements; j++) { // copy all existing elements
```

```
162    temp[j] = array[j];
163    }
164   temp[numElements] = newElement; // add new one at end
165   }
166
167   // this case handles an insertion when the index is too small
168   else {
169    temp[0] = newElement;        // insert new on at front
170    for (j=0; j<numElements; j++) { // copy all others after it
171     temp[j+1] = array[j];
172    }
173   }
174
175   // for all cases, delete current array, assign new one and
176   // increment the number of elements in the array
177   if (array) delete [] array;
178   array = temp;
179   numElements++;
180   return true;
181 }
182
183 /*****************************************************************/
184 /*                                                             */
185 /* GetAt: returns the element at index i                       */
186 /*        if i is out of range, returns 0                      */
187 /*                                                             */
188 /*****************************************************************/
189
190 template<class UserData>
191 UserData* Array<UserData>::GetAt (long i) const {
192  if (i < numElements && i >=0)
193   return &array[i];
194  else
195   return 0;
196 }
197
198 /*****************************************************************/
199 /*                                                             */
200 /* RemoveAt: removes the element at subscript i                */
201 /*                                                             */
202 /* If i is out of range, an error is displayed on cerr         */
203 /*                                                             */
204 /* Note that what the element actually points to is not        */
205 /*        deleted                                              */
206 /*                                                             */
207 /*****************************************************************/
208
209 template<class UserData>
210 bool Array<UserData>::RemoveAt (long i) {
211  UserData* temp;
212  if (numElements > 1) {
213   if (i >= 0 && i < numElements) {  // if the index is in range,
214    temp = new UserData [numElements - 1]; // alloc smaller array
215    long j;
216    for (j=0; j<i; j++) {                // copy all elements up to
217     temp[j] = array[j];                 // the desired one to be
```

```
   }                                   // removed
   for (j=i+1; j<numElements; j++) {// then copy all the elements
    temp[j-1] = array[j];              // that remain
   }
   numElements--;                 // decrement number of elements
   if (array) delete [] array; // delete the old array
   array = temp;                  // and assign the new one
   return true;
  }
 }
 cerr << "Array: RemoveAt Error - element out of range\n"
      << "         It was " << i << " and numElements is "
      << numElements << endl;
 return false;
}

/***************************************************************/
/*                                                             */
/* RemoveAll: empties the entire array, resetting it to       */
/*            an empty state ready for reuse                   */
/*                                                             */
/***************************************************************/

template<class UserData>
void Array<UserData>::RemoveAll () {
 if (array) delete [] array; // remove all elements
 numElements = 0;            // reset number of elements
 array = 0;                  // and reset array to 0
}

/***************************************************************/
/*                                                             */
/* GetNumberOfElements: returns the number of elements        */
/*                      currently in the array                 */
/*                                                             */
/***************************************************************/

template<class UserData>
long Array<UserData>::GetSize () const {
 return numElements;
}

/***************************************************************/
/*                                                             */
/* Array: copy constructor, makes a duplicate copy of a       */
/*                                                             */
/* Note: what the elements actually point to are not          */
/* duplicated only our pointers are duplicated                 */
/*                                                             */
/***************************************************************/

template<class UserData>
Array<UserData>::Array (const Array<UserData>& a) {
 Copy (a);
}

```

```
/***************************************************************/
/*                                                             */
/* operator=: makes a duplicate array of passed array a       */
/*                                                             */
/* Note: what the elements actually point to are not          */
/* duplicated only our pointers are duplicated                */
/*                                                             */
/***************************************************************/

template<class UserData>
Array<UserData>& Array<UserData>::operator= (
                                      const Array<UserData>& a) {
 if (this == &a) // avoids silly a = a assignemnts
  return *this;
 delete [] array; // remove existing array
 Copy (a);        // duplicate array a
 return *this;    // return us for chaining assignments
}

/***************************************************************/
/*                                                             */
/* Copy: helper function to actual perform the copy           */
/*                                                             */
/***************************************************************/

template<class UserData>
void Array<UserData>::Copy (const Array<UserData>& a) {
 if (a.numElements) { // be sure array a is not empty
  numElements = a.numElements;
  // allocate a new array the size of a
  array = new void* [numElements];

  // check for out of memory condition
  if (!array) {
   cerr << "Array: Copy function - Error out of memory\n";
   numElements = 0;
   return;
  }

  // copy all of a's pointers into our array
  for (long i=0; i<numElements; i++) {
   array[i] = a.array[i];
  }
 }
 else { // a is empty, so make ours empty too
  numElements = 0;
  array = 0;
 }
}
```

Please notice that for simplicity, I have ignored all out of memory situations with dynamic memory.

Review Questions

1. Describe three different types of user application programs for which the graph would be an ideal data structure. Be sure to explain why the graph is well suited for each of these.

2. Make a diagram showing how the two different graph traversal methods actually work. Under what kind of circumstances would a depth traversal be more desirable than a breadth traversal?

3. Explain why the largest value item must be stored in element 0 of the Heap implementation. How can the user do this when the most important item is the lesser value item? Explain in detail the difference.

4. Diagram how a priority queue could be used to hold a series of dictionary words for a spelling checker program.

5. Draw a diagram illustrating how the shortest path algorithm works using the **Pgm13b** graph when flying from Peoria to Burbank.

6. Draw an example of a digraph and an undirected graph. Show an example of a network graph.

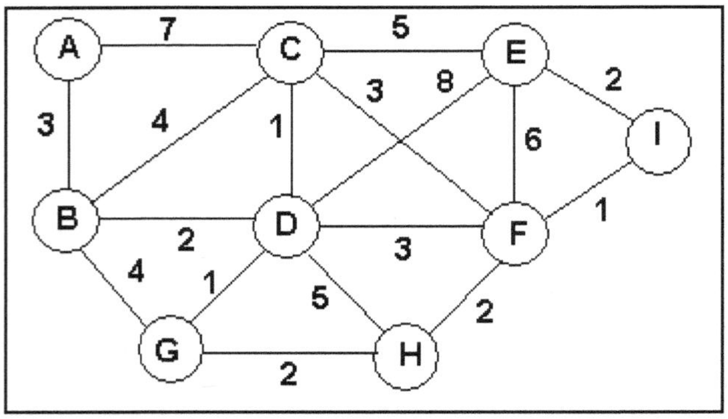

Figure 13.22 A Network

7. Using the network in Figure 13.22, draw a minimum spanning tree.

8. Using the network in Figure 13.22, what is the shortest path from A to I? From A to H?

9. Draw the vertices and edges if a graph were constructed to hold the data shown in Figure 13.22 as linked lists.

10. Draw the vertices and edges if a graph were constructed to hold the data shown in Figure 13.22 as arrays instead.

Stop! Do These Exercises Before Programming

There is another type of graph situation that is commonly needed, **topological sorting** in which a vertex B appears after vertex A, if there is a path from A to B. Of course, the graph cannot have a path from B to A if there is one from A to B or it would be circular.

Suppose that we needed to store a list of college courses. However, we must list all prerequisite courses before the course that needs those prerequisite courses. Thus, an edge from A to B means that course A must be taken prior to taking B.

Another powerful use is in the construction industry. Building a new road has many separate actions that must be done. Before certain ones can be undertaken, others must have already been completed. For example, the purchase of the right-of-ways must occur before you do the initial grading, which, in turn, must be done before the road bed can be formed, which must be done before the concrete can be poured, and so on. Here, **critical path analysis** is used to determine the scheduling of all of the tasks to get a project completed. The amount of time to accomplish a task is stored in the vertices which represent the tasks. The edges only indicate that a task must be completed before the next one can begin. With a critical path analysis, the two key questions are: What is the earliest completion date and what portions can be delayed a bit without impacting the completion date?

This series of exercises attempts to solve the following problem. Acme Construction wishes to make a bid on a construction project of a new building. They need first to know the minimum time it will take them to build the building. Secondarily, when troubles occur, they need to know which activities can be delayed without impacting that minimum completion time.

A Vertex node contains the string description of the task and its length to perform in days. If another task B depends upon this task A being finished first, then there is an Edge structure between them from A to B only but not from B to A.

1. Our programmer has devised the following pseudo coding to accomplish the task of performing a topological sort based upon depth first. The method is that each vertex must ahead of all other vertices that are its successors in the directed graph. Thus, we begin by finding a vertex that has no successors. It is then placed last into the ordered list. Then, recursively place all of the successors into the ordered list and finally place this one into the list.

```
void Graph::TopologicalSort (List& order)
    Clear the visited flags
    for all vertices v from the beginning to the end
        If ( ! Visited) RecursiveSort (v, order)

void Graph::RecursiveSort (Vertex& v, List& order)
    Mark v as visited
    for all of its edges
        If that edge's vertex is not yet visited
            RecursiveSort (that not yet visited one, order)
    end for
    insert this vertex v into the order at element 0
```

Convert this pseudo coding into working functions as part of our **Graph** template class. Note that you will need to create a different **Vertex** and **Edge** structure definitions from that used in **Pgm13b**.

2. Check out the solution by using the following input file that defines a construction project. The last two numbers represent the months to complete each of the two actions on that line, respectively.

```
From "Plans Drawn" To "Survey" is 2 1
From "Plans Drawn" To "Land Acquisition" is 2 3
From "Survey" To "Initial Grading" is 1 2
From "Land Acquisition" To "Initial Grading" is 3 2
From "Initial Grading" To "Fine Grading" is 2 1
From "Initial Grading" To "Bed Preparations" is 2 2
From "Fine Grading" To "Lay Road Bed" is 1 3
From "Bed Preparations" To "Lay Road Bed" is 2 3
From "Lay Road Bed" To "Final Landscaping" is 3 2
```

The resultant ordered list should contain the following.

```
Plans Drawn  2
Survey  1
Land Acquisition  3
Initial Grading  2
Fine Grading  1
Bed Preparations  2
Lay Road Bed  3
Final Landscaping  2
```

3. Next, devise an algorithm to display the critical path through the ordered list. The "Plans Drawn" vertex has two edges. The critical one is that edge which takes the longest time to accomplish. Thus, the "Land Acquisition" becomes the determining task before "Initial Grading" can occur. The routine should display the critical path and the accumulated total time through the project. The results should be something like the following.

```
The Critical Path to Follow
```

```
Plans Drawn          2
Land Acquisition     5
Initial Grading      7
Bed Preparations     9
Lay Road Bed        12
Final Landscaping 14
```

Programming Problems

Problem Pgm13-1—The Grand Vacation

You have decided to take the summer off and visit a large number of US National Parks and Forests out west. The order that they are visited is important because you only have two summer months for the trip. You cannot visit them in a random order because of the excessive driving time. For example, it would not be wise to visit Glacier National Park in Montana, then drive to the Grand Canyon and then back up to the Tetons. So a minimum spanning tree would be helpful.

First, examine an US map and pick out 20 national parks, forest and lake resorts located in the western states. Assume that you are leaving from Denver, Colorado on your trip and that you intend to end up in Denver when you are finished.

Create an input file similar to that used in **Pgm13b** for the key routes among all of the parks and Denver. Now write an application program that loads in the graph and displays an optimum sequence of the visitation of these parks. It should also display the total miles traveled.

Problem Pgm13-2—Cabling the Company's New Network

Assume that Figure 13.22 above represents your company's new proposed network of computers, where each vertex represents a computer installation. Assume that a weight of 1 shown in the figure represents 10 feet of cable. Your job is to cable those computers using the smallest amount of cabling. Write a program that determines how these computers should be cabled and the total amount of cable required.

Problem Pgm13-3—Delivery Routes

Assume that Figure 13.22 above represents your company's delivery routes. Each vertex represents a city that you service. A distance unit of 1 represents 10 miles; a weight of 1 means 10 miles. Assume that any single service truck can cover 60 miles one way a day. Further, node D is the city from which your company operates.

Write a program that determines how the minimum number of service trucks your company will need to properly service each city in the network.

Problem Pgm13-4 —Airline Routes with Departure/Arrival Times

Of course, **Pgm13b** is overly simplistic. We know that departure/arrival times are vital to making travel plans. For example, the shortest route from A to B might require spending the night at C because of the arrival and departure times. Most travelers wish to avoid sleeping in an airport. So we really must add in support for timings.

For each Edge, which represents a flight from A to B, add two more variables: the float time of day that the flight leaves from the "from" city, or A, and the float time of day the flight arrives in the "to" city, B. Notice that if there are several flights from A to B throughout the day, there can be several Edge instances for these two cities.

Modify the input file for **Pgm13b** to handle a number of daily flights from each of the cities. Specifically, add in four flights scattered throughout the day from Peoria to Chicago and St. Louis. Add in only 1 morning flight from New York to Chicago. Add in a morning and evening flight from Chicago to the two West Coast cities and Denver. Similarly, add in two flights from St. Louis to the West Coast cities.

Now modify the shortest path functions of **Pgm13b** to handle this new consideration that for a connection to exist, any arrival to a node must occur before any departure from that city. That is, if going from A to B to C, then you must arrive at B before B's flight to C takes off.

Chapter 14—Of Sets and Maps

Introduction

The set is a basic building block of mathematics. A set is a nonlinear collection of objects called **elements**. An example is the set of all positive, even integers. The **universe** consists of all possible positive even integers. The number 2, an object, would be a member of that set, while the number 3 would not be a member. A set of items implies no specific ordering, just a pile of items that are in the set universe.

From set theory, we have three properties.

1. All elements of a set belong to some universe that represents all possible values that are potential elements.
2. For any given object, either it is a member or it is not a member of the universe.
3. There is no particular order of the elements within the set.

From property 2, a specific element can appear in the set only once. Thus, these two sets are the same set:

{2, 4, 6} = {4, 2, 6, 2, 6, 4, 4}

Remember that order does not matter. If a set is currently empty, it is denoted { }; it is also called the **null** set.

Another term associated with sets is the **cardinality** of a set. The cardinality is the number of distinct elements that are present in a particular set. The cardinality of a null set is 0. If a set has potentially an infinite number of elements, its cardinality is infinity. However, if the set has a finite number of elements, then its cardinality is finite and is expressed as a positive integer. Obviously, when we program a set, the cardinality must be finite since there is not an infinite amount of computer memory available to store an infinite number of elements.

A set has three binary operations that can be performed with it. Binary operations are those actions that involve two sets, in this case, two = binary. The **intersection** of two sets consists of those elements that are held in common between the two sets. For example, the intersection of the set of all integers from 1 to 10 with the set of all even integers between 4 and 8 would include the elements 4, 6, and 8. The **union** of two sets represents those elements that are in at least one of the two sets. For example, the union of the set of the integers 1 through 3 with the set of integers 3 through 5 would be the set of elements 1 through 5. The **difference** between set A and set B would be all elements of set A that are not in set B. The difference between the set of integers 1 through 3 and the set of integers 3 through 5 would be 1 and 2.

A set also has a couple of relational operations that can be performed. Set **equality** tests whether or not set A equals set B; two sets are equal if they contain the same elements. The other relational operation is the **subset**. Set B is considered a subset of set A if all of set B's elements are found in set A.

An element is a member of a set, if that set contains that element. This operation is called **membership**.

While this text is not concerned about writing mathematical applications where set theory abounds, there are some circumstances where a set data structure is useful in representing the real-world situation. Consider for a moment what classes you plan to take next semester. Obviously, you can only take those classes that are actually offered, for not every class that a college has is taught each semester, particularly during the summer semester. Thus, we could use a set data structure to contain all of the classes that were to be offered in a given semester. Any given class the college potentially could offer is in either the set of offerings this semester or it is not. Table 14.1 shows the definition of a set data structure.

Data Type	Set
Domain	A set is a collection of component whose values are all of the same data type
Structure	A nonlinear collection of items that correspond to a mathematical set
Operations	
Initialize()	Creates an empty set
Insert()	Add a new element to the set

Delete()	Remove an element from the set
IsAMember()	Is an item an element in the set
Intersection ()	Constructs a resultant set that represents the intersection of this set with another set
Union()	Constructs a resultant set that represents the union of this set with another set
IsEmpty()	Returns true if the set contains no elements
Difference()	Constructs a resultant set that represents the difference between this set and another set
Cardinality()	Returns the cardinality number of this set

Table 14.1 The Set Data Structure Definition

Implementations of a Set

There are many ways of implementing a **Set** data structure. One common approach is to store the elements in a growable **array**. Another common approach, where memory reduction is a factor, is to let a single bit represent whether or not an element is in the set; this is called a **bit-vector** set. On the other hand, if the application is heavily dependent upon rapidly finding an element in the set, the set can be constructed as a searchable tree. Let's examine the first two approaches, the array and the bit-vector.

To begin, what exactly do we wish to store in a **Set** object? First, suppose that we wish to create a **Set** object that stores even integers. We could store each integer that is added to the set in an array of integers. If we do so, then we are storing the actual client's object. Alternatively, we could store only the true/false aspect of whether or not a specific integer was in the set. This true/false aspect could be stored in a single bit as a 1 or 0. Thus, given the integer, we could map it to a specific bit within an array or vector of such bits and test or set or clear that corresponding bit. This then is the major difference between the two approaches, the **Set** as an array and the **Set** as a bit-vector, storing the object itself or storing only whether or not an element is present.

Note that if we are storing an element presence, we are not storing the element or object itself. This is the major design factor. Do we want to store the client's object or merely its presence in the **Set** object? Another example helps clarify this issue.

Suppose that the client wishes to create a set of all recent customers. The customer data resides in the client's **Customer** class, one member of which is the **long customerId**. We either can then store **Customer** instances in the **Set** or we can store a **Customer**'s presence in the **Set** based upon the **customerId**. Which should we store? The client applications most certainly have the **Customer** objects stored elsewhere, in a database, in a list, or in an array, for example. It would be redundant to also store additional copies of the data within the **Set** object. Thus, a **Set** object usually stores only the **presence** of an indicated element.

If we implement the **Set** as an array, then we can store the presence or not as an array of **bool** values. On the other hand, if we implemented the **Set** as a bit-vector, then we store only a 1/0 for the presence or absence of a given customer. With either, the **Set** operations functions must be given the **customerId** in order to be able to find the corresponding bit or the array's **bool** to test or set.

Again, notice that with the **Set** implementations, we do not save the user's data items, but rather an indicator of whether or not that item is present in the **Set**.

The Set as an Array Implementation

At first thought, we can seemingly reuse the **Array** template class from Chapter 12 to store the array of **bool** values.

```
Array<bool> array;
```

This would be our single **Set** data member.

Here comes the next problem. How big is the array to be initially? Suppose that we wanted to store the presence of a set of **Customer** records. The **customerId** member is used to uniquely identify a record. Then, the array of **bool** values must span the range of id numbers. If the id numbers ranged from 1 to 100, then we need to allocate an array of one hundred **bool** values, perhaps ignoring element 0, since a **customerId** cannot contain zero.

On the other hand, suppose that the social security number is the identifier of the client's data? Now how big is the array? Enormous to say the least! Clearly, the design of the **Set** must be different if the range of id values becomes huge. That is the topic of the second half of this chapter—how to handle a **Set** when the range of possibilities becomes overwhelmingly large. So for now, the user must have a clear idea of the range of id values to be stored in the **Set** and tell us at **Set** construction time.

The **Set** ctor is passed the number of elements to create. The client passes the various **Set** operations an id which we take to be an index into the array of **bool** values. The ctor dynamically allocates the array of **bool** values and initializes them all to **false**. The two data members of the **Set** class are as follows.

```
bool* array; // a true = the corresponding element is in the set
long  count; // the number of elements in the array
long  cardinality; // number items in the set currently
```

We can immediately code the ctor and dtor functions as well as the copy constructor and the assignment operator. However, to handle error situations, let's use the C++ error handling mechanism, try-catch logic.

```
Set::Set (long max) throw (const char*) {
 if (max < 1) {
  throw "Set Error: ctor must be passed a positive number";
 }
 array = new (std::nothrow) bool [max];
 if (!array) {
  throw "Set Error: ctor - out of memory";
 }
 count = max;
 cardinality = 0;
 for (long i=0; i<max; i++)
  array[i] = false;
}
Set::~Set () {
 if (array) delete [] array;
}
Set::Set (const Set& s) throw (const char*) {
 try {
  Copy (s);
 }
 catch (const char* msg) {
  throw msg;
 }
}
Set& Set::operator= (const Set& s) throw (const char*) {
 if (this == &s) return *this;
 if (array) delete [] array;
 try {
  Copy (s);
 }
 catch (const char* msg) {
  throw msg;
 }
 return *this;
}
void Set::Copy (const Set& s) throw (const char*) {
 array = new (std::nothrow) bool [s.count];
 if (!array) {
  throw "Set Error: copy ctor - out of memory";
 }
 count = s.count;
 cardinality = s.cardinality;
 for (long i=0; i<count; i++) {
  array[i] = s.array[i];
 }
}
```

With the basic shell coded, let's examine how to implement the **Insert**, **Delete**, and **IsAMember** functions.

The **Insert** function is used to add a new item to the **Set**. It is passed its id number. All that we must do is to ensure that id is within range and set the corresponding **bool** to **true**. Similarly, to implement the **Delete** function that removes an item from the **Set**, we must be given the id. Again, if the id is within range, we set the corresponding **bool** to **false**. To implement the **IsAMember** function, we are passed the id and return its corresponding **bool**. But again, we need to ensure that the id is within range. Since we need to check the range numerous times, let's add a helper function, **RangeCheck**.

```
bool Set::RangeCheck (long num) const {
 if (num < 1)
 return false;
 return num > count ? false : true;
}
void Set::Insert (long num) throw (const char*) {
 if (RangeCheck(num)) {
  if (!array[num]){
   cardinality++;
   array[num] = true;
  }
 }
 else
  throw "Set Error: Insert index out of range";
}
void Set::Delete (long num) throw (const char*) {
 if (RangeCheck (num)) {
  if (array[num]) {
   cardinality- -;
   array[num] = false;
  }
 }
 else
  throw "Set Error: Delete index out of range";
}
bool Set::IsAMember (long num) const throw (const char*) {
 if (RangeCheck (num))
  return array[num];
 else
  throw "Set Error: IsAMember index out of range";
}
```

Finally, we need to implement the **Set** operations: union, intersection, and difference. Certainly we can create functions of these names, but a union is adding in the other set's items and a difference is basically a subtraction. Thus, I am going to overload the math operators to provide these functions. Specifically, a union is **operator+**, a difference is **operator–**, and the intersection of two sets is **operator***.

The union is simple to code. The first action is to verify that both sets have the same count or array size. If they do not, then we will have to create a new result that is large enough to hold the combined merged results. Here, **newcount** holds the largest array size.

```
Set Set::operator+ (const Set& s) const throw (const char*) {
 long newcount = count > s.count ? count : s.count;
 Set result (newcount);
```

With a union, if either set has an element present, then it is present in the union. So first I visit all elements that the two sets have in common. I do this by first obtaining the smallest array size of the two sets.

```
 newcount = count < s.count ? count : s.count;
 for (long i=0; i<newcount; i++) {
  result.array[i] = array[i] || s.array[i];
 }
```

Once this loop finishes, there is the possibility that one or the other set is larger than this minimum size, so we must add in those as well.

```
 if (count > newcount) {
  for (i=newcount; i<count; i++) {
   result.array[i] = array[i];
  }
 }
 if (s.count > newcount) {
  for (i=newcount; i<s.count; i++) {
```

```
    result.array[i] = s.array[i];
   }
  }
 result.SetCardinality ();
 return result;
}
```

Notice that we must reset the result set's cardinality. Since this must be done in several places, I have made it a protected, helper function.

```
void Set::SetCardinality (Set& s) {
 cardinality = 0;
 for (long i=0; i<s.count; i++) {
  if (s.array[i])
   s.cardinality++;
 }
}
```

To implement the difference operator, here **operator–**, I follow the same procedure and find the largest new array size and build a result set of the maximum size. To find the difference between this set and the passed set, we want a true result for elements that are in this set but not in the passed set, or **array[i] && !s.array[i]**. If the other array is smaller, then certainly any elements in this array which lies above **s.count** are in the difference set.

```
Set Set::operator- (const Set& s) const throw (const char*) {
 long newcount = count > s.count ? count : s.count;
 Set result (newcount);
 newcount = count < s.count ? count : s.count;
 for (long i=0; i<newcount; i++) {
  result.array[i] = array[i] && !s.array[i];
 }
 if (count > newcount) {
  for (i=newcount; i<count; i++) {
   result.array[i] = array[i];
  }
 }
 result.SetCardinality ();
 return result;
}
```

To find the intersection of this set and another set s, the resultant set contains only those elements present in both sets. So this function is even simpler.

```
Set Set::operator* (const Set& s) const throw (const char*) {
 long newcount = count > s.count ? count : s.count;
 Set result (newcount);
 newcount = count < s.count ? count : s.count;
 for (long i=0; i<newcount; i++) {
  result.array[i] = array[i] && s.array[i];
 }
 result.SetCardinality ();
 return result;
}
```

Finally, are there any other operator functions that a client program may need? Well, yes, the client program might like to inquire if one set is the same as another set. This is **operator==**. Also, the client might like to know if set T is a subset of set S. Set T is a subset of set S if every item of T is also present in set S. This function can be called **IsThisASubsetOf**. However, we could also use **operator<=** to represent this action.

```
bool Set::operator== (const Set& s) const{
 if (count != s.count)
  return false;
 for (long i=0; i<count; i++) {
  if (array[i] != s.array[i])
   return false;
 }
 return true;
}
bool Set::operator<= (const Set& s) const {
 if (count > s.count)
```

```
  return false;
 long i, is;
 for (i=0, is=0; i<count && is<s.count; i++, is++) {
  if (array[i] && !s.array[i])
   return false;
 }
 for (; i<count; i++) {
  if (array[i])
   return false;
 }
 return true;
}
```

Here are the **Set** definition and implementation file along with a simple tester program and its output.

SetAsArray Class Definition

```
#pragma once

/***************************************************************/
/*                                                             */
/* SetAsArray: encapsulates a set as an array of bools         */
/*             the user items are not stored, only their       */
/*             presence in the set is maintained               */
/*                                                             */
/***************************************************************/

class SetAsArray {
protected:
 bool* array; // a true = the corresponding element is in the set
 long  count; // the number of elements in the array
 long  cardinality; // the number of items in the set currently

public:
 SetAsArray (long max) throw (const char*);
 SetAsArray (const SetAsArray& s) throw (const char*);
~SetAsArray ();
 SetAsArray& operator= (const SetAsArray& s) throw (const char*);

 void Insert (long num) throw (const char*);
 void Delete (long num) throw (const char*);
 bool IsAMember (long num) const;
 long GetCardinality () const;

 // union function
 SetAsArray  operator+ (const SetAsArray& s) const
                       throw (const char*);

 // difference function
 SetAsArray  operator- (const SetAsArray& s) const
                       throw (const char*);

 // intersection function
 SetAsArray  operator* (const SetAsArray& s) const
                       throw (const char*);

 // are two sets equal
 bool operator== (const SetAsArray& s) const;
```

```

 // is this a subset of set s?
 bool operator<= (const SetAsArray& s) const;

protected:
 SetAsArray (); // disallow default ctor
 void Copy (const SetAsArray& s) throw (const char*);// deep copy
 bool RangeCheck (long num) const; // idx in range?
 void SetCardinality (); // recalcs a set's cardinality
};
```

SetAsArray Class Implementation

```
#include <iostream>
#include <iomanip>
using namespace std;

#include "SetAsArray.h"

/***************************************************************/
/*                                                             */
/* SetAsArray: allocates and initializes the array of max bools*/
/*        can throw exceptions if max out of range or no memory  */
/*                                                             */
/***************************************************************/

SetAsArray::SetAsArray (long max) throw (const char*) {
 if (max < 1) {
  throw"SetAsArray Error: ctor must be passed a positive number";
 }
 try {
  array = new bool [max];
 }
 catch (std::bad_alloc e) {
  count = 0;
  array = 0;
  throw "SetAsArray Error: ctor - out of memory";
 }
 count = max;
 cardinality = 0;
 for (long i=0; i<max; i++)
  array[i] = false;
}

/***************************************************************/
/*                                                             */
/* ~SetAsArray: dtor deletes the array                         */
/*                                                             */
/*                                                             */
/***************************************************************/

SetAsArray::~SetAsArray () {
 if (array) delete [] array;
}

```

```
/***************************************************************/
/*                                                             */
/* SetAsArray copy ctor: can throw an out of memory exception  */
/*                                                             */
/***************************************************************/

SetAsArray::SetAsArray (const SetAsArray& s) throw (const char*){
 try {
  Copy (s);
 }
 catch (const char* msg) {
  throw msg;
 }
}

/***************************************************************/
/*                                                             */
/* operator= assignment op makes this a dupe of s              */
/*           can throw out of memory exception                 */
/*                                                             */
/***************************************************************/

SetAsArray& SetAsArray::operator= (const SetAsArray& s)
                                   throw (const char*) {
 if (this == &s) return *this;
 if (array) delete [] array;
 try {
  Copy (s);
 }
 catch (const char* msg) {
  throw msg;
 }
 return *this;
}

/***************************************************************/
/*                                                             */
/* Copy: make a duplicate copy of a SetAsArray                 */
/*       can throw an out of memory exception                  */
/*                                                             */
/***************************************************************/

void SetAsArray::Copy (const SetAsArray& s) throw (const char*) {
 try {
  array = new bool [s.count];
 }
 catch (std::bad_alloc e) {
  count = 0;
  array = 0;
  throw "SetAsArray Error: copy ctor - out of memory";
 }
 count = s.count;
 cardinality = s.cardinality;
 for (long i=0; i<count; i++) {
  array[i] = s.array[i];
 }
```

```
}

/***************************************************************/
/*                                                             */
/* GetCardinality: returns the number of items in the set now  */
/*                                                             */
/***************************************************************/

long SetAsArray::GetCardinality () const {
 return cardinality;
}

/***************************************************************/
/*                                                             */
/* RangeCheck: return true if num is within the array bounds   */
/*                                                             */
/***************************************************************/

bool SetAsArray::RangeCheck (long num) const {
 if (num < 1)
  return false;
 return num > count ? false : true;
}

/***************************************************************/
/*                                                             */
/* Insert: adds a new item to the SetAsArray                   */
/*         can throw an exception if num is out of range       */
/*                                                             */
/***************************************************************/

void SetAsArray::Insert (long num) throw (const char*) {
 if (RangeCheck(num)) {
  if (!array[num]) {
   cardinality++;
   array[num] = true;
  }
 }
 else
  throw "SetAsArray Error: Insert index out of range";
}

/***************************************************************/
/*                                                             */
/* Delete: removes this item from the SetAsArray               */
/*         can throw an exception if num is out of range       */
/*                                                             */
/***************************************************************/

void SetAsArray::Delete (long num) throw (const char*) {
 if (RangeCheck (num)) {
  if (array[num]) {
   cardinality--;
   array[num] = false;
  }
 }
```

```
 else
  throw "SetAsArray Error: Delete index out of range";
}

/***************************************************************/
/*                                                             */
/* IsAMember: returns true if this item is in the SetAsArray   */
/*                                                             */
/***************************************************************/

bool SetAsArray::IsAMember (long num) const {
 if (RangeCheck (num))
  return array[num];
 else
  return false;
}

/***************************************************************/
/*                                                             */
/* SetAsArrayCardinality: calcs the number of items in set now */
/*                                                             */
/***************************************************************/

void SetAsArray::SetCardinality () {
 cardinality = 0;
 for (long i=0; i<count; i++) {
  if (array[i])
   cardinality++;
 }
}

/***************************************************************/
/*                                                             */
/* operator+ returns the union of this set and the passed set s*/
/*           can throw an out of memory exception              */
/*                                                             */
/***************************************************************/
SetAsArray SetAsArray::operator+ (const SetAsArray& s) const
                                    throw (const char*) {
 long newcount = count > s.count ? count : s.count;
 SetAsArray result (newcount);
 newcount = count < s.count ? count : s.count;
 for (long i=0; i<newcount; i++) {
  result.array[i] = array[i] || s.array[i];
 }
 if (count > newcount) {
  for (long i=newcount; i<count; i++) {
   result.array[i] = array[i];
  }
 }
 if (s.count > newcount) {
  for (i=newcount; i<s.count; i++) {
   result.array[i] = s.array[i];
  }
 }
 result.SetCardinality();
```

```
 return result;
}

/***************************************************************/
/*                                                             */
/* operator- returns the difference set of this one and set s  */
/*           can throw an exception if out of memory           */
/*                                                             */
/***************************************************************/

SetAsArray SetAsArray::operator- (const SetAsArray& s) const
                                          throw (const char*) {
 long newcount = count > s.count ? count : s.count;
 SetAsArray result (newcount);
 newcount = count < s.count ? count : s.count;
 for (long i=0; i<newcount; i++) {
  result.array[i] = array[i] && !s.array[i];
 }
 if (count > newcount) {
  for (i=newcount; i<count; i++) {
   result.array[i] = array[i];
  }
 }
 result.SetCardinality();
 return result;
}

/***************************************************************/
/*                                                             */
/* operator*: returns the intersection set of this set with    */
/*            the passed set s - can throw an exception if out */
/*                                 of memory                   */
/*                                                             */
/***************************************************************/

SetAsArray SetAsArray::operator* (const SetAsArray& s) const
                                          throw (const char*) {
 long newcount = count > s.count ? count : s.count;
 SetAsArray result (newcount);
 newcount = count < s.count ? count : s.count;
 for (long i=0; i<newcount; i++) {
  result.array[i] = array[i] && s.array[i];
 }
 result.SetCardinality();
 return result;
}

/***************************************************************/
/*                                                             */
/* Operator==: is this set equal to the passed set?            */
/*                                                             */
/***************************************************************/

bool SetAsArray::operator== (const SetAsArray& s) const{
 if (count != s.count)
  return false;
```

```
 for (long i=0; i<count; i++) {
  if (array[i] != s.array[i])
   return false;
 }
 return true;
}

/***************************************************************/
/*                                                             */
/* Operator<=: IsThisOneASubSet of passed set?                 */
/*                                                             */
/***************************************************************/

bool SetAsArray::operator<= (const SetAsArray& s) const {
 if (count > s.count)
  return false;
 long i, is;
 for (i=0, is=0; i<count && is<s.count; i++, is++) {
  if (array[i] && !s.array[i])
   return false;
 }
 for (; i<count; i++) {
  if (array[i])
   return false;
 }
 return true;
}
```

Pgm14a SetAsArray Tester Program

```
#include <iostream>
#include <iomanip>
#include <crtdbg.h>

using namespace std;

#include "SetAsArray.h"

int main () {
{
 SetAsArray s (100);
 SetAsArray t (100);
 SetAsArray u (90);
 long i;
 for (i=2; i<100; i+=2) {
  s.Insert (i);
  t.Insert (i);
 }

 cout << "Set s has a cardinality of " << s.GetCardinality ()
      << endl;
 if (s == t)
  cout << "Set s equals set t\n";
 else
  cout << "Set s does not equal set t which is an error\n";
```

```

  try {
   u.Insert (100);
  }
  catch (const char* msg) {
   cout << "Correctly caught a range exception. It was"
        << endl << "   " << msg << endl;
  }

  u.Insert (2);
  u.Insert (4);
  if (u <= s)
   cout << "Set u is a subset of set s\n";
  else
   cout << "Set u is not a subset of set s - but it should be\n";

  t.Delete (98);
  t.Delete (96);
  cout << "Set s has a cardinality of " << s.GetCardinality ()
       << endl;
  cout << "Set t has a cardinality of " << t.GetCardinality ()
       << endl;
  if (s == t)
   cout << "Set s equals set t - this is an error\n";
  else
   cout << "Set s does not equal set t which is correct\n";

  SetAsArray r = s + t;
  SetAsArray v = s - t;
  SetAsArray w = s * u;
  cout << "Set r has a cardinality of " << r.GetCardinality ()
       << endl;
  cout << "Set v has a cardinality of " << v.GetCardinality ()
       << endl;
  cout << "Set w has a cardinality of " << w.GetCardinality ()
       << endl;
  cout << "Number 98 is " << (w.IsAMember(98) ? " " : "not ")
       << "a member of set w - should be not\n";
 }

  // check for memory leaks
  if (_CrtDumpMemoryLeaks())
   cerr << "Memory leaks occurred!\n";
  else
   cerr << "No memory leaks.\n";

  return 0;
 }
```

Output of Pgm14a

```
Set s has a cardinality of 49
Set s equals set t
Correctly caught a range exception. It was
   Set Error: Insert index out of range
```

```
Set u is a subset of set s
Set s has a cardinality of 49
Set t has a cardinality of 47
Set s does not equal set t which is correct
Set r has a cardinality of 49
Set v has a cardinality of 2
Set w has a cardinality of 2
Number 98 is not a member of set w - should be not
No memory leaks.
```

A Set Implemented as a Bit Vector

When saving the presence status as a **bool**, eight bits are used to save a true/false result. However, this boolean value could more efficiently be represented by a single bit, 1/0. If so, then a byte could contain eight different bit presence flags. This is the basis of implementations of the **Set** as a bit vector.

Rather than retaining a single byte as the array elements, it is also more efficient to use an **unsigned long**. The 32-bit processors are designed to fetch 32 bits from any given memory fetch, not a single byte. So less hardware manipulation is required when accessing 32-bit values than other sizes. Of course, the implementation difficulties center around the absence of any direct bit access instructions. That is, we cannot define a variable that is a bit in size. Rather, we have to use boolean logic to test and set and clear a specific bit within a byte or **unsigned long**.

Bit Manipulation Operations

AND, OR, and NOT boolean operations are used to preform the various operations on a bit within a byte. You are used to seeing logical AND, OR, and NOT operations within test conditions—that is, the operators `&&`, `||` and `!`. The boolean versions, or bitwise versions, are the operators &, |, and ~. Notice that it is a single & and a single |; the bitwise not is the ~ character.

Rule: OR bitwise operations are used to turn on a bit
Rule: AND bitwise operations are used to turn off a bit
Rule: AND bitwise operations are also used to test if a bit is on

Let's see how this is done. Remember, with OR logic, if either or both bits are on, the result is on; and with AND logic, if both bits are on, the result is on.

For simplicity, let's assume that a byte contains eight different flags. Suppose that the second bit of the byte contains a flag that we wish to turn on. Figure 14.1 shows the layout of a single byte and the corresponding bit numbers that we use to identify each specific bit. Again, the bit numbers are offsets, really, and bit 0 is the rightmost bit of the field.

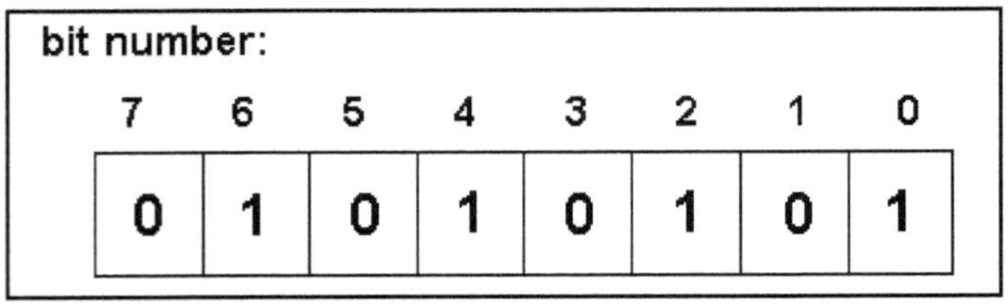

Figure 14.1 The Numbering of Bits within a Byte

Ok suppose that we wish to turn on bit 1, the second from the right, which currently contains a 0. We would OR with a value that contains a 1 bit in that corresponding bit position. However, the OR operation affects all of the bits within the flag. We must be careful not to alter the remaining bit values as we turn on bit 1. So our mask value must be the following.

```
0 0 0 0 0 0 1 0
```

The OR operation is done like this.

```
Bit flag:       0  1  0  1  0  1  0  1
OR mask:        0  0  0  0  0  0  1  0
                ----------------------
Result:         0  1  0  1  0  1  1  1
```

```
unsigned char flag;
unsigned char mask = 2;
flag = (unsigned char) (flag | mask);
```

The OR mask is a 2 in decimal, because that is what a 1 bit in the second position represents, if the mask is a number. Specifically, the decimal numbers that correspond to each of the bit positions from right to left are: 1, 2, 4, 8, 16, 32, 64, and 128. However, we will shortly see an easier way to create the OR mask for a specific bit. In the instructions above, C++ promotes all smaller sized values to an **int** which is really 4-bytes in size on the Win32 platform. Thus, to assign the result back into **flag**, a typecast is required to remove the compiler warning message.

Now suppose that we wish to turn our bit 1 flag off. We would need to AND that bit with a bit containing a 0 bit so that both bits would not be on, resulting in bit 1 being turned off. However, when we perform the AND operation, we must not alter any other bit flags in this byte, only bit 1. Thus, we must use a mask that contains all 1 bits except for that bit we wish to turn off.

The AND operation is done like this.

```
Bit flag:       0  1  0  1  0  1  1  1
AND mask:       1  1  1  1  1  1  0  1
                ----------------------
Result:         0  1  0  1  0  1  0  1
```

Thus, the AND mask is the opposite of the OR mask, or the reverse of it. This can be accomplished by using the ~ operator. The ~ reverses all bit values in the item. Originally, the mask contains the following.

```
mask:           0  0  0  0  0  0  1  0
```

After the ~ operation, it contains this.

```
mask:           1  1  1  1  1  1  0  1
        unsigned char flag;
        unsigned char mask = 2;
        flag = (unsigned char) (flag & ~mask);
```

Since a typecast is always required for these smaller values, it only makes sense to use a larger size field to store our presence flags, an **unsigned long**. But rather than continually coding this, I substituted a typecast of **unsigned long** to a **uint32**.

Next, suppose that each of these eight bit flags corresponds to the presence of an item in the set whose key identifiers, indices, are the integers 0 through 7. To add say item 1 to the set, how can we create the mask value that corresponds to that key identifier? Bit shifting is the answer. We put a 1 bit into the right most bit position of an **unsigned char** and then shift that bit to the left by the number of times the index contains. If the index was the 1 as above, then we would shift that 1-bit to the left one bit position as illustrated below.

```
int index = 1;
unsigned char mask = (unsigned char) (1 << index);
```

or

```
0 0 0 0 0 0 0 1
```

is shifted 1 position left to yield

```
0 0 0 0 0 0 1 0
```

Left bit shifting is done by using the << operator. Right bit shifting is done by using the >> operator. The bit shifting operation is extremely fast on Pentium class machines; the barrel shifter, as the machine instructions are called, takes only a few machine clock cycles to perform. Thus, bit shifting can be done in a minimal amount of time.

Obviously, we need to store the flags in an **unsigned long** to avoid all of the conversion problems. To implement this method of storing an item's presence in the **Set** class, we store the flags as an array of **unsigned longs**. Each of the **unsigned long** values contains then 32 separate presence flags. The real problem that we face in implementing this is twofold: given the user's index identifier, how do we determine which **unsigned long** actually contains the flag that we need and, secondly, how do we create a bit mask to identify that specific bit within that **unsigned long**?

Since an unsigned long is 32 bits in size, simple divide the user's index number by 32 to obtain the index of the unsigned long in our array actually contains that item's presence flag.

```
  long idx = num / 32; // which uint32 is this one in?
```

For example, suppose the user's number was 14. Then, that item's flag is located in our **unsigned long** array element 0. If the number was 33, then it is located in out array element 1.

To obtain the bit position within our flag unsigned long, we take the remainder of the user's number with 32.

```
position = num & 32;
```

Using the above two examples, the position of the user's item numbered 14 is bit 14. The position of the item 33 is 1.

We can then create the needed OR flag by shifting a 1 position number of bits to the left. Usually, we combine both of these operations in a single statement as follows.

```
uint32 flag = 1 << num % 32; // which bit is this one?
```

Given the flag mask, we can then test this specific bit within the unsigned long by using the bitwise or boolean & operator which returns the AND result and then tests it to see if it is not zero.

```
if (!(array[idx] & flag)) {  // if it is not on,
 array[idx] |= flag;         // then turn this bit on
 cardinality++;
}
```

Then, to turn on this presence bit, we can use the |= operator which ORs the array element value with the flag and then stores the result back into the array element. The above sequence is what is needed to **Insert** the presence of an item in the set.

To delete an item from the set, we follow the same basic sequence to obtain the index and the mask. Then, to handle the deletion of an item, or to turn off its corresponding bit, we code the following.

```
if (array[idx] & flag) { // is bit on?
 cardinality--;          // yes, this one is present, so remove
 array[idx] &= ~flag;
}
```

Notice that we are ANDing the ~flag value (or reverse of the flag bits) to the array element and then storing the result back into the array element using the &= operator.

The other functions are implemented similarly. The only other tricky feature is how to determine the number of array elements we must allocate given the maximum item number index of the user? For example, if the user constructs a set that is to contain 100 items, how many **unsigned long**s do we allocate in our array? If we just divided 100 by 32 bits per **unsigned long**, we would get 3. But 3 **unsigned long**s only hold 96 items. Thus, we must round up to the nearest **unsigned long**. This is done easily by adding 31 to the user's maximum before dividing by 32.

```
count = (max + 32 -1) / 32;
array = new uint32 [count];
```

To make the class operations easier to do, I also store the maximum number of user items, which is count * 32. This way, a range check of any given user id number can easily be done.

Here are the **SetAsBitVector** class definition and implementation files. The coding is totally parallel to that of the previous class version. I have not shown the **Pgm14b** tester program because it is the same as **Pgm14a** except for the data type of the set class instances. Its output is identical to **Pgm14a**.

SetAsBitVector Class Definition

```
#pragma once

typedef unsigned long uint32;

/***************************************************************/
/*                                                             */
/* SetAsBitVector: encapsulates a set as an array of bools     */
/*                 the user items are not stored, only their   */
/*                 presence in the set is maintained           */
/*                                                             */
/***************************************************************/

class SetAsBitVector {
protected:
 uint32* array;      // 1b = true - a uint32 holds 32 items
 long  count;        // the number of elements in the array
 long  numItems;     // the max items that can be stored
 long  cardinality;  // the number of items in the set currently

```

```
public:
 SetAsBitVector (long max) throw (const char*);
 SetAsBitVector (const SetAsBitVector& s) throw (const char*);
~SetAsBitVector ();
 SetAsBitVector& operator= (const SetAsBitVector& s)
                            throw (const char*);

 void Insert (long num) throw (const char*);
 void Delete (long num) throw (const char*);
 bool IsAMember (long num) const;
 long GetCardinality () const;

 // union function
 SetAsBitVector  operator+ (const SetAsBitVector& s) const
                       throw (const char*);

 // difference function
 SetAsBitVector  operator- (const SetAsBitVector& s) const
                       throw (const char*);

 // intersection function
 SetAsBitVector  operator* (const SetAsBitVector& s) const
                       throw (const char*);

 // are two sets equal
 bool operator== (const SetAsBitVector& s) const;

 // is this a subset of set s?
 bool operator<= (const SetAsBitVector& s) const;

protected:
 SetAsBitVector (); // disallow default ctor
 void Copy (const SetAsBitVector& s) throw (const char*);
 bool RangeCheck (long num) const; // idx in range?
 void SetCardinality (); // recalcs a set's cardinality
};
```

SetAsBitVector Class Implementation

```
#include <iostream>
#include <iomanip>
using namespace std;

#include "SetAsBitVector.h"

/***************************************************************/
/*                                                             */
/* SetAsBitVector: allocate and inits the array of uint32 flags*/
/*      can throw exceptions if max out of range or no memory  */
/*                                                             */
/***************************************************************/

SetAsBitVector::SetAsBitVector (long max) throw (const char*) {
 if (max < 1) {
  throw "SetAsBitVector Error: ctor must be passed "
```

```
        "a positive number";
 }
 // calc number of uint32 flags by rounding up
 count = (max + 32 -1) / 32;
 try {
  array = new uint32 [count];
 }
 catch (std::bad_alloc e) {
  count = 0;
  array = 0;
  throw "SetAsBitVector Error: ctor - out of memory";
 }
 numItems = count * 32; // the number of items is 32 per uint32
 cardinality = 0;
 for (long i=0; i<count; i++)
  array[i] = 0;
}

/***************************************************************/
/*                                                             */
/* ~SetAsBitVector: dtor deletes the array                     */
/*                                                             */
/*                                                             */
/***************************************************************/

SetAsBitVector::~SetAsBitVector () {
 if (array) delete [] array;
}

/***************************************************************/
/*                                                             */
/* SetAsBitVector copy ctor: can throw an out of memory ex     */
/*                                                             */
/***************************************************************/

SetAsBitVector::SetAsBitVector (const SetAsBitVector& s)
                                throw (const char*) {
 try {
  Copy (s);
 }
 catch (const char* msg) {
  throw msg;
 }
}

/***************************************************************/
/*                                                             */
/* operator= assignment op makes this a dupe of s              */
/*           can throw out of memory exception                 */
/*                                                             */
/***************************************************************/

SetAsBitVector& SetAsBitVector::operator= (
                   const SetAsBitVector& s) throw (const char*) {
 if (this == &s) return *this;
 if (array) delete [] array;
```

```
 try {
  Copy (s);
 }
 catch (const char* msg) {
  throw msg;
 }
 return *this;
}

/***************************************************************/
/*                                                             */
/* Copy: make a duplicate copy of a SetAsBitVector             */
/*       can throw an out of memory exception                  */
/*                                                             */
/***************************************************************/

void SetAsBitVector::Copy (const SetAsBitVector& s)
                           throw (const char*) {
 count = s.count;
 numItems = s.numItems;
 cardinality = s.cardinality;
 try {
  array = new uint32 [count];
 }
 catch (std::bad_alloc e) {
  count = 0;
  array = 0;
  throw "SetAsBitVector Error: copy ctor - out of memory";
 }
 for (long i=0; i<count; i++) {
  array[i] = s.array[i];
 }
}

/***************************************************************/
/*                                                             */
/* GetCardinality: returns the number of items in the set now  */
/*                                                             */
/***************************************************************/

long SetAsBitVector::GetCardinality () const {
 return cardinality;
}

/***************************************************************/
/*                                                             */
/* RangeCheck: return true if num is within the array bounds   */
/*             checks the max number of items in array         */
/*             not the array size                              */
/*                                                             */
/***************************************************************/

bool SetAsBitVector::RangeCheck (long num) const {
 if (num < 1)
  return false;
 return num > numItems ? false : true;
```

```
}

/***************************************************************/
/*                                                             */
/* Insert: adds a new item to the SetAsBitVector               */
/*         can throw an exception if num is out of range       */
/*                                                             */
/***************************************************************/

void SetAsBitVector::Insert (long num) throw (const char*) {
 if (RangeCheck(num)) {
  long idx = num / 32; // which uint32 is this one in?
  uint32 flag = 1 << num % 32; // which bit is this one?
  if (!(array[idx] & flag)) {  // if not on, then turn on
   array[idx] |= flag;
   cardinality++;
  }
 }
 else
  throw "SetAsBitVector Error: Insert index out of range";
}

/***************************************************************/
/*                                                             */
/* Delete: removes this item from the SetAsBitVector           */
/*         can throw an exception if num is out of range       */
/*                                                             */
/***************************************************************/

void SetAsBitVector::Delete (long num) throw (const char*) {
 if (RangeCheck (num)) {
  long idx = num / 32; // which uint32 is this one in?
  uint32 flag = 1 << num % 32; // which bit is this one?
  if (array[idx] & flag) { // is bit on?
   cardinality--;          // yes, this one is present, so remove
   array[idx] &= ~flag;
  }
 }
 else
  throw "SetAsBitVector Error: Delete index out of range";
}

/***************************************************************/
/*                                                             */
/* IsAMember: returns true if this item is in SetAsBitVector   */
/*                                                             */
/***************************************************************/

bool SetAsBitVector::IsAMember (long num) const {
 if (RangeCheck (num)) {
  long idx = num / 32; // which uint32 is this one in?
  uint32 flag = 1 << num % 32; // which bit this one in?
  return array[idx] & flag ? true : false;
 }
 else
  return false;
```

```
}

/*****************************************************************/
/*                                                               */
/* SetCardinality: calcs the number of items in set now         */
/*                                                               */
/*****************************************************************/

void SetAsBitVector::SetCardinality () {
 cardinality = 0;
 long i, j;
 uint32 flag;
 for (i=0; i<count; i++) { // for each uint32
  for (j=0; j<32; j++) {   // for each bit in the unit32
   flag = 1 << j;          // make its location flag
   if (array[i] & flag)    // it this bit is on, inc cardinality
    cardinality++;
  }
 }
}

/*****************************************************************/
/*                                                               */
/* operator+ returns the union of this set and the passed set s*/
/*           can throw an out of memory exception                */
/*                                                               */
/*****************************************************************/
SetAsBitVector SetAsBitVector::operator+ (
             const SetAsBitVector& s) const throw (const char*) {
 long newcount = count > s.count ? count : s.count;
 SetAsBitVector result (newcount*32);
 newcount = count < s.count ? count : s.count;
 for (long i=0; i<newcount; i++) { // if either is on, turn on
  result.array[i] = array[i] | s.array[i];
 }
 if (count > newcount) {            // add in any extras in us
  for (long i=newcount; i<count; i++) {
   result.array[i] = array[i];
  }
 }
 if (s.count > newcount) {          // add in any extras in s
  for (i=newcount; i<s.count; i++) {
   result.array[i] = s.array[i];
  }
 }
 result.SetCardinality();
 return result;
}

/*****************************************************************/
/*                                                               */
/* operator- returns the difference set of this one and set s   */
/*           can throw an exception if out of memory             */
/*                                                               */
/*****************************************************************/

```

```
SetAsBitVector SetAsBitVector::operator- (
             const SetAsBitVector& s) const throw (const char*) {
 long newcount = count > s.count ? count : s.count;
 SetAsBitVector result (newcount*32);
 newcount = count < s.count ? count : s.count;
 for (long i=0; i<newcount; i++) {
  // leave on any bits which are on in ours and off in theirs
  result.array[i] = array[i] & ~s.array[i];
 }
 if (count > newcount) { // add in any extras in ours
  for (i=newcount; i<count; i++) {
   result.array[i] = array[i];
  }
 }
 result.SetCardinality();
 return result;
}

/***************************************************************/
/*                                                             */
/* operator*: returns the intersection set of this set with    */
/*            the passed set s - can throw an exception if out */
/*                              of memory                      */
/*                                                             */
/***************************************************************/

SetAsBitVector SetAsBitVector::operator* (
             const SetAsBitVector& s) const throw (const char*) {
 long newcount = count > s.count ? count : s.count;
 SetAsBitVector result (newcount*32);
 newcount = count < s.count ? count : s.count;
 for (long i=0; i<newcount; i++) {
  // turn on if any bit is present in both
  result.array[i] = array[i] & s.array[i];
 }
 result.SetCardinality();
 return result;
}

/***************************************************************/
/*                                                             */
/* Operator==: is this set equal to the passed set?            */
/*                                                             */
/***************************************************************/

bool SetAsBitVector::operator== (const SetAsBitVector& s) const{
 if (count != s.count)
  return false;
 for (long i=0; i<count; i++) {
  if (array[i] != s.array[i])
   return false;
 }
 return true;
}

/***************************************************************/
```

```
/*                                                                   */
/* Operator<=: IsThisOneASubSet of passed set?                       */
/*                                                                   */
/*********************************************************************/

bool SetAsBitVector::operator<= (const SetAsBitVector& s) const {
 if (count > s.count)
  return false;
 long i, is;
 for (i=0, is=0; i<count && is<s.count; i++, is++) {
  if (array[i] & ~s.array[i])
   return false;
 }
 for (; i<count; i++) {
  if (array[i])
   return false;
 }
 return true;
}
```

Both set classes suffer from a significant design defect. Have you spotted the flaw or performance problem in the design? If not, consider how large the array of present flags would have to be if the user intended to use the social security numbers as the item identifiers?

Our design allocates space for each possible user index value, assuming that they are in sequential order from zero to the maximum value and that any one of these may be present. However, suppose that a company had no more than 1,000 customers but that they used the social security numbers as their identifiers? We cannot allocate arrays whose limits are in the hundreds of millions!

Further, suppose that the identifiers were not easily expressible as an array subscript as all have been thus far. What if the client program wanted to use the city names as the item identifiers, as the program from the graph chapter did in the airline routes problem? As it stands, neither problem can be immediately handled with either of the two set classes presented thus far. There just is not enough memory available and the user's item identifiers had to be an index that we use to access the array of presence flags.

The Map Data Structure

The map data structure provides a convenient method to "map" any given identifier into a more usable index type of identifier. If the identifier were the social security number, the map data structure can map it into a simple index-type of numerical value. If the identifier was a string, such as the city name, the map can convert it into an index value. A map data structure stores a collection of ordered entries consisting of user keys and their values. The keys must be unique. Usually the values are also unique, but do not have to be so, necessarily. In this chapter, I assume all values are also unique.

Essentially, the map data structure stores a table of values. Each element in the table consists of the user's identifier and the index assigned number. For example, using the social security number problem, the map entries might look something like this.

Social Security Number	Index Value
111-11-1111	0
222-22-2222	1
111-22-3333	2
444-11-2222	3
221-00-1234	4

Here, any given social security number is mapped into an index value that can be used in any manner desired, such as in our set classes. Conversely, any index value can be mapped back to the user identifier it represents.

Thus, a map structure is essentially a set of pairs of values. The operational functions include the following: insert a new pair, delete a pair, given a key find the value, and given a value, find the key. Quite often, operator[] is overloaded to provide a more convenient user interface as shown below.

```
long index = map["Chicago, IL"];
```

or

```
char* name = map[42];
```

Here the map instance is mapping a string to an **int** and the **int** back into its string.

There are numerous ways the map data structure can be implemented. Each has its pros and cons. If the map contains a large number of items and the map is expected to be heavily used, then storing the table entries in a binary search tree makes good sense. If the number of items is very small and few table look ups are required, then a simple unsorted array of entries would suffice. For something in between, perhaps a sorted array with a binary search might work well.

The table look up process must go both ways. That is, given a social security number or city name, find its assigned index; given an index, find its associated social security number or city name. Here in lies the real problem. If we maintain the collection of table entries sorted into social security number order, then the reverse search—given an index, find its social security number—would have terrible response time when the table is large because the search would have to visit every entry sequentially looking for a match. So a method of efficiently handling the reverse searching must be found, assuming that a binary search on the sorted list can be done on the user's item values. In the Map class here, the reverse search is sequential for simplicity.

Another consideration is how are the index values assigned? When the user inserts a new key values, they could be asked to provide the next index value. On the other hand, the map class could keep track of index values and assign each new addition with the next sequential number. If the map class does the assignment, then fewer mapping errors may occur since the user is relieved of the responsibility of maintaining the index values. However, if the map class does the assignments of the index values, then the user is precluded from "reusing" an index value after they have deleted a key and is attempting to insert another key and reuse the original index value. Further, we would be restricting even the type of data to which a key maps. Hence, we cannot assign index values; they are given to the **Map** by the client.

How should the **Map** class store the pairs of user items? A convenient way is to store them in a **Pair** structure. Thus, the **Map** class maintains a growable, sorted array of **Pair** structures. The sorting is on the user's "key" item not its corresponding index or value item. A template **Map** class is used so that it is independent of the user's actual data types. Since the array is maintained in a sorted order, a fast binary search can be done to find a "key" item and return it's corresponding value or index that the user has associated with this key.

Here is the **Map** class. It is actually a rather simple template class. It depends for its operation upon some key properties of the user's key and value data types. Specifically, those user types must support the comparison operators: <, >, and ==.

Map Class Template

```
#pragma once

/***************************************************************/
/*                                                             */
/* Map class: maps user type T to user type V                  */
/* user types must be able to support operators > and < and == */
/*                                                             */
/***************************************************************/

template<class T, class V>
struct Pair { // storing pairs of user T and corresponding V sets
 T data;
 V value;
};

template<class T, class V>
class Map {

protected:
 Pair<T, V>* map;        // the array of Pair objects
 long        mapSize;    // the number in the array
 long        iterator;   // the next subscript when iterating
```

```

public:
      Map ();
     ~Map ();

 bool Insert (const T& data, const V& idx);// add new pair to map
 bool Delete (const T& data);       // remove a pair by finding T
 bool ReverseDelete (const V& idx); // remove a pair by finding V

 // find the V that corresponds to a specific T
 V& operator[] (const T& data) throw (const char*);
 // find the T that corresponds to a specific V
 T& ReverseFind (const V& idx);

 long GetSize () const; // returns the number of Pairs in the map

 void ResetIterator (); // reset iterator back to the beginning
 bool GetNextMapPair (T&, V&); // get the next Pair of values

protected:
 bool BinarySearch (const T& findId, long& foundIndex);

};

/***************************************************************/
/*                                                             */
/* Map: initialize to an empty array                           */
/*                                                             */
/***************************************************************/

template<class T, class V>
Map<T, V>::Map (){
 map = 0;
 mapSize = 0;
 iterator = 0;
}

/***************************************************************/
/*                                                             */
/* ~Map: delete any allocated map array                        */
/*                                                             */
/***************************************************************/

template<class T, class V>
Map<T, V>::~Map () {
 if (map) delete [] map;
}

/***************************************************************/
/*                                                             */
/* Insert: add a new T,V pair to map in sorted by T order      */
/*                                                             */
/***************************************************************/

template<class T, class V>
bool Map<T, V>::Insert (const T& data, const V& idx) {
```

```
 if (!mapSize) {           // here there are no items in the map
  map = new Pair<T, V>[1];
  map[0].data = data;
  map[0].value = idx;
  mapSize = 1;
  return true;
 }
 long hereIdx; // Find where this one should go in sorted map
 if (BinarySearch (data, hereIdx)) {
  cerr << "Map Error: item already exists at index of "
       << idx << endl << "  It has not been added to the map.\n";
  return false;
 }
 // allocate a larger array of Pairs
 Pair<T, V>* temp = new Pair<T, V>[mapSize+1];
 long i;
 for (i=0; i<hereIdx; i++) { // copy those up to where it goes
  temp[i] = map[i];
 }
 temp[i].data = data;       // insert new one
 temp[i++].value = idx;
 for (; i<=mapSize; i++) { // copy those below it
  temp[i] = map[i-1];
 }
 if (map) delete [] map; // remove old map array
 map = temp;             // save as new array
 mapSize++;              // inc array size
 return true;
}

/***************************************************************/
/*                                                             */
/* Delete: given a T, find it and delete its Pair              */
/*                                                             */
/***************************************************************/

template<class T, class V>
bool Map<T, V>::Delete (const T& data) {
 if (!mapSize) { // cannot delete if nothing is in array
  return false;
 }
 long hereIdx;   // find this item
 if (!BinarySearch (data, hereIdx))
  return false;  // item not found

 if (mapSize == 1) { // if there is only one item left in map,
  mapSize = 0;       // remove all traces of map
  delete [] map;
  map = 0;
  return true;
 }

 // allocate a smaller array of Pairs
 Pair<T, V>* temp = new Pair<T, V>[mapSize-1];
 for (long i=0; i<hereIdx; i++) {// copy all Pairs upto this one
  temp[i] = map[i];
```

```
  }
  for (; i<mapSize-1; i++) {       // copy all Pairs after this one
   temp[i] = map[i+1];
  }
  mapSize--;       // reduce array size
  delete [] map;  // remove old map
  map = temp;      // save new map
  return true;
 }

/***************************************************************/
/*                                                             */
/* ReverseDelete: given a V, find it and delete that pair      */
/*                                                             */
/***************************************************************/

template<class T, class V>
bool Map<T, V>::ReverseDelete (const V& value) {
 if (!mapSize) return false; // nothing to delete

 // find the one to delete by sequential search
 long hereIdx;
 for (hereIdx=0; hereIdx<mapSize; hereIdx++) {
  if (map[hereIdx].value == value) break;
 }
 // if not found, quit
 if (hereIdx == mapSize) return false;

 // if only one left in array, reset to empty map
 if (mapSize == 1) {
  mapSize = 0;
  delete [] map;
  map = 0;
  return true;
 }

 // allocate a new map one smaller than before
 Pair<T, V>* temp = new Pair<T, V>[mapSize-1];
 for (long i=0; i<hereIdx; i++) { // copy those before this one
  temp[i] = map[i];
 }
 for (; i<mapSize-1; i++) {        // copy those after this one
  temp[i] = map[i+1];
 }
 mapSize--;       // dec array size
 delete [] map;  // remove old map
 map = temp;      // save as new map
 return true;
}

/***************************************************************/
/*                                                             */
/* operator[] given a T, find its V from sorted list of Ts     */
/*                                                             */
/***************************************************************/

```

```
template<class T, class V>
V& Map<T, V>::operator[] (const T& data) throw (const char*) {
 if (!mapSize) {
  throw "Map Error: attempting to access an empty map";
 }
 long hereIdx;
 if (BinarySearch (data, hereIdx))
  return map[hereIdx].value;
 else
  throw "Map Error: item not found in the map";
}

/***************************************************************/
/*                                                             */
/* ReverseFind: given a V, sequential search to find its T     */
/*                                                             */
/***************************************************************/

template<class T, class V>
T& Map<T, V>::ReverseFind (const V& idx) {
 if (!mapSize) {
  throw "Map Error: attempting to access an empty map";
 }
 for (long i=0; i<mapSize; i++) {
  if (map[i].value == idx)
   return map[i].data;
 }
 throw "Map Error: item not found in the map";
}

/***************************************************************/
/*                                                             */
/* BinarySearch: find T in the map or where it should be after */
/*                                                             */
/***************************************************************/

template<class T, class V>
bool Map<T, V>::BinarySearch (const T& findId, long& foundIndex){
 long firstidx = 0;
 long lastidx = mapSize - 1;
 long middleidx;
 bool foundMatch = false;
 bool goesBefore = false;
 while (lastidx >= firstidx && !foundMatch) {
  middleidx = (firstidx + lastidx) / 2;
  if (findId < map[middleidx].data) {
   lastidx = middleidx - 1;
   goesBefore = true;
  }
  else if (findId > map[middleidx].data) {
   firstidx = middleidx + 1;
   goesBefore = false;
  }
  else foundMatch = true;
 }
 foundIndex = middleidx;
```

```
 if (!foundMatch && !goesBefore) foundIndex++;
 return foundMatch;
}

/***************************************************************/
/*                                                             */
/* GetSize: returns the number of pairs in the map             */
/*                                                             */
/***************************************************************/

template<class T, class V>
long Map<T, V>::GetSize () const{
 return mapSize;
}

/***************************************************************/
/*                                                             */
/* ResetIterator: reset it back to 0 to restart through map    */
/*                                                             */
/***************************************************************/

template<class T, class V>
void Map<T, V>::ResetIterator (){
 iterator = 0;
}

/***************************************************************/
/*                                                             */
/* GetNextMapPair: gets the next pair of values                */
/*                                                             */
/***************************************************************/

template<class T, class V>
bool Map<T, V>::GetNextMapPair (T& t, V& v) {
 if (!mapSize || iterator < 0 || iterator >= mapSize)
  return false;
 t = map[iterator].data;
 v = map[iterator].value;
 iterator++;
 return true;
}
```

Putting a Map to Use—the Beginnings of Data Compression Theory

One of the many uses of a Map structure is to store a dictionary of words or symbols. And one of the uses of a dictionary is in the arena of data compression. The purpose of this sample program is twofold—show how a dictionary of words can be built and to illustrate the very beginnings of a data compression routine.

The basic idea of data compression is to somehow compress the original document into a smaller sized compressed file and to be able to recover that document. There are many such programs available on the market, such as WinZip and PKZip. Many of the data compression schemes utilize a dictionary of repeated symbols and words.

For example, suppose that the document contained 15 occurrences of the word "appliances." In a compressed form, one may find a single occurrence of "appliances" in the dictionary and 15 numerical references to that dictionary item within the text portion of the compressed file. In other words, the 15 occurrences are replaced with an index number that points to the single occurrence of the word. This reduces the total size of the document accordingly.

One of the first actions of a compression routine is to build the dictionary of words and symbols contained within the document to be compressed. In this example, we are only going to explore the most fundamental approach, building a dictionary of symbols and words. Obviously, a far better compression algorithm would look for repeated sequences. In this basic approach, no attempt is made to get a high degree of compression nor in the actual storing of the numerical indices of those symbols.

The indices of the symbols cannot be stored in an **unsigned char** because of the limitation of only 256 words. So let's use a **short** which can hold up to 65, 536 values. In reality, a short is also way too large. So much more commonly, a 12-bit number is used, that is a byte and a half. Since one cannot access 1.5 bytes at a time, a deal of bit-shifting is required to insert and retrieve such numbers. Thus, for this first look, I am storing **short** integer values.

Instead of looking for repeated sequences, I am looking for words and symbol strings. This way, you can see the coding required to build an actual dictionary of words contained in a document, which also has other uses, such as spelling dictionaries and vocabulary analyses. For the test document, I took the first eight pages of this chapter saved as a DOS text file to remove the word processing special values.

Here I define a "word" as a consecutive series of letters (A-Z and a-z) only. The series of non-letters that appear between words I refer to as a series of non-words. These non-words series can consist of CRLFs and of " ." and so on. The basic table for the first eight chapters contains a little more than 600 items. I maintain an index **short** which starts at 0. As I sequentially search the input file, every time that a word or on-word series is not in the dictionary map set, I add it and increment the associated index.

The basic compressed format consists then of the complete dictionary with each word and its associated index followed by a huge series of short indexes, each of which represents the corresponding dictionary item.

Here is an example of the compressed format idea. The original document contains the following line.

```
The black cat.
```

The dictionary contains three words (The, black, cat) and two non-word series: (a blank and a period). The first two bytes of the file contain the total number of dictionary items, five in this case. This is followed by the dictionary items and their indices. Then, comes the text where each item has been replaced by the index to which it corresponds in the dictionary.

```
5 blank-0, .-1, black-2, cat-3, The-4, 4, 0, 2, 0, 3, 5
```

Let's examine the resultant compressed file size. Each short occupies 2 bytes. Thus, the above compressed string occupies a total of 42 bytes (12 shorts for 24 bytes and 5 strings with their null terminators for 18 bytes). The original message contains 15 bytes including its null terminator. Oops. Instead of data compression, we have expanded the file size!

But in the above line, there are no duplicated words, except the blank. So let's try another one. Suppose that the message was as follows.

```
The black cat? The black cat? Did you say black cat?
```

Now we add four more items to the dictionary (? -1, Did-5, you-6, say-7). Here is the compressed version.

```
9 blank-0, .-1, black-2, cat-3, The-4, Did-5, you-6, say-7, ? -8 4, 0, 2, 0, 3,
8, 4, 0, 2, 0, 3, 8, 5, 0, 6, 0, 7, 0, 2, 0, 3, 8
```

The compressed size is now 96 bytes long while the original is 53 bytes in length. Certainly, storing the indices as a two-byte number is adding to the file size.

Certainly, if we used repeated sequences, we could achieve a much better compression. The series " black cat?" is repeated three times. Rather than going this route of repeated sequences as a good compression routine might, let's stay with our dictionary of words. We'll live with the fact that our data compression routine actually does not compress the file without further refinements.

When **Pgm14c** runs, it builds two **Map** dictionaries. One consists of the actual words and the other contains the non-word series. Since the map is maintained in alphabetical order, if we display the map, we have an alphabetical listing of all words in the document. The list is shown below. Notice that all capitalized words appear before the lowercase versions. If we wanted a spelling type dictionary, the case of a word would likely be ignored when the map is built. Since there are 532 words in this dictionary, I have omitted a major portion of the results listing.

The Words Map Listing from Pgm14c

```
1. |A|
2. |Add|
3. |Again|
4. |All|
5. |Also|
```

```
  6   6. |Alternatively|
  7   7. |An|
  8   8. |Another|
  9   9. |Any|
 10  10. |Array|
 11  11. |At|
 12  12. |B|
 13  13. |Binary|
 14  14. |But|
 15  15. |C|
 16  16. |Cardinality|
...
 94  94. |a|
 95  95. |able|
 96  96. |abounds|
 97  97. |about|
 98  98. |above|
 99  99. |absence|
100 100. |action|
101 101. |actions|
102 102. |actual|
103 103. |actually|
104 104. |add|
105 105. |added|
106 106. |adding|
107 107. |additional|
108 108. |again|
109 109. |all|
110 110. |allocate|
111 111. |allocates|
112 112. |also|
113 113. |am|
114 114. |amount|
115 115. |an|
116 116. |and|
117 117. |another|
118 118. |any|
119 119. |appear|
120 120. |application|
121 121. |applications|
122 122. |approach|
123 123. |approaches|
124 124. |are|
125 125. |array|
126 126. |as|
127 127. |aspect|
128 128. |assignment|
129 129. |associated|
130 130. |at|
131 131. |available|
...
529 529. |writing|
530 530. |yes|
531 531. |you|
532 532. |zero|
```

In order to accurately perform the processing, the input file, although it is actually a text file, must be input as a binary file. This eliminates the problem of C++ removing all CR codes leaving only the LF codes from the <CRLF> pairs. The squished output file is also binary because of all of the **short** integers and null terminated strings.

There is an implementation detail that cannot be overlooked. I wish to store character strings in the map. I cannot store them directly, as in the following.

```
Map<char*, short> words;
```

or

```
Map<char [], short> words;
```

Why? Because this data type does not support the assignment operator nor the comparison operators. Hence, I must either store the strings as a structure member and overload these operators as structure member functions or use a form of string class. Here, we can finally make excellent use of the **string** template class.

Pgm14c also illustrates the use of the **string** template class to encapsulate character strings. The **string** class provides a convenient user interface to string processing. Strings are constructed in a similar manner to other classes. The ctor is overloaded to also take a **const char*** string.

```
        string s ("Hello");
        char myOrdinaryString[100];
        ... fill up myOrdinaryString
        string t = myOrdinaryStirng;
```

One can assign a new value to an existing string using the assignment operator.

```
        t = "A new Value";
```

The **string** class also implements the relational operators and the insertion and extraction operators. Operator+ is used to concatenate two strings. The **getline** function is also provided for input operations. However, there are times when one needs the **string** as an array of characters. **Pgm14c** needs to output the string in binary format. The **c_str()** function returns a **const char*** pointer to a null terminated array of char. (Note, if you go on and take the next course, Windows MFC (Microsoft Foundation Classes) Programming I, you will find that Microsoft provides a far, far better string class called **CString**.)

Pgm14c contains quite a bit of more unusual coding. As you look over the program, pay attention to the use of the new string class, the methods of inserting/extracting binary numbers into a string, the use of our new Map class, and the use of the try-catch logic.

Pgm14c - File Compress/Decompress Program

```
#include <iostream>
#include <iomanip>
#include <fstream>
#include <string>
#include <cctype>
#include <crtdbg.h>
#include "Map.h"

using namespace std;

/***************************************************************/
/*                                                             */
/* Pgm14c Using a Map to build a Dictionary of Words           */
/*        elementary file compression theory                   */
/*                                                             */
/***************************************************************/

void CompressFile ();
string GetString (const char* inbuffer, long& inIdx, bool word);
void MoveIndexValueToBuffer (char* outbuffer, long& outIdx,
                             short index);
void ReadSqzFile ();
void LoadDictionary (Map<string, short>& dict, const char* buf,
                     long& inIdx);
void Display (Map<string, short>& words);
```

```

int main () {

 CompressFile ();
 ReadSqzFile ();

 // check for memory leaks
 if (_CrtDumpMemoryLeaks())
  cerr << "Memory leaks occurred!\n";
 else
  cerr << "No memory leaks.\n";

 return 0;
}

/***************************************************************/
/*                                                             */
/* CompressFile: builds a dictionary of words/nonwords and     */
/*               constructs a compressed file from these       */
/*                                                             */
/***************************************************************/

void CompressFile () {
 // open the input file
 ifstream infile ("c14-pgs.txt", ios::in | ios::binary);
 if (!infile) {
  cerr << "Error: cannot open c14-pgs.txt file\n";
  exit (1);
 }

 // get file size
 infile.seekg (0, ios::end);
 long filesize = infile.tellg();
 infile.seekg (0, ios::beg);

 // create a new input and output buffer - note that the output
 // buffer does not contain the actual dictionaries - only the
 // short indexes
 char* inbuffer = new char[filesize+1];
 char* outbuffer = new char[filesize+1];
 if (!inbuffer || !outbuffer) {
  infile.close ();
  cerr << "Error: out of memory\n";
  if (inbuffer) delete [] inbuffer;
  exit (2);
 }

 // input the whole file
 infile.read (inbuffer, filesize);
 inbuffer[filesize] = 0;

 long inIdx = 0;
 long outIdx = 0;
 short nextIndex = 0;
 short index;
 Map<string, short> words;
```

```
Map<string, short> nonwords;
string s;

// process all characters in the input buffer
while (inbuffer[inIdx]) {
 // get the first non word string, if any
 s = GetString (inbuffer, inIdx, false);
 if (s.length() != 0) { // see if it is already in the map
  try {
   index = nonwords[s];
  }
  catch (const char*) { // not in the map, so add it
   nonwords.Insert (s, nextIndex);
   index = nextIndex++;
  }
  // and move its index value into the output buffer
  MoveIndexValueToBuffer (outbuffer, outIdx, index);
 }

 // now get any word string
 if (inbuffer[inIdx] == 0) break;
 s = GetString (inbuffer, inIdx, true);
 try {
  index = words[s];           // see if it is already in the map
 }
 catch (const char*) {
  words.Insert (s, nextIndex); // no, so add to words map
  index = nextIndex++;
 }
 // and move its index into the output buffer
 MoveIndexValueToBuffer (outbuffer, outIdx, index);
}
infile.close ();
delete [] inbuffer;

// now write the output file
ofstream outfile ("c14-pgs.sqz", ios::out | ios::binary);
if (!outfile) {
 cerr << "Error: cannot open the output file c14-pgs.sqz\n";
 delete [] outbuffer;
 exit (3);
}

// display the table of words for debugging purposes
Display (words);

// write the total number of words to the file
long ct = words.GetSize ();
outfile.write ((char*) &ct, sizeof (ct));

// now write out all the pairs of words and indices
words.ResetIterator ();
while (words.GetNextMapPair (s, index)) {
 const char* ss = s.c_str ();
 outfile.write (ss, (int)(strlen(ss)+1));
 outfile.write ((char*) &index, sizeof (index));
```

```
 }

 // repeat for the nonwords map
 ct = nonwords.GetSize ();
 outfile.write ((char*) &ct, sizeof (ct));
 nonwords.ResetIterator ();
 while (nonwords.GetNextMapPair (s, index)) {
  const char* ss = s.c_str ();
  outfile.write (ss, (int)(strlen(ss)+1));
  outfile.write ((char*) &index, sizeof (index));
 }

 // write out the text now converted to a series of indices
 outfile.write (outbuffer, outIdx);
 outfile.close ();
 delete [] outbuffer;
}

/***************************************************************/
/*                                                             */
/* Display: print the contents of a Map which holds words      */
/*                                                             */
/***************************************************************/

void Display (Map<string, short>& words) {
 string s;
 short index;
 long i = 1;
 words.ResetIterator ();
 while (words.GetNextMapPair (s, index)) {
  const char* ss = s.c_str ();
  cout << setw(3) << i << ". |" << ss << "|\n";
  i++;
 }
}

/***************************************************************/
/*                                                             */
/* GetString: extracts a word string from the input buffer     */
/*                                                             */
/* when word is true, looks for alphabetical letters           */
/* when word is false, looks not non-letter strings            */
/*                                                             */
/***************************************************************/

string GetString (const char* inbuffer, long& inIdx, bool word) {
 char s[500];
 long iend = inIdx;
 if (!word) {
  while (inbuffer[iend] && !isalpha(inbuffer[iend])) iend++;
 }
 else {
  while ((inbuffer[iend] >= 'A' && inbuffer[iend] <= 'Z') ||
         (inbuffer[iend] >= 'a' && inbuffer[iend] <= 'z')) {
   iend++;
  }
```

```
 }
 long len = iend - inIdx;
 memcpy (s, &inbuffer[inIdx], len); // copy the string's chars
 s[len] = 0;                        // null terminate it
 string str = s;                    // turn into a string object
 inIdx = iend;
 return str;
}

/***************************************************************/
/*                                                             */
/* MoveIndexValueToBuffer: stores a short into the buffer      */
/*                                                             */
/***************************************************************/

void MoveIndexValueToBuffer (char* outbuffer, long& outIdx,
                             short index) {
 memcpy (&outbuffer[outIdx], &index, sizeof (index));
 outIdx += sizeof (index);
}

/***************************************************************/
/*                                                             */
/* ReadSqzFile: input squished file and output it as a txt file*/
/*                                                             */
/***************************************************************/

void ReadSqzFile () {
 ifstream infile ("c14-pgs.sqz", ios::in | ios::binary);
 if (!infile) {
  cerr << "Error: cannot open input c14-pgs.sqz file\n";
  exit (4);
 }
 // obtain filesize so that we can allocate an input buffer
 infile.seekg (0, ios::end);
 long filesize = infile.tellg();
 infile.seekg (0, ios::beg);

 // create a buffer to hold the entire file
 char* inbuffer = new char[filesize+1];
 // input the entire file at one time
 infile.read (inbuffer, filesize);
 infile.close ();
 inbuffer[filesize] = 0;

 string s;
 short index;
 Map<string, short> words;
 Map<string, short> nonwords;

 // open the resultant output text file
 ofstream outfile ("c14-pgs-new.txt", ios::out | ios::binary);
 if (!outfile) {
  cerr << "Error: cannot open c14-pgs-new.txt file\n";
  delete [] inbuffer;
  exit (4);
```

```
 }

 // load the words dictionary, load the nonwords dictionary
 long inIdx = 0;
 long endIdx = filesize;
 LoadDictionary (words, inbuffer, inIdx);
 LoadDictionary (nonwords, inbuffer, inIdx);

 // now translate each short of the body of the document
 while (inIdx < filesize) {
  // get the short index
  memcpy (&index, &inbuffer[inIdx], sizeof (index));
  inIdx += sizeof (index);
  // check if it is in the words map
  try {
   s = words.ReverseFind (index);
  }
  catch (const char*) {
   // not in the words map, so try the nonwords map
   try {
    s = nonwords.ReverseFind (index);
   }
   catch (const char* msg) {
    cerr << "Error: bad dictionary - "
         << msg << endl;
    delete [] inbuffer;
    outfile.close ();
    exit (5);
   }
  }
  // we have the word, so convert to char* and output it
  const char* ss = s.c_str ();
  outfile.write (ss, (int) strlen (ss));
 }
 // clean up actions, close the output file and delete the buffer
 outfile.close();
 delete [] inbuffer;
}

/***************************************************************/
/*                                                             */
/* LoadDictionary: load a dictionary Map from compressed file  */
/*                                                             */
/***************************************************************/

void LoadDictionary (Map<string, short>& dict, const char* buf,
                     long& inIdx) {
 // get the number of words in the dictionary
 long ct;
 memcpy (&ct, &buf[inIdx], sizeof (ct));
 inIdx += sizeof (ct);

 // retrieve all of the words and add to the map
 for (long i=0; i<ct; i++) {
  char str[500];
  long j = 0;
```

```
    // extract the string portion from the file buffer
    while (str[j++] = buf[inIdx++]) ;
    string s = str; // build the string object
    // extract the short index from the file buffer
    short index;
    memcpy (&index, &buf[inIdx], sizeof(index));
    inIdx += sizeof (index);
    // add the pair to the map
    dict.Insert (s, index);
  }
}
```

If you are interested in data compression, read Mark Nelson, The Data Compression Book, M&T Books, ISBN: 1-55851-434-1, 1995. His book covers this topic in great detail.

Review Questions

1. Describe the difference between a set and a map.

2. Describe two applications that could make use of a set data structure. Describe two other applications that could make use of a map structure.

3. What is meant by the cardinality of a set?

4. Show an example of performing an intersection of two sets, the union of two sets, and the difference between two sets.

5. Describe the difference of the **SetAsArray** and **SetAsBitVector** classes. What are the pros and cons of each? When would you use one version over the other version? Why?

6. Explain how a bit can be turned on without affecting other bits within a field? How can that same bit be turned off? How can a specific bit within a byte be tested to see if it is on or not?

7. Assume that bit number 5 of an **unsigned long** is the EOF bit and that the remaining bits represent additional flags, show the instructions to turn on the EOF bit, to turn it off and to test whether or not it is on.

8. What advantage, if any, is there to having the **Set** class not store the actual user's data but only its presence?

9. Why does the **Map** class store pairs of values?

10. What is the **string** class? How is it more useful than the ordinary array of char?

Stop! Do These Exercises Before Programming

1. A Math teacher wishes to illustrate the concepts of Set theory to her students. The program creates a random set of 10 integers between 1 and 20. This is called the master set. The program then prompts the student to make five guesses for integers that could be in the set. Store these five integers in the student set.

Next, the program displays the intersection of the two sets, indicating the percentage of correct guesses that were found. Show also both sets and the intersection set clearly labeled. Then, the program displays the union of the two sets clearly labeled. Finally, it shows the difference between the master set and the student guess set.

Our programmer began his coding this way, but it does not even compile. Baffled, he asks for your assistance. Correct his design and coding errors.

```
...
int main () {
  Map<int> master;
  Map<int> student;
```

```
  srand (time(0);
  for (j=0; j<10; j++) {
   master.Insert (rand() %20);
  }
...
```

2. Wondering how he could have made such a wild set of errors, our programmer now continues.

```
  Array<int> array;
  j = 0;
  while (j<5) {
   cout << "Enter Next Guess (between 1 and 20): ";
   cin >> array[i];
  }
```

This, of course, works no better than before, and he again asks you for assistance. Correct his design errors and coding.

3. Our programer just got transferred to another non-programing department primarily because of his enormous difficulties in performing his job. You are given the task of finishing this math teacher's project. Code a function, Intersection, that performs that task as described in question 1 above.

4. Code another function, Union, that performs that task as described in question 1 above.

5. Code the final function, Difference, that performs that task as described in question 1 above.

Programming Problems

Problem Pgm14-1 —The Grand Vacation Revisited

In Problem Pgm13-1—The Grand Vacation, you have decided to take the summer off and visit a large number of US National Parks and Forests out west. The order that they are visited is important because you only have two summer months for the trip. You cannot visit them in a random order because of the excessive driving time. For example, it would not be wise to visit Glacier National Park in Montana, then drive to the Grand Canyon and then back up to the Tetons. So a minimum spanning tree would be helpful.

First, examine an US map and pick out 20 national parks, forest and lake resorts located in the western states. Assume that you are leaving from Denver, Colorado on your trip and that you intend to end up in Denver when you are finished.

Create an input file similar to that used in **Pgm13b** for the key routes among all of the parks and Denver. Now write an application program that loads in the graph and displays an optimum sequence of the visitation of these parks. It should also display the total miles traveled.

In this variation, you are to use a **Map** data structure to store the character strings and an arbitrary index value. The **Graph** is given this index value and not the character string name. Thus, the performance should be improved because short integers can be assigned, compared and so on much faster than character strings.

Problem Pgm14-2—Delivery Routes —Revisited

Rework Pgm13-3 to use a Map structure to store the city names. Then, modify the Graph to use the short index values instead of the character string names. The problem definition was as follows.

Assume that Figure 13.22 above represents your company's delivery routes. Each vertex represents a city that you service. A distance unit of 1 represents 10 miles; a weight of 1 means 10 miles. Assume that any single service truck can cover 60 miles one way a day. Further, node D is the city from which your company operates.

Write a program that determines how the minimum number of service trucks your company will need to properly service each city in the network.

Chapter 15—An Introduction to the STL—Standard Template Library

Introduction

The compiler comes with the Standard Template Library or STL as it is called. The STL provides the new C++ standard implementation of the iostreams, the data structure container classes, and even sorting and other runtime libraries. The emphasis of this chapter is upon the use of the built-in STL container classes for the various data structures that we have been studying. Using the STL, we can store and retrieve data in a standard uniform way. We do not have to implement our own stack, list, or queue classes, for example. The STL provides them for us by providing reusable software.

The STL is a collection of template classes and functions that implement the commonly needed data structures and processing algorithms such as sorting. The STL is now standardized into the C++ language and is readily available with most compilers.

A **container**, as we have seen, is an object that holds other objects, such as an array (vector) or list. The list, stack, and queue are sequence type containers while the map is an associative type of container. Each container class defines a set of functions that can be applied to it, such as push and pop for a stack.

An **algorithm** in STL terms is a method that acts upon a container allowing you to manipulate the contents of the container in some way. Sorting and searching are two common algorithms.

An **iterator** is an object that provides you the ability to cycle through the contents of a container. For example, we use a subscript to access the items in an array. We use the current pointer to cycle through the items in a list. Iterators come in five forms depending upon their usage. **Random** access iterators provide the ability to store and retrieve values in a random manner. **Bidirectional** iterators provide the ability to store and retrieve values in a forward or backward fashion, much like our forward and backward pointers in a linked list. A **forward** iterator only allows for storage and retrieval in a forward direction as in a single linked list. An **input** iterator is a forward-moving iterator that allows for retrieval only. The **output** iterator provides for storing values in the forward direction only. Additionally, there are **reverse** iterators for both random access and bidirectional iterators that move through the container in the backwards direction.

An iterator can be handled just as we would a pointer. Namely, it can be incremented or decremented. If you dereference them, you get the object in the container to which it is pointing.

Every container has an **allocator** which manages memory for the container. The allocator is much like the constructor/destructor functions.

To handle the generic comparison operations and basic math operations, the STL defines a series of **function** objects. Some examples of these predefined function objects include the following: **greater**, **less**, **plus**, **minus**, **multiplies**, and **divides**. From our studies of the various data structures, the **less** function is often used, particularly when sorting.

Finally, the STL has **adaptors** which transform one thing into another. Adaptors can modify iterators, containers, and functions. The STL has a **deque** container. An adaptor is used to turn it into a queue type container.

Finally, the C++ Standard specifies minium execution speeds for all the containers. The standard does not specify how that container is to be internally implemented, but the manufacturer must adhere to the performance issues. Thus, when using an STL object, you can be assured that you are using one whose execution speed is up to industry standards.

The Container Classes

Table 15.1 shows the more commonly used template container classes defined by the STL and the required header files.

Table 15.1 Commonly Used STL Template Container Classes

Container	Description	Header File
deque	a double-ended queue	<deque>
list	a linked list	<list>
map	stores pairs of keys and their values - associative container	<map>
priority_queue	a priority queue - container adaptor	<queue>
queue	a queue - container adaptor	<queue>
set	a set with each element being unique - associative container	<set>
stack	a stack - container adaptor	<stack>
vector	a growable array	<vector>

Typically, these container classes are defined similarly to the following.

```
template<class T, class Allocator = allocator<T>>
class deque {
```

Remember that the allocator function handles the dynamic memory allocation of the container. Notice that there is a default value assigned which is the default allocator for the specific class. Unless you have some very special allocation scheme to be implemented, the default is perfect.

The **stack**, **queue**, and **priority_queue** classes are container adaptors because they use one of the sequence containers to hold their data. Hence, they are adapting another container for their purposes. The sequence containers are the **vector**, **list**, and **deque** while the associative containers are the **map** and **set**.

Finally, because of the generic type T in the definitions, the STL defines some **typedef** names for our convenience. One of these is called **iterator** which represents an iterator for this type. Its use will be shown shortly.

All containers automatically grow as needed when elements are added to it. Likewise, the containers shrink when elements are removed. Most containers provide an **insert** function to insert a new element into the container. The **erase** function removes elements from the container. Additionally, the sequence containers also provide **push_back** and **pop_back** functions which add or remove an element from the end of the container. The **list** and **deque** also provide **push_front** and **pop_front** functions to add or remove elements from the front of the container. Thus, the STL containers maintain a uniform approach to the member functions from one container to the next.

To iterate through a container, an iterator is used with the functions **begin** and **end.** These are similar to our **ResetToHead** and **ResetToTail** functions of the linked list classes. To move sequentially through all elements in a container, you would first call **begin** which gives you an iterator to the first element. Then, you would increment that iterator until its value was equal to the return value from the **end** function. For **vector** classes only (arrays), the operator[] is provided so that simple subscripting can be used. For the **set** and **map** containers only, the **find** function can be used to find an element given its key. Now let's see how the STL containers can be used. We start with the simplest, the **vector** class (array).

The vector STL Class

The vector class implements a growable array. It has several constructors including a default ctor. The overloaded versions are passed first the initial number of elements to allocate and second, if present, the initial value for all of those elements. The following represents the definition of several arrays.

```
...
#include <vector>
```

```
using namespace std;

struct COSTREC {
 int itemNum;
 short quantity;
 double cost;
};

int main () {
 vector<long> longArray;         // default an array of long values
 vector<short> shortArray(50);  // an array of initially 50 short
 vector<char> types(10, ' ');   // create an array of 5 characters
                                // each initialized to a blank
 vector<COSTREC> arec(100);     // create an array of 100 COSTREC
                                // structures
```

All six of the comparison operators are implemented, such as == and <=. The operator[] is provided as well. Table 15.2 shows some of the often used functions supported by the **vector** class.

Table 15.2 Commonly Used Functions of the vector Class

Function	Meaning
iterator begin ();	Returns an iterator to the first element of the vector
iterator end();	Returns an iterator to the last element of the vector
bool empty() const;	Returns true if the vector is empty - no elements
iterator insert (iterator I, const T& value);	Inserts the new item, value, immediately before the element specified by I. It returns an iterator to this newly added element.
iterator erase (iterator I);	Removes the element at I and returns an iterator to the element after the one deleted.
iterator erase (iterator start, iterator end);	Removes all elements from start to end and returns an iterator to the next element after the last element that was removed.
void pop_back();	Removes the last element from the array.
void push_back (const T& value);	Adds the element value at the end of the array.
size_type size() const;	Returns the number of elements in the array as an unsigned int.

Here is a simple example showing the basic usage of a **vector** and the output from **Pgm15a**. Notice that the <**vector**> header is included along with **using namespace std**. Lines 14, 15, and 16 create three arrays. The current number of elements of each array is displayed by lines 18 through 21. Notice that the **size** function returns the number of elements currently in the array. This eliminates our need for keeping track of the number or passing it to other functions that use the array. However, to avoid warning messages, the returned value of **size_t** is typecast to an **int**.

Notice lines 24 and 25. Here I am altering the stored values of all ten characters. These lines represent typical looping and access operations.

```
for (i=0; i< (int) carray.size(); i++) {
 carray[i] = (char) ('A' + I);
```

Lines 34 through 36 show how new elements can easily be added to the end of the array by using the **push_back** function, thereby growing the array in size. Similarly, lines 46 and 47 show how elements can be removed from the end of the array using **pop_back**.

Lines 57 and 58 show how to pass a reference to a **vector** to a function with the prototypes shown on lines 9 and 10. You can use a **typedef** name to make passing easier. You can also allocate vector instances using the **typedef** name, **cArray**.

```
cArray carray;
```

Please note that you cannot grow an array or vector by using the [] operator specifying a subscript larger than the current size of the vector. Doing so yields a "subscript out of range" runtime error. To add new elements either use

push_back or the **insert** functions.

Pgm15a - A Simple Vector Example

```
#include <iostream>
#include <iomanip>
#include <vector>

using namespace std;

void Fun (vector<char>& array);

typedef vector<char> cArray;
void Fun2 (cArray& array);

int main () {

 vector<long> larray;
 vector<short> sarray(100);
 vector<char> carray(10, ' ');

 cout << "The size of the three arrays are:\n"
  << "  larray: " << (int) larray.size() << endl
  << "  sarray: " << (int) sarray.size() << endl
  << "  carray: " << (int) carray.size() << endl << endl;

 int i;
 for (i=0; i< (int) carray.size(); i++) {
  carray[i] = (char) ('A' + i);
 }

 cout << "carray now contains the following letters\n";
 for (i=0; i< (int) carray.size(); i++) {
  cout << carray[i] << " ";
 }
 cout << endl << endl;

 for (i=0; i<5; i++) {
  char c = (char) ('Z' - i);
  carray.push_back(c);
 }

 cout << "carray after adding five letters at the end of the"
      <<" array\nnow contains the following letters\n";
 for (i=0; i<(int) carray.size(); i++) {
  cout << carray[i] << " ";
 }
 cout << endl << endl;

 for (i=0; i<5; i++) {
  carray.pop_back();
 }

 cout << "carray after removing five letters at the end of the"
      <<" array\nnow contains the following letters\n";
 for (i=0; i<(int) carray.size(); i++) {
```

```
   cout << carray[i] << " ";
  }
  cout << endl << endl;

  Fun (carray);
  Fun2 (carray);

  return 0;
 }

void Fun (vector<char>& array) {
  cout << "carray passed by reference contains\n";
  for (int i=0; i<(int) array.size(); i++) {
   cout << array[i] << " ";
  }
  cout << endl << endl;
 }

void Fun2 (cArray& array) {
  cout << "carray passed by reference using typedef contains\n";
  for (int i=0; i<(int) array.size(); i++) {
   cout << array[i] << " ";
  }
  cout << endl << endl;
 }
```

```
Output of Pgm15a - Simple Vector Example
```

```
The size of the three arrays are:
  larray: 0
  sarray: 100
  carray: 10

carray now contains the following letters
A B C D E F G H I J

carray after adding five letters at the end of the array
now contains the following letters
A B C D E F G H I J Z Y X W V

carray after removing five letters at the end of the array
now contains the following letters
A B C D E F G H I J

carray passed by reference contains
A B C D E F G H I J

carray passed by reference using typedef contains
A B C D E F G H I J
```

While subscript notation, **array[i]**, is ideal for many array or vector applications, most all of the other containers use iterators to gain access to the next item. So let's examine how the iterators work with the vector class.

Iterators

The array style access of elements is available only with a few containers, such as the vector and set. All containers do provide an iterator method of access. The vector supports the most powerful iterator class, the random access iterator which supports operators ++, – –, + and –. That is, with a random access iterator, you can go sequentially forward or backwards through the list as well as jump from one point to another by adding or subtracting an integer amount.

A list supports the second most powerful iterator, the bidirectional iterator, which supports ++, – – only. A bidirectional iterator can go forward or backwards sequentially through the list. But it cannot jump around with the + and – operators.

The operation of an iterator instance is much like that of a pointer. Most importantly, to obtain the element to which the iterator is pointing, you dereference the iterator just as you would a pointer. The iterator is defined by the specific class. Thus, to create an instance of an iterator, we must use the class qualifier, just as we do when we work with class enumerated data types.

Returning to **Pgm15a**, if we wished to use an iterator for the array access, then an instance is defined this way.

```
vector<char> carray(10, ' ');
vector<char>::iterator iterC;
```

To move sequentially through the elements, initialize the iterator to the first element by calling the **begin** function. The **end** function is used to find the end of the list. The increment operator is used to move to the next element. The dereference operator is used to access the **char** element that the **vector** is storing at this location. The following sequence initializes the ten elements to successive letters beginning with A.

```
iterC = carray.begin();
int i = 0;
while (iterC != carray.end()) {
 *iterC = (char) ('A' + i);
 iterC++;
 i++;
}
```

The following sequence displays the series of characters the **vector** now holds. Notice how a specific character in the vector is accessed and sent to **cout**.

```
cout << "carray now contains the following letters\n";
iterC = carray.begin();
while (iterC != carray.end()) {
 cout << *iterC << " ";
 iterC++;
}
```

Details of the begin and end Functions

The **begin** returns an iterator value that points to the first item in the container. So to begin a sequential traversal of all elements in a container, we set our iterator variable to the return value of **begin** which returns the required iterator value of the first element in the container.

The **end** function operates in a rather unexpected way. One might think that **end** would return a pointer to the last item in the container. But no, the **end** function returns a value that points to an element ***past*** the last item in the container! Do not attempt to actually dereference or use the iterator value that **end** returns because it is pointing to a nonexistent element! Therefore, our loop continues as long as the iterator value does not equal that given by the **end** function. Another way of looking at this is to realize that there are **end() – 1** items in the container. Also, do not use less than or equal as frequently is done when using a pointer to traverse an array.

```
while (iterC <= carray.end()) { // error - use != instead
```

Remember that there is no guarantee that the elements are located in successive memory locations. And they are very likely not in such order in lists and queues.

There are some occasions when the list must be traversed in reverse order. With ordinary arrays, we are used to seeing the following.

```
j = numElements - 1;
while (j >= 0) {
  . . .
  j--;
```

```
}
```

This sequence is not going to work with iterators. In fact, we cannot code the following either.

```
iterC = carray.end() - 1;
while (iterC != carray.begin()) { // error - omits item 0
  . . .
  iterC--;
}
```

If we use the above coding, we omit processing the first element in the container.

To iterate in the reverse order, we set the iterator to the end value which is one too many and inside the loop, decrement it before using it.

```
iterC = carray.end();
while (iterC != carray.begin()) { // error - omits item 0
  iterC--;
  . . . // use *iterC here
}
```

Initially, **iterC** is one too large, so we decrement it before using it within the loop.

Well, what happens if we use the above style loop and that there are no elements in the container? If the container is empty, both **end** and **begin** return the same value, a null pointer. Thus, the **while** clause fails at once.

Using a Range of Iterators

Iterators are a vital portion of the STL. The **erase** and **insert** functions use iterators to point to the insertion or deletion point. Recall their prototypes from Table 15.2 above.

```
iterator insert (iterator I, const T& value);
iterator erase (iterator I);
iterator erase (iterator start, iterator end);
```

Using the vector of character items from the above examples, we can delete the element that contains the letter B as follows.

```
iterC = carray.begin();
while (iterC != carray.end()) {
 if (*iterC == 'B') {
   carray.erase (iterC);
   break;
 }
 iterC++;
}
```

Or we can delete from the letter B through D using the alternate form of **erase**.

```
while (iterC != carray.end()) {
 if (*iterC == 'B') {
   carray.erase (iterC, iterC+3);
   break;
 }
 iterC++;
}
```

We could insert the letter Q after the letter B in the array using the **insert** function.

```
while (iterC != carray.end()) {
 if (*iterC == 'B') {
   carray.insert (iterC, 'Q');
   break;
 }
 iterC++;
}
```

Thus, the use of iterators plays a vital role in our usage of STL and its containers. Now let's examine another of the containers, the linked list.

The list Container

The STL containers often share the same or similar functions. The **list** container supports a bidirectional linked list. The simplest constructor is quite similar to the **vector**. Its header file is **<list>**.

```
list<COSTREC> costRecList; // a list of COSTREC structures
list <short> shortLst(10); // a list with 10 short items
                           // whose values are 0
list <short> sList(10,42); // a list with 10 short items
                           // whose values are 42
```

The **list** supports the six relational operators, such as ==. The **begin** and **end** functions are used to support iteration. Table 15.3 shows the commonly used **list** functions.

Table 15.3 Commonly Used Functions of the list Class

Function	Meaning
iterator begin ();	Returns an iterator to the first element of the list.
iterator end();	Returns an iterator to the end of the list.
bool empty() const;	Returns true if the list is empty - no elements.
iterator insert (iterator I, const T& value);	Inserts the new item, value, immediately before the element specified by I. It returns an iterator to this newly added element.
iterator erase (iterator I);	Removes the element at I and returns an iterator to the element after the one deleted.
iterator erase (iterator start, iterator end);	Removes all elements from start to end and returns an iterator to the next element after the last element that was removed.
void pop_back();	Removes the last element from the list.
void push_back (const T& value);	Adds the element value at the end of the list.
void pop_front ();	Removes the first element from the list.
void push_front (const T& value);	Adds the element value to the front of the list.
void sort ();	Sorts the list.
template<class Comp> void sort (Comp compare);	Sorts the list but uses the comparison function to determine which of two elements is smaller.
size_type size() const;	Returns the number of elements in the list as an unsigned int.

The **push_front** function is identical to what we have been calling **AddAtHead** in our list classes, while the **push_back** function is our **AddAtTail** function. In addition to the functions shown in the table above, the **list** also supports two other operations. It is possible to splice an element or series of elements of one list onto another list. It is possible to merge two lists into one list.

To illustrate the **list** class, let's input a file of song titles and their durations. Then, let's sort the list and display a simple report. Further, let's encapsulate the songs into the class **Song** so that we can see how the **list** works when we store objects instead of simple intrinsic data types.

The **Song** class handles input and output of a song. **Pgm15b** inputs a file of **Song** objects by calling the **Song**'s extraction operator. A copy of each **Song** object is then placed into a **list**. Next, the **list**'s **sort** function is called. Since the **list** does not know how to sort our ADT, we must provide the comparison function. The **list** is sorted into alphabetical order on song titles and then again by song duration. A report of each sorted order is made iterating sequentially through the sorted **list**. First, look at the simple **Song** ADT.

Song Class Definition

```
#pragma once
#include <iostream>
using namespace std;

/***************************************************************/
/*                                                             */
/* Song: a simple class to encapsulate a music song            */
/*                                                             */
/***************************************************************/

class Song {
protected:
 char  songName[21];
 float duration;

public:
 Song ();
 Song (const char* name, float dur);

 const char* GetName () const;
 float GetDuration () const;
 friend istream& operator>> (istream& is, Song& s);
 friend ostream& operator<< (ostream& os, const Song& s);
};

#endif
```

Song Class Implementation

```
#include <iostream>
#include <iomanip>
#include "Song.h"

/***************************************************************/
/*                                                             */
/* Song: set up a default unknown song                         */
/*                                                             */
/***************************************************************/

Song::Song () {
 strcpy_s (songName, sizeof(songName), "Unknown");
 duration = 0;
}

/***************************************************************/
/*                                                             */
/* Song: setup a specific song                                 */
/*                                                             */
/***************************************************************/

Song::Song (const char* name, float dur) {
 if (!name)
  strcpy_s (songName, sizeof(songName), "Unknown");
```

```
 else if (strlen (name) < sizeof (songName) - 1)
  strcpy_s (songName, sizeof(songName), name);
 else {
  strncpy_s (songName, sizeof(songName), name,
             sizeof (songName) - 1);
  songName[sizeof (songName) - 1] = 0;
 }
 duration = dur;
}

/***************************************************************/
/*                                                             */
/* GetName: returns the song's name                            */
/*                                                             */
/***************************************************************/

const char* Song::GetName () const {
 return songName;
}

/***************************************************************/
/*                                                             */
/* GetDuration: returns the song's play time duration          */
/*                                                             */
/***************************************************************/

float Song::GetDuration () const {
 return duration;
}

/***************************************************************/
/*                                                             */
/* operator>> input a song from a stream                       */
/*                                                             */
/***************************************************************/

istream& operator>> (istream& is, Song& s) {
 char c;
 is >> c;
 if (!is) return is;
 is.getline (s.songName, sizeof (s.songName), '\"');
 is >> s.duration;
 return is;
}

/***************************************************************/
/*                                                             */
/* operator<< output a song to a stream                        */
/*                                                             */
/***************************************************************/

ostream& operator<< (ostream& os, const Song& s) {
 os << fixed << left << setw (sizeof(s.songName) + 3)
    << s.songName << right << setprecision (2) << setw (5)
    << s.duration << endl;
 return os;
```

```
}

```

When we call the **sort** function of the list container, it must be able to determine which of two elements is the smaller. It the list contains an intrinsic data type, then **sort** can automatically make the determination. However, if the list contains an ADT, then we must provide a callback comparison function. Its prototype is as follows where T is the ADT type or class.

```
bool compare (const T& object1, const T& object2);
```

The key lines of the list processing are highlighted in boldface.

Pgm15b Illustrates list Container Processing

```
#include <iostream>
#include <iomanip>
#include <fstream>
#include <list>
#include <algorithm>
#include <crtdbg.h>
#include "Song.h"

using namespace std;

/***************************************************************/
/*                                                             */
/* Pgm14b: illustrates list processing                         */
/*                                                             */
/***************************************************************/

// the comparison functions
bool CompareName (const Song& s1, const Song& s2);
bool CompareTime (const Song& s1, const Song& s2);

// count_if algorithm tester function
bool AtLeastDuration (const Song& s);

void DisplayReport (list<Song>& songs, const char* title);

int main () {
{
 ifstream infile ("songs.txt");
 if (!infile) {
  cerr << "Error: cannot open file songs.txt\n";
  exit (1);
 }

 list<Song> songs; // the list of songs
 Song s;

 // fill up a list with a file of songs
 while (infile >> s) {
  songs.push_back (s);
 }

 infile.close ();

 // sort the list into name order and display all songs
```

```
 songs.sort (CompareName);
 DisplayReport (songs, "Songs in Alphabetical Order");

 cout << endl << endl;

 // sort the list into play time order and display report
 songs.sort (CompareTime);
 DisplayReport (songs, "Songs in Duration of Play Order");

 long ct = (long) count_if (songs.begin(), songs.end(),
                            AtLeastDuration);
 cout << endl << endl << "The number of songs that last for at"
  " least 5 minutes are: " << ct << endl;
}

 // check for memory leaks
 if (_CrtDumpMemoryLeaks())
  cerr << "Memory leaks occurred!\n";
 else
  cerr << "No memory leaks.\n";

 return 0;
}

// the list comparison function for alphabetical order
bool CompareName (const Song& s1, const Song& s2) {
 return _stricmp (s1.GetName(), s2.GetName()) < 0;
}

// the list comparison function for duration order
bool CompareTime (const Song& s1, const Song& s2) {
 return s1.GetDuration() < s2.GetDuration();
}

// the count_if helper function - returns true if duration
// is 5 minutes or larger
bool AtLeastDuration (const Song& s) {
 return s.GetDuration() > 5.0;
}

// a simple report of all items in the list's current order
void DisplayReport (list<Song>& songs, const char* title) {
 cout << title << endl << endl;
 list<Song>::iterator iter = songs.begin();
 while (iter != songs.end()) {
  cout << *iter;
  iter++;
 }

```

Output of Pgm15b

```
Songs in Alphabetical Order

Alto Rhapsody            9.60
```

```
Christmas Concerto       18.60
German Dances             5.45
Hungarian Dances          6.25
La Follia Variations     10.50
Moonlight Sonata         14.50
Romance in F              6.30
Sextet in B-flat         12.40


Songs in Duration of Play Order

German Dances             5.45
Hungarian Dances          6.25
Romance in F              6.30
Alto Rhapsody             9.60
La Follia Variations     10.50
Sextet in B-flat         12.40
Moonlight Sonata         14.50
Christmas Concerto       18.60

The number of songs that last for at least 5 minutes are: 8

No memory leaks.
```

Algorithms

In addition to member functions that support the basic container operations, the STL provides a set of template functions called **algorithms** that handle more complex operations on one or more containers at the same time. They also allow you to operate on different containers at the same time. Thus, an algorithm function can be thought of as spanning across all containers. Table 15.4 shows some of the algorithms that are available. To use any, include the header <**algorithm**>.

Table 15.4 Some of the Available Algorithms

Algorithm Function	Action Performed
binary_search	Does a binary search on an ordered container.
count	Determines the number of elements in the sequence.
find	Searches a range of elements looking for a value and returns an iterator to the first matching element.
for_each	Applies a function to a range of elements like a for loop.
includes	Determines if one sequence includes all of the elements of another sequence.
iter_swap	Swaps the values pointed to by the two iterators.
make_heap	Makes a heap from a sequence.
max_element	Returns an iterator to the maximum element within a range.
min_element	Returns an iterator to the minimum element within a range.
merge	Merges two ordered sequences into a third sequence.

Algorithm Function	Action Performed
random_shuffle	Randomizes a sequence, such as shuffling a card deck.
set_difference	Makes a set of the differences between two sequences.
set_intersection	Makes a set of the intersection of two sequences.
set_union	Makes a set of the union of two sequences.
sort	Sort a sequence into order.
swap	Swaps two values.

The **count** function counts the number of elements within the indicated range that match the passed value. Its prototype is

```
template<class Iter, class T>
size_t count (Iter start, Iter end, const T& value);
```

In the songs **list**, this version is not too useful unless we wanted to count the number of duplicated songs.

An alternate version is more useful in this application; it is **count_if**.

```
template<class Iter, class T>
size_t count_if (Iter start, Iter end, const T boolFunct);
```

The third parameter is a function that is passed one item from the container and is to return a **bool true** or **false** indicating whether or not this item match the desired counting scheme.

For example, I can use **count_if** to find the number of songs whose duration is at least five minutes. I need to add the following to **Pgm15b**.

```
#include <algorithm>

// count_if algorithm tester function prototype
bool AtLeastDuration (const Song& s);
```

in the main function:

```
 long ct = (long) count_if (songs.begin(), songs.end(),
                            AtLeastDuration);
 cout << endl << endl << "The number of songs that last for at"
      " least 5 minutes are: " << ct << endl;

// the count_if helper function - returns true if duration
// is 5 minutes or larger
bool AtLeastDuration (const Song& s) {
 return s.GetDuration() > 5.0;
}
```

The above produces the following line.

```
The number of songs that last for at least 5 minutes is: 8
```

The deque Container

This general purpose container represents a double ended queue in which values can be added at either end, values can be removed at either end, and values can be inserted and removed from any point within the queue. I think you can see why the queue and stack containers are derived from this more general class. Its header file is <**deque**>. Some common ctor functions include these.

```
deque<COSTREC> costRecQue; // a deque of COSTREC structures
deque <short> shortQue(10);// a deque with 10 short items
                           // whose values are 0
deque <short> sQue(10,42); // a deque with 10 short items
                           // whose values are 42
```

The **deque** supports the six relational operators, such as ==. It also supports operator[] so that it can be accessed like an array. The **begin** and **end** functions are used to support iteration. Table 15.5 shows the commonly used **deque** functions.

Table 15.5 Commonly Used Functions of the deque Class

Function	Meaning
iterator begin ();	Returns an iterator to the first element of the deque.
iterator end();	Returns an iterator to the end of the deque.
bool empty() const;	Returns true if the deque is empty - no elements.
iterator insert (iterator I, const T& value);	Inserts the new item, value, immediately before the element specified by I. It returns an iterator to this newly added element.
iterator erase (iterator I);	Removes the element at I and returns an iterator to the element after the one deleted.
iterator erase (iterator start, iterator end);	Removes all elements from start to end and returns an iterator to the next element after the last element that was removed.
void pop_back();	Removes the last element from the deque.
void push_back (const T& value);	Adds the element value at the end of the deque.
void pop_front ();	Removes the first element from the deque.
void push_front (const T& value);	Adds the element value to the front of the deque.
size_t max_size () const;	Returns the maximum number of elements the deque cn hold.
size_t size () const;	Returns the current number of elements in the deque.

To illustrate the **deque** in operation, let's modify the Song Application. This time, the input file represents the order of play. **Pgm15c** should load the file, enqueueing each song in the input file. Then, we must determine the song-commercial mix script for the DJ. The algorithm is
there should be a commercial of two minutes every twenty minutes. If the next song will take us over that limit and if we have not just already done a commercial, break for a commercial before playing that next selection.

Here are **Pgm15c** and the output. The new **deque** instructions are boldfaced.

Pgm15c Illustrates a Deque in Operation - DJ Playlist

```
#include <iostream>
#include <iomanip>
#include <fstream>
#include <deque>
#include <algorithm>
#include <crtdbg.h>
#include "Song.h"

using namespace std;

/***************************************************************/
/*                                                             */
/* Pgm15c: Scheduling songs and commercials for the DJ         */
/*                                                             */
/***************************************************************/

int main () {
{
 ifstream infile ("songs.txt");
```

```
 if (!infile) {
  cerr << "Error: cannot open file songs.txt\n";
  exit (1);
 }

 deque<Song> songs; // the list of songs
 Song s;

 // fill up deque with a file of songs
 while (infile >> s) {
  songs.push_back (s);
 }
 infile.close ();
 cout << fixed << setprecision (2);

 double time = 0;                    // the clock time
 double nextBreakAt = 15;            // the time of the next break
 bool   justHadCommercial = true;
 long   count = 1;

 cout << "            DJ's Schedule\n\n"
      << "   Activity               Duration   Time\n\n"
      << setw(2) << count++
      << ". Break for Commercial             "
      << setw(5) << time << endl;
 time += 2;

 while (!songs.empty()) { // repeat until deque is empty
  s = songs[0];           // get next song possibility
  // if we have not just had a commercial, check if there is time
  // to play the next song before the next commercial
  if (!justHadCommercial) {
   if (time > nextBreakAt) {
    // not enough time, so break for a commercial message
    nextBreakAt += 15;
    cout << setw(2) << count++
         << ". Break for Commercial             "
         << setw(5) << time << endl;
    justHadCommercial = true;
    time += 2;
   }
  }
  // now display this song and remove it from the deque
  cout << setw(2) << count++ << ". " << s << "   "
       << setw(5) << time << endl;
  justHadCommercial = false;
  time += s.GetDuration();
  songs.pop_front ();
 }
}

 // check for memory leaks
 if (_CrtDumpMemoryLeaks())
  cerr << "Memory leaks occurred!\n";
 else
```

```
  cerr << "No memory leaks.\n";

 return 0;
}
```

```
Output from Pgm15c
```

```
              DJ's Schedule

    Activity                Duration    Time

 1. Break for Commercial                 0.00
 2. Moonlight Sonata           14.50     2.00
 3. Break for Commercial                16.50
 4. Romance in F                6.30    18.50
 5. German Dances               5.45    24.80
 6. Break for Commercial                30.25
 7. Hungarian Dances            6.25    32.25
 8. Sextet in B-flat           12.40    38.50
 9. Break for Commercial                50.90
10. Alto Rhapsody               9.60    52.90
11. Break for Commercial                62.50
12. La Follia Variations       10.50    64.50
13. Christmas Concerto         18.60    75.00
No memory leaks
```

By now, you should be seeing the uniformity and consistency of the STL implementation across the container classes. Once you have the basics of STL operations learned, you can easily utilize any of these containers in your applications.

To learn more about the STL and how to use it, I recommend reading Herbert Schildt's book, *STL Programming from the Ground Up*, 1999, Osborne, ISBN 0-07-882507-5. It is an excellent book on the STL.

Review Questions

1. What is the STL?

2. After studying the chapter, what do you consider the major benefit(s) of the STL and what are its drawbacks, if any?

3. What is meant by a container?

4. What is meant by an algorithm?

5. What is meant by an iterator?

6. Describe how an iterator is acquired and how it operates? How does one gain access to the container's elements?

7. Describe the five types of iterators and detail the differences between them.

8. What is a **deque** container? How does it work? Why is it the base class for the **queue** and **stack** classes?

9. Describe the steps needed to sequentially access each element in a **list**?

10. Describe what the **end** function returns and how it impacts our coding for container traversals?

Stop! Do These Exercises Before Programming

1. Our programmer must implement the Boat Docking Application for one of our clients. The problem specifications read as follows.

Acme Holiday Harbor needs a list application written to assist them in managing small crafts that are docking at their harbor. The harbor has assigned slip numbers to all docking areas. They have a total of 200 slips available which limits them to docking a maximum of 200 boats at one time.

When a boat is docked, they need to store the following information.
boat name—a string of 20 characters
boat id—a string of 10 characters
owner's name—a string of 30 characters

Create a **Boat** class to store the data. Use the STL **list** container to store the **Boat** objects.

When the program begins, it calls the **LoadAllBoats** function passing it the name of the file to load. This function then inputs the file of boat data, storing each in the list. Then the program goes into its main processing loop. The program displays a small menu as follows.

```
Acme Holiday Harbor

1. Dock a new boat
2. Undock an existing boat
3. Display all docked boats
4. Write new master file
5. Terminate the program

Enter the number of your choice: __
```

When "Dock a new boat" is chosen, prompt the user for the three data fields and then add that boat to the list. Keep in mind that there cannot ever be more than 200 boats docked at any one time. When "Undock an existing boat" is chosen, prompt for the boat id number and then delete that boat from the list. When "Display all docked boats" is made, traverse the boat list and display a nicely formatted report. For convenience, send the output to a file on disk to later print. When "Write new master file" is chosen, prompt the user for the new file name and pass it to the corresponding function.

The programmer created the **Boat** class and has it working. Briefly, his **Boat** class is as follows.

```
class Boat {
protected:
 char name[21];
 char id[11];
 char owner[31];
public:
 Boat();
const char* GetName() const;
const char* GetId() const;
const char* GetOwner() const;
friend istream& operator>> (istream& is, Boat& b);
frienf ostream& operator<< (ostream& os, const Boat& b);
};
```

His first difficulty lies in the **main** and **LoadAllBoats** functions. Correct his errors in coding.

```
#include <list>
using namespace std;

void LoadAllBoats (const char* filename, list boatList);

int main () {
 list boatList;
 LoadAllBoats ("TestFile.txt", boatList);
 return 0;
}
void LoadAllBoats (const char* filename, list boatList) {
 Boat b;
```

```
 ifstream is (filename);
 while (is >> b) {
  boatList.Add (b);
 }
 is.close ();
}
```

2. With the **LoadAllBoats** function working, the programmer now gets the menu displayed and valid choices inputted. His attempt to dock a boat ended in failure. Correct his **DockNewBoat** function.

```
void DockNewBoat (list& boatList) {
 Boat b;
 . . . successful coding to input a new boat set of data is ok
 boatList.Insert (b);
}
```

3. Believing that he now understands the STL, he embarks on coding the **DisplayAllDockedBoats** function. Correct his errors in this function.

```
void DisplayAllDockedBoats (list<Boat>& boatList) {
 iterator iter = begin ();
 while (iter <= end()) {
  cout << boatList[iter] << endl;
 }
}
```

4. Now he has written the **UndockBoat** function. It also does not work. Correct his coding so that it does work.

```
Boat UndockBoat (list<Boat>& boatList) {
 char id[100];
 cout << "Enter boat id: ";
 cin.getline (id, sizeof (id));
 if (!cin) return Boat();

 list::iterator iter = list.begin();
 while (iter != list.end()) {
  if (*iter == id) {
   list.erase (iter);
   return *iter;
  }
 }
 return Boat();
}
```

5. The programmer gives up and asks you to write the **WriteNewMasterFile** function.

```
void WriteNewMasterFile (list<Boat>& boatList) {
 char filename[_MAX_PATH];
 cout << "Enter new master file name: ";
 cin.getline (filename, sizeof(filename));
 if (!cin) return;
 ofstream os (filename);
 if (!os) {
  cerr << "Error: cannot open the output file\n";
  return;
 }
 list::iterator iter = begin();
 while (iter

 os.close();
}
```

Programming Problems

Problem Pgm15-1—Reworking of Pgm07-4 Announcing the Galactic Treaty Game

The Galactic Omega Confederation, consisting of a number of planets scattered across a vast space, was at war. However, at Planet X, a peace treaty was signed. However, none of the rulers of the various planets will believe the treaty unless they see it with their own eyes. Thus, you have been hired to fly a space ship to each planet, showing the signed treaty to each planetary ruler. The objective is to travel the minimum total distance and thus complete the process in the shortest amount of time thereby ending the war as fast as possible. Simplifying the process, all of the planetary systems lie in a common two-dimensional plane of the galaxy.

Each planet is located by its (x, y) coordinates. The distance between planet1 and planet2 whose coordinates are (x1, y1) and (x2, y2) respectively, is given by the following formula.

```
Distance = sqrt ( (x2-x1)^2 + (y2-y1)^2 )
```

The program inputs a file of planet information and then displays the minimum total distance traveled along with the order of the planets.

Each line contains the planet's name, x and y coordinates. All coordinate values are in the same units. The name is abstract, such as "Planet 1" and can contain nine characters. All coordinates are doubles. Further, the very first line is the location of Planet X, the starting point where the treaty was signed.

The program output should be something like the following.

```
Planet Visited    Total Distance Thus Far
Planet X                    0.0
Planet A                   10.3
Planet E                   15.3
...
Total Distance Traveled: 1000.2
```

Test your program using the provided file called **Planets.txt** which is located in the **TestDataForAssignments** folder under the **Pgm07-4** folder.

Note: you must use one of the STL container classes for this solution.

Problem Pgm15-2—Reworking Pgm07-5 The Veterinarian's Patient Processing Program

Rework this problem using the **deque** STL container class. Alternatively, you can use the STL **priority_queue** class. A veterinarian needs a program to manage his processing of his patients. When a person arrives with their pet, the pet information is input into a **Pet** structure. Next, the pet record is entered into his queue of patients at the proper location. The pet information consists of the owner's name (20 characters), the pet's name (20 characters), and an integer emergency code (0 = normal, 1 = emergency).

When the vet finishes with a patient, that animal is removed from the queue. The vet then takes the next patient in the queue unless there is an emergency patient in the queue. His algorithm to choose the next patient is to take the next patient in the queue unless there is another patient in the queue whose emergency code is 1. Should there be more than one emergency, he handles them in the order that they arrived.

To simulate the day's operations, a transaction file is used. Each record in the file consists of four fields:

action code (1 character) A (add this patient) or H (handle next patient)
owner's name
pet's name
emergency code (0 or 1)

If the action code is H, then the other three fields are not present. If the action code is A, then the other three fields are present.

In the **TestDataForAssignments** folder under the **Pgm07-5** folder is a test data file called **patients.txt**. Your program should input this file and process them. Your program output should be similar to the following.

```
Added:   Samuel Spade          Fido          0
Added:   John Jones            Rover         0
```

```
Added:    Betsy Ann Smithville  Jenny            0
Treated:  Samuel Spade          Fido             0
Treated:  John Jones            Rover            0
Added:    Lou Ann deVille       Kitty            1
Treated:  Lou Ann deVille       Kitty            1
Added:    Tom Smythe            Fifi             0
Added:    Marie Longfellow      Jack             1
Treated:  Marie Longfellow      Jack             1
Treated:  Betsy Ann Smithville  Jenny            0
Treated:  Tom Smythe            Fifi             0
```

Problem Pgm15-3—The Acme Music Store's Sheet Music in Stock Program

Acme Music Store carries a wide line of sheet music, much of which is always in stock. They desire a program to allow them to perform real time inquiries while the customer is waiting.

Each piece of sheet music carries their stock number on it. They maintain a data base of sheet music in stock called **music.txt** located in the **Pgm15-3** folder. Each line contains the stock number (4 numerical digits), composer's name (21 characters), the title (31 characters), the quantity in stock at the moment and the cost of the music.

Design a simple class called **SheetMusic** to encapsulate a piece of music. It should support insertion and extraction from a stream.

When the program begins, it should allocate an instance of the **list** STL class. Input the file of music in stock into that linked list instance, always adding at the tail. Then, display the main menu.

```
Acme Music Store - Sheet Music Inventory Program

1. Check on availability of a piece of music by stock number
2. Find a piece of music given the composer
3. Find a piece of music given the title
4. Exit the program

Enter the number of your choice: _
```

When choice 1 is made, prompt the user to enter the four digit stock number and then look it up in the list. If the item is found, display its information nicely formatted on the screen. If it is not found, so state.

When choice 2 or 3 is made, prompt the user to enter the composer or music title. Then search the list for any matches. The search should be case insensitive. If one is found, display that item's information nicely formatted along with an option to continue the search. Remember, that there can be more than one piece of music written by any specific composer and some works may have duplicate titles.

Thoroughly test your program. You may add additional data to the **music.txt** file to ensure that your program is working perfectly.

Chapter 16—Complex Analysis

Introduction

In the days of old DOS and Windows 3.1, a programmer had to face two conflicting situations of efficiency when implementing a program. Either the program was optimized for speed of execution or it was optimized to take the smallest amount of memory. The two were mutually exclusive, for the most part, because what one did to make a program occupy less memory tended to slow a program's execution speed. And what one did to make a program run faster generally involved an increase in its overall memory requirements. Under old DOS, a program had to fit into conventional memory, memory below the 640K boundary. In general, it was difficult to implement any application that required more than around 600K total. With larger programs, the programmer was forced to make takeoffs in speed of execution with code size. This operation is often called **program tuning**, a process in which an optimum version of a program is created to fit operational requirements of speed and size.

This program tuning operation changed remarkably when Windows 95 appeared because Windows applications and DOS Console applications no longer had memory requirements that were restrictive. Indeed, now a program can utilize up to 2G of memory, assuming that there is a combination of real memory and swap drive space to equal that total amount required. The result has been the total de-emphasis on code size with full emphasis on speed of execution.

With today's amazingly fast PCs, one must use some common sense with regarding tuning programs for speed of execution. The modern compilers all generate a highly optimized for speed set of machine instructions for a program. One does not indiscriminately code certain actions for speed. For example, suppose that a program must input 100 customer order records and display a sales report. Tweaking the program for speed of execution is utterly pointless because such a program executes in less than a second of time!

However, we are studying data structure container classes designed to be utilized by many applications. Suppose that an application wishes to store two hundred thousand customer records in one of our list data structures. It should be obvious to you that speed of execution in this case is an important consideration we must examine.

In this chapter, we explore ways of measuring the efficiency of algorithms. This is not a chapter on how to fine-tune a program or methods of coding that run faster. Rather, we are discussing large scale algorithm performances so that we can evaluate which approach yields a faster implementation. We are then dealing with generalities and not specific coding techniques that impact program execution speed.

Beginning Axioms of Program Execution Efficiency

In all but the simplest problems to be solved with computer programs, there is seldom a single algorithm available for your use. Often, there are many different possibilities. If we can find a way to roughly determine that one algorithm is an order of magnitude slower in its execution than another, then if speed is a concern, we can pick the faster algorithm.

The first axiom deals with a linear series of instructions which is one that contains no loops of any kind.

> **Axiom 1. If a series is linear, then its speed depends only on the number and type of instructions it contains.**

How fast a given sequence executes is dependent upon the speed of the computer. Here I assume that the compiler has optimized this sequence for speed. True, a given sequence could be reworked into several versions, one of which may execute more quickly. However, this is the province of program tuning. There are tools on the market that monitor lines of coding producing a histogram of which lines are using the greater percentage of the program execution time. From these, one could attempt to alter the sequence so that it ran faster. But this is not our objective here. (If you are interested in these aspects, see *Zen of Code Optimization*, Abrash, Coriolis Books, 1994, ISBN: 1-883577-03-9.)

On the other hand, if we place this same sequence of instruction within a loop, then the overall speed of loop execution can vary widely, depending upon the loop itself. And this is the factor we wish to consider here. In abstract terms, we can say that this sequence of instructions has an efficiency function, f (n), where n is the number of repetitions or elements to be done. In general, we can say the following.

f (n) = an efficiency factor of some kind

As we examine different kinds of loops, we can make comparisons of their efficiencies. These are relative or proportional efficiencies, not absolute values.

Linear Loops

A linear loop is a loop that goes from a starting control value to an ending value in steps of +1 or –1. Consider the following linear loop.

```
for (k=0; k<100; k++) {
  an application sequence
}
```

How many times is the application sequence executed? 100 times.

Axiom 2. A linear loop has an efficiency f (n) = n, where n is the number of times the loop is repeated.

The efficiency is directly proportional to the number of times the loop is executed. Thus, if the limit were raised to 200, we would expect that the loop would take twice as long. If the limit were raised to 1000, we would expect the loop to take 10 times as long to be executed. The execution time of the linear loop is then linear as well. Or we can say the following.

f (n) = n

where n is the number of times the loop is to execute.

Now suppose that we were summing all of the odd integers from 1 to limit. We might have the following loop.

```
for (k=0; k<100; k+=2) {
  an application sequence
}
```

Here, the limit is 100. While one could say that f (n) = n / 2, realize that if you actually count the number of iterations, the sequence really only gets executed 50 times. However, if we talk in terms of the limit, then when comparing the first loop to the above loop, the first loop is f (n) = n while the second is **f (n) = n / 2.**

Logarithmic Loops

Now suppose that our loop control variable is either multiplied by 2 or divided by two. In terms of the limit, n, being 100, we have a very different total number of loop executions.

```
for (k=1; k<=100; k*=2) {
  an application sequence
}
for (k=100; k>0; k/=2) {
  an application sequence
}
```

Let's work out the actual number of times the body of these loops gets executed.

iteration	k for multiply	k for divide
1	1	100
2	2	50
3	4	25
4	8	12
5	16	6
6	32	3
7	64	1

Notice that when the limit n is 100, in these two cases, the actual number of times the loop is executed is far less than n. I chose to multiply or divide by 2 so that we can easily write an expression to represent their efficiency. We can write their efficiencies as follows.

Multiply: $2^n < 100$

Divide: $100 / 2^n > 0$

Or we can say that they take $\log_2 (n)$ iterations. So that if we compared f (n) from the first linear loop to the multiply loop, we can see the relative efficiencies.

f (n) linear loop = n

f (n) multiply loop = $\log_2 (n)$

If n was 100, then the linear loop requires 100 iterations while the multiply loop requires $\log_2(100)$ or 7 (if rounded). Thus, one could say that the multiply loop runs much faster than the linear loop.

Axiom 3. For logarithmic loops, $f(n) = \log_2(n)$.

What has this to do with data structures? Well, consider the problem of finding an item in an array or vector. If we have 100 items in the array to search and if we do a sequential search and the item we are looking for is the last element in the array, the linear search takes 100 tries to find it. However, if the array of 100 items is in sorted order and we can do a binary search for the requested item, then the number of iterations required is given by $\log_2(n)$ or 7 in this case.

Nested Linear Loops

Suppose that we are dealing with a two-dimensional array. How many times is the body of the loops executed in the following sample?

```
for (k=0; k<100; k++) {
  for (m=0; m<10; m++) {
    an application sequence
  }
}
```

The inner loop executes the application sequence ten times for each outer loop iteration. Thus, we get the next axiom.

Axiom 4. A Nested loop efficiency f (n) = #inner loop iterations * #outer loop iterations.

If both the inner and outer loops have the same number of iterations, n, then the efficiency formula is given as follows.

$$f(n) = n^2$$

Nested Linear Logarithmic Loops

Next, suppose that we combine a linear loop and a logarithmic loop in a nested fashion.

```
for (k=0; k<100; k++) {
  for (m=1; m<100; m*=2) {
    an application sequence
  }
}
```

Certainly the outer loop is linear and the efficiency is $f(n) = n$, where n is 100 in this case. However, the inner loop is logarithmic taking only $\log_2(n)$ per each invocation. If we combine these two terms using Axiom 4, we get the linear logarithmic loop efficiency function as follows.

$$f(n) = n * \log_2(n)$$

Dependent Quadratic Loops

This kind of looping situation occurs when the inner loop depends upon the outer loop's control variable for its beginning value. We have seen this occurring in the sorting process. The simple selection sort of n elements uses two loops. The outer loop runs from 0 to n – 1, while the inner loop runs from current value of the outer loop control variable + 1 to n.

```
for (k=0; k<9; k++) {
  for (m=k+1; m<10; m++) {
    an application sequence
  }
}
```

Here, I have lowered the limits so we can see the effect. The first time that the inner loop is executed, it runs from 1 through 9. The second time, it runs from 2 through 9 and the last time, it runs from 9 through 9. Thus, the number of iterations goes from 9, 8, 7, . . . 1. If we look at the average number of iterations of this inner loop, it is 5 (9+8+7+...1)/9. Mathematically, the average number of iterations is given by (n+1)/2 or (10+1)/2 = 5.

Using Axiom 4 once more, the total efficiency of this approach is given by the following.

$f(n) = n(n+1)/2$

In summary, we have seen that the efficiency of loops can be expressed as efficiency functions whose values included the following ranked from lowest to highest.

$\log_2(n)$ n $n \log_2(n)$ n^2

In designing solutions to problems, we can get an estimate of an algorithm's efficiency by examining its looping mechanism. Based upon an approximation of an algorithm's efficiency, we can then choose to use those algorithms that execute the fastest.

Big O Notation

These approximate efficiency functions that we have been creating are actually called big-O analysis and the factors are called big-O. Big-O means "on the order of." These are just approximations of the efficiency. Notice that we really are not concerned with absolute speed measurements, but larger scale approximations so that we can make intelligent choices among different algorithms that accomplish the same task.

The big-O notation is derived from our efficiency functions in a simple manner. If there is a constant coefficient, such as 2, set it to 1. If there are multiple terms, keep the largest term as given in the summary above.

Suppose we wanted to convert the dependent quadratic efficiency into big-O notation. We would expand our result as follows.

$f(n) = n * (n+1)/2 = n^2 * ½ + n * ½$

Remove the coefficients to get

$n^2 + n$

Keep only the highest ranking term

n^2

Thus, in big-O notation, an algorithm that followed the dependent quadratic route would be given as

$O(f(n)) = O(n^2)$

In big-O analysis, seven categories of algorithm efficiencies are defined. We have already examined four of these. Table 16.1 shows the seven categories. The difference in run time between algorithms that follow these seven categories can be dramatic.

Table 16.1 Big-O Algorithms

Efficiency	Big-O Expressions	Iterations where n = 10,000
Logarithmic	$O(\log_2 n)$	14
Linear	$O(n)$	10,000
Linear Logarithmic or n log n	$O(n \log_2 n)$	140,000
Quadratic	$O(n^2)$	100,000,000
Polynomial	$O(n^k)$ where k is the highest polynomial power	huge
Exponential	$O(c^k)$ where c is the base	really enormous
Factorial	$O(n!)$	gargantuan

Keep these estimates in perspective. Suppose that n is 5 and that a single iteration takes a microsecond to carry out. In such a case, it makes no observable difference to the user which algorithm is used. But if n is 100,000, then we must avoid quadratic or higher efficiency algorithms because the program might never finish execution before the user cancels the program out of frustration with the immense delay.

Let's put this to use on some very simple algorithms where we can easily see the process for determining big-O. In my first ebook on C++ programming, I introduced you to matrix algebra operations involving two-dimensional arrays. Here is a quick review.

Matrix Algebra

Specifically, matrices can be stored in two-dimensional arrays. Matrices can be used to solve linear simultaneous equations, such as **n** equations in **n** unknowns. The starting point is a brief review of the rules of Matrix Algebra.

Suppose that we had the following simultaneous equations.

$5x + 4y + 3z = 40$
$9y + 3z + 8x = 10$
$4z + 3x + 6y = 20$

They must be rearranged into the proper format.

$5x + 4y + 3z = 40$
$8x + 9y + 3z = 10$
$3x + 6y + 4z = 20$

In matrix notation, this becomes the following.

$$\begin{pmatrix} 5 & 4 & 3 \\ 9 & 3 & 8 \\ 4 & 3 & 6 \end{pmatrix} x \begin{pmatrix} x \\ y \\ z \end{pmatrix} = \begin{pmatrix} 40 \\ 10 \\ 20 \end{pmatrix}$$

Or **A X** = **B**; so the solution is **X** = **B/A**

The normal matrix notation for this case of 3 equations in 3 unknowns is show below.

$$\begin{pmatrix} a11 & a12 & a13 \\ a21 & a22 & a23 \\ a31 & a32 & a33 \end{pmatrix} . \begin{pmatrix} x1 \\ x2 \\ x3 \end{pmatrix} = \begin{pmatrix} b1 \\ b2 \\ b3 \end{pmatrix}$$

Notice that the math matrix notation parallels C++ subscripts, but begins with subscript 1 not 0. Always remember to subtract 1 from the matrix math indices to get a C++ array subscript.

In this example, the **a** matrix is composed of 3 rows or row vectors, and 3 columns or column vectors. In general a matrix is said to be an **m** by **n** matrix, **m** rows and **n** columns. When **m** = **n**, it is called a **square** matrix. A matrix with only one row is a **row** matrix; one with only one column is a **column** matrix. The **x** and **b** matrices are both column matrices.

Matrix Math Operations Summary

1. Two matrices are said to be equal if and only if they have the same dimensions and all corresponding elements are equal.

aij = **bij** for all **i**=1,**m** and **j**=1,**n**

2. Addition and Subtraction operations require that the matrices involved have the same number of rows and columns. To compute **C** = **A** + **B** or **C** = **A** – **B**, simply add or subtract all corresponding elements. This can be implemented in C++ as follows.

```
for (int I=0; I<M; I++) {
 for (int J=0; J<N; J++) {
  C(I,J) = A(I,J) + B(I,J);
 }
}
```

3. Multiplication of a matrix by a number is commutative. That is, **rA** is the same as **Ar.** The result is given by **r** times each element.

```
for (int I=0; I<M; I++) {
 for (int J=0; J<N; J++) {
  A(I,J) = A(I,J) * r;
 }
}
```

For example, assume **A** is defined to be the following.

$$A = \begin{pmatrix} 2.7 & -1.8 \\ 0.9 & 3.6 \end{pmatrix}$$

Then 2**A** would be

$$A = \begin{pmatrix} 5.4 & -3.6 \\ 1.8 & 7.2 \end{pmatrix}$$

and 10/9**A** would be

$$A = \begin{pmatrix} 3 & -2 \\ 1 & 4 \end{pmatrix}$$

4. A **diagonal** matrix is one whose elements above and below the principal diagonal are 0: namely **aij**=0 for all **i**!=**j**

$$diagonal \begin{pmatrix} 3 & 0 & 0 \\ 0 & 4 & 0 \\ 0 & 0 & 5 \end{pmatrix}$$

5. An **identity** matrix is a diagonal matrix whose principal diagonal elements are all 1.

$$identity \begin{pmatrix} 1 & 0 & 0 \\ 0 & 1 & 0 \\ 0 & 0 & 1 \end{pmatrix}$$

6. Matrix multiplication says that the product of a square matrix times a column matrix is another column matrix. It is computed as follows: for each row in the square matrix, sum the products of each element in the square matrix's row by the corresponding element in the column matrix's column.

$$\begin{pmatrix} a11 & a12 & a13 \\ a21 & a22 & a23 \\ a31 & a32 & a33 \end{pmatrix} . \begin{pmatrix} b1 \\ b2 \\ b3 \end{pmatrix} = \begin{pmatrix} a11*b1+a12*b2+a13*b3 \\ a21*b1+a22*b2+a23*b3 \\ a31*b1+a32*b2+a33*b3 \end{pmatrix}$$

For a square matrix times a square matrix, the result is a square matrix of the same dimensions, each element of the result is the sum of the products of each element of the corresponding row of one matrix times each element of the corresponding column of the other matrix

C = A * B

where **Cij** = i^{th} row of **A** * j^{th} column of **B** or in coding

```
for (int I=0; I<3; I++) {
 for (int J=0; J<3; J++) {
  C(I,J) = 0;
  for (int K=0; K<3; K++) {
   C(I,J) = C(I,J) + A(I,K)*B(K,J);
  }
 }
}
```

Matrix Addition

Let's implement the matric addition as a function and then determine its big-O. Assume that the matrices are of integer type.

```
void AddMatrices (int A[M][N], int B[M][N], int C[M][N]) {
  for (int I=0; I<M; I++) {
```

```
    for (int J=0; J<N; J++) {
      C(I,J) = A(I,J) + B(I,J);
    }
  }
}
```

This is an example of nested linear loops. The efficiency is M * N. If we let M = N for our approximation, then the efficiency of the AddMatrices function is O (n^2).

Matrix Multiplication

If we implement the matrix multiplication operation, we get the following simple routine.

```
void MultiplyMatrices (int A[N][N], int B[N][N], int C[N][N]) {
  for (int I=0; I<N; I++) {
    for (int J=0; J<N; J++) {
      C(I,J) = 0;
      for (int K=0; K<N; K++) {
        C(I,J) = C(I,J) + A(I,K)*B(K,J);
      }
    }
  }
}
```

This is also an example of nested linear loops. The efficiency is N * N * N. The efficiency of the MultiplyMatrices function is O (n^3).

A Pitfall of Big-O Analysis

Sometimes, a reader has a misunderstanding of the big-O notation. For example in mathematics, if we have the following equations

$f1\ (n) = g\ (n);$

$f2\ (n) = g\ (n);$

one can assume that f1 (n) = f2 (n). But with big-O analysis, one is easily misled.

$f1\ (n) = O\ (n);$

$f2\ (n) = O\ (n);$

Here f1 (n) does not equal f2 (n) at all. The big-O equations are just saying that these two functions have the same approximate efficiency. They are not the same function. Remember that big-O means on the order of.

There are a number of mathematical theorems concerning big-O analysis and the equations. (If you are interested in the mathematical background, consult Data Structures and Algorithms with Object-oriented Design Patterns in C++, Preiss, Wiley, 1999, ISBN: 0-471-24134-2.)

Applications of Big-O

To see big-O analysis in operation, let's return to the five sorting algorithms from chapter 11 and determine their O functions.

The Straight Selection Sort is the first of our sort routines. Here is its implementation.

```
void StraightSelectionSort (int array[], long count) {
 long currentSmallestIndex; // stores idx of current smallest one
 int  temp;
 long j, k;
 // outer loop traverses all elements except the last one
 for (j=0; j<count-1; j++) {
  // assume that the current j contains the smallest value
  currentSmallestIndex = j;
  // inner loop traverses all elements below j looking for the
  // next smallest one - notice we avoid swapping each time a
  // smaller one is found - just keep track of its index
  for (k=j+1; k<count; k++) {
```

```
    if (array[k] < array[currentSmallestIndex])
     currentSmallestIndex = k;
   }
   // now see if the new smallest one is in the correct position
   if (currentSmallestIndex != j) {
    // no, so one time only, swap the smallest into the correct
    // position in the array
    temp = array[j];
    array[j] = array[currentSmallestIndex];
    array[currentSmallestIndex] = temp;
   }
  }
}
```

To analyze it, let's remove the unnecessary coding, leaving the loops.

```
void StraightSelectionSort (int array[], long count) {
 for (j=0; j<count-1; j++) {
  for (k=j+1; k<count; k++) {
   ...
  }
 }
}
```

The outer loop is done effectively n times; remember we throw away the constants (n-1). You should recognize this as a dependent quadratic form whose efficiency function is

f (n) = n(n+1)/2

The big-O conversion above yields the following for the Straight Selection Sort.

$O(n) = n^2$

Next, the Bubble sort was coded this way.

```
void BubbleSort (int array[], int count) {
 int  temp;
 long j;
 long lastSwapIndex;          // the idx of the last one swapped
 long bottomIdx = count - 1; // the current ending idx
 while (bottomIdx > 0) { // repeat until only the top idx is left
  lastSwapIndex = 0;
  // rearrange all elements to current bottom
  for (j=0; j<bottomIdx; j++) {
   if (array[j] > array[j+1]) {
    // swap these two into increasing order
    temp = array[j];
    array[j] = array[j+1];
    array[j+1] = temp;
    lastSwapIndex = j; // reset the last idx swapped
   }
  }
  // since several lower ones might already be in increasing
  // order, we may not need to further check these - thus,
  // reposition bottom accordingly
  bottomIdx = lastSwapIndex;
 }
}
```

Again, remove the extraneous coding, leaving the basic looping.

```
void BubbleSort (int array[], int count) {
 long bottomIdx = count - 1; // the current ending idx
 while (bottomIdx > 0) { // repeat until only the top idx is left
  for (j=0; j<bottomIdx; j++) {
   if (array[j] > array[j+1]) {
   }
  }
  bottomIdx = lastSwapIndex;
 }
}
```

Now what do we do? The number of swaps is highly variable. Big-O always determines the worst case scenario. So we should examine this as the worst case. If we had the worst case on the inner loop swaps, then count number of them would occur. Thus, we get the big-O for the Bubble Sort.

$O(n) = n^2$

Next, comes the Quick Sort whose coding is as follows.

```
void QuickSort (int array[], long count, long lowIndex,
                long highIndex) {
 int  pivot;
 int  temp;
 long lowSwapIndex;
 long highSwapIndex;

 if (lowIndex >= highIndex) // 0 or 1 item to sort, we are done
  return;

 if ((highIndex - lowIndex) == 1) { // only two items to sort
  if (array[lowIndex] > array[highIndex]) { // we must swap them
   temp = array[lowIndex];
   array[lowIndex] = array[highIndex];
   array[highIndex] = temp;
  }
  return;
 }

 // here we have 3 or more items to swap
 // pick the value in the middle to be the pivot value for the
 // dividing vlaue between the two portions
 long mid = (lowIndex + highIndex) / 2;
 pivot = array[mid];
 // and swap this value into lowIndex postion
 array[mid] = array[lowIndex];
 array[lowIndex] = pivot;
 // divide into two portions in which one portion's array values
 // are all greater than the pivot value and the other one's
 // values are all <= to it
 lowSwapIndex = lowIndex + 1;
 highSwapIndex = highIndex;
 do {
  while (lowSwapIndex <= highSwapIndex &&
         array[lowSwapIndex] <= pivot) {
   lowSwapIndex++;
  }
  while (array[highSwapIndex] > pivot) {
   highSwapIndex--;
  }
  if (lowSwapIndex < highSwapIndex) {
   // here we have encountered an array value that belongs in the
   // other partition, so we must swap these two array values to
   // get them into the correct portions
   temp = array[lowSwapIndex];
   array[lowSwapIndex] = array[highSwapIndex];
   array[highSwapIndex] = temp;
  }
  // and repeat the process until these two points cross
 } while (lowSwapIndex < highSwapIndex);
 // here highSwapIndex has crossed, so all values in the
 // range of highSwapIndex through highIndex, are larger than
 // pivot. Thus, we put the value of pivot into its correct
 // position at point highSwapIndex. It is currently stored in
 // position lowIndex

 array[lowIndex] = array[highSwapIndex];
```

```
 array[highSwapIndex] = pivot;
 QuickSort (array, count, lowIndex, highSwapIndex-1);
 QuickSort (array, count, highSwapIndex+1, highIndex);
}
```

This one is more complicated because of the recursion. Again, let's strip it down to the looping instructions.

```
void QuickSort (int array[], long count, long lowIndex,
                long highIndex) {
 if (lowIndex >= highIndex) // 0 or 1 item to sort, we are done
  return;

 if ((highIndex - lowIndex) == 1) { // only two items to sort
  if (array[lowIndex] > array[highIndex]) { // we must swap them
  }
  return;
 }
 ...
 do {
  while (lowSwapIndex <= highSwapIndex &&
         array[lowSwapIndex] <= pivot) {
   lowSwapIndex++;
  }
  while (array[highSwapIndex] > pivot) {
   highSwapIndex--;
  }
  ...
 } while (lowSwapIndex < highSwapIndex);
 ...
 QuickSort (array, count, lowIndex, highSwapIndex-1);
 QuickSort (array, count, highSwapIndex+1, highIndex);
}
```

If the pivot does not divide the array evenly, the performance suffers. What happens if, at the indicated pivot element, we always end up finding the largest value or the smallest value? In such as case, we end up with one partition of size 0 and the rest of the array in the other partition! In this situation, we would end up with a running time proportional to $\mathbf{n^2}$ once again. The best case situation can be described by **n log n**. Thus, Quicksort runs between the following.

O(n) = $\mathbf{n^2}$

O(n) = n log n

Next, is the Shellsort whose coding is as follows.

```
void ShellSort (int array[], long count) {
 long gap, i, j;
 int temp;
 for (gap=count/2; gap>0;
      gap = (gap==2) ? 1 : (long)(gap/2.2)) {
  for (i=gap; i<count; i++) {
   temp = array[i];
   for (j=i; j>=gap && temp<array[j-gap]; j-=gap) {
    array[j] = array[j-gap];
   }
   array[j] = temp;
  }
 }
}
```

Since each time, the gap is halved, instead of $\mathbf{n^2}$, the performance is more like a dependent quadratic or **n log n**. So the Shellsort has a big-O of

O(n) = n log n

Finally, the Heapsort used the RebuildHeapDownward function.

```
void HeapSort (int array[], long count) {
 int temp;
 long i;
 for (i=count/2 - 1; i>=0; i--) {
  RebuildHeapDownward (array, i, count-1);
```

```
 }
 for (i=count-1; i>=1; i--) {
  temp = array[0];
  array[0] = array[i];
  array[i] = temp;
  RebuildHeapDownward (array, 0, i-1);
 }
}
void RebuildHeapDownward (int array[], long root, long bottom) {
 int temp;
 long maxChild;
 long leftChild  = root * 2 + 1;
 long rightChild = root * 2 + 2;
 if (leftChild <= bottom) {
  if (leftChild == bottom)
   maxChild = leftChild;
  else {
   if (array[leftChild] <= array[rightChild])
    maxChild = rightChild;
   else
    maxChild = leftChild;
  }
  if (array[root] < array[maxChild]) {
   temp = array[root];
   array[root] = array[maxChild];
   array[maxChild] = temp;
   RebuildHeapDownward (array, maxChild, bottom);
  }
 }
}
```

Again, reduce it to the basic looping instructions.

```
void HeapSort (int array[], long count) {
 for (i=count/2 - 1; i>=0; i--) {
  RebuildHeapDownward (array, i, count-1);
 }
 for (i=count-1; i>=1; i--) {
  RebuildHeapDownward (array, 0, i-1);
 }
}
void RebuildHeapDownward (int array[], long root, long bottom) {
  if (array[root] < array[maxChild]) {
   RebuildHeapDownward (array, maxChild, bottom);
  }
 }
}
```

Observe that there is a count/2 loop and a count loop. Thus, the Heapsort is at least

O(n) = n log n

ignoring any possible effects of the recursion.

The following summarizes the big-O results and shows the second required to sort 100,000 integers that are in random order.

Straight Selection	**O(n) = n^2**	18.787
Bubble Sort	**O(n) = n^2**	47.368
Quicksort	**O(n) = n log n**	0.020
Shellsort	**O(n) = n log n**	0.030
Heapsort	**O(n) = n log n**	0.040

From these, you can see that the big-O estimates are fairly predictive of just how that sort performs.

Review Questions

1. Explain the difference between tuning a program for speed and for smallest size. Why are both of these different from determining an algorithm's efficiency?

2. Axiom 1 said that if a series is linear, then its speed depends only on the number and type of instructions it contains. Explain what this means. Give an example of this principle.

3. What is meant by a linear loop? Give an example of one that was not shown in this chapter.

4. Explain what is meant by a linear loop having an efficiency of n, where n is the number of times the loop is executed.

5. What is a logarithmic loop? Give an example that was not shown in this chapter.

6. Why does a logarithmic loop execute more quickly than a linear loop?

7. How do we measure the efficiency of nested loops? Give an example that was not shown in this chapter.

8. What is a dependent quadratic loop? Give an example that was not shown in this chapter.

9. What is meant by big-O notation? How is it useful?

10. How is big-O calculated? How does big-O relate to a function's efficiency?

Stop! Do These Exercises Before Programming

1. Determine the big-O function for the following coding.
```
ostream& Plot (int array[MAX][MAX], ostream& os) {
 for (long j=0; j<MAX; j++) {
  os << "|";
  for (long k=0; k<MAX; k++) {
   os << setw(3) << array[j][k];
  }
 os << "|" << endl;
 return os;
}
```

2. Determine the big-O function for the following coding assuming n additions are required.
```
template<class T>
void  DoubleLinkedList<T>::AddAtHead (T* ptrdata) {
 // allocate a new node and fill it up
 LinkNode* ptrnew = new LinkNode;
 ptrnew->dataptr = ptrdata; // copy the passed client pointer
 ptrnew->backptr = 0;       // back pointer is 0 because at head
 count++;                   // increment total number of nodes
 // now chain this one into the list
 if (headptr) {             // if headptr exists, then the new
  ptrnew->fwdptr = headptr; // fwdptr contains the previous one
  headptr->backptr = ptrnew;// prev node's backptr is us now
  headptr = ptrnew;         // set headptr to newly added node
 }
 else {                     // empty list, so all ptrs point to
  headptr = tailptr = ptrnew; // this new node
  ptrnew->fwdptr = 0;       // and no forward nodes yet
 }
 currentptr = ptrnew; // leave the current one at the new one
}
```

3. Determine the big-O function for the following coding assuming insertions are required.

```
template<class T>
void DoubleLinkedList<T>::InsertAfterCurrentNode(T* ptrdata){
 if (!headptr)          // list is empty so add at head
  AddAtHead (ptrdata);
 else if (!currentptr) // current ptr is 0, so also add at head
  AddAtHead (ptrdata);
 else if (IsTail())     // current ptr is the last node, so
  AddAtTail (ptrdata); // reuse add at the tail
 else {                 // here we are inserting in the middle
  LinkNode* ptrnew = new LinkNode;
  ptrnew->dataptr = ptrdata;
  count++;
  // set new node's back pointer to current node to insert us
  ptrnew->backptr = currentptr;
  // set new node's forward ptr to the next node to the right
  ptrnew->fwdptr = currentptr->fwdptr;
  // set current's forward ptr to us to insert us
  currentptr->fwdptr = ptrnew;
  // set the node to the right of us to point back to us
  ptrnew->fwdptr->backptr = ptrnew;
  currentptr = ptrnew; // make the newly added node the current
 }
}
```

4. Determine the big-O function for the following coding assuming n deletions in random order are required.

```
template<class T>
bool  DoubleLinkedList<T>::DeleteCurrentNode () {
 if (!currentptr) // if no current node, abort
  return false;
 T* ptrdatadel;
 count--;
 if (!count) { // will list now be empty? if so reset to 0
  ptrdatadel = currentptr->dataptr;
  delete currentptr;
  delete ptrdatadel;
  headptr = tailptr = currentptr = 0;
  return true;
 }
 LinkNode* ptrtodelete = currentptr;
 ptrdatadel = currentptr->dataptr;
 if (IsHead()) {                    // deleting first node? if so,
  currentptr->fwdptr->backptr = 0;// set next node's back to none
  headptr = currentptr->fwdptr;    // set head to next node
  currentptr = headptr;            // and current to next node
 }
 else if (IsTail()) {               // deleting last one, if so,
  currentptr->backptr->fwdptr = 0;// set prev node's fwd to none
  tailptr = currentptr->backptr;   // set tail to prev node
  currentptr = tailptr;            // set current to prev node
 }
 else { // here the node to delete is in the middle
  // set next node's back to previous node
  currentptr->fwdptr->backptr = currentptr->backptr;
  // set previous node's fwd to next node
  currentptr->backptr->fwdptr = currentptr->fwdptr;
  // leave current pointing to previous node
  currentptr = currentptr->backptr;
 }
 delete ptrtodelete; // now delete the requested node
 delete ptrdatadel;  // delete the client's data too
 return true;
```

```
}
```

5. Determine the big-O function for the following coding assuming n random insertions.

```
bool Array::InsertAt (long i, void* ptrNewElement) {
 void** temp;
 long j;
 // allocate a new array one element larger
 temp = new void* [numElements + 1];

 // check if out of memory
 if (!temp) {
  cerr << "Array: InsertAt - Error out of memory\n";
  return false;
 }

 // this case handles an insertion that is within range
 if (i < numElements && i >= 0) {
  for (j=0; j<i; j++) { // copy all elements below insertion
   temp[j] = array[j];  // point
  }
  temp[i] = ptrNewElement; // insert new element
  for (j=i; j<numElements; j++) { // copy remaining elements
   temp[j+1] = array[j];
  }
 }

 // this case handles an insertion when the index is too large
 else if (i >= numElements) {
  for (j=0; j<numElements; j++) { // copy all existing elements
   temp[j] = array[j];
  }
  temp[numElements] = ptrNewElement; // add new one at end
 }

 // this case handles an insertion when the index is too small
 else {
  temp[0] = ptrNewElement;         // insert new on at front
  for (j=0; j<numElements; j++) { // copy all others after it
   temp[j+1] = array[j];
  }
 }

 // for all cases, delete current array, assign new one and
 // increment the number of elements in the array
 if (array) delete [] array;
 array = temp;
 numElements++;
 return true;
}
```

6. Determine the big-O function for the following coding assuming n Pushes.

```
void Stack::Push (void* ptrdata) {
 StackNode* ptrnew = new StackNode;
 ptrnew->dataptr = ptrdata;
 ptrnew->fwdptr = headptr;
 headptr = ptrnew;
 count++;
}
```

7. Determine the big-O function for the following coding assuming n enqueues.

```
void  Queue::Enqueue (void* ptrdata) { // Add at Tail
 QueueNode* ptrnew = new QueueNode;     // make new node
 ptrnew->dataptr = ptrdata;      // insert user's object
 count++;                        // increment number of nodes
 if (tailptr) {                  // if there are other nodes,
  tailptr->fwdptr = ptrnew;      // last one now points to us
  ptrnew->backptr = tailptr;     // us points to previous last one
  ptrnew->fwdptr = 0;            // us points to none
  tailptr = currentptr = ptrnew;// reset tail to us
 }
 else { // queue is currently empty, so just add us
  headptr = tailptr = currentptr = ptrnew;
  ptrnew->fwdptr = ptrnew->backptr = 0;
 }
}
```

8. Acme Construction has a master file of Part records arranged in part number order. Their online parts look up program needs to match a user-entered part number with the master file to obtain additional availability and cost information. Should the MatchPartNumber function use a linear search or a binary search? Assume that there are going to be 50 part records in the master file. Would your answer change if the number of parts was 50,000? Why? Defend your choices.